DESERET NEWS
1989-90 CHURCH
ALMANAC

GENERAL AUTHORITIES, OFFICERS

AREAS OF THE WORLD

HISTORICAL FACTS, STATISTICS

STAKES, MISSIONS

HISTORICAL CHRONOLOGY

About the cover: Top left, President Ezra Taft Benson and his counselors President Gordon B. Hinckley and President Thomas S. Monson; top right, recently dedicated Germany Frankfurt Temple; lower left, Elizabeth Nielsen and Ashley Anderson celebrate U.S. Constitution's Bicentennial; lower right, members of Tabernacle Choir enjoy Grand Teton National Park following choir performance.

GENERAL AUTHORITIES, OFFICERS

AREAS OF THE WORLD

HISTORICAL FACTS, STATISTICS

STAKES, MISSIONS

HISTORICAL CHRONOLOGY

FOREWORD

Get the facts!

How often we hear this statement, but how difficult it sometimes is to get the important facts that we need.

For those needing facts and figures about The Church of Jesus Christ of Latter-day Saints, this book is *the* source.

The 1989-90 *Deseret News Church Almanac* is an authoritative, reliable resource book, continuing the series of Almanacs published by the *Deseret News* and its *Church News* supplement since 1973.

No other volume available contains the wealth of information about the Church that is found in this Almanac.

This volume contains historical facts, Church statistics and information, and provides highlights of the two-year growth of the Church from October 1986 to October 1988. Brief biographical information is provided on all General Authorities, past and present.

Sincere appreciation for the preparation of the material in this Almanac is expressed to the staff of the *Church News* who have worked so diligently in its production. Also, without the cooperation and assistance of the Historical Department at Church headquarters this volume would not have been possible.

It is the continuing desire of the staff and management of the Deseret News Publishing Company that this Almanac will prove a valuable resource about the true Church, its glorious past, its vibrant present, and its promising future.

Wm. James Mortimer,
President and Publisher, *Deseret News*

The Deseret News Church Almanac is prepared and edited by the staff of the *Church News*, a section of the Deseret News, in cooperation with the staff of the Historical Department of The Church of Jesus Christ of Latter-day Saints.

Deseret News President and Publisher	Wm. James Mortimer
Deseret News Managing Editor	LaVarr G. Webb
Deseret News Assistant Managing Editor	Don C. Woodward
Church News Editor	Dell Van Orden
Church News Assistant Editor	Gerry Avant
Almanac Coordinating Editor	John L. Hart
Church News Staff	Kevin Stoker
	R. Scott Lloyd
	Mike Cannon
	Kellene Ricks
	Lee Warnick
	Jodee Gates
Deseret News Art Department	Robert Noyce
	Cory Maylett
	Christie Jackson Meyer
	Heather Tuttle
Deseret News Pagination Department	Steve Hawkins
	Mike Montrose
	David Croft
	B. Douglas Osborn
	Jean Cassidy

Historical Department:

Executive Director	Elder Dean L. Larsen
Managing Director	Elder John K. Carmack
Assistant Managing Director	Richard E. Turley Jr.
Director, Museum Division	Glen M. Leonard
Director, Library-Archives	Glenn N. Rowe
Chairman	Grant A. Anderson
Staff contributions:	Melvin L. Bashore
	Vivian C. Duvall
	Kim B. Farr
	Mary S. Kiessling
	James L. Kimball Jr.
	Veneese C. Nelson
	Larry Skidmore
	William W. Slaughter
	F. Annette Tucker

CONTENTS

A Statistical Profile of

THE CHURCH OF JESUS CHRIST OF LATTER-DAY SAINTS

CHURCH MEMBERSHIP
(Est. Dec. 31, 1988)

Total membership 6,650,000

CHURCH UNITS
(As of Oct. 15, 1988)

Number of stakes 1,700
Number of missions 221
Number of wards and branches 16,026
Number of countries with organized wards or branches 97
Number of territories, colonies and possessions
   with organized wards or branches 25

CHURCH GROWTH
(For year ending Dec. 31, 1987)

Children blessed 99,000
Children of record baptized 75,000
Converts baptized 227,284

TEMPLES
(As of Oct. 30, 1988)

Number of temples in use 41
Number of temples approved or under construction 6
(Temples are in use or planned in 26 countries)

LANGUAGES
(As of Oct. 30, 1988)

Number of established languages spoken by members 20
Number of emerging languages spoken by members 129
Number of complete Book of Mormon translations available 35
Total of complete Book of Mormon translations 41
Number of translated selections of Book of Mormon available 40
Total of selections of Book of Mormon translated 48
Total number of language translations 80

MISSIONARIES
(Sept. 27, 1988)

Single male missionaries serving 27,059
Single female missionaries serving 6,317
Total single missionaries serving 33,376
Married couples serving 1,215
Total missionaries serving 35,806

EDUCATION
(1987-88 school year)

Cumulative total of continuing education enrollment 376,427
Number of students in seminary and institute programs 363,350
Number of students at primary and secondary Church schools 9,018
Number of students Church colleges and universities (Fall, 1987) 36,758

MAJOR EVENTS OCTOBER 1986 — OCTOBER 1988

(For a more detailed listing, see News in Review, page 307)

Changes in leadership

GENERAL AUTHORITIES

The Council of the Twelve

• President Howard W. Hunter, acting president of the Council of the Twelve since Nov. 10, 1985, was set apart as president of the Twelve on June 2, 1988, succeeding President Marion G. Romney, who died May 20, 1988.

• Elder Richard G. Scott was sustained to the Council of the Twelve Oct. 1, 1988, filling the vacancy created with the death of President Marion G. Romney.

Presidency of the First Quorum of the Seventy

• Elder James M. Paramore was called to the Presidency of the First Quorum of the Seventy, and began service Aug. 15, 1987. He filled the vacancy created with the release of Elder Jack H. Goaslind.

• Elder J. Richard Clarke was sustained to the Presidency of the First Quorum of the Seventy on Oct. 1, 1988, filling the vacancy created with the call of Elder Richard G. Scott to the Council of the Twelve.

First Quorum of the Seventy

• Elder Jack H. Goaslind, called to the Presidency of the First Quorum of the Seventy Oct. 6, 1985, was released to become president of the United Kingdom/Ireland/Africa Area on Aug. 15, 1987.

• Fourteen new members of the First Quorum of the Seventy were called. Elders George R. Hill III, 65; John R. Lasater, 55; Douglas J. Martin, 59; Alexander B. Morrison, 56; L. Aldin Porter, 55; Glen L. Rudd, 68; Douglas H. Smith, 65; and Lynn A. Sorensen, 67, were sustained April 4, 1987. Elders Robert E. Sackley, 65, and L. Lionel Kendrick, 56, were sustained April 2, 1988. Monte J. Brough, 49; Albert Choules Jr., 62; Lloyd P. George, 68; and Gerald E. Mel-

chin, 67, were sustained Oct. 1, 1988.

General Authority Emeritus

• On Oct. 26, 1986, Elder Joseph Anderson reached the age of 96 years and 340 days, becoming the oldest General Authority in the 156-year history of the Church. Elder Anderson was born Nov. 20, 1889. He surpassed Elder LeGrand Richards, who died in 1983, as the oldest General Authority. Elder Richards of the Council of the Twelve was 96 years and 339 days at the time of his death.

General Authority Deaths

• President Marion G. Romney of the Council of the Twelve died May 20, 1988.

• Elder Franklin D. Richards of the First Quorum of the Seventy died Nov. 13, 1987.

• Elder A. Theodore Tuttle of the First Quorum of the Seventy died Nov. 28, 1986.

• Elder Henry D. Taylor, General Authority emeritus, died Feb. 24, 1987.

AUXILIARIES

• Dwan J. Young, general president of the Primary since April 5, 1980, was released April 2, 1988, along with her counselors, Virginia B. Cannon and Michaelene P. Grassli.

• Michaelene Grassli was sustained as general Primary president April 2, 1988. Called as her counselors were Betty Jo Jepsen and Ruth B. Wright.

• Jayne B. Malan, second counselor in the general presidency of the Young Women, was sustained as first counselor on April 4, 1987. She succeeded Maureen J. Turley, released to serve with her husband, Robert S., who was called as a mission president.

• Elaine Jack of the Relief Society General Board was sustained as second counselor in the general presidency of the Young Women on April 4, 1987.

Administrative Changes

● In a letter from the First Presidency, dated Oct. 3, 1988, minor modifications in the Sunday consolidated meeting schedule were announced. Sunday School opening exercises conducted by the Sunday School presidency will be held for 10 minutes and will include a hymn-singing period. Time for class periods will remain the same; only the break periods will be shortened.

● An official Young Women logo with a young woman's face stylized in the flames of a torch, and mission statements and symbols for the Beehive, Mia Maid and Laurel age groups, were introduced Oct. 18, 1987, at a Young Women satellite fireside.

● In a change of terminology, the First Presidency announced Aug. 15, 1987, that the Church Genealogical Department would be known as the Family History Department, and its library would be renamed the Family History Library.

● The Young Women program was strengthened in a letter from the First Presidency, sent June 20, 1987, to priesthood leaders defining the organizational structure of ward Young Women presidencies and calling for consistent midweek activities for Young Women.

Anniversaries

● Stakes, wards and branches across the United States took part in a year-long commemoration of the bicentennial of the U.S. Constitution, with musicals, programs and dances. The commemoration by the Church and the nation came to a climax in September 1987, the 200th anniversary of the signing of the "miracle" document. President Ezra Taft Benson delivered a stirring fireside address at Valley Forge, Pa., on Sept. 13, 1987. On the anniversary date of Sept. 17, the Tabernacle Choir sang the national anthem on the steps of Independence Hall in Philadelphia, Pa., to start the official parade, and performed that evening at the nation's "We the People 200 Constitutional Gala. That same day, 700 LDS teenagers performed a musical tribute, "Ring the Bells of Freedom," at the Jefferson Memorial in Washington, D.C.

On Sept. 18, Church leaders gathered at Hotel Utah in Salt Lake City for the Church's Constitutional Bicentennial Ball. President Benson was the guest of honor at the colonial-type ball, which was telecast over the Church satellite system as a live addition to stake constitutional balls throughout the United States.

● President Benson traveled to Great Britain with 12 other General Authorities for a gala celebration of the 150th anniversary of the first missionaries in the British Isles. Joining President Benson and President Gordon B. Hinckley, first counselor in the First Presidency, at an anniversary dinner on July 24, 1987, was former British Prime Minister Edward Heath. A videotaped message was relayed from U.S. President Ronald Reagan, and the queen's trumpeters performed at the dinner. In addition, markers were dedicated at eight historically significant locations throughout the British Isles, and conferences were held in London and Birmingham, England; Edinburgh, Scotland; Cardiff, Wales; Dublin, Ireland; and Belfast, Northern Ireland.

Other anniversaries during the two-year period included:

● The 100th anniversary of the Church in western Canada, May 2, 1987.

● The 75th anniversary of the founding of the seminary program, May 2, 1987.

● The 140th anniversary of Mormon Battalion's first raising of the United States flag over the city of Los Angeles, Calif., July 4, 1987.

● The 50th anniversary of "America's Witness for Christ," July 24-Aug. 1, 1987, the Church-sponsored pageant on the Hill Cumorah in New York, attended annually by 100,000 people.

● The 150th anniversary of the

Church in New Jersey, a summer-long celebration that began in Wayne, N.J., on May 14, 1988.

● The 100th anniversary of the dedication of the Manti Temple, May 21, 1988.

● The 10th anniversary of the revelation giving the priesthood to all worthy male members, regardless of race, June 9, 1988.

● The 100th anniversary of the first missionaries in Samoa, June 13-26, 1988.

News events

● On Oct. 10, 1986, a severe earthquake in El Salvador killed an estimated 1,200 people, including two Church members. Homes of nearly 250 LDS families were destroyed or severely damaged.

● On Jan. 23, 1987, former documents dealer Mark W. Hofmann was imprisoned after admitting in court under a plea bargain agreement that he was responsible for the bombing deaths of two people in October 1985, and that he forged the so-called Martin Harris "salamander letter." Another 24 documents not included in the plea bargain agreement were listed by the Salt Lake County Attorney's office as being forged or fraudulent. These included the 1828 Charles Anthon transcript, the Joseph Smith III blessing of 1844, the Lucy Mack Smith letter of 1829, and the Josiah Stowell letter of 1825.

● On March 12, 1987, the First Presidency announced that the Church-owned Hotel Utah, a landmark in downtown Salt Lake City for 76 years, would be closed, refurbished, and used as a meetinghouse and to house various Church departments.

● Ten new missions were announced March 14, 1987, to be established in Brazil Fortaleza, Dominican Republic Santiago, Florida Jacksonville, Mexico Mazatlan, Mexico Mexico City East, New Hampshire Manchester, New Jersey Newark, Philippines Cebu East, Portugal Porto and Zimbabwe Harare.

● On April 25, 1987, two more new missions were announced — the Zaire Kinshasa Mission in Africa and the Spain Bilbao Mission in Europe.

● The Frankfurt Germany Temple

was dedicated by President Ezra Taft Benson on Aug. 28, 1987, in the first of 11 dedicatory sessions.

● Ground was broken Oct. 10, 1987, by President Thomas S. Monson for the Toronto Ontario Temple.

● On Nov. 27, 1987, three members of the Church were killed by a typhoon in southern Luzon in the Philippines.

● Seven new missions were announced Dec. 19, 1987, to be located in Argentina Salta, Bolivia La Paz, Guatemala Guatemala City North, Mexico Chihuahua, Mexico Tuxtla-Gutierrez, Peru Lima East and Philippines Cagayan de Oro.

● Eleven stakes became 18 stakes in one of the largest divisions in Church history at Lima, Peru, Jan. 30-31, 1988.

● Ground was broken for the San Diego California Temple by President Ezra Taft Benson on Feb. 27, 1988, and the site was dedicated the same day by President Thomas S. Monson.

● Nine new missions were announced March 19, 1988. The new missions are: Brazil Belo Horizonte, Chile Antofagasta, Colombia Barranquilla, Liberia Monrovia, Mascarene Islands, Mexico Puebla, Mexico Tampico, Philippines Quezon City and Spain Las Palmas. All began functioning July 1, 1988, except for the Liberia Monrovia Mission, which started March 1, 1988.

● On June 4, 1988, the First Presidency announced that the block surrounding the Carthage Jail would be renovated into a park-like appearance, expanding the visitors center and adding exhibits.

● The Tabernacle Choir made a tour to Hawaii, Australia and New Zealand June 14-July 4, 1988.

Appointments

● Joe J. Christensen was inaugurated as the 12th president of Ricks College in Rexburg, Idaho, on Oct. 10, 1986.

● Kenneth H. Beesley was inaugurated as the ninth president of LDS Business College in Salt Lake City on Nov. 15, 1986.

● Alton L. Wade was inaugurated as the seventh president of BYU-Hawaii campus at Laie, Hawaii, on Feb. 20, 1987.

● Joseph F. Horne, 64 became the new director of Temple Square, following Arch L. Madsen on June 20, 1987.

● Richard T. Bretzing, 49, special agent in charge of the Federal Bureau of Investigation's Los Angeles, Calif., office, was named managing director of the Church's Security Department on April 2, 1988.

● James P. Christensen, 54, was appointed president and general manager of the Church-owned Polynesian Cultural Center in Laie, Hawaii on April 16, 1988.

Awards and honors

● Jason Buck, defensive lineman for the BYU football team, was awarded the Outland Trophy on Nov. 29, 1986, as the best college lineman in the nation.

● Janet Bird, an LDS mother of four from Medford, Ore., was named national Young Mother representative on April 10, 1987.

● On Dec. 21, 1987, *Sports Illustrated* magazine named LDS baseball player Dale Murphy one of eight "Sportsmen and Sportswomen of the Year."

● LDS quarterback Todd Santos of San Diego State University set a college football record for career passing of 10,660 yards during a game against BYU on Nov. 7, 1987.

Deaths

● Beverly Johnson Call, wife of Elder Waldo P. Call of the First Quorum of the Seventy, Oct. 7, 1986, in Salt Lake City.

● Howard S. McDonald, 92, president of BYU from 1945-49, Oct. 25, 1986, in San Luis Obisbo, Calif.

● Avard T. Fairbanks, 89, who sculpted the statue of the Angel Moroni atop the Jordan River, Seattle Washington and Washington D.C. temples, Jan. 1, 1987, in Salt Lake City.

● J. Martell Bird, managing director of the Church Security Department, Jan. 31, 1987, in Salt Lake City.

● George Carlos Smith Jr., 76, former general superintendent of the Young Men's Mutual Improvement Association from 1963-69, March 29, 1987, in Salt Lake City.

● Elva Taylor Cowley, widow of Elder Matthew Cowley of the Council of the Twelve, Aug. 18, 1987, in Glendale, Calif.

● Alexander Schreiner, 86, Tabernacle organist from 1924 to 1977, Sept. 15, 1987, in Salt Lake City.

● Camilla Eyring Kimball, 92, widow of President Spencer W. Kimball, Sept. 20, 1987, in Salt Lake City.

● Robert W. Barker, 68, president of the Washington D.C. Temple since 1985, Dec. 31, 1987, of a heart attack while visiting Southern California.

● A. Ray Curtis, 77, former president of the Salt Lake Temple, YMMIA General Board member, died Sept. 10, 1988, in Holladay, Utah.

GENERAL AUTHORITIES, OFFICERS

(Information in this section is as of Oct. 15, 1988)

THE FIRST PRESIDENCY

President Ezra Taft Benson

President Ezra Taft Benson was ordained and set apart as the 13th president of the Church on Nov. 10, 1985, 42 years after he became an apostle.

During his administration, he has emphasized the Book of Mormon and focused upon the theme, "Come Unto Christ," in emphasizing missionary and temple work, and the strengthening of families. A great-grandson and namesake of apostle Ezra T. Benson, President Benson was reared in a religious tradition, and in an agricultural setting, in Whitney, Idaho. From that foundation, he rose to the highest position of agriculture, and in the Church.

He was born Aug. 4, 1899, to George T. and Sarah Dunkley Benson, the oldest of 11 children. He began helping with the farm work at age 4, and was doing a man's work at 14. At this time, he shouldered increased responsibility as his father began a three-year full-time mission. All 11 of the Benson children later served full-time missions.

Despite severe economic conditions, he attended and graduated from Oneida Academy in Preston, Idaho, in 1914, and fulfilled a full-time mission to Great Britain from 1921-23.

He returned from his mission and graduated from BYU in 1926. The same year, on Sept. 10, he married Flora Smith Amussen, for whom he had waited to complete a mission to the Hawaiian Islands. They are the parents of two sons and four daughters, and have 18 grandchildren and 34 great-grandchildren.

Returning to the family farm in Idaho after earning a master's degree from Iowa State College in 1927, he became the county agent. That started a career in agriculture that took him to the Idaho state capital in 1930, the nation's capital in 1939, and finally to the U.S. Cabinet in 1952.

He was called to the Council of the Twelve on Oct. 7, 1943, at age 44, after serving as president of the Boise (Idaho) stake from 1938-40, and president of the Washington D.C. Stake, 1940-43. As an apostle, he returned to Europe after World War II to visit members and distribute supplies. In 1952, he was asked to become U.S. Secretary of Agriculture in President Eisenhower's Cabinet and received President David O. McKay's permission to accept.

After his eight-year term was over, he returned to full-time Church service. Highly popular, he was in constant demand as a speaker. He frequently shared his views in the same forthright style he used in Washington. However, he resisted several efforts to draft him into political office.

He presided over the European Mission from 1963-68, and in Asia, 1968-71. He became president of the Council of the Twelve on Dec. 30, 1973, when President Spencer W. Kimball was named president of the Church. Twelve years later, after the death of President Kimball, President Benson became president of the Church.

He has received 11 honorary degrees from American universities.

In addition to his other assignments as president of the Church, he is chairman of the Church Board of Education and of BYU and Ricks boards of trustees.

Gordon B. Hinckley

President Gordon B. Hinckley was set apart as first counselor to President Ezra Taft Benson on Nov. 10, 1985. He served previously in the First Presidency with President Spencer W. Kimball, called as a counselor on July 23, 1981, and as second counselor on Dec. 2, 1982.

President Hinckley is a member of the Church board of education, chairman of the Church Education Executive Committee, a vice chairman of the boards of trustees of BYU and Ricks College, and member of the General Welfare Services Committee. He is chairman of the board and of the executive committee of Bonneville International Corp. In 1981, he was chairman of the Church's Sesquicentennial executive committee.

Born June 23, 1910, in Salt Lake City, to Bryant S. and Ada Bitner Hinckley, President Hinckley was sustained an Assistant to the Twelve April 6, 1958, and ordained an apostle Oct. 5, 1961, at age 51.

He served for 20 years as secretary of the Radio, Publicity and Literature Committee of the Church, and was one of the pioneers in adapting modern electronic media to Church uses. He has been a stake president, and is a graduate of the University of Utah.

He has filled numerous special assignments, including the dedication of 18 temples from 1983-86.

President Hinckley and his wife, the former Marjorie Pay, have five children.

Thomas S. Monson

President Thomas S. Monson was called as second counselor to President Ezra Taft Benson on Nov. 10, 1985. He previously served 22 years in the Council of the Twelve, being called as an apostle on Oct. 4, 1963, at age 36.

He is vice chairman of the General Welfare Services Committee and is chairman of the Welfare Services Executive Committee. He is chairman of the Information and Communications Systems Committee, vice chairman of the Church Board of Education and of the Church Education Executive Committee, and a vice chairman of the BYU and Ricks College boards of trustees. He is also on the National Executive Board of Boy Scouts of America.

He is chairman of the board of *Deseret News* Publishing Co., and vice president of Newspaper Agency Corp. Before being called as a General Authority, he was general manager of Deseret Press.

Born Aug. 21, 1927, in Salt Lake City, to G. Spencer and Gladys Condie Monson, he graduated cum laude from the University of Utah in business management, and received an MBA degree from BYU. He served in the Navy during World War II.

President Monson was a counselor in a stake presidency when called as president of the Canadian Mission in 1959. He was ordained a bishop of a Salt Lake City Ward at age 22. He and his wife, the former Frances Beverly Johnson, are parents of three children.

**The Council
of the Twelve**

(as of October 15, 1988)

Front row, from left, President Howard W. Hunter and Elders Boyd K. Packer, Marvin J. Ashton, L. Tom Perry; back row, from left, Elders David B. Haight, James E. Faust, Neal A. Maxwell, Russell M. Nelson, Dallin H. Oaks, M. Russell Ballard, Joseph B. Wirthlin and Richard G. Scott.

COUNCIL OF THE TWELVE

Set apart as president of the Council of the Twelve June 2, 1988, after serving as acting president since Nov. 10, 1985; sustained to the Council of the Twelve Oct. 10, 1959, and ordained an apostle Oct. 15, 1959, at age 51. Graduated from Southwestern University Law School in Los Angeles with a degree of juris doctor, cum laude. A leading corporation attorney in Southern California when called to the Twelve. Served as chairman of the Southern California Welfare Region and Los Angeles Welfare Region, stake president and bishop. Has been president of the Genealogical Society and the Polynesian Cultural Center in Laie, Hawaii. Born Nov. 14, 1907, in Boise, Idaho, to John William and Nellie Rasmussen Hunter. Wife, Clara May Jeffs Hunter; parents of three children, two of whom are living. She died Oct. 9, 1983.

Howard W. Hunter

Boyd K. Packer

Chairman of the Temple and Family History Executive Council, adviser to the Historical Department, serves on the Board of Education of the Church and on BYU's Board of Trustees. Named an Assistant to the Twelve Sept. 30, 1961; sustained to the Council of the Twelve April 5, 1970, and ordained an apostle April 9, 1970, at age 45. Former supervisor of Seminaries and Institutes of Religion; educator; former president of the New England Mission. Received his bachelor's and master's degrees from Utah State University, and Ph.D. in educational administration from BYU. Pilot in the Pacific Theater during World War II. Born Sept. 10, 1924, in Brigham City, Utah, a son of Ira Wright and Emma Jensen Packer. Wife, Donna Smith Packer, parents of 10 children.

Chairman of the Priesthood Executive Council, member of the Church Board of Education and a trustee of BYU. Chairman of the board of Deseret Book Co., ZCMI and Zions Securities. Sustained an Assistant to the Twelve Oct. 3, 1969; ordained an apostle Dec. 2, 1971, at age 56, and sustained to the Council of the Twelve April 6, 1972. Former Utah State senator who spearheaded legislation for improved juvenile detention facilities. Served on the national committee of Boy Scouts of America. A graduate of the University of Utah in business administration. Received honorary doctorate of laws from University of Utah. Born May 6, 1915, in Salt Lake City, Utah, a son of Marvin O. and Rachel Grace Jeremy Ashton. Wife, Norma Bernston Ashton, parents of four children.

Marvin J. Ashton

Chairman of the Missionary Executive Council, serves on the Church Board of Education and on its executive committee, on the General Authority and Missionary assignments committes, and the Correlation Executive and Information Communications Systems committees. Sustained as Assistant to the Twelve Oct. 6, 1972; sustained to the Council of the Twelve on April 6, 1974; ordained an apostle April 11, 1974, at age 51. Former stake president's counselor and stake president. Served in the Marines in the Pacific during World War II. Graduated from Utah State University with a B.S. degree in finance; was vice president and treasurer of department store chain in Boston, Mass. Born Aug. 5, 1922, in Logan, Utah, to L. Tom and Nora Sonne Perry. Wife, Virginia Lee Perry, parents of three children. She died in 1974. Married the former Barbara Dayton in 1976.

L. Tom Perry

Serves on the Missionary Executive Council, chairman of Special Affairs Committee, on the board of directors and Executive Committee of Bonneville International Corp., and Deseret Management Corp., board of advisers of the University of Utah College of Business and the Utah State University National Advisory Board. Sustained an Assistant to the Twelve April 6, 1970, and to the Council of the Twelve April 3, 1976; ordained an apostle Jan. 8, 1976, at age 69. Former regional representative, president of Scottish Mission and stake president. Graduated from Albion State Normal School in Idaho, and attended Utah State University. Former mayor of Palo Alto, Calif. District and regional manager of large retail store chain; assistant to president of BYU, and a commander in the Navy during World War II. Born Sept. 2, 1906, at Oakley, Idaho, to Hector C. and Clara Tuttle Haight. wife, Ruby Olsen Haight, parents of three children.

David B. Haight

Serves on the Temple and Family History Executive Council and on the Special Affairs and General Welfare Services Executive committees; chairman of the Leadership Training Committee and Legal Oversight Committee; vice chairman of board and chairman of executive committee of the Deseret *News.* Sustained an Assistant to the Twelve Oct. 6, 1972, and to the Presidency of the First Quorum of the Seventy Oct. 1, 1976. Sustained to the Council of the Twelve on Sept. 30, 1978, and ordained an apostle Oct. 1, 1978, at age 58. Attorney and former state legislator. Served as regional representative, stake president and bishop; served in Air Force during World War II. Graduated from University of Utah with B.A. and juris doctor degrees; was adviser to the American Bar Journal and president of Utah Bar Association. Born July 31, 1920, in Delta, Utah, a son of George A. and Amy Finlinson Faust. Wife, Ruth Wright Faust, parents of five children.

James E. Faust

Serves on Priesthood Executive Council and the Appropriations and Leadership Training committees, Church Board of Education and BYU Board of Trustees executive committee.Called as an Assistant to the Twelve April 6, 1974, to Presidency of the First Quorum of the Seventy Oct. 1, 1976; ordained an apostle July 23, 1981, at age 55; and sustained to Council of the Twelve Oct. 3, 1981. Former Church commissioner of education; former YMMIA general board member, regional representative, bishop. Received bachelor's degree in political science and a master's degree from the University of Utah; has received four honorary doctorates. Former executive vice president of the University of Utah and legislative assistant to former U.S. Sen. Wallace F. Bennett of Utah. Born in Salt Lake City, Utah, on July 6, 1926, to Clarence H. and Emma Ash Maxwell. Wife, Colleen Hinckley Maxwell, parents of four children.

Neal A. Maxwell

Russell M. Nelson

Serves on the Priesthood Executive Council, the Welfare Services Executive Special Affairs, and the General Authorities Assignment committees. Sustained to the Council of the Twelve April 7, 1984; ordained an apostle April 12, 1984, at age 59. Former stake president, general president of the Sunday School, and regional representative. Renowned surgeon and medical researcher. Received B.A. and M.D. degrees from University of Utah, and Ph.D. from University of Minnesota. Former president of the Society for Vascular Surgery, former chairman of the Council on Cardiovascular Surgery for the American Heart Association. Born in Salt Lake City, Utah, on Sept. 9, 1924, a son of Marion C. and Edna Anderson Nelson. Wife, Dantzel White Nelson, parents of 10 children.

Serves on the Temple and Family History Executive Council, and is chairman of the board of Polynesian Cultural Center in Laie, Hawaii.Sustained to the Council of the Twelve April 7, 1984; ordained an apostle on May 3, 1984, at age 51. Former stake president's counselor and regional representative. Graduate of BYU in accounting; received J.D. degree cum laude from University of Chicago, later a professor of law there. Was law clerk to U.S. Supreme Court Chief Justice Earl Warren, practiced law in Chicago for three years specializing in corporate litigation; was executive director of the American Bar Association. Former president of BYU; former Utah Supreme Court justice; former national chairman of the board of Public Broadcasting Service (PBS), and former president of the American Association of Presidents of Independent Colleges and Universities. Born Aug. 12, 1932, in Provo, Utah, a son of Dr. Lloyd E. and Stella Harris Oaks. wife, June Dixon Oaks, parents of six children.

Dallin H. Oaks

M. Russell Ballard

Serves on the Missionary Executive Council and the Leadership Training, Personnel, and Information Communications Systems committees. Sustained to the First Quorum of the Seventy April 3, 1976, and to the presidency of the quorum Feb. 21, 1980. Sustained to the Council of the Twelve Oct. 6, 1985, and ordained an apostle Oct. 10, 1985, at age 57. Attended the University of Utah; Previously engaged in various business enterprises, including automotive, real estate, and investments. President of the Canada Toronto Mission and while there called as a General Authority; also served as counselor in a mission presidency and bishop twice. Has been executive director of the Missionary, Curriculum and Correlation departments. The grandson of late Apostles Melvin J. Ballard and Hyrum Mack Smith, he was born in Salt Lake City, Utah, on Oct. 8, 1928, to Melvin Russell Sr. and Geraldine Smith Ballard. Wife, Barbara Bowen Ballard, parents of seven children.

Serves on the Priesthood Executive Council and the Personnel and Leadership Training committees, and is chairman of the Curriculum Committee. Former president of Europe Area. Sustained as an Assistant to the Twelve April 4, 1975, to the First Quorum of the Seventy on Oct. 1, 1976, and to the presidency of the quorum on Aug. 28, 1986. Sustained to the Council of the Twelve Oct. 4, 1986, and ordained an apostle Oct. 9, 1986, at age 69. Served in the Sunday School general presidency and in a stake presidency and was a bishop. Graduate of University of Utah in business management. Former president of trade association in Utah, active in business affairs. A son of former Presiding Bishop of the Church, he was born June 11, 1917, in Salt Lake City, Utah, to Joseph L. and Madeline Bitner Wirthlin. Wife, Elisa Young Rogers Wirthlin, parents of eight children.

Joseph B. Wirthlin

Richard G. Scott

Serves on Temple and Family History Executive Council. Called to the First Quorum of the Seventy April 2, 1977, and to the presidency of the quorum Oct. 1, 1983. Sustained to the Council of the Twelve on Oct. 1, 1988, ordained an apostle Oct. 6, 1988, at age 59. Former president of the Argentina North Mission, former regional representative, stake president's counselor. Received B.S. degree in mechanical engineering from George Washington University, later completed the equivalent to a doctorate in nuclear engineering at Oakridge, Tenn. Worked 12 years on the staff of Adm. Hyman Rickover, developing nuclear submarines, and with power companies for possible use of nuclear power reactors. Born Nov. 7, 1928, at Pocatello, Idaho, to Kenneth Leroy and Mary Eliza Whittle Scott. Wife, Jeanene Watkins Scott, parents of seven children, five of whom are living.

The First Quorum of the Seventy
(as of October 15, 1988)

Front row, from left, Elders Joseph Anderson, Dean L. Larsen, Marion D. Hanks, Wm. Grant Bangerter, Robert L. Backman, Hugh W. Pinnock, James M. Paramore and J. Richard Clarke.

Second row, from left, Elders Sterling W. Sill, Theodore M. Burton, Angel Abrea, John Sonnenberg, Alexander B. Morrison, Helio R. Camargo, Francis M. Gibbons, Robert E. Sackley, Hans B. Ringger, George P. Lee, John R. Lasater, John K. Carmack, William R. Bradford, Glen L. Rudd, Robert B. Harbertson, Robert L. Simpson, Charles Didier, Keith W. Wilcox.

Third row, from left, Elders Paul H. Dunn, Ronald E. Poelman, H. Burke Peterson, Russell C. Taylor, Spencer H. Osborn, Jack H. Goaslind, Adney Y. Komatsu, Devere Harris, J. Thomas Fyans, Derek A. Cuth-

bert, Victor L. Brown, Waldo P. Call, L. Lionel Kendrick, Gerald E. Melchin, Ted E. Brewerton, Douglas H. Smith, Douglas J. Martin, Hartman Rector Jr., Albert Choules Jr., and John H. Groberg.

Fourth row, from left, Elders Vaughn J. Featherstone, Rex D. Pinegar, Rex C. Reeve, Gardner H. Russell, Gene R. Cook, Philip T. Sonntag, George I. Cannon, L. Aldin Porter, F. Enzio Busche, Carlos E. Asay, Jacob de Jager, Loren C. Dunn, F. Arthur Kay, F. Burton Howard, George R. Hill III, Royden G. Derrick, Lynn A. Sorensen, H. Verlan Andersen, Lloyd P. George, Monte J. Brough, and Robert E. Wells.

Not pictured, Elder Yoshihiko Kikuchi, and General Authorities Emeritus, Bernard P. Brockbank and John H. Vandenberg.

PRESIDENCY OF THE FIRST QUORUM OF THE SEVENTY

Church Historian and Recorder; executive director of the Historical Department and Correlation Department. Sustained to the First Quorum of the Seventy Oct. 1, 1976, and to the quorum presidency Feb. 22, 1980; served as president of the Texas South Mission, regional representative, member of the Sunday School general board, secretary of Adult Correlation Committee, member of Priesthood Missionary Committee. Graduated from Utah State University, was basketball coach and seminary teacher. Born May 24, 1927, at Hyrum, Utah, to Edgar Nels and Gertrude Prouse Larsen. Wife, Geneal Johnson Larsen, parents of five children.

Dean L. Larsen

Marion D. Hanks

Executive director of the Priesthood Department. Called to the Presidency of the First Quorum of the Seventy for the second time Oct. 6, 1984; previously served in the quorum presidency, 1976-1980; called to the First Council of the Seventy Oct. 4, 1953, and as Assistant to the Twelve April 6, 1968; former president of the Salt Lake Temple, president of the British Mission, and oversaw development of Church's refugee program in Asia. Holds a juris doctor degree from the University of Utah, was an educator; served in the Navy on a submarine chaser during World War II; served on two presidential advisory committees. Born Oct. 13, 1921, in Salt Lake City, Utah, to Stanley Alonzo and Maude Frame Hanks. Wife, Maxine Christensen Hanks, parents of four daughters and a son.

Executive director of the Temple Department, which oversees operation of the Church's temples. Called to the Presidency of the First Quorum of the Seventy for the second time Feb. 17, 1985; previously served in the quorum presidency, 1978-80; called as Assistant to the Twelve April 4, 1975, and to the First Quorum of the Seventy Oct. 1, 1976; served as president of the Brazilian, Portugal Lisbon and International missions, and twice as stake president. Received bachelor's degree from the University of Utah. Born June 8, 1918, at Granger, Utah, to William Henry and Isabelle Bawden Bangerter. Married to Mildred Schwantes Bangerter, who died in 1952; he married Geraldine Hamblin in 1953. He has 10 children.

Wm. Grant Bangerter

Robert L. Backman

Executive director of the Missionary Department, former president of North America West Area. Sustained to the First Quorum of the Seventy April 1, 1978, and to the quorum presidency Oct. 6, 1985; Young Men general president, 1979-1985; former general president and counselor, and general board member of the Aaronic Priesthood MIA and YMMIA; former president of the Northwestern States Mission, regional representative, and counselor in a stake presidency. Was attorney and Utah state legislator; graduated from the University of Utah; World War II veteran. Born March 22, 1922, in Salt Lake City, Utah, to LeGrand P. and Edith Price Backman. Wife, Virginia Pickett Backman, parents of seven children.

Executive director of the Curriculum Department and editor of the Church magazines, former president of Utah South Area. Sustained to the First Quorum of the Seventy Oct. 1, 1977, and to the quorum presidency Oct. 4, 1986; general president of the Sunday School, 1979-1986; former regional representative and president of Pennsylvania Harrisburg Mission. Graduate of University of Utah, former area general agent for insurance company, served on underwriter associations, president of Deseret Foundation of LDS Hospital, was appointed to serve on several governmental boards. Born Jan. 15, 1934, in Salt Lake City, Utah, to Lawrence Sylvester and Florence Boden Pinnock. Wife, Anne Hawkins Pinnock, parents of six children.

Hugh W. Pinnock

James M. Paramore

Executive director of the Priesthood Auxiliaries, former president of Utah North Area. Sustained to the First Quorum of the Seventy April 2, 1977, and to the quorum presidency Aug. 15, 1987; former executive secretary to the Council of the Twelve; former president of Belgium Brussels Mission, regional representative, stake president, and served on General Missionary Committee. Graduate of BYU, former executive director of Utah Committee on Children and Youth, and was on board of directors of National Committee on Children and Youth. Born May 6, 1928, in Salt Lake City, Utah, to James F. and Ruth C. Martin Paramore. Wife, Helen Heslington Paramore, parents of six children.

Executive director of the Family History Department. Sustained as second counselor in Presiding Bishopric Oct. 1, 1976, to the First Quorum of the Seventy April 6, 1985, and to the Presidency of the First Quorum of the Seventy Oct. 1, 1988; former president of the South Africa Cape Town Mission, regional representative, stake president, counselor in a stake presidency. Graduate of BYU with B.S. in marketing, did graduate work at Stanford University; former agency manager for life insurance company in Boise, Idaho. Born April 4, 1927, at Rexburg, Idaho, to John Roland and Nora L. Redford Clarke. Wife, Barbara Jean Reed Clarke, parents of eight children.

J. Richard Clarke

ADDITIONAL MEMBERS OF THE
FIRST QUORUM OF THE SEVENTY

Sustained Assistant to the Twelve Oct. 8, 1960, and to First Quorum of the Seventy Oct. 1, 1976; former managing director of the Genealogical Department; spent many years in Europe supervising Church programs and in government service; former president of West German and European missions. Graduated from University of Utah with bachelor's and master's degrees, and received doctorate in chemistry at Purdue University; former Utah State University (USU) chemistry professor; composed the USU alma mater hymn. Born March 27, 1907, in Salt Lake City, Utah, to Theodore T. and Florence Moyle Burton. Wife, Minnie Susan Preece Burton, parents of one son.

Theodore M. Burton

Paul H. Dunn

First counselor in the Utah South Area presidency. Called to the First Council of the Seventy April 6, 1964, and served in the Presidency of First Quorum of the Seventy, 1976-1980. Received bachelor's degree in religion from Chapman College, master's degree in educational administration and doctorate from University of Southern California. Served in the infantry in World War II; former professional baseball player; career Church educator, was coordinator of LDS Institutes of Religion in Southern California; author of 28 books. Born April 24, 1924, in Provo, Utah, to Joshua Harold and Geneve Roberts Dunn. Wife, Jeanne Alice Cheverton Dunn, parents of three daughters.

Second counselor in the South America North Area presidency. Called to First Council of the Seventy April 6, 1968, and to the First Quorum of the Seventy Oct. 1, 1976; former president of California San Diego and Alabama-Florida missions; converted to the Church in 1952. Attended University of Georgia and University of Southern California; naval aviator for 26 years, retiring with rank of captain; was also financial analyst in budget office of U.S. Department of Agriculture; author of two books and co-author of series of books recounting conversion stories. Born Aug. 20, 1924, at Moberly, Mo., to Hartman and Vivian Fay Garvin Rector. Wife, Constance Kirk Daniel Rector, parents of nine children.

Hartman Rector Jr.

Loren C. Dunn

President of the North America Central Area; former president of the North America Northwest Area. Sustained to the First Council of the Seventy April 6, 1968, and to the First Quorum of the Seventy Oct. 1, 1976; has lived in Brazil, Australia and New Zealand while in Church leadership positions; former counselor in mission presidency. Received degree in journalism and economics from BYU and M.S. in public relations from Boston University; former executive with economic development board in Boston, where he was noted for his work in regional economic planning; author of two books on gospel and missionary themes. Born June 12, 1930, in Tooele, Utah to Alex F. and Carol Horsfall Dunn. Wife, Sharon Longden Dunn, parents of five children.

Robert L. Simpson

General Sunday School president. Former president of the Pacific Area. Called as first counselor in Presiding Bishopric Sept. 30, 1961, as Assistant to the Twelve April 6, 1972, and to First Quorum of the Seventy Oct. 1, 1976; former president of Los Angeles Temple and of New Zealand and East London missions. Graduate of Santa Monica City College; employed by Bell Telephone for nearly 20 years; served in World War II as Air Force captain. Received Silver Antelope award from Boy Scouts of America. Born Aug. 8, 1915, in Salt Lake City, Utah, to Heber Chase and Lillian Leatham Simpson. Wife, Jelaire Chandler Simpson, parents of four children, three of whom are living

First counselor in the General Young Men presidency and president of the North America Southeast Area. Called to First Council of the Seventy Oct. 6, 1972, while president of Virginia-North Carolina Mission; sustained to First Quorum of the Seventy Oct. 1, 1976; served as counselor in stake mission presidency. Received bachelor's degree at BYU, master's degree at San Francisco State College, and doctorate in education at University of Southern California; former chairman of the educational psychology department at BYU. Born Sept. 18, 1931, in Orem, Utah, to John F. and Grace Murl Ellis Pinegar. Wife, Bonnie Lee Crabb Pinegar, parents of six children.

Rex D. Pinegar

J. Thomas Fyans

President of the Utah Central Area, former president of the Utah North and South America South areas. Called as Assistant to the Twelve April 6, 1974; served in the Presidency of the First Quorum of the Seventy, 1976-85; former executive director of Correlation and Genealogy departments; lived in South America and Mexico for several years while in Church service; was regional representative and president of the Uruguay Mission, member of a stake presidency and a bishop. Former executive with ZCMI, director of Church Distribution and Translation, and administrative director for the Presiding Bishopric. Born May 17, 1918, at Moreland, Idaho, to Joseph and Mae Farnsworth Fyans. Wife, Helen Cook Fyans, parents of five daughters.

First counselor in the Asia Area presidency. Sustained an Assistant to the Twelve April 4, 1975, and to First Quorum of the Seventy Oct. 1, 1976; first General Authority and regional representative of Japanese descent; former president of the Tokyo Temple and of Northern Far East Mission; served as branch president, bishop, high councilor. Served in World War II as counterintelligence officer; former senior vice president of savings and loan association in Honolulu. Born in Honolulu, Hawaii, Aug. 2, 1923, to Jizaemon and Misao Tabata Komatsu; converted from Buddhism at 17. Wife, Judy Nobue Fujitani Komatsu, parents of four children.

Adney Y. Komatsu

President of the North American West Area, former president of Mexico/Central America Area. Called to First Council of the Seventy Oct. 3, 1975, and to the First Quorum of the Seventy Oct. 1, 1976; former executive secretary to First Council of the Seventy, president of Uruguay-Paraguay Mission, and lived in Latin American countries for several years. Previously was consultant, agency manager and trainer for life insurance firm, was management trainer for Church employment. Received bachelor's and master's degrees in business administration from Arizona State University. Born Sept. 1, 1941, at Lehi, Utah, to Clarence H. and Myrl Johnson Cook. Wife, Janelle Schlink Cook, parents of eight children.

Gene R. Cook

Charles Didier

President of the South America North Area, former president of the North America Southeast Area and the South America North Area. Sustained to the First Quorum of the Seventy Oct. 3, 1975; was president of French/Switzerland Mission and served as regional representative; former Church area manager for distribution and translation for the European Area; converted to Church in 1957; fluent in five languages. Received bachelor's degree in economics from University of Liege in Belgium; served as officer in the Belgian Air Force Reserve. Born Oct. 5, 1935, at Ixelles, Belgium, to Andre and Gabrielle Colpaert Didier. Wife, Lucie Lodomez Didier, parents of two sons.

President of the Utah North Area, former president of the Asia Area. Sustained to the First Quorum of the Seventy Oct. 3, 1975, while president of Chile Mission; lived in Latin America and Asia for several years while in Church leadership positions. Was in fruit growing and shipping business in Texas, and owner of a company that grew citrus and tropical fruits in Texas, Mexico and Central America for distribution in the United States and other countries; attended BYU. Born Oct. 25, 1933, in Springville, Utah, to Rawsel W. and Mary Waddoups Bradford. Wife, Mary Ann Bird Bradford, parents of six children.

William R. Bradford

George P. Lee

Sustained to the First Quorum of the Seventy Oct. 3, 1975. A Navajo, he was first Indian to be called as a General Authority; former president, Arizona Holbrook Mission. Received bachelor's degree from BYU, master's from Utah State University and doctorate in educational administration from BYU. Former coach, guidance counselor, teacher, and president of College of Ganado on Navajo reservation; recipient of the Spencer W. Kimball Lamanite Leadership Award. Born March 23, 1943, at Towaoc, Colo., to Pete and Mae K. Asdzaatchii Lee. Wife, Katherine Hettich Lee, parents of seven children.

Carlos E. Asay

President of the Europe Area. Sustained to First Quorum of the Seventy April 3, 1976, and served in quorum presidency, 1980-86; former executive director of the Missionary and Curriculum departments and editor of Church magazines; former regional representative, president of the Texas North Mission, high councilor and bishop, and served on the Sunday School general board. Graduate, University of Utah with a doctorate in educational administration, was professor of education at BYU and assistant dean at BYU-Hawaii. Born June 12, 1926, in Sutherland, Utah, to A. E. Lyle and Elsie Egan Asay. Wife, Colleen Webb Asay, parents of eight children, seven of whom are living.

First counselor in the South America South Area presidency. Sustained to the First Quorum of the Seventy April 3, 1976; Former president of the Tonga Mission, regional representative and bishop. Has lived in South America and Hawaii while in Church leadership positions. Received bachelor's degree from BYU, master of business administration degree from Indiana University, where he also taught; formerly in real estate, development and construction; was vice president of Idaho State Real Estate Association. Born June 17, 1934, in Idaho Falls, Idaho, to Delbert V. and Jennie Holbrook Groberg. Wife, Jean Sabin Groberg, parents of 11 children.

John H. Groberg

Jacob de Jager

First counselor in the North America Central Area presidency, former president of the Asia Area. Sustained to the First Quorum of the Seventy April 3, 1976; former regional representative and counselor to three mission presidents; lived in Far East for several years while in Church leadership positions; converted to the Church in 1960; speaks six languages, Dutch, German, English, French, Spanish and Indonesian. Former vice president of an electronics company, for whom he served in five countries, was interpreter for Canadian Army in Europe after World War II. Born Jan. 16, 1923, at The Hague, Netherlands, to Alexander Philippis and Marie Jacoba Cornelia Scheele de Jager. Wife, Bea Lim de Jager, parents of two children.

General president of the Young Men and president of the Utah South Area, former president of the North America Southeast Area. Sustained as second counselor in Presiding Bishopric April 6, 1972, and to the First Quorum of the Seventy Oct. 1, 1976; served as president of Texas San Antonio Mission, member of the YMMIA general board and stake president; member, Boy Scouts of America National Executive Board, recipient of Silver Antelope and Silver Buffalo awards; former corporate training manager of supermarket chain based in Boise, Idaho. Born March 26, 1931, at Stockton, Utah, to Stephen E. and Emma M. Johnson Featherstone. Wife, Merlene Miner Featherstone, parents of seven children.

Vaughn J. Featherstone

Second counselor in the Asia Area presidency. Sustained to the First Quorum of the Seventy Oct. 1, 1976, and served in the quorum presidency, 1980-84; was executive director of Genealogical Department; former president of the Seattle Temple, and served in Sunday School general superintendency and as president of Ireland Dublin Mission. Attended University of Utah and served as chairman of the university's governing body; former president and general manager of steel company and chairman of the board of a branch of the Federal Reserve Bank. Born Sept. 7, 1915, at Salt Lake City, Utah, to Hyrum H. and Margaret Glade Derrick. Wife, Allie Jean Olson Derrick, parents of four children.

Royden G. Derrick

President of the Mexico/Central America Area. Sustained to the First Quorum of the Seventy Oct. 1, 1976; former mission president in Mexico; served as branch president, district president, regional representative and executive administrator in Latin America. Graduate of BYU; was former head of Central Purchasing for the Church, and former banking executive in South America for 18 years for New York City-based bank. Born Dec. 28, 1927, in Las Vegas, Nev., to Robert Stephen and Zella Verona Earl Wells. Married Meryl Leavitt, who died in 1960. Married Helen Walser Wells, parents of seven children, including Sharlene Wells Hawkes, Miss America of 1985.

Robert E. Wells

President of the Frankfurt Germany Temple. Sustained to the First Quorum of the Seventy Oct. 1, 1977; former president of Germany Munich Mission, regional representative and district president; converted to the Church in 1958. Graduate in economics and management from Bonn and Freiburg universities, and did graduate studies in technical printing; former chief executive officer of large printing and publishing firm in West Germany. Born April 5, 1930, at Dortmund, Germany, to Friedrich and Anna Weber Busche. Wife, Jutta Baum Busche, parents of four children.

F. Enzio Busche

President of the Hawaii Honolulu Mission, former counselor in the Utah North Area presidency. Sustained to the First Quorum of the Seventy Oct. 1, 1977; first native-born Japanese to be called as General Authority; was stake president, counselor to mission president and branch president; converted to the Church in 1955. Graduated from Asia University of Tokyo; former sales manager over Japan for a cookware company, president of a Japanese food storage company. Born July 25, 1941, to Hatsuo Kikuchi and Koyo Ideda Kikuchi at Horoizumi, Japan. Wife, Toshiko Koshiya Kikuchi, parents of four children.

Yoshihiko Kikuchi

Ronald E. Poelman

First counselor in the North America Southwest Area presidency. Sustained to the First Quorum of the Seventy April 1, 1978; served in general Sunday School presidency. Graduate of University of Utah with juris doctor degree; also graduated from Harvard University's Graduate School of Business Administration, Advanced Management Program; was vice president, secretary and director of trucking company. Born May 10, 1928, in Salt Lake City, Utah, to Hendrick and Ella May Perkins Poelman. Married Claire Howell Stoddard, parents of four children; she died in May 1979. Married Anne G. Osborn in June 1982.

Second counselor in the General Sunday School presidency and second counselor in the North America West Area presidency. Sustained to the First Quorum of the Seventy April 1, 1978, while president of Scotland Edinburgh Mission; was regional representative, stake president, district president, counselor to four mission presidents, and filled four stake and district missions; converted to the Church in 1951. Graduated in economics and law from University of Nottingham; was commercial manager of chemical and plastics company; served in British Royal Air Force during World War II. Born Oct. 5, 1926, at Nottingham, England, to Harry and Hilda May Freck Cuthbert. Wife, Muriel Olive Mason Cuthbert, parents of 10 children.

Derek A. Cuthbert

Rex C. Reeve

President of the North America Northwest Area, former president of the North America Northeast Area. Sustained to the First Quorum of the Seventy April 1, 1978, while serving as president of California Anaheim Mission; served as regional representative, stake president, counselor in four stake presidencies, patriarch, bishop and youth leader. Graduate of Snow College and LDS Business College; was executive of dairy firm and was on the board of directors of several businesses and organizations; served on executive committee of Boy Scout council. Born Nov. 23, 1914, at Hinckley, Utah, to Arthur H. and Mary A. Cropper Reeve. Wife, Phyllis Mae Nielson Reeve, parents of seven children.

Second counselor in the North America Northeast Area presidency, former president of the South America North Area. Sustained to the First Quorum of the Seventy Sept. 30, 1978; former president of Uruguay Montevideo Mission and stake president; was special representative for First Presidency in Latin American affairs. Graduate of Utah State University, received law degree from the University of Utah; former assistant attorney general for Utah, chief counsel for Utah Tax Commission, legal counsel for Mexico in Intermountain Area and managing partner of Salt Lake City law firm. Born March 24, 1933, at Logan, Utah, to Fred P. and Beatrice Ward Howard. Wife, Caroline Heise Howard, parents of five children.

F. Burton Howard

First counselor in the North America West Area presidency. Sustained to the First Quorum of the Seventy Sept. 30, 1978; former president of Central American Mission, and has lived for several years in Latin America on Church assignments; former regional representative, stake president, and stake president's counselor. Graduate of University of Alberta in pharmacology; former pharmacist in Calgary, Alberta, area; veteran of the Royal Canadian Air Force during World War II. Born March 30, 1925, at Raymond, Alberta, to Lee and Jane Fisher Brewerton. Wife, Dorothy Hall Brewerton, parents of six children.

Ted E. Brewerton

President of the United Kingdom/Ireland/Africa Area. Called to the First Quorum of the Seventy Sept. 30, 1978, and served in the Presidency of the First Quorum of the Seventy, 1985-87; former counselor in Aaronic Priesthood MIA general presidency, former president of the Arizona Tempe Mission, regional representative, stake president and bishop. Graduate of University of Utah; was vice president of a metals corporation, also served as officer in U.S. Air Force. Born April 18, 1928, in Salt Lake City, Utah, to Jack H. and Anita Jack Goaslind. Wife, Gwen Caroline Bradford Goaslind, parents of six children.

Jack H. Goaslind

First counselor in the South America North Area presidency. Sustained to the First Quorum of the Seventy April 4, 1981; first Argentine General Authority; former president of Argentina Rosario Mission and of the Buenos Aires Argentina Temple, stake president and regional representative. Graduate of University of Buenos Aires; was a certified public accountant; served as secretary of the treasury in San Miguel, Argentina. Born Sept. 13, 1933, in Buenos Aires, Argentina, to Edealo and Zulema Estrada Abrea. Wife, Maria Victoria Chiapparino de Abrea, parents of three daughters.

Angel Abrea

President of the North America Northeast Area, former president of the North America West Area. Sustained to the First Quorum of the Seventy April 7, 1984, while president of Idaho Boise Mission; former regional representative, president of the Los Angeles California Stake. Received B.A. degree from BYU, law degree from University of California at Los Angeles; an attorney, he was legislative assistant in California Legislature; Was president of a law firm in Los Angeles and past president of Westwood Bar Association. Born May 10, 1931, in Winslow, Ariz., to Cecil E. and Gladys Carmack. Wife, Shirley Fay Allen Carmack, parents of five children.

John K. Carmack

Russell C. Taylor

Second counselor in the Utah South Area presidency, former counselor in the Europe Area presidency. Sustained to the First Quorum of the Seventy April 7, 1984; former regional representative, chairman of Denver Colorado Temple Committee, president of the Georgia Atlanta Mission and stake president. Graduate, BYU in economics; was executive vice president and director of employee benefit company in Denver, Colo.; served in U.S. Navy during World War II. Born Nov. 25, 1925, in Red Mesa, Colo., to Leo S. and Stella Dean Taylor. Wife, Joyce Elaine Mortensen Taylor, parents of six children.

Second counselor in the Young Men general presidency and first counselor in the North America Northwest Area presidency. Sustained to the First Quorum of the Seventy April 7, 1984; was regional representative, president of California Fresno Mission, temple sealer and member of the General Aaronic Priesthood Committee. Graduate and former All-Conference and Small All-American basketball player at Utah State University; former executive vice president of hardware company, partner of fastener company. Born in Ogden, Utah, April 19, 1932, to Brigham Y. and Gladys L. Harbertson. Wife, Norma Creer Harbertson, parents of five children.

Robert B. Harbertson

Devere Harris

First counselor in the General Sunday School presidency and second counselor in the North America Southwest Area presidency. Sustained to the First Quorum of the Seventy April 7, 1984, while serving as president of the Idaho Falls Temple; served as regional representative, stake president, stake mission president and bishop. Attended Stevens-Henager College of Business in Salt Lake City; was regional manager for an insurance company. Born in Portage, Utah, May 30, 1916, to Robert C. and Sylvia Green Harris. Wife, Velda Gibbs Harris, parents of five children.

First counselor in the North America Southeast Area presidency. Sustained to First Quorum of the Seventy April 7, 1984, while serving as counselor in the Salt Lake Temple presidency; was full-time regional representative in the Philippines, president of Florida Tallahassee Mission, stake president and stake president's counselor. Attended UCLA and USC; chairman of the board of apparel manufacturing company in Salt Lake City. Born in Salt Lake City, Utah, on July 8, 1921, to William W. and Alice Hamlin Osborn. Wife, Avanelle Richards Osborn, parents of seven children.

Spencer H. Osborn

Second counselor in the Philippines/Micronesia Area presidency, former counselor in the General Sunday School presidency and in the North America Central Area. Sustained to the First Quorum of the Seventy April 7, 1984; former director of Temple Square, mission president in New Zealand and Connecticut, full-time regional representative in the Philippines and stake president. Served in U.S. Navy during World War II; attended University of Utah; was wholesale jeweler. Born in Salt Lake City, Utah, July 13, 1921, to Richard P. and Lena Tadje Sonntag. Wife, Voloy Andreasen Sonntag, parents of three children.

Philip T. Sonntag

Second counselor in the North America Central Area presidency, former president of the Pacific Area. Sustained to the First Quorum of the Seventy Oct. 6, 1984. Served as regional representative, chairman of the Chicago Temple committee, president of two stakes and high councilor. Was dentist; graduate of BYU, received dental training at University of Louisville School of Dentistry, and has served on several local and national dental societies. Born April 11, 1922, in Schneidemuhle, Germany, to Otto Paul and Lucille Mielke Sonnenberg. Wife, Joyce C. Dalton Sonnenberg, parents of seven children.

John Sonnenberg

President of the Pacific Area. Sustained to the First Quorum of the Seventy Oct. 6, 1984; prominent leader in the Northwest at the time of his calling. Was first president of the Seattle Temple, former regional representative, stake president, and counselor in stake presidency and bishop. Was dentist, graduate of Oregon Dental College in Portland; former U.S. dental officer in Heidelberg, Germany for two years. Born in Annabella, Utah, July 15, 1916, to Samuel A. and Medora Hooper Kay. Wife, Eunice D. Nielsen Kay, parents of six children.

F. Arthur Kay

First counselor in the North America Northeast Area presidency. Sustained to First Quorum of the Seventy Oct. 6, 1984; former president of the Ogden Temple, regional representative, president of the Indiana Indianapolis Mission, and stake president. Was architect, designer of Washington Temple and Missionary Training Center in Provo, Utah; served in Utah House of Representative for 10 years. Received bachelor's degree, University of Utah, master's, University of Oregon; served in U.S. Navy during World War II. Born May 15, 1921, in Hyrum, Utah, to Irving C. and Nancy Wilson Wilcox. Wife, Viva May Gammell Wilcox, parents of six daughters.

Keith W. Wilcox

Victor L. Brown

First counselor in the Utah North Area presidency. Sustained as second counselor in Presiding Bishopric Sept. 30, 1961; served as Presiding Bishop from April 6, 1972 until call to First Quorum of the Seventy April 6, 1985; former president of the Salt Lake Temple, stake president's counselor, bishop. Attended University of Utah, LDS Business College; former airline executive. Born July 31, 1914, at Cardston, Alberta, Canada, to Gerald Stephen and Maggie Calder Lee Brown. Wife, Lois Kjar Brown, parents of five children.

President of the North America Southwest Area. Sustained as first counselor in Presiding Bishopric April 6, 1972, and to the First Quorum of the Seventy April 6, 1985; former regional representative, stake president, and president of Jordan River Temple. Received bachelor's degree in civil engineering from University of Arizona, master's degree from Utah State University; was partner in engineering company and consulting civil engineer; served in U.S. Navy Seabees during World War II. Born Sept. 19, 1923, in Salt Lake City, Utah, to Harold A. and Juna Tye Peterson. Wife, Brookie Cardon Peterson, parents of five daughters.

H. Burke Peterson

Hans B. Ringger

First counselor in the Europe Area presidency. Sustained to the First Quorum of the Seventy April 6, 1985; first native of Switzerland to become a General Authority; was regional representative and stake president in Zurich, Switzerland, bishop and elders quorum president. Retired colonel in the Swiss army; was electrical engineer, architect, industrial designer and planner for laboratories and factories. Born Nov. 2, 1925, in Zurich, Switzerland, to Carl and Maria Reif Ringger. Wife, Helene Suzy Zimmer Ringger, parents of four children.

President of the South America South Area, former counselor in the same area. Sustained to the First Quorum of the Seventy April 6, 1985; former president of the Uruguay Montevideo Mission, regional representative, and stake president. A former self-employed orchardist, he holds a bachelor's degree from BYU in agronomy and horticulture. Born in Colonia Juarez, Mexico, Feb. 5, 1928, to Charles Helaman and Hannah Skousen Call. Married Beverly Johnson, parents of seven children, she died in 1986; married LaRayne Whetten in 1987.

Waldo P. Call

First counselor in the Brazil Area presidency. Sustained to the First Quorum of the Seventy on April 6, 1985; first Brazilian to be called as a General Authority; served as regional representative, stake president; converted to the Church in 1957. Graduate of Colegio Paulistano and Agulhas Negras Military Academy in Resende, Brazil, and received graduate degree of business from Fundacao Getull Vargas in Sao Paulo, Brazil; farmer and retired army officer. Born Feb. 1, 1926, in Resende, Brazil, to Jose Medeiros and Else Ferreira da Rocha Camargo Wife, Nair Belmira de Gouvea Camargo, parents of six children.

Helio R. Camargo

First counselor in the Mexico/Central America Area presidency. Sustained to the First Quorum of the Seventy April 6, 1986; served as patriarch, counselor in stake presidency, bishop, and high councilor in four stakes. Graduated from Gila Junior College in Thatcher, Ariz., received bachelor's degree from BYU, law degree from Stanford University Law School, and master of law from Harvard University; was CPA and former professor in accounting at BYU; served in Utah State Legislature. Born Nov. 6, 1914, in Logan, Utah to Hans and Mynoa Richardson Andersen Wife, Shirley Hoyt Andersen, parents of 11 children.

H. Verlan Andersen

President of the Philippines/Micronesia Area. Sustained to the First Quorum of the Seventy April 6, 1986; served as mission president, regional representative, in Young Men general presidency, on Young Men general board, and as stake president and patriarch. Graduate of BYU; was vice president of life insurance company. Born March 9, 1920, in Salt Lake City, Utah, to George Jenkins Cannon and Lucy Grant Cannon. Wife, Isabel Hales Cannon, parents of seven children.

George I. Cannon

President of the Brazil Area. Sustained to the First Quorum of the Seventy April 6, 1986; was secretary to the First Presidency for 16 years; served as stake president, patriarch and bishop. Graduate of Stanford University and received juris doctorate from University of Utah; Was attorney in Salt Lake City; author of eight biographies on Church presidents. Born April 10, 1921, in St. Johns, Ariz., to Andrew Smith Gibbons and Adeline Christensen Gibbons. Wife, Helen Bay Gibbons, parents of four children.

Francis M. Gibbons

Gardner H. Russell

Second counselor in the Mexico/Central America Area presidency. Sustained to the First Quorum of the Seventy April 6, 1986; former president of the Uruguay-Paraguay Mission, regional representative, counselor in a stake presidency and district president in Florida. Received bachelor's degree from Miami University in Oxford, Ohio; was manufacturer and financial consultant. Born Aug. 12, 1920, in Salt Lake City, Utah, to Harry J. and Agnes Gardner Russell. Wife, Dorothy Richardson Russell, parents of four children.

First counselor in the Philippines/Micronesia Area presidency. Sustained to the First Quorum of the Seventy April 4, 1987; former regional representative, bishop of two wards, and longtime volunteer with Scouting. Received bachelor's degree from BYU and doctorate from Cornell University; prize-winning scientist known for his work with coal; professor of chemical engineering and fuels engineering at the University of Utah; recipient of the Henry H. Storch Award of the American Chemical Society, author of many scientific papers. Born Nov. 24, 1921, in Ogden, Utah, to George Richard Jr. and Elizabeth O. McKay Hill. Wife, Melba Parker, parents of seven children.

George R. Hill III

John R. Lasater

Second counselor in the Europe Area presidency. Sustained to the First Quorum of the Seventy April 4, 1987, while serving as president of the New Zealand Auckland Mission; former stake president in Germany, and branch president in Vietnam, France, England. Graduate of Omaha University, earned master's degree at University of Southern California; was career officer in the U.S. Air Force until his retirement. Born Dec. 8, 1931, in Farmington, Utah, to Robert B. and Rowena Saunders Lasater. Wife, Marilyn Jones Lasater, parents of five children.

Second counselor in the Pacific Area presidency. Sustained to the First Quorum of the Seventy April 4, 1987; first native New Zealander to be a General Authority; former regional representative, president of the Hamilton New Zealand Stake, patriarch, twice as stake president's counselor, temple sealer, and bishop. Was manager of the largest injection and molding plastics company in New Zealand. Born April 20, 1927, in Hastings, New Zealand; Wife, Amelia Wati Crawford, parents of four children.

Douglas J. Martin

First counselor in the United Kingdom/Ireland/Africa Area presidency. Sustained to the First Quorum of the Seventy on April 4, 1987; former regional representative, bishop, and welfare regional agent. Former assistant deputy minister of the Department of National Health and Welfare, in Ottawa, Canada; former professor and chairman of the Food Science Department, University of Guelph, Ontario, Canada, and is internationally known scientist. Born Dec. 22, 1930, in Edmonton, Alberta, Canada, to Alexander S. Morrison and Christina Wilson Morrison. Wife, Shirley E. Brooks Morrison, parents of eight children.

Alexander B. Morrison

Second counselor in the South America South Area presidency. Sustained to the First Quorum of the Seventy April 4, 1987, while serving as president of the Louisiana Baton Rouge Mission; former regional representative, stake president, counselor in the Boise Idaho Temple presidency, and bishop. Employed by life insurance company. Born June 30, 1931, in Salt Lake City, Utah, to J. Lloyd and Revon Hayward Porter. Wife, Shirley Palmer Porter, parents of six children.

L. Aldin Porter

First counselor in the Pacific Area presidency. Called to First Quorum of the Seventy April 4, 1987, while president of the New Zealand Temple; former president of Florida and New Zealand Wellington missions; director of Welfare Square for 25 years, and former director of zone operations for Welfare Services, member of the General Church Welfare Committee and General Priesthood Missionary Committee, and was stake president's counselor. Born May 18, 1918, in Salt Lake City, Utah, to Charles P. and Gladys Harman Rudd. Wife, Marva Sperry Rudd, parents of eight children.

Glen L. Rudd

President of the Asia Area. Sustained to the First Quorum of the Seventy April 4, 1987; former regional representative, stake president, counselor in a stake presidency, high councilor, and bishop. Graduate of University of Utah; former president of Beneficial Life Insurance and Utah Home Fire Insurance Co. in Salt Lake City. Born May 11, 1921, in Salt Lake City, Utah, to Virgil H. and Winifred Pearl Hill Smith. Wife, Barbara Jean Bradshaw Smith, former Relief Society general president, parents of seven children.

Douglas H. Smith

Lynn A. Sorensen

Second counselor in the Brazil Area presidency. Sustained to the First Quorum of the Seventy April 4, 1987; former director of temporal affairs for the Church in Brazil, mission president, member of general board of the Young Men's Mutual Improvement Association, Melchizedek Priesthood General Board, executive secretary of the International Mission, patriarch and bishop. Graduated from the University of Utah; Served in Army Air Force during World War II; previously employed by Litton Industries, and was plant manager of Deseret Press. Born Sept. 25, 1919, in Salt Lake City to Ulrich Andrew and Fannie Goodman Boam Sorensen. Wife, Janet Elaine Weech Sorensen, parents of nine children.

Second counselor in the United Kingdom/Ireland/Africa Area presidency. Sustained to the First Quorum of the Seventy April 2, 1988; former president of Philippines Quezon City and Baguio missions, 1979-82, and was president of the Nigeria Lagos Mission when called as a General Authority. Served in the Australian commando forces during World War II, and was converted to the Church while recovering from combat injuries. Born Dec. 17, 1922, in Lismore, New South Wales, Australia, to Cecil James and Mary Sackley. He and his wife, Marjorie Orth, immigrated to Canada from Australia in 1954 and retired as president of Medicine Hat College in 1979; parents of five children.

Robert E. Sackley

L. Lionel Kendrick

Second counselor in the North America Northwest Area presidency. Sustained to the First Quorum of the Seventy April 2, 1988; former president of Florida Tampa Mission, regional representative, and stake president; converted to Church while an officer in the U.S. Air Force in 1954. Received bachelor's, master's and doctorate of education from Louisiana State University; was professor of health education and director of the Regional Training Center at East Carolina University. Born Sept. 19, 1931, in Baton Rouge, La., to Bonnie Delen and Edna Campbell Forbes Kendrick; Wife, Myrtis Lee Noble, parents of four children.

Second counselor in the Utah Central Area presidency. Sustained to the First Quorum of the Seventy Oct. 1, 1988; former regional representative, president of the Minnesota Minneapolis Mission, member of the Young Men General Board, and bishop. Graduate of University of Utah; was assets manager; former president and founder of national financial management company that pioneered direct computer billing, and former owner of a holding firm of wholesale office equipment companies. Born June 11, 1939, in Randolph, Utah, to Richard Muir and Gwendolyn Kearl Brough. Wife, Lanette Barker Brough, parents of seven children.

Monte J. Brough

First counselor in the Utah Central Area presidency. Sustained to the First Quorum of the Seventy Oct. 1, 1988; former regional representative, president of the New York New York City Mission, stake president, temple officiator, and active in Boy Scout affairs. Graduate of BYU and Harvard Graduate School of Business; personal investment, former president of international hotel chain, and former finance executive. Born Feb. 15, 1926, in Driggs, Idaho, to Albert and Rula Wilson Choules. Married Rosemary Phillips, parents of three sons; she died in 1984, married Marilyn Jeppson in 1987.

Albert Choules Jr.

Second counselor in the North America Southeast Area presidency. Sustained to the First Quorum of the Seventy Oct. 1, 1988; former regional representative, president of the Arizona Tempe Mission, stake president and bishop. Attended BYU; was an Army pilot during World War II; retired rancher, mercantile businessman, and real estate broker. Born Sept. 17, 1920, in Kanosh, Utah, to Preal and Artemisia Palmer George. Wife, Leola Stott George, parents of three children.

Lloyd P. George

Second counselor in the Utah North Area presidency. Sustained to the First Quorum of the Seventy Oct. 1, 1988; former regional representative, president of the California Arcadia Mission, stake president, region welfare agent, bishop. Graduate of Angus Business College in Calgary, served in the Royal Canadian Air Force during World War II; former self-employed businessman. Born May 24, 1921, in Kitchener, Ontario, Canada, to Arthur and Rosetta Willis Melchin. Wife, Evelyn Knowles Melchin, parents of seven children.

Gerald E. Melchin

PRESIDING BISHOPRIC

Called as Presiding Bishop April 6, 1985. Sustained as Assistant to the Twelve April 4, 1975, and to the First Quorum of the Seventy Oct. 1, 1976; former first counselor in the Sunday School general presidency, president of England London Mission, regional representative, served in various leadership positions, including stake president, in the United States, England, Germany and Spain. Graduate of University of Utah, with master of business administration degree from Harvard; served in the U.S. Air Force as a jet fighter pilot; was an executive with four major national companies. Born Aug. 24, 1932, in New York City, to John Rulon and Vera Marie Holbrook Hales. Wife, Mary Elene Crandall Hales, parents of two sons.

Robert D. Hales

Henry B. Eyring

Sustained first counselor in the Presiding Bishopric April 6, 1985; former regional representative, member of the Sunday School general board, and bishop. Graduate of University of Utah, received master's and doctorate of business administration from Harvard University, was on faculty at Stanford University Graduate School of Business; formerly deputy commissioner and Church Commissioner of Education, and former president of Ricks College. Born May 31, 1933, in Princeton, N.J., to Henry and Mildred Bennion Eyring. Wife, Kathleen Johnson Eyring, parents of six children.

Sustained as second counselor in the Presiding Bishopric April 6, 1985; former bishop's counselor, stake clerk, and elders quorum president. Received bachelor's and master's degrees from BYU; was a certified public accountant, employed by a national accounting firm and was chief financial officer for a land development company; managing director of Welfare Services for nearly four years. Born March 21, 1940, in Provo, Utah, to Kenneth LeRoy and Elizabeth A. Wilde Pace. Wife, Jolene Clayson Pace, parents of six children.

Glenn L. Pace

EMERITUS GENERAL AUTHORITIES

Eldred G. Smith

Named emeritus Oct. 6, 1979; called as Patriarch to the Church April 10, 1947; has given 18,000 recorded blessings. Attended University of Utah; was an engineer for the Manhattan Atomic Energy project in Oak Ridge, Tenn. A great-great-great-grandson of Joseph Smith Sr., first Church patriarch. Born Jan. 9, 1907, at Lehi, Utah, to Hyrum Gibbs and Martha Electa Gee Smith. Married Jeanne Ness Smith who died in 1977, parents of five children; married Hortense Child in 1978.

Named emeritus Sept. 30, 1978. Sustained an Assistant to the Twelve April 6, 1954, and to the First Quorum of the Seventy Oct. 1, 1976. Attended Utah State University; retired insurance executive; for many years was the speaker on KSL Radio's Sunday Evening from Temple Square; was member of the University of Utah board of regents. Born March 31, 1903, in Layton, Utah, to Joseph Albert and Marcetta Welling Sill. Wife, Doris Mary Thornley Sill, parents of three children.

Sterling W. Sill

Named emeritus Oct. 4, 1980. Sustained an Assistant to the Twelve Oct. 6, 1962, and to the First Quorum of the Seventy Oct. 1, 1976; former stake president and president of Scottish and International missions; served as managing director of the Mormon pavilions at world's fairs in 1960, 1968, 1970 and 1974. Attended University of Utah, George Washington University; former building contractor. Born May 24, 1909, in Salt Lake City, Utah, to Taylor P. and Sarah Le Cheminant Brockbank. Married Nada Rich Brockbank who died in 1967, parents of six children; married Frances Morgan in 1968.

Bernard P. Brockbank

Joseph Anderson

Named emeritus Sept. 30, 1978. Sustained an Assistant to the Twelve April 6, 1970, and to the First Quorum of the Seventy Oct. 1, 1976; served as secretary to First Presidency, 1923-1972; was managing director of the Church Historical Department; is the oldest living General Authority ever. Graduate of Weber Academy. Born Nov. 20, 1889, in Salt Lake City, Utah, to George and Isabella Watson Anderson. Married Norma Peterson Anderson who died in 1985, parents of three children.

Named an emeritus Sept. 30, 1978. Sustained as Presiding Bishop Sept. 30, 1961, as an Assistant to the Twelve April 6, 1972, and to the First Quorum of the Seventy Oct. 1, 1976. Previously, engaged in wool and livestock merchandising, as well as textile manufacturing and ranching. Born Dec. 18, 1904, in Ogden, Utah, to Dirk and Maria Alkema Vandenberg. Wife, Ariena Stok Vandenberg, parents of two daughters.

John H. Vandenberg

PRESIDENTS OF THE CHURCH

1. Joseph Smith — Born Dec. 23, 1805, in Sharon, Windsor Co., Vermont, a son of Joseph Smith Sr. and Lucy Mack. Received the Melchizedek Priesthood (ordained an apostle) in May 1829, by Peter, James and John, (D&C 20:2, 27:12); sustained as First Elder (and Oliver Cowdery as Second Elder) of the Church April 6, 1830, at age 24; ordained high priest June 3, 1831, by Lyman Wight, sustained as president of the High Priesthood Jan. 25, 1832, at a conference at Amherst, Loraine Co., Ohio, martyred June 27, 1844, at Carthage Jail, Carthage, Hancock Co., Illinois, at age 38.

2. Brigham Young — Born June 1, 1801, at Whitingham, Windham Co., Vermont, a son of John Young and Abigail Howe. Ordained an apostle Feb. 14, 1835, by the Three Witnesses to the Book of Mormon: Oliver Cowdery, David Whitmer and Martin Harris; sustained as president of the Quorum of the Twelve Apostles April 14, 1840; sustained as president of the Church Dec. 27, 1847, at age 46; died Aug. 29, 1877, in Salt Lake City, Salt Lake Co., Utah, at age 76.

3. John Taylor — Born Nov. 1, 1808, at Milnthrop, Westmoreland Co., England, a son of James Taylor and Agnes Taylor. Ordained an apostle Dec. 19, 1838, under the hands of Brigham Young and Heber C. Kimball at age 30; sustained as president of the Quorum of the Twelve Apostles Oct. 6, 1877; sustained as president of the Church Oct. 10, 1880, at age 71; died July 25, 1887, in Kaysville, Davis Co., Utah, at age 78.

4. Wilford Woodruff — Born March 1, 1807, at Avon (Farmington), Hartford Co., Connecticut, a son of Aphek Woodruff and Beulah Thompson. Ordained an apostle April 26, 1839, by Brigham Young; sustained as president of the Quorum of the Twelve Apostles Oct. 10, 1880; sustained as president of the Church April 7, 1889, at age 82; died Sept. 2, 1898, in San Francisco, San Francisco Co., California at age 91.

5. Lorenzo Snow — Born April 3, 1814, at Mantua, Portage Co., Ohio, a son of Oliver Snow and Rosetta Leonora Pettibone. Ordained an apostle Feb. 12, 1849, by Heber C. Kimball; sustained as counselor to President Brigham Young April 8, 1873; sustained as assistant counselor to President Brigham Young May 9, 1874; sustained as president of the Quorum of the Twelve Apostles April 7, 1889; sustained as president of the Church Sept. 13, 1898, at age 84; died Oct. 10, 1901, in Salt Lake City, Salt Lake Co., Utah, at age 87.

6. Joseph Fielding Smith — Born Nov. 13, 1838, at Far West, Caldwell Co., Missouri, a son of Hyrum Smith and Mary Fielding. Ordained an apostle and counselor to the First Presidency July 1, 1866, by Brigham Young; set apart as a member of the Quorum of the Twelve Apostles Oct. 8, 1867; released as counselor to the First Presidency at the death of President Young Aug. 29, 1877; sustained as second counselor to President John Taylor Oct. 10, 1880; released at the death of President Taylor July 25, 1887; sustained as second counselor to President Wilford Woodruff April 7, 1889; sustained as second counselor to President Lorenzo

Snow Sept. 13, 1898; sustained as first counselor to Lorenzo Snow Oct. 6, 1901, not set apart to this position; released at the death of President Snow Oct. 10, 1901; sustained as president of the Church Oct. 17, 1901, at age 62; died Nov. 19, 1918, in Salt Lake City, Salt Lake Co., Utah, at age 80.

7. Heber Jeddy Grant — Born Nov. 22, 1856, in Salt Lake City, Salt Lake Co., Utah, a son of Jedediah Morgan Grant and Rachel Ridgeway Ivins. Ordained an apostle Oct. 16, 1882, by George Q. Cannon; sustained as president of the Quorum of the Twelve Apostles Nov. 23, 1916; sustained as president  of the Church Nov. 23, 1918, at age 62; died May 14, 1945, in Salt Lake City, Salt Lake Co., Utah, at age 88.

8. George Albert Smith — Born April 4, 1870, in Salt Lake City, Salt Lake Co., Utah, a son of John Henry Smith and Sarah Farr. Married Lucy Emily Woodruff May 25, 1892 (she died Nov. 5, 1937); they had three children. Ordained an apostle Oct. 8, 1903, by Joseph F. Smith; sustained as president of the Quo-  rum of the Twelve Apostles July 1, 1943; sustained as president of the Church May 21, 1945, at age 75; died April 4, 1951, in Salt Lake City, Salt Lake Co., Utah, at age 81.

9. David Oman McKay — Born Sept. 8, 1873, at Huntsville, Weber Co., Utah, a son of David McKay and Jennette Eveline Evans. Married to Emma Ray Riggs Jan. 2, 1901 (she died Nov. 14, 1970); they had seven children. Ordained an apostle April 9, 1906, by Joseph F. Smith; sustained as second coun-  selor to President Heber J. Grant Oct 6,

1934; sustained as second counselor to President George Albert Smith May 21, 1945; sustained as president of the Quorum of the Twelve Apostles Sept. 30, 1950; sustained as president of the Church April 9, 1951, at age 77; died Jan. 18, 1970, in Salt Lake City, Salt Lake Co., Utah at age 96.

10. Joseph Fielding Smith — Born July 19, 1876, in Salt Lake City, Salt Lake Co., Utah, a son of Joseph Fielding Smith and Julina Lambson. Married Louie E. Shurtliff April 26, 1898 (she died March 30, 1908); they had two children. Married Ethel G. Reynolds Nov. 2, 1908 (she died Aug. 26, 1937); they  had nine children; Married Jessie Ella Evans April 12, 1938 (she died Aug. 3, 1971). Ordained an apostle April 7, 1910, by Joseph F. Smith, at Salt Lake City, Utah; sustained as acting president of the Quorum of the Twelve Apostles Sept. 30, 1950; sustained as president of the Quorum of the Twelve Apostles April 9, 1951; sustained as counselor in the First Presidency Oct. 29, 1965; sustained as president of the Church Jan. 23, 1970, at age 93; died July 2, 1972, in Salt Lake City, Salt Lake Co., Utah, at age 95.

11. Harold Bingham Lee — Born March 28, 1899, at Clifton, Oneida Co., Idaho, a son of Samuel M. Lee and Louisa Bingham. Married Fern Lucinda Tanner Nov. 14, 1923 (she died Sept. 24, 1962); they had two children. Married Freda Joan Jensen June 17, 1963. Ordained an  apostle April 10, 1941, by Heber J. Grant; sustained as president of the Quorum of the Twelve Apostles Jan. 23, 1970; sustained as first counselor to President Joseph Fielding Smith Jan. 23, 1970, at age 70; sustained as president of the Church July 7, 1972, at age 73; died Dec. 26, 1973, in Salt Lake City, Salt Lake Co., Utah, at age 74.

12. Spencer Woolley Kimball — Born March 28, 1895, in Salt Lake City, Utah,

Andrew and Olive Woolley Kimball. Married Camilla Eyring on Nov. 16, 1917; they had three sons and a daughter. Ordained an apostle Oct. 7, 1943, by President Heber J. Grant; became acting president of the Council of the Twelve Apostles after the death of President David O. McKay in 1970; sustained as president of the Quorum of the Twelve Apostles July 7, 1972; sustained as president of the Church Dec. 30, 1973, at age 78. Died Nov. 5, 1985, in Salt Lake City, Salt Lake Co., Utah, at age 90.

13. Ezra Taft Benson — See p. 12.

PROGRESS DURING ADMINISTRATIONS
OF THE PRESIDENTS

	At beginning		At end	
	Stakes	*Members	Stakes	*Members
JOSEPH SMITH	0	280	2	26,146
BRIGHAM YOUNG	2	34,694	20	115,065
JOHN TAYLOR	23	133,628	31	173,029
WILFORD WOODRUFF	32	180,294	40	267,251
LORENZO SNOW	40	267,251	50	292,931
JOSEPH F. SMITH	50	292,931	75	495,962
HEBER J. GRANT	75	495,962	149	954,004
GEORGE ALBERT SMITH	149	954,004	184	1,111,314
DAVID O. MCKAY	184	1,111,314	500	2,807456
JOSEPH FIELDING SMITH	500	2,807,456	581	3,218,908
HAROLD B. LEE	581	3,218,908	630	3,306,658
SPENCER W. KIMBALL	630	3,306,658	1,570	5,920,000
EZRA TAFT BENSON	1,570	5,920,000	**1,700	†6,389,000

* Nearest year-end totals
** To Oct. 15, 1988.
† Year-end, 1987

ASSISTANT PRESIDENTS OF THE CHURCH

1. Oliver Cowdery — Born Oct. 3, 1806, at Wells, Rutland Co., Vermont, a son of William Cowdery and Rebecca Fuller. Received Melchizedek Priesthood (ordained an apostle) in May 1829, by Peter, James, and John (D&C 20:2, 27:12) at age 22; sustained as second elder of the Church April 6, 1830; ordained a high priest Aug. 28, 1831, by Sidney Rigdon; ordained assistant president of the High Priesthood Dec. 5, 1834, at age 27; sustained as assistant counselor in the First Presidency Sept. 3, 1837; excommunicated April 11, 1838; baptized again Nov. 12, 1848; died March 3, 1850 at Richmond, Mo., at the age of 43.

2. Hyrum Smith — Born Feb. 9, 1800, at Tunbridge, Orange Co., Vermont, a son of Joseph Smith Sr. and Lucy Mack. Ordained high priest in June 1831, by Joseph Smith; sustained as assistant counselor to the First Presidency Sept. 3, 1837; sustained as second counselor to President Joseph Smith Nov. 7, 1837; given all the priesthood formerly held by Oliver Cowdery (including apostle); ordained Patriarch to the Church and assistant president Jan. 24, 1841, by Joseph Smith, at age 40; martyred June 27, 1844, at age 44 at Carthage Jail, Hancock Co., Illinois.

FIRST COUNSELORS IN THE FIRST PRESIDENCY

1. Sidney Rigdon — Born Feb. 19, 1793, at Saint Clair Township, Allegheny Co., Pennsylvania, a son of William Rigdon and Nancy Bryant. Ordained a high priest in June 1831, by Lyman Wight; set apart as first counselor to President Joseph Smith by Joseph Smith March 18, 1833, at age 40; excommunicated Sept. 8, 1844; died July 14, 1876, at Friendship, Allegheny Co., New York, at age 83.

2. Heber Chase Kimball — Born June 14, 1801, at Sheldon, Franklin Co., Vermont, a son of Solomon Farnham Kimball and Anna Spaulding. Ordained apostle Feb. 14, 1835, under the hands of Oliver Cowdery, David Whitmer and Martin Harris at age 33; sustained as first counselor to President Brigham Young Dec. 27, 1847, at age 46; died June 22, 1868, at Salt Lake City, Salt Lake Co., Utah, at age 67.

3. George Albert Smith — Born June 26, 1817, at Potsdam, Saint Lawrence Co., New York, a son of John Smith and Clarissa Lyman. Ordained apostle April 26, 1839, by Heber C. Kimball at age 21; sustained as first counselor to President Brigham Young Oct. 7, 1868, at age 51; died Sept. 1, 1875, at Salt Lake City, Salt Lake Co., Utah, at age 58.

4. John Willard Young — Born Oct. 1, 1844, at Nauvoo, Hancock Co., Illinois, a son of Brigham Young and Mary Ann Angell. Sustained as counselor to President Brigham Young April 8, 1873; sustained as assistant counselor to President Young May 9, 1874; sustained as first counselor to President Young Oct. 7, 1876, at age 32; released at death of President Young; sustained as a counselor to the Twelve Apostles Oct. 6, 1877; released Oct. 6, 1891; died Feb. 11, 1924, at New York City, New York at age 79.

5. George Quayle Cannon — Born Jan. 11, 1827, at Liverpool, Lancashire Co., England, a son of George Cannon and Ann Quayle. Ordained apostle Aug. 26, 1860, by Brigham Young at age 33; sustained as counselor to President Young April 8, 1873; sustained as assistant counselor to President  Young May 9, 1874; released at death of President Young Aug. 29, 1877; sustained as first counselor to President John Taylor Oct. 10, 1880, at age 53; released at death of President Taylor July 25, 1887; sustained as first counselor to President Wilford Woodruff April 7, 1889; sustained as first counselor to President Lorenzo Snow Sept. 13, 1898; died April 12, 1901, at Monterey, Monterey Co., California at age 74.

6. Joseph F. Smith — See PRESIDENTS OF THE CHURCH, No. 6.

7. John Rex Winder — Born Dec. 11, 1821, at Biddenham, Kent Co., England, a son of Richard Winder and Sophia Collins. Ordained high priest March 4, 1872, by Edward Hunter; sustained as second counselor to the Presiding Bishop April 8, 1887 at age 65; sustained as first counselor to President Joseph F. Smith Oct. 17, 1901, at age 79; died March 27, 1910, at Salt Lake City, Salt Lake Co., Utah, at age 88.

8. Anthon Henrik Lund — Born May 15, 1844, at Aalborg, Jutland Amt., Denmark, a son of Henrik Lund and Anne C. Andersen. Ordained apostle Oct. 7, 1889, by George Q. Cannon at age 45; sustained as second counselor to President Joseph F. Smith Oct. 17, 1901; sustained as first counselor to President  Smith April 7, 1910, at age 65; sustained as first counselor to President Heber J. Grant Nov. 23, 1918; died March 2, 1921, at Salt Lake City, Salt Lake Co., Utah, at age 76.

9. Charles William Penrose — Born Feb. 4, 1832, at London, Surrey Co., England, a son of Richard Penrose and Matilda Sims. Ordained apostle July 7, 1904, by Joseph F. Smith at age 72; sustained as second counselor to President Smith Dec. 7, 1911; sustained as second counselor to President Heber  J. Grant Nov. 23, 1918; sustained as first counselor to President Grant March 10, 1921, at age 89; died May 16, 1925, at Salt Lake City, Salt Lake Co., Utah at age 93.

10. Anthony Woodward Ivins — Born Sept. 16, 1852, at Toms River, Ocean Co., New Jersey, a son of Israel Ivins and Anna Lowrie. Ordained apostle Oct. 6, 1907, by Joseph F. Smith at age 55; sustained as second counselor to President Heber J. Grant March 10, 1921; sustained as first counselor to President  Grant May 28, 1925, at age 72; died Sept. 23, 1934, at Salt Lake City, Salt Lake Co., Utah at age 82.

11. Joshua Reuben Clark, Jr. — Born Sept. 1, 1871, at Grantsville, Tooele Co., Utah, a son of Joshua Reuben Clark and Mary Louise Woolley. Sustained as second counselor to President Heber J. Grant, April 6, 1933, at age 61; sustained as first counselor to President Grant, Oct. 6, 1934, at age 63; or-  dained apostle Oct. 11, 1934, by President Grant; sustained as first counselor to President George Albert Smith May 21, 1945; sustained as second counselor to President David O. McKay April 9, 1951; sustained as first counselor to President David O. McKay June 12, 1959; died Oct. 6, 1961, at Salt Lake City, Salt Lake Co., Utah at age 90.

12. Stephen L Richards — Born June 18, 1879, at Mendon, Cache Co., Utah, a son of

Stephen Longstroth Richards and Emma Louise Stayner. Ordained apostle Jan. 18, 1917, by Joseph F. Smith at age 37; sustained as first counselor to President David O. McKay April 9, 1951, at age 71; died May 19, 1959, at Salt Lake City, Salt Lake Co., Utah, at age 79.

13. Joshua Reuben Clark, Jr. — See No. 11 above.

14. Henry Dinwoodey Moyle — Born April 22, 1889, at Salt Lake City, Salt Lake Co., Utah, a son of James H. Moyle and Alice E. Dinwoodey. Ordained apostle April 10, 1947, by George Albert Smith at age 57; sustained as second counselor to President David O. McKay June 12, 1959, at age 70; sustained as first counselor to President McKay Oct. 12, 1961; died Sept. 18, 1963, at Deer Park, Osceola Co., Florida, at age 74.

15. Hugh Brown Brown — Born Oct. 24, 1883, at Granger, Salt Lake Co., Utah, a son of Homer Manly Brown and Lydia Jane Brown. Sustained as Assistant to the Quorum of the Twelve Apostles Oct. 4, 1953, at age 70; ordained apostle April 10, 1958, by David O. McKay; sustained as second counselor to President McKay Oct. 12, 1961; sustained as first counselor to President McKay Oct. 4, 1963,

at age 79; released at death of President McKay Jan. 18, 1970; died Dec. 2, 1975, at Salt Lake City, Salt Lake Co., Utah at age 92.

16. Harold Bingham Lee — See PRESIDENTS OF THE CHURCH, No. 11.

17. Nathan Eldon Tanner — Born May 9, 1898, at Salt Lake City, Salt Lake Co., Utah, a son of Nathan William Tanner and Sarah Edna Brown. Sustained as Assistant to the Quorum of the Twelve Apostles Oct. 8, 1960, at age 62; ordained apostle Oct. 11, 1962; sustained as second counselor to President David O. Mc-

Kay Oct. 4, 1963; sustained as second counselor to President Joseph Fielding Smith Jan. 23, 1970; sustained as first counselor to President Harold B. Lee July 7, 1972, at age 74; sustained as first counselor to President Spencer W. Kimball Dec. 30, 1973 at age 75; died Nov. 27, 1982, at Salt Lake City, Salt Lake Co., Utah, at age 84.

18. Marion George Romney — Born Sept. 19, 1897, in Colonia Juarez, Mexico, to George Samuel and Teressa Artemesia Redd Romney. Sustained Church's first Assistant to the Twelve April 6, 1941 at age 43; sustained to Council of the Twelve Oct. 4, 1951; ordained an apostle Oct. 11, 1951; sustained

as second counselor to President Harold B. Lee on July 7, 1972; second counselor to President Spencer W. Kimball on Dec. 30, 1973; first counselor to President Kimball Dec. 2, 1982; president of the Council of the Twelve Nov. 10, 1985; died May 20, 1988, at Salt Lake City, Salt Lake Co., Utah, at age 90.

19. Gordon Bitner Hinckley — See p. 13.

SECOND COUNSELORS IN THE FIRST PRESIDENCY

1. Frederick Granger Williams — Born Oct. 28, 1787, at Suffield, Hartford, Co., Connecticut, a son of William Wheeler Williams and Ruth Zodack. Called by revelation March 1832, to be a high priest and counselor to President Joseph Smith; ordained high priest by Miles H. Jones; set apart as second counselor to President Smith March 18, 1833, at age 45; rejected Nov. 7, 1837; ex-

communicated March 17, 1839; restored to fellowship April 8, 1840; died Oct. 25, 1842, at Quincy, Adams Co., Illinois, at age 54.

2. Hyrum Smith — See ASSISTANT PRESIDENTS OF THE CHURCH, No. 2.

3. William Law — Born Sept. 8, 1809. Set apart as second counselor to President Joseph Smith Jan. 24, 1841, at age 31; excommunicated April 18, 1844; died Jan. 19, 1892, at Shullsburg, LaFayette Co., Wisconsin, at age 82.

4. Willard Richards — Born June 24, 1804, at Hopkinton, Middlesex Co., Massachusetts, a son of Joseph Richards and Rhoda Howe. Ordained apostle April 14, 1840, by Brigham Young at age 36; sustained as second counselor to President Young Dec. 27, 1847, at age 43; died March 11, 1854, at Salt Lake City, Salt Lake Co., Utah, at age 49.

5. Jedediah Morgan Grant — Born Feb. 21, 1816, at Windsor, Broome Co., New York, a son of Joshua Grant and Athalia Howard. Set apart as one of the first seven presidents of the Seventy Dec. 2, 1845, at age 29; ordained apostle April 7, 1854, by Brigham Young, sustained as second counselor to President Young April 7, 1854, at age 38; died Dec. 1, 1856, at Salt Lake City, Salt Lake Co., Utah, at age 40.

6. Daniel Hanmer Wells — Born Oct. 27, 1814, at Trenton, Oneida Co., New York, a son of Daniel Wells and Catherine Chapin. Ordained a high priest Dec. 15, 1857, by Brigham Young; set apart as second counselor to President Young Jan. 4, 1857, by President Young, at age 42; released at the death of President Young Aug. 29, 1877; sustained as a counselor to the Twelve Apostles Oct. 6, 1877; died March 24, 1891, at Salt Lake City, Salt Lake Co., Utah, at age 76.

7. Joseph Fielding Smith — See PRESIDENTS OF THE CHURCH, No. 6.

8. Rudger Clawson — Born March 12, 1857, at Salt Lake City, Salt Lake Co., Utah, a son of Hiram Bradley Clawson and Margaret Gay Judd. Ordained apostle Oct. 10, 1898, by Lorenzo Snow at age 41; sustained as second counselor to President Snow Oct. 6, 1901, not set apart to this position; released at death of President Snow Oct. 10, 1901; sustained as president of the Council of the Twelve March 17, 1921; died June 21, 1943, in Salt Lake City, Salt Lake Co., Utah, at age 86.

9. Anthon Henrik Lund — See FIRST COUNSELORS IN THE FIRST PRESIDENCY, No. 8.

10. John Henry Smith — Born Sept. 18, 1848, at Carbunca (now Council Bluffs), Pottawattamie, Iowa, a son of George Albert Smith and Sarah Ann Libby. Ordained apostle Oct. 27, 1880, by Wilford Woodruff at age 32; sustained as second counselor to President Joseph F. Smith April 7, 1910, at age 61; died Oct. 13, 1911, at Salt Lake City, Salt Lake Co., Utah, at age 63.

11. Charles William Penrose — See FIRST COUNSELORS IN THE FIRST PRESIDENCY, No. 9.

12. Anthony Woodward Ivins — See FIRST COUNSELORS IN THE FIRST PRESIDENCY, No. 10.

13. Charles Wilson Nibley — Born Feb. 5, 1849, at Hunterfield, Midlothian Co., Scotland, a son of James Nibley and Jane Wilson. Ordained a high priest June 9, 1901, by Joseph F. Smith; sustained as Presiding Bishop of the Church Dec. 4, 1907; sustained as second counselor to President Heber J. Grant, May 28, 1925, at age 76; died Dec. 11, 1931, at Salt Lake City, Salt Lake Co., Utah, at age 82.

14. Joshua Reuben Clark, Jr. — See FIRST COUNSELORS IN THE FIRST PRESIDENCY, NO. 11, 13.

15. David Oman McKay — See PRESIDENTS OF THE CHURCH, NO. 9.

16. Joshua Reuben Clark, Jr. — See FIRST COUNSELORS IN THE FIRST PRESIDENCY, Nos. 11, 13.

17. Henry Dinwoodey Moyle — See FIRST COUNSELORS IN THE FIRST PRESIDENCY, No. 14.

18. Hugh Brown Brown — See FIRST COUNSELORS IN THE FIRST PRESIDENCY, No. 15.

19. Nathan Eldon Tanner — See FIRST COUNSELORS IN THE FIRST PRESIDENCY, No. 17.

20. Marion George Romney — See FIRST COUNSELORS IN THE FIRST PRESIDENCY, No. 18.

21. Gordon Bitner Hinckley — See p. 13.

22. Thomas S. Monson — See p. 13.

OTHER COUNSELORS IN THE FIRST PRESIDENCY

1. Jesse Gause — No biographical information available. Evidently convert from Shaker community, possibly in late 1830; ordained a counselor to Joseph Smith March 8, 1832; service in this capacity unconfirmed by historical records. Sent on mission Aug. 1, 1832, from which he evidently never returned.

2. John Cook Bennett — Born Aug. 3, 1804, at Fair Haven, Bristol Co., Massachusetts, a son of J. and N. Bennett. Presented as assistant president with the First Presidency April 8, 1841, at age 36; disfellowshipped May 25, 1842; excommunicated latter part of 1842; died in Polk City, Iowa.

3. Amasa Mason Lyman — Born March 30, 1813, at Lyman, Crafton Co., New Hampshire, a son of Roswell Lyman and Martha Mason. Ordained apostle Aug. 20, 1842, by Brigham Young at age 29; replaced in the Quorum of the Twelve Apostles Jan. 20, 1843, due to reinstatement of Orson Pratt; appointed  counselor to the First Presidency about Feb. 4, 1843; retired from the First Presidency with death of Joseph Smith June 27, 1844; returned to the Quorum of the Twelve Apostles Aug. 12, 1844; deprived of apostleship Oct. 6, 1867; excommunicated May 12, 1870; died Feb. 4, 1877, at Fillmore, Millard Co., Utah, at age 63.

4. Joseph F. Smith — See PRESIDENTS OF THE CHURCH, No. 6.

5. Lorenzo Snow — See PRESIDENTS OF THE CHURCH, No. 5.

6. Brigham Young Jr. — Born Dec. 18, 1836, at Kirtland, Geauga Co., Ohio, a son of Brigham Young and Mary Ann Angell. Ordained apostle Feb. 4, 1864, at age 27, by President Young; sustained to the Quorum of the Twelve Apostles Oct. 9, 1868; sustained as counselor to President Young April 8,  1873, at age 36; sustained as assistant counselor to President Young May 9, 1874; released at President Young's death Aug. 29, 1877; sustained president of the Quorum of the Twelve Apostles Oct. 17, 1901; died April 11, 1903 in Salt Lake City, Salt Lake Co., Utah, at age 66.

7. Albert Carrington — Born Jan. 8, 1813, at Royalton, Windsor Co., Vermont, a son of Daniel Van Carrington and Isabella Bowman. Ordained apostle July 3, 1870, by Brigham Young at age 57; sustained as counselor to President  Young April 8, 1873, at age 60; sustained as assistant counselor to President Young May 9, 1874; released at death of President Young Aug. 29, 1877; excommunicated Nov. 7, 1885; baptized again Nov. 1, 1887; died Sept. 19, 1889, at Salt Lake City, Salt Lake Co., Utah, at age 75.

8. John Willard Young — See FIRST COUNSELORS IN THE FIRST PRESIDENCY, No. 4.

9. George Quayle Cannon — See FIRST COUNSELORS IN THE FIRST PRESIDENCY, No. 5.

10. Hugh Brown Brown — See FIRST COUNSELORS IN THE FIRST PRESIDENCY, No. 15.

11. Joseph Fielding Smith — See PRESIDENTS OF THE CHURCH, No. 10.

12. Henry Thorpe Beal Isaacson — Born Sept. 6, 1898, at Ephra-im, Sanpete Co., Utah, a son of Martin Isaacson and Mary Jemima Beal. Ordained a high priest Oct. 1, 1941, by Charles A. Callis; sustained as second counselor to the Presiding Bishop Dec. 12, 1946. at age 48; sustained as first counselor to the Presiding Bishop April 6, 1952; sustained as Assistant to the Quorum of the Twelve Apostles Sept. 30,

1961; sustained as counselor in the First Presidency Oct. 28, 1965, at age 67; released at death of President McKay Jan. 18, 1970; resumed position as Assistant to the Quorum of the Twelve Apostles Jan. 23, 1970; died Nov. 9, 1970, at Salt Lake City, Salt Lake Co., Utah, at age 72.

13. Alvin Rulon Dyer — Born Jan. 1, 1903, at Salt Lake City, Salt Lake Co., Utah, a son of Alfred R. Dyer and Harriet Walsh. Ordained a high priest Oct. 2, 1927, by Joseph Fielding Smith; sustained an Assistant to the Quorum of the Twelve Apostles Oct. 11, 1958; ordained apostle Oct. 5, 1967, by

David O. McKay at age 64; sustained as counselor in the First Presidency April 6, 1968; released at death of President McKay Jan. 18, 1970; resumed position as Assistant to the Quorum of the Twelve Apostles Jan. 23, 1970; sustained a member of the First Quorum of Seventy Oct. 1, 1976; died March 6, 1977, at Salt Lake City, Salt Lake Co., Utah, at age 74.

14. Gordon Bitner Hinckley — See p. 13.

ASSISTANT COUNSELORS IN THE FIRST PRESIDENCY

1. Oliver Cowdery — See ASSISTANT PRESIDENTS OF THE CHURCH, No. 1.

2. Joseph Smith Sr. — Born July 12, 1771, at Topsfield, Essex Co., Massachusetts, a son of Asael Smith and Mary Duty. Ordained a high priest June 3, 1831, by Lyman Wight; ordained Patriarch to the Church Dec. 18, 1833, at age 62; also sustained as assistant counselor to the First Presidency Sept. 3, 1837, at age 66; died Sept. 14, 1840, at Nauvoo, Hancock Co., Illinois, at age 69.

3. Hyrum Smith — See ASSISTANT PRESIDENTS OF THE CHURCH, No. 2.

4. John Smith — Born July 16, 1781, at Derryfield, Hillsboro Co., New Hampshire, a son of Asael Smith and Mary Duty. Ordained a high priest June 3, 1833, by Lyman Wight; sustained as assistant counselor in the First Presidency Sept. 3, 1837, at age 56;

released at the death of Joseph Smith June 27, 1844; set apart as Patriarch to the Church Jan. 1, 1849, at age 67; died May 23, 1854, at Salt Lake City, Salt Lake Co., Utah, at age 72.

5. Lorenzo Snow — See PRESIDENTS OF THE CHURCH, No. 5.

6. Brigham Young Jr. — See OTHER COUNSELORS IN THE FIRST PRESIDENCY, No. 6.

7. Albert Carrington — See OTHER COUNSELORS IN THE FIRST PRESIDENCY, No. 7.

8. John Willard Young — See FIRST COUNSELORS IN THE FIRST PRESIDENCY, No. 4.

9. George Quayle Cannon — See FIRST COUNSELORS IN THE FIRST PRESIDENCY, No. 5.

THE COUNCIL OF THE TWELVE

1. Thomas Baldwin Marsh — Born Nov. 1, 1799, at Acton, Middlesex Co., Massachusetts, a son of James Marsh and Molly Law. Ordained apostle April 26, 1835, under the hands of Oliver Cowdery, David Whitmer and Martin Harris, at Kirtland, Ohio, at age 35; sustained as president of the Quorum of the Twelve Apostles May 2, 1835; excommunicated for apostasy March 17, 1839; baptized again in July 1857; died January 1866 at Ogden, Weber Co., Utah at age 66.

2. David Wyman Patten — Born Nov. 14, 1799, at Theresa, Jefferson Co., New York, a son of Benenio Patten and Abigail Cole. Ordained apostle Feb. 15, 1835, under the hands of Oliver Cowdery, David Whitmer and Martin Harris, at Kirtland, Ohio, at age 35; killed Oct. 25, 1838, at the Battle of Crooked River, Missouri, at age 38.

3. Brigham Young — See PRESIDENTS OF THE CHURCH, No. 2.

4. Heber Chase Kimball — See FIRST COUNSELORS IN THE FIRST PRESIDENCY, No. 2.

5. Orson Hyde — Born Jan. 8, 1805, at Oxford, New Haven Co., Connecticut, a son of Nathan Hyde and Sally Thorp. Ordained apostle Feb. 15, 1835, under the hands of Oliver Cowdery, David Whitmer and Martin Harris, at Kirtland, Ohio, at age 30; sustained as president of the Quorum of the Twelve Apostles  Dec. 27, 1847; dropped from Quorum May 4, 1839; restored to Quorum June 27, 1839; Brigham Young, April 10, 1875, took him from his original position in the Quorum and placed him in the order he would have been in when he was restored to fellowship had he come into the Quorum at that time (See: "Succession in the Priesthood" by John Taylor, p. 16.); died Nov. 28, 1878, at Spring City, Sanpete Co., Utah, at age 73.

6. William E. M'Lellin — Born 1806, in Tennessee. Ordained apostle Feb. 15, 1835, under the hands of Oliver Cowdery and David Whitmer, at Kirtland, Ohio, at age 29; excommunicated May 11, 1838; died April 24, 1883, at Independence, Jackson Co., Missouri, at age 77.

7. Parley Parker Pratt — Born April 12, 1807, at Burlington, Otsego Co., New York, a son of Jared Pratt and Charity Dickinson. Ordained apostle Feb. 21, 1835, under the hands of Joseph Smith, Oliver Cowdery, and David Whitmer, at Kirtland, Ohio, at age 27; assassinated May 13, 1857, at Van Buren, Crawford Co., Arkansas, at age 50.

8. Luke S. Johnson — Born Nov. 3, 1807, at Pomfret, Windsor Co., Vermont, a son of John Johnson and Elsa Jacobs. Ordained apostle Feb. 15, 1835, under the hands of Oliver Cowdery, David Whitmer and Martin Harris, at Kirtland, Ohio, at age 27; excommunicated April 13, 1838; baptized again in 1846 in Nauvoo; died Dec. 9, 1861, at Salt Lake City, Salt Lake Co., Utah, at age 53.

9. William Smith — Born March 13, 1811, at Royalton, Windsor Co., Vermont, a son of Joseph Smith Sr. and Lucy Mack. Ordained apostle Feb. 15, 1835, under the hands of Oliver Cowdery, David Whitmer and Martin Harris, at Kirtland, Ohio, at age 23; dropped from the Quorum May 4, 1839; restored to Quorum May 25, 1839; dropped from the Quorum Oct. 6, 1845; excommunicated Oct. 19, 1845; died Nov. 13, 1893, at Osterdock, Clayton Co., Iowa, at age 82.

10. Orson Pratt — Born Sept. 19, 1811, at Hartford, Washington, Co., New York, a son of Jared Pratt and Charity Dickinson. Ordained apostle April 26, 1835, under the hands of Oliver Cowdery, David Whitmer and Martin Harris, at Kirtland, Ohio, at age 23; excommunicated Aug. 20, 1842; baptized again June 20, 1843, and ordained to former office in the

Quorum of the Twelve Apostles. Brigham Young took him from his original position in the quorum in 1875 and placed him in the order he would have been in when he was restored to fellowship had he come into the quorum at that time; died Oct. 3, 1881, at Salt Lake City, Salt Lake Co., Utah, at age 70.

11. John Farnham Boynton — Born Sept. 20, 1811, at Bradford, Essex Co., Massachusetts, a son of Eliphalet Boynton and Susannah Nicholas. Ordained apostle Feb. 15, 1835, under the hands of Oliver Cowdery, David Whitmer and Martin Harris, at Kirtland, Ohio, at age 23; disfellowshipped Sept. 3, 1837; excommunicated 1837; died Oct. 20, 1890, at Syracuse, Onodago Co., New York, at age 79.

12. Lyman Eugene Johnson — Born Oct. 24, 1811, at Pomfret, Windsor Co., Vermont, the son of John Johnson and Elsa Jacobs. Ordained apostle Feb. 14, 1835, under the hands of Oliver Cowdery, David Whitmer and Martin Harris, at Kirtland, Ohio at age 23; excommunicated April 13, 1838; died December 1856, at Prairie du Chien, Crawford Co., Wisconsin, at age 45.

13. John Edward Page — Born Feb. 25, 1799, at Trenton Township, Oneida Co., New York, a son of Ebenezer and Rachel Page. Ordained apostle Dec. 19, 1838, under the hands of Brigham Young and Heber C. Kimball at Far West, Missouri, at age 39; disfellowshipped Feb. 9, 1846; excommunicated June 27, 1846; died in the fall of 1867, at De Kalb Co., Illinois, at age 68.

14. John Taylor — See PRESIDENTS OF THE CHURCH, No. 3.

15. Wilford Woodruff — See PRESIDENTS OF THE CHURCH, No. 4.

16. George Albert Smith — See FIRST COUNSELORS IN THE FIRST PRESIDENCY, No. 3.

17. Willard Richards — See SECOND COUNSELORS IN THE FIRST PRESIDENCY, No. 4.

18. Lyman Wight — Born May 9, 1796, at Fairfield, Herkimer Co., New York, a son of Levi Wight and Sarah Corbin. Ordained apostle April 8, 1841, by Joseph Smith, at Nauvoo, Illinois, at age 44. Excommunicated Dec. 3, 1848; died March 31, 1858, in Mountain Valley, Texas, at age 63.

19. Amasa Mason Lyman — see OTHER COUNSELORS IN THE FIRST PRESIDENCY, No. 3.

20. Ezra Taft Benson — Born Feb. 22, 1811, at Mendon, Worcester Co., Massachusetts, a son of John Benson and Chloe Taft. Ordained apostle July 16, 1846, by Brigham Young at Council Bluffs, Iowa, at age 35, died Sept. 3, 1869, at Ogden, Weber Co., Utah, at age 58.

21. Charles Coulsen Rich — Born Aug. 21, 1809, at Campbell Co., Kentucky, a son of Joseph Rich and Nancy O. Neal. Ordained apostle Feb. 12, 1849, by Brigham Young, at Salt Lake City, Utah, at age 39; died Nov. 17, 1883, at Paris, Bear Lake, Idaho, at age 74.

22. Lorenzo Snow — See PRESIDENTS OF THE CHURCH, No. 5.

23. Erastus Snow — Born Nov. 9, 1818, at Saint Johnsbury, Caledonia Co., Vermont, a son of Levi Snow and Lucina Streeter. Ordained apostle Feb. 12, 1849, by Brigham Young, at Salt Lake City, Utah, at age 30; died May 27, 1888, at Salt Lake City, Salt Lake Co., Utah, at age 69.

24. Franklin Dewey Richards — Born April 2, 1821, at Richmond, Berkshire co., Massachusetts, a son of Phinehas Richards and Wealthy Dewey. Ordained apostle Feb. 12, 1849, by Heber C. Kimball, at Salt Lake City, Utah, at age 27; sustained as president of the Quorum of the Twelve Apostles Sept. 13, 1898; died Dec. 9, 1899, at Ogden, Weber Co., Utah, at age 78.

25. George Quayle Cannon — See FIRST COUNSELORS IN THE FIRST PRESIDENCY, No. 5.

26. Brigham Young Jr. — See OTHER COUNSELORS IN THE FIRST PRESIDENCY, No. 6.

27. Joseph F. Smith — See PRESIDENTS OF THE CHURCH, No. 6.

28. Albert Carrington — See OTHER COUNSELORS IN THE FIRST PRESIDENCY, No. 7.

29. Moses Thatcher — Born February 1842, Sangamon Co., Illinois, a son of Hezekiah Thatcher and Alley Kitchen. Ordained apostle April 9, 1879, by John Taylor, at Salt Lake City, Utah, at age 37; dropped from the Quorum of the Twelve Apostles, April 6, 1896; died Aug. 21, 1909, at Logan, Cache Co., Utah, at age 67.

30. Francis Marion Lyman — Born Jan. 12, 1840, at Good Hope, McDonough Co., Illinois, a son of Amasa Mason Lyman and Maria Louisa Tanner. Ordained apostle Oct. 27, 1880, by John Taylor, at Salt Lake City, Utah, at age 40; sustained as president of the Quorum of the Twelve Apostles Oct. 6, 1903; died Nov.

18, 1916, Salt Lake City, Salt Lake Co., Utah, at age 76.

31. John Henry Smith — See SECOND COUNSELORS IN THE FIRST PRESIDENCY, No. 10.

32. George Teasdale — Born Dec. 8, 1831, at London, Middlesex Co., England, a son of William Russell Teasdale and Harriett H. Tidey. Ordained apostle Oct. 16, 1882, by John Taylor, at Salt Lake City, Utah, at age 50; died June 9, 1907, at Salt Lake City, Salt Lake Co., Utah, at age 75.

33. Heber Jeddy Grant — See PRESIDENTS OF THE CHURCH, No. 7.

34. John Whittaker Taylor — Born May 15, 1858, at Provo, Utah Co., Utah, a son of John Taylor and Sophia Whittaker. Ordained apostle April 9, 1884, by John Taylor at Salt Lake City, Utah, at age 25; resigned Oct. 28, 1905; excommunicated March 28, 1911; died Oct. 10, 1916, at Salt Lake City, Salt Lake Co., Utah, at age 58.

35. Marriner Wood Merrill — Born Sept. 25, 1835, at Sackville, Westmoreland Co., New Brunswick, a son of Nathan Alexander Merrill and Sarah Ann Reynolds. Ordained apostle Oct. 7, 1889, by Wilford Woodruff at Salt Lake City, Utah, at age 57; died Feb. 6, 1906, at Richmond, Cache Co., Utah, at age 73.

36. Anthon Henrik Lund — See FIRST COUNSELORS IN THE FIRST PRESIDENCY, No. 8.

37. Abraham Hoagland Cannon — Born March 12, 1859, at Salt Lake City, Utah, a son of George Quayle Cannon and Elizabeth Hoagland.  Sustained as one of the first seven presidents of the Seventy Oct. 8, 1882; ordained apostle Oct. 7, 1889, by Joseph F. Smith, at Salt Lake City, Salt Lake Co., Utah, at age 30; died July 19, 1896, at Salt Lake City, Salt Lake Co., Utah, at age 37.

38. Matthias Foss Cowley — Born Aug. 25, 1858, at Salt Lake City, Utah, a son of Matthias and Sarah Elizabeth Foss Cowley. Ordained an apostle Oct. 7, 1897, by George Q. Cannon, at Salt Lake City, Utah, at age 39; resigned Oct. 28, 1905; priesthood suspended May 11, 1911; restored to full membership April 3, 1936; died June 16, 1940, at Salt Lake City, Salt Lake Co., Utah, at age 81.

39. Abraham Owens Woodruff — Born Nov. 23, 1872, at Salt Lake City, Utah, a son of Wilford Woodruff and Emma Smith. Ordained an apostle Oct. 7, 1897, by Wilford Woodruff, at Salt Lake City, at age 24; died June 20, 1904, at El Paso, El Paso Co., Texas, at age 31.

40. Rudger Clawson — See SECOND COUNSELORS IN THE FIRST PRESIDENCY, No. 8.

41. Reed Smoot — Born Jan. 10, 1862, at Salt Lake City, Utah, a son of Abraham Owen Smoot and Anne Kestine Morrison. Ordained apostle April 8, 1900, by Lorenzo Snow, at Salt Lake City, at age 38; died Feb. 9, 1941, at St. Petersburg, Pinellas Co., Florida, at age 79.

42. Hyrum Mack Smith — Born March 21, 1872, at Salt Lake City, Utah, a son of Joseph Fielding Smith and Edna Lambson. Ordained apostle Oct. 24, 1901, by Joseph F. Smith, at Salt Lake City, at age 29; died Jan. 23, 1918, at Salt Lake City, Salt Lake Co., Utah, at age 45.

43. George Albert Smith — See PRESIDENTS OF THE CHURCH, No. 8.

44. Charles William Penrose — See FIRST COUNSELORS IN THE FIRST PRESIDENCY, No. 9.

45. George Franklin Richards — Born Feb. 23, 1861, at Farmington, Davis Co., Utah, a son of Franklin D. Richards and Nanny Longstroth. Ordained apostle April 9, 1906, by Joseph F. Smith at Salt Lake City, Utah, at age 45; sustained as acting patriarch to the Church Oct. 8, 1937; released from this position Oct.  3, 1942; sustained as president of the Quorum of the Twelve Apostles May 21, 1945; died Aug. 8, 1950, at Salt Lake City, Salt Lake Co., Utah, at age 89.

46. Orson Ferguson Whitney — Born July 1, 1855, at Salt Lake City, Utah, a son of Horace Kimball Whitney and Helen Mar Kimball. Ordained apostle April 9, 1906, by Joseph F. Smith, at Salt Lake City, at age 50; died May 16, 1931, at Salt Lake City, Salt Lake Co., Utah, at age 75.

47. David Oman McKay — See PRESIDENTS OF THE CHURCH, No. 9.

48. Anthony Woodward Ivins — See FIRST COUNSELORS IN THE FIRST PRESIDENCY, No. 10.

49. Joseph Fielding Smith — See PRESIDENTS OF THE CHURCH, No. 10.

50. James Edward Talmage — Born Sept. 21, 1862, at Hungerford, Berkshire Co., England, a son of James J. Talmage and Susannah Preater. Ordained apostle Dec. 8, 1911, by Joseph F. Smith at Salt Lake City, Utah, at age 49; died July 27, 1933, at Salt Lake City, Salt Lake Co., Utah, at age 70.

51. Stephen L Richards — See FIRST COUNSELORS IN THE FIRST PRESIDENCY, No. 12.

52. Richard Roswell Lyman — Born Nov. 23, 1870, at Fillmore, Millard Co., Utah, a son of Francis Marion Lyman and Clara Caroline Callister. Ordained apostle April 7, 1918, by Joseph F. Smith, at Salt Lake City, Utah, at age 47; excommunicated Nov. 12, 1943; baptized again Oct. 27, 1954; died Dec. 31, 1963, at Salt Lake City, Salt Lake Co., Utah, at age 93.

53. Melvin Joseph Ballard — Born Feb. 9, 1873, at Logan, Cache Co., Utah, a son of Henry Ballard and Margaret McNiel. Ordained apostle Jan. 7, 1919, by Heber J. Grant, at Salt Lake City, Utah, at age 45; died July 30, 1939, at Salt Lake City, Salt Lake Co., Utah, at age 66.

54. John Andreas Widtsoe — Born Jan. 31, 1872, at Daloe, Island of Froyen, Trondhjem, Norway, a son of John A. Widtsoe and Anna Karine Gaarden. Ordained apostle March. 17, 1921, by Heber J. Grant, at Salt Lake City, Utah, at age 49; died Nov. 29, 1952, at Salt Lake City, Salt Lake Co., Utah, at age 80.

55. Joseph Francis Merrill — Born Aug. 24, 1868, at Richmond, Cache Co., Utah, a son of Marriner Wood Merrill and Mariah Loenza Kingsbury. Ordained apostle Oct. 8, 1931, by Heber J. Grant at Salt Lake City, Utah, at age 63; died Feb. 3, 1952, at Salt Lake City, Salt Lake Co., Utah, 83.

56. Charles Albert Callis — Born May 4, 1865, at Dublin, Dublin Co., Ireland, a son of John Callis and Susanna Charlotte Quillam. Ordained apostle Oct. 12, 1933, by Heber J. Grant, at Salt Lake City, Utah, at age 68. Died Jan. 21, 1947, in Jacksonville, Duval Co., Florida, at age 81.

57. Joshua Reuben Clark Jr. — See FIRST COUNSELORS IN THE FIRST PRESIDENCY, No. 11.

58. Alonzo Arza Hinckley — Born April 23, 1870, at Cove Fort, Millard Co., Utah, a son of Ira Nathaniel Hinckley and Angeline Wilcox Noble. Ordained apostle Oct. 11, 1934, by Heber J. Grant, at Salt Lake City, Utah, at age 64; died Dec. 22, 1936, at Salt Lake City, Salt Lake Co., Utah, at age 66.

59. Albert Ernest Bowen — Born Oct. 32, 1875, at Henderson Creek, Oneida Co., Idaho, a son of David Bowen and Annie Schackelton. Ordained apostle April 8, 1937, by Heber J. Grant, at Salt Lake City, Utah, at age 61; died July 15, 1953, at Salt Lake City, Salt Lake Co., Utah, at age 77.

60. Sylvester Quayle Cannon — Born

June 10, 1877, at Salt Lake City, Utah, a son of George Quayle Cannon and Elisabeth Hoagland. Sustained as Presiding Bishop of the Church June 4, 1925; sustained as Associate to the Quorum of the Twelve Apostles April 6, 1938; ordained apostles April 14, 1938, by  Heber J. Grant, at Salt Lake City at age 60; sustained as a member of the Quorum of the Twelve Apostles April 6, 1939, at age 62; died May 29, 1943, at Salt Lake City, Salt Lake Co., Utah, at age 65.

61. Harold Bingham Lee — See PRESIDENTS OF THE CHURCH, No. 11.

62. Spencer Woolley Kimball — See PRESIDENTS OF THE CHURCH, No. 12.

63. Ezra Taft Benson — See p. 12.

64. Mark Edward Petersen — Born Nov. 7, 1900, at Salt Lake City, Utah, to Christian Petersen and Christine M. Andersen. Ordained apostle April 20, 1944, by Heber J. Grant at age 43; died Jan 11, 1984, at Salt Lake City, Salt Lake Co., Utah, at age 83.

65. Matthew Cowley — Born Aug. 2, 1897, at Preston, Franklin Co., Idaho, a son of Matthias Foss Cowley and Abbie Hyde. Ordained apostle Oct. 11, 1945, by George Albert Smith, at Salt Lake City, Utah, at age 48; died Dec. 13, 1953, at Los Angeles, Los Angeles Co., California, at age 56.

66. Henry Dinwoodey Moyle — See FIRST COUNSELORS IN THE FIRST PRESIDENCY, No 14.

67. Delbert Leon Stapley — Born Dec.

11, 1896, at Mesa, Maricopa Co., Ariz., a son of Orley S. Stapley and Polly M. Hunsaker. Ordained an apostle Oct. 5, 1950, by George Albert Smith, at Salt Lake City, Utah, at age 53; died Aug. 19, 1978, at Salt Lake City, Salt Lake Co., Utah, at age 81.

68. Marion George Romney — See FIRST COUNSELORS IN THE FIRST PRESIDENCY, No. 18.

69. LeGrand Richards — Born Feb. 6, 1886, at Farmington, Davis Co., Utah, a son of George Franklin Richards and Alice Almira Robinson. Sustained Presiding Bishop of the Church April 6, 1938; ordained apostle April 10, 1952, at age 66 by David O. McKay; died Jan. 11, 1983, at Salt Lake City, Salt Lake Co., Utah, at age 96.

70. Adam Samuel Bennion — Born Dec. 2, 1886, at Taylorsville, Salt Lake Co., Utah, a son of Joseph Bennion and Mary A. Sharp. Ordained apostle April 9, 1953, by David O. McKay at Salt Lake City, Utah, at age 66; died Feb. 11, 1958, at Salt Lake City, Salt Lake Co., Utah, at age 71.

71. Richard Louis Evans — Born March 23, 1906, at Salt Lake City, Utah, a son of John A. Evans and Florence Neslen. Sustained as a member of the First Council of the Seventy Oct. 7, 1938; ordained apostle Oct. 8, 1953, by David O. McKay, at Salt Lake City, at age 47; died Nov. 1, 1971, at Salt Lake City, Salt Lake Co., Utah, at age 65.

72. George Quayle Morris — Born Feb. 20, 1874, at Salt Lake City, Utah, a son of Elias Morris and Mary L. Walker. Sustained as Assistant to the Quorum of the Twelve Apostles Oct. 6, 1951, ordained apostle April 8, 1954, by David O. McKay, at Salt Lake City at age 80; died April 23, 1962, at Salt Lake City, Salt Lake Co., Utah, at age 88.

73. Hugh Brown Brown — See FIRST COUNSELORS IN THE FIRST PRESIDENCY, No. 15.

74. Howard William Hunter — See p. 15.

75. Gordon Bitner Hinckley — See p. 13.

76. Nathan Eldon Tanner — See FIRST COUNSELORS IN THE FIRST PRESIDENCY, No. 17.

77. Thomas Spencer Monson — See p. 13.

78. Boyd Kenneth Packer — See p. 15.

79. Marvin Jeremy Ashton — See p. 15.

80. Bruce Redd McConkie — Born July 29, 1915, to Oscar Walter and Vivian Redd McConkie at Ann Arbor, Washtenaw Co., Mich. Sustained to First Council of the Seventy Oct. 6, 1946; ordained an apostle Oct. 12, 1972, by Harold B. Lee, at age 57; died April 19, 1985, at Salt Lake City, Salt Lake Co., Utah, at age 69.

81. Lowell Tom Perry — See p. 16.

82. David Bruce Haight — See p. 16.

83. James Esdras Faust — See p. 16.

84. Neal Ash Maxwell — See p. 17.

85. Russell Marion Nelson — See p. 17.

86. Dallin Harris Oaks — See p. 17.

87. Melvin Russell Ballard — See p. 18

88. Joseph Bitner Wirthlin — See p. 18.

89. Richard Gordon Scott — See p. 18.

APOSTLES

(Who served other than as members of the Quorum of the Twelve Apostles)

1. Joseph Smith — See PRESIDENTS OF THE CHURCH, No. 1.

2. Oliver Cowdery — See ASSISTANT PRESIDENTS OF THE CHURCH, No. 1.

3. Hyrum Smith — See ASSISTANT PRESIDENTS OF THE CHURCH, No. 2.

4. Amasa Mason Lyman — See OTHER COUNSELORS IN THE FIRST PRESIDENCY, No. 3.

5. Jedediah Morgan Grant — See SECOND COUNSELORS IN THE FIRST PRESIDENCY, No. 5

6. John Willard Young — See FIRST COUNSELORS IN THE FIRST PRESIDENCY, No. 4

7. Daniel Hanmer Wells — See SECOND COUNSELORS IN THE FIRST PRESIDENCY, No. 6

8. Joseph Angell Young — Born Oct. 14, 1834, in Kirtland, Geauga Co., Ohio, a son of Brigham Young and Mary Ann Angell. Ordained apostle Feb. 4, 1864, by Brigham Young, at age 29; died Aug. 5, 1875, at Manti, Sanpete Co., Utah, at age 40.

9. Brigham Young Jr. — See OTHER COUNSELORS IN THE FIRST PRESIDENCY, No. 6.

10. Joseph F. Smith — See PRESIDENTS OF THE CHURCH, No. 6.

11. Sylvester Quayle Cannon — See THE TWELVE APOSTLES OF THE CHURCH, No. 60.

12. Alvin Rulon Dyer — See OTHER COUNSELORS IN THE FIRST PRESIDENCY, No. 13.

PATRIARCHS TO THE CHURCH

1. Joseph Smith Sr. — See ASSISTANT COUNSELORS IN THE FIRST PRESIDENCY, No. 2.

2. Hyrum Smith — See ASSISTANT PRESIDENTS OF THE CHURCH, No. 2.

William Smith — See COUNCIL OF THE TWELVE, No. 9. Ordained Patriarch to the Church May 24, 1845, by the Twelve and then gave patriarchal blessings, but was rejected by the Church membership at the General Conference held Oct. 6, 1845.

3. John Smith — See ASSISTANT COUNSELORS IN THE FIRST PRESIDENCY, No. 4.

4. John Smith — Born Sept. 22, 1832, at Kirtland, Geauga Co., Ohio, the oldest son of Hyrum Smith and Jerusha Barden. Ordained patriarch to the Church Feb. 18, 1855, by Brigham Young, at age 22; died Nov. 6, 1911, at Salt Lake City, Salt Lake Co., Utah, at age 79.

5. Hyrum Gibbs Smith — Born July 8, 1879, at South Jordan, Salt Lake Co., Utah, the oldest son of Hyrum Fisher Smith and Annie Maria Gibbs. Ordained a high priest and patriarch to the Church May 9, 1912, by Joseph F. Smith, at age 32; died Feb. 4, 1932, at Salt Lake City, Salt Lake Co., Utah, at age 52.

(From 1932 to 1937, no patriarch to the Church was sustained.)

George Franklin Richards — See THE COUNCIL OF THE TWELVE, No. 45.

6. Joseph Fielding Smith — Born Jan. 30, 1899, at Salt Lake City, Utah, the oldest son of Hyrum Mack Smith and Ida E. Bowman. Ordained a high priest and patriarch to the Church Oct. 8, 1942, by Heber J. Grant; at age 43; released Oct. 6, 1946, due to ill health; died Aug. 29, 1964, in Salt Lake City, Salt Lake Co., Utah, at age 65.

7. Eldred Gee Smith — See p. 37.

(No patriarch to the Church has been sustained since Oct. 6, 1979.)

ASSISTANTS TO THE TWELVE

1. Marion George Romney — See FIRST COUNSELORS IN THE FIRST PRESIDENCY, No. 18.

2. Thomas Evans McKay — Born Oct. 29, 1875, at Huntsville, Weber Co., Utah, a son of David McKay and Jennette Eveline Evans. Ordained a high priest July 26, 1908, by George F. Richards; sustained as Assistant to the Quorum of the Twelve Apostles April 6, 1941, and set apart May 23, 1941, by Heber J. Grant, at Salt Lake City, at age 65; died Jan. 15, 1958, at Salt Lake City, Salt Lake Co., Utah, at age 82.

3. Clifford Earl Young — Born Dec. 7, 1883, at Salt Lake City, Utah, a son of Seymour Bicknell Young and Ann Elizabeth Riter. Ordained a high priest July 1, 1928, by Heber J. Grant; sustained as Assistant to the Quorum of the Twelve Apostles April 6, 1941, and set apart May 23, 1941, by President Grant, at Salt Lake City, at age 57; died Aug. 21, 1958, at Salt Lake City, Salt Lake Co., Utah, at age 74.

4. Alma Sonne — SEE FIRST QUORUM OF THE SEVENTY, No. 8.

5. Nicholas Groesbeck Smith — Born June 20, 1881, at Salt Lake City, Utah, the son of John Henry Smith and Josephine Groesbeck. Ordained a high priest Aug. 1, 1921, by Rudger Clawson; sustained an Assistant to the Quorum of the Twelve Apostles April 6, 1941, set apart Oct. 1, 1941, by Heber J. Grant at Salt Lake City, at age 60; died Oct. 27, 1945, at Salt Lake City, Salt Lake Co., Utah, at age 64.

6. George Quayle Morris — See THE COUNCIL OF THE TWELVE, No. 72.

7. Stayner Richards — Born Dec. 20, 1885, at Salt Lake City, Utah, a son of Stephen L Richards and Emma Louise Stayner. Ordained a high priest Feb. 24, 1914, by George F. Richards; sustained as Assistant to the Quorum of the Twelve Apostles Oct. 6, 1951, and set apart Oct. 11, 1951, by David O. McKay at Salt Lake City, at age 65; died May 28, 1953, at Salt Lake City, Salt Lake Co., Utah, at age 67.

8. ElRay LaVar Christiansen — Born July 13, 1897, at Mayfield, Sanpete Co., Utah, a son of Parley Christiansen and Dorthea C. Jensen. Ordained a high priest Oct. 22, 1933, by George F. Richards; sustained as Assistant to the Quorum of the Twelve Apostles Oct. 6, 1951, and set apart Oct. 11, 1951, by Stephen L Richards at Salt Lake City, at age 54; died Dec. 1, 1975, at Salt Lake City, Salt Lake Co., Utah, at age 78.

9. John Longden — Born Nov. 4, 1898, at Oldham, Lancashire Co., England, a son of Thomas Johnson Longden and Lizetta Taylor. Ordained a high priest Sept. 27, 1925, by Rudger Clawson; sustained as Assistant to the Quorum of the Twelve Apostles Oct. 6, 1951, and set apart Oct. 11, 1951, by J. Reuben Clark at Salt Lake City, at age 52; died Aug.

30, 1969, at Salt Lake City, Salt Lake Co., Utah, at age 70.

10. Hugh Brown Brown — See FIRST COUNSELORS IN THE FIRST PRESIDENCY, No. 15.

11. Sterling Welling Sill — See p. 37.

12. Gordon Bitner Hinckley — See p. 13.

13. Henry Dixon Taylor — See FIRST QUORUM OF THE SEVENTY, NO. 10.

14. William James Critchlow Jr. — Born Aug. 21, 1892, at Brigham City, Box Elder Co., Utah, a son of William James Critchlow and Anna C. Gregerson. Ordained a high priest Dec. 16, 1934, by George F. Richards; sustained as Assistant to the Quorum of the Twelve Apostles Oct. 11, 1958, and set apart Oct. 16, 1958, by David O. McKay, at Salt Lake City, at age 66; died Aug. 29, 1968, at Ogden, Weber Co., Utah, at age 76.

15. Alvin Rulon Dyer — See OTHER COUNSELORS IN THE FIRST PRESIDENCY, No. 13.

16. Nathan Eldon Tanner — See FIRST COUNSELORS IN THE FIRST PRESIDENCY, No. 17.

17. Franklin Dewey Richards — See PRESIDENCY OF THE FIRST QUORUM OF THE SEVENTY, No. 1.

18. Theodore Moyle Burton — See p. 22.

19. Henry Thorpe Beal Isaacson — See OTHER COUNSELORS IN THE FIRST PRESIDENCY, No. 12.

20. Boyd Kenneth Packer — See p. 15.

21. Bernard Park Brockbank — See p. 38.

22. James Alfred Cullimore — See FIRST QUORUM OF THE SEVENTY, No. 14.

23. Marion Duff Hanks — See p. 20.

24. Marvin Jeremy Ashton — See p. 15.

25. Joseph Anderson — See p. 38.

26. David Bruce Haight — See p. 16.

27. William Hunter Bennett — See FIRST QUORUM OF THE SEVENTY, No. 16.

28. John Henry Vandenberg — See p. 38.

29. Robert Leatham Simpson — See p. 23.

30. Oscar Leslie Stone — See FIRST

QUORUM OF THE SEVENTY, No. 19.

31. James Esdras Faust — See p. 16.

32. Lowell Tom Perry — See p. 16.

33. John Thomas Fyans — See p. 23.

34. Neal Ash Maxwell — See p. 17.

35. William Grant Bangerter — See p. 20.

36. Robert Dean Hales — See p. 36.

37. Adney Yoshio Komatsu — See p. 23.

38. Joseph Bitner Wirthlin — See p. 18.

FIRST COUNCIL OF THE SEVENTY

1. Hazen Aldrich — Chosen and ordained one of the first Seven Presidents Feb. 28, 1835; released April 6, 1837, having previously been ordained a high priest.

2. Joseph Young — Born April 7, 1797, at Hopkinton, Middlesex Co., Massachusetts, a son of John Young and Abigail Howe. Ordained a seventy Feb. 28. 1835, under the hands of Joseph Smith, Sidney Rigdon and Frederick G. Williams; chosen and ordained one of the First Seven Presidents Feb. 28, 1835, at age 37; died July 16, 1881, at Salt Lake City, Salt Lake Co., Utah, at age 84.

3. Levi Ward Hancock — Born April 7, 1803, at Springfield, Hampden, Co., Massachusetts, a son of Thomas Hancock and Amy Ward. Ordained a seventy Feb. 28, 1835, under the hands of Joseph Smith, Sidney Rigdon and Frederick G. Williams; chosen and ordained one of the First Seven Presidents Feb. 28, 1835, at age 31; released April 6, 1837, having supposedly previously been ordained a high priest; restored to former place in the First Council Sept. 3, 1837, as he had not been ordained a high priest; died June 10, 1882, at Washington, Washington Co., Utah, at age 79.

4. Leonard Rich — Chosen and ordained one of the first Seven Presidents Feb. 28, 1835; released April 6, 1837, having previously been ordained a high priest.

5. Zebedee Coltrin — Born Sept. 7, 1804, at Ovid, Seneca Co., New York, a son of John Coltrin, Jr. and Sarah Graham. Chosen and ordained one of the First Seven Presidents Feb. 28, 1835, at age 30; released April, 6 1837, having previously been ordained a high priest; died July 20, 1887, at Spanish Fork, Utah Co., Utah, at age 82.

6. Lyman Royal Sherman — Born May 22, 1804, at Salem, Essex Co., Massachusetts, a son of Elkanah Sherman and Asenath Hulbert. Chosen and ordained one of the First Seven Presidents Feb. 28, 1835, at age 30, released April 6, 1837, having previously been ordained a high priest; died Jan. 27, 1839, at age 34.

7. Sylvester Smith — Chosen and ordained one of the First Seven Presidents Feb. 28, 1835; released April 6, 1837; having previously been ordained a high priest.

8. John Gould — Born May 11, 1808. Ordained a seventy and set apart as one of the First Seven Presidents April 6, 1837, at age 28 by Sidney Rigdon and Hyrum Smith; released Sept. 3, 1837, to become a high priest. Died May 9, 1851, at age 42.

9. James Foster — Born April 1, 1775, at Morgan Co., New Hampshire. Ordained a seventy April 6, 1837, under the hands of Sidney Rigdon and Hyrum Smith; set apart as one of the First Seven Presidents April 6, 1837, at age 62; died Dec. 21, 1841, at Morgan Co., Illinois, at age 66.

10. Daniel Sanborn Miles — Born July 23, 1772, at Sanbornton, Belknap Co., New Hampshire, a son of Josiah Miles and Marah Sanborn. Ordained a seventy April 6, 1837, by Hazen Aldrich; set apart as one of the First Seven Presidents April 6, 1837, at age 64, by Sidney Rigdon and Hyrum Smith; died in fall of 1845, at Hancock Co., Illinois, at age 73.

11. Josiah Butterfield — Born March 13 or 18, 1795, at Saco, Maine, a son of Abel Butterfield and Mary or Mercy -----. Ordained a seventy April 6, 1837, under the hands of Sidney Rigdon and Hyrum Smith; set apart as one of the First Seven Presidents April 6, 1837, at age 42; excommunicated Oct. 7, 1844, died at Monterey Co., Calif., April 1871, at age 76.

12. Salmon Gee — Born Oct. 16, 1792, at Lyme, New London Co., Connecticut, a son of Zopher Gee and Esther Beckwith. Ordained a seventy April 6, 1837, under the hands of Sidney Rigdon and Hyrum Smith; set apart as one of the First Seven Presidents April 6, 1837, at age 44; fellowship withdrawn March 6, 1838; died Sept. 13, 1845, at Ambrosia, Lee Co., Iowa, at age 52; posthumously reinstated Sept. 14, 1967.

13. John Gaylord — Born July 12, 1797, in Pennsylvania, a son of Chauncey Gaylord. Ordained a seventy Dec. 20, 1836, by Hazen Aldrich; set apart as one of the First Seven Presidents April 6, 1837, at age 39 by Sidney Rigdon and others; excommunicated Jan. 13, 1838; rejoined the Church at Nauvoo, Illinois, Oct. 5, 1839; died July 17, 1878, at age 81.

14. Henry Harriman — Born June 9, 1804, at Rowley, Essex Co., Massachusetts, a son of Enoch Harriman and Sarah Brocklebank. Ordained a seventy March 1835, under the hands of Joseph Smith and Sidney Rigdon; set apart as one of the First Seven Presidents Feb. 6, 1838, at age 33, by Joseph Young and others; died May 17, 1891, at Huntington, Emery Co., Utah, at age 86.

15. Zera Pulsipher — Born June 24, 1789, at Rockingham, Windham Co., Vermont, a son of John Pulsipher and Elizabeth Dutton. Ordained a seventy March 6, 1838, under the hands of Joseph Young and James Foster; set apart as one of the First Seven Presidents March 6, 1838, at age 48; released April 12, 1862; died Jan. 1, 1872, Hebron, Washington Co., Utah, at age 81.

Roger Orton was excommunicated Nov. 30, 1837; returned to the Church; sustained as one of the First Seven Presidents April 7, 1845, but was never set apart and did not function; dropped from this position Oct. 6, 1845.

16. Albert Perry Rockwood — Born June 5, 1805, at Holliston, Middlesex Co., Massachusetts, a son of Luther Rockwood and Ruth Perry. Ordained a seventy Jan. 5, 1839, under the hands of Joseph Young, Henry Harriman and Zera Pulsipher; set apart as one of the First Seven Presidents Dec. 2, 1845, at age 40, by Brigham Young and others; died Nov. 26, 1879, at Sugar House, Salt Lake Co., Utah, at age 74.

17. Benjamin Lynn Clapp — Born Aug. 19, 1814, at West Huntsville, Madison Co., Alabama, a son of Ludwig Lewis Clapp and Margaret Ann Loy. Ordained a seventy Oct. 20, 1844, under the hands of Joseph Young and Levi W. Hancock; set apart as one of the First Seven Presidents Dec. 2, 1845, at age 31, by Brigham Young and others; excommunicated April 7, 1859; died in 1860 in California, at age 46.

18. Jedediah Morgan Grant — See SECOND COUNSELORS IN THE FIRST PRESIDENCY, No. 5.

19. Horace Sunderlin Eldredge — Born Feb. 6, 1816, at Brutus, Cayuga Co., New York, a son of Alanson Eldredge and Esther Sunderlin. Ordained a seventy Oct. 13, 1844, by Joseph Young; sustained as one of the First Seven Presidents Oct. 7, 1854, at age 38; died Sept. 6, 1888, at Salt Lake City, Salt Lake Co., Utah, at age 72.

20. Jacob Gates — Born March 9, 1811, at Saint Johnsbury, Caledonia Co., Vermont, a son of Thomas Gates and Patty Plumley. Ordained a seventy Dec. 19, 1838, under the hands of Joseph Smith and Sidney Rigdon; sustained as one of the First Seven Presidents April 6, 1860, at age 51; set apart Oct. 8, 1862, by Orson Hyde; died April 14, 1892, at Provo, Utah Co., Utah, at age 81.

21. John Van Cott — Born Sept. 7, 1814, at Canaan, Columbia Co, New York, a son of Losee Van Cott and Lovinia Pratt. Ordained a seventy Feb. 25, 1847, by Joseph Young; sustained as one of the First Seven Presidents Oct. 8, 1862, at age 48; set apart by John Taylor; died Feb. 18, 1883, at Salt Lake City, Salt Lake Co., Utah, at age 68.

22. William Whittaker Taylor — Born Sept. 11, 1853, at Salt Lake City, Utah, a son of John Taylor and Harriet Whittaker. Ordained a seventy Oct. 11, 1875, by Orson Pratt; sustained as one of the First Seven Presidents April 7, 1880, at age 26; set apart by John Taylor; died Aug. 1, 1884, at Salt Lake City, Salt Lake Co., Utah, at age 30.

23. Abraham Hoagland Cannon — See

THE COUNCIL OF THE TWELVE, No. 37.

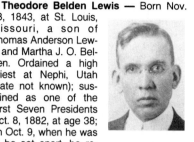

Theodore Belden Lewis — Born Nov. 18, 1843, at St. Louis, Missouri, a son of Thomas Anderson Lewis and Martha J. O. Belden. Ordained a high priest at Nephi, Utah (date not known); sustained as one of the First Seven Presidents Oct. 8, 1882, at age 38; on Oct. 9, when he was to be set apart, he reported that he was already a high priest, so he was not set apart and did not function in this position.

24. Seymour Bicknell Young — Born Oct. 3, 1837, at Kirtland, Geauga Co., Ohio, a son of Joseph Young and Jane Adeline Bicknell. Ordained a seventy Feb. 18, 1857, by Edmund Ellsworth; set apart as one of the First Seven Presidents Oct. 14, 1882, at age 45; sustained as one of the First Seven Presidents April 8, 1883; set apart by Franklin D. Richards; died Dec. 15, 1924, at Salt Lake City, Salt Lake Co., Utah, at age 87.

25. Christian Daniel Fjelsted — Born Feb. 20, 1829, at Amagar, Sundbyvester Co., Copenhagen, Denmark, a son of Hendrick Ludvig Fjelsted and Ann Catrine Hendriksen. Ordained a seventy Feb. 5, 1859, by William H. Walker; sustained as one of the First Seven Presidents April 6, 1884, at age 55; set apart by Wilford Woodruff; died Dec. 23, 1905, at Salt Lake City, Salt Lake Co., Utah, at age 76.

26. John Morgan — Born Aug. 8, 1842, at Greensburg, Decatur Co., Indiana, a son of Gerrard Morgan and Ann Eliza Hamilton. Ordained a seventy Oct. 8, 1875, by Joseph Young; sustained as one of the First Seven Presidents Oct. 5, 1884, at age 42; set apart by Wilford Woodruff; died Aug. 14, 1894, at Preston, Franklin Co., Idaho, at age 52.

27. Brigham Henry Roberts — Born March 13, 1857, at Warrington, Lancashire Co., England, a son of Benjamin Roberts and Ann Everington. Ordained a seventy March 8, 1877, by Nathan T. Porter. Sustained as one of the First Seven Presidents Oct. 7, 1888, at age 31; died Sept. 27, 1933, at Salt Lake City, Salt Lake Co., Utah, at age 76.

28. George Reynolds — Born Jan. 1, 1842, at Marylebone, London Co., London, England, a son of George Reynolds and Julia Ann Tautz. Ordained a seventy March 18, 1866, by Israel Barlow; sustained as one of the First Seven Presidents April 5, 1890, at age 48; set apart by Lorenzo Snow; died Aug. 9, 1909, at Salt Lake City, Salt Lake Co., Utah, at age 67.

29. Jonathan Golden Kimball — Born June 9, 1853, at Salt Lake City, Utah, a son of Heber Chase Kimball and Christeen Golden. Ordained a seventy July 21, 1886, by William M. Allred; sustained as one of the First Seven Presidents April 5, 1892, at age 38; set apart by Francis M. Lyman; killed in an automobile accident Sept. 2, 1938, near Reno, Nevada, at age 85.

30. Rulon Seymour Wells — Born July 7, 1854 at Salt Lake City, Utah, a son of Daniel Hanmer Wells and Louisa Free. Ordained a seventy Oct. 22, 1875, by Brigham Young; sustained as one of the First Seven Presidents April 5, 1893, at age 38; set apart by George Q. Cannon; died May 7, 1941, at Salt Lake City, Salt Lake Co., Utah, at age 86.

31. Edward Stevenson — Born May 1, 1820, at Gibraltar, Spain, a son of Joseph Stevenson and Elizabeth Stevens. Ordained a seventy May 1, 1844, by Joseph Young; sustained as one of the First Seven Presidents Oct. 7, 1894, at age 74; set apart by Brigham Young; died Jan. 27, 1897, at Salt Lake City, Salt Lake Co., Utah, at age 76.

32. Joseph William McMurrin — Born Sept. 5, 1858, at Tooele, Tooele Co., Utah, a son of Joseph McMurrin and Margaret Leaning. Ordained a seventy April 21, 1884, by Royal Barney; sustained as one of the First Seven Presidents Oct. 5, 1897, and set apart Jan. 21, 1898, at Liverpool, England, at age 39, by Anthon H. Lund; died Oct. 24, 1932, at Los Angeles, Los Angeles Co., California, at age 74.

33. Charles Henry Hart — Born July 5, 1866, at Bloomington, Bear Lake Co., Idaho, a son of James Henry Hart and Sabina Scheib. Ordained a seventy Aug. 10, 1890, by John Henry Smith; sustained as one of the First Seven Presidents April 9, 1906, at age 39; set apart by Joseph F. Smith; died Sept. 29, 1934, at Salt Lake City, Salt Lake Co., Utah, at age 68.

34. Levi Edgar Young — Born Feb. 2, 1874, at Salt Lake City, Utah, a son of Seymour Bicknell Young and Ann Elizabeth Riter. Ordained a seventy June 18, 1897, by Seymour B. Young; sustained as one of the First Seven Presidents Oct. 6, 1909; set apart Jan. 23, 1910, at age 36, by John Henry Smith; died Dec. 13, 1963, at Salt Lake City, Salt Lake Co., Utah, at age 89.

35. Rey Lucero Pratt — Born Oct. 11, 1878, at Salt Lake City, Utah, a son of Helaman Pratt and Emeline Victoria Billingsley. Ordained a seventy Sept. 23, 1911, by Rulon S. Wells; sustained as one of the First Seven Presidents Jan. 29, 1925, and set apart April 7, 1925, at age 46, by Anthony W. Ivins; died April 14, 1931, at Salt Lake City, Salt Lake Co., Utah, at age 52.

36. Antoine Ridgeway Ivins — Born May 11, 1881, at St. George, Washington Co., Utah, a son of Anthony Woodward Ivins and Elizabeth A. Snow. Ordained a seventy Dec. 28, 1913, by Fred E. Barker; sustained as one of the First Seven Presidents Oct. 4, 1931, at age 50; ordained a high priest June 11, 1961, by David O. McKay; died Oct. 18, 1967, at Salt Lake City, Salt Lake Co., Utah, at age 86.

37. Samuel Otis Bennion — Born June 9, 1874, at Taylorsville, Salt Lake Co., Utah, a son of John Rowland Bennion and Emma Jane Terry. Ordained a seventy March 14, 1904, by Samuel Gerrard; sustained as one of the First Seven Presidents April 6, 1933, at age 58; set apart by Heber J. Grant; died March 8, 1945, at Salt Lake City, Salt Lake Co., Utah, at age 70.

38. John Harris Taylor — Born June 28, 1875, at Salt Lake City, Utah, a son of Thomas E. Taylor and Emma L. Harris. Ordained a seventy Jan. 24, 1896, by Heber J. Grant; sustained as one of the First Seven Presidents Oct. 6, 1933, at age 58; set apart by Heber J. Grant; died May 28, 1946, at Salt Lake City, Salt Lake Co., Utah, at age 71.

39. Rufus Kay Hardy — Born May 28, 1878, at Salt Lake City, Utah, a son of Rufus H. Hardy and Annie Kay. Ordained a seventy July 2, 1897, by John Henry Smith; sustained a member of the First Council of the Seventy Oct. 6, 1934, and set apart Feb. 7, 1935, at age 56, by Heber J. Grant; died March 7, 1945, at Salt Lake City, Salt Lake Co., Utah, at age 66.

40. Richard Louis Evans — See THE COUNCIL OF THE TWELVE, No. 71.

41. Oscar Ammon Kirkham — Born Jan. 22, 1880, at Lehi, Utah Co., Utah, a son of James Kirkham and Martha Mercer. Ordained a seventy Feb. 26, 1905, by Joseph W. McMurrin; sustained a member of the First Council of the Seventy Oct. 5, 1941, at age 61; set apart by Heber J. Grant; died March 10, 1958; at Salt Lake City, Salt Lake Co., Utah, at age 78.

42. Seymour Dilworth Young — SEE FIRST QUORUM OF THE SEVENTY, No. 24.

43. Milton Reed Hunter — Born Oct. 25, 1902, at Holden, Millard Co., Utah, a son of John E. Hunter and Margaret Teeples. Ordained a seventy Aug. 31, 1928, by Rulon S. Wells; sustained a member of the First Council of the Seventy April 6, 1945, at age 42; ordained a high priest June 11, 1961, by David O. McKay; died June 27, 1975, at Salt Lake City, Salt Lake Co., Utah, at age 72.

44. Bruce Redd McConkie — See THE COUNCIL OF THE TWELVE, No. 80.

45. Marion Duff Hanks — See p. 20.

46. Albert Theodore Tuttle — See THE PRESIDENCY OF THE FIRST QUORUM OF THE SEVENTY, NO. 4.

47. Paul Harold Dunn — See p. 22.

48. Hartman Rector Jr. — See p. 22.

49. Loren Charles Dunn — See p. 22.

50. Rex Dee Pinegar — See p. 23.

51. Gene Raymond Cook — See p. 24.

On Oct. 3, 1975, the First Quorum of the Seventy was reconstituted with the sustaining of three members, Elders Charles Didier, William R. Bradford, and George P. Lee. Four additional members, Elders Carlos E. Asay, M. Russell Ballard, John H. Groberg, and Jacob de Jager, were sustained April 3, 1976.

On Oct. 1, 1976, the members of the First Council of the Seventy and the Assistants to the Twelve were released and added to the First Quorum of the Seventy. A new presidency of the First Quorum of the Seventy was sustained, and the position of members of the quorum revised.

PRESIDENCY OF THE FIRST QUORUM OF THE SEVENTY

1. Franklin Dewey Richards — Born Nov. 17, 1900, in Ogden, Weber Co., Utah, to Charles C. Richards and Louisa L. Peery. Sustained as Assistant to the Twelve Oct. 8, 1960, at age 59; sustained to First Quorum of the Seventy Oct. 1, 1976; served in Presidency of the First Quorum of the Seventy, Oct. 1, 1976, to Oct. 1, 1983; died Nov. 13, 1987, at Salt Lake City, Salt Lake Co., Utah, at age 86.

2. James Esdras Faust — See p. 16.

3. John Thomas Fyans — See p. 23.

4. Albert Theodore Tuttle — Born March 2, 1919, in Manti, Sanpete Co., Utah, to Albert M. Tuttle and Clarice Beal.Sustained to First Council of the Seventy April 6, 1958, at age 39, and to First Quorum of the Seventy Oct. 1, 1976; served in Presidency of the First Quorum of the Seventy from Oct. 1, 1976 to Feb. 22, 1980; died Nov. 28, 1986, at Salt Lake City, Salt Lake Co., Utah, at age 67.

5. Neal Ash Maxwell — See p. 17.

6. Marion Duff Hanks — See p. 20.

7. Paul Harold Dunn — See p. 22.

8. William Grant Bangerter — See p. 20.

9. Carlos Egan Asay — See p. 25.

10. Melvin Russell Ballard Jr. — See p. 18.

11. Dean LeRoy Larsen — See p. 20.

12. Royden Glade Derrick — See p. 26.

13. George Homer Durham — Born Feb. 4, 1911, at Parowan, Iron Co., Utah, to George H. Durham and Mary Ellen Marsden. Sustained to First Quorum of the Seventy April 2, 1977, at age 66; sustained to presidency of quorum on Oct. 1, 1981; died Jan. 10, 1985, at Salt Lake City, Salt Lake County, Utah, at age 73.

14. Richard Gordon Scott — See p. 18.

15. Marion Duff Hanks — See p. 20.

16. William Grant Bangerter — See p. 20.

17. Jack H Goaslind Jr. — See p. 28.

18. Robert LeGrand Backman — See page 21.

19. Joseph Bitner Wirthlin — See p. 18.

20. Hugh Wallace Pinnock — See p. 21.

21. James Martin Paramore — See p. 21.

22. John Richard Clarke — See p. 21.

FIRST QUORUM OF THE SEVENTY

1. Franklin Dewey Richards — See PRESIDENCY OF THE FIRST QUORUM OF THE SEVENTY, No. 1

2. James Esdras Faust — See p. 16.

3. John Thomas Fyans — See p. 23.

4. Albert Theodore Tuttle — See PRESIDENCY OF THE FIRST QUORUM OF THE SEVENTY, No. 4

5. Neal Ash Maxwell — See p. 17.

6. Marion Duff Hanks — See p. 20.

7. Paul Harold Dunn — See p. 22.

8. Alma Sonne — Born March 5, 1884, at Logan, Cache Co., Utah, a son of Niels C. Sonne and Elisa Peterson. Ordained a high priest Feb. 2, 1913, by Anthony W. Ivins; sustained as Assistant to the Quorum of the Twelve Apostles April 6, 1941, and set apart May 26, 1941, by Heber J. Grant at Salt Lake City, at age 57;  sustained a member of the First Quorum of the Seventy Oct. 1, 1976; died Nov. 27, 1977, at Logan, Cache Co., Utah, at age 93.

9. Sterling Welling Sill — See p. 37.

10. Henry Dixon Taylor — Born Nov. 22, 1903, in Provo, Utah Co., Utah, to Arthur N. Taylor and Maria Dixon. Sustained Assistant to the Twelve April 6, 1958, at age 55; to First Quorum of the Seventy Oct. 1, 1976. Named emeritus General Authority Sept. 30, 1978;  died Feb. 24, 1987, at Salt Lake City, Salt Lake Co., Utah, at age 84.

11. Alvin Rulon Dyer — See OTHER COUNSELORS IN THE FIRST PRESIDENCY, No. 13.

12. Theodore Moyle Burton — See p. 22.

13. Bernard Park Brockbank — See p. 38.

14. James Alfred Cullimore — Born Jan. 17, 1906, at Lindon, Utah Co.,Utah, to Albert Lorenzo Cullimore and Luella Keetch. Sustained an Assistant to the Quorum of the Twelve Apostles April 6, 1966, at age 60, and to the First Quorum of the Seventy Oct. 1, 1976.  Named emeritus General Authority Sept. 30, 1978; died June 14, 1986, at Salt Lake City, Salt Lake Co., Utah, at age 80.

15. Joseph Anderson — See p. 38.

16. William Hunter Bennett — Born Nov. 5, 1910, at Taber, Alberta, Canada, a son of William Alvin Bennett and Mary Walker. Sustained as Assistant to the Quorum of Twelve Apostles, April 6, 1970; sustained to First Quorum of the Seventy Oct. 1, 1976, at age 65; died July 23, 1980, at Bountiful, Davis Co., Utah, at age 69.

17. John Henry Vandenberg — See p. 38.

18. Robert Leatham Simpson — See p. 23.

19. Oscar Leslie Stone — Born May 28, 1903, at Chapin, Idaho, to Frank J. Stone and Mable Crandall. Sustained Oct. 6, 1972, as an Assistant to the Quorum of the Twelve Apostles at age 69, and Oct. 1, 1976, to the First Quorum of the Seventy at age 73. Named emeritus General Authority Oct. 4, 1980. Died April

26, 1986, at Salt Lake City, Salt Lake Co., Utah, at age 82.

20. William Grant Bangerter — See p. 20.

21. Robert Dean Hales — See p. 36.

22. Adney Yoshio Komatsu — See p. 23.

23. Joseph Bitner Wirthlin — See p. 18.

24. Seymour Dilworth Young — Born Sept. 7, 1897, at Salt Lake City, Salt Lake Co., Utah, a son of Seymour Bicknell Young Jr. and Carlie Louine Clawson. Sustained a member of the First Council of the Seventy April 6, 1945, at age 47; sustained a member of the First Quorum of the Seventy Oct. 1, 1976; named  emeritus General Authority Sept. 30, 1978; died July 9, 1981, at Salt Lake City, Salt Lake Co., Utah, at age 84.

25. Hartman Rector Jr. — See p. 22.

26. Loren Charles Dunn — See p. 22.

27. Rex Dee Pinegar — See p. 23.

28. Gene Raymond Cook — See p. 24.

29. Charles Amand Andre Didier — See p. 24.

30. William Rawsel Bradford — See p. 24.

31. George Patrick Lee — See p. 24.

32. Carlos Egan Asay — See p. 25.

33. Melvin Russell Ballard Jr. — See p. 18.

34. John Holbrook Groberg — See p. 25.

35. Jacob deJager — See p. 25.

36. Vaughn J Featherstone — See p. 25.

37. Dean Le Roy Larsen — See p. 20.

38. Royden Glade Derrick — See p. 26.

39. Robert Earl Wells — See p. 26.

40. George Homer Durham — See PRESIDENCY OF THE FIRST QUORUM OF THE SEVENTY, No. 13

41. James Martin Paramore — See p. 21.

42. Richard Gordon Scott — See p. 18.

43. Hugh Wallace Pinnock — See p. 21.

44. Friedrich Enzio Busche — See p. 26.

45. Yoshihiko Kikuchi — See p. 26.

46. Ronald Eugene Poelman — See p. 27.

47. Derek Alfred Cuthbert — See p. 27.

48. Robert LeGrand Backman — See p. 21.

49. Rex Cropper Reeve Sr. — See p. 27.

50. Fred Burton Howard — See p. 27.

51. Teddy Eugene Brewerton — See p. 28.

52. Jack H Goaslind Jr. — See p. 28.

53. Angel Abrea — See p. 28.

54. John Kay Carmack — See p. 28.

55. Russell Carl Taylor — See p. 29.

56. Robert B Harbertson — See p. 29.

57. Devere Harris — See p. 29.

58. Spencer Hamlin Osborn — See p. 29.

59. Philip Tadje Sonntag — See p. 30.

60. John Sonnenberg — See p. 30.

61. Ferril Arthur Kay — See p. 30.

PRESIDING BISHOPS

1. Edward Partridge — Born Aug. 27, 1793, at Pittsfield, Berkshire Co., Massachusetts, a son of William Partridge and Jemima Bidwell. Ordained a high priest June 6, 1831, by Lyman Wight; called by revelation to be the First Bishop of the Church Feb. 4, 1831, at age 38 (D&C 41:9); died May 27, 1840, at Nauvoo, Hancock Co., Illinois, at age 47.

2. Newel Kimball Whitney — Born Feb. 5, 1795, at Marlborough, Windham Co., Vermont, a son of Samuel Whitney and Susanna Kimball. Called by revelation to be the First Bishop of Kirtland (D&C 72:8); sustained as First Bishop in the Church Oct. 7, 1844, at age 49; sustained as Presiding Bishop of the Church April 6, 1847; died Sept. 23, 1850, at Salt Lake City, Salt Lake Co., Utah, at age 55.

George Miller — Born Nov. 25, 1794, at County of Orange, Virginia, a son of John Miller and Margaret Pfeiffer. Sustained as Second Bishop of the Church Oct. 7, 1844, at age 49; dropped prior to 1847; disfellowshipped Oct. 20, 1848.

3. Edward Hunter — Born June 22, 1793, at Newton, Delaware Co., Pennsylvania, a son of Edward Hunter and Hannah Maris.

Ordained a high priest Nov. 23, 1844, by Brigham Young; sustained as Presiding Bishop of the Church April 7, 1851, at age 58; died Oct. 16, 1883, at Salt Lake City, Salt Lake Co., Utah, at age 90.

4. William Bowker Preston — Born Nov. 24, 1830, at Halifax, Franklin Co., Virginia, a son of Christopher Preston and Martha Mitchell Clayton. Ordained a high priest Nov. 14, 1859, by Orson Hyde; sustained as Presiding Bishop of the Church April 6, 1884, at age 53; released due to ill health Dec. 4, 1907; died Aug. 2, 1908, at Salt Lake City, Salt Lake Co., Utah, at age 78.

5. Charles Wilson Nibley — See SECOND COUNSELORS IN THE FIRST PRESIDENCY, No. 13.

6. Sylvester Quayle Cannon — See THE COUNCIL OF THE TWELVE, No. 60.

7. LeGrand Richards — See THE COUNCIL OF THE TWELVE, No. 69.

8. Joseph Leopold Wirthlin — Born Aug. 14, 1893, at Salt Lake City, Salt Lake Co., Utah, a son of Joseph Wirthlin and Emma Hillstead. Ordained a high priest Feb. 24, 1926, by Charles W. Nibley; sustained as second counselor to the Presiding Bishop April 6, 1938, at age 44; sustained as first counselor to the Presiding Bishop Dec. 12, 1946; sustained as Presiding Bishop of the Church April 6, 1952, at age 58; released Sept. 30, 1961; died Jan. 25, 1963, at Salt Lake City, Salt Lake Co., Utah, at age 69.

9. John Henry Vandenberg — See p. 38.

10. Victor Lee Brown — See p. 31.

11. Robert Dean Hales — See p. 36.

FIRST COUNSELORS TO PRESIDING BISHOPS

1. Isaac Morley — Born March 11, 1786, at Montague, Hampshire Co., Massachusetts, a son of Thomas Morley and Editha Marsh. Ordained a high priest June 3, 1831, by Lyman Wight; set apart as first counselor to the Presiding Bishop June 6, 1831, at age 45; released at the death of Bishop Edward Partridge May 27, 1840; died June 24, 1865, at Fairview, Sanpete Co., Utah, at age 79.

2. Leonard Wilford Hardy — Born Dec. 31, 1805, at Bradford, Essex Co., Massachusetts, a son of Simon Hardy and Rhoda Hardy. Ordained a high priest April 6, 1856, by John Taylor; sustained as first counselor to the Presiding Bishop Oct. 6, 1856, at age 50; died July 31, 1884, at Salt Lake City, Salt Lake Co., Utah, at age 78.

3. Robert Taylor Burton — Born Oct. 25, 1821, at Amherstburg, Essex Co., Ontario, Canada, a son of Samuel Burton and Hannah Shipley. Ordained a high priest Sept. 2, 1875, by Edward Hunter; sustained as second counselor to the Presiding Bishop Oct. 9, 1874 at age 52; sustained as first counselor to the Presiding Bishop Oct. 5, 1884, at age 62; died Nov. 11, 1907, at Salt Lake City, Salt Lake Co., Utah, at age 86.

4. Orrin Porter Miller — Born Sept. 11, 1858, at Mill Creek, Salt Lake Co., Utah, a son of Reuben G. Miller and Ann Craynor. Ordained a high priest Aug. 8, 1886, by Angus M. Cannon; sustained as second counselor to the Presiding Bishop Oct. 24, 1901 at age 43; sustained as first counselor to the Presiding Bishop Dec. 4, 1907, at age 49; died July 7, 1918, at Salt Lake City, Salt Lake Co., Utah, at age 59.

5. David Asael Smith — Born May 24, 1879, at Salt Lake City, Utah, a son of Joseph Fielding Smith and Julina Lambson. Ordained a high priest Dec. 11, 1907, by Anthon H. Lund; sustained as second counselor to the Presiding Bishop Dec. 4, 1907, at age 28; sustained as first counselor to the Presiding Bishop July 18, 1918, at age 39; released April 6, 1938; died April 6, 1952, at Salt Lake City, Salt Lake Co., Utah, at age 73.

6. Marvin Owen Ashton — Born April 8, 1883, at Salt Lake City, Utah, a son of Edward T. Ashton and Effie W. Morris. Ordained a high priest June 22, 1917, by Heber J. Grant; sustained as first counselor to the Presiding Bishop April 6, 1938, at age 55; died Oct. 7, 1946, at Salt Lake City, Salt Lake Co., Utah, at age 63.

7. Joseph Leopold Wirthlin — See PRESIDING BISHOPS, No. 8.

8. Henry Thorpe Beal Isaacson — See OTHER COUNSELORS IN THE FIRST PRESIDENCY, No. 12.

9. Robert Leatham Simpson — See p. 23.

10. Harold Burke Peterson — See p. 31.

11. Henry B. Eyring — See p. 37.

SECOND COUNSELORS TO PRESIDING BISHOPS

1. John Corrill — Born Sept. 17, 1794, at Worcester Co., Massachusetts. Ordained a high priest June 6, 1831, by Edward Partridge; set apart as second counselor to the Presiding Bishop June 6, 1831, at age 36; released Aug. 1, 1837; excommunicated March 17, 1839.

2. Titus Billings — Born March 25, 1793, at Greenfield, Franklin Co., Massachusetts, a son of Ebenezer Billings and Esther Joyce. Ordained a high priest Aug. 1, 1837, by Edward Partridge; set apart as second counselor to the Presiding Bishop Aug. 1, 1837, at age 44; released at the death of Bishop Edward Partridge May 27,1840; died Feb. 6, 1866, at Provo, Utah Co., Utah, at age 73.

3. Jesse Carter Little — Born Sept. 26, 1815, at Belmont, Waldo Co., Maine, a son of Thomas Little and Relief White. Ordained a high priest April 17, 1845, by Parley P. Pratt; sustained as second counselor to the Presiding Bishop Oct. 6, 1856, at age 41; resigned summer of 1874; died Dec. 26, 1893, at Salt Lake City, Salt Lake Co., Utah, at age 78.

4. Robert Taylor Burton — See FIRST COUNSELORS IN THE PRESIDING BISHOPRIC, No. 3.

5. John Quayle Cannon — Born April 19, 1857, at San Francisco, San Francisco Co., California, a son of George Quayle Cannon and Elizabeth Hoagland. Ordained a high priest Oct. 1884 by John Taylor; sustained as second counselor to the Presiding Bishop Oct. 5, 1884, at age 27; excommunicated Sept. 5, 1886; baptized again May 6, 1888; died Jan. 14, 1931, at Salt Lake City, Salt Lake Co., Utah, at age 74.

6. John Rex Winder — See FIRST COUNSELORS IN THE FIRST PRESIDENCY, No. 7.

7. Orrin Porter Miller — See FIRST

COUNSELORS IN THE PRESIDING BISHOPRIC, No. 4.

8. David Asael Smith — See FIRST COUNSELORS IN THE PRESIDING BISHOPRIC, No. 5.

9. John Wells — Born Sept. 16, 1864, at Carlton, Nottinghamshire, England, a son of Thomas Potter Wells and Sarah Cook. Ordained a high priest Feb. 12, 1911, by Richard W. Young; sustained as second counselor to the Presiding Bishop July 18, 1918, at age 53; released April 6, 1938; died April 18, 1941, at Salt Lake City, Salt Lake Co., Utah, at age 76.

10. Joseph Leopold Wirthlin — See PRESIDING BISHOPS, No. 8.

11. Henry Thorpe Beal Isaacson — See OTHER COUNSELORS IN THE FIRST PRESIDENCY, No. 12.

12. Carl William Buehner — Born Dec. 27, 1898, at Stuttgart, Wuertemberg, Germany, a son of Carl F. Buehner and Anna B. Geigle. Ordained a high priest Dec. 9, 1935, by Richard R. Lyman; sustained as second counselor to the Presiding Bishop April 6, 1952, at age 54; released Sept. 30, 1961; died Nov. 18, 1974, at Salt Lake City, Salt Lake Co., Utah, at age 75.

13. Victor Lee Brown — See p. 31.

14. Vaughn J. Featherstone — See p. 25.

15. John Richard Clarke — See p. 21.

16. Glenn Leroy Pace — See page 37.

LENGTH OF SERVICE IN THE
FIRST PRESIDENCY AND COUNCIL OF TWELVE

(As of October 1988)

Name	Dates of Service, Age at Time	Length of Service	Total Years as General Authority†
David O. McKay	Apr 1906 (32) - Jan 1970 (96)	63 yrs 9 mos	
Heber J. Grant	Oct 1882 (25) - May 1945 (88)	62 yrs 7 mos	
Joseph Fielding Smith	Apr 1910 (33) - Jul 1972 (95)	62 yrs 3 mos	
Wilford Woodruff	Apr 1839 (32) - Sept 1898 (91)	59 yrs 5 mos	
Lorenzo Snow	Feb 1849 (34) - Oct 1901 (87)	52 yrs 8 mos	
Joseph F. Smith	Jul 1866 (27) - Nov 1918 (80)	52 yrs 4 mos	
Franklin D. Richards	Feb 1849 (27) - Dec 1899 (78)	50 yrs 10 mos	
John Taylor	Dec 1838 (30) - Jul 1887 (78)	48 yrs 7 mos	
George Albert Smith	Oct 1903 (33) - Apr 1951 (81)	47 yrs 6 mos	
Orson Pratt	Apr 1835 (23) - Aug 1842 Jan 1843 - Oct 1881 (70)	46 yrs 1 mo	
● **Ezra Taft Benson**	Oct 1943 (44) - present	45 yrs	
Rudger Clawson	Oct 1898 (41) - Jun 1943 (86)	44 yrs 8 mos	
George F. Richards	Apr 1906 (45) - Aug 1950 (89)	44 yrs 4 mos	
Orson Hyde	Feb 1835 (30) - Nov 1878 (73)	43 yrs 9 mos	
Brigham Young	Feb 1835 (33) - Aug 1877 (76)	42 yrs 6 mos	
Stephen L Richards	Jan 1917 (37) - May 1959 (79)	42 yrs 4 mos	
Spencer W. Kimball	Oct 1943 (48) - Nov 1985 (90)	42 yrs 1 mo	
Reed Smoot	Apr 1900 (38) - Feb 1941 (79)	40 yrs 10 mos	
George Q. Cannon	Aug 1860 (33) - Apr 1901(74)	40 yrs 8 mos	
Mark E. Petersen	Apr 1944 (43) - Jan 1984 (83)	39 yrs 9 mos	
Erastus Snow	Feb 1849 (30) - May 1888 (69)	39 yrs 3 mos	
Marion G. Romney	Oct 1951 (54) - May 1988 (90)	36 yrs 7 mos	47 yrs 1 mo
George A. Smith	Apr 1839 (21) - Sept 1875 (58)	36 yrs 5 mos	
Francis M. Lyman	Oct 1880 (40) - Nov 1916 (76)	36 yrs 1 mo	
Charles C. Rich	Feb 1849 (39) - Nov 1883 (74)	34 yrs 9 mos	
Brigham Young Jr.	Oct 1868 (31) - April 1903 (66)	34 yrs 6 mos	
# Daniel H. Wells	Jan 1857 (42) - Mar 1891 (76)	34 yrs 2 mos	
Heber C. Kimball	Feb 1835 (33) - Jun 1868 (67)	33 yrs 4 mos	
Harold B. Lee	Apr 1941 (42) - Dec 1973 (74)	32 yrs 8 mos	
John A. Widtsoe	Mar 1921 (49) - Nov 1952 (80)	31 yrs 8 mos	
Anthon H. Lund	Oct 1889 (45) - Mar 1921 (76)	31 yrs 5 mos	
John Henry Smith	Oct 1880 (32) - Oct 1911 (63)	31 yrs	
LeGrand Richards	Apr 1952 (66) - Jan 1983 (96)	30 yrs 9 mos	44 yrs 9 mos
● Howard W. Hunter	Oct 1959 (51) - present	29 yrs	
J. Reuben Clark Jr.	Apr 1933 (61) - Oct 1961 (90)	28 yrs 6 mos	
Delbert L. Stapley	Oct 1950 (53) - Aug 1978 (81)	27 yrs 10 mos	
● Gordon B. Hinckley	Oct 1961 (51) - present	27 yrs	30 yrs 6 mos
Anthony W. Ivins	Oct 1907 (55) - Sept 1934 (82)	26 yrs 11 mos	
Richard R. Lyman	Apr 1918 (47) - Nov 1943 (72)	25 yrs 7 mos	
Amasa M. Lyman	Aug 1842 (29) - Oct 1867 (54)	25 yrs 2 mos	
Orson F. Whitney	Apr 1906 (50) - May 1931 (75)	25 yrs 1 mo	
● Thomas S. Monson	Oct 1963 (36) - present	25 yrs	
George Teasdale	Oct 1882 (50)- Jun 1907 (75)	24 yrs 8 mos	
Ezra T. Benson	Jul 1846 (35) - Sept 1869 (58)	23 yrs 2 mos	
Parley P. Pratt	Feb 1835 (27)- May 1857 (50)	22 yrs 3 mos	
James E. Talmage	Dec 1911 (49) - Jul 1933 (70)	21 yrs 7 mos	
John W. Taylor	Apr 1884 (25) - Oct 1905 (47)	21 yrs 6 mos	
Charles W. Penrose	Jul 1904 (72) - May 1925 (93)	20 yrs 10 mos	
Melvin J. Ballard	Jan 1919 (45) - Jul 1939 (66)	20 yrs 6 mos	
Joseph F. Merrill	Oct 1931 (63) - Feb 1952 (83)	20 yrs 4 mos	

Bold Face denotes Church President
● Currently serving
† Includes service in the First Council of the Seventy, Assistants to the Twelve, First Quorum of the Seventy, Presiding Bishopric or as Church patriarch.
# Served in the First Presidency under Brigham Young, after his death sustained as a counselor to the Twelve Apostles

Name	Dates of Service, Age at Time	Length of Service	Total Years as General Authority†
N. Eldon Tanner	Oct 1962 (64) - Nov 1982 (84)	20 yrs 1 mo	22 yrs 1 mo
● Boyd K. Packer	Apr 1970 (45) - present	18 yrs 6 mos	27 yrs
#John Willard Young	Apr 1873 (28) - Oct 1891 (47)	18 yrs 6 mos	
Richard L. Evans	Oct 1953 (47) - Nov 1971 (65)	18 yrs 1 mo	33 yrs 1 mo
Hugh B. Brown	Apr 1958 (74) - Dec 1975 (92)	17 yrs 8 mos	22 yrs 2 mos
Moses Thatcher	Apr 1879 (37) - Apr 1896 (54)	17 yrs	
● Marvin J. Ashton	Dec 1971 (56) - present	16 yrs 10 mos	19 yrs
Henry D. Moyle	Apr 1947 (57) - Sept 1963 (74)	16 yrs 5 mos	
Marriner W. Merrill	Oct 1889 (57) - Feb 1906 (73)	16 yrs 4 mos	
Hyrum Mack Smith	Oct 1901 (29) - Jan 1918 (45)	16 yrs 3 mos	
Albert E. Bowen	Apr 1937 (61) - Jul 1953 (77)	16 yrs 3 mos	
Albert Carrington	Jul 1870 (57) - Nov 1885 (72)	15 yrs 4 mos	
● L. Tom Perry	Apr 1974 (51) - present	14 yrs 6 mos	16 yrs
Joseph Smith	Apr 1830 (24) - Jun 1844 (38)	14 yrs 2 mos	
Willard Richards	Apr 1840 (35) - Mar 1854 (49)	13 yrs 11 mos	
Charles A. Callis	Oct 1933 (68)- Jan 1947 (81)	13 yrs 3 mos	
● David B. Haight	Jan 1976 (69) - present	12 yrs 9 mos	18 yrs 6 mos
Bruce R. McConkie	Oct 1972 (57) - Apr 1985 (69)	12 yrs 6 mos	38 yrs 6 mos
Sidney Rigdon	Mar 1833 (40) - Jun 1844 (51)	11 yrs 3 mos	
William Smith	Feb 1835 (23) - Oct 1845 (34)	10 yrs 8 mos	
● James E. Faust	Oct 1978 (58) - present	10 yrs	16 yrs
John R. Winder	Oct 1901 (79) - Mar 1910 (88)	8 yrs 5 mos	22 yrs 11 mos
Matthew Cowley	Oct 1945 (48) - Dec 1953 (56)	8 yrs 2 mos	
Matthias F. Cowley	Oct 1897 (39) - Oct 1905 (47)	8 yrs	
George Q. Morris	Apr 1954 (80) - Apr 1962 (88)	8 yrs	10 yrs 6 mos
Lyman Wight	Apr 1841 (44) - Dec 1848 (52)	7 yrs 8 mos	
Oliver Cowdery	Apr 1830 (23) - Apr 1838 (31)	7 yrs 6 mos	
John E. Page	Dec 1838 (39) - Jun 1846 (47)	7 yrs 6 mos	
● Neal A. Maxwell	Jul 1981 (55) - present	7 yrs 3 mos	14 yrs 6 mos
Abraham H. Cannon	Oct 1889 (30) - Jul 1896 (37)	6 yrs 9 mos	13 yrs 9 mos
Hyrum Smith	Sep 1837 (37) - Jun 1844 (44)	6 yrs 9 mos	
* John Smith	Sep 1837 (56) - Jun 1844 (62)	6 yrs 9 mos	
Abraham O. Woodruff	Oct 1897 (24) - Jun 1904 (31)	6 yrs 8 mos	
Charles W. Nibley	May 1925 (76) - Dec 1931 (82)	6 yrs 7 mos	24 yrs
Sylvester Q. Cannon	Apr 1938 (60) - May 1943 (65)	5 yrs 1 mo	18 yrs
Adam S. Bennion	Apr 1953 (66) - Feb 1958 (71)	4 yrs 10 mos	
Frederick G. Williams	Mar 1833 (45) - Nov 1837 (50)	4 yrs 8 mos	
● Russell M. Nelson	Apr 1984 (59) - present	4 yrs 6 mos	
● Dallin H. Oaks	Apr 1984 (51) - present	4 yrs 6 mos	
Thorpe B. Isaacson	Oct 1965 (67) - Jan 1970 (71)	4 yrs 3 mos	23 yrs 1 mo
Thomas B. Marsh	Apr 1835 (35) - Mar 1839 (39)	3 yrs 11 mos	
David W. Patten	Feb 1835 (35) - Oct 1838 (38)	3 yrs 8 mos	
William E. M'Lellin	Feb 1835 (29) - May 1838 (32)	3 yrs 3 mos	
William Law	Jan 1841 (31) - Apr 1844 (34)	3 yrs 3 mos	
Luke S. Johnson	Feb 1835 (27) - Apr 1838 (30)	3 yrs 2 mos	
Lyman E. Johnson	Feb 1835 (23) - Apr 1838 (26)	3 yrs 2 mos	
● M. Russell Ballard	Oct 1985 (57) - present	3 yrs	12 yrs 6 mos
* Joseph Smith Sr.	Sep 1837 (66) - Sep 1840 (69)	3 yrs	6 yrs 9 mos
Jedediah M. Grant	Apr 1854 (38) - Dec 1856 (40)	2 yrs 8 mos	11 yrs
John F. Boynton	Feb 1835 (23) - Sep 1837 (25)	2 yrs 7 mos	
Alonzo A. Hinckley	Oct 1934 (64) - Dec 1936 (66)	2 yrs 2 mos	
● Joseph B. Wirthlin	Oct 1986 (69) - present	2 yrs	13 yrs 6 mos
Alvin R. Dyer	Apr 1968 (65) - Jan 1970 (67)	1 yr 9 mos	18 yrs 5 mos
● Richard G. Scott	Oct 1988 (59) - present		11 yrs 6 mos

Bold Face denotes Church President
● Currently serving
† Includes service in the First Council of the Seventy, Assistants to the Twelve, First Quorum of the Seventy, Presiding Bishopric or as Church patriarch.
* Served as assistant counselor in the First Presidency
# Served in the First Presidency under Brigham Young, after his death sustained as a counselor to the Twelve Apostles

GENERAL OFFICERS OF THE CHURCH

SUNDAY SCHOOL

President
Robert L. Simpson, Aug 1986 - present, see p. 23.
First Counselor
Adney Y. Komatsu, Aug 1986 - Aug 1987
Devere Harris, Aug 1987 - present, see p. 29.
Second Counselor
A. Theodore Tuttle, Aug 1986 - Nov 1986
Devere Harris, Jan 1987 - Aug 1987
Phillip T. Sonntag, Aug 1987 - Aug 1988
Derek A. Cuthbert, Aug 1988 - present, see p. 27.

GENERAL SUPERINTENDENCIES AND PRESIDENCIES OF THE SUNDAY SCHOOL

Superintendent
George Q. Cannon, Nov 1867 - Apr 1901
First Assistant
George Goddard, Jun 1872 - Jan 1899
Karl G. Maeser — Jan 1899 - Feb 1901
Second Assistant
John Morgan, Jun 1883 - Jul 1894
Karl G. Maeser, Jul 1894 - Jan 1899
George Reynolds, Jan 1899 - May 1901

Superintendent
Lorenzo Snow, May 1901 - Oct 1901
First Assistant
George Reynolds, May 1901 - Oct 1901
Second Assistant
J.M. Tanner — May 1901 - Oct 1901

Superintendent
Joseph F. Smith, Nov 1901 - Nov 1918
First Assistant
George Reynolds, Nov 1901 - May 1909
David O. McKay, May 1909 - Nov 1918
Second Assistant
Jay M. Tanner, Nov 1901 - April 1906
David O. McKay, Jan 1907 - May 1909
Stephen L Richards, May 1909 - Nov 1918

Superintendent
David O. McKay, Dec 1918 - Oct 1934
First Assistant
Stephen L Richards — Dec 1918 - Oct 1934
Second Assistant
George D. Pyper, Dec 1918 - Oct 1934

Superintendent
George D. Pyper — Oct 1934 - Jan 1943
First Assistant
Milton Bennion, Oct 1934 - May 1943

Second Assistant
George R. Hill, Oct 1934 - May 1943

Superintendent
Milton Bennion, May 1943 - Sep 1949
First Assistant
George R. Hill, May 1943 - Sep 1949
Second Assistant
Albert Hamer Reiser, May 1943 - Sep 1949

Superintendent
George R. Hill, Sep 1949 - Nov 1966
First Assistant
Albert Hamer Reiser, Sep 1949 - Oct 1952
David Lawrence McKay, Oct 1952 - Nov 1966
Second Assistant
David Lawrence McKay, Sep 1949 - Oct 1952
Lynn S. Richards, Oct 1952 - Nov 1966

Superintendent
David Lawrence McKay, Nov 1966 - Jun 1971
First Assistant
Lynn S. Richards, Nov 1966 - Jun 1971
Second Assistant
Royden G. Derrick, Nov 1966 - Jun 1971

President
Russell M. Nelson, Jun 1971 - Oct 1979
First Counselor
Joseph B. Wirthlin, Jun 1971 - Apr 1975
F. Lloyd Poelman, Apr 1975 - Mar 1978
Joe J. Christensen, Mar 1978 - Aug 1979
Second Counselor
Richard L. Warner, Jun 1971 - Apr 1975
Joe J. Christensen, Apr 1975 - Mar 1978
William D. Oswald, May 1978 - Aug 1979
J. Hugh Baird, Aug 1979 - Oct 1979

President
Hugh W. Pinnock, Oct 1979 - Aug 1986
First Counselor
Ronald E. Poelman, Oct 1979 - Jul 1981
Robert D. Hales, Jul 1981 - Jul 1985
Adney Y. Komatsu, Jul 1985 - Aug 1986

Second Counselor
Jack H. Goaslind Jr., Oct 1979 - Jul 1981
James M. Paramore, Jul 1981 - Jan 1983
Loren C. Dunn, Jan 1983 - Jul 1985
Ronald E. Poelman, Jul 1985 - Aug 1986

YOUNG MEN

President
Vaughn J. Featherstone, Nov. 1985 - present, see p. 25.
First Counselor
Rex D. Pinegar, Nov 1985 - present, see p. 23.
Second Counselor
Robert L. Simpson, Nov 1985 - 15 Aug 1986
Hartman Rector Jr., Aug. 15, 1986 - October 1988
Robert B. Harbertson, October 1988 - present, see p. 29

GENERAL SUPERINTENDENCIES AND PRESIDENCIES
OF THE YOUNG MEN'S MUTUAL IMPROVEMENT ASSOCIATION

Superintendent
Junius F. Wells, 1876 - 1880
First Counselor
M.H. Hardy
Second Counselor
Rodney C. Badger

Superintendent
Wilford Woodruff (President of the Church), 1880 - 1898
First Assistant
Joseph F. Smith
Second Assistant
Moses Thatcher

Superintendent
Lorenzo Snow (President of the Church), 1898 - 1901
First Assistant
Joseph F. Smith
Second Assistant
Heber J. Grant
Assistant
B.H. Roberts

Superintendent
Joseph F. Smith (President of the Church), 1901-1918
First Assistant
Heber J. Grant
Second Assistant
B.H. Roberts

Superintendent
Anthony W. Ivins (Counselor in First Presidency), 1918 - 1921

First Assistant
B.H. Roberts
Second Assistant
Richard R. Lyman

Superintendent
George Albert Smith (Apostle), 1921 1935
First Assistant
B.H. Roberts
Second Assistant
Richard R. Lyman
Melvin J. Ballard

Superintendent
Albert E. Bowen, 1935 - 1937
First Assistant
George Q. Morris
Second Assistant
Franklin West

Superintendent
George Q. Morris, 1937 - 1948
First Assistant
Joseph J. Cannon
John D. Giles
Second Assistant
Burton K. Farnsworth
Lorenzo H. Hatch

Superintendent
Elbert R. Curtis, 1948 - 1958
First Assistant
A. Walter Stevenson
Second Assistant
Ralph W. Hardy
David S. King

Superintendent
Joseph T. Bentley, 2 Jul 1958 - 6 Oct 1962
First Assistant
Alvin R. Dyer, 2 Jul 1958 - 6 Dec 1958
G. Carlos Smith, 6 Dec 1958 - 9 Jun 1961
Marvin J. Ashton, 9 Jun 1961 - 6 Oct 1962
Second Assistant
Marvin J. Ashton, 6 Dec 1958 - 9 Jun 1961
Verl F. Scott, 9 Jun 1961 - 4 Oct 1961
Carl W. Buehner, 25 Oct 1961 - Oct 1962

Superintendent
G. Carlos Smith, 6 Oct 1962 - 17 Sep 1969
First Assistant
Marvin J. Ashton, 6 Oct 1962 - 17 Sep 1969
Second Assistant
Carl W. Beuhner, 6 Oct 1962 - Oct 1967
George Richard Hill — 6 Oct 1967 - 17 Sep 1969

Superintendent
W. Jay Eldredge, 17 Sep 1969 - 25 Jun 1972
First Assistant
George Richard Hill, 17 Sep 1969 - 24 Jun 1972
Second Assistant
George I. Cannon — 17 Sep 1969 - 25 Jun 1972

President
W. Jay Eldredge, 25 Jun 1972 - 9 Nov 1972
First Counselor
George I. Cannon, 25 Jun 1972 - 9 Nov 1972
Second Counselor
Robert L. Backman, 25 Jun 1972 - 9 Nov 1972

President
Robert L. Backman, 9 Nov 1972 - 23 Jun 1974
First Counselor
LeGrand R. Curtis, Nov 1972 - 23 Jun 1974
Second Counselor
Jack H. Goaslind, Jr., 9 Nov 1972 - 23 Jun 1974

Note: On June 23, 1974, the Aaronic Priesthood MIA was dissolved and was replaced by the Aaronic Priesthood and the Young Women, coming directly under the stewardship of the Presiding Bishop.

In April 1977, the Aaronic Priesthood organization was renamed the Young Men, and both it and the Young Women came under the direction of the Priesthood Department.

YOUNG MEN

President
Neil D. Schaerrer, 7 Apr 1977 - Oct 1979
First Counselor
Graham W. Doxey, 7 Apr 1977 - Oct 1979
Second Counselor
Quinn G. McKay, 7 Apr 1977 - Oct 1979

President
Robert L. Backman, Oct 1979 - Nov 1985
First Counselor
Vaughn J. Featherstone, Oct 1979 - Nov 1985
Second Counselor
Rex D. Pinegar, Oct 1979 - Nov 1985

PRIMARY

Betty Jo Jepsen
First Counselor

Michaelene P. Grassli
President

Ruth B. Wright
Second Counselor

President — Michaelene P. Grassli, April 2, 1988 - to present; served as second counselor in the general Primary presidency from April 5, 1980 to April 2, 1988. Born in Salt Lake City to Clyde Dean and Dottie McKinley Packer; attended BYU, studying child development and family relations; was stake Primary president before being called to the general Primary presidency; married to Leonard M. Grassli, parents of three daughters.

First Counselor — Betty Jo N. Jepsen, April 2, 1988 - to present; served on Primary General Board from 1985 to 1988. Born to Douglas L. Nelson and Edna Brown Nelson in Boise, Idaho; earned bachelor's and master's degrees from Utah State University, and has taught on elementary, secondary and university levels; former stake Primary president, ward Relief Society president; married Glen F. Jepsen, parents of four children.

Second Counselor — Ruth B. Wright, April 2, 1988 - to present; served on Primary General Board from 1985 to 1988. Born to Benn E. and Louie Gill Richards Broadbent Wright at Bingham, Utah; received bachelor's degree from University of Utah, school teacher; former ward and stake Primary president, ward and stake Relief Society president; married Gary E. Wright, parents of five children.

GENERAL PRESIDENCIES OF THE PRIMARY ASSOCIATION

President
Louie B. Felt, 19 Jun 1880 - 6 Oct 1925
First Counselor
Matilda W. Barrett, 19 Jun 1880 - Oct 1888
Lillie T. Freeze, Oct 1888 - 8 Dec 1905
May Anderson, 29 Dec 1905 - 6 Oct 1925
Second Counselor
Clare C.M. Cannon, 19 Jun 1880 - 4 Oct 1895
Josephine R. West, 15 Dec 1896 - 24 Nov 1905
Clara W. Beebe, 29 Dec 1906 - 6 Oct 1925

President
May Anderson, 6 Oct 1925 - 11 Sep 1939
First Counselor
Sadie Grant Pack, 6 Oct 1925 - 11 Sep 1929
Isabelle Salmon Ross, 11 Sep 1929 - 31 Dec 1939
Second Counselor
Isabelle Salmon Ross, 6 Oct 1925 - 11 Sep 1929
Edna Harker Thomas, 11 Sep 1929 - 11 Dec 1933
Edith Hunter Lambert, 11 Dec 1933 - 31 Dec 1939

President
May Green Hinckley, 1 Jan 1940 - 2 May 1943
First Counselor
Adele Cannon Howells, 1 Jan 1940 - 2 May 1943
Second Counselor
Janet Murdock Thompson, 1 Jan 1940 - May 1942
LaVern Watts Parmley, May 1942 - 2 May 1943

President
Adele Cannon Howells, 29 Jul 1943 - 14 Apr 1951
First Counselor
LaVern Watts Parmley, 20 Jul 1943 - 14 Apr 1951
Second Counselor
Dessie Grant Boyle, 20 Jul 1943 - 14 Apr 1951

President
LaVern Watts Parmley, 16 May 1951 - 5 Oct 1974
First Counselor
Arta M. Hale, 16 May 1951 - 6 Apr 1962
Leone W. Doxey — 6 Apr 1962 - 23 Oct 1969
Lucille C. Reading, 8 Jan 1970 - 6 Aug 1970
Naomi W. Randall, 4 Oct 1970 - 5 Oct 1974
Second Counselor
Florence H. Richards, 16 May 1951 - 11 Jun 1953
Leone W. Doxey, 10 Sep 1953 - 6 Apr 1962
Eileen R. Dunyon, 6 Apr 1962 - 3 Jun 1963
Lucile C. Reading, 23 Jul 1963 - 8 Jan 1970
Florence R. Lane, 8 Jan 1970 - 5 Oct 1974

President
Naomi M. Shumway, 5 Oct 1974 - 5 Apr 1980
First Counselor
Sara B. Paulsen, 5 Oct 1974 - 2 Apr 1977
Colleen B. Lemmon, 2 Apr 1977 - 5 Apr 1980
Second Counselor
Collen B. Lemmon, 5 Oct 1974 - 2 April 1977
Dorthea C. Murdock, 2 Apr 1977 - 5 Apr 1980

President
Dwan J. Young, 5 Apr 1980 - 2 Apr 1988
First Counselor
Virginia B. Cannon, 5 Apr 1980 - 2 Apr 1988
Second Counselor
Michaelene P. Grassli, 5 Apr 1980 - 2 Apr 1988

YOUNG WOMEN

Jayne B. Malan
First Counselor

Ardeth G. Kapp
President

Elaine L. Jack
Second Counselor

President — Ardeth G. Kapp, April 7, 1984 - present. Born in Glenwood, Alberta, Canada, to Edwin Kent and Julia Leavitt Greene; received bachelor's degree in education from University of Utah and master's degree from BYU; served as second counselor to Ruth H. Funk in Young Women general presidency Nov. 9, 1972 to July 12, 1978; married to Heber B. Kapp.

First Counselor — Jayne B. Malan, April 4, 1987 - present; previously served as second counselor from April 6, 1986 to April 4, 1987. Born in Heber City, Utah, to Sylvester and Maggie Josephine Murdock Broadbent; freelance writer and producer; served on general boards of Relief Society, Young Women, YWMIA, and as national officer of LDS college sorority Lambda Delta Sigma; married to Terry Malan, parents of two children.

First Counselor

Patricia T. Holland, 11 May 1984 - 6 Apr 1986

Maurine J. Turley, 6 Apr 1986 - 4 Apr 1987

Second Counselor — Elaine L. Jack, April 4, 1987 - present. Born to Sterling O. and Lavina Anderson Low at Cardston, Alberta, Canada; attended University of Utah; served on Relief Society general board from 1972 to 1984, former stake Relief Society president, and ward and branch Young Women president; married Joseph E. Jack, parents of four sons.

Second Counselor

Maurine J. Turley, 11 May 1984 - 6 Apr 1986

Jayne B. Malan, 6 Apr 1986 - 4 Apr 1987

GENERAL PRESIDENCIES OF YOUNG WOMEN'S MUTUAL IMPROVEMENT ASSOCIATION

President
Elmina Shephard Taylor, 19 Jun 1880 - 6 Dec 1904
First Counselor
Margaret Young Taylor, 19 Jun 1880 - 1887
Maria Young Dougall, 1887 - 6 Dec 1904
Second Counselor
Martha Horne Tingey, 19 Jun 1880 - 6 Dec 1904

President
Martha Horne Tingey, 5 Apr 1905 - 28 Mar 1929
First Counselor
Ruth May Fox, 5 Apr 1905 - 28 Mar 1929

Second Counselor
Mae Taylor Nystrom, 5 Apr 1905 - 15 Jul 1923
Lucy Grant Cannon, 15 Jul 1923 - 28 Mar 1929

President
Ruth May Fox, 28 Mar 1929 - Oct 1937
First Counselor
Lucy Grant Cannon, 28 Mar 1929 - Oct 1937
Second Counselor
Clarissa A. Beesley, 30 Mar 1929 - Oct 1937

President
Lucy Grant Cannon, Nov 1937 - 6 Apr 1948
First Counselor
Helen S. Williams, Nov 1937 - 17 May 1944
Verna W. Goddard, Jul 1944 - 6 Apr 1948
Second Counselor
Verna W. Goddard, Nov 1937 - Jul 1944
Lucy T. Anderson, 6 Jul 1944 - 6 Apr 1948

President
Bertha S. Reeder, 6 Apr 1948 - 30 Sep 1961
First Counselor
Emily H. Bennett, 13 Jun 1948 - 30 Sep 1961
Second Counselor
LaRue C. Longden, 13 Jun 1948 — 30 Sep 1961

President
Florence S. Jacobsen, 30 Sep 1961 - 9 Nov 1972
First Counselor
Margaret R. Jackson, 30 Sep 1961 - 9 Nov 1972
Second Counselor
Dorothy P. Holt, 30 Sep 1961 - 9 Nov 1972

AARONIC PRIESTHOOD MIA (YOUNG WOMEN)

President
Ruth H. Funk, 9 Nov 1972 - 23 Jun 1974
First Counselor
Hortense H. Child, 9 Nov 1972 - 23 Jun 1974
Second Counselor
Ardeth G. Kapp, 9 Nov 1972 - 23 Jun 1974

YOUNG WOMEN

President
Ruth H. Funk, 23 Jun 1974 - 12 Jul 1978
First Counselor
Hortense H. Child, 23 Jun 1974 - 12 Jul 1978
Second Counselor
Ardeth G. Kapp, 23 Jun 1974 - 12 Jul 1978

President
Elaine A. Cannon, 12 Jul 1978 - 7 Apr 1984
First Counselor
Arlene B. Darger, 12 Jul 1978 - 7 Apr 1984
Second Counselor
Norma B. Smith, 12 Jul 1978 - 7 Apr 1984

RELIEF SOCIETY

Joy F. Evans
First Counselor

Barbara W. Winder
President

Joanne B. Doxey
Second Counselor

President — Barbara W. Winder, April 7, 1984 - present. Born in Midvale, Utah, to Willard Verl and Marguerite Hand Woodhead; attended University of Utah; served on Relief Society General Board from 1977 until her husband, Richard W. Winder, was called as president of the California San Diego Mission in 1982; former national president of Lambda Delta Sigma; parents of three sons, one daughter.

First Counselor — Joy F. Evans, May 21, 1984 - present. Born in Salt Lake City to Sidney H. and Ruby Taylor Frewin; received nursing education degree from University of Utah; served 8½ years on Relief Society General Board before call to general Relief Society presidency; married to David C. Evans, parents of five sons, three of whom are living, and five daughters, four of whom are living.

Second Counselor — Joanne B. Doxey, May 21, 1984 - present. Born in Salt Lake City to

Bliss L and Eva Murdoch; received bachelor's degree from University of Utah in interior design and child development; was serving on Primary General Board at time of her present call; married to David W. Doxey, parents of five sons, three daughters.

GENERAL PRESIDENCIES OF THE RELIEF SOCIETY

President
Emma Hale Smith, 17 May 1842 - 16 Mar 1844
First Counselor
Sarah M. Cleveland, 17 Mar 1842 - 16 Mar 1844
Second Counselor
Elizabeth Ann Whitney, 17 May 1842 - 16 Mar 1844

President
Eliza Roxey Snow, 1866 - 5 Dec 1887
First Counselor
Zina Diantha Young, 19 Jun 1880 - Apr 1888
Second Counselor
Elizabeth Ann Whitney — 19 Jun 1880 - 15 Feb 1882

President
Zina Diantha Young, 8 Apr 1888 - 28 Aug 1901
First Counselor
Jane S. Richards, 11 Oct 1888 - 10 Nov 1901
Second Counselor
Bathsheba W. Smith, 11 Oct 1888 - 10 Nov 1901

President
Bathsheba W. Smith, 10 Nov 1901 - 20 Sep 1910
First Counselor
Annie Taylor Hyde, 10 Nov 1901 - 2 Mar 1909
Second Counselor
Ida Smooth Dusenberry, 10 Nov 1901 - 20 Sep 1910

President
Emmeline B. Wells, 3 Oct 1910 - 2 Apr 1921
First Counselor
Clarissa Smith Williams, 3 Oct 1910 - Apr 1921
Second Counselor
Julina L. Smith, 3 Oct 1910 - 2 Apr 1921

President
Clarissa Smith Williams, 2 Apr 1921 - 7 Oct 1928
First Counselor
Jennie Brimhall Knight, 2 Apr 1921 - 7 Oct 1928
Second Counselor
Louise Yates Robison, 2 Apr 1921 - 7 Oct 1928

President
Louise Y. Robison, 7 Oct 1928 - Dec 1939
First Counselor
Amy Brown Lyman, 7 Oct 1928 - Dec 1939
Second Counselor
Julia A. Child, 7 Oct 1928 - 23 Jan 1935
Kate M. Barker, 3 Apr 1935 - Dec 1939

President
Amy Brown Lyman, 1 Jan 1940 - 6 Apr 1945
First Counselor
Marcia K. Howells, Apr 1940 - 6 Apr 1945
Second Counselor
Donna D. Sorensen, Apr 1940 - 12 Oct 1942
Belle S. Spafford, Oct 1942 - Apr 1945

President
Belle S. Spafford, 6 Apr 1945 - 3 Oct 1974
First Counselor
Marianne C. Sharp, 6 Apr 1945 - 3 Oct 1974
Second Counselor
Gertrude R. Garff, 6 Apr 1945 - 30 Sep 1947
Velma Simonsen, 3 Oct 1947 - 17 Dec 1956
Helen W. Anderson, Jan 1957 - Aug 1958
Louise W. Madsen, Aug 1958 - 3 Oct 1974

President
Barbara B. Smith, 3 Oct 1974 - 7 Apr 1984
First Counselor
Janath R. Cannon, 3 Oct 1974 - Nov 1978
Marian R. Boyer, Nov 1978 - 7 Apr 1984
Second Counselor
Marian R. Boyer, 3 Oct 1974 - Nov 1978
Shirley W. Thomas, 28 Nov 1978 - 24 Jun 1983
Ann S. Reese, 1 Oct. 1983 - 7 Apr 1984

AREAS OF THE WORLD

'TO ALL THE WORLD'

The International Church — 18 areas

On Nov. 1, 1988, the Utah Central Area was created from the Utah North and Utah South areas. The new area includes Salt Lake, Tooele and Summit counties in Utah. Elder J. Thomas Fyans, president; and Elders Albert Choules Jr. and Monte J. Brough, counselors; comprise the area presidency.

"Go ye to all the world" has been a commandment taken seriously by the Church since the Restoration. As early as 1832, just two years after the Church was organized, missionaries left the United States for Canada. During the next two decades, missionaries preached the gospel in Great Britain, Ireland, the Nordic countries, much of Europe, the Pacific Islands, Chile, parts of Asia, the Holy Land, and other areas.

Today, that commandment continues to motivate Church leaders. In January 1984, the First Presidency announced that headquarters would be decentralized and the administration of the world would be placed under the direction of General Authority presidencies supervising 13 areas: Europe, Pacific, Asia, Mexico/Central America, South America North, South America South, Utah North, Utah South, North America West, North America Northwest, North America Northeast, North America Southwest, and North America Southeast.

In 1987, an additional four areas were created to supervise the work in the Brazil, United Kingdom/Ireland/Africa, Philippines/Micronesia and the North America Central areas.

The 1989-90 *Church Almanac* looks at the Church's growing international presence through administration by areas.

Particularly significant strides have been made in the past two years. Among them was the establishment of 28 new missions in 17 nations, with almost all in developing countries. The International Mission was discontinued and its vast area divided among the 17 administrative areas of the world, with Europe, British Isles and Asia taking the bulk of it.

Six of the 28 missions were created in Mexico, and another eight were created in Latin areas of Guatemala, Colombia, Peru, Brazil, Bolivia, Argentina and Chile.

Three new missions were created in the rapidly growing area of the Philippines, three in Europe's most prolific areas of Portugal and Spain, and another in the Dominican Republic.

Four were the first to be established in the African nations of Zimbabwe, Zaire, Liberia, and the outlying Mascarene Islands.

Other progress in Africa has been made in several areas. The Aba Nigeria Stake was created May 15, 1988. The nations of Zaire, Liberia and the Ivory Coast were dedicated for the preaching of the gospel by Elder Marvin J. Ashton.

In some of these countries, the Church has given humanitarian aid. On Nov. 11, 1986, the Church disbursed more than $6.5 million in fast offering funds to organizations fighting hunger in Africa. And two years later, on June 25, 1988, the Church donated $250,000 to Rotary International PolioPlus to provide more than a million polio immunizations to young people in Kenya and Ivory Coast.

During the past two years, the Church also made progress in translation of the Book of Mormon into other languages. In 1987, the Book of Mormon was translated into Greek, Arabic and Aymara (a South American Indian language). In 1988, selections of the Book of Mormon were translated Pacific Island and African languages of Papiamento, Tagalog, Pohnpeian, Trukese, Lingala, Akan (Fante), and Zulu. With these translations, the Book of Mormon is available in 80 languages, which are spoken by some 85-90 percent of the world's population, some 4.25 billion people.

Other developments of international significance were:

— Eleven stakes were divided into 18 stakes in Lima, Peru, on Jan. 30-31, 1988.

— A renewable 49-year lease for BYU's Jerusalem Center for Near Eastern Studies was signed May 18, 1988, by BYU Pres. Jeffrey R. Holland.

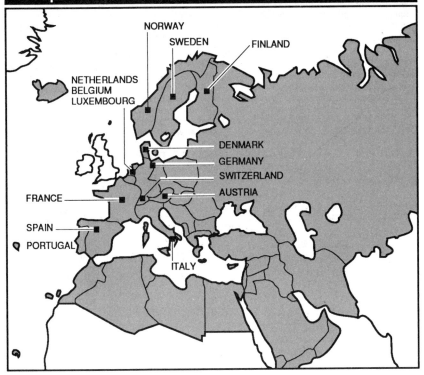

EUROPE AREA

AREA: 14.7 million square miles

POPULATION: Denmark, 5.1 million; Finland, 4.9 million; Iceland, 244,000; Norway, 4.2 million; Sweden, 8.4 million; Austria, 7.5 million; Belgium, 9.9 million; Bulgaria, 9 million; Czechoslavakia, 15.5 million; France, 55.2 million; German Democratic Republic, 16.7 million; Greece, 10 million; Italy, 57.2 million; Netherlands, 14.5 million; Portugal, 10 million; Romania, 22.8 million; Spain, 39 million; Switzerland, 6.5 million; West Germany, 60.7 million; Total, 357.4 million

AREA PRESIDENCY: Elders Carlos E. Asay, Hans B. Ringger and John R. Lasater

LDS POPULATION: 129,800

THE LANDS AND THE PEOPLES: Europe varies from frigid, expansive lowlands of northern continent to mountain ranges of the south. Most citizens are Christian, but there are sizable Moslem and Jewish populations, and many smaller religions.

CHURCH HISTORY: Countries in the present-day Europe Area opened their doors to missionaries in the early 1840s. The first missionary work in Germany was done in 1843, but did not begin in earnest until 1851. The first missionary to France arrived in 1849. The Scandinavian Mission was formed in 1850, and Sweden and Denmark also received their first missionaries that year, followed by Norway in 1851. Missionary work began in France, Italy and Switzerland in 1850, in the Netherlands in 1861, and in Belgium in the late 1880s.

In 1914, war broke out in Europe, and missionaries were evacuated. Many had presided over branches, and their departure created a leadership void that had to be filled with native missionaries and members. During the war, German membership actually increased from about 7,500 to 8,000.

In the decade after World War I, LDS membership in Europe increased by about 4,000, even while many members immigrated to the United States. By 1930, there were about 29,000 saints scattered throughout Europe. During the 1930s, the missionary program in Europe was augmented by local missionaries serving on a part-time basis. At one point in the German-Austrian Mission, there were 138 U.S. missionaries and 152 local missionaries.

On Aug. 24, 1939, one week before Hitler invaded Poland, the First Presidency ordered the evacuation of all U.S. missionaries in Europe. For the duration of the war, contact between Church leaders and saints in most war-affected areas was impossible. When the war ended in 1945, Church leaders quickly moved to re-establish contact with the saints there. Elder Ezra Taft Benson of the Council of the Twelve, called to preside over the European Mission, arrived in Europe in February 1946, and by December had traveled 60,000 miles in an effort to reach the saints. Missionaries, many fresh out of military service, soon began arriving, and by the end of 1946 there were 311 in Europe. By 1950 there were 1,200 in Europe

1987 units and membership†

Country	Stakes	Wards	Stake branches	Missions	Districts	Mission branches	Total wards, branches	Membership	Per cent of Pop.	1 LDS in:
NORDIC COUNTRIES										
Denmark	2	12	10	1			22	4,300	.080	1,250
Finland	2	10	7	1	3	11	28	4,100	.081	1,235
Greenland					1		1	*		
Iceland					1	3	3	200	.082	1,220
Norway	1	7	2	1	3	14	23	3,700	.086	1,157
Sweden	2	12	14	1	4	14	40	7,100	.092	1,085
EUROPE										
Austria	1	7	11	2			18	3,100	040	2,516
Belgium	1	5	7	1	1	11	23	4,000	.036	2,741
GDR	2	9	18				27	3,600	.022	4,638
France	4	19	23	1	8	50	92	18,100	.033	3,069
Greece					1	3	3	200	.002	50,000
Italy	2	10	13	3	8	61	84	13,000	.023	4,403
Netherlands	2	11	20	1		2	33	6,700	.046	2,174
Portugal	3	16	14	2	8	35	65	12,000	.119	840
Spain	3	11	12	5	11	84	107	14,000	.036	2,792
Switzerland	3	15	16	2			31	5,700	.087	1,155
W. Germany	14	83	54	3	1	10	147	30,000	.049	2,025

* Fewer than 100 members

† Membership totals rounded off, some include partial estimates; stakes, missions as of Oct. 16, 1988.

STAKES — 42

DENMARK—2
945 Aarhus Denmark
648 Copenhagen Denmark

FINLAND—2
865 Helsinki Finland
1408 Tampere Finland

NORWAY—1
835 Oslo Norway

SWEDEN—2
880 Goteborg Sweden
691 Stockholm Sweden

AUSTRIA—1
1126 Vienna Austria

BELGIUM—1
813 Brussels Belgium

GERMAN DEMOCRATIC REPUBLIC—2
1358 Freiberg German Democratic Republic
1475 Leipzig German Democratic Republic

FRANCE—4
1669 Lille France
1413 Nancy France
1130 Nice France
731 Paris France

ITALY—2
1274 Milan Italy

1556 Venice Italy

NETHERLANDS—2
326   The Hague Netherlands
933   Utrecht Netherlands

PORTUGAL—3
1276 Lisbon Portugal
1613 Porto Portugal
1652 Setubal Portugal

SPAIN—3
1370 Barcelona Spain
1327 Madrid Spain
1687 Seville Spain

SWITZERLAND—3
1261 Bern Switzerland
1352 Geneva Switzerland

341   Zurich Switzerland

WEST GERMANY—14
334   Berlin Germany
768   Dortmund Germany
577   Duesseldorf Germany
766   Frankfurt Germany
824   Frankfurt Germany Servicemen
342   Hamburg Germany
845   Hannover Germany
466   Kaiserslautern Germany Servicemen
1324 Mannheim Germany
870   Munich Germany
1305 New Muenster Germany
1651 Nuremberg Germany Servicemen
340   Stuttgart Germany
765   Stuttgart Germany Servicemen

MISSIONS — 24

NORDIC COUNTRIES — 4

DENMARK COPENHAGEN MISSION
Tornerosevej 127
2730 Herlev
Denmark
Phone: (011-45-2) 84-39-99

FINLAND HELSINKI MISSION
Neitsytpolku 3 A 4
SF-00140 Helsinki 14
Finland
Phone: (011-358-0) 177-311

NORWAY OSLO MISSION
Drammensveien 96 G
Postboks 7583, Skillebekk
0205 Oslo 2
Norway
Phone: (011-47-2) 44-79-85

SWEDEN STOCKHOLM MISSION
Box 2087
S-183 02 Taby 2
Sweden
Phone: (011-46-8) 768-03-35

EUROPE — 20

AUSTRIA VIENNA MISSION
Fuerfanggasse 4
A-1190 Vienna
Austria
Phone: (011-43-222) 37-32-57

AUSTRIA VIENNA EAST MISSION
Keylwerthgasse 20/I/1
A-1190 Vienna
Austria
Phone: (011-43-222) 44-28-410

BELGIUM BRUSSELS MISSION
87, Blvd. Brand Whitlock
B-1040 Bruxelles
Belgium
Phone: (011-32-2) 736-99-33

FRANCE PARIS MISSION
23, rue du onze novembre
F-78110 Le Vesinet
France
Phone: (011-33-1) 3976-5588

GERMANY FRANKFURT MISSION
Klaus Groth Strasse #12
D-6000 Frankfurt Am Main 1
West Germany
Phone: (011-49-69) 56-80-38

GERMANY HAMBURG MISSION
Eimsbuettelerstrasse 53/55
D-2000 Hamburg 50
West Germany
Phone: (011-49-40) 4390-010

GERMANY MUNICH MISSION
Machtlfingerstrasse 5
D-8000 Munich 70
West Germany
Phone: (011-49-89) 788-071

ITALY CATANIA MISSION
Corso Sicilia 48
I-95131 Catania
Italy
Phone: (011-39-95) 317-759

ITALY MILAN MISSION
Via Pavoni, 1/3
I-20052 Monza (MI)
Italy
Phone: (011-39-39) 365-218

ITALY ROME MISSION
Via Cimone 103
I-00141 Rome
Italy
Phone: (011-39-6) 898-394

NETHERLANDS AMSTERDAM MISSION
Noordsebosje 16
1211 BG Hilversum
Netherlands
Phone: (011-31-35) 48-346

PORTGUAL LISBON MISSION
Largo Com. Augusto Madureira, 7-B
1495 Alges
Portugal
Phone: (011-351-1) 410-2064

PORTUGAL PORTO MISSION
Rua de Amalia Luazes, 23 - Sala 1
4200 Porto
Portugal
Phone: (011-351-2) 481-575

SPAIN BARCELONA MISSION
Calle Calatrava 10-12, bajos
08017 Barcelona
Spain
Phone: (011-34-3) 211-6558

SPAIN BILBAO MISSION
c/Las Mercedes 31, Abra 3, 3a
48930 Las Arenas (Vizcaya)
Spain
Phone: (011-34-4) 464-8687

SPAIN LAS PALMAS MISSION
Avenida Rafael Cabrera 4 6th A
35002 Las Palmas de Gran Canaria
Spain
Phone: (011-34-28) 36-87-62

SPAIN MADRID MISSION
Calle San Telmo, 26
E-28016 Madrid
Spain
Phone: (011-34-1) 458-2634

SPAIN SEVILLE MISSION
Calle Virgen de Regla 1-1st, 1
41011 Seville
Spain
Phone: (011-34-54) 27-63-73

SWITZERLAND GENEVA MISSION
8, Chemin William-Barbey
CH-1292 Chambesy (GE)
Switzerland
Phone: (011-41-22) 58-15-35

SWITZERLAND ZURICH MISSION
Pilatusstrasse 11
CH-8032 Zurich
Switzerland
Phone: (011-41-1) 252-51-14

TEMPLES — 4

FRANKFURT

GERMANY

TEMPLE

Location: In the center of Friedrichdorf, a small town nine miles north of Frankfurt that was settled in 1687 by Huguenot refugees in 1687; Talstrasse 10, D-6382 Friedrichdorf, Federal Republic of Germany, 5.2 acres. Phone: 011-49-61-72-72066.

Exterior Finish: white granite, copper roof.

Temple Design: Modern

Architects: Church architectural staff; local architect, Borchers-Metzner-Kramer; Hanno Luschin, project architect

Construction Advisor: Henry Haurand

Contractor: Hochtief AG

Number of Rooms: Four ordinance rooms, five sealing rooms; a total of 63 rooms.

Total Floor Area: 24,757 square feet.

District and membership: Federal Republic of Germany, Belgium, Netherlands, Luxemburg, parts of France and Austria, 41,000 members.

Groundbreaking, site dedication: July 1, 1985, by President Gordon B. Hinckley

Dedication: Aug. 28-30, 1987, by President Ezra Taft Benson, 11 sessions.

Dedicatory Prayer excerpt: *"The presence of this house, on the soil of this nation, is an answer to the prayers of of thy people, and a fulfillment of the words of thy prophets."*

FREIBERG DDR TEMPLE

Location: About 150 miles south of Berlin, in southern part of German Democratic Republic.

Exterior Finish: Modern design with old world German influence; exterior white German stucco over 24-inch thick brick walls, blue-gray slate stone slab roof; two high arches, reminiscent of Gothic style, are parallel with front of building and bisected by two similar arches to form a single spire.

Temple Design: Modern adaptation of earlier six-spire design.

Architect: Emil B. Fetzer.

Government Construction Advisor: Dr. Dieter Hantzche, architect director of Bauakademie of Dresden.

Number of Rooms: One ordinance room, two sealing rooms; total rooms, 32.

Total Floor Area: 7,840 square feet.

Groundbreaking, Site Dedication: April 23, 1983, by Elder Thomas S. Monson.

District and membership: German Democratic Republic; 4,000 members.

Temple Dedication: June 29-30, 1985, by President Gordon B. Hinckley, seven sessions.

Dedicatory Prayer excerpt: *"On this day of dedication our hearts turn to thee. We thank thee for this holy temple in this land and nation. We thank thee for all who have made possible its building — the officers of the government who have given encouragement and made available land and materials, the architects and the builders, and all who have made possible this glorious day of dedication."*

SWEDEN STOCKHOLM TEMPLE

Location: Vasterhaninge, about 13 miles southeast of Stockholm, Sweden, at Tempelgatan 5; 4.5 acres. Phone: (011-46) 750-265-20

Exterior Finish: Swedish rendering.

Temple Design: Modern adaptation of earlier six-spire design 178 feet by 71 feet; Angel Moroni statue is atop tallest spire at 112 feet.

Architects: Church architectural staff; local architect, John Sjostrom.

Construction Advisor: Henry Haurand

Contractor: J.C.C.

Number of Rooms: Four ordinance rooms; three sealing rooms.

Total Floor Area: 14,508 square feet.

District and membership: Sweden, Finland, Denmark, Norway, and Iceland; 19,400 members.

Groundbreaking, site dedication: March 17, 1984, by Elder Thomas S. Monson.

Dedication: July 2-4, 1985, by President Gordon B. Hinckley, 11 sessions.

Dedicatory Prayer excerpt: *"Bless this nation where is found thy temple, and its sister nations. . . .*

"Save these nations from war and oppression, and may their people look to thee and open their doors and hearts to thy messengers of eternal truth."

SWISS TEMPLE

Location: Tempelstrasse 4, 3052 Zollikofen, a northern suburb of Bern, with Bern, the Aare River, the Jural Mountains and the Alps on the south, and on the north and west deeply wooded forests. Phone: (011 + 41 + 31 57-09-12)

Site Selected: July 1952, by President Samuel E. Bringhurst of the Swiss-Austrian Mission and President David O. McKay; 7 acres.

Exterior Finish: Built of reinforced concrete with a creamish gray terra cotta facing trimmed in white. Tower is white at base and spire is gold-colored.

Temple Design: Modern-contemporary, but similar to lines of early Church temples.

Architect: Edward O. Anderson, Church architect. Re-drawn into German by Wilhelm Zimmer of Bercher and Zimmer Architects.

Supervising Architects: Wihelm Zimmer and Kurt Liggenstorfer.

Contractor: Hans Jordi of Bern.

Number of Rooms: 81.

Total Floor Area: 34,750 square feet.

Dimensions of Building: 152 feet long by 84 feet wide; top of tower rises 140 feet.

District and membership: Switzerland, Spain, Portugal, Italy, and parts of France; 56,000 members.

Groundbreaking, Site Dedication: Aug. 5, 1953, site dedicated and ground broken by President David O. McKay.

Temple Dedication: Sept. 11, 1955, and nine additional sessions by President David O. McKay. President McKay addressed group and gave dedicatory prayer at each. Tabernacle Choir participated.

Dedicatory Prayer excerpt: *"Increase our desire, O Father, to put forth even greater effort towards the consummation of thy purpose to bring to pass the immortality and eternal life of all thy children. This edifice is one more means to aid in bringing about this divine consummation."*

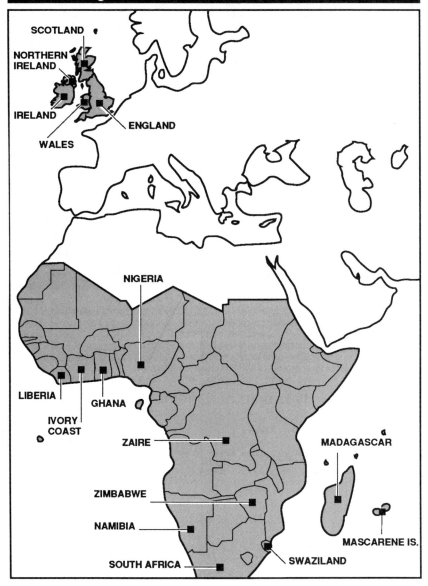

United Kingdom/Ireland/Africa Area

AREA: 9,604,274 square miles
POPULATION: 492,776,000
AREA PRESIDENCY: Elders Jack H. Goaslind, Alexander B. Morrison, Robert E. Sackley.
LDS POPULATION: 163,800

THE LANDS AND THE PEOPLES: In addition to England, Scotland, Wales, and Ireland, the United Kingdom/Ireland/Africa Area covers 49 countries, republics, dominions and principalities on and around the continent of Africa. The area comprises about 10.1 percent of the world geographical area, and about 10.4 percent of the world's population.

English is the dominant language, being spoken throughout the United Kingdom and Ireland, and being the official or secondary language of several African nations. Other widely used languages are French, Afrikaans, Bantu, Creole, Ibo, and Swahili. The exact number of languages is difficult to determine since each village, township or nation may have its own official language and several dialects.

The cultural and geographical diversities of the area are immense — from bustling cities with high-rise offices and apartments to small villages where dwellings are constructed of grass or mud. The area is diverse also in its sources of incomes, having industrial centers, fertile farmlands, rich mineral deposits and abundant natural resources. The terrain is just as diverse, with high mountain ranges, tropical rain forests and arid plains.

In the United Kingdom and Ireland, Christianity is dominant, with Protestants and Catholics comprising most of the population. In Africa, there are large Christian populations in South Africa, Zaire, Ghana, Kenya, and Nigeria. Traditional tribal religions are abundant; the Moslem religion also has a large following in Africa.

CHURCH HISTORY: The first missionaries arrived in Liverpool, England, on July 20, 1837. They were Elders Heber C. Kimball and Orson Hyde of the Quorum of the Twelve; Willard Richards, Joseph Fielding, Isaac Russell, John Goodson and John Snyder. By April 1840, the LDS membership in Britain was 1,677. The first missionaries to Scotland, Samuel Mulliner and Alexander Wright (native Scots who joined the Church in England), arrived in Glasgow on Dec. 21, 1839; their first converts were baptized Jan. 14, 1840. On May 23, 1840, Elder John Taylor landed in Belfast, becoming the first-known Latter-day Saint to go to Ireland. The gospel was preached in Wales at least from 1841. In the early years, missionaries confined their preaching in Wales mostly to counties that bordered England.

Missionaries first taught in South Africa in 1853, but by 1865 most members and missionaries had left and the country wasn't reopened to missionary work until 1903. For decades after missionary work resumed on the continent, most of the Church emphasis was placed on South Africa. On May 15, 1988, (less than a month before the 10th anniversary of the June 9, 1978, revelation making it possible for all worthy male members to be ordained to the priesthood) the Aba Nigeria Stake was created; it is the first stake in western Africa. The Church has become established also in Ghana, Ivory Coast, Liberia, Namibia, Swaziland, Zaire and Zimbabwe.

1987 units and membership†

Country	Stakes	Wards	Stake bran- ches	Mis- sions	Dist- ricts	Total Mission wards, bran- ches	wards, bran- ches	Memb- ership	Per cent of Pop.	1 LDS in:
AFRICA										
Ghana				1	8	50	50	5,500	.04	2,564
Kenya				1	1	1	1	*		
Liberia				1						
Mascarene Islands				1						
Mauritius				1		1	1	*		
Namibia						1	1	*		
Nigeria	1	6		2	8	50	50	8,000	.001	126,582
Reunion						3	3	*		
Somalia						1	1	*		
South Africa	5	28	23	2	1	9	60	14,000	.04	2,558
Zaire				1	1	3	3	400	.001	78,740
Zimbabwe					1	6	6	1,300	.01	6,911
UNITED KINGDOM, IRELAND										
England	32	199	71	6	0	0	270	110,000	.3	347
Ireland	0	0	0	1	2	8	8	2,000	.210	476
Northern Ireland	1	7	6	0	0	0	13	3,700	.05	1,908

Scotland	5	28	27	1	0	0	55	13,000	.253	395
Wales	2	13	9	0	0		22	6,400	.221	452

* Fewer than 100 members

† Membership totals rounded off, some include partial estimates; stakes, missions as of Oct. 16, 1988.

STAKES — 46

NIGERIA — 1

1695 Aba Nigeria

SOUTH AFRICA— 5

1662 Benoni South Africa
1469 Cape Town South Africa
1314 Durban South Africa
506 Johannesburg South Africa
969 Pretoria South Africa

ENGLAND—32

1345 Ashton England
760 Billingham England
494 Birmingham England
609 Bristol England
1331 Cheltenham England
1346 Chester England
856 Crawley England
327 Huddersfield England
608 Hull England
1423 Ipswich England
780 Leeds England
325 Leicester England
814 Lichfield England
748 Liverpool England
928 London England Hyde Park
929 London England Wandsworth

930 Maidstone England
294 Manchester England
677 Newcastle-Under-Lyme England
810 Northampton England
549 Norwich England
597 Nottingham England
885 Plymouth England
1343 Poole England
762 Preston England
615 Reading England
666 Romford England
932 St. Albans England
1376 Sheffield England
600 Southampton England
931 Staines England
374 Sunderland England

NORTHERN IRELAND — 1

647 Belfast Northern Ireland

SCOTLAND — 5

1186 Aberdeen Scotland
734 Dundee Scotland
1187 Edinburgh Scotland
356 Glasgow Scotland
1188 Paisley Scotland

WALES — 2

1341 Cardiff Wales
676 Merthyr Tydfil Wales

MISSIONS — 17

AFRICA — 9

GHANA ACCRA MISSION
P.O. Box 9461 Airport
Accra
Ghana
Phone: (010-233) 223362
(No direct dial)

LIBERIA MONROVIA MISSION
P.O. Box 3945
Monrovia
Liberia
Phone: (011-231) 261-668

MASCARENE ISLANDS MISSION
13 Bis, Route De La Riviere
Des Pluies
97490 Ste. Clotilde
La Reunion, Indian Ocean
Phone: 29-14-54
(No direct dial)

NIGERIA ABA MISSION
P.O. Box 3636
Aba, Imo State
Nigeria
Phone: (011-234-82) 225-360

NIGERIA LAGOS MISSION
P.O. Box 9028
Ikeja, Lagos
Nigeria
Phone: (011-234-1) 961-647

SOUTH AFRICA CAPE TOWN MISSION
P.O. Box 217 Howard Place
Cape Town, 7450
South Africa
Phone: (011-27-21) 536-903

SOUTH AFRICA JOHANNESBURG
MISSION
P.O. Box 1517
Florida 1710

Republic of South Africa
Phone: (011-27-11) 672-6693

ZAIRE KINSHASA MISSION
B.P. 20572
KIN 15 CCIZ
Kinshasa
Zaire
Phone: (011-243-12) 80-589

ZIMBABWE HARARE MISSION
67 Enterprise Road
Highlands, Harare
Zimbabwe
Phone: (011-263-4) 737-297

UNITED KINGDOM — 7

ENGLAND BRISTOL MISSION
Southfield House #2
Southfield Road
Westbury on Trym
Bristol, BS9 3BH
England
Phone: (011-44-272) 621-939

ENGLAND COVENTRY MISSION
4 Copthall House, Station Square
Coventry, West Midlands, CV1 2PP
England
Phone: (011-44-203) 26-568

ENGLAND LEEDS MISSION
Techno Centre, Station Road
Horsforth Leeds LS18 5BJ
West Yorkshire
England
Phone: (011-44-532) 584-221

ENGLAND LONDON MISSION
64/68 Exhibition Road
South Kensington, London SW7 2PA
England
Phone: (011-44-1) 584-7553

ENGLAND LONDON SOUTH MISSION
484 London Road
Mitcham, Surrey CR4 4ED
England
Phone: (011-44-1) 640-6018

ENGLAND MANCHESTER MISSION
Paul House
Stockport Road, Timperley
Altrincham, Cheshire WA15 7UP
England
Phone: (011-44-61) 980-8015

SCOTLAND EDINBURGH MISSION
"Boroughfield," 32 Colinton Rd.
Edinburgh, EH10 5DG
Scotland
Phone: (011-44-31) 337-1283

NORTHERN IRELAND — 1

IRELAND DUBLIN MISSION
The Willows, Finglas Road
Glasnevin, Dublin 11
Ireland
Phone: (011-353-1) 30-68-99

Training Center

ENGLAND MISSIONARY TRAINING
CENTER
London Temple
New Chapel, Surrey RH7 6HW
England
Phone: (011-44-342) 83-4484

TEMPLES — 2

JOHANNESBURG SOUTH AFRICA TEMPLE

Location: 7 Jubilee Rd., Parktown, South Africa. Phone: (011-27-11) 642-4952.
Area of Site: One acre.
Exterior Finish: Masonry exterior.
Temple Design: Modern adaptation of earlier six-spire design.
Architects: Church architectural staff; local architect, Halford & Halford.
Construction Advisor: Stan Smith.
Contractor: Tiber Bonvac.
Number of Rooms: Four ordinance rooms; three sealing rooms.
Total Floor Area: 13,025 square feet.
Dimensions of Building: 178 feet by 71 feet; Angel Moroni statue is atop tallest spire at 112 feet.
  District and membership: South Africa and adjacent nations; 21,000 members.

Groundbreaking, site dedication: Nov. 27, 1982, by Elder Marvin J. Ashton.
Dedication: Aug. 24-25, 1985, by President Gordon B. Hinckley, four sessions.

Dedicatory Prayer excerpt: *"Almighty God, wilt thou overrule for the blessing and safety of thy faithful saints. We pray for peace in this troubled land. Bless this nation which has befriended thy servants. May those who rule in the offices of government be inspired to find a basis for reconciliation among those who now are in conflict one with another. May the presence of thy house on the soil of this land bring blessings to the entire nation."*

LONDON TEMPLE

Location: Newchapel, N. Lingfield, Surrey, England, 25 miles south of London, formerly Elizabethan farm. Phone: (011+44+342-83-2759)

Site: In June 1952, President David O. McKay and Elder Stayner Richards, president of the British Mission, selected Newchapel. Purchased several months later in 1953; 32 acres.

Exterior Finish: Reinforced concrete and structural steel skeleton, walls of brick masonry faced with cut Portland limestone, white in color. Spire sheathed in lead-coated copper.

Temple Design: Modern-contemporary.

Architect: Edward O. Anderson, Church architect.

Supervising Architects: T.T. Bennett and Son, London.

Contractors: Kirk and Kirk, Ltd., London

Number of Rooms: 63.

Total Floor Area: 34,000 square feet. Basement and 3 floors above.

Dimensions of Building: 84 feet wide, 159 feet long, 56 feet to the square. The tower rises 156 feet 9½ inches from ground level, spire 33 feet above that.

District and membership: England, Scotland, Wales, Ireland, and parts of Belgium and France: 135,400 members

Groundbreaking, Site Dedication: Aug. 10, 1953, site dedicated by David O. McKay, who broke ground on Saturday, Aug. 27, 1955.

Temple Dedication: Sept. 7-9, 1958, by President David O. McKay. Six sessions with 12,000 attending were held.

Dedicatory Prayer excerpt: *"With humility and deep gratitude we acknowledge thy nearness, thy divine guidance and inspiration. Help us, we pray thee, to become even more susceptible in our spiritual response to thee.*

"Temples are built to thy holy name as a means of uniting thy people, living and dead, in bonds of faith, of peace and of love throughout eternity."

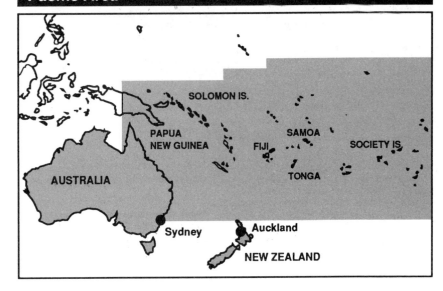

PACIFIC AREA

AREA: About 5 million square miles
POPULATION: 21 million
AREA PRESIDENCY: Elders F. Arthur Kay, Glen L. Rudd and Douglas J. Martin
LDS POPULATION: 213,000

THE AREA AND THE PEOPLES: The distance from the area's eastern to western boundaries is about 6,000 miles. Geographers estimate there are at least 20,000 islands, some covering thousands of square miles while others are little more than volcanic rock or sand barely poking out of the ocean. Not all islands are inhabited. The island continent of Australia is the largest land mass; the next largest is New Zealand. Other islands in the area include American Samoa, Western Samoa, Tonga, Fiji, Papua New Guinea, New Caldeonia, Solomon Islands, Cook Islands, Fiji and Tahiti and other islands of French Polynesia. Some islands have hills and mountain ranges.

The population is a mixture of many races: Polynesians, Maoris, Melanesians, and Micronesians, as well as descendants of peoples from Europe and immigrants from India.

Sydney, on Australia's southeastern coast, is the area's largest city. Life styles, occupations and activities in large cities and towns of the Pacific Area are much the same as in other parts of the world. The skyscrapers of Australia and New Zealand are as impressive as high-rise buildings anywhere. However, there are many places that modern-day society has not reached. While some cities maintain important positions in international finances, there are places where the average income is less than $500 a year, and people depend on a harvest from the land and fish from the sea.

CHURCH HISTORY: Wards and branches have been established throughout the area, some on very remote islands and atolls. Some branches are accessible only by boat; travel to some may take four or five days, using a combination of airplanes and boats.

Elders Addison Pratt, Noah Rogers, Benjamin F. Grouard and Knowlton F. Hanks were the first missionaries to the Pacific Islands. They left Nauvoo, Ill., May 23, 1843, and booked passage on a whaling ship in Massachusetts on Oct. 10, 1843. They sailed down the Atlantic Ocean and around the Cape of Good Hope to reach the Pacific Ocean. Elder Hanks died and was buried at sea Nov. 3, 1843. The ship reached Tubai, about 350 miles south of Tahiti, on April 30, 1844. Elder Pratt remained on Tubuai, while Elders Rogers and Grouard went on to Tahiti to begin their missionary labors.

In later years, missionaries went to other parts of the Pacific: Hawaii (now part of the North America West Area), Dec. 12, 1850; Australia, Oct. 30, 1851; and New Zealand, Oct. 27, 1854.

Some missionary work began in Samoa in 1862; official missionary work began there June 21, 1888. Missionaries arrived in the Tongan Islands July 15, 1891. Work did not begin in Fiji until Sept. 4, 1954.

1987 units and membership†

Country	Stakes	Wards	Stake bran- ches	Mis- sions	Dist- ricts	Mission bran- ches	Total wards, bran- ches	Memb- ership	Per cent of Pop.	1 LDS in:
American Samoa	2	16	5				21	6,900	17	5.8
Australia	18	112	28	5	14	58	198	66,000	.42	239
Cook Islands					1	7	7	700	.56	179
Fiji Islands	1	9	1	1		6	16	4,000	.56	179
Kiribati					1	12	12	1,200	1.9	52
Nauru						1	1	*		
New Caledonia					1	4	4	600	.27	373
New Zealand	16	92	47	2	2	10	149	60,000	1.8	57
Niue					1	7	7	300	8.8	11
Papua New Guinea					1	12	12	1,700	.05	1,997
Tahiti	2	17	4	1	4	22	43	8,600	4.8	21
Tonga	10	63	53	1			116	29,000	27.9	3.6
Tuvalu						1	1	*		
Vanuatu						1	1	*		
Western Samoa	9	67	25	1			92	34,000	.15	680

* Fewer than 100 members

† Membership totals rounded off, some include partial estimates; stakes, missions as of Oct. 16, 1988.

STAKES — 58

AMERICAN SAMOA—2
488 Pago Pago Samoa
1169 Pago Pago Samoa West

AUSTRALIA—18
414 Adelaide Australia Marion
907 Adelaide Australia Modbury
306 Brisbane Australia
1684 Brisbane Australia North
892 Brisbane Australia South
860 Hobart Australia
1279 Ipswich Australia
551 Melbourne Australia Dandenong
1175 Melbourne Australia Deer Park
307 Melbourne Australia Fairfield
1617 Melbourne Australia Waverly
1106 Newcastle Australia
447 Perth Australia Dianella
1159 Perth Australia Southern River
293 Sydney Australia Greenwich
1105 Sydney Australia Hebersham
435 Sydney Australia Mortdale

495 Sydney Australia Parramatta

FIJI ISLANDS—1
1426 Suva Fiji

NEW ZEALAND—16
630 Auckland New Zealand Harbour
1304 Auckland New Zealand Henderson
861 Auckland New Zealand Manukau
455 Auckland New Zealand Manurewa
264 Auckland New Zealand Mt. Roskill
1664 Auckland New Zealand Tamaki
953 Christchurch New Zealand
1104 Gisborne New Zealand
310 Hamilton New Zealand
313 Hastings New Zealand
475 Kaikohe New Zealand
1012 Palmerstown North New Zealand
884 Rotorua New Zealand
445 Temple View New Zealand
853 Upper Hutt New Zealand
407 Wellington New Zealand

TAHITI—2
573 Papeete Tahiti

1355 Pirae Tahiti

TONGA—10

1430 Ha'apai Tonga
737 Neiafu Vava'u Tonga
1172 Neiafu Vava'u Tonga North
463 Nuku'alofa Tonga
550 Nuku'alofa Tonga East
1173 Nuku'alofa Tonga Liahona
1445 Nuku'alofa Tonga North
519 Nuku'alofa Tonga South
1431 Nuku'alofa Tonga Vaini

520 Nuku'alofa Tonga West

WESTERN SAMOA—9

353 Apia Samoa
1045 Apia Samoa East
513 Apia Samoa West
538 Savai'i Samoa
1366 Savai'i Samoa South
619 Savai'i Samoa West
868 Upolu Samoa East
645 Upolu Samoa South
545 Upolu Samoa West

MISSIONS — 11

AUSTRALIA ADELAIDE MISSION
P.O. Box 97
Marden, South Australia 5070
Australia
Phone: (011-61-8) 332-2588

AUSTRALIA BRISBANE MISSION
146 Racecourse Road, Suite 7
Ascot, Brisbane, Queensland 4007
Australia
Phone: (011-61-7) 268-7077

AUSTRALIA MELBOURNE MISSION
1216 Old Burke Road
North Balwyn 3104, Victoria
Australia
Phone: (011-61-3) 859-6826

AUSTRALIA PERTH MISSION
P.O. Box 185
Tuart Hill, Western Australia 6060
Australia
Phone: (011-61-9) 275-7177

AUSTRALIA SYDNEY MISSION
P.O. Box 905
Crows Nest, N.S.W. 2065
Australia
Phone: (011-61-2) 438-3733

FIJI SUVA MISSION
GPO Box 215
Suva

Fiji Islands
Phone: (011-679) 314-277

NEW ZEALAND AUCKLAND MISSION
P.O. Box 33-840
Takapuna, Auckland 9
New Zealand
Phone: (011-64-9) 495-102

NEW ZEALAND CHRISTCHURCH MISSION
53 First Floor Victoria Street
Christchurch 1
New Zealand
Phone: (011-64-3) 650-582

SAMOA APIA MISSION
P.O. Box 1865
Apia
Western Samoa
Phone: 20311

TAHITI PAPEETE MISSION
B.P. 93
Papeete
Tahiti
Phone: (011-689) 42-03-84

TONGA NUKU'ALOFA MISSION
P.O. Box 58
Nuku'alofa
Tonga
Phone: 21-577

Training Centers

NEW ZEALAND MISSIONARY TRAINING
CENTER
Temple View P.O.
Hamilton
New Zealand
Phone: (011-64-71) 73-722

SAMOA MISSIONARY TRAINING CENTER
P.O. Box 197

Apia
Western Samoa
Phone: 20-299

TONGA MISSIONARY TRAINING CENTER
P.O. Box 58
Nuku'alofa
Tonga
Phone: 41-188

TEMPLES — 5

APIA SAMOA TEMPLE

Location: Address: P.O. Box 1621, Apia,

Samoa, 1.7 acres. Telephone: 9-00 operator
Operator (for non-direct dialing), 160-685,
#24-461.

Exterior Finish: "R-wall" exterior finish and insulation system on concrete block; split cedar shake shingles on roof.

Temple Design: Modern.

Architect: Emil B. Fetzer, Church architect.

Construction Advisor: Dale Cook and Richard Rowley.

Contractor: Utah Construction and Development.

Number of Rooms: Three sealing rooms, two ordinance rooms; total rooms 31.

Total Floor Area: 13,020 square feet.

Dimensions of Building: 142.88 feet by 115.32 feet.

District and membership: Islands of Western Samoa and American Samoa; 40,000 members.

Groundbreaking, Site Dedication: Feb. 19, 1981, by President Spencer W. Kimball, assisted by the head of state, Malieotoa Tanumafil II. Nearly 4,000 people attended, sitting through a torrential downpour.

Temple Dedication: Aug. 5, 1983, by President Gordon B. Hinckley, who conducted four of the seven dedicatory sessions.

NEW ZEALAND TEMPLE

Location: Temple site and college property are in Temple View, Hamilton, New Zealand. Hamilton is 75 miles south of Auckland. (011+64+71-77169)

Area of Site: Temple site and college grounds, 86 acres.

Exterior Finish: Reinforced concrete block, structural steel, painted white. (Concrete block manufactured at site.)

Temple Design: Modern-contemporary. Plan and lines similar to Swiss and London Temples, but with different dimensions and exterior designs.

Architect: Edward O. Anderson, Church architect.

Construction Chairman: Wendell B. Mendenhall.

Construction Supervisor: E. Albert Rosenvall and George R. Biesinger.

Number of Rooms: 75 rooms; 3 floors.

Total Floor Area: 34,000 square feet.

Dimensions of Building: 159 feet by 84 feet, total height of tower, 215 feet above highway, 157 feet above ground line.

District and membership: New Zealand

and Fiji; 64,000 members

Groundbreaking, Site Dedication: Dec. 21, 1955. First sod turned by Ariel Ballif, Wendell B. Mendenhall, and George R. Biesinger.

Temple Dedication: April 20, 1958, by President David O. McKay.

Dedicatory Prayer excerpt: *"We invoke thy blessing particularly upon the men and women who have so willingly and generously contributed their means, time and effort to the completion of this imposing and impressive structure. Especially we mention all those who have accepted calls as labor missionaries and literally consecrated their all upon the altar of service."*

NUKU'ALOFA TONGA TEMPLE

Area of Site: 5 acres.

Location: P.O. Box 40; Nuku'Alofa, Tonga; on 5 acres. Telephone — operator assisted, 9-00; 160-676, #41-055.

Exterior Finish: "R-wall" exterior finish and insulation system on concrete block; split cedar shake shingles on roof.

Temple Design: Modern.

Architect: Emil B. Fetzer, Church architect.

Construction Advisor: Richard Westover and Richard Rowley.

Contractor: Utah Construction & Development.

Number of Rooms: Three sealing rooms, two ordinance rooms; total rooms 31.

Total Floor Area: 13,020 square feet.

Dimensions of Building: 142.88 feet by 115.32 feet.

District and membership: Tonga; 29,000 members.

Groundbreaking, Site Dedication: Feb. 18, 1981, by President Spencer W. Kimball, with Tonga's King Taufa'ahau Tupou IV. Nearly 7,000 people attended the groundbreaking, after which President Kimball was honored with a feast attended by thousands.

Temple Dedication: Aug. 9-11, 1983, in seven sessions with President Gordon B. Hinckley presiding over the services.

Dedicatory Prayer excerpt: *'We ask that*

thou wilt accept this temple as the gift of thy people presented unto thee with love for the accomplishments of thy holy purposes with reference to thy children. It is thy house. It is the house of thy Son. May it always be held in reverence by thy people."

PAPEETE TAHITI TEMPLE

Location: Address — Rua de Pierri Loti, B.P. 5682; Pirae, Tahiti. Phone: (011 + 689) 4-31349.

Exterior Finish: Stucco, using imported white sand.

Temple Design: Shows some European elements of French influence as well as Polynesian culture.

Architect: Emil B. Fetzer, adapted by Temples and Special Projects Architecture.

Construction Advisor: George Bonnet.

Contractor: Comtrol Inc., a Midvale, Utah, construction firm.

Area of Site: About 1.7 acres.

Number of Rooms: Two ordinance

rooms, two sealing rooms; total 29 rooms.

Total Floor Area: 10,658 square feet.

Dimensions of Building: 125 feet by 105 feet, with an eight-foot statue of Angel Moroni on a 66-foot spire.

District and membership: Tahiti; 8,000 members.

Groundbreaking, Site Dedication: Feb. 13, 1981, by President Spencer W. Kimball, who also offered a prayer of dedication that the temple would be "a light to all in these islands."

Temple Dedication: Oct. 27-29, 1983, by President Gordon B. Hinckley in the first of six sessions, attended by 2,500 members.

Dedicatory Prayer excerpt: *"We ask that thou wilt preserve [the temple] . . . as thy house. May it be protected by thy power from any who would defile it. May it stand against the winds and the rains . . . ."*

SYDNEY AUSTRALIA TEMPLE

Location: Address — Pennant Hill Road & Moseley Street; Carlingford, NSW Australia; 3 acres. Telephone: 011-61-2-872-2447.

Exterior Finish: Precast panels, white quartz finish, terra cotta roof tiles.

Temple Design: Modern.

Architect: Emil B. Fetzer, Church architect, and R. Lindsay Little.

Construction Advisor: D. Crosbie and Richard Rowley.

Contractor: J. P. Cordukes Pty. Ltd.

Number of Rooms: Three sealing rooms, two ordinance rooms; total rooms 31.

Total Floor Area: 13,020 square feet.

Dimensions of Building: 145.11 feet by 115.14 feet.

District and membership: Australia; 66,000 members.

Groundbreaking, Site Dedication: Aug. 13, 1982, by Elder Bruce R. McConkie of the Council of the Twelve.

Temple Dedication: Sept. 20-23, 1984, by President Gordon B. Hinckley, 14 dedicatory sessions.

Dedicatory Prayer excerpt: *"May this temple with its grounds be a place of beauty to all who look upon it. May they be touched by thy spirit . . . ."*

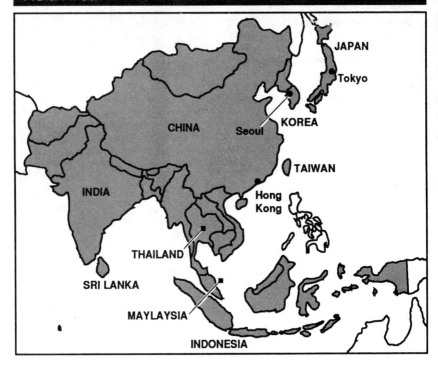

ASIA AREA

AREA: Approximately 2,607,136 square miles.

POPULATION: (1986 estimates) Hong Kong — 5,000,000; India — 777,804,000; Indonesia — 181,381,000; Japan — 127,899,000; Malaysia — 16,155,000; Singapore —2,639,000; South Korea — 44,116,000; Sri Lanka — 16,429,000; Taiwan — 19,929,000; Thailand — 56,465,000.

AREA PRESIDENCY: — Elders Douglas H. Smith, Adney Y. Komatsu and Royden G. Derrick

LDS POPULATION: 166,000

THE LANDS AND THE PEOPLES: Asia is comprised of a diverse mixture of mountains, plateaus, rain forests and islands. The area generally has a humid, wet climate with extremely hot summers and mild, wet winters (except the Japan and Korean areas, where winters are often accompanied by snow and low temperatures.) Religions in the area vary widely. A majority of the people are Buddhist and Muslim, with some Hindu, Shintoists, and Christians. Languages are even more varied. English is spoken in many of the countries, although it is not the major language in any of them.

Lifestyles in the Asia Area also vary greatly. Many Asians work on small farms and live in small villages, although growing Western influence and industrial opportunities encourage an increase in city dwellers. There are few places with such a marked contrast between old and new, modern and traditional societies.

CHURCH HISTORY: Pioneer wagon trains were still arriving in the Salt Lake Valley when the first LDS missionaries were sent to some Asian countries in the early 1850s.

However, these forerunners encountered almost insurmountable language, culture and religion barriers. By 1856, the last missionaries in Asia were called home, and it wasn't until almost 50 years later that the work was started up again. Elder Heber J. Grant, then of the Council of the Twelve, dedicated Japan for the preaching of the gospel on Sept. 1, 1901. Elder Grant, Horace S. Ensign, Louis A. Kelsch and Alma O. Taylor opened the country to missionary work, but 23 years and 166 baptisms later, the mission was closed. It was reopened in 1937, but work was limited to Japanese living in Hawaii.

After World War II, full-time missionaries — aided by the work of LDS servicemen stationed in Asia — returned to Japan in 1948. Hong Kong was opened briefly in 1950, then permanently in 1955. Taiwan was also opened in 1955. In April 1956, missionaries arrived in South Korea, three years after the end of the Korean War, and a mission was established there in July 1962.

The gospel was first introduced in Thailand in 1854. Four missionaries set out from San Francisco, Calif., but only one, Elam Luddington, reached the country. Arriving April 6, 1854, he spent only four months in Thailand. It wasn't until Feb. 2, 1968, that missionaries again set foot in Thailand. They have been there ever since.

President Ezra Taft Benson, then an apostle, dedicated Singapore April 14, 1969, and Indonesia Oct. 26, 1969, to the preaching of the gospel.

Missionary work began as early as 1853 in India, but despite some success, the last missionary left in May 1856. The Church now has representatives and native missionaries in India as well as representatives in Sri Lanka.

In 1988, the Asia area was divided and the new Philippines/Micronesia Area was formed.

1987 units and membership†

Country	Stakes	Wards	Stake bran- ches	Mis- sions	Dist- ricts	Mission wards, bran- ches	Total wards, bran- ches	Memb- ership	Per cent of Pop.	1 LDS in:
Diego Garcia						1	1	*		
Hong Kong	4	23	1	1	0	0	24	14,000	.03	386
India					2	9	9	700		
Indonesia				1	3	18	18	3,600		49,261
Japan	23	114	63	9	15	81	258	85,000	.07	1,429
Macao			1				1	300	.07	1,443
Malaysia					1	3	3	300		52,910
Singapore				1	1	5	5	1,300	.05	1,998
South Korea	14	68	47	4	2	24	139	44,000	.1	980
Sri Lanka					1	1	1	*		
Taiwan	3	19	7	2	2	21	47	14,000	.08	1,299
Thailand				1	1	17	17	2,800		18,762

* Fewer than 100 members

† Membership totals rounded off, some include partial estimates; stakes, missions as of Oct. 16, 1988.

STAKES — 44

HONG KONG—4
756 Hong Kong Island
1141 Hong Kong Kowloon
1502 Hong Kong Kowloon North
1503 Hong Kong New Territories

JAPAN—23
1018 Fukuoka Japan
1271 Hiroshima Japan
1120 Kobe Japan
1197 Machida Japan
919 Nagoya Japan
1203 Nagoya Japan West
1195 Naha Okinawa Japan
1404 Okayama Japan

586 Osaka Japan
872 Osaka Japan North
949 Sapporo Japan
1328 Osaka Japan Sakai
1154 Sapporo Japan West
1202 Sendai Japan
1255 Shizuoka Japan
1257 Takamatsu Japan
1164 Takasaki Japan
505 Tokyo Japan
1121 Tokyo Japan East
869 Tokyo Japan North
1270 Tokyo Japan South
1329 Tokyo Japan West

662 Yokohama Japan

SOUTH KOREA—14

1385 Chong Ju Korea
1435 Daegu Korea
1306 Inchon Korea
1596 Jeon Ju Korea
1196 Kwang Ju Korea
1059 Pusan Korea
1382 Pusan Korea West
 604 Seoul Korea

1412 Seoul Korea Dongdaemun
1017 Seoul Korea East
1386 Seoul Korea Kang Seo
1060 Seoul Korea North
 834 Seoul Korea West
1387 Seoul Korea Yong Dong

TAIWAN—3

1303 Kaohsiung Taiwan
1326 Taipei Taiwan East
 755 Taipei Taiwan West

MISSIONS — 19

HONG KONG MISSION
No. 2 Cornwall Street
Kowloon-Tong, Kowloon
Hong Kong
Phone: (011-852-3) 361-261

INDONESIA JAKARTA MISSION
J1. Senopati 115
Kebayoran Baru
Jakarta 12190, Indonesia
Phone: (011-62-21) 713-035

JAPAN FUKUOKA MISSION
46 Josui-machi, Hirao, Chuo-ku
Fukuoka, 810
Japan
Phone: (011-81-92) 522-0386

JAPAN KOBE MISSION
6-18 4-Chome, Shinohara Honmachi
Nada Ku, Kobe, T 657
Japan
Phone: (011-81-78) 881-2712

JAPAN NAGOYA MISSION
1-304 Itakadai
Meito-ku Nagoya-shi T 465
Japan
Phone: (011-81-52) 773-0755

JAPAN OKAYAMA MISSION
87-4 Kokufu-ichiba
Okayama-Shi, Okayama-Ken, T 703
Japan
Phone: (011-81-862) 75-4833

JAPAN OSAKA MISSION
Osaka Fu, Hirakata Shi
Asahigaoka-Cho 15-12, T 573
Japan
Phone: (011-81-720) 46-5551

JAPAN SAPPORO MISSION
Kita 2 Jo Nishi 24 Chome
245 Banchi 14 Chuo-Ku
Sapporo, Hokkaido 064
Japan
Phone: (011-81-11) 643-6411

JAPAN SENDAI MISSION
Yagiyama Minami 3 Chome 1-5
Sendai 982
Japan

Phone: (011-81-222) 45-8851

JAPAN TOKYO NORTH MISSION
4-25-12 Nishi Ochiai
Shinjuku-ku
Tokyo 161
Japan
Phone: (011-81-3) 952-6802

JAPAN TOKYO SOUTH MISSION
1-7-7 Kichijoji-Higashi Machi
Musashino-shi
Tokyo 180
Japan
Phone: (011-81-422) 21-2619

KOREA PUSAN MISSION
Tongnae P.O. Box 73
Pusan 607
Korea
Phone: (011-82-51) 552-7011

KOREA SEOUL MISSION
Gwang Hwa Moon
KPO 210
Seoul, 110
Korea
Phone: (011-82-2) 94-9785

KOREA SEOUL WEST MISSION
Yong Dong Post Office Box 62
Seoul, 135
Korea
Phone: (011-82-2) 585-2361

KOREA TAEJON MISSION
Taejon P.O. Box 38
Taejon, 300
Korea
Phone: (011-82-42) 524-9220

SINGAPORE MISSION
1 Goldhill Plaza #03-05
Podium Block, Newton Road
Singapore, 1130
Singapore
Phone: (011-65) 253-3722

TAIWAN TAICHUNG MISSION
No. 498-11 Wu Chuan Road
Taichung 40316
Taiwan, ROC
Phone: (011-886-4) 226-7181

TAIWAN TAIPEI MISSION
Floor 4, No. 24, Lane 183
Chin Hua Street
Taipei 10606
Taiwan, ROC
Phone: (011-886-2) 393-3285

THAILAND BANGKOK MISSION
15th Floor, Sino-Thai Tower
32/56 Soi 21 (Asoke) Sukhumvit Road
Bangkok 10110
Thailand
Phone: (011-66-2) 260-1279

Training Centers

JAPAN TOKYO MISSIONARY TRAINING CENTER
10-30 Minami-Azabu
5 Chome, Minato-Ku
Tokyo 106
Japan
Phone: (011-81-3) 444-6256

KOREA MISSIONARY TRAINING CENTER
No. 500-23 Changchun-Dong
Seodaemoon-Ku
Seoul 120
Korea
Phone: (011-82-2) 95-4104

TEMPLES — 3

SEOUL

KOREA

TEMPLE

Location: 500-23 Chang-Chun-Dong, Seo-dae-Moon, Ku, Seoul, Korea. Phone: (011-82-2) 322-9526.

Exterior Finish: Granite exterior.

Temple Design: Modern adaptation of earlier six-spire design 178 feet by 71 feet; Angel Moroni statue is atop tallest spire at 112 feet.

Architects: Church architectural staff; local architect, Komerican Architects.

Construction Advisor: Calvin Wardell.

Contractor: Woo Chang.

Area of Site: One acre.

Number of Rooms: Four ordinance rooms; three sealing rooms.

Total Floor Area: 12,780 square feet.

District and membership: South Korea; 44,000 members.

Groundbreaking, site dedication: May 9, 1983, by Elder Marvin J. Ashton.

Dedication: Dec. 14-15, 1985, by President Gordon B. Hinckley, six sessions.

Dedicatory Prayer excerpt: *"Our hearts are filled with gratitude for this long-awaited day. This is the first such house of the Lord ever constructed on the mainland of Asia, this vast continent where dwell more than a billion of thy sons and daughters, and where through the generations of the past have lived unnumbered hosts whose lives have not been touched by the saving principles of the gospel."*

TAIPEI TAIWAN TEMPLE

Location: On half-acre site at 256 AI KUO East Rd., in Taipei, Taiwan business district. Phone: (011+886+2) 351-0218.

Exterior Finish: White ceramic tile.
Temple Design: Modern adaptation of earlier six-spire design.

Architect: Church architectural staff with assistance from Philip Fei & Associates of Taipei.

Construction Advisor: Harold Smith.

Contractor: I. Cheng Construction & Development Corp.

Area of Site: About .5 acre.

Number of Rooms: Three sealing rooms, four ordinance rooms; total rooms 32.

Total Floor Area: 16,214 square feet.

Dimensions of Building: 178 feet by 72 feet, six spires; statue of Angel Moroni rises to height of 126 feet atop front arched spire.

District and membership: Taiwan and Hong Kong; 28,000 members.

Groundbreaking, Site Dedication: Aug. 26, 1982, by President Gordon B. Hinckley.

Temple Dedication: Nov. 17-18, 1984, by President Gordon B. Hinckley, five sessions.

Dedicatory Prayer excerpt: *"We thank thee for the firm foundation on which thy Church is now established in this part of the earth. We thank thee for this day . . . ."*

TOKYO TEMPLE

Location: Opposite the Arisugawa Park at 5-8-10 Minami Azabu in Minato-Ku, Tokyo, Japan. Phone: (011-813-422-8171.

Exterior Finish: Structural steel and reinforced concrete faced with 289 panels of precast stone, having the appearance of light gray granite. Building exceeds rigid Tokyo codes for earthquake and typhoon protection.

Architect: Emil B. Fetzer, Church architect. Architect's local representative, Masao Shiina.

Resident Engineer: Sadao Nagata

Construction Superintendent: Yuji Morimura for the Kajima Corporation.

Area of Site: 18,000 square feet, or slightly less than one-half acre.

Number of Rooms: Two ordinance rooms, five sealing rooms.

Total Floor Area: 58,000 square feet.

Dimensions of Building: Ground floor is 103 feet by 134 feet, upper levels are 103 by 105. Height to square is 70½ feet, to top of finial, 178½ feet.

District and membership: Japan; 85,000 members.

Groundbreaking, Site Dedication: Neither a groundbreaking nor a site dedication were held.

Temple Dedication: Oct. 27-29, 1980, by President Spencer W. Kimball.

Dedicatory Prayer excerpt: *"Kind Father, bless all those who come to this temple, that they may do so with humble hearts, in cleanliness, and honor, and integrity. We are grateful for these saints, for their devotion and their faith, for their worthiness and their determination to be pure and holy."*

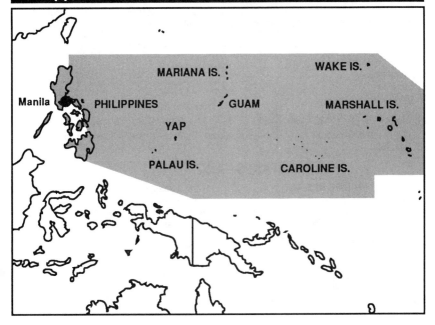

Philippines/Micronesia Area

AREA: 118,000 square miles

POPULATION: 58.3 million

AREA PRESIDENCY: Elders George I. Cannon, George R. Hill, Philip T. Sonntag

LDS POPULATION: 153,700

THE AREA AND THE PEOPLES: The Philippines/Micronesia Area covers a vast area of the South Pacific, and it's land mass consists of thousands of islands. The largest is Luzon with 43,308 square miles, and the smallest are Pacific atolls no more than a few miles across. About 58 million people reside on the Philippines' 7,000 islands, only 463 are larger than 1 square mile. About 250,000 of the area's population reside in the seven independent island nations of Micronesia-Guam. The area's climate is warm and humid, with heavy rainfall, especially during the typhoon season.

CHURCH HISTORY: President Joseph Fielding Smith dedicated the Philippine Islands to the preaching of the gospel Aug. 21, 1955, but the first missionaries didn't arrive until 1961. That year, Elder Gordon B. Hinckley officially opened the country for missionary work when he offered a prayer at Manila's American War Memorial Cemetery. Since then, the Church has expanded steadily. However, in the last few years, the Philippines has been the site of explosive growth, with nearly 23,000 Filipinos joining the Church last year. The faithfulness of the people is reflected in the number of home-grown missionaries serving in the country's nine missions. As of October 1988, 82 percent of the missionaries serving in this island nation were Filipinos. The work in Micronesia-Guam has been slower but no less significant as more and more islands are opened for missionary work.

1987 units and membership†

Country	Stakes	Wards	Stake bran- ches	Mis- sions	Dist- ricts	Mission bran- ches	Total wards, bran- ches	Memb- ership	Per cent of Pop.	1 LDS in:
Guam				1	1	4	4	1,500	.1	151
Marshall Islands					1	4	4	1,100	2.3	44
Micronesia					0	16	16	1,700	1.4	71
N. Marianas Is.						1	1	*		
Palau						1	1	200	.9	110
Philippines	32	186	80	8	32	231	497	149,000	.26	385

† Membership totals rounded off, some include partial estimates; stakes, missions as of Oct. 16, 1988.

STAKES — 32

PHILIPPINES—32

1226 Angeles Philippines	1551 Legaspi Philippines
1281 Bacolod Philippines	1557 Lingayen Philippines
1323 Bacolod Philippines North	841 Makati Philippines
1573 Baguio Philippines	1546 Makiling Philippines
1340 Cabanatuan Philippines	613 Manila Philippines
1572 Cadiz Philippines	1210 Marikina Philippines
1535 Cagayan de Oro Philippines	1577 Munoz Philippines
1238 Caloocan Philippines	1546 Naga Philippines
1220 Cebu City Philippines	1309 Paranaque Philippines
1330 Cebu City Philippines South	1554 Pasig Philippines
1229 Dagupan Philippines	842 Quezon City Philippines
1307 Davao Philippines	1315 San Fernando Philippines La Union
1544 Davao Philippines Buhangin	1552 San Pablo Philippines
1508 Iloilo Philippines	1321 Tarlac Philippines
1547 La Carlota Philippines	1558 Urdaneta Philippines
1555 Las Pinas Philippines	1571 Zamboanga Philippines

MISSIONS — 9

MICRONESIA GUAM MISSION
P.O. Box 21749 GMF
Barrigada, 96921
Guam
Phone: (011-671) 734-3526

PHILIPPINES BAGUIO MISSION
3rd Floor La Azotea Bldg.
112 Session Road
Baguio City, Benguet
Philippines
Phone: (011-63-74) 442-6030

PHILIPPINES CAGAYAN DE ORO MISSION
c/o State Investment
Cor. Tiano/Hayes Sts.
Cagayan de Oro 9000
Philippines
Phone: (011-63-88) 22-2410

PHILIPPINES BACOLOD MISSION
Box 489
Cebu City, Cebu 6401
Philippines
Phone: (011-63-32) 9-43-18

PHILIPPINES CEBU MISSION
P.O. Box 338
Cebu City, Cebu 6000
Philippines
Phone: (011-63-32) 6-10-13

PHILIPPINES DAVAO MISSION
P.O. Box 494
Davao City, 9501
Philippines
Phone: (011-63-82) 7-22-36

PHILIPPINES MANILA MISSION
Makati Central P.O. Box 801
Makati, Metro Manila, 3117
Philippines
Phone: (011-63-2) 818-7749

PHILIPPINES QUEZON CITY MISSION
MRF Arcade - P.O. Box 10206
Makati Commercial Center
Metro Manila 3117
Philippines
Phone: (011-63-2) 673-6364

PHILIPPINES QUEZON CITY
WEST MISSION
Hanston Bldg. 3rd Floor
Emerald Ave., Ortigas Commercial Complex
Pasig, Metro Manila 3130
Philippines
Phone: (011-63-2) 673-6340

Training Center
MANILA MISSIONARY TRAINING CENTER
17 La Salle Street
Northwest Greenhills Village
1500 San Juan, Metro Manila
Philippines
Phone: (011-63-2) 79-88-72

TEMPLES — 1

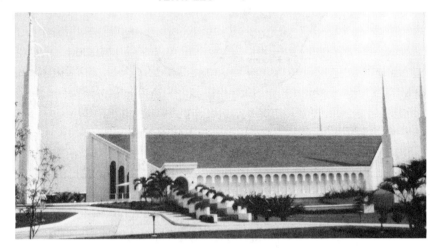

MANILA PHILIPPINES TEMPLE

Location: On Temple Drive in Quezon City. Address — P.O. Box 373, Greenmeadows; Metro Manila, Philippines. Phone: (011-63-2) 722-2821.

Area of Site: About 3.5 acres.

Exterior Finish: Ceramic tile.

Temple Design: Modern adaptation of earlier six-spire design.

Architect: Church architectural staff with assistance from Felipe M. Mendoza & Partners, Manila.

Construction Advisor: Wayne Tuttle.

Contractor: A. C. K. Construction, of Manila

Number of Rooms: Three sealing rooms, four ordinance rooms; total rooms 34.

Total Floor Area: 19,388 square feet.

Dimensions of Building: 200 feet by 75 feet, six spires; tallest is 115 feet high including statue of Angel Moroni.

District and membership: Philippines, Indonesia, Singapore, and Thailand; 156,000 members.

Groundbreaking, Site Dedication: Aug. 25, 1982, by President Gordon B. Hinckley. A typhoon threatened to strike, but even that did not dissuade 2,000 members from attending the groundbreaking.

Temple Dedication: Sept. 25-27, 1984, by President Gordon B. Hinckley in the first of nine sessions, who explained, "Never has there been a time that I've felt such a surge of emotion and been touched by the Spirit than I feel now."

Dedicatory Prayer excerpt: *"Lift the blight of poverty for which so many suffer. Particularly bless thy faithful saints who live honestly with thee in the payment of their tithes and offerings. Bless them that neither they nor their generations after them will go hungry, nor naked, nor without shelter from the storms that beat about them.*

"We thank thee for this beautiful edifice and for all who have worked to make it possible. May it stand as a pillar of truth and as an invitation to all who look upon it to learn of the purposes for which it has been created."

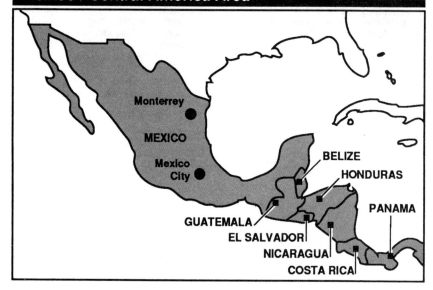

Mexico / Central America Area

MEXICO/CENTRAL AMERICA AREA

AREA: 954,000 square miles.

POPULATION: Mexico, 81.7 million; Guatemala, 8.6 million; El Salvador, 5.1 million; Honduras, 4.6 million; Nicaragua, 3.3 million; Costa Rica, 2.7 million; Panama, 2.2. million.

AREA PRESIDENCY: Elders Robert E. Wells, H. Verlan Andersen, and Gardner H. Russell.

LDS POPULATION: 495,700

THE LANDS AND THE PEOPLES: Much of the area is arid, with temperate highlands and tropical coastal areas, though containing many natural resources. Mexico has a wide range of geography, from desert plains to volcanic mountains and tropical lowlands. Central American nations have mountains and wide fertile valleys. Many Indian populations such as the Toltecs, Aztecs, Mayans flourished anciently. Today, many people live in large cities, although villages are scattered throughout the area. The people are predominantly Roman Catholic and speak Spanish as well as many Indian dialects.

CHURCH HISTORY: In 1874 Daniel W. Jones and Militon G. Trejo translated selections of the Book of Mormon into Spanish and published them in pamphlet form. In 1875 Jones led a small group of missionaries to Mexico City and distributed the tracts to government leaders. One fell into the hands of Plotino Rhodocanaty, an instructor of Greek in Mexico City. In 1878 he requested more information and a year later a second group of missionaries came, this time with Trejo and under the direction of Elder Moses Thatcher of the Council of the Twelve. They arrived Nov. 15, 1879, and soon baptized Rhodocanaty and a group with whom he studied. The Mexico City Branch was organized a week later. Mexico was dedicated for the preaching of the gospel April 6, 1881, by Elder Thatcher.

Mormon colonists came to the country five years later. The next two decades brought revolution and turmoil and missionary work was sporadic at best. Restrictions against foreign missionaries hindered proselyting. During one period shortly before World War II, a group broke off from the Church but was reconciled in 1946 after a visit from President George Albert Smith.

In the 1970s, the deep roots of nearly a century began to produce more abundantly and stakes and wards were divided rapidly.

The first expansion into Central America came in 1941 when John O'Donnal, who was reared in the Mexican colonies, went to work in Guatemala City for the U.S. Department of Agriculture. Six years later, after O'Donnal's efforts, four missionaries were sent to Guatemala and Costa Rica to begin proselyting. On Sept. 7, 1947, the first sacrament meeting was held in Central America. The Central American Mission was dedicated for preaching the gospel in Nov. 16, 1952, by Elder Spencer W. Kimball, then of the Council of the Twelve. On Aug. 1, 1965, the Guatemala-El Salvador Mission was created from the Central American Mission.

Since that time, inroads have been made in Panama, Nicaragua, Honduras, and to a lesser extent, Belize.

1987 units and membership†

Country	Stakes	Wards	Stake branches	Mis-sions	Dist-ricts	Total Mission wards, branches	branches	Memb-ership	Per cent of Pop.	1 LDS in:
Belize					1	5	5	900	.48	211
Costa Rica	2	12	12	1	2	7	31	8,900	.27	366
El Salvador	6	41	26	1			67	24,000	.35	283
Guatemala	13	86	51	3	12	78	215	63,000	.86	116
Honduras	5	24	22	1	7	27	73	23,000	.45	221
Mexico	92	531	249	14	35	209	989	360,000	.44	228
Nicaragua	1	4	5				9	3,900	.1	980
Panama	3	15	10		3	12	37	12,000	.49	202

† Membership totals rounded off, some include partial estimates; stakes, missions as of Oct. 16, 1988.

STAKES — 122

COSTA RICA—2
803 San Jose Costa Rica
917 San Jose Costa Rica La Sabana

EL SALVADOR—6
1223 San Miguel El Salvador
618 San Salvador El Salvador
1035 San Salvador El Salvador Cuzcatlan
741 San Salvador El Salvador Ilopango
1217 Santa Ana El Salvador Modelo
1088 Santa Ana El Salvador El Molino

GUATEMALA—13
1611 Chilmaltenango Guatemala
436 Guatemala City Guatemala
1618 Guatemala City Guatemala Atlantico
1619 Guatemala City Guatemala Central
1681 Guatemala City Guatemala Escuintla
1620 Guatemala City Guatemala Florida
778 Guatemala City Guatemala Las Victorias
1040 Guatemala City Guatemala Mariscal
699 Guatemala City Guatemala Utatlan
713 Quetzaltenango Guatemala
1497 Quetzaltenango Guatemala West
1168 Retalhuleu Guatemala
1498 San Marcos Guatemala

HONDURAS—5
1383 Comayaguela Honduras
1647 La Ceiba Honduras
1601 La Lima Honduras
820 San Pedro Sula Honduras
947 Tegucigalpa Honduras

MEXICO—92
1640 Aguascalientes Mexico
1474 Campeche Mexico
941 Celaya Mexico
722 Chalco Mexico
782 Chihuahua Mexico
1633 Chihuahua Mexico East
783 Ciudad Juarez Mexico
1109 Ciudad Juarez Mexico East
1699 Ciudad Juarez Mexico North
1301 Ciudad Mante Mexico
772 Ciudad Obregon Mexico
1500 Ciudad Obregon Mexico Yaqui
797 Ciudad Victoria Mexico
1043 Coatzacoalcos Mexico
37 Colonia Juarez Mexico
721 Cuautla Mexico
1428 Cuernavaca Mexico
838 Culiacan Mexico
1644 Culiacan Mexico Tamazula
1228 Durango Mexico
935 Gomez Palacio Mexico
1183 Guadalajara Mexico Independencia
683 Guadalajara Mexico Union

771	Hermosillo Mexico	1114	Monterrey Mexico Moderna
1636	Hermosillo Mexico Pitic	1144	Monterrey Mexico Morelos
1589	Jalapa Mexico	908	Monterrey Mexico Paraiso
1232	Leon Mexico	773	Monterrey Mexico Roma
1139	Los Mochis Mexico	1615	Monterrey Mexico Valle Verde
795	Madera Mexico	1280	Oaxaca Mexico
1131	Matamoros Mexico	1685	Oaxaca Mexico Monte Alban
804	Merida Mexico	801	Orizaba Mexico
923	Merida Mexico Lakin	857	Piedras Negras Mexico
819	Mexicali Mexico	730	Poza Rica Mexico
1626	Mexicali Mexico Los Pinos	799	Poza Rica Mexico Palmas
1603	Mexico City Mexico Anahuac	1293	Puebla Mexico Fuertes
617	Mexico City Mexico Aragon	680	Puebla Mexico La Paz
658	Mexico City Mexico Arbolillo	898	Puebla Mexico Popocateptl
1317	Mexico City Mexico Azteca	681	Puebla Mexico Valsequillo
719	Mexico City Mexico Camarones	1132	Reynosa Mexico
1357	Mexico City Mexico Chapultepec	1155	Saltillo Mexico
716	Mexico City Mexico Churubusco	1231	San Luis Potosi Mexico
1663	Mexico City Mexico Ecatepec	567	Tampico Mexico
718	Mexico City Mexico Ermita	951	Tapachula Mexico
723	Mexico City Mexico Industrial	757	Tijuana Mexico
1070	Mexico City Mexico Iztapalapa	1587	Tijuana Mexico La Mesa
965	Mexico City Mexico Linda Vista	781	Torreon Mexico
726	Mexico City Mexico Moctezuma	1532	Torreon Mexico Jardin
727	Mexico City Mexico Netzahualcoyotl	725	Tula Mexico
1433	Mexico City Mexico Oriental	1174	Tuxtla Gutierrez Mexico
1466	Mexico City Mexico Pachuca	1653	Valle del Mezquital Mexico
717	Mexico City Mexico Tacubaya	628	Valle Hermosa Mexico
720	Mexico City Mexico Tlalnepantla	700	Veracruz Mexico
1356	Mexico Mexico Mexico Tlalpan	800	Veracruz Mexico Reforma
1579	Mexico City Mexico Valle Dorado	1166	Villahermosa Mexico
724	Mexico City Mexico Villa de las Flores		
715	Mexico City Mexico Zarahemla		**NICARAGUA—1**
829	Minatitlan Mexico	1246	Managua Nicaragua
644	Monclova Mexico		**PANAMA—3**
774	Monterrey Mexico Anahuac	1634	David Panama
572	Monterrey Mexico Libertad	1081	Panama City Panama
508	Monterrey Mexico Mitras	1596	San Miguelito Panama

MISSIONS — 20

COSTA RICA SAN JOSE MISSION
Apartado Postal 2339
San Jose
Costa Rica, C.A.
Phone: (011-506) 34-19-40

EL SALVADOR SAN SALVADOR MISSION
Apartado Postal 367
San Salvador
El Salvador, C.A.
Phone: (011-503) 235-654

GUATEMALA GUATEMALA CITY
NORTH MISSION
Apartado Postal 119-C
Guatemala
Guatemala, C.A.
Phone: (011-502-2) 31-69-51

GUATEMALA GUATEMALA CITY
SOUTH MISSION
Apartado Postal 119-C
Guatemala
Guatemala, C.A.

Phone: (011-502-2) 76-15-08

GUATEMALA QUETZALTENANGO
MISSION
Apartado Postal 206
Quetzaltenango
Guatemala, C.A.
Phone: (011-502-9) 61-6736

HONDURAS TEGUCIGALPA MISSION
Apartado Postal 556
Tegucigalpa
Honduras, C.A.
Phone: (011-504) 32-8923

MEXICO CHIHUAHUA MISSION
Calle Maria Luisa
Colonia Jardines de Sacturio
Apartado E41
Chihuahua
Mexico
Phone: (011-52-14) 13-88-94

MEXICO GUADALAJARA MISSION

Ricardo Palma 2660
Col. Lomas de Guevara
Guadalajara, Jalisco 44640
Mexico
Phone: (011-52-36) 41-00-58

MEXICO HERMOSILLO MISSION
Apartado Postal 557
Hermosillo, Sonora, C.P. 83000
Mexico
Phone: (011-52-621) 4-15-02

MEXICO MAZATLAN MISSION
Rio Culiacan #49
Fracc. Tellerias
Mazatlan, Tellerias Sin. C.P. 23000
Mexico
Phone: (011-52-678) 23-703

MEXICO MERIDA MISSION
Apartado Postal #26 y 27 Sucursal C
97000, Merida, Yucatan
Mexico
Phone: (011-52-99) 24-51-08

MEXICO MEXICO CITY EAST MISSION
Calle Leibnitz No. 166
Colonia Nueva Anzures
C.P. 11590 Mexico, D.F.
Mexico
Phone: (011-52-5) 531-9245

MEXICO MEXICO CITY NORTH MISSION
Legaria 779-101, Col. Irrigacion
Del. Hidalgo
11500 Mexico 10 D.F.
Mexico
Phone: (011-52-5) 395-1871

MEXICO MEXICO CITY SOUTH MISSION
Monte Caucaso 1110

Lomas de Chapultepec
Mexico City D.F., C.P. 11000
Mexico
Phone: (011-52-5) 540-3797

MEXICO MONTERREY MISSION
Apartado Postal 862
Monterrey, Nuevo Leon, 64000
Mexico
Phone: (011-52-83) 58-10-44

MEXICO PUEBLA MISSION
Calle 25 Sur #907
Colonia La Paz
Puebla, Puebla 72160
Mexico
Phone: (011-52-22) 49-88-07

MEXICO TAMPICO MISSION
Ejercito Mexicano 74
Col. Loma del Gallo
Cd. Madero, Tampico 89460
Phone: (011-52-121) 52-208

MEXICO TORREON MISSION
Apartado Postal 792
Torreon, Coahuila
Mexico C.P. 27000
Phone: (011-52-171) 23392

MEXICO TUXTLA-GUTIERREZ MISSION
Apartado 278
Tuxtla Gutierrez, Chiapas
Mexico C.P. 29000
Phone: (011-52-961) 21-441

MEXICO VERACRUZ MISSION
Apartado Postal 103
Veracruz, Veracruz CP 91700
Mexico
Phone: (011-52-293) 1-35-66

Training Centers

GUATEMALA MISSIONARY TRAINING
CENTER
23 Avenida 6-83 Zona L5
Vista Hermosa I
Apartado Postal 4-C
Guatemala
Guatemala, C.A.
Phone: (011-502-2) 690-836/693-426

MEXICO CITY MISSIONARY TRAINING
CENTER
Apartado Postal 135-027
Unidad Aragon
07970 Mexico, D.F.
Mexico
Phone: (905) 551-3273

TEMPLES — 2

MEXICO CITY TEMPLE

Location: Bounded on three sides by following streets: Calle Ignacio Allende, Calle Emiliano Capata, and Avenida 510 in Mexico City's Aragon area near Aragon public park and zoological gardens. (905) 551-1784

Exterior Finish: White cast stone, ornate with adaptions of ancient Mayan designs, especially on upper portion of the structure.

Temple Design: Modern adaption of ancient Mayan architecture.

Architect: Emil B. Fetzer, Church architect.

Resident Project Inspector: Ricardo Espiriti.

Construction Superintendent: Jose Ortiz for Urbec Construction Co.

Area of Site: 7 acres.

Number of Rooms: Four ordinance rooms, 11 sealing rooms.

Total Floor Area: 117,133 square feet.

Dimensions of Building: Basement and first floors, 178 by 214½ feet; two upper levels, 119½ by 157 feet. Height to square, 70 feet; to top of tower, 152 feet. Sculptured figure of Angel Moroni was placed atop the apex of tower.

District and membership: Mexico; 360,000 members.

Groundbreaking, Site Dedication: Nov. 25, 1979, by Elder Boyd K. Packer of the Council of the Twelve, who addressed the 10,000 persons who attended.

Temple Dedication: Dec. 2-4, 1983, the first of nine sessions. President Gordon B.

Hinckley offered the dedicatory prayer. About 40,000 members participated in the dedicatory sessions.

Dedicatory Prayer excerpt: *"Bless thy saints in this great land and those from other lands who will use this temple. Most have in their veins the blood of Father Lehi. Thou hast kept thine ancient promises."*

GUATEMALA CITY TEMPLE

Location: 24 Avenida 2-20, at foot of hills in the southeastern part of Guatemala City. (011+502+2) 69-3426.

Exterior Finish: Natural white Guatemala marble.

Temple Design: Modern adaptation of

earlier six-spire design.

Architect: Church architectural staff with assistance from Jose Asturias, architect, Guatemala City.

Construction Advisor: David Judd.

Contractor: Isa Constructors Aires Y Cia Ltd.

Area of Site: About 1.4 acres.

Number of Rooms: Three sealing rooms, four ordinance rooms; total rooms, 32.

Total Floor Area: 11,610 square feet.

Dimensions of Building: 178 feet by 72 feet, six spires; statue of Angel Moroni rises to height of 126 feet atop front arched spire.

District and membership: Guatemala, Nicaragua, Costa Rica, El Salvador, Honduras; 122,000 members.

Announced: April 1, 1981, by President Spencer W. Kimball.

Groundbreaking, Site Dedication: Sept. 12, 1982, by Elder Richard G. Scott of the First Quorum of the Seventy.

Temple Dedication: Dec. 14-16, 1984, by President Gordon B. Hinckley, 10 sessions.

"Bless our land, O Father, this nation of Guatemala where stands thy holy house. May those who govern do so in righteousness. Bless them as they act to preserve the liberties and enhance the prosperity of the people. May there be peace in the land."

BRAZIL AREA

AREA: 3.2 million square miles

POPULATION: 135.5 million

LDS POPULATION: 249,000

AREA PRESIDENCY: Elders Francis M. Gibbons, Helio Camargo, and Lynn A. Sorenson.

THE LANDS AND THE PEOPLES: Brazil covers almost half the continent of South America and is almost as long as it is wide. The Amazon Region, with many rain forests that drain into the Amazon River, the Northeast Region with a mostly rural population, and the Central and Southern Plateau Region, the nation's heartland, make up Brazil.

Most of Brazil is hot all year, with rainfall ranging from 50 inches to much less. More than half the population is of European ancestry with a high percentage of mixed nationalities. They are predominantly Catholics in a land where Brazilian law provides freedom of worship. Most of the population is urban. Brazilians enjoy sports and frequent family gatherings. Brazil is also known for its festivals.

CHURCH HISTORY: The first proselyting in Brazil was an extension of the South American Mission in Argentina. Elders William F. Heinz and Emil A. J. Schindler, accompanied for a short time by Pres. Reinhold Stoof of the South American Mission, arrived by boat and began proselyting in Brazil in September 1928.

The Brazilian Mission was later established under Pres. Rulon S. Howells on May 15, 1935. The first converts were in Joinville among German emigrants.

1987 units and membership†

Country	Stakes	Wards	Stake branches	Mis-sions	Dist-ricts	Total Mission wards, branches	branches	Memb-ership	Per cent of Pop.	1 LDS in:
Brazil	57	331	101	10	16	85	517	249,000	.174	575

† Membership totals rounded off, some include partial estimates; stakes, missions as of Oct. 16, 1988.

STAKES — 57

BRAZIL—57

1292 Alegrete Brazil	1604 Passo Fundo Brazil
970 Araraquara Brazil	1658 Pelotas Brazil
1234 Belo Horizonte Brazil	1377 Petropolis Brazil
1332 Boa Viagem Brazil	1182 Ponta Grossa Parana Brazil
1189 Brasilia Brazil	601 Porto Alegre Brazil
1393 Brasilia Brazil Alvorada	1256 Porto Alegre Brazil North
1442 Campina Grande Brazil	1201 Recife Brazil
621 Campinas Brazil	1645 Ribeirao Preto Brazil
1586 Campinas Brazil Castelo	1135 Rio Claro Brazil
552 Curitiba Brazil	589 Rio de Janeiro Brazil
1302 Curitiba Brazil Bacacheri	1028 Rio de Janeiro Brazil Andarai
1243 Curitiba Brazil East	1378 Rio de Janeiro Brazil Madureira
1470 Curitiba Brazil Iquacu	769 Rio de Janeiro Brazil Niteroi
1030 Curitiba Brazil North	1516 San Jose Dos Campos Brazil
893 Curitiba Brazil South	1136 Santo Andre Brazil
1569 Florianopolis Brazil	620 Santos Brazil
1284 Fortaleza Brazil	523 Sao Bernardo Brazil
1454 Fortaleza Brazil Montese	417 Sao Paulo Brazil
1578 Fortaleza Brazil West	467 Sao Paulo Brazil East
1641 Goiania Brazil	1536 Sao Paulo Brazil Interlagos
1185 Joao Pessoa Brazil	1137 Sao Paulo Brazil Ipiranga
1338 Joinville Brazil	815 Sao Paulo Brazil North
1080 Londrina Brazil	1138 Sao Paulo Brazil Perdizes
1322 Maceio Brazil	1082 Sao Paulo Brazil Santo Amaro
1700 Manaus Brazil	1441 Sao Paulo Brazil Taboao
1449 Marilia Brazil	622 Sao Paulo Brazil West
987 Novo Hamburgo Brazil	1291 Sao Vincente Brazil
1282 Olinda Brazil	989 Sorocaba Brazil
	1630 Vitoria Brazil

MISSIONS — 10

BRAZIL BELO HORIZONTE MISSION
Rua Sao Paulo, 1781, 10 Andar
Edificio 17 de Maio, Sala 1001
30170 Belo Horizonte - MG
Brazil
Phone: (011-55-31) 335-7770

BRAZIL BRASILIA MISSION
SEPS EQ 714/914 - Bl. A Sala 110
70.390 Brasilia - DF
Brazil
Phone: (011-55-61) 245-5399

BRAZIL CAMPINAS MISSION
Caixa Postal 1814
13100 - Campinas - SP
Brazil
Phone: (011-55-192) 51-50-99

BRAZIL CURITIBA MISSION
Caixa Postal 9191
80311 - Curitiba - Parana
Brazil
Phone: (011-55-41) 244-1821

BRAZIL FORTALEZA MISSION
Rua Barao de Aracati, No. 1145

Aldeota - Fortaleza
Brazil
Phone: (011-55-85) 221-1335

BRAZIL PORTO ALEGRE MISSION
Caixa Postal 4089
90.620 Porto Alegre - RS
Brazil
Phone: (011-55-512) 23-0748

BRAZIL RECIFE MISSION
Caixa Postal 1620 - Centro
50.000 Recife - PE
Brazil
Phone: (011-55-81) 231-6496

BRAZIL RIO DE JANEIRO MISSION
Rua Muniz Barreto, 581
Botofogo
22.251 Rio de Janeiro - RJ
Brazil

Phone: (011-55-21) 266-0201
BRAZIL SAO PAULO NORTH MISSION
Caixa Postal 26095
05599 Sao Paulo - SP
Brazil
Phone: (011-55-11) 814-2277

BRAZIL SAO PAULO SOUTH MISSION
Caixa Postal 26023
01.000 Sao Paulo - SP
Brazil
Phone: (011-55-11) 814-2277

Training Center

SAO PAULO MISSIONARY TRAINING
CENTER
Av. Prof. Francisco Morato, 2.430 - Caxingui
CEP: 05512 - Sao Paulo - S.P.
Brazil
Phone: (011-55-11) 211-0236

TEMPLES — 1

SAO PAULO TEMPLE

Location: Avenida Prof. Francisco Morato 2390 in the Butanta section of Sao Paulo, Brazil. Phone: (011+55+11 813-9354)

Exterior Finish: Reinforced concrete faced with cast stone composed of quartz and marble aggregates set in special white-base cement.

Temple Design: Modern design with Spanish influence.

Architect: Emil B. Fetzer, Church architect.

Construction Chairman: Christiani Nielsen, general contractor.

Construction Supervisor:

Ross Jensen and James Magleby.
Number of Rooms: 76.
Total Floor Area: 51,279 square feet.
Dimensions of Building: 116 feet by 256 feet, with tower reaching 101 feet, 4 inches.

District and membership: Brazil and Paraguay; 257,000 members.

Groundbreaking: March 20, 1976; Elder James E. Faust, then an Assistant to the Twelve, presided, broke ground and spoke to more than 2,000 Church members present. He was assisted by Asael T. Sorensen and Walter Spat who also addressed the group, and by Antonio Carlos de Camargo

and Osiris Grobel Cabral, who offered prayers.

Temple Dedication: Oct. 30, 1978, in the first of 10 dedicatory sessions, President Spencer W. Kimball offered the dedicatory prayer in the celestial room of the temple. He repeated the prayer in the additional nine sessions that were held in the Sao Paulo Stake Center.

Dedicatory Prayer excerpt: *"Our Father, may peace abide in all the homes of thy saints. May holy angels guard them. May prosperity shine upon them and sickness and disease be rebuked from their midst."*

South America North Area

SOUTH AMERICA NORTH AREA

AREA: 1,821,748 square miles

POPULATION: Bolivia, 6.2 million; Colombia, 29.9 million; Ecuador, 9.6 million; Peru, 20.2 million; Venezuela, 17.8 million.

AREA PRESIDENCY: Elders Charles Didier, Angel Abrea and Hartman Rector Jr.

LDS POPULATION: 312,000

THE LANDS AND THE PEOPLES: Most of the countries are split by the Andes range, with highlands in the center, humid lowlands on the coast, and temperate highlands and tropical lowlands to the east. A high percentage of the people are of Indian descent, or of mixed European-Indian decent. Spanish is the official language, but such Indian dialects as Quechua, Aymara, and Jivaroan are used by many people. More than 90 percent of the people are Roman Catholics. Per capita income ranges from $2,629 in the north to $536 in the south.

CHURCH HISTORY: Although several members lived in these lands in the 1940s and possibly earlier, the first branch was organized July 8, 1956, in Lima, Peru, with Frederick S. Williams, former president of the South America and Uruguay missions, as president. Elder Henry D. Moyle, then of the Council of the Twelve, organized the branch and delivered a blessing on the land. The first Sunday School was held on July 8, 1956, in the Williams' home in Lima with Elder Moyle presiding.

The Church became established in Bolivia through the efforts of the North American families of Duane Wilcox and Dube Thomas, then living in La Paz, and Norval Jesperson of Cochabamba in 1963. After legal permission for the Church to operate was obtained, missionaries came in 1964, and the baptism of Victor Walter Vallejos, the first in the country, came about Christmas time.

Ecuador was opened next, prompted by a letter to Pres. J. Averil Jesperson in Lima from Elder Spencer W. Kimball, then of the Council of the Twelve. Two missionaries were dispatched to Quito and three weeks later, Elder Kimball dedicated the land on Oct. 8, 1965. The Ecuador Mission was created Aug. 1, 1970, and divided in 1978.

Colombia was dedicated a year later by Elder Kimball. Venezuela was visited that year by Elder Marion G. Romney, then of the Council of the Twelve, who dedicated the land on Nov. 2, 1966. Mission Pres. Ted E. Brewerton opened the country, and under his direction, missionaries concentrated on families and potential members with leadership ability. By July 1, 1968, enough members had joined that Venezuela was taken from the Central America Mission and the Colombia-Venezuela Mission was created. Three years later, The Venezuela Maracaibo Mission was created.

1987 units and membership*

State	Stakes	Wards	Stake bran- ches	Mis- sions	Dis- tricts	Total Mission wards, bran- ches	wards, bran- ches	Mem- bership	Per cent of Pop.	1 LDS in:
Bolivia	9	55	26	2	7	43	124	40,000	.645	155
Colombia	9	45	20	3	17	65	130	60,000	.200	500
Ecuador	8	46	7	2	6	31	84	52,000	.539	186
Netherlands Antilles						4	4	100		
Peru	31	181	55	5	16	110	346	125,000	.619	162
Venezuela	5	35	13	2	12	54	102	35,000	.197	508

* Membership totals rounded off, some include partial estimates; stakes, missions as of Oct. 16, 1988.

STAKES — 62

BOLIVIA—9

1465 Cochabamba Bolivia Cobija
1062 Cochabamba Bolivia Universidad
1112 La Paz Bolivia Constitucion
1227 La Paz Bolivia El Alto
1007 La Paz Bolivia Miraflores
1670 La Paz Bolivia Sopocachi
1213 Oruro Bolivia
 993 Santa Cruz Bolivia Canoto
1235 Santa Cruz Bolivia Paraiso

COLOMBIA—9

1537 Barranquilla Colombia
 805 Bogota Colombia
1113 Bogota Colombia Ciudad Jardin
1659 Bogota Colombia El Dorado
1008 Bogota Colombia Kennedy
1308 Bucaramanga Colombia
 937 Cali Colombia
1054 Cali Colombia Americas
1697 Medellin Colombia

ECUADOR—8

1117 Guayaquil Ecuador North
1006 Guayaquil Ecuador South
 939 Guayaquil Ecuador West
1316 Otavalo Ecuador
1224 Portoviejo Ecuador
1259 Quevedo Ecuador
1053 Quito Ecuador Colon
1225 Quito Ecuador Santa Ana

PERU—31

1540 Arequipa Peru Manuel Prado
1108 Arequipa Peru Umacollo
1145 Chiclayo Peru
1567 Chiclayo Peru Central
1122 Chimbote Peru
1527 Cuzco Peru
1471 Huancayo Peru
1162 Iquitos Peru
1541 Iquitos Peru Sacha Chorro
1063 Lima Peru Callao
 789 Lima Peru Central
1679 Lima Peru Chorrillos
1675 Lima Peru Comas
1680 Lima Peru El Olivar
 788 Lima Peru Lamanita
1677 Lima Peru Las Flores
1674 Lima Peru Las Palmeras
 503 Lima Peru Limatambo
 670 Lima Peru Magdalena
1678 Lima Peru Maranga
1486 Lima Peru Palao
1439 Lima Peru San Felipe
1064 Lima Peru San Juan
1440 Lima Peru San Luis
1065 Lima Peru San Martin
1553 Lima Peru Villa Maria
1676 Lima Peru Vivarte
1400 Piura Peru
1399 Tacna Peru
 887 Trujillo Peru North
1487 Trujillo Peru Palermo

827   Caracas Venezuela
1585   Guayana Venezuela
1181   Maracaibo Venezuela

1414   Maracaibo Venezuela South
1050   Valencia Venezuela

MISSIONS — 14

BOLIVIA COCHABAMBA MISSION
Casilla de Correo 1375
Cochabamba
Bolivia
Phone: (011-591-42) 42-509

BOLIVIA LA PAZ MISSION
20 de Octubre 2550
Casilla 4789
La Paz
Bolivia
Phone: (011-591-2) 327-062

COLOMBIA BARRANQUILLA MISSION
Calle 72, No. 54-35, Ofc. 6A
A.A. 50710
Barranquilla - Atlantico
Colombia
Phone: (011-57-58) 45-4018

COLOMBIA BOGOTA MISSION
Apartado Aereo 90746
Bogota 8, D.E.
Colombia
Phone: (011-57-1) 218-4484

COLOMBIA CALI MISSION
Apartado Aereo 4892
Cali, Valle
Colombia
Phone: (011-57-23) 671-816

ECUADOR GUAYAQUIL MISSION
Casilla 8750
Guayaquil
Ecuador
Phone: (011-593-4) 386-680

ECUADOR QUITO MISSION
Casilla 78-A
Quito
Ecuador
Phone: (011-593-2) 525-583

PERU AREQUIPA MISSION
Casilla 1884
Arequipa
Peru
Phone: (011-51-54) 22-34-63

PERU LIMA EAST MISSION
Casilla de Correo 14-0196
Lima 14
Peru
Phone: (011-51-14) 318-654

PERU LIMA NORTH MISSION
Casilla de Correo 11-0123
Lima 11
Peru
Phone: (011-51-14) 221-129

PERU LIMA SOUTH MISSION
Casilla de Correo 14-0293
Lima 14
Peru
Phone: (011-51-14) 31-9235

PERU TRUJILLO MISSION
Los Sauces 792
Urbanizacion California
Trujillo
Peru
Phone: (011-51-44) 24-44-82

VENEZUELA CARACAS MISSION
Apartado 80425
Caracas 1080-A
Venezuela
Phone: (011-58-2) 77-30-09

VENEZUELA MARACAIBO MISSION
Apartado 10020 Bella Vista
Maracaibo, Estado Zulia CP 4002A
Venezuela
Phone: (011-58-61) 515-320

Training Centers

LIMA PERU MISSIONARY TRAINING
CENTER
Jorge Basadre 1210
Casilla de Correo 14-0125
Lima 14
Peru
Phone: (01-51-14) 42-8723

BOGOTA COLOMBIA TEMPLE

Announced: April 7, 1984, by President Gordon B. Hinckley.

Site announced: May 28, 1988, by the First Presidency

Temple district: 87,000 members in Colombia, Venezuela, and Panama.

Status: Pending groundbreaking.

GUAYAQUIL ECUADOR TEMPLE

Announced: President Gordon B. Hinckley, March 31, 1982.

Initial plans: Six-spired international temple of 10,000 square feet.

Temple district: about 36,000 members in Ecuador.

Status: Pending groundbreaking.

LIMA PERU TEMPLE

Location: Southwest part of Lima, Peru, in the Molina district. Avenida Javier Prado, Esq. Av. de Los Ingenieros, Urb. STA Patricia 3a Etapa, Lima Peru. Phone (011-51-14) 37-3022.

Announced: April 1, 1981, by President Spencer W. Kimball.

Exterior Finish: Local granite; Oriental design.

Temple Design: Modern adaptation of earlier six-spire design 178 feet by 71 feet; Angel Moroni statue is atop tallest spire at 112 feet.

Construction Advisor: Sergio Gomez.

Contractor: Grana y Montero.

Architects: Church architectural staff; local architect, Jose Asturias.

Area of Site: 4.5 acres.

Number of Rooms: Four ordinance rooms, three sealing rooms.

Total Floor Area: 10,052 square feet.

District and membership: Peru, Bolivia; 165,000 members.

Dedication: Jan. 10-12, 1986, by President Gordon B. Hinckley, 11 sessions.

Dedicatory Prayer excerpt: *"We are particularly mindful this day of the sons and daughters of Lehi. They have known so much of suffering and sorrow in their many generations. They have walked in darkness and in servitude. Now thou hast touched them by the light of the everlasting gospel. The shackles of darkness are falling from their eyes as they embrace the truths of thy great work."*

SOUTH AMERICA SOUTH AREA

AREA: 1,582,530 square miles.

POPULATION: Argentina, 31.2 million; Chile, 12.3 million; Paraguay, 4.1 million; Uruguay, 2.9 million.

AREA PRESIDENCY: Elders Waldo P. Call, John H. Groberg and L. Aldin Porter

LDS POPULATION: 360,000

THE LANDS AND THE PEOPLES: The area contains the Andes mountain chain that runs through Chile, the plains and highlands of Argentina, as well as the tropical forests of interior Paraguay and the temperate, grassy, well-watered plains of Uruguay. Most dwell in large, modern cities, such as Buenos Aires or Montevideo. The major religion in the area is Roman Catholic, and religious freedom is permitted. The climate is temperate to frigid.

CHURCH HISTORY: Parley P. Pratt and his wife Phebe Soper Pratt, and Elder Rufus C. Allen were the first missionaries to South America. They arrived in Valparaiso, Chile, via the bark Henry Kelsey on Nov. 8, 1851. The visit was unsuccessful, and they returned after five months. Seventy-four years later, in 1925, Wilhelm Friedrichs and Emil Hoppe, converts from Germany living on the other side of the continent in Buenos Aires, Argentina, were visited by Elder Melvin J. Ballard of the Council of the Twelve. He opened a mission and on Dec. 13, 1925, presided at the baptism of six converts. He dedicated South America for the preaching of the gospel on Christmas Day, 1925.

Work next extended to Uruguay in 1940 when Rolf Larson, a former missionary, played basketball in a national tournament. His influence led the way for contacts and converts, who were visited by Pres. Frederick S. Williams of the Argentine Mission. The first branch was opened in 1944, and in 1947, when Pres. Williams was a resident of Uruguay, he was called as president of the Uruguay Mission.

Missionary work began in Paraguay in 1948 when returned missionaries employed by the Paraguayan government baptized a convert.

Proselyting began in Chile almost a century after Elder Pratt's visit. The E.L. Folsoms from Salt Lake City, Utah, lived in the country from 1928 to 1944, and they were followed by the William Fotheringham family in 1952. This family was visited by President David O. McKay on Feb. 9, 1954. Two years later, Elders Joseph Bentley and Verle Allred crossed the Andes to Chile. They stayed with the Fotheringhams and soon baptized Ricardo and Perla Garcia, on Nov. 25, 1956, as well as several others.

In each of these countries, the work progressed slowly at first, then with increasing tempo. The Church in Argentina is the most established since the work was started there first. However, Chile has the largest number of members and is growing more rapidly. Membership in Uruguay has also rapidly increased. In Paraguay, growth has continued at a measured pace.

1987 units and membership†

Country	Stakes	Wards	Stake bran- ches	Mis- sions	Dist- ricts	Total Mission wards, bran- ches	wards, bran- ches	Memb- ership	Per cent of Pop.	1 LDS in:
Argentina	26	148	81	6	13	118	347	114,000	.366	273
Chile	48	293	139	6	18	112	544	196,000	1.599	63
Paraguay	2	10	9	1	5	22	41	8,000	.194	515
Uruguay	13	61	37	1			98	42,000	1.425	70

† Membership totals rounded off, some include partial estimates; stakes, missions as of Oct. 16, 1988.

STAKES — 89

ARGENTINA—26

1097 Bahia Blanca Argentina
920 Buenos Aires Argentina Banfield
1143 Buenos Aires Argentina Castelar
423 Buenos Aires Argentina East
1178 Buenos Aires Argentina Litoral
950 Buenos Aires Argentina Merlo
1405 Buenos Aires Argentina Moreno
995 Buenos Aires Argentina North
639 Buenos Aires Argentina West
569 Cordoba Argentina
1021 Cordoba Argentina North
1036 Godoy Cruz Argentina
1642 Jujuy Argentina
1207 La Plata Argentina
997 Mar del Plata Argentina
570 Mendoza Argentina
1250 Parana Argentina
694 Quilmes Argentina
1237 Resistencia Argentina
636 Rosario Argentina

1177 Rosario Argentina North
1260 Salta Argentina
1096 San Juan Argentina
1001 San Nicolas Argentina
1161 Santa Fe Argentina
1095 Tucuman Argentina

CHILE—48

1499 Achupallas Chile
1075 Andalien Chile
1165 Antofagasta Chile
1100 Arica Chile
1598 Arica Chile El Morro
1522 Calama Chile
1501 Caliche Chile
1398 Chillan Chile
808 Concepcion Chile
1264 Curico Chile
1146 Hualpen Chile
1621 Iquique Chile
1694 Linares Chile
1599 Los Angeles Chile

1267	Osorno Chile		1083	Talca Chile
1320	Penaflor Chile		866	Talcahuano Chile
1268	Penco Chile		1245	Temuco Chile
1339	Puerto Montt Chile		1667	Valdivia Chile
1478	Punta Arenas Chile		882	Valparaiso Chile
1275	Quillota Chile		1230	Valparaiso Chile South
791	Quilpue Chile		1037	Villa Alemana Chile
1285	Rancagua Chile		671	Vina del Mar Chile
1286	San Pedro Chile			

PARAGUAY—2

1002	Asuncion Paraguay
1142	Fernando de la Mora Paraguay

URUGUAY—13

1038 Santiago Chile Cinco de Abril
1077 Santiago Chile Conchali
1216 Santiago Chile El Bosque
1205 Santiago Chile Huechuraba
1024 Santiago Chile Independencia
 672 Santiago Chile La Cisterna
1039 Santiago Chile La Florida
1379 Santiago Chile Las Canteras
1402 Santiago Chile Las Condes
 792 Santiago Chile Nunoa
1403 Santiago Chile Pudahuel
1548 Santiago Chile Puente Alto
 590 Santiago Chile Quinta Normal
1492 Santiago Chile Renca
 754 Santiago Chile Republica
1003 Santiago Chile San Bernardo
1549 Santiago Chile San Miguel

1123	Artigas Uruguay
1098	Durazno Uruguay
1033	Melo Uruguay
836	Minas Uruguay
1058	Montevideo Uruguay Cerro
631	Montevideo Uruguay East
1034	Montevideo Uruguay Maronas
890	Montevideo Uruguay North
444	Montevideo Uruguay West
833	Paysandu Uruguay
832	Rivera Uruguay
1019	Salto Uruguay
840	Santa Lucia Uruguay

MISSIONS — 14

ARGENTINA BAHIA BLANCA MISSION
Casilla de Correo 70
8000 Bahia Blanca, Buenos Aires
Argentina
Phone: (011-54-91) 28-175

ARGENTINA BUENOS AIRES
NORTH MISSION
Ituzaingo 355, C.C. 46
1642 San Isidro, Buenos Aires
Argentina
Phone: (011-54-1) 743-2450

ARGENTINA BUENOS AIRES
SOUTH MISSION
Casilla de Correo 35
1828 Banfield, Buenos Aires
Argentina
Phone: (011-54-1) 242-7403

ARGENTINA CORDOBA MISSION
Casilla de Correo 17
Sucursal 9
5009 Cordoba
Argentina
Phone: (011-54-51) 910-699

ARGENTINA ROSARIO MISSION
Casilla de Correo 341
2000 Rosario, Santa Fe
Argentina
Phone: (011-54-41) 560-601

ARGENTINA SALTA MISSION
C.C. 429

4400 Salta
Argentina
Phone: (011-54-87) 21-75-83

CHILE ANTOFAGASTA MISSION
Sucre 220, Oficina 504
Edificio Bulnes
Antofagasta
Chile
Phone: (011-56-83) 222-841

CHILE CONCEPCION MISSION
Casilla 2210
Concepcion
Chile
Phone: (011-56-41) 229-641

CHILE OSORNO MISSION
Casilla 798
Osorno
Chile
Phone: (011-56-642) 2754

CHILE SANTIAGO NORTH MISSION
Casilla 16053
Providencia
Santiago 9
Chile
Phone: (011-56-2) 223-6466

CHILE SANTIAGO SOUTH MISSION
Casilla 28
Las Condes
Santiago 10
Chile
Phone: (011-56-2) 223-5366

CHILE VINA DEL MAR MISSION
Casilla 24-D
Vina del Mar
Chile
Phone: (011-56-32) 976-080

PARAGUAY ASUNCION MISSION
Casilla de Correo 818
Asuncion
Paraguay
Phone: (011-595-21) 601-392

URUGUAY MONTEVIDEO MISSION
San Carlos de Bolivar 6148
Carrasco, Montevideo
Uruguay
Phone: (011-598-2) 50-44-11

Training Centers

BUENOS AIRES MISSIONARY
TRAINING CENTER
Dolores 818
1704 Ramos Mejia
Buenos Aires
Argentina
Phone: (011-54-1) 654-5537

SANTIAGO CHILE MISSIONARY TRAINING
CENTER
Av. Pocuro 1940
Clasificador 54
Santiago 9
Chile
Phone: (011-56-2) 225-8901, ext. 108

TEMPLES — 2

BUENOS AIRES ARGENTINA TEMPLE

Location: On three-acre site on south-west outskirts of Buenos Aires, Argentina, on the Autopista Richieri y Calle Italia, 6230 Villegas in Ciudad Evita. Phone, 011-54-1-620-0883.

Exterior Finish: Light gray native granite.

Temple Design: Modern adaptation of earlier six-spire design 178 feet by 71 feet; Angel Moroni statue is atop tallest spire at 112 feet.

Construction Advisor: Gary Holland.

Contractor: Benito Roggio and Sons.

Architects: Church architectural staff; local architect, Ramon Paez.

Number of Rooms: Four ordinance rooms, three sealing rooms.

Total Floor Area: 11,980 square feet.

Area of Site: Three acres.

District and membership: Argentina, Uruguay; 117,000 members.

Groundbreaking, site dedication: April 20, 1983, by Elder Bruce R. McConkie.

Dedication: Jan. 17-19, 1986, by President Thomas S. Monson, 11 sessions.

Dedicatory Prayer excerpt: *"We remember that it was in this very city of Buenos Aires, on Christmas Day in the year 1925, just 60 years ago, that Elder Melvin J. Ballard, an apostle of the Lord, dedicated all of South America for the preaching of the gospel. What a fulfillment to an inspired prayer is evident today."*

SANTIAGO
CHILE
TEMPLE

Location: At former Church school and PBIO headquarters in Providencia, an exclusive section of the city. Address — Pedro de Valdivia 1423; Clasificador 54; Santiago 9, Chile. Phone — (011 + 56 + 2) 225-8910.

Exterior Finish: Stucco on concrete block.

Temple Design: Modern.

Architect: Emil B. Fetzer, Church architect.

Construction Advisor: Gary Holland.

Contractor: H. Briones Y. Cia & The Church of Jesus Christ of Latter-day Saints.

Number of Rooms: Three sealing rooms, two ordinance rooms; total rooms 31.

Total Floor Area: 13,020 square feet.

Dimensions of Building: 142.88 feet by 115.32 feet.

Area of Site: 2.61 acres.

District and membership: Chile; 196,000 members.

Groundbreaking, Site Dedication: May 30, 1981, by President Spencer W. Kimball. The groundbreaking took place in the midst of a cold rain, but more than 6,000 Chilean members stood for the hour-and-a-half meeting to hear the prophet and other General Authorities speak.

Temple Dedication: Sept. 15-17, 1983, by President Gordon B. Hinckley in the first of 10 sessions; 15,370 members attended the dedication.

Dedicatory Prayer excerpt: *"Bless thy work upon this great continent of South America which is part of the land of Zion. Bless thy work in this nation of Chile. May all that has been done in the past be but a prologue to a far greater work in the future. May thy people be recognized for the virtue of their lives."*

UNITED STATES AND CANADA

UNITED STATES*

State	Stakes	Wards	Stake bran-ches	Mis-sions	Dis-tricts	Mission bran-ches	Total wards, bran-ches	Mem-bership	Per cent of Pop.	1 LDS in:
Alabama	6	33	27	1	0	0	60	19,000	.5	213
Alaska	5	33	8	1	3	20	61	21,000	4	25
Arizona	56	396	45	2	0	0	441	226,000	6.8	15
Arkansas	3	20	20	1	0	0	40	13,000	.6	182
California	153	1,064	128	11	0	0	1,192	681,000	2.5	40
Colorado	23	156	28	1	0	1	185	84,000	2.6	39
Connecticut	2	20	2	1	0	0	22	9,000	.3	57
Delaware	1	3	1	0	0	0	4	2,200	.35	286
District of Columbia	1	1	0	2	0	0	1	400		
Florida	18	120	29	4	0	0	149	76,000	.65	154
Georgia	10	59	23	1	0	0	82	36,000	.6	167
Hawaii	13	91	6	1	0	1	98	45,000	4.3	24
Idaho	94	619	30	1	0	0	649	289,000	28.81	3.5
Illinois	10	67	19	2	0	0	86	35,000	.3	333
Indiana	8	49	19	1	0	0	68	24,000	.4	227
Iowa	3	22	14	1	0	0	36	11,000	.4	263
Kansas	4	30	10	0	1	9	49	17,000	.7	145
Kentucky	3	25	17	1	1	5	47	16,000	.4	233
Louisiana	7	36	20	1	0	0	56	21,000	.5	213
Maine	3	15	7	0	0	0	22	6,900	.6	169
Maryland	6	43	8	0	0	0	51	25,000	.6	179
Massachusetts	3	25	4	1	0	0	29	12,000	.2	500
Michigan	8	49	21	2	1	5	75	27,000	.3	333
Minnesota	4	26	11	1	1	5	42	15,000	.4	278
Mississippi	3	24	22	1	0	0	46	13,000	.5	200
Missouri	10	64	25	2	0	0	89	32,000	.6	159
Montana	10	61	35	1	2	12	108	34,000	4.2	24
Nebraska	3	16	7	0	1	13	36	11,000	.7	145
Nevada	23	140	22	1	0	0	162	95,000	9.9	10
New Hampshire	2	11	5	1	0	0	16	5,300	.5	192
New Jersey	4	24	7	1	0	0	31	15,000	.2	500
New Mexico	12	76	31	1	0	0	107	47,000	3.2	31
New York	10	56	36	2	0	0	92	35,000	.2	500
North Carolina	12	67	43	2	0	0	110	41,000	.65	154
North Dakota	1	3	2	0	1	10	15	4,600	.68	147
Ohio	11	65	22	3	1	4	91	35,000	.33	303
Oklahoma	8	43	24	1	0	1	68	26,000	.79	127
Oregon	32	193	29	1	0	0	222	106,000	3.9	25
Pennsylvania	9	55	19	3	1	6	80	26,000	.22	455
Rhode Island	1	5	1	0	0	0	6	1,700	.17	588
South Carolina	4	37	14	1	0	0	51	21,000	.62	161
South Dakota	2	11	9	1	3	16	36	7,300	1	97
Tennessee	7	34	18	1	0	0	52	21,000	.44	227
Texas	34	235	77	4	0	0	312	139,000	.83	120
Utah	382	2,683	72	2	0	0	2,755	1,277,000	76.7	1.3
Vermont	1	4	5	0	0	0	9	2,700	.5	200
Virginia	15	81	22	1	1	3	106	50,000	.86	116
Washington	46	309	26	2	0	0	335	172,000	3.85	26
West Virginia	3	17	11	1	0	2	30	10,000	.52	192
Wisconsin	3	22	12	1	1	7	41	11,000	.23	435
Wyoming	16	118	13	0	0	0	131	52,000	10.26	9.7
Total	**1,108**	**7,456**	**1,106**	**71**	**18**	**120**	**8,682**	**4,001,000**	**1.66**	**60**

CANADA*

Alberta	16	117	31	1	1	8	156	53,000	2.267	44
British Columbia	5	33	9	1	3	23	65	22,000	.76	131
Manitoba	1	5	5	1			10	3,400	.32	313
New Brunswick	1				1	9	9	1,600	.22	448
Newfoundland					1	3	3	400	.07	1,449
Northwest Territories					1		1	100	.2	505
Nova Scotia	1	6	6	1		1	13	3,200	.36	275
Ontario	7	42	18	1	3	12	72	25,000	.28	361
Prince Edward Island					3		3	300	.24	422
Quebec	2	9	5	1	1	6	20	5,700	.09	1,149
Saskatchewan	1	5	9		1	3	17	4,200	.41	242
Yukon					1		1	200	.88	114
Totals	**34**	**217**	**83**	**6**	**11**	**70**	**370**	**118,000**	**.460**	**217**

* Membership totals rounded off, some include partial estimates.

Utah North Area

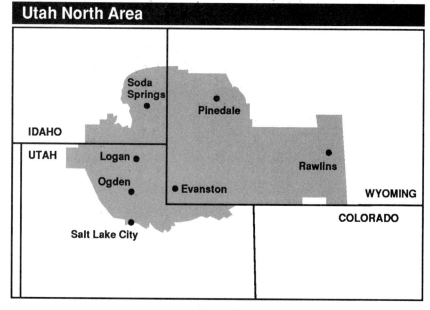

UTAH NORTH AREA*

*On Nov. 1, 1988, the Utah Central Area was created from parts of this area.

AREA: Approximately 80,000 square miles

POPULATION: Utah — 611,000; Wyoming — 144,000; Idaho — 26,500; total: 781,500.

AREA PRESIDENCY: Elders William R. Bradford, Victor L. Brown, and Gerald E. Melchin.

LDS POPULATION: 561,000

THE LAND AND ITS PEOPLE: The Utah North Area includes the northern part of the Uintah Range and the fertile Cache, Bear Lake and Star valleys in Utah, Idaho and Wyoming. It includes most of the northern section of the Salt Lake Valley and sparsely populated mountainous areas, rangeland and farmland in southeastern Idaho and southwestern Wyoming. The area is predominantly LDS and the main language is English. Winters are normally harsh with mild to moderate summers. Beautiful colors cover the mountains and fields during the fall season.

CHURCH HISTORY: Following the arrival of the first pioneer company in the Salt Lake Valley in 1847, exploration of surrounding valleys began almost immediately. In the fall of 1847, several families settled in Bountiful and Farmington. Ogden was settled in 1848. The city soon became one of the largest and most prosperous colonies of the Latter-day Saints.

The first stake in what is now the Utah North Area was organized in the Salt Lake Valley in the fall of 1847. In 1849, the valley was divided into four wards south, and east of the Jordan River, the Sugar House, Cottonwood, Cottonwood Creek, and Caanan wards. Three wards also were created north of the city and east of the Great Salt Lake. These wards included the settlements as far north as Ogden. A few days later, Salt Lake City was divided into 19 wards of nine blocks each.

Brigham City was settled in 1849, followed by the movement of saints into the Cache Valley in 1859. The Cache Valley Stake was created in November 1859 with a ward in Logan. In 1864, LDS settlements were established in the Bear Lake Valley in Paris and St. Charles, Idaho. These settlements led to expansion into Wyoming and the Snake River Valley of Southeastern Idaho. More settlements were opened up with the coming of the railroad.

STAKES — 163

IDAHO—9 (in area)
(See also North America Northwest)

1419 Franklin Idaho
39 Grace Idaho
32 Malad Idaho
75 Montpelier Idaho
1020 Montpelier Idaho South
8 Paris Idaho
29 Preston Idaho North
81 Preston Idaho South
73 Soda Springs Idaho

UTAH—146 (in area)
(See also Utah South, North America Southwest)

918 Benson Utah
193 Bountiful Utah
539 Bountiful Utah Central
383 Bountiful Utah East
546 Bountiful Utah Heights
1127 Bountiful Utah Mueller Park
260 Bountiful Utah North
1206 Bountiful Utah North Canyon
71 Bountiful Utah Orchard
262 Bountiful Utah South
1269 Bountiful Utah Stone Creek
501 Bountiful Utah Val Verda
382 Brigham City Utah
148 Brigham City Utah Box Elder
147 Brigham City Utah North
375 Brigham City Utah South
1242 Brigham City Utah West
575 Centerville Utah
1335 Centerville Utah North
903 Centerville Utah South
277 Clearfield Utah
966 Clearfield Utah North
728 Clinton Utah
1467 Clinton Utah East
18 Coalville Utah
152 Farmington Utah
1342 Farmington Utah North
1531 Fielding Utah

1568 Fruit Heights Utah
1494 Harrisville Utah
141 Hooper Utah
924 Huntsville Utah
59 Garland Utah
1559 Hyde Park Utah
46 Hyrum Utah
1046 Hyrum Utah North
106 Kamas Utah
1635 Kanesville Utah
350 Kaysville Utah
1027 Kaysville Utah Crestwood
568 Kaysville Utah East
1010 Kaysville Utah South
203 Layton Utah
449 Layton Utah East
957 Layton Utah Holmes Creek
1529 Layton Utah North
1657 Layton Utah Northridge
1629 Layton Utah South
858 Layton Utah West
80 Logan Utah
13 Logan Utah Cache
1422 Logan Utah Cache West
1241 Logan Utah Central
164 Logan Utah East
160 Logan Utah Mt. Logan
1347 Logan Utah South
259 Logan Utah University 1st
427 Logan Utah University 2nd
785 Logan Utah University 3rd
16 Morgan Utah
1240 Morgan Utah North
528 North Logan Utah
146 North Ogden Utah
956 North Ogden Utah Ben Lomond
1016 North Salt Lake Utah
57 Ogden Utah
998 Ogden Utah Burch Creek
1133 Ogden Utah Canyon View
458 Ogden Utah College
199 Ogden Utah East
198 Ogden Utah Lorin Farr
140 Ogden Utah Mound Fort

1157 Ogden Utah Mt. Lewis	145 Salt Lake Park
87 Ogden Utah Mt. Ogden	273 Salt Lake Parleys
314 Ogden Utah North	54 Salt Lake Pioneer
201 Ogden Utah Riverdale	130 Salt Lake Riverside
798 Ogden Utah Terrace View	222 Salt Lake Rose Park
520 Ogden Utah Weber	412 Salt Lake Rose Park North
272 Ogden Utah Weber Heights	144 Salt Lake Sugar House
58 Ogden Utah Weber North	178 Salt Lake University 1st
1191 Ogden Utah Weber South	433 Salt Lake University 2nd
1520 Park City Utah	1488 Salt Lake University 3rd
876 Plain City Utah	236 Salt Lake Valley View
	105 Salt Lake Wells
559 Pleasant View Utah	182 Salt Lake Wilford
561 Providence Utah	274 Salt Lake Winder
1351 Providence Utah South	706 Salt Lake Winder West
47 Richmond Utah	119 Smithfield Utah
328 Roy Utah	1384 Smithfield Utah North
1485 Roy Utah Central	139 South Ogden Utah
438 Roy Utah North	138 South Salt Lake
1673 Roy Utah South	424 Sunset Utah
942 Roy Utah West	70 Syracuse Utah
1 Salt Lake	173 Tremonton Utah
	1004 Tremonton Utah South
115 Salt Lake Bonneville	371 Washington Terrace Utah
204 Salt Lake Cannon	1043 Wellsville Utah
237 Salt Lake Canyon Rim	578 West Bountiful Utah
291 Salt Lake Central	1128 West Point Utah
1607 Salt Lake Eagle Gate	1506 Willard Utah
150 Salt Lake East Millcreek	498 Woods Cross Utah
996 Salt Lake East Millcreek North	1333 Woods Cross Utah East
129 Salt Lake Emigration	**WYOMING—8 (in area)**
55 Salt Lake Ensign	(See also North America Central)
249 Salt Lake Foothill	
42 Salt Lake Granite	33 Afton Wyoming
1457 Salt Lake Granite Park	38 Evanston Wyoming
92 Salt Lake Grant	1493 Evanston Wyoming South
	660 Green River Wyoming
114 Salt Lake Highland	708 Kemmerer Wyoming
154 Salt Lake Hillside	790 Lyman Wyoming
227 Salt Lake Holladay	95 Rock Springs Wyoming
891 Salt Lake Holladay North	975 Thayne Wyoming
460 Salt Lake Holladay South	
53 Salt Lake Liberty	
68 Salt Lake Millcreek	

MISSIONS — 1

UTAH SALT LAKE CITY NORTH MISSION
57 West South Temple, Suite 452
Salt Lake City, Utah 84101
Phone: (801) 321-4660

187 Salt Lake Monument Park	
393 Salt Lake Mt. Olympus	
904 Salt Lake Mt. Olympus North	
267 Salt Lake Olympus	

TEMPLES — 3

LOGAN TEMPLE

Location: 175 N. 300 East, Logan, Utah overlooking Cache Valley. (801-752-3611)

Exterior Finish: Dark-colored, siliceous limestone, extremely hard and compact in texture, was used for the major portion of the temple. Buff-colored limestone, more easily carved, was used wherever intricate shaping was necessary.

Temple Design: Castellated style.

Architect: Truman O. Angell.

Construction Heads: Superintendent of construction, Charles O. Card; master mason, John Parry; plastering foreman, William Davis. Temple districts were organized within the stakes to provide the labor and construction needs during a certain period; 25,000 persons worked on the Logan Temple.

Number of Rooms: Five stories, 60 rooms.

Total Floor Area: Originally 59,130 square feet; 115,507 square feet after remodeling.

Dimensions of Building: 171 feet long, 95 feet wide, 86 feet high. The east tower is 170 feet high; west tower, 165 feet high; four octagonal towers, each 100 feet high.

Site: Nine-acre site selected by Brigham Young May 18, 1877.

District and membership: 25 stakes in northern Utah, 13 in southern Idaho; 98,000 members.

Temple Dedication: May 17-19, 1884; Saturday the dedicatory prayer was given by President John Taylor; Sunday it was read by President George Q. Cannon; and on Monday by President Joseph F. Smith.

On March 13-15, 1979, after extensive remodeling, the temple was rededicated by President Spencer W. Kimball.

Dedicatory Prayer excerpt: *"We ask that in this house a more full knowledge of thee and thy laws may be developed...."*

"And, as all wisdom dwells with thee, and, as all light, truth and intelligence, . . . we humbly seek unto thee for thy learning under thy guidance, direction and inspiration."

OGDEN TEMPLE

Location: Ogden Temple Square, 350-22nd St., between Grant Avenue and Washington Boulevard, Ogden, Utah. (801-621-6880)

Site: In late 1967, Presidents Hugh B. Brown and N. Eldon Tanner met with the Church Building Committee and a committee of stake presidencies. Site selected was approved by President David O. McKay and announced Aug. 14, 1967; 18.3 acres.

Exterior Finish: White cast stone with a fluted appearance, gold anodized aluminum grillwork; gold directional glass windows; and single tower of 180 feet.

Temple Design: Modern and functional.

Architect: Emil B. Fetzer, Church architect.

Construction Chairman: Mark B. Garff and Fred A. Baker, vice chairman.

Contractor: Okland Construction Company.

Number of Rooms: Four floors, 283 rooms.

Total Floor Area: 115,000 square feet.

Dimensions of Building: 200 feet by 184 feet; tower 180 feet above ground level.

District and membership: 57 stakes in northern Utah, seven in southwestern Wyoming; 222,000 members.

Groundbreaking, Site Dedication:

Sept. 8, 1969, by members of the First Presidency; President N. Eldon Tanner conducted; prayers were given by President Alvin R. Dyer and President Joseph Fielding Smith; ground broken by President Hugh B. Brown.

Temple Dedication: Jan. 18-20, 1972, with two sessions each day. President Joseph Fielding Smith gave dedicatory prayer.

Dedicatory Prayer excerpt: *"It has been our privilege, as guided by the whisperings of thy Spirit, to build unto thee this temple, which we now present unto thee as another of thy holy houses."*

SALT LAKE TEMPLE

Location: Temple Square located in the heart of Salt Lake City, Utah (801-531-2640)

Site: Selected July 28, 1847, by Brigham Young, 10 acres.

Exterior Finish: Granite from Little Cottonwood Canyon, 20 miles to the southeast of Salt Lake City. The chapel and office annex is reinforced concrete faced with Utah granite.

Temple Design: Suggestive of Gothic and other classical styles, but unique and distinctive.

Architect: Truman O. Angell, Church architect, worked out plans under direction of Brigham Young. During Angell's illness, William Folsom temporarily filled his post. After Angell's death in 1887, Don Carlos Young completed work on the temple.

Construction: The "Public Works" was organized Jan. 26, 1850, to provide necessary labor and materials.

Construction Supervisor: Daniel H. Wells was appointed to supervise the building of the temple and the Public Works.

District and membership: 60 stakes in north central Utah and two in northern Nevada; 211,000 members.

Groundbreaking, Site Dedication: Feb. 14, 1853, President Brigham Young broke ground and Heber C. Kimball dedicated the site.

Temple Dedication: From April 6 to April 24, 1893, 31 dedicatory sessions were held. President Wilford Woodruff gave the dedicatory prayer at the first service.

On April 5, 1893, more than 600 non-member residents of Salt Lake City toured the completed temple.

Area of Site: Ten-acre square.

Number of Rooms: 177.

Total Floor Area: 253,015 square feet in the temple including the annex.

Dimensions of Building: From north to south, 118 feet 6-3/4 inches; from east to west 181 feet 7-1/4-3/8 inches. At east end of the building are three pinnacled towers, the height of the center one being 210 feet. There are three similar towers on the west end, the center one being 204 feet high.

"When thy people . . . are oppressed and in trouble, surrounded by difficulties or assailed by temptation and shall turn their faces towards this thy holy house . . . we beseech thee, to look down from thy holy habitation in mercy and tender compassion upon them, and listen to their cries."

● A site was announced May 28, 1988, for a temple in Bountiful, Utah, although no temple was announced as of Oct. 15, 1988.

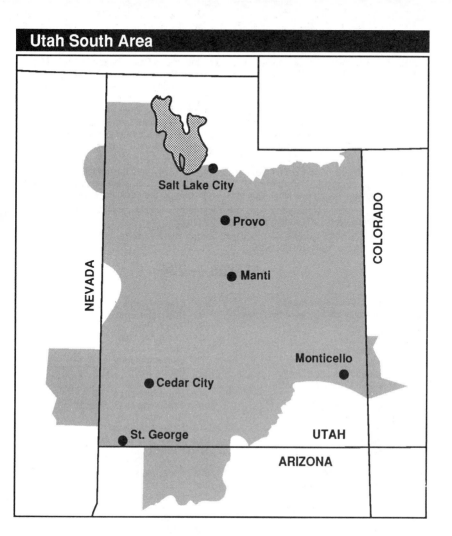

UTAH SOUTH AREA*

* On Nov. 1, 1988, the Utah Central Area was created from parts of this area.

AREA: 55,000 square miles (est.).

POPULATION: 1,070,000

AREA PRESIDENCY: Elders Vaughn J. Featherstone, Paul H. Dunn and Russell C. Taylor

LDS POPULATION: 763,000

THE LAND AND ITS PEOPLE: Shortly after the arrival of the pioneers in the Salt Lake Valley on July 24, 1847, President Brigham Young issued a call to establish settlements throughout much of the Rocky Mountain region. Many of these communities are in the Utah South Area, which includes the southern part of the Salt Lake Valley south to the Arizona border and small parts of three other states.

The area sits atop a high plateau cut by brilliantly colored canyons in the southeast; broad, flat desert in the south and west; and valleys and plateaus along the Wasatch Front. Most of the population is of European descent, with pockets of Latin and Indian with some Asian subgroups. Some 70 percent of the population is LDS (1980 figures for state of Utah); Catholics and most Protestant denominations area also represented.

CHURCH HISTORY: Colonization of the area by Latter-day Saints began in 1849, when a company directed by John Rowberry arrived in Tooele Valley. Provo was established by a company under John Higbee March 18, 1849. Manti was founded by LDS settlers in November 1849.

Colonization missionaries arrived in St. George in southwest Utah on Dec. 1, 1861, and settlers soon followed. The area was visited by President Brigham Young in September 1862. Cedar City was settled in November 1861, and soon became a center of commerce. Kanab was settled in 1864, but problems with Indians held back its growth. It was disrupted in 1866 and resettled by Jacob Hamblin, who visited area Indians as early as 1858.

Ground for the St. George Temple was broken in 1871, and the temple was partially completed and dedicated in January 1877. Final dedication took place April 6, 1877, with President Brigham Young presiding. Daniel H. Wells offered the dedicatory prayer.

The Manti Temple was started in April 1877. The temple was dedicated in May 1888, with President Wilford Woodruff offering the dedicatory prayer.

The area's two other temples — Provo and Jordan River — were dedicated in February 1972 and November 1981, respectively.

STAKES — 234

UTAH—234 (in area)
(See Also Utah North, North America Southwest)

44	Alpine Utah
1526	Altamont Utah
376	American Fork Utah
1022	American Fork Utah East
624	American Fork Utah North
1218	American Fork Utah West
7	Beaver Utah
1482	Bennion Heights Utah
664	Bennion Utah
1459	Bennion Utah East
875	Bennion Utah West
1690	Bloomington Utah
1623	Bloomington Hills Utah
1521	Bluffdale Utah
225	Brigham Young University 1st
295	Brigham Young University 2nd
296	Brigham Young University 3rd
395	Brigham Young University 4th
396	Brigham Young University 5th
397	Brigham Young University 6th
431	Brigham Young University 7th
432	Brigham Young University 8th
478	Brigham Young University 9th
479	Brigham Young University 10th
688	Brigham Young University 11th
689	Brigham Young University 12th
973	Brigham Young University 13th
974	Brigham Young University 14th
1605	Brigham Young University 15th
1688	Brigham Young University 16th
23	Castle Dale Utah
172	Cedar City Utah
413	Cedar City Utah College
901	Cedar City Utah North
316	Cedar City Utah West
65	Delta Utah
1068	Delta Utah West
142	Draper Utah
1319	Draper Utah North
62	Duchesne Utah
1564	Enoch Utah
134	Enterprise Utah
1524	Ephraim Utah
83	Escalante Utah
1336	Ferron Utah
6	Fillmore Utah
147	Grantsville Utah
1069	Grantsville Utah West
89	Gunnison Utah
19	Heber City Utah
649	Heber City Utah East
1170	Helper Utah
1167	Highland Utah
871	Huntington Utah
104	Hurricane Utah
11	Kanab Utah
1638	Kanab Utah South
255	Kearns Utah
1055	Kearns Utah Central
990	Kearns Utah East
256	Kearns Utah North
653	Kearns Utah South
1462	Kearns Utah West
1258	Kearns Utah Western Hills
1294	La Verkin Utah
100	Lehi Utah
637	Lehi Utah North
1416	Lehi Utah West
1392	Lindon Utah
34	Loa Utah
90	Magna Utah
1013	Magna Utah Central
410	Magna Utah East
1510	Magna Utah South
43	Manti Utah
714	Mapleton Utah
246	Midvale Utah
457	Midvale Utah East

96	Midvale Utah Ft. Union	1067	Riverton Utah North
1278	Midvale Utah Ft. Union South	82	Roosevelt Utah
1561	Midvale Utah North	1458	Roosevelt Utah East
1407	Midway Utah	685	Roosevelt Utah West
553	Moab Utah	9	St. George Utah
85	Monroe Utah	759	St. George Utah College
27	Monticello Utah	322	St. George Utah East
102	Moroni Utah	895	St. George Utah West
42	Mt. Pleasant Utah	686	Salem Utah
183	Murray Utah	84	Salina Utah
543	Murray Utah East	576	Salt Lake Big Cottonwood
1009	Murray Utah North	603	Salt Lake Brighton
240	Murray Utah South	361	Salt Lake Butler
468	Murray Utah West	418	Salt Lake Butler West
5	Nephi Utah	133	Salt Lake Cottonwood
1538	Nephi Utah North	936	Salt Lake Cottonwood Heights
166	Orem Utah	266	Salt Lake Granger
1668	Orem Utah Aspen	636	Salt Lake Granger Central
1518	Orem Utah Canyon View	491	Salt Lake Granger East
812	Orem Utah Central	324	Salt Lake Granger North
271	Orem Utah Cherry Hill	764	Salt Lake Granger South
1490	Orem Utah College	497	Salt Lake Granger West
751	Orem Utah East	390	Salt Lake Hunter
251	Orem Utah Geneva Heights	982	Salt Lake Hunter Central
867	Orem Utah Lakeridge	1533	Salt Lake Hunter Copperhill
1184	Orem Utah Lakeview	839	Salt Lake Hunter East
533	Orem Utah North	1539	Salt Lake Hunter South
1682	Orem Utah Northridge	582	Salt Lake Hunter West
1176	Orem Utah Park	863	Salt Lake Jordan
103	Orem Utah Sharon	162	Salt Lake Jordan North
1581	Orem Utah Sharon South	345	Salt Lake South Cottonwood
862	Orem Utah Suncrest	1111	Salt Lake Wasatch
554	Orem Utah Sunset Heights	276	Sandy Utah
1048	Orem Utah Timp View	1489	Sandy Utah Alta View
905	Orem Utah Windsor	955	Sandy Utah Central
12	Panguitch Utah	968	Sandy Utah Cottonwood Creek
5	Parowan Utah	627	Sandy Utah Crescent
45	Payson Utah	1110	Sandy Utah Crescent North
634	Payson Utah East	1639	Sandy Utah Crescent Park
1297	Payson Utah South	981	Sandy Utah Crescent South
1310	Payson Utah West	775	Sandy Utah Crescent West
529	Pleasant Grove Utah	365	Sandy Utah East
894	Pleasant Grove Utah East	972	Sandy Utah Granite
1124	Pleasant Grove Utah Manila	1367	Sandy Utah Granite South
101	Pleasant Grove Utah Mt. Timpanogos	1612	Sandy Utah Granite View
61	Price Utah	811	Sandy Utah Hillcrest
151	Price Utah North	611	Sandy Utah North
127	Provo Utah	579	Sandy Utah West
1437	Provo Utah Bonneville	623	Sandy Utah Willow Creek
3	Provo Utah Central	1361	Santa Clara Utah
165	Provo Utah East	74	Santaquin Utah
541	Provo Utah Edgemont	1525	Snow College Utah
1692	Provo Utah Edgemont North	482	South Jordan Utah
899	Provo Utah Edgemont South	1491	South Jordan Utah East
1209	Provo Utah Grandview	1192	South Jordan Utah West
547	Provo Utah North	138	South Salt Lake
821	Provo Utah Oak Hills	233	Spanish Fork Utah
200	Provo Utah Sharon East	94	Spanish Fork Utah Palmyra
1090	Provo Utah South	1115	Spanish Fork Utah South
1424	Provo Utah Sunset	900	Spanish Fork Utah West
167	Provo Utah West	235	Springville Utah
10	Richfield Utah	1483	Springville Utah Hobble Creek
848	Richfield Utah East	93	Springville Utah Kolob
303	Riverton Utah	705	Springville Utah North

217	Taylorsville Utah	1311	West Jordan Utah Oquirrh
598	Taylorsville Utah Central	1686	West Jordan Utah Prairie
629	Taylorsville Utah North	1443	West Jordan Utah River
1473	Taylorsville Utah North Central	614	West Jordan Utah South
1461	Taylorsville Utah South	1511	West Jordan Utah Southeast
411	Taylorsille Utah West	1509	West Jordan Utah Welby
809	Taylorsville Utah West Central	929	West Jordan Utah West
15	Tooele Utah		
206	Tooele Utah North		
928	Tooele Utah South		
239	Vernal Utah Ashley		
1434	Vernal Utah Glines		
913	Vernal Utah Maeser		
30	Vernal Utah Uintah		
991	Washington Utah		
1625	Washington Utah West		
193	Wellington Utah		
97	West Jordan Utah		
1099	West Jordan Utah Central		
735	West Jordan Utah East		
1512	West Jordan Utah North		

MISSIONS — 1

UTAH SALT LAKE CITY SOUTH MISSION
7938 South 3500 East
Salt Lake City, Utah 84121
Phone: (801) 942-7983

Training Center

MISSIONARY TRAINING CENTER
(PROVO)
2005 North 900 East
Provo, Utah 84604
Phone: (801) 378-4565

TEMPLES — 4

JORDAN RIVER TEMPLE

Location: 10200 S. 1300 West in South Jordan with access from Redwood Road and 13th West. (801-254-3003)

Site: 15-acre site, announced Feb. 3, 1978, by the First Presidency.

Exterior Finish: Cast stone containing white marble chips. Tower appears same as the rest of the building, but in order to reduce weight it contains fiberglass in a product called cemlite.

Temple Design: Modern.

Architect: Emil B. Fetzer, Church architect.

Resident Project Inspector: Jerry Sears.

Construction Superintendent: Lawrence O. Dansie for Layton Construction Co.

Number of Rooms: Six ordinance rooms, 17 sealing rooms.

Total Floor Area: 153,641 square feet.

Dimensions of Building: Basement and main floor, 211 by 218 feet; two upper levels, 140 by 166 feet. Height to square is 58 feet, to top of tower, 199½ feet. Tower topped with a 20-foot sculptured figure of the Angel Moroni.

District and membership: Ninety-two stakes in Salt Lake and Tooele counties in Utah; 323,000 members.

Groundbreaking, Site Dedication: June 9, 1979, by President Spencer W. Kimball broke ground (with a large power scoop shovel instead of the traditional shovel).

Temple Dedication: Nov. 16-20, 1981, by President Marion G. Romney, acting under President Spencer W. Kimball's direction. An estimated 163,000 members attended 15 dedicatory sessions.

Dedicatory Prayer excerpt: *"May all who enter have clean hands and pure hearts, and may they participate with faith in the ordinances to be given herein."*

MANTI TEMPLE

Location: Hill above U.S. Highway 89 in Sanpete Valley in the city of Manti, Utah, 120 miles south of Salt Lake City. (801-835-2291)

Site: "Manti Stone Quarry" has been prophesied as site for a temple since the settlement in 1849. President Brigham Young on June 25, 1875, announced the temple would be built there; 27 acres. It then became "Temple Hill."

Exterior Finish: Fine-textured, cream-colored oolite limestone obtained from quarries in hill upon which it is built.

Temple Design: Of the castellated style reflecting influence of Gothic Revival, French Renaissance Revival, French Second Empire, and colonial architecture.

Architect: William H. Folsom appointed Oct. 15, 1877.

Construction Heads: William H. Folsom from Oct. 15, 1877, to Aug. 7, 1888, when Daniel H. Wells took his place as supervisor; master mason, Edward L. Parry.

Number of Rooms: Four floors including basement, 43 rooms.

Total Floor Area: 86,809 square feet.

Dimensions of Building: 171 feet long, 95 feet wide, 86 feet high. The east tower is 179 feet high, west tower 169 feet high, building at ground level 60 feet above highway below.

District and membership: 27 stakes in central and southeastern Utah and one in western Colorado; 80,000 members.

Temple Dedication: May 17, 1888, private dedication held. President Wilford Woodruff offered dedicatory prayer. First of three public dedicatory services held Monday, May 21, 1888. Lorenzo Snow read prayer given by President Wilford Woodruff

on May 17. Additional services held following two days.

Rededicated June 14-16, 1985 by President Gordon B. Hinckley with 20,231 in attendance.

Dedicatory Prayer excerpt: "*May this holy temple be to them as one of the gates of heaven, opening into the straight and narrow path that leads to endless lives and eternal dominion.*"

PROVO TEMPLE

Location: 2200 N. West Temple Drive, at the entrance Rock Canyon, Provo, Utah. (801-375-5775)

Site: In 1967, several sites considered by the First Presidency, Building Committee, and stake presidencies. Announced by President David O. McKay on Aug. 14, 1967; 17 acres.

Exterior Finish: White cast stone, gold anodized aluminum grilles, bronze glass panels, and single spire finished in gold and anodized aluminum.

Temple Design: Modern and functional.

Architect: Emil B. Fetzer, Church architect.

Construction Chairman: Mark B. Garff, and Fred A. Baker, vice chairman.

Construction Supervisor: General contractors, Hogan and Tingey.

Number of Rooms: 283.

Total Floor Area: 115,000 square feet.

Dimensions of Building: 200 feet by 184 feet; 175 feet high with a 118-foot spire on top of the building.

District and membership: 85 stakes in central and eastern Utah; 256,000 members.

Groundbreaking, Site Dedication: Sept. 15, 1969, ground broken by President Hugh B. Brown and invocation offered by President Joseph Fielding Smith, counselors in the First Presidency.

Temple Dedication: Feb. 9, 1972, 2 p.m. and 7 p.m. Dedicatory prayer written by President Joseph Fielding Smith and read by President Harold B. Lee.

Dedicatory Prayer excerpt: *". . . We dedicate this temple to thee, the Lord. We dedicate it as a house of baptism, a house of endowment, a house of marriage, a house of righteousness for the living and the dead.*

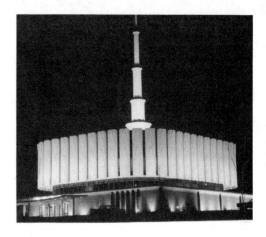

ST. GEORGE TEMPLE

Location: 200 E. 400 South, St. George, Utah. (801-673-3533)

Site: Selected by Brigham Young in 1871; 6 acres.

Exterior Finish: Native red sandstone quarried north of the city was used for the temple which was then plastered white.

Temple Design: Castellated Gothic style.

Architect: Truman O. Angell.

Construction Superintendent: Miles P. Romney, Edward L. Parry, head stone mason.

Number of Rooms: 64 rooms in original structure; 135 rooms after remodeling.

Total Floor Area: 56,062 square feet in original building; 110,000 square feet after remodeling completed in 1975.

Dimensions of Building: Outside measurements of temple proper are 142 feet long by 96 feet wide. To the top of the buttresses, the height is 80 feet, and to the top of the vane, 175 feet.

District and membership: 19 stakes in southwestern Utah, one in Nevada, one in Arizona; 70,000 members.

Temple Dedication: January 1877, completed portions were dedicated. On April 6, 1877, final dedication took place with President Brigham Young presiding. Daniel H. Wells offered the dedicatory prayer.

On Nov. 11 and 12, 1975, after extensive remodeling, the temple was rededicated by President Spencer W. Kimball.

Dedicatory Prayer excerpt: *"We implore thy blessings upon the various congregations of thy people who may assemble in this house from time to time.*

NORTH AMERICA WEST AREA

AREA: 165,143 square miles

POPULATION: 27,365,000

AREA PRESIDENCY: Elders Gene R. Cook, Ted E. Brewerton and Derek A. Cuthbert

LDS POPULATION: 728,000

THE LAND AND ITS PEOPLE: The area covers the eight islands that comprise Hawaii, most of California (small sections along the Nevada and Oregon borders are in the North America Southwest and North America Northwest areas) and a small portion of western

Arizona. Located about 2,400 miles west of California, Hawaii was admitted as a U.S. state in 1959. English is the official language throughout the area. Other widely spoken languages include Spanish, Samoan, Tongan, Japanese, Korean, Mandarin, Cantonese and Vietnamese.

CHURCH HISTORY: The LDS influence began during the war between the United States and Mexico (1846-48) when the Mormon Battalion made the longest infantry march in U.S. history. The battalion traveled through what is now New Mexico and Arizona to San Diego, Calif.

During the summer of 1848, when thousands flocked to California in search of gold, most of the Mormon Battalion men who had been stationed in San Diego were heading home with their families in the Great Salt Lake Valley. The common explanation was, "They chose God rather than gold." Later, some of the battalion members and their families helped found the LDS settlement of San Bernardino in Southern California. During the same period of time, in 1850, a number of elders who had been involved with the gold rush were called by Apostle Charles C. Rich to open up a mission in Hawaii.

The Hawaiian Mission began in 1850 with the arrival of 10 elders, including George Q. Cannon, later to be counselor to four Church presidents. California was not organized into a mission until 1892, with Karl G. Maeser serving as mission president.

STAKES — 166

ARIZONA—1 (in area)
(See also North America Southwest)

263 Yuma Arizona

CALIFORNIA—153 (in area)
(See also North America Southwest)

402 Anaheim California
1514 Anaheim California East
1042 Anderson California
1263 Antioch California
864 Arcadia California
1032 Auburn California
186 Bakersfield California
944 Bakersfield California East
1622 Bakersfield California South
288 Barstow California
750 Blythe California
763 Camarillo California
309 Carlsbad California
1505 Carmichael California
269 Cerritos California
656 Cerritos California West
565 Chico California
1072 Chino California
770 Chula Vista California
1150 Citrus Heights California
378 Concord California
983 Corona California
226 Covina California
502 Cypress California
1151 Davis California
279 Downey California
261 El Cajon California
1119 El Centro California
984 El Dorado California
588 Escondido California
338 Eureka California
428 Fair Oaks California
682 Fairfield California
1602 Fontana California
425 Fremont California
1584 Fremont California South
185 Fresno California

381 Fresno California East
1463 Fresno California North
1464 Fresno California West
707 Fullerton California
330 Garden Grove California
175 Glendale California
786 Glendora California
107 Gridley California
442 Hacienda Heights California
948 Hanford California
228 Hayward California
961 Hemet California
1632 Hesperia California
420 Huntington Beach California
802 Huntington Beach California North
1477 Huntington Park California West
1633 Irvine California
518 La Crescenta California
347 La Verne California
1354 Laguna Niguel California
794 Lancaster California
1107 Lawndale California
1654 Livermore California
822 Lodi California
1649 Lompoc California
117 Long Beach California
177 Long Beach California East
1683 Long Beach California North
704 Los Altos California
98 Los Angeles California
337 Los Angeles California Canoga Park
230 Los Angeles California Chatsworth
179 Los Angeles California East
817 Los Angeles California Granada Hills
129 Los Angeles California Inglewood
231 Los Angeles California North Hollywood
642 Los Angeles California Santa Clarita
188 Los Angeles California Santa Monica
116 Los Angeles California Van Nuys
1249 Manteca California

156	Menlo Park California
659	Merced California
826	Mission Viejo California
399	Modesto California
716	Modesto California North
258	Monterey California
1656	Moreno Valley California
831	Morgan Hill California
1693	Murrieta California
297	Napa California
652	Newbury Park California
453	Newport Beach California
227	Oakland California
1092	Ontario California
251	Orange California
441	Palm Springs California
459	Palmdale California
739	Palos Verdes California
128	Pasadena California
1608	Penasquitos California
215	Placentia California
675	Pleasanton California
1056	Poway California
1648	Rancho Cucamonga California
319	Redding California
938	Redlands California
415	Rialto California
521	Ridgecrest California
196	Riverside California
430	Riverside California West
515	Roseville California
108	Sacramento California
1691	Sacramento California Antelope
290	Sacramento California East
219	Sacramento California North
1152	Sacramento California Rancho Cordova
487	Sacramento California South
111	San Bernadino California
136	San Diego California
736	San Diego California East
489	San Diego California North
360	San Diego California Sweetwater
99	San Francisco California
1515	San Francisco California West

202	San Jose California
693	San Jose California East
450	San Jose California South
329	San Leandro California
248	San Luis Obispo California
462	San Rafael California
787	Santa Ana California
184	Santa Barbara California
585	Santa Clara California
823	Santa Cruz California
384	Santa Maria California
181	Santa Rosa California
1582	Santee California
387	Saratoga California
448	Simi Valley California
171	Stockton California
1624	Thousand Oaks California
282	Torrance California
220	Torrance California North
1591	Turlock California
877	Ukiah California
583	Upland California
548	Ventura California
1397	Victorville California
492	Visalia California
967	Vista California
281	Walnut California
229	Walnut Creek California
1587	Walnut Creek California East
280	Whittier California
1079	Yuba City California

Hawaii—13

807	BYU-Hawaii 1st
1313	BYU-Hawaii 2nd
473	Hilo Hawaii
222	Honolulu Hawaii
348	Honolulu Hawaii West
729	Kahului Hawaii
560	Kaneohe Hawaii
851	Kauai Hawaii
669	Kona Hawaii
113	Laie Hawaii
1395	Laie Hawaii North
1103	Mililani Hawaii
566	Waipahu Hawaii

MISSIONS — 12

CALIFORNIA ANAHEIM MISSION
760 North Euclid, Suite 213
Anaheim, California 92801
Phone: (714) 776-2725

CALIFORNIA ARCADIA MISSION
P.O. Box 3028
Arcadia, California 91006-0940
Phone: (818) 446-8519

CALIFORNIA FRESNO MISSION
2350 West Shaw Avenue, Suite 123
Fresno, California 93711
Phone: (209) 431-5510

CALIFORNIA LOS ANGELES MISSION
1591 East Temple Way
P.O. Box 24089
Los Angeles, California 90024
Phone: (213) 474-2593

CALIFORNIA OAKLAND MISSION
4945 Lincoln Way
Oakland, California 94602
Phone: (415) 531-3881

CALIFORNIA SACRAMENTO MISSION
7806 Madison Avenue, Suite 128
Fair Oaks, California 95628
Phone: (916) 967-1921

CALIFORNIA SAN BERNARDINO MISSION
2724 North Waterman Ave., Suite D
San Bernardino, California 92404
Phone: (714) 886-4772

CALIFORNIA SAN DIEGO MISSION
3835 Avocado Blvd., #260
La Mesa, California 92041-7383
Phone: (619) 461-7882

CALIFORNIA SAN JOSE MISSION
6489 Camden, #107
San Jose, California 95120
Phone: (408) 268-9411

CALIFORNIA SANTA ROSA MISSION
2777 Cleveland Ave., #105
Santa Rosa, California 95401
Phone: (707) 579-9411

CALIFORNIA VENTURA MISSION
P.O. Box 3692
Ventura, California 93006-3692
Phone: (805) 644-1034

HAWAII HONOLULU MISSION
1500 So. Beretania St., Suite 410
Honolulu, Hawaii 96826
Phone: (808) 942-0050

TEMPLES — 4 (1 under construction)

HAWAII TEMPLE

Location: On the northeast side of the island of Oahu, at 55-600 Lanihuli Pl., Laie, formerly a 6,000-acre plantation purchased by the Church in 1865, 32 miles from Honolulu. (808-293-2427)

Site: In 1915 October general conference, motion presented by President Joseph F. Smith that a temple be built at Laie, Oahu, Hawaii; the motion was unanimously sustained; 11.4 acres, a portion of original property purchased by Church.

Exterior Finish: Built of concrete made from the crushed lava rock of the area, reinforced with steel. After hardening, it was dressed on the exterior by pneumatic stone-cutting tools that produced a cream white finish.

Temple Design: The first of three temples built with no tower, it is in the shape of a Grecian Cross and suggestive of the ancient temples found in South America.

Architects: Hyrum C. Pope and Harold W. Burton.

General Superintendent: Samuel E. Woolley, president, Hawaiian Mission.

Construction Supervisor: Ralph E. Woolley. Much of the work on this temple was done by the Polynesian Saints.

Number of Rooms: 163 rooms after remodeling.

Total Floor Area: 10,500 square feet originally, approximately 40,971 square feet after remodeling.

Dimensions of Building: 140 feet from east to west, 282 feet from north to south, rising to a height of 50 feet above the upper terrace. Very similar "cubical contents" as ancient Temple of Solomon.

District and membership: Hawaii and Guam; 46,000 members.

Groundbreaking, Site Dedication: June 1, 1915, site dedicated by President Joseph F. Smith, accompanied by Elder Reed Smoot, and Presiding Bishop Charles W. Nibley.

Cornerstone Laying: Apparently there was no formal cornerstone laying ceremony.

Temple Dedication: Thanksgiving Day, Nov. 27, 1919, by President Heber J. Grant.

Rededicated June 13-15, 1978, by President Spencer W. Kimball after extensive remodeling.

Dedicatory Prayer excerpt: *"May thy*

peace ever abide in this holy building, that all who come here may partake of the spirit of peace, and of the sweet and heavenly influence that thy saints have experienced in other temples. . . . May all who come upon the grounds which surround this temple, in the years to come, whether members of the Church or Christ or not, feel the sweet and peaceful influence of this blessed and hallowed spot.''

LOS ANGELES TEMPLE

Location: 10777 Santa Monica Blvd., atop a hill near Westwood Village, two miles west of Beverly Hills in Los Angeles, Calif. (213-474-5569)

Site: March 23, 1937, President Heber J. Grant completed negotiations for purchase of the Harold Lloyd Motion Picture Company property; 13 of the original 24.23 acres were used for the temple.

Exterior Finish: Built of reinforced concrete and structural steel, building is fireproof and quake resistant. Exterior covered with 146,000 square feet of Mo-Sai stone facing, a mixture of crushed quartz and white Portland cement quarried in Utah and Nevada. Wainscot around exterior is Rockville granite from Minnesota.

Temple Design: Modern.

Architect: Edward O. Anderson, Church architect. Millard F. Malin, sculptor of 15 foot, 5½ inch gold leaf-covered statue of Angel Moroni.

Superintendent: Vern Loder.

Contractor: Soren N. Jacobsen.

Number of Rooms: 90.

Total Floor Area: 190,614 square feet or approximately 4½ acres.

Dimensions of Building: 364 feet wide, 241 feet deep; overall height of building including tower is 257 feet 1½ inches.

District and membership: 68 stakes in Southern California; 248,000 members.

Groundbreaking, Site Dedication: Saturday, Sept. 22, 1951, by President David O. McKay, who broke ground and offered dedi-

catory prayer.

Temple Dedication: March 11-14, 1956, by President David O. McKay. Eight sessions held. All General Authorities present at one or more of the sessions.

Dedicatory Prayer excerpt: *"May all who come within these sacred walls feel a peaceful, hallowed influence. Cause, O Lord, that even people who pass the grounds, or view the temple from afar, may lift their eyes from the groveling things of sordid life and look up to thee and thy providence."*

OAKLAND TEMPLE

Location: 4700 Lincoln Ave., Oakland, Calif., near intersection of Lincoln Avenue and Warren Boulevard Freeway. (415-531-3200)

Site: Located 1934, but property was not for sale. Inspected and approved by President David O. McKay in 1942. Purchased 14½ acres Jan. 28, 1943; additional land acquired later to make 18.3 acres; situated on hills overlooking Oakland, Berkeley, San Francisco and Bay.

Exterior Finish: Reinforced concrete faced with Sierra white granite from Raymond, Calif.

Temple Design: Modern, with an Oriental motif.

Architect: Harold W. Burton. Resident architect supervisor, Arthur Price.

Construction Chairman: W.B. Mendenhall.

Construction Supervisor: Robert C. Loden. Contractors: Leon M. Wheatley Co., Palo Alto, Calif., and Jacobsen Construction Co., Salt Lake City.

Number of Rooms: 265.

Total Floor Area: 82,417 square feet.

Dimensions of Building: Temple proper, 210 feet by 190 feet with a central tower rising 170 feet, other towers 96 feet.

District and membership: Fifty-six stakes in northern California and five in western Nevada; 219,000 members.

Groundbreaking, Site Dedication: Saturday, May 26, 1962, President David O. McKay broke ground and dedicated the site.

Temple Dedication: Nov. 17-19, 1964. President David O. McKay presided and offered dedicatory prayer. He addressed all six sessions and gave dedicatory prayer in four.

Dedicatory Prayer excerpt: *"This temple . . . is a monument testifying to the faith and loyalty of the members of thy Church . . . ."*

SAN DIEGO TEMPLE

Announced: April 7, 1984, by President Gordon B. Hinckley.

Site: In north San Diego City near the suburb of La Jolla.

Groundbreaking, site dedication: Ground broken by President Ezra Taft Benson on Feb. 27, 1988; site dedicated same day by President Thomas S. Monson.

Temple district: includes 14 stakes in Southern California and two in Mexico, 65,000 members.

Status: Under construction.

NORTH AMERICA CENTRAL AREA

AREA: 3.6 million square miles

POPULATION: 42.1 Million

AREA PRESIDENCY: Elders Loren C. Dunn, Jacob de Jager and John Sonnenberg.

LDS POPULATION: 334,000

THE LAND AND ITS PEOPLE: The North America Central Area is huge geographically, extending from Colorado, Kansas, and Missouri on the south to the North Pole on the north. It includes all or parts of 12 western and mid-western states of the United States, and five Canadian provinces, plus the Northwest Territories. The area is characterized by contrast and variety. Topographically, the area ranges from the Rocky Mountains to the plains and prairies of the United States and Canada to the frozen Arctic tundra. The area is predominantly populated by descendants of emigrants from Europe and the British Isles. Many Indian tribes are located throughout the area. Mainly in the larger cities have increasing populations of black, Asian, Hispanic and other cultures. There is a wide variation in population density, including such urban centers as Chicago, Ill.; Milwaukee, Wis.; and Kansas City, Mo.; and the rural regions of the Dakotas.

CHURCH HISTORY: Many landmark events in the early history of the Church occurred in the Central Area. In June 1831, elders were sent from Kirtland, Ohio, to Jackson County, Mo. There, on Aug. 2, 1831, the land of Zion was dedicated, and a temple site dedicated the following day. On May 8, 1834, Zion's Camp commenced its march from New Portage, Ohio, to Clay County Missouri to assist exiled saints. Mob violence forced the exodus of the saints from Kirtland July 6, 1838, ending at Far West, Mo. Oct. 2. On May 10, 1839, the saints founded Nauvoo, Ill.

On June 27, 1844, the Prophet Joseph Smith and his brother Hyrum were killed at Carthage, Ill. The exodus of the saints to the Rocky Mountains commenced Feb. 4, 1846. During their trek, they founded Winter Quarters, Neb. The formation of the Indian Territory Mission in 1855 led to the establishment of the Church in some of the areas now in the Central Area. It was renamed the Central States Mission on March 29, 1898. The organization of the North Central States Mission on July 12, 1925, gave the Church a greater foothold in the central United States and central provinces of Canada.

Western Canada was settled by Latter-day Saints in 1887-88, and in 1895, the first stake outside the United States was organized in Cardston, Alberta.

STAKES — 95

Canada—19 (in area)
(See also North America Northwest,
North America Northeast)

211	Calgary Alberta
416	Calgary Alberta North
1101	Calgary Alberta South
1031	Calgary Alberta West
35	Cardston Alberta
1455	Cardston Alberta West
994	Cranbrook British Columbia
665	Edmonton Alberta Bonnie Doon
1453	Edmonton Alberta Millwoods
312	Edmonton Alberta Riverbend
1560	Ft. Macleod Alberta
189	Lethbridge Alberta
667	Lethbridge Alberta East
1199	Magrath Alberta
51	Raymond Alberta
1350	Red Deer Alberta
978	Saskatoon Saskatchewan
302	Taber Alberta
980	Winnipeg Manitoba

COLORADO—20 (in area)
(See also North America Southwest)

1655	Arapahoe Colorado
287	Arvada Colorado
1318	Aurora Colorado
595	Boulder Colorado
301	Colorado Springs Colorado
1134	Colorado Springs Colorado North
1214	Columbine Colorado

132	Denver Colorado
596	Denver Colorado North
470	Ft. Collins Colorado
1452	Golden Colorado
223	Grand Junction Colorado
1415	Grand Junction Colorado West
1528	Greeley Colorado
394	Lakewood Colorado
625	Littleton Colorado
320	Meeker Colorado
977	Montrose Colorado
632	Pueblo Colorado
1534	Willow Creek Colorado

ILLINOIS—10

370	Champaign Illinois
646	Chicago Heights Illinois
749	Fairview Heights Illinois
1672	Long Grove Illinois
368	Naperville Illinois
1000	Nauvoo Illinois
1163	Peoria Illinois
1334	Rockford Illinois
1094	Schaumberg Illinois
118	Wilmette Illinois

IOWA—3

419	Cedar Rapids Iowa
902	Davenport Iowa
525	Des Moines Iowa

KANSAS—4

1610	Olathe Kansas
1696	Salina Kansas
747	Topeka Kansas

355 Wichita Kansas

MINNESOTA—4

1562 Anoka Minnesota
317   Minneapolis Minnesota
910   Rochester Minnesota
744   St. Paul Minnesota

MISSOURI—8 (in area)
(See also North America Southwest)

1563 Cape Girardeau Missouri
511   Columbia Missouri
544   Independence Missouri
234   Kansas City Missouri
1071 Liberty Missouri
265   St. Louis Missouri
1634 St. Louis Missouri North
1118 St. Louis Missouri South

MONTANA—10

369   Billings Montana
849   Billings Montana East
1066 Bozeman Montana
208   Butte Montana
244   Great Falls Montana
976   Great Falls Montana East
464   Helena Montana
535   Kalispell Montana

243   Missoula Montana
1074 Stevensville Montana

NEBRASKA—3

663   Lincoln Nebraska
318   Omaha Nebraska
1614 Papillion Nebraska

NORTH DAKOTA—1

852   Fargo North Dakota

SOUTH DAKOTA—2

592   Rapid City South Dakota
1085 Sioux Falls South Dakota

WYOMING—8 (in area)
(See also Utah North)

357   Casper Wyoming
286   Cheyenne Wyoming
593   Cody Wyoming
1158 Gillette Wyoming
1420 Laramie Wyoming
48   Lovell Wyoming
358   Riverton Wyoming
1194 Worland Wyoming

WISCONSIN—3

1597 Appleton Wisconsin
702   Madison Wisconsin
367   Milwaukee Wisconsin

MISSIONS — 12

CANADA CALGARY MISSION
6940 Fisher Road S.E., #122
Calgary, Alberta T2H 0W3
Canada
Phone: (403) 252-1141

CANADA WINNIPEG MISSION
1661 Portage Ave., Suite 306
Winnipeg, Manitoba R3J 3T7
Canada
Phone: (204) 775-0466

COLORADO DENVER MISSION
Box 2674
Littleton, Colorado 80122
Phone: (303) 794-6457

ILLINOIS CHICAGO MISSION
1319 Butterfield Road, Suite 522
Downers Grove, Illinois 60515
Phone: (312) 969-2145

ILLINOIS PEORIA MISSION
4700 North Sterling, Suite 100
Peoria, Illinois 61615
Phone: (309) 685-1116

IOWA DES MOINES MISSION
8515 Douglas Ave., Suite 19
Des Moines, Iowa 50322
Phone: (515) 278-9637

MINNESOTA MINNEAPOLIS MISSION
5931 West 96th Street
Bloomington, Minnesota 55438
Phone: (612) 835-7788

MISSOURI INDEPENDENCE MISSION
517 West Walnut, Box 455
Independence, MO. 64051
(816) 252-6050

MISSOURI ST. LOUIS MISSION
745 Craig Road, Suite 206
Creve Coeur, MO. 63141
(314) 872-8510

MONTANA BILLINGS MISSION
Box 1797
Billings, Montana 59103
Phone: (406) 245-6146

SOUTH DAKOTA RAPID CITY MISSION
2525 West Main, Suite 311
Rapid City, South Dakota 57702
Phone: (605) 348-1520

WISCONSIN MILWAUKEE MISSION
5651 Broad Street
Greendale, Wisconsin 53129-1889
Phone: (414) 421-7506

ALBERTA TEMPLE

Location: Cardston, in the southern part of the province of Alberta, in western Canada. (403-653-3552)

Site: In 1887, eight-acre site laid out and given to the Church by Charles Ora Card, leader of the first group of Mormons to Canada. It was then called the Tabernacle Block.

Exterior Finish: White granite quarried near Kootenai Lakes in Nelson, British Columbia. Each stone was hand-hewn at the quarry or temple site.

Temple Design: Octagonal shape, similar to Maltese cross, with no spire.

Architects: Hyrum C. Pope and Harold W. Burton.

Chairman Temple Committee: Bishop James P. Brown.

Number of Rooms: Approximately 40 in original structure.

Dimensions of Building: Originally 29,471 square feet; height 85 feet.

Total Floor Area: 60,360

District and membership: Alberta, Saskatchewan, Manitoba, southeastern British Columbia, and northern Montana; 64,000 members.

Groundbreaking, Site Dedication: July 27, 1913, by President Joseph F. Smith, in the presence of about 1,500 people. Ground broken Nov. 9, 1913, by Daniel Kent Greene of Glenwoodville, Alberta.

Temple Dedication: Aug. 26-29, 1923, by President Heber J. Grant in 11 sessions. Rededicated after remodeling July 2, 1962, by President Hugh B. Brown of the First Presidency.

Dedicatory Prayer excerpt: *"We especially pray thee, O Father in Heaven, to bless the youth of thy people in Zion and in all the world. Shield them from the adversary and from wicked and designing men. Keep the youth of thy people, O Father, in the straight and narrow path that leads to thee, preserve them from the pitfalls and snares that are laid for their feet."*

CHICAGO ILLINOIS TEMPLE

Location: Glenview, 20 miles north of Chicago, Ill., at 4151 West Lake Ave. Phone: (312) 299-6500.

Exterior Finish: Gray buff marble, gray slate roof.

Description: Modern adaptation of earlier six-spire design; exterior, gray buff marble;

Temple Design: Modern adaptation of earlier six-spire design.

Architects: Church architectural staff; local architect, Wight & Co.

Construction Advisor: Virgil Roberts.

Contractor: Pora Construction Co., Des Plaines, Ill., with Utah Construction and Development Co.

Area of Site: 13 acres.

Number of Rooms: Four ordinance rooms; three sealing rooms.

Total Floor Area: 17,850 square feet.

Dimensions of Building: 236 feet long and 78 feet wide; seven-foot tall Angel Moroni statue is atop tallest spire, 112 feet high.

District and membership: Illinois, North Dakota, Wisconsin, parts of Nebraska, Indiana, Iowa, Michigan, Minnesota, Missouri, Ohio, South Dakota; 123,000 members.

Groundbreaking, site dedication: Aug. 13, 1983, by President Gordon B. Hinckley.

Dedication: Aug. 9-13, 1985, by President Gordon B. Hinckley, 19 sessions.

Dedicatory Prayer excerpt: *"We are mindful that thy Prophet Joseph, and his brother Hyrum, were martyred in Carthage, Ill., at a time of terrible conflict and persecution. May there now be peace and goodwill in the land. Bless the officers of this state and nation that they shall stand firmly for those principles of freedom and equity which were written into the Constitution of the United States under thine inspiration."*

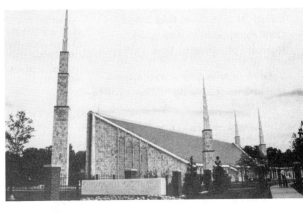

DENVER COLORADO TEMPLE

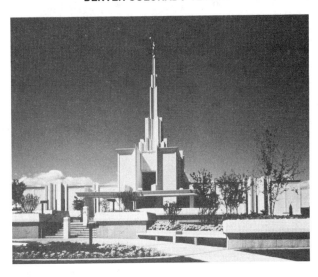

Location: Hilltop site at County Line Road and South University Boulevard, 2001 E. Phillips Circle, in Littleton, Colo., a suburban community in Arapahoe County, about 18 miles south of Denver. Phone: (303) 730-0220.

Site: 7.5 acres.

Exterior Finish: Modern design, similar to Atlanta Georgia Temple; single spire capped with statue of Angel Moroni 90 feet high; precast stone walls and built-up roof.

Temple Design: Modern.

Architects: Church architectural staff; local architect, Bobby R. Thomas.

Temple Dedication: October 24-28, 1986, by President Ezra Taft Benson in 18 sessions.

Dedicatory Prayer excerpt: *"Touch the hearts of thy people that they may look to this temple as a refuge from the evil and turmoil of the world. May they ever live worthy of the blessings here to be found. May they be prompted to seek the records of their forebears and to serve here in their behalf, under that plan which thou has revealed for the salvation and exaltation of thy children of all generations"*

Construction Advisor: Mike Enfield.

Contractor: Langley Constructors.

Number of Rooms: Four ordinance rooms, six sealing rooms; total of 54 rooms.

Total Floor Area: 29,117 square feet.

Dimensions of Building: 166 feet by 184 feet.

District and membership: Most of Colorado, eastern Wyoming, southwestern South Dakota, one stake in New Mexico; 85,000 members.

Groundbreaking, site dedication: May 19, 1984, by President Gordon B. Hinckley.

NAUVOO TEMPLE*

*No longer exists

Location: In Nauvoo, Ill., on a high bluff on the east side of the Mississippi River. Temple block bounded by Woodruff, Mulholland, Knight and Wells streets.

Site: Selected in October 1840 by Joseph Smith on property known as the Wells addition, slightly less than 4 acres.

Exterior Finish: Light gray limestone quarried to the north and south of the city.

Temple Design: Incorporated several types of architecture, no single style dominating.

Architect: William Weeks.

Temple Building Committee: Alpheus Cutler, Elias Higbee and Reynolds Cahoon. After the death of Elias Higbee in 1843, Hyrum Smith replaced him until his own death.

Number of Rooms: Approximately 60.

Total Floor Area: Approximately 50,000 square feet.

Dimensions of Building: Approximately 128 feet long, by 88 feet wide, by 65 feet high, with the tower and spire reaching to 165 feet.

Temple Dedication: Portions of the temple were dedicated and used as soon as completed. To avoid possible violence, a private dedication was held April 30, 1846, with Orson Hyde and Joseph Young officiating. The temple was dedicated publicly, May 1-3, 1846, with the dedicatory prayer offered by Orson Hyde.

Dedicatory Prayer excerpt: *"We thank thee that thou hast given us strength to accomplish the charges delivered by thee. Thou hast seen our labors and exertions to accomplish this purpose. By the authority of the Holy Priesthood now we offer this building as a sanctuary to thy worthy name. We ask thee to take the guardianship into thy hands and grant thy spirit shall dwell here and may all feel a sacred influence on their hearts that His Hand has helped this work."*

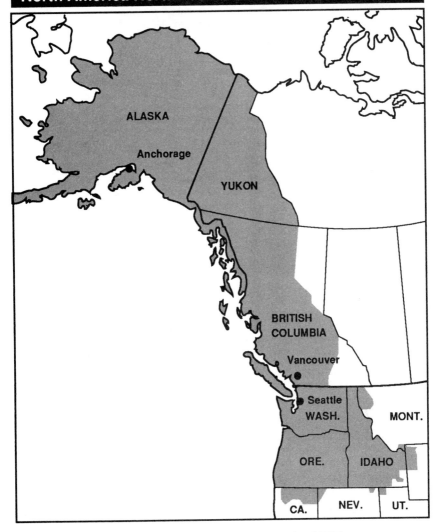

NORTH AMERICA NORTHWEST AREA

AREA: 1.4 million square miles
POPULATION: 10.2 million
AREA PRESIDENCY: Elders Rex C. Reeve, Robert B. Harbertson, L. Lionel Kendrick.

LDS POPULATION: 589,000

THE LAND AND ITS PEOPLE: The North America Northwest Area covers some of the most rugged country on earth. It reaches from Idaho, Oregon and Washington in the United States through British Columbia to the wide expanses of Alaska and the stark wilderness of the Yukon Territory. The climate varies from dry and seasonal in the southeastern end of the area to the rainy west coast and the frigid Arctic Circle. Most of this broad expanse is sparsely populated, but it still possesses one of the largest concentrations of Latter-day Saints in the World.

CHURCH HISTORY: In the early 1850s, the first LDS missionaries were sent from the Mormon settlement in San Bernardino, Calif., to the Oregon Territory by Apostle Charles C. Rich. Mob violence and ill treatment of missionaries and members led to temporary abandonment of proselyting efforts in Oregon. But eventually the Church took hold, and a stake was established in 1901.

After the missionaries arrived in Washington in 1855, they experienced persecution but were able to stimulate interest and build a foundation for steady growth. By 1930, the state had 2,000 members.

Southern Idaho became part of the saints' colonizing effort and those settlements supplied many of the future members for growth throughout the state. A branch of more than 100 members was established in the capital of Boise in 1903 by Elder Melvin J. Ballard, then president of the Northwestern States Mission.

Alaska's first recorded conversion occurred June 25, 1902, when a member, Dr. Edward G. Cannon, baptized K.N. Winner near Nome. The pair proselyted in the gold settlements, using a wagon for transportation and as a meetinghouse. Missionaries arrived in the territory in 1928, but the first stake wasn't established until 1974. In British Columbia, a meetinghouse was purchased in 1925 in Vancouver, and a stake formed in 1960.

STAKES — 172

British Columbia—4 (in area)
(See also North America Central)

315 Vancouver British Columbia
1014 Vancouver British Columbia South
709 Vernon British Columbia
679 Victoria British Columbia

ALASKA—5
331 Anchorage Alaska
962 Anchorage Alaska North
1033 Fairbanks Alaska
1507 Soldotna Alaska
1456 Wasilla Alaska

IDAHO—85 (in area)
(See also Utah North)

170 American Falls Idaho
1481 Arimo Idaho
695 Ashton Idaho
52 Blackfoot Idaho
1391 Blackfoot Idaho East
914 Blackfoot Idaho Northwest
214 Blackfoot Idaho South
504 Blackfoot Idaho West
66 Boise Idaho
1460 Boise Idaho Central
1041 Boise Idaho East
409 Boise Idaho North
701 Boise Idaho South
218 Boise Idaho West
77 Burley Idaho
1421 Burley Idaho West
564 Caldwell Idaho
1446 Caldwell Idaho North
78 Carey Idaho
960 Chubbuck Idaho
359 Coeur d'Alene Idaho
69 Declo Idaho
50 Driggs Idaho
661 Emmett Idaho

1147 Filer Idaho
655 Firth Idaho
36 Idaho Falls Idaho
343 Idaho Falls Idaho Ammon
825 Idaho Falls Idaho Ammon West
1448 Idaho Falls Idaho Central
1665 Idaho Falls Idaho Eagle Rock
285 Idaho Falls Idaho East
1149 Idaho Falls Idaho Lincoln
112 Idaho Falls Idaho North
157 Idaho Falls Idaho South
602 Idaho Falls Idaho West
607 Iona Idaho
192 Jerome Idaho
1015 Kimberly Idaho
268 Lewiston Idaho
72 McCammon Idaho
1125 Menan Idaho
580 Meridian Idaho
847 Meridian Idaho East
1401 Meridian Idaho South
79 Moore Idaho
641 Mountain Home Idaho
125 Nampa Idaho
874 Nampa Idaho South
32 Oakley Idaho
587 Paul Idaho
278 Pocatello Idaho
40 Pocatello Idaho Alameda
1484 Pocatello Idaho Central
971 Pocatello Idaho East
377 Pocatello Idaho Highland
207 Pocatello Idaho North
1444 Pocatello Idaho Tyhee
406 Pocatello Idaho University
149 Pocatello Idaho West
28 Rexburg Idaho
1369 Rexburg Idaho Center
405 Rexburg Idaho College 1st
480 Rexburg Idaho College 2nd

690	Rexburg Idaho College 3rd
1689	Rexburg Idaho College 4th
697	Rexburg Idaho East
153	Rexburg Idaho North
56	Rigby Idaho
158	Rigby Idaho East
1140	Ririe Idaho
606	Roberts Idaho
91	Rupert Idaho
1476	Rupert Idaho West
60	St. Anthony Idaho
211	Salmon Idaho
952	Sandpoint Idaho
67	Shelley Idaho
1180	Shelley Idaho South
1129	Sugar City Idaho
76	Twin Falls Idaho
490	Twin Falls Idaho West
1156	Ucon Idaho
126	Weiser Idaho
1005	Wendell Idaho

OREGON—32

386	Beaverton Oregon
472	Bend Oregon
1373	Cedar Mill Oregon
1325	Central Point Oregon
493	Coos Bay Oregon
385	Corvallis Oregon
191	Eugene Oregon
1410	Eugene Oregon Santa Clara
767	Eugene Oregon West
779	Grants Pass Oregon
643	Gresham Oregon
1365	Gresham Oregon South
1200	Hermiston Oregon
710	Hillsboro Oregon
743	Keizer Oregon
205	Klamath Falls Oregon
49	La Grande Oregon
1468	Lake Oswego Oregon
1102	Lebanon Oregon
1300	McMinnville Oregon
400	Medford Oregon
999	Milwaukie Oregon
176	Nyssa Oregon
1504	Ontario Oregon
563	Oregon City Oregon
123	Portland Oregon
190	Portland Oregon East
1239	Redmond Oregon

830	Roseburg Oregon
321	Salem Oregon
1171	Salem Oregon East
850	The Dalles Oregon

WASHINGTON—46

1388	Auburn Washington
388	Bellevue Washington
1266	Bellingham Washington
1312	Bothell Washington
299	Bremerton Washington
958	Centralia Washington
1299	Colville Washington
1438	Elma Washington
1148	Ephrata Washington
532	Everett Washington
883	Federal Way Washington
776	Kennewick Washington
1374	Kennewick Washington East
1495	Kent Washington
1565	Lakewood Washington
599	Longview Washington
925	Lynnwood Washington
1251	Marysville Washington
213	Moses Lake Washington
379	Mt. Vernon Washington
440	Olympia Washington
1049	Othello Washington
437	Pasco Washington
638	Pullman Washington
542	Puyallup Washington
1389	Puyallup Washington South
844	Redmond Washington
514	Renton Washington
1244	Renton Washington North
180	Richland Washington
124	Seattle Washington
242	Seattle Washington North
1496	Seattle Washington Shoreline
1023	Selah Washington
1057	Silverdale Washington
168	Spokane Washington
556	Spokane Washington East
992	Spokane Washington North
195	Tacoma Washington
1052	Tacoma Washington South
389	Vancouver Washington
1570	Vancouver Washington North
979	Vancouver Washington West
1011	Walla Walla Washington
426	Wenatchee Washington
284	Yakima Washington

MISSIONS — 6

ALASKA ANCHORAGE MISSION
201 Danner Ave., Suite 140
Anchorage, Alaska 99518
Phone: (907) 344-4561

CANADA VANCOUVER MISSION
P.O. Box 442
Point Roberts, Washington 98281
Phone: (604) 278-3585

IDAHO BOISE MISSION
2710 Sunrise Rim Road, Suite 220
Boise, Idaho 83705
Phone: (208) 343-9883

OREGON PORTLAND MISSION
13635 N.W. Cornell Road, Suite 100
Portland, Oregon 97229
Phone: (503) 643-1696

WASHINGTON SEATTLE MISSION
P.O. Box 3887
Bellevue, Washington 98009
Phone: (206) 641-5050

WASHINGTON SPOKANE MISSION
P.O. Box 14808
Spokane, Washington 99214
Phone: (509) 924-8932

TEMPLES — 4 (1 under construction)

BOISE IDAHO TEMPLE

Location: Just off Interstate 84 on South Cole Road in the west end of Boise; address, 1211 S. Cole Road, Boise, Idaho 83709. Telephone: (208)-322-4422.

Exterior Finish: The temple is faced with light colored marble and has a slate roof. It is surrounded by three detached towers on each end, and an 8-foot, gold-leafed statue of the Angel Moroni stands atop the highest spire.

Temple Design: Modern adaptation of six-spire design.

Architect: Church Architectural Staff, with assistance from Ron Thurber & Associates of Boise.

Construction Advisor: Jerry Sears.

Contractor: Comtrol Inc. of Midvale, Utah.

Number of Rooms: Three sealing rooms, four ordinance rooms; total rooms 42.

Total Floor Area: 32,269 square feet.

Dimensions of Building: 236 feet by 78 feet.

Area of Site: 4.8 acres.

District and membership: 29 stakes in Idaho, two in eastern Oregon; 88,000 members.

Groundbreaking, Site Dedication: Dec. 18, 1982, by Elder Mark E. Petersen of the Council of the Twelve. About 4,500 people attended.

Temple Dedication: May 25-30, 1984, by President Gordon B. Hinckley in the first of 24 sessions. About 29,000 members attended.

Dedicatory Prayer excerpt: *"May thy faithful saints of this and future generations look to this beautiful structure as a house to which they will be made welcome for their washings and anointings, for endowments and sealings, for instruction, for meditation, for worship, for the making of eternal covenants with thee, for inspiration and sanctification, as they serve unselfishly in assisting thee in bringing to pass thine eternal purposes for the salvation and exaltation of thy sons and daughters."*

PORTLAND OREGON TEMPLE

Announced: April 7, 1984, by President Gordon B. Hinckley.

Location: In a thickly wooded suburb about 10 miles southwest of downtown Portland, in the northwest corner of Oswego, adjacent to Interstate 5 freeway.

Site: The land was purchased by the Church 25 years ago for a junior college, but 7.3 acres was later chosen as a temple site.

Total square feet: 82,000

Architects: Leland A. Gray, temple architect; Lee/Ruff/Waddle, site and local architects.

Contractor: Zwick Construction Co.

Temple district and membership: Includes most of Oregon and parts of Washington, 90,000 members.

Groundbreaking: by President Gordon B. Hinckley on Sept. 20, 1986.

Status: Under construction, completion expected in 1989.

IDAHO FALLS TEMPLE

Location: 1000 Memorial Dr., in northwestern part of Idaho Falls, Idaho, on the banks of the Snake River. (208-522-7669)

Site: March 3, 1937, the First Presidency, announced that a temple would be built in Idaho Falls. In 1938, the city donated a seven-acre site.

Exterior Finish: Built of reinforced concrete. A mixture of white quartz aggregate and white cement known as cast stone covers the 16-inch exterior walls in slabs two inches thick. A 12-foot gold-leaf, fiberglass statue of Angel Moroni was added Sept. 5, 1983.

Temple Design: Modern-contemporary.

Architect: Church board of temple architects. Edward O. Anderson, Georgius Y. Cannon, Ramm Hansen, John Fetzer, Hyrum C. Pope, Lorenzo S. Young.

Construction Adviser: Arthur Price.

Contractor: Birdwell Finlayson of Pocatello, Idaho.

Number of Rooms: 38 in original plans; 84 at present.

Total Floor Area: 86,972 square feet.

Dimensions of Building: 175 feet by 190 feet; tower 148 feet high. There are two annexes that were built later and added 7,700 square feet of floor space.

District and membership: Southeastern Idaho, and parts of Montana and Wyoming;

173,000 members.

Groundbreaking, Site Dedication: Dec. 19, 1939, ground broken by President David Smith, North Idaho Falls Stake. Site dedicated Saturday, Oct. 19, 1940, by President David O. McKay of the First Presidency.

Temple Dedication: Sept. 23 through 25, 1945, in a total of eight sessions by President George Albert Smith.

Dedicatory Prayer excerpt: *"We pray now that thou wilt accept this temple as a freewill offering from thy children, that it will be sacred unto thee. We pray that all that has* been accomplished here may be pleasing in thy sight and that thou wilt be mindful of this structure at all times that it may be preserved from the fury of the elements and wilt thou, our Heavenly Father, let thy presence be felt here always, that all who assemble here may realize that they are thy guests and that this is thy house."*

SEATTLE TEMPLE

Location: 2808-148th Ave. S.E. across from Bellevue Community College, near the Eastgate Interchange on Interstate 90. (206) 643-5144

Site Selected: 23.5 acre site selected June 1975.

Exterior Finish: Reinforced concrete faced with white marble aggregate and cast stone.

Temple Design: Modern.

Architect: Emil B. Fetzer, Church architect.

Resident Project Inspector: Mike Enfield.

Construction Superintendent: Kent Carter for Jacobsen Construction Co. of Salt Lake City.

Number of Rooms: 4 ordinance rooms, 12 sealing rooms.

Total Floor Area: 110,000 square feet.

Dimensions of Building: Ground level is 142 feet by 194 feet; upper levels are 117 feet by 163 feet. Height to square is 70 feet, to top of the Angel Moroni, 179 feet.

District and membership: Washington, Alaska, northern Idaho, and most of British Columbia; 161,000 members.

Groundbreaking, Site Dedication: May 27, 1978, President Marion G. Romney of the First Presidency presided and broke ground and offered the dedicatory prayer.

Temple Dedication: Nov. 17-21, 1980, by President Spencer W. Kimball. Thirteen dedicatory sessions held.

Dedicatory Prayer excerpt: *"Bless, we pray thee, the presidency of this temple and the matron and all the officiators herein. Help them to create a sublime and holy atmosphere so that all ordinances may be performed with love and a sweet, spiritual tone that will cause the members to greatly desire to be here, and to return again and again."*

NORTH AMERICA NORTHEAST AREA

AREA: approximately 2,275,000 square miles
POPULATION: Estimated 140 million
AREA PRESIDENCY: Elders John K. Carmack, Keith W. Wilcox and F. Burton Howard.
LDS POPULATION: 331,000

THE LAND AND ITS PEOPLE: The North America Northeast Areas consists of parts of Canada (Quebec, Newfoundland, Prince Edward Island, New Brunswick, Nova Scotia and part of Ontario), Greenland, and 17 states plus the District of Columbia. Appalachian highlands, interior plains, the Great Lakes, and rolling hills make up the land formations. Thousands of lakes dot the landscape. Excluding Greenland (which remains snow-covered year-round except for coastal areas), most of the area experiences four seasons throughout the year. Winters are harsh and summers are fairly mild.

The population is predominantly Christian, although there are sizeable numbers of Jewish, Moslem, Buddhist, and Hindu believers. A large majority of the population speaks English. Other widely spoken languages include French, Spanish, Italian, German, Polish, Greek,

Chinese, Japanese and Korean.

CHURCH HISTORY: The North America Northeast Area has the distinction of being the setting for the restoration of the gospel and the base from which the Church spread throughout the earth.

The Church was organized April 6, 1830, at Fayette, N.Y., and branches were soon established in New York, Pennsylvania and New England. Apostle Parley P. Pratt established branches in 1837 in New York City, Brooklyn, and on Long Island. In 1843, Apostle John E. Page set up a branch in Washington, D.C.

Meanwhile, in Canada, the gospel had been preached since June 1832, beginning at Ernesttown near Kingston, Ontario. Eastern Canada was a fertile field for the growth of the Church and opened the way for missionary work in the British Isles.

By the time of the martyrdom of the Prophet Joseph Smith, the apostles were preaching the gospel in nearly all the Eastern states. Then came the exodus of most of the saints to the Mountain West.

In 1854, Apostle John Taylor, a former resident of Canada, was appointed to preside over the approximately 10,000 saints east of the Mississippi River.

But Church leaders emphasized gathering to the Rocky Mountains, and most of the Eastern branches were dissolved. In 1893, missionary work was reopened in New York City, and by the turn of the century, there were mission conferences (districts) in New York, Maryland, Pennsylvania, Virginia and New England, with a total of 975 members.

By 1919, missionary work was formally reopened in Canada with the organization of the Canadian Mission.

STAKES — 101

CANADA—11 (in area)
(See also North America Northwest, North America Central)

1222	Brampton Ontario
1530	Dartmouth Nova Scotia
524	Hamilton Ontario
1600	Kitchener Ontario
752	London Ontario
943	Montreal Quebec
1160	Montreal Quebec Mt. Royal
761	Oshawa Ontario
796	Ottawa Ontario
1698	Saint John New Brunswick
300	Toronto Ontario

CONNECTICUT—2
421	Hartford Connecticut
1288	New Haven Connecticut

DELAWARE—1
673	Wilmington Delaware

DISTRICT OF COLUMBIA-1
131	Washington D.C.

INDIANA—8
1078	Bloomington Indiana
712	Evansville Indiana
352	Ft. Wayne Indiana
283	Indianapolis Indiana
624	Indianapolis Indiana North
1417	Lafayette Indiana
1368	New Albany Indiana
873	South Bend Indiana

KENTUCKY—2 (in area)
(See also North America Southeast)

571	Lexington Kentucky
540	Louisville Kentucky

MAINE—3
461	Augusta Maine
1595	Bangor Maine
1290	Portland Maine

MARYLAND—6
674	Baltimore Maryland
1429	Columbia Maryland
1390	Frederick Maryland
1566	Seneca Maryland
526	Silver Spring Maryland
1051	Suitland Maryland

MASSACHUSETTS—3
354	Boston Massachusetts
1287	Hingham Massachusetts
1646	Springfield Massachusetts

MICHIGAN—8
854	Ann Arbor Michigan
197	Bloomfield Hills Michigan
940	Grand Blanc Michigan
684	Grand Rapids Michigan
1091	Kalamazoo Michigan
349	Lansing Michigan
469	Midland Michigan
474	Westland Michigan

NEW HAMPSHIRE—2
1289	Concord New Hampshire
507	Nashua New Hampshire

NEW JERSEY—4
1252	Caldwell New Jersey
1084	Cherry Hill New Jersey
429	East Brunswick New Jersey
292	Morristown New Jersey

NEW YORK—10
485	Albany New York
657	Buffalo New York

483	Ithaca New York
110	New York New York
1574	New York New York East
439	Plainview New York
346	Rochester New York
1543	Rochester New York Palmyra
711	Syracuse New York
909	Yorktown New York

OHIO—11

696	Akron Ohio
270	Cincinnati Ohio
1523	Cincinnati Ohio North
336	Cleveland Ohio
351	Columbus Ohio
793	Columbus Ohio East
1609	Columbus Ohio North
516	Dayton Ohio
1029	Dayton Ohio East
1447	Kirtland Ohio
1204	Toledo Ohio

PENNSYLVANIA—9

946	Altoona Pennsylvania
1592	Erie Pennsylvania
1047	Harrisburg Pennsylvania
304	Philadelphia Pennsylvania
481	Pittsburgh Pennsylvania
985	Pittsburgh Pennsylvania East
1373	Reading Pennsylvania

| 1044 | Scranton Pennsylvania |
| 510 | York Pennsylvania |

RHODE ISLAND—1

| 818 | Providence Rhode Island |

VERMONT—1

| 753 | Montpelier Vermont |

VIRGINIA—15

512	Annandale Virginia
922	Bluefield Virginia
1671	Chesapeake Virginia
740	Fairfax Virginia
1198	Fredericksburg Virginia
1325	McLean Virginia
1583	Mt. Vernon Virginia
846	Newport News Virginia
392	Norfolk Virginia
372	Oakton Virginia
245	Richmond Virginia
1450	Richmond Virginia Chesterfield
499	Roanoke Virginia
934	Waynesboro Virginia
837	Winchester Virginia

WEST VIRGINIA—3

522	Charleston West Virginia
1025	Fairmont West Virginia
1375	Huntington West Virginia

MISSIONS — 23

CANADA HALIFAX MISSION
Commerce Building
73 Tacoma Drive, Suite 202
Dartmouth, Nova Scotia B2W 3Y6
Canada
Phone: (902) 434-2722

CANADA MONTREAL MISSION
8885 Lacordaire Blvd.
St. Leonard Montreal, P.Q. H1R 2B4
Canada
Phone: (514) 322-3130

CANADA TORONTO MISSION
338 Queen Street East, Suite 214
Brampton, Ontario L6V 1C5
Canada
Phone: (416) 451-7511

CONNECTICUT HARTFORD MISSION
P.O. Box 378
Bloomfield, Connecticut 06002
Phone: (203) 242-2099

INDIANA INDIANAPOLIS MISSION
P.O. Box 495
Carmel, Indiana 46032
Phone: (317) 844-3964

KENTUCKY LOUISVILLE MISSION
P.O. Box 4247 Baxter Ave. Station

Louisville, Kentucky 40204
Phone: (502) 451-3010

MASSACHUSETTS BOSTON MISSION
4 Longfellow Park
Cambridge, Massachusetts 02138-4895
Phone: (617) 868-0630

MICHIGAN DEARBORN MISSION
33505 State Street, Suite 101
Farmington, Michigan 48024
Phone: (313) 478-8588

MICHIGAN LANSING MISSION
1400 Abbott, Suite 460
East Lansing, Michigan 48823
Phone: (517) 351-3430

NEW HAMPSHIRE MANCHESTER
MISSION
Bedford Farms, Bldg. #6
Bedford, New Hampshire 03102-2177
Phone: (603) 622-0429

NEW JERSEY MORRISTOWN MISSION
2 Ridgedale Avenue, #210
Cedar Knolls, New Jersey 07927
Phone: (201) 326-9494

NEW YORK NEW YORK MISSION
55 Northern Blvd., Suite 206

Great Neck, New York 11021
Phone: (516) 829-1920

NEW YORK ROCHESTER MISSION
P.O. Box 263
Pittsford, New York 14534
Phone: (716) 248-8570

OHIO AKRON MISSION
931 North Main Street, Suite 101
North Canton, Ohio 44720
Phone: (216) 494-2164

OHIO CLEVELAND MISSION
24600 Center Ridge Road, #450
Westlake, Ohio 44145
Phone: (216) 871-0937

OHIO COLUMBUS MISSION
P.O. Box 20130
Columbus, Ohio 43220
Phone: (614) 451-6183

PENNSYLVANIA HARRISBURG MISSION
3607 Rosemont Avenue
Camp Hill, Pennsylvania 17011-6943
Phone: (717) 761-3611

PENNSYLVANIA PHILADELPHIA MISSION
280 North Providence Road
Media, Pennsylvania 19063
Phone: (215) 565-1150

PENNSYLVANIA PITTSBURGH MISSION
2589 Washington Road, Suite 410
Pittsburgh, Pennsylvania 15241
Phone: (412) 831-7557

VIRGINIA ROANOKE MISSION
P.O. Box 4758
Roanoke, Virginia 24015
Phone: (703) 774-7262

WASHINGTON D.C. NORTH MISSION
12520 Prosperity Drive, Suite 330
Silver Spring, Maryland 20904
Phone: (301) 622-9373

WASHINGTON D.C. SOUTH MISSION
5618-D Ox Road
Fairfax Station, Virginia 22039
Phone: (703) 250-0111

WEST VIRGINIA CHARLESTON MISSION
Box 2187
Charleston, West Virginia 25328
Phone: (304) 342-8332

TEMPLES — 3 (1 under construction, 1 no longer used)

KIRTLAND TEMPLE*

*No longer operating

Location: Kirtland, Ohio, 25 miles east of Cleveland, on a hill west of the Chagrin River.

Site: Selected March 1833; deed for temple site not recorded until Aug. 4, 1834.

Exterior Finish: Sandstone covered with stuccoed plaster.

Temple Design: An adaption of Federal Georgian and New England Colonial.

Architect: Joseph Smith.

Building Committee: Hyrum Smith, Reynolds Cahoon and Jared Carter.

Master Builder: Artemis Millett.

Number of Rooms: Originally 15.

Total Floor Area: Approximately 15,000 square feet.

Dimensions of Building: 79 feet long; 59 feet wide; walls 50 feet high; tower height above ground, 110 feet.

Groundbreaking, Site Dedication: Hauling of sandstone to site began June 5, 1833.

Temple Dedication: March 27, 1836, by President Joseph Smith.

Dedicatory Prayer excerpt: *"And we ask thee, Holy Father, that thy servants may go forth from this house, armed with thy power, and that thy name may be upon them . . . ."*

WASHINGTON TEMPLE

Location: 9900 Stoneybrook Dr., wooded, 57-acre site in Kensington, Md., near Exit 20 of the Capitol Beltway (I-495), and one-half hour's drive from Washington, D.C. (301-588-0650)

Site: Purchased in 1962 for $850,000; 52 acres.

Exterior Finish: Reinforced concrete sheathed in 173,000 square feet of Alabama white marble.

Temple Design: The total design portrays the Church as "a light to the world," with three towers to the east representing the Melchizedek Priesthood leadership, and those to the west, the Aaronic Priesthood leadership, said principal architect Keith W. Wilcox.

Architects: Fred L. Markham, Henry P. Fetzer, Harold K. Beecher, Keith W. Wilcox, under general direction of Church architect Emil B. Fetzer.

Contractors: Jacobson, Okland, and Sidney Foulger construction companies.

Groundbreaking, Site Dedication: Dec. 7, 1968, by President Hugh B. Brown.

Number of Rooms: Seven floors, 294 rooms.

Total Floor Area: 160,000 square feet; 108,000 square feet of landscaping around temple.

Dimensions of Building: 248 feet long, 136 feet wide, not including annex or bridge to temple proper. Statue of Angel Moroni on highest spire 288 feet above ground.

District and membership: Most of eastern United States, Puerto Rico and Dominican Republic; 185,000 members.

Temple Dedication: Nov. 19-22, 1974, by President Spencer W. Kimball in 10 sessions.

Dedicatory Prayer excerpt: *"We are so grateful, our Father, that thy Son has thrown wide open the doors of the prisons for the multitudes who are waiting in the spirit world."*

TORONTO ONTARIO TEMPLE

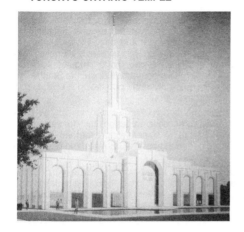

Announced: April 7, 1984, by President Gordon B. Hinckley.

Site: Announced June 22, at the creation of the Kitchener Ontario Stake by President Thomas S. Monson; 13.4 acres.

Location: The temple is being built in Brampton, a city of about 195,000 people about 20 miles west of Toronto.

Groundbreaking: Oct. 10, 1987, by President Thomas S. Monson.

Contractor: Milne & Nicholls Ltd.

Temple District: The temple district includes about 63,000 members from Ontario, Nova Scotia, Quebec, and parts of Ohio, Michigan, New York and Vermont.

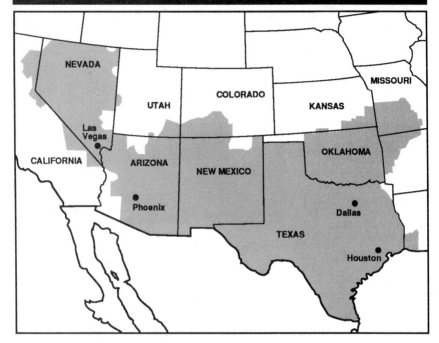

NORTH AMERICA SOUTHWEST AREA

AREA: 717,000

POPULATION: About 26.7 million

AREA PRESIDENCY: Elders H. Burke Peterson, Ronald E. Poelman, and Devere Harris.

LDS POPULATION: 553,000

THE LAND AND ITS PEOPLE: All or part of 12 states comprise the area. The Rocky Mountain range splits the North America Southwest Area; includes a broad coastal plain of Texas along the Gulf of Mexico; the Great Basin encompasses most of Nevada; the Colorado Plateau covers the northern part of Arizona, which is cut by many deep canyons, including the Grand Canyon; Mediterranean-type climate of warm summers and rainy winters, with arid deserts is characteristic of the southern part of the area. Languages spoken are English with Spanish as a second language in parts of Texas and New Mexico; Indian languages among tribes in New Mexico, Arizona and Nevada. Catholics predominate throughout the Southwest, with a significant number of Protestants. In Nevada, one-fifth of the population is LDS, and in Arizona, Mormons make up the second largest religious group.

CHURCH HISTORY: The Southwest was first mentioned in Church history as early as 1844 when the Prophet Joseph Smith suggested Texas as a possible gathering place for saints from the Southern states. Early historical reports showed that missionaries there met with considerable success, although missionary work in Texas halted during the Civil War, and resumed in 1875.

Texas' sister state, New Mexico, first became known to members through the march of the Mormon Battalion from Ft. Leavenworth, Kan., to the Pacific Coast in 1846. The battalion also marched through Arizona, where two decades later, LDS settlers would begin colonizing the state.

In 1873, missionaries were called to locate sites for settlements in Arizona. The first stake was organized among the Little Colorado River communities in 1878. In all, about 30 communities in Arizona were settled by Mormons, in the 1870s and early 1880s.

The first white settlers in Nevada were members of the Church. Mormon Station in Genoa, Nev., located near what is now the state's capital of Carson City, was established in 1848 by seven men who were part of a company headed for the California mines. A number of families from Utah were later called by the Church to settle there during the 1850s under the direction of Apostle Orson Hyde. The settlement project was known as the Carson Valley Mission.

In 1855, 30 brethren were called to settle in Las Vegas. Soon afterwards a company was formed, and upon arriving in Las Vegas on June 14, 1855, the brethren planted crops and built cabins, a bowery and an adobe fort. The Las Vegas settlement was frequently visited by companies of missionaries traveling to and from California.

Prior to the creation of Oklahoma, missionary work to the Indians was sporadic, and the elders suffered from lack of proper food and clothing. Considerable progress was made in 1885 when Andrew Kimball, father of President Spencer W. Kimball, began presiding over the Indian Territory Mission. Branches were formed and several meetinghouses erected. In 1907, the U.S. Indian Territory became the state of Oklahoma, and missionary work there was carried out under the direction of the Indian Territory Mission.

Missionary work in New Mexico among the Zuni Indians was particularly successful in 1875-76. Two years later later, members were called to settle areas of New Mexico. They found the land fertile and established successful colonies in Fruitland in the northeast, Ramah in the north central area and Luna Valley in the southeast.

STAKES — 141

ARIZONA—55 (in area)
(See also North America West)

1616	Apache Junction Arizona
1666	Buckeye Arizona
888	Camp Verde Arizona
988	Chandler Arizona
1513	Chandler Arizona Alma
963	Duncan Arizona
1627	Eagar Arizona
232	Flagstaff Arizona
703	Gilbert Arizona Greenfield
1295	Gilbert Arizona Stapley
1661	Gilbert Arizona Val Vista
612	Glendale Arizona
1236	Glendale Arizona North
650	Globe Arizona
536	Holbrook Arizona
1436	Kingman Arizona
161	Mesa Arizona
1265	Mesa Arizona Central
224	Mesa Arizona East
1087	Mesa Arizona Kimball
1026	Mesa Arizona Lehi
24	Mesa Arizona Maricopa
1628	Mesa Arizona Mountain View
558	Mesa Arizona North
1479	Mesa Arizona Pueblo
745	Mesa Arizona Salt River
362	Mesa Arizona South
555	Mesa Arizona West
633	Page Arizona
1061	Paradise Valley Arizona
1631	Peoria Arizona
121	Phoenix Arizona
1248	Phoenix Arizona Camelback
1233	Phoenix Arizona Deer Valley
212	Phoenix Arizona East
253	Phoenix Arizona North
380	Phoenix Arizona West

896	Phoenix Arizona West Maricopa
517	Prescott Arizona
120	Safford Arizona
137	St. David Arizona
31	St. Johns Arizona
364	Scottsdale Arizona
668	Show Low Arizona
1348	Sierra Vista Arizona
31	Snowflake Arizona
1212	Taylor Arizona
391	Tempe Arizona
738	Tempe Arizona South
25	Thatcher Arizona
238	Tucson Arizona
878	Tucson Arizona East
477	Tucson Arizona North
1517	Tucson Arizona Rincon
959	Winslow Arizona

ARKANSAS—1 (in area)
(See also North America Southeast)

911	Ft. Smith Arkansas

CALIFORNIA—1 (in area)
(See also North America West)

1073	Quincy California

COLORADO—3 (in area)
(See also North America Central)

1425	Alamosa Colorado
26	Manassa Colorado
557	Durango Colorado

OKLAHOMA—8

777	Lawton Oklahoma
1418	Muskogee Oklahoma
531	Norman Oklahoma
305	Oklahoma City Oklahoma
1381	Oklahoma City Oklahoma South
1277	Stillwater Oklahoma
298	Tulsa Oklahoma

912 Tulsa Oklahoma East

NEVADA—23

906 Carson City Nevada
143 Elko Nevada
96 Ely Nevada
500 Fallon Nevada
1650 Fallon Nevada South
228 Henderson Nevada
605 Henderson Nevada West
216 Las Vegas Nevada
451 Las Vegas Nevada Central
915 Las Vegas Nevada East
1519 Las Vegas Nevada Green Valley
1542 Las Vegas Nevada Lakes
401 Las Vegas Nevada Paradise
855 Las Vegas Nevada Redrock
509 Las Vegas Nevada South
1576 Las Vegas Nevada Sunrise
1406 Las Vegas Nevada West
64 Logandale Nevada
308 North Las Vegas Nevada
135 Reno Nevada
635 Reno Nevada North
339 Sparks Nevada
1296 Winnemucca Nevada

NEW MEXICO—12

250 Albuquerque New Mexico
422 Albuquerque New Mexico East
1353 Albuquerque New Mexico South
742 Bloomfield New Mexico
63 Farmington New Mexico
687 Gallup New Mexico
1298 Grants New Mexico
1363 Kirtland New Mexico
654 Las Cruces New Mexico
816 Roswell New Mexico
1219 Santa Fe New Mexico
1409 Silver City New Mexico

MISSOURI—2 (in area)

(See also North America Central)

859 Joplin Missouri

610 Springfield Missouri

TEXAS—34

1262 Abilene Texas
1272 Amarillo Texas
1594 Arlington Texas
626 Austin Texas
333 Beaumont Texas
1076 Conroe Texas
398 Corpus Christi Texas
1451 Cypress Texas
210 Dallas Texas
828 Dallas Texas East
194 El Paso Texas
1359 El Paso Texas Mt. Franklin
443 Ft. Worth Texas
843 Friendswood Texas
1394 Gilmer Texas
1247 Harlingen Texas
209 Houston Texas
456 Houston Texas East
733 Houston Texas North
1211 Houston Texas South
784 Hurst Texas
986 Killeen Texas
1337 Kingwood Texas
1253 Lewisville Texas
496 Longview Texas
446 Lubbock Texas
692 McAllen Texas
471 Odessa Texas
1360 Orange Texas
616 Plano Texas
1396 Richardson Texas
252 San Antonio Texas
758 San Antonio Texas East
1427 San Antonio Texas West

UTAH—2 (in area)

(See also Utah South, Utah North)

897 Blanding Utah
1283 Blanding Utah West

MISSIONS — 9

ARIZONA PHOENIX MISSION
6265 North 82nd Street
Scottsdale, Arizona 85253
Phone: (602) 951-8098

ARIZONA TEMPE MISSION
P.O. Box 27056
Tempe, Arizona 85282
Phone: (602) 838-0659

NEVADA LAS VEGAS MISSION
4161 Pecos-McLeod, Suite B-140
Las Vegas, Nevada 89121
Phone: (702) 435-0025

NEW MEXICO ALBUQUERQUE MISSION
6100 Seagull Street, N.E., #109
Albuquerque, New Mexico 87109
Phone: (505) 888-0225

OKLAHOMA TULSA MISSION
5215 East 71st Street, Suite 300

Tulsa, Oklahoma 74136
Phone: (918) 496-0056

TEXAS DALLAS MISSION
13747 Montfort Drive, #120
Dallas, Texas 75240-4454
Phone: (214) 239-5621

TEXAS FT. WORTH MISSION
3301 West Airport Freeway, Suite 114
Bedford, Texas 76021
Phone: (817) 354-7444

TEXAS HOUSTON MISSION
16333 Hafer Road
Houston, Texas 77090
Phone: (713) 440-6770

TEXAS SAN ANTONIO MISSION
1015 Jackson-Keller, Suite 114
San Antonio, Texas 78213
Phone: (512) 349-3268

TEMPLES — 3 (1 under construction)

ARIZONA TEMPLE

Location: 121 S. Lesueur, Mesa, Ariz., 16 miles east of Phoenix, in central Arizona's Valley of the Sun. Apache Trail or the Bankhead Highway (Highway 60-70-80-90) passes the site on the north. (602-833-1211)

Site: Twenty-acre site selected Feb. 1, 1920, by President Heber J. Grant, Apostles David O. McKay and George F. Richards. Purchased in 1921.

Exterior Finish: Concrete reinforced with 130 tons of steel. Exterior is faced with a terra cotta glaze that is egg-shell in color and tile-like in finish.

Temple Design: Modification of the classic style, suggestive of pre-Columbian temples and even of the Temple of Herod.

Architects: Don C. Young and Ramm Hansen.

Construction Chairman: Executive building committee, J.W. Lesueur, chairman; O.S. Stapley, John Cummard, Andrew Kimball.

Construction Supervisor: Arthur Price.

Number of Rooms: 193.

Total Floor Area: 72,712 square feet.

Dimensions of Building: 128 feet north and south, 184 feet east and west, and 50 feet in height above the foundation.

District and membership: Most of Arizona and of New Mexico; a stake in California; and two in Texas; 217,000 members.

Groundbreaking, Site Dedication: Nov. 28, 1921, President Heber J. Grant dedicated site. Ground broken April 25, 1922.

Temple Dedication: Sunday, Oct. 23, 1927, by President Heber J. Grant. Services broadcast by radio from Station KFAD at Phoenix. Rededicated April 15, 1975, in seven sessions by President Spencer W. Kimball; more than 30,000 in attendance.

Dedicatory Prayer excerpt: "... *Accept the dedication of this house, and these grounds, which we have dedicated unto thee by virtue of the Priesthood of the Living God which we hold.*"

DALLAS TEXAS TEMPLE

Location: Address — 6363 Willow Lane; Dallas, Texas 75248. Phone: (214) 991-1273.

Exterior Finish: Light colored marble tile walls, dark gray slate roof.

Temple Design: Modern adaptation of earlier six-spire design.

Architect: Church architectural staff with assistance from West & Humphries of Dallas.

Construction Advisor: Virgil Roberts.

Contractor: Comtrol Inc. of Midvale, Utah.

Number of Rooms: Three sealing rooms, four ordinance rooms; total rooms 42.

Total Floor Area: 17,850 square feet.

Dimensions of Building: 236 by 78 feet.

Area of Site: 6 acres.

District and membership: Oklahoma, Arkansas, Kansas, most of Texas and parts of Missouri and Louisiana; 155,000 members.

Groundbreaking, Site Dedication: Jan. 22, 1983, by President Gordon B. Hinckley.

Temple Dedication: Oct. 19-24, 1984 in

23 sessions by President Gordon B. Hinckley.

Dedicatory Prayer excerpt: *"May this beautiful temple, standing in this community, become a declaration to all who shall look upon it, of the faith of thy saints in the revealed things of eternity, and may they be led to respect that which is sacred unto us, thy people."*

LAS VEGAS NEVADA TEMPLE

Location: The temple is in a sparsely populated residential area on the slope of Sunrise Mountain on the east side of Las Vegas.

Announced: Announced April 7, 1984 by President Gordon B. Hinckley.

Site: 10.3 acres

Architects: Tate & Snyder

Contractor: Hogan & Tingey

District and membership: The district includes Nevada, parts of Arizona and California, and has about 54,000 members.

Total square feet: 80,900

Groundbreaking: Nov. 30, 1985, by President Gordon B. Hinckley.

North America Southeast Area

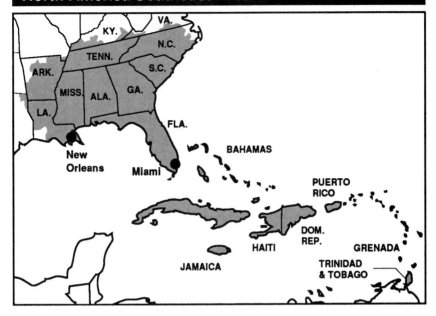

NORTH AMERICA SOUTHEAST AREA

AREA: 4.7 million square miles

POPULATION: 65 million

AREA PRESIDENCY: Elders Rex D. Pinegar, Spencer H. Osborn, and Lloyd P. George

LDS POPULATION: 294,000

THE LAND AND ITS PEOPLE: From the southern half of the Appalachian Mountains to the tropical climes of the Gulf of Mexico and the Caribbean Sea, the North America Southeast Area is full of contrasting peoples, cultures and religions. The southeastern United States is the heart of the Protestant Bible Belt, while Puerto Rico, Dominican Republic and West Indies are predominantly Roman Catholic. The weather ranges from hot and humid tropical weather to the seasonal weather of Kentucky, Virginia and Arkansas.

CHURCH HISTORY: Missionary work began in Mississippi in 1839 under the direction of Benjamin L. Clapp and others. But not until many years after the exodus of the saints to the Rocky Mountains was the Church established in the Southeast. The Southeastern States Mission was formed in 1875 with Henry G. Boyle serving as president. By 1883, 25 branches had been organized in the area with a membership of about 1,000.

From 1890 to 1930, the Southeast was one of the most successful proselyting areas, but also the site of some of the greatest persecution. But the Church has gained acceptance through the years and headquarters for stakes can be found in almost every major city in the area.

The first missionaries were sent to Puerto Rico in the mid-1960s, and a dependent branch was established in 1970. In 1977, the first all-Puerto Rican district presidency was sustained to preside over 1,306 members. Two years later a mission was formed in Puerto Rico, and the next year, the San Juan District became a stake. Most of the islands of the West Indies were opened to missionary work in 1978 and 1979.

Elder Thomas S. Monson, then of the Council of the Twelve, dedicated Haiti for the preaching of the gospel in April 1983, and three months later, the West Indies Mission was formed. There are now missions in Haiti, Jamaica and the Dominican Republic.

1987 units and membership†

Country	Stakes	Wards	Stake bran- ches	Mis- sions	Dist- ricts	Mission wards, bran- ches	Total wards, bran- ches	Memb- ership	Per cent of Pop.	1 LDS in:
Antigua						1	1	*		
Barbados						5	5	*		
Bermuda						1	1	*		
Cayman Island					1	1	*			
Cuba						1	1	*		
Dominican Republic	1	5	8	2	7	47	60	15,000	.221	452
Grenada						1	1	*		
Guadeloupe						1	1	*		
Haiti				1	1	15	15	2,200	.037	2,703
Jamaica				1	2	10	10	1,200	.052	1,923
Martinique						1	1	*		
Puerto Rico	4	23	24	1			47	1,300	.396	253
Saint Kitts Nevis						1	1	*		
Sant Lucia						2	2	*		
Saint Vincent						1	1	200		
St. Martin						1	1	*		
Trinidad, Tobago						2	2	*		
Virgin Islands						2	2	200		

* Fewer than 100 members
† Membership totals rounded off, some include partial estimates; stakes, missions as of Oct. 16, 1988.

STAKES — 75

DOMINICAN REPUBLIC—1
1593 Santo Domingo Dominican Republic

PUERTO RICO—4
1480 Carolina Puerto Rico
1580 Mayaquez Puerto Rico
1349 Ponce Puerto Rico
1215 San Juan Puerto Rico

ALABAMA—6
1362 Bessemer Alabama
678 Birmingham Alabama
1588 Dothan Alabama
452 Huntsville Alabama
964 Mobile Alabama
717 Montgomery Alabama

ARKANSAS—2 (in area)
(See also North America Southwest)
1432 Jacksonville Arkansas
484 Little Rock Arkansas

FLORIDA—18
879 Cocoa Florida
530 Ft. Lauderdale Florida
1472 Ft. Myers Florida
746 Gainesville Florida
465 Jacksonville Florida East
1660 Jacksonville Florida North
163 Jacksonville Florida West
1590 Lake City Florida
1380 Lake Mary Florida
1153 Lakeland Florida
311 Miami Florida
257 Orlando Florida
732 Panama City Florida
486 Pensacola Florida
651 St. Petersburg Florida
594 Tallahassee Florida
289 Tampa Florida
1190 West Palm Beach Florida

GEORGIA—10
921 Atlanta Georgia
889 Augusta Georgia
886 Columbus Georgia
715 Douglas Georgia
373 Macon Georgia
1208 Marietta Georgia
1643 Marietta Georgia East
640 Roswell Georgia
916 Savannah Georgia
241 Tucker Georgia

KENTUCKY—1 (in area)
(See also North America Northeast)

926   Hopkinsville Kentucky

LOUISIANA—7

954   Alexandria Louisiana
476   Baton Rouge Louisiana
1254 Denham Springs Louisiana
1550 Monroe Louisiana
221   New Orleans Louisiana
254   Shreveport Louisiana
1575 Slidell Louisiana

MISSISSIPPI—3

1364 Gulfport Mississippi
408   Hattiesburg Mississippi
404   Jackson Mississippi

NORTH CAROLINA—12

1086 Asheville North Carolina
1606 Charlotte North Carolina Central
591   Charlotte North Carolina South
1637 Durham North Carolina

698   Fayetteville North Carolina
1344 Goldsboro North Carolina
335   Greensboro North Carolina
1371 Hickory North Carolina
332   Kinston North Carolina
363   Raleigh North Carolina
574   Wilmington North Carolina
881   Winston-Salem North Carolina

SOUTH CAROLINA—4

584   Charleston South Carolina
169   Columbia South Carolina
454   Florence South Carolina
366   Greenville South Carolina

TENNESSEE—7

927   Chattanooga Tennessee
1089 Franklin Tennessee
1093 Kingsport Tennessee
581   Knoxville Tennessee
403   Memphis Tennessee
1179 Memphis Tennessee North
537   Nashville Tennessee

MISSIONS — 19

ALABAMA BIRMINGHAM MISSION
1560 Montgomery Hwy., Suite 204
Birmingham, Alabama 35216
Phone: (205) 979-0686

ARKANSAS LITTLE ROCK MISSION
University Tower, Suite 210
12th and University
Little Rock, Arkansas 72204
Phone: (501) 664-3765

DOMINICAN REPUBLIC SANTIAGO
MISSION
Apartado 1240
Santiago
Dominican Republic
Phone: (809) 581-3232

DOMINICAN REPUBLIC SANTO
DOMINGO MISSION
Apartado 30103 Ensanche La Fe
Santo Domingo
Dominican Republic
Phone (809) 562-6969

FLORIDA FT. LAUDERDALE MISSION
1350 N.E. 56th Street, Suite A
Ft. Lauderdale, Florida 33308
Phone: (305) 491-2447

FLORIDA JACKSONVILLE MISSION
P.O. Box 17723
Jacksonville, Florida 32245
Phone: (904) 363-0224

FLORIDA TALLAHASSEE MISSION
P.O. Box 12984

Tallahassee, Florida 32317
Phone: (904) 893-4243

FLORIDA TAMPA MISSION
P.O. Box 151685
Tampa, Florida 33684-1685
Phone: (813) 932-5372

GEORGIA ATLANTA MISSION
2215 Perimeter Park, Bldg. 1, #3
Atlanta, Georgia 30341
Phone: (404) 457-0234

HAITI PORT-AU-PRINCE MISSION
Boite Postale 15319
Petionville
Haiti
Phone: (011-509-1) 60-876

JAMAICA KINGSTON MISSION
#4 Ellesmere Road
Kingston 10, Jamaica
West Indies
Phone: (809) 929-2249

LOUISIANA BATON ROUGE MISSION
11816 Sunray Avenue, Suite A
Baton Rouge, Louisiana 70816
Phone: (504) 293-6060

MISSISSIPPI JACKSON MISSION
5200 Keele Street
Jackson, Mississippi 39206
Phone: (601) 362-1518

NORTH CAROLINA CHARLOTTE MISSION
6407 Idlewild, Suite 533

Charlotte, North Carolina 28212
Phone: (704) 563-1560

NORTH CAROLINA RALEIGH MISSION
1300 Paddock Drive, Suite G-15
Raleigh, North Carolina 27609
Phone: (919) 876-2091

PUERTO RICO SAN JUAN MISSION
1590 Ponde de Leon Avenue
General Computer Bldg., #210
Rio Piedras
Puerto Rico 00926
Phone: (809) 751-1030

SOUTH CAROLINA COLUMBIA MISSION
14 Calendar Court, Suite D
Columbia, South Carolina 29206
Phone: (803) 787-6162

TENNESSEE NASHVILLE MISSION
P.O. Box 1287
Brentwood, Tennessee 37024-1287
Phone: (615) 373-1836

WEST INDIES MISSION
Carleigh House, Suite #3
Golf Club Road
Christ Church, Barbados
West Indies
Phone: (809) 427-8753

TEMPLES — 1

ATLANTA GEORGIA TEMPLE

Location: 6450 Barfield Road; Atlanta, Georgia 30328. Phone: (404) 393-3698

Area of Site: 5.9 acres.

Exterior Finish: Precast stone walls, built-up roof.

Temple Design: Modern.

Architect: Emil B. Fetzer, Church architect.

Construction Advisor: Michael Enfield and Ronald Prince.

Contractor: Cube Construction Company.

Number of Rooms: Five sealing rooms, four ordinance rooms; total rooms 54.

Total Floor Area: 27,360 square feet.

Dimensions of Building: 187 feet 8 inches by 166 feet three inches.

District and membership: Most of southeastern U.S., Haiti, Jamaica, and West Indies; 180,000 members.

Groundbreaking, Site Dedication: March 7, 1981, with President Spencer W. Kimball turning the first shovelful of dirt. Previous to the groundbreaking, President Kimball addressed the 10,000-strong crowd, then dedicated the site for the building of a temple.

Temple Dedication: June 1-4, 1983, by President Gordon B. Hinckley, who spoke at five of the 11 dedicatory sessions and gave the prayer in five others.

"May the very presence of this temple in the midst of thy people become a reminder of the sacred and eternal covenants made with thee. May they strive more diligently to banish from their lives those elements which are inconsistent with the covenants they have made with thee.

"May all who enter these holy precincts feel of thy spirit and be bathed in its marvelous, sanctifying influence. May they come . . . in a spirit of love and dedication."

HISTORICAL FACTS, STATISTICS

LATTER-DAY SAINT EMIGRANTS SAILING TO AMERICA

Note: Most information is from manscript History of the British Mission or Church Emigration Books.

Code for ports: L = Liverpool, B = Bristol, H = Hamburg, Le = Le Harve
Lo = London, A = Amsterdam, NY = New York, NO = New Orleans
Q = Quebec, Bo = Boston, P = Philadelphia.
*some figures and dates are estimates.

No.	Date of Sailing	Port of Sailing	Name of Ship	Company Leader	Total* Persons	Port of Entry
1.	6 Jun 1840	L	Britannia	John Moon	41	NY
	Up to April 1841, about 1000 Saints had emigrated, according to Parley P. Pratt					
2.	8 Sep 1840	L	North America	Theodore Turley	200	NY
3.	15 Oct 1840	L	Isaac Newton	Samuel Mulliner	50*	NO
4.	7 Feb 1841	L	Sheffield	Hiram Clark	235	NO
5.	1841	?	Caroline	Thomas Clark	?	?
6.	16 Feb 1841	L	Echo	Daniel Browett	109	NO
7.	17 Mar 1841	L	Uleste or Alesto	Thomas Smith	54	NO
8.	21 Apr 1841	L	Rochester	Brigham Young	130	NY
	Heber C. Kimball, John Taylor, assistants					
	10 May 1841	B	Harmony	Thomas Kingston	50	Q
	8 Aug 1841	B	Caroline	Thomas Richardson	100*	Q
9.	21 Sep 1841	L	Tyrean	Joseph Fielding	207	NO
10.	8 Nov 1841	L	Chaos	Peter Melling	170	NO
11.	12 Jan 1842	L	Tremont	?	143	NO
12.	5 Feb 1842	L	Hope	James Burnham	270	NO
13.	20 Feb 1842	L	John Cummins	?	200*	NO
14.	12 Mar 1842	L	Hanover	Amos Fielding	200*	NO
15.	17 Sep 1842	L	Sidney	Levi Richards	180	NO
	George D. Watt, 1st person baptized in England, on board ship. Roster in Church Emigration book for 1842 under ship "Sidney".					
16.	25 Sep 1842	L	Medford	Orson Hyde	214	NO
17.	29 Sep 1842	L	Henry	John Snider	157	NO
18.	29 Oct 1842	L	Emerald	Parley P. Pratt	250	NO
19.	16 Jan 1843	L	Swanton	Lorenzo Snow	212	NO
20.	8 Mar 1843	L	Yorkshire	Thomas Bullock	83	NO
21.	21 Mar 1843	L	Claiborne	?	106	NO
22.	5 Sep 1843	L	Metoka	?	280	NO
23.	21 Oct 1843	L	Champion	?	91	NO
24.	23 Jan 1844	L	Fanny	William Kay	210	NO
25.	6 Feb 1844	L	Isaac Allerton	?	60	NO
26.	11 Feb 1844	L	Swanton	?	81	NO
27.	5 Mar 1844	L	Glasgow	Hiram Clark	150	NO
28.	19 Sep 1844	L	Norfolk	?	143	NO
29.	17 Jan 1845	L	Palmyra	Amos Fielding	200*	NO
30.	Feb 1845	L	?	?	86?	NO
31.	Sep 1845	L	Oregon	?	125(?)	NO
32.	16 Jan 1846	L	Liverpool	Hiram Clark	45	NO
	Misc.	L	Misc.		137*	
	6 Jul 1847	L	Empire	Lucius N. Scovil	24	NY
33.	20 Feb 1848	L	Carnatic	Franklin D. Richards	120	NO
34.	9 Mar 1848	L	Sailor Prince	Moses Martin	80*	NO
35.	7 Sep 1848	L	Erin's Queen	Simeon Carter	232	NO
36.	24 Sep 1848	L	Sailor Prince	L.D. Butler	311	NO
	Nov 1848	L	Lord Sandon	?	11	NO
37.	29 Jan 1849	L	Zetland	Orson Spencer	358	NO
38.	6 Feb 1849	L	Ashland	John Johnson	187	NO
39.	7 Feb 1849	L	Henry Ware	Robert Martin	225	NO
40.	25 Feb 1849	L	Buena Vista	Dan Jones	249	NO
41.	5 Mar 1849	L	Hartley	William Hulme	220	NO
42.	12 Mar 1849	L	Emblem	Robert Deans	100*	NO
43.	2 Sep 1849	L	James Pennell	Thomas H. Clark	236	NO

No.	Date of Sailing	Port of Sailing	Name of Ship	Company Leader	Total* Persons	Port of Entry
44.	10 Nov 1849	L	Zetland	Samuel H. Hawkins	250*	NO
45.	18 Feb 1850	L	Berlin	James G. Brown	253	NO
46.	10 Jan 1850	L	Argo	Jeter Clinton	402	NO
47.	18 Feb 1850	L	Josiah Bradlee	Thomas Day	263	NO
48.	2 Mar 1850	L	Hartley	David Cook	109	NO
49.	4 Sep 1850	L	North Atlantic	David Sudworth	357	NO
50.	2 Oct 1850	L	James Pennell	Christopher Layton	254	NO
51.	17 Oct 1850	L	Joseph Badger	John Morris	227	NO
52.	8 Jan 1851	L	Ellen	James W. Cummings	456 or 466	NO
53.	9 Jan 1851	L	George W. Bourne	William Gibson	281	NO
54.	1 Feb 1851	L	Ellen Maria	George D. Watt	378	NO
55.	4 Mar 1851	L	Olympus	William Howell	245	NO
56.	10 Jan 1852	L	Kennebec	John S. Higbee	333	NO
57.	10 Feb 1852	L	Ellen Maria	Isaac C. Haight	369	NO
	6 Mar 1852	L	Niagara	John Taylor	20*	Bo
58.	6 Mar 1852	L	Rockaway	Elias Morris?	30	NO
59.	11 Mar 1852	L	Italy	Ole U.C. Munster	28	NO
60.	16 Jan 1853	L	Forest Monarch	John E. Forsgren	297	NO
61.	17 Jan 1853	L	Ellen Maria	Moses Clawson	332	NO
62.	23 Jan 1853	L	Golcondo or Golconda	Jacob Gates	321	NO
63.	5 Feb 1853	L	Jersey	George Halliday	314	NO
64.	15 Feb 1853	L	Elvira Owen	Joseph W. Young	345	NO
65.	28 Feb 1853	L	International	Christopher Arthur	425	NO
66.	26 Mar 1853	L	Falcon	Cornelius Bagnell	324	NO
67.	6 Apr 1853	L	Camillus	Curtis E. Bolton	228	NO
68.	24 Aug 1853	L	Page	Brother Bender	17	NO
	1853	L	Misc.	Misc.	23	NO
69.	3 Jan 1854	L	Jesse Munn	Christian J. Larsen or B.C. Larsen	335	NO
	302 Scandinavians, 33 German Saints					
70.	28 Jan 1854	L	Benjamin Adams	Hans Peter Olsen	384	NO
71.	4 Feb 1854	L	Golcondo or Golconda	Dorr P. Curtis	464	NO
72.	22 Feb 1854	L	Windermere	Daniel Garn	477	NO
73.	5 Mar 1854	L	Old England	John O. Angus	45	NO
74.	12 Mar 1854	L	John M. Wood	Robert Campbell	397	NO
75.	4 Apr 1854	L	Germanicus	Richard Cook	220	NO
76.	8 Apr 1854	L	Marshfield	William Taylor	366	NO
77.	24 Apr 1854	L	Clara Wheeler	?	29	NO
	1854	L	Misc.	Misc.	34	NO
78.	27 Nov 1854	L	Clara Wheeler	Henry E. Phelps	422	NO
79.	6 Jan 1855	L	Rockaway	Samuel Glasgow	24	NO
80.	7 Jan 1855	L	James Nesmith	Peter O. Hansen	440	NO
81.	9 Jan 1855	L	Neva	Thomas Jackson	13	NO
82.	17 Jan 1855	L	Charles Buck	Richard Ballantyne	403 or 401	NO
83.	3 Feb 1855	L	Isaac Jeans	George C. Riser	16	P
84.	27 Feb 1855	L	Siddons	John S. Fullmer	430	P
85.	31 Mar 1855	L	Juventa	William Glover	573	P
86.	17 Apr 1855	L	Chimborazo	Edward Stevenson	431	P
87.	22 Apr 1855	L	Samuel Curling	Israel Barlow	581	NY
88.	36 Apr 1855	L	William Stetson	Aaron Smethurst	293	NY
89.	29 Jul 1855	L	Cynosure	George Seager	159	NY
90.	30 Nov 1855	L	Emerald Isle	Philomen C. Merrill	350	NY
91.	12 Dec 1855	L	John J. Boyd	Knud Peterson	509 or 512	NY
	Misc.	L	Misc.	Misc.	319	Misc.
92.	18 Feb 1856	L	Caravan	Daniel Taylor	457	NY
93.	23 Mar 1856	L	Enoch Train	James Ferguson	534	Bo
94.	19 Apr 1856	L	Samuel Curling	Dan Jones	707	Bo
95.	4 May 1856	L	Thornton	James C. Willie	764	NY
96.	25 May 1856	L	Horizon	Edward Martin	856	Bo

No.	Date of Sailing	Port of Sailing	Name of Ship	Company Leader	Total* Persons	Port of Entry
97.	31 May 1856	L	Wellfleet	John Aubrey	146	Bo
	5 Jul 1856	L	Lucy Thornton	James Thompson	14	NY
98.	18 Nov 1856	L	Columbia	John Williams	223	NY
	Misc.	L	Misc.		69	
99.	28 Mar 1857	L	George Washington	James P. Park	817	Bo
100.	25 Apr 1857	L	Westmoreland	Matthias Cowley	544	P
	(Mostly Scandinavians)					
101.	30 May 1857	L	Tuscarora	Richard Harper	547	P
102.	18 Jul 1857	L	Wyoming	Charles Harmon	36	P
	Misc.	Misc.	Misc.		50	

According to the *Millennial Star*, Vol. 19: p. 479; 2, 181 emigrants came from July 6, 1856 to July 1, 1857.

	21 Jan 1858	L	Underwriter	Henry Harriman	25	NY
	19 Feb 1858	L	Empire	Jesse Hobson	64	NY
103.	22 Mar 1858	L	John Bright	Iver N. Iversen	89	NY

80 Scandinavians, 9 English plus about 600 Irish non-Mormon emigrants.

104.	11 Apr 1859	L	William Tapscott	Robert F. Neslen	726 or 725	NY
105.	10 Jul 1859	L	Antarctic	James Chaplow	30	NY
106.	20 Aug 1859	L	Emerald Isle	Henry Hug	54	NY
	50 from Swiss and Italian Mission, 4 British					
	1860	L	Misc.		84	
107.	30 Mar 1860	L	Underwriter	James D. Ross	594	NY
108.	11 May 1860	L	Tapscott	Asa Calkin	731	NY
109.	16 Apr 1861	L	Manchester	Claudius V. Spencer	380	NY
110.	23 Apr 1861	L	Underwriter	Milo Andrus	624	NY

Note: *Millennial Star*, of October 6, 1860 reports that 2,433 persons emigrated on the Wyoming (1857), William Tapscott (1859), Emerald Isle (1859), Underwriter (1860), William Tapscott (1860), and Miscellaneous ships from July 1, 1857 to June 30, 1860 carrying 263 people.

111.	16 May 1861	L	Monarch of the Sea	Jabez Woodard	955	NY
112.	9 Apr 1862	H	Humbolt	Hans C. Hansen	323	NY
113.	15 Apr 1862	H	Franklin	Christian A. Madsen	413	NY
114.	18 Apr 1862	H	Electric	Soren Christoffersen	336	NY
115.	21 Apr 1862	H	Athenia	Ola N. Liljenquist	484 or 486	NY
116.	23 Apr 1862	L	John J. Boyd	James S. Brown	702	NY
117.	6 May 1862	L	Manchester	John D.T. McAllister	376	NY
118.	14 May 1862	L	William Tapscott	William Gibson	807	NY
119.	15 May 1862	Le	Windermere	Serge L. Ballif	110	NY
120.	18 May 1862	L	Antarctic	William C. Moody	38	NY
	Misc.	L	Misc.		8	NY

Between July 1, 1860 and June 30, 1862; 5,556 had emigrated from Europe — see *Millenial Star* Vol. 24, p. 510.

The "Rowena' sailed from Port Elizabeth, Cape of Good Hope, South Africa for New York March 14, 1863 with 15 Saints on board under the charge of Elder Robert Grant. The ship "Henry Ellis' sailed from Algoa Bay, Cape of Good Hope, South Africa March 31, 1863 with a company of 32 Saints in charge of Elders Stock and Zyderlaam.

121.	30 Apr 1863	L	John J. Boyd	William W. Cluff	763 or 767	NY
122.	8 May 1863	L	B.S. Kimball	Hans Peter Lund	654 or 657	NY
123.	8 May 1863	L	Consignment	Anders Christensen	38	NY
124.	23 May 1853	L	Antarctic	John Needham	483 or 486	NY
125.	30 May 1863	L	Cynosure	David M. Stuart	755 or 775	NY
126.	4 Jun 1863	Lo	Amazon	William Bramall	882 or 895	NY
	Misc.	L	Misc.		72	NY

On April 5, 1864, 9 LDS emigrants left Port Elizabeth, South Africa on the ship "Echo' for Boston in charge of Elder John Talbot and another company of 18 emigrating Saints left the same port April 10th in charge of Elders William Fotheringham and Henry A. Dixon and arrived at Boston June 12, 1864 — see *Millennial Star* Vol. 26, p. 475.

127.	28 Apr 1864	L	Monarch of the Sea	John Smith (patriarch)	974	NY
128.	21 May 1864	L	General McClellan	Thomas E. Jeremy	802	NY
129.	3 Jun 1864	Lo	Hudson	John M. Kay	853	NY
	Misc.	L	Misc		58	NY

No.	Date of Sailing	Port of Sailing	Name of Ship	Company Leader	Total* Persons	Port of Entry
	From October 1, 1863 to December 31, 1864, 2,697 Saints had emigrated from Liverpool and London. The "Mexicana" left Port Elizabeth, South Africa April 12, 1865 with 47 emigrating Saints in charge of Elder Miner Grant Atwood and counselors Adolphus H. Noon and Henry Smith. Sailed to New York. *Millennial Star* Vo. 27, p. 442-445.					
130.	29 Apr 1865	L	Belle Wood	William H. Shearman	636	NY
131.	8 May 1865	H	B.S. Kimball	Anders W. Winberg	558	NY
132.	10 May 1865	L	David Hoadley	William Underwood	23 or 24	NY
	Misc.	L	Misc.		83	
	From January 1, 1865 to December 31, 1865, 1,301 Saints had emigrated from Liverpool and Hamburg.					
133.	30 Apr 1866	L	John Bright	Collins M. Gillet	747	NY
134.	5 May 1866	Lo	Caroline	Samuel H. Hill	389	NY
135.	23 May 1866	Lo	American Congress	John Nicholson	350	NY
136.	25 May 1866	H	Kenilworth	Samuel L. Sprague	684	NY
137.	30 May 1866	L	Arkwright	Justin C. Wixom	450	NY
138.	30 May 1866	Lo	Cornelius Grinnell	Ralph Harrison	26 or 27	NY
139.	1 Jun 1866	H	Cavour	Niels Nielsen	201	NY
140.	2 Jun 1866	H	Humboldt	George M. Brown	328	NY
141.	6 Jun 1866	L	Saint Mark	Alfred Stevens	105	NY
	Misc.	L	Misc.		56	
	Perhaps included in the Miscellaneous ships for 1867 — 20 Saints sailed from London June 1, 1867 in the ship Hudson bound for New York, *Millennial Star* Vol. 29, p. 53.					
142.	21 Jun 1867	L	Manhattan	Archibald N. Hill	482	NY
143.	Misc.	L&Lo	Misc.		178	NY
	660 Saints had emigrated from January 1, 1867 to December 31, 1867 from Europe.					
144.	4 Jun 1868	L	John Bright	James McGaw	720	NY
145.	20 Jun 1868	L	Emerald Isle	Hans Jensen Hals	876	NY
146.	24 Jun 1868	L	Constitution	Harvey H. Cluff	457 or 449	NY
147.	30 Jun 1868	L	Minnesota	John Parry	534 or 530	NY
148.	14 Jul 1868	L	Colorado	William B. Preston	600 or 597	NY
	Misc.	L	Misc.		43	
149.	2 Jun 1869	L	Minnesota	Elias Morris	338	NY
	1st group that could take the railroad all the way to Ogden, Utah from the Eastern U.S.					
150.	15 Jul 1869	L	Minnesota	Ole C. Olsen	598	NY
151.	28 Jul 1869	L	Colorado	John E. Pace	365	NY
152.	25 Aug 1869	L	Minnesota	Marius Ensign	443	NY
153.	22 Sep 1869	L	Manhattan	Joseph Lawson	242 or 239	NY
154.	6 Oct 1869	L	Minnesota	James Needham	294	NY
	20 Oct 1869	L	Colorado	Charles Wilden	16	NY
	Misc.	L	Misc.		41	
	"During the present season, a trifle more than 2,300 Saints have emigrated", from Liverpool (*Mill. Star* 31:674).					
155.	28 Jun 1870	L	Colorado	?	20	NY
156.	13 Jul 1870	L	Manhattan	Karl G. Maeser	269	NY
157.	20 Jul 1870	L	Minnesota	Jesse N. Smith	357	NY
158.	7 Sep 1870	L	Idaho	Frank H. Hyde	186	NY
159.	14 Sep 1870	L	Nevada	B.N. Walter?	26	NY
160.	16 Nov 1870	L	Manhattan	Ralph Thompson	59	NY
	Misc.	L	Misc.			
161.	10 May 1871	L	Wyoming	Joseph Parry	10	NY
162.	21 Jun 1871	L	Wyoming	George Lake	248	NY
163.	28 Jun 1871	L	Minnesota	William W. Cluff	397	NY
164.	12 Jul 1871	L	Colorado	Hamilton G. Park	146	NY
165.	26 Jul 1871	L	Nevada	Lot Smith	93	NY
166.	9 Aug 1871	L	Minnesota	William Douglass	60	NY
167.	6 Sep 1871	L	Nevada	John I. Hart	263	NY
	1871	L	Misc.		?	NY
168.	18 Oct 1871	L	Nevada	George H. Peterson	300	NY
169.	12 Jun 1872	L	Manhattan	David Brinton	221	NY
170.	26 Jun 1872	L	Nevada	Erik Peterson	426	NY
171.	31 Jul 1872	L	Wisconsin	George P. Ward	179	NY

No.	Date of Sailing	Port of Sailing	Name of Ship	Company Leader	Total* Persons	Port of Entry
172.	4 Sep 1872	L	Minnesota	George W. Wilkins	602	NY
173.	16 Oct 1872	L	Minnesota	Thomas Dobson	203	NY
174.	4 Dec 1872	L	Manhattan	Daniel Kennedy	35	NY
	Misc.	L	Misc.		?	NY
175.	4 Jun 1873	L	Nevada	Charles H. Wilcken	246	NY
176.	2 Jul 1873	L	Wisconsin	David O. Calder	976	NY
177.	10 Jul 1873	L	Nevada	Elijah A. Box	283	NY
178.	3 Sep 1873	L	Wyoming	John B. Fairbanks	510	NY
179.	22 Oct 1873	L	Idaho	John I. Hart	522	NY
	Misc.	L	Misc.			
180.	6 May 1874	L	Nevada	Lester J. Herrick	155 or 139	NY
181.	11 Jun 1874	L	Nevada	Joseph Birch	243	NY
182.	24 Jun 1874	L	Idaho	Peter C. Carstensen	806 or 810	NY
183.	8 Jul 1874	L	Minnesota	John Keller	81	NY
184.	2 Sep 1874	L	Wyoming	John C. Graham	558 or 553	NY
185.	14 Oct 1874	L	Wyoming	William N. Fife	155 or 152	NY
	Misc.	L	Misc.		11	NY?
186.	12 May 1875	L	Wyoming	Hugh S. Gowans	176	NY
187.	16 Jun 1875	L	Wisconsin	Robert T. Burton	167	NY
188.	30 Jun 1875	L	Idaho	Christen G. Larsen	765	NY
189.	15 Sep 1875	L	Wyoming	Richard V. Morris	300	NY
190.	14 Oct 1875	L	Dakota	Bedson Eardley	120	NY
191.	19 Jan 1876	L	Montana	Isaiah M. Coombs	20	NY
	Misc.	L	Misc.		?	NY?
192.	24 May 1876	L	Nevada	John Woodhouse	131 or 122	NY
193.	28 Jun 1876	L	Idaho	Nils C. Flygare	628	NY
	23 Aug 1876		Nevada	?	5	NY
	From Iceland, 2 missionaries, 3 emigrants					
194.	13 Sep 1876	L	Wyoming	William L. Binder	322	NY
195.	25 Oct 1876	L	Wyoming	Peter Barton	118	NY
	Misc.	L	Misc.	various names	62	NY
196.	13 Jun 1877	L	Wyoming	David K. Udall	186	NY
197.	27 Jun 1877	L	Wisconsin	John Rowberry	714	NY
198.	19 Sep 1877	L	Wisconsin	Hamilton G. Park	482	NY
199.	17 Oct 1877	L	Idaho	William Paxman	150	NY
	Misc.	L	Misc.	various names	47	NY
200.	25 May 1878	L	Nevada	Thomas Judd	363 or 354	NY
201.	15 Jun 1878	L	Montana	Theodore Braendli	221	NY
202.	29 Jun 1878	L	Nevada	John Cook	569	NY
203.	14 Sep 1878	L	Wyoming	Henry W.Naisbitt	609	NY
204.	19 Oct 1878	L	Wyoming	Aurelius Miner	145 or 132	NY
	Misc.	L	Misc.		145	
205.	19 Apr 1879	L	Wyoming	Charles W. Nibley	170	NY
206.	24 May 1879	L	Wyoming	Alexander F. McDonald	162 or 170	NY
207.	28 Jun 1879	L	Wyoming	William N. Williams	622	NY
208.	6 Sep 1879	L	Wyoming	Nils C. Flygare	336	NY
209.	18 Oct 1879	L	Arizona	William Bramall	224	NY
	Misc.	L	Misc.		3	NY?
210.	10 Apr 1880	L	Wyoming	James L. Bunting	120	NY
211.	5 Jun 1880	L	Wisconsin	John G. Jones	332	Entry
212.	10 Jul 1880	L	Wisconsin	Niels P. Rasmussen	727	NY
213.	4 Sep 1880	L	Nevada	John Rider	337	NY
214.	23 Oct 1880	L	Wisconsin	John Nicholson	258	NY
	Misc.	L	Misc.		63	NY?
215.	16 Apr 1881	L	Wyoming	David C. Dunbar	186	NY
	27 Saints left Auckland, New Zealand April 26, 1881 on the steamship "City of Sidney" in charge of Elder George Batt landing in San Francisco. Roster see Deseret Weekly News vol. 30, p. 265.					
216.	21 May 1881	L	Wyoming	Joseph R. Mathews	297	NY
	11 Jun 1881	L	Nevada	Runolf Runolfsen	11	NY
217.	25 Jun 1881	L	Wyoming	Samuel Roskelly	775	NY

No.	Date of Sailing	Port of Sailing	Name of Ship	Company Leader	Total* Persons	Port of Entry
218.	16 Jul 1881	L	Nevada	John Eyvindson	22	NY
219.	3 Sep 1881	L	Wyoming	James Finlayson	644	NY
220.	22 oct 1881	L	Wisconsin	Lyman R. Martineau	396	NY
	Misc.	L	Misc.	various names		NY?
221.	12 Apr 1882	L	Nevada	John Donaldson	342	NY
222.	17 May 1882	L	Nevada	William R. Webb	392	NY
223.	21 Jun 1882	L	Nevada	Robert R. Irvine	933	NY
224.	22 Jul 1882	L	Arizona		18	
225.	2 Sep 1882	L	Wyoming	William Cooper	662	NY
	Misc.	L	Misc.			
226.	21 Oct 1882	L	Abyssinia	George Stringfellow	416	NY
227.	11 Apr 1883	L	Nevada	David McKay	352	NY
228.	10 May 1883	L	Nevada	Ben E. Rich	427	NY
	British, Swiss, German, Scandinavian					
229.	20 Jun 1883	L	Nevada	Hans O. Magleby	697	NY
230.	14 July 1883	L	Wisconsin	John A. Sutton	18	NY
	A company from Iceland					
231.	29 Aug 1883	L	Nevada	P.F. Goss	682	NY
232.	27 Oct 1883	L	Wisconsin	John Picket	369	NY
	Misc.	L	Misc.		?	
	2,460 emigrants in 1883 not counting the returning misionaries					
233.	9 Apr 1884	L	Nevada	Christian D. Fjeldsted	319	NY
234.	17 May 1884	L	Arizona	Eph. H. Williams	287	NY
235.	14 Jun 1884	L	Arizona	Ephriam H. Nye	531	NY
236.	2 Aug 1884	L	Nevada	Henry W. Attley	14	NY
237.	30 Aug 1884	L	Wyoming	Benjamin Bennett	496	NY
238.	23 Oct 1884	L	City of Berlin	Carl A. Ek	93	NY
239.	1 Nov 1884	L	Arizona	J. Alma Smith	163	NY
	Misc.	L	Misc.		?	
240.	11 Apr 1885	L	Wisconsin	Louis P. Lund	187	NY
241.	16 May 1885	L	Wisconsin	Nathaniel M. Hodges	274	NY
	10 Jul 1885	L	Alaska	?	23	NY
242.	20 Jun 1885	L	Wisconsin	Jorgen Hansen	541	NY
243.	29 Aug 1885	L	Wisconsin	John W. Thornley	329	NY
244.	24 Oct 1885	L	Nevada	Anthon H. Lund	313	NY
	Misc.	L	Misc.		23	NY
245.	17 Apr 1886	L	Nevada	Edwin T. Woolley	179	NY
	15 May 1886	L	Arizona	Isaac C. Gadd	15	NY?
246.	22 May 1886	L	Nevada	Moroni L. Pratt	279	NY
247.	26 Jun 1886	L	Nevada	C.F. Olsen	426	NY
248.	21 Aug 1886	L	Wyoming	David Kunz	301	NY
249.	13 Oct 1886	L	British King	Joshua Greenwood	307	P
	Misc.	L	Misc.		?	
250.	16 Apr 1887	L	Nevada	D.P. Callister	194	NY
251.	21 May 1887	L	Nevada	Edward Davis	187	NY
252.	4 Jun 1887	L	Wyoming	J.C.Nielsen	159	NY
253.	18 Jun 1887	L	Wisconsin	Quincy B. Nichols	646	NY
	536 left Liverpool, 110 boarded at Queenstown, Ireland, 646 total					
254	27 Aug 1887	L	Wisconsin	John I. Hart	406	NY
255.	8 Oct 1887	L	Nevada	Joseph S. Wells	278	NY
	Misc.	L	Misc.		?	
256.	28 Apr 1888	L	Wisconsin	Franklin S. Bramwell	74	NY
257.	16 May 1888	L	Wyoming	William Wood	137	NY
	26 May 1888	L	Arizona	?	11	?
258.	2 Jun 1888	L	Wisconsin	C.A. Dorius	210	NY
259.	9 Jun 1888	L	Nevada	J.S. Stucki	70	NY?
260.	23 Jun 1888	L	Wyoming	Henry E. Bowring	118	NY?
	7 Jul 1888	L	Wisconsin	Robert Lindsay	&	NY?
261.	28 Jul 1888	L	Wyoming	H.J. Christiansen	136	NY
262.	11 Aug 1888	L	Wisconsin	Levi W. Naylor	155	NY
	925 persons had emigrated so far this year.					

No.	Date of Sailing	Port of Sailing	Name of Ship	Company Leader	Total* Persons	Port of Entry
263.	1 Sep 1888	L	Wyoming	Abraham Johnson	83	NY
264.	15 Sep 1888	L	Wisconsin	William G. Phillips	145	NY
265.	6 Oct 1888	L	Wyoming	N.P. Lindelof	123	NY
266.	20 Oct 1888	L	Wisconsin	John Quigley	125	NY
	17 Nov 1888	L?	Arizona	?	7	
	Misc.	L	Misc.			
267.	27 Apr 1889	A	?	Martinus F. Krumperman	26	NY
	11 May 1889	?	Arizona	H.C. Barrell	?	NY
268.	18 May 1889	L	Wisconsin	Mayhew H. Dailey	142	NY
269.	8 Jun 1889	L	Wyoming	Lars S. Anderson	359	NY
270.	22 Jun 1889	L	Wisconsin	John W.F. Volker	172	NY
271.	17 Aug 1889	L	Wyoming	J.P. Toolson or or J.C.A. Werbye	191	NY
272.	31 Aug 1889	L	Wisconsin	William P. Payne	172	NY
273.	21 Sep 1889	L	Wyoming	Rasmus Larsen	113	NY
274.	5 Oct 1889	L	Wisconsin	Edward Bennett	142	NY
275.	26 Oct 1889	L	Wyoming	A.L. Skanchy	161	NY
276.	16 Nov 1889	L	Nevada	Richard Morse	11	NY
	Misc.	L	Misc.			
277.	19 Apr 1890	L	Wisconsin	Orson H. Worthington	52	NY
278.	3 May 1890	L	Wyoming	Adolf Anderson	156	NY
279.	24 May 1890	L	Wisconsin	John H. Hayes	122	NY
280.	7 Jun 1890	L	Wyoming	Erastus C. Willardson	304	NY
281.	28 Jun 1890	L	Wisconsin	Abraham Maw	113	NY
282.	2 Aug 1890	L	Wisconsin	Leonard J. Jordan	86	NY
283.	16 Aug 1890	L	Wyoming	J. Ostlund	128	NY
284.	6 Sep 1890	L	Wisconsin	John U. Stucki	116	NY
285.	20 Sep 1890	L	Wyoming	Jens Jensen	197	NY
286.	11 Oct 1890	L	Wisconsin	Joseph J. Golightly	?	NY

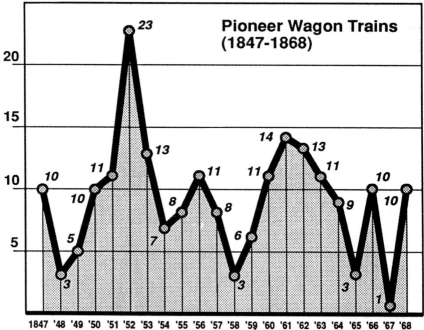

Pioneer Wagon Trains (1847-1868)

PIONEER COMPANIES THAT CROSSED THE PLAINS, 1847-1868

(J.H. is Journal History of the Church)

Outfitting post	Date of departure	Captain of company, company no.	Number leaving Outfitting Post: People—Wagons	Date Arrived	Roster (* means partial roster)
	1847				
Winter Quarters, Neb (Omaha)	14 Apr (last date in 1847 that Brigham Young left Winter Quarters)	Brigham Young (Original)	148 72	21-24 Jul 1847 (Brigham Young entered 24th)	Church Emigration Book, (CEB) D.U.P. lesson for Apr 1959; and Andrew Jenson's *Biographical Encyclopedia*, vol. 4, p. 693-725.
Winter Quarters, Neb (Left camp on Elkhorn River - abt. 27 mi. west of Winter Quarters)	17 Jun 18 Jun	Daniel Spencer Capt. 1st Hundred Peregrine Sessions Capt. 1st Fifty (1)	185 75	24-25 Sep 1847	J.H. 21 Jun 1847, p. 6-11.
Elkhorn River	17 Jun	Ira Eldredge Capt. 2nd Fifty (2) [Also known as Parley P. Pratt Co.]	177 76 (or 174)	19-22 Sep 1847	J.H. 21 Jun 1847, p. 11-16.
Winter Quarters, Neb		Edward Hunter Capt. 2nd Hundred			
Elkhorn River	17 Jun	Joseph Horne Capt. 1st Fifty (3) [Also known as John Taylor Co.]	197 72	29 Sep 1847	J.H. 21 Jun 1847, p. 17-22
Elkhorn River	19 Jun	Jacob Foutz (4) Capt. 2nd Fifty	155 59	abt. 1 Oct 1847	J.H. 21 Jun 1847, p. 23-27
Winter Quarters, abt. 17 Jun Neb.		Jedediah M. Grant Capt. 3rd Hundred		29 Sep 1847	
Elkhorn River	17 Jun	Joseph B. Noble Capt. 1st Fifty (5)	171	abt. 2 Oct 1847 (and during week)	J.H. 21 Jun 1847, p. 28-32
Elkhorn River	19 Jun	Willard Snow Capt. 2nd Fifty (6)	160	abt. 4 Oct 1847 (and during week)	J.H. 21 Jun 1847, p. 33-37
Winter Quarters, abt. 17 Jun Neb.		*Abraham O. Smoot* Capt. 4th Hundred			
Elkhorn River	18 Jun	George B. Wallace Capt. 1st Fifty (7)	223	25,26,29 Sep 1847	J.H. 21 Jun 1847, p. 38-44
Elkhorn River	17 Jun?	Samuel Russell Capt. 2nd Fifty (8)	95	25 Sep 1847	J.H. 21 Jun 1847, p. 44-47
Winter Quarters, 21 Jun Neb. Elkhorn River		Charles C. Rich (9)	126	2 Oct 1847	J.H. 21 Jun 1847, p. 48-51

1848					
Winter Quarters, Abt. 6 Jun Neb.	Brigham Young Capt. 1st Division	1220		20-24 Sep 1848	J.H. Supp. after 31 Dec 1848, p. 1-10.
Winter Quarter Neb. 29 May	Heber C. Kimball Capt. 2nd Division	662		24 Sep and later	J.H. Supp. 1848, p. 11-16.
Winter Quarters Neb. 3 Jul Richard's Section; 30 or 31 Jun Lyman Section	Willard Richards Capt. 3rd Division (Amasa Lyman Part of co.)	526		Richard's 12, 17,19 Oct; Lyman 10 Oct	J.H. Supp. after 31 Dec 1848, p. 17-20.
1849					
Kanesville, Iowa Abt. 6 Jun (present day Council Bluffs)	Orson Spencer and Samuel Gully (1)		100	22 Sep 1949	J.H. Supp. after 31 Dec 1849, p. 1-2.*
Kanesville, Iowa abt. 12 Jul	Allen Taylor (2)	abt. 500	100	abt. 10 Oct 1849	J.H. Supp. after 31 Dec 1849, p. 3-4.*
Kanesville, Iowa 10 Jul Elkhorn River	Silas Richards (3)		abt. 100	abt. 27 Oct 1849	J.H. Supp. after 31 Dec 1849, p. 5A-51.*
Kanesville, Iowa 4 Jul	George A. Smith (4) [included Capt. Dan Jones' Welsh Company]	370 or 447	120	27 and Oct 28 1849 [Smith, Benson combined as their companies traveled close together]	J.H. Supp. after 31 Dec 1849, p. 6-8G.
Kanesville, Iowa 4 Jul	Ezra T. Benson (5)			abt. 28 Oct	J.H. Supp. after 31 Dec 1849, p. 9-12H.*
Pottawattamie Co., Iowa 18 Apr	Howard Egan (independent Company	57	22	7 Aug	J.H. Supp. after 31 Dec 1849, p. 13-14 also CEB, 1849)
1850					
Kanesville, Iowa 3 Jun	Milo Andrus (1)	206	51	30 Aug	J.H. Supp. after 31 Dec 1850, p. 1.*
Kanesville, Iowa Before 7 Jun	Benjamin Hawkins (2)		150	9 Sep 1850	J.H. Supp. after 31 Dec 1850, p. 2-3.*
Kanesville, Iowa Before 12 Jun	Aaron Johnson(3)		100	12 Sep 1850	J.H. Supp. after 31 Dec 1850, p. 3-5.*
Kanesville, Iowa Before 7 Jun	James Pace (4)		100	abt. 20 Sep 1850	J.H. Supp. after 31 Dec 1850, p. 5-6.*
Kanesville, Iowa 4 Jul (organized at 12-mile Creek near Missouri River)	Edward Hunter (5) [1st Perpetual Emigration Fund Company]	261	67	13 Oct 1850	J.H. Supp. after 31 Dec 1850, p. 7-12.*
Kanesville, Iowa 15 Jun (organized near Missouri River	William Snow(6) and Joseph Young		42	1 Oct 1850	J.H. Supp. after 31 Dec 1850, p. 13-14.*

Kanesville, Iowa 15 Jun (organized 12 Jun)	Warren Foote (7)	abt. 540	104	17 sep 1850	J.H. Supp. after 31 Dec 1850, p. 15-16. [heads of families in Church Emigration Book, CEB 1850]
Kanesville, Iowa organized camp 20 Jun	Wilford Woodruff (8)	abt. 209	abt. 44	14 Oct 1850	J.H. Supp. after 31 Dec 1850, p. 17-18.*
Kanesville, Iowa abt. 20 Jun	Stephen Markham (9)		50	1 Oct 1850	J.H. Supp. after 31 Dec 1850, p. 19.*
Kanesville, Iowa abt. middle Jun. 1850	David Evans (10)		54	15 Sep 1850	J.H. Supp. after 31 Dec 1850, p. 20, also J.H. Supp. after 31 Dec 1850, p. 21-25, for emigrants not in above 10 companies.*
1851					
Kanesville, Iowa abt. 1 May	John G. Smith (1)		150	some 23 Sep 1851	J.H. Supp. after 31 Dec. 1851, p. 1.*
Kanesville, Iowa abt. 10 Jun; turned back due to Indian trouble, left again 29 Jun	Easton Kelsey, Luman A. Shurtleff, Capt. 1st Fifty; Isaac Allred, Capt. 2nd Fifty (3)		100	Shurtleff's group, 23 Sep; Allred's group, 2 Oct 1851	J.H. Supp. after 31 Dec 1851, p. 4-5.*
Kanesville, Iowa 21 Jun	James W. Cummings (2)	abt. 150	100	some 5 Oct 1851	J.H. Supp. after 31 Dec 1851, p. 2-3.* See CEB 1851.
Kanesville, Iowa 7 Jul	John Brown [a P.E.F. Company] (4)		50	28 Sep 1851	J.H. Supp. after 31 Dec 1851, p. 6A-6-G.*
Kanesville, Iowa Left Garden Grove, Iowa 17 May	Garden Grove Co. Harry Walton, Capt.	21 Families from Garden Grove plus others	60	24 Sep 1851	J.H. Supp. after 31 Dec 1851, p. 7-9, also CEB 1851 under Garden Grove Co.
Kanesville, Iowa	George W. Oman			1 Sep 1851	Some names in J.H. Supp. after 31 Dec 1851, p. 10-12 may be from this company
Kanesville, Iowa before 7 Jul	Morris Phelps			abt. 28 Sep 1851	J.H. Supp. after 31 Dec 1851, p. 10-12.
Kanesville, Iowa before 12	Wilkins Freight		10	abt. 28 Sep	J.H. Supp.

	Aug	(Train includes Scottish emigrants)		1851	after 31 Dec 1851, p. 10-12.
		Ben Holliday's Freight Train		10 Aug 1851	J.H. Supp. after 31 Dec 1851; p. 10-12.
Kanesville, Iowa 3 Aug		Thomas A. Williams' Freight Train		25 Aug 1851	J.H. Supp. after 31 Dec 1851, p. 10-12.
		Livingston and Kincade's Freight Company			J.H. Supp. after 31 Dec 1851, p. 10-12.

1852

Kanesville, Iowa 30 May	John S. Higbee (1)	abt. 190		abt. 13 Aug 1852	J.H. Supp.* after 31 Dec 1852, p. 1-6.
Kanesville, Iowa abt. 29 May	James J. Jepson (2)	abt. 220	abt. 32	some arrived 10 Sep	J.H. Supp.* after 31 Dec 1852, p. 7-11.
Kanesville, Iowa 7 Jun	Thomas C.D. Howell (3)	293 plus 10 families	abt. 65	27 Sep 1852	J.H. Supp.* after 31 Dec 1852, p. 12-18.
Kanesville, Iowa abt. 10 Jun	Joseph Outhouse (4)	230	50	6 Sep 1852	J.H. Supp.* after 31 Dec 1852, p. 19-24.
Kanesville, Iowa early Jun	John Tidwell (5)	abt. 340	abt. 54	15 Sep 1852	J.H. Supp.* after 31 Dec 1852, p. 19-24.
Kanesville, Iowa	David Wood (6)	abt. 288	abt. 58	1 Oct 1852	J.H. Supp.* after 31 Dec 1852, p. 34-40.
Kanesville, Iowa early Jun	Henry Bryant Manning Jolly (7)	abt. 340	abt. 64	15 Sep 1852	J.H. Supp.* after 31 Dec 1852, p. 41-49.
	Warren Snow (8th Company)				No report
Kanesville, Iowa Jun	Isaac M. Stewart (9)	abt. 245	53	28 Aug 1852	J.H. Supp.* after 31 Dec 1852, p. 55-61.
Kanesville, Iowa May	Benjamin Gardner (10)	241	45	24 and 27 Sep 1852	J.H. Supp.* after 31 Dec 1852, p. 61B; J.H. Supp. 24 and 27 Sep 1852.
Kanesville, Iowa Jun	James McGaw (11)	239	54	20 Sep 1852	J.H. Sup.* after 31 Dec 1852, p. 67-73.
Kanesville, Iowa Jun	Harmon Cutler (12)	262	63	Sep 1852	J.H. Sup.* after 31 Dec 1852, p. 79-84.
	William Morgan (13th Company)		50	30 sep 1852	

Location	Departure	Captain	Persons	Wagons	Arrival	Reference
Kanesville, Iowa	5 Jul	John B. Walker (14)	abt. 258		3 Oct 1852	J.H. Supp.* after 31 Dec 1852, p. 89-95.
Kanesville, Iowa	Beginning of Jul	Robert Weimer (15)	230	130?	15 Sep 1852	J.H. Supp.* after 31 Dec 1852, p. 96-100.
Kanesville, Iowa	shortly after 24 Jun	Uriah Curtis (16)	abt. 365	51	1 Oct 1852	J.H. Supp.* after 31 Dec 1852, p. 101-107.
Kanesville, Iowa		Isaac Bullock (17)	Abt. 175		21 Sep 1852	J.H. Supp.* after 31 Dec 1852, p. 198-111.
Kanesville, Iowa	Middle of June	James C. Snow (18)	250	abt. 55	9 Cot 1852	J.H. Supp.* after 31 Dec 1852, p. 112-117.
Kanesville, Iowa	early July	Eli B. Kelsey (19) [includes first 28 saints from Scandinavia.].	Abt. 100		16 Oct 1852	J.H. Supp.* after 31 Dec 1852, p. 120-122.
Kanesville, Iowa		Henry W. Miller (20)	abt. 229	63	abt. 21 Sep 1852	J.H. Supp.* after 31 Dec 1852, p. 123-128.
Kanesville, Iowa	July	Allen Weeks (21)	abt. 226		12 Oct 1852	J.H. Supp.* after 31 Dec 1852, p. 129-136.
Organized in St. Louis	4 Jun (left Independence, Mo)	Thomas Marsden (22nd Company)		10	2 Sep 1852	J.H. Supp.* after 31 Dec 1852, p. 144.
	1 Jun (left Kansas City Mo.)	Abraham O. Smoot [first company to cross by P.E.F.]	abt. 250	33	3 Sep 1852	J.H. Supp.* after 31 Dec 1852, p. 137-143.
1853						
Six-Mile Grove, Iowa or Neb. (6 miles from Winter Quarters)	1 Jun	David Wilkin (1)	122	28	abt. 9 Sep 1853	J.H. 15 Jul 1853, p. 2-5.
Six-Mile Grove, Iowa or Neb.	9 Jun	Daniel A. Miller and John W. Cooley (2)	282	70	some 9 Sep 1853	J.H. 9 Sep 1853, p. 2-24. See also J.H. 9 Aug 1853, p. 2-20.
Keokuk, Iowa	18 May (left Kanesville, Iowa, 1 Jul)	Jesse W. Crosby (3)	79	12	abt. 10 Sep 1853	J.H. 19 Aug 1853, p. 2
Keokuk, Iowa (organized at Kanesville)	16 May (left Kanesville, 29 Jun)	Moses Clawson (4) [St. Louis Co.]	295	56	abt. 15 Sep 1853	J.H. 19 Aug 1853, p. 3-7. See also J.H. 7 Aug 1853, p. 4-5.
Keokuk, Iowa	abt. 3 Jun	Jacob Gates (5)	262	33	26 Sep 1853	J.H. 9 Sep 1853, p. 25-28
Keokuk, Iowa	21 May	John E. Forsgren (6)	294	34	30 Sep 1853	J.H. 30 Sep 1853, p. 307.*

Keokuk, Iowa	1 Jul (left Missouri River)	Henry Ettleman (7)	40	11	abt. 1 Oct 1853	J.H. 19 Aug 1853, p. 1B.
Kanesville, Iowa	13 Jul (crossed Missouri River at Council Bluffs)	Vincent Shurtleff (8) [merchandise wagons and a few emigrants]			abt. 30 Sep 1853	no roster See J.H. 17 Jul 1853, and 31 Aug 1853 for mention.
Keokuk, Iowa	3 Jun (crossed Missouri River 11 Jul)	Joseph W. Young (9)	402	abt. 54	10 Oct 1853	J.H. 22 Sep 1853, p. 1B-9.
Keokuk, Iowa	3 Jun (crossed Missouri River 11 Jul)	Cyrus H. Wheelock (10) [included a California company]	abt. 400	52	16 Oct 1853	J.H. 19 Sep 1853, p. 2-7.
Keokuk, Iowa or Kanesville, Iowa	3 Jun (crossed Missouri River)	Claudius V. Spencer (11)	abt. 250	40	abt. 24 Sep 1853	J.H. 17 Sep 1853, p. 1B-4.
Keokuk, Iowa or Kanesville, Iowa	14 Jul (Crossed Missiouri River)	Appleton M. Harmon (12)	abt. 200	abt. 22	16 Oct 1853	no roster
Keokuk, Iowa	1 Jul	John Brown (13)	abt. 303		17 Oct 1853	No roster, see roster for ship Campillus in "Ms. History of British Mission" 6 Apr 1853
	1854					
Westport, Mo. (Kansas City area)	15 Jun	Hans Peter Olsen (1)	abt. 550	69	5 Oct 1854	partial roster, J.H. 31 Dec 1854, Supp.,p. 7-9. ,p. 7-9.
Westport, Mo.	abt. 17 Jun	James Brown (2)	abt. 300	42	3 Oct 1854	partial roster, J.H. 31 Dec.1854, Supp., p.10
Westport, Mo.	abt. 17 Jun	Darwin Richardson (3)	abt. 300	40	30 Sep 1854	partial roster J.H. 31 Dec 1854, P. 10.
Westport, Mo.	16 Jun	Job Smith (4) [Independent company]	217	45	23 Sep 1854	no roster.
Westport, Mo.	2 Jul	Daniel Garn (5) [many members crossed ocean on ship Windermere]	477	abt. 40	1 Oct 1854	no roster, see Ms. History of British Mission, 22 Feb 1854.
Westport, Mo.	14 Jul	Robert L. Campbell (6th Company)	397		28 Oct 1854	partial roster, J.H. 31 Dec 1854, Supp. p. 13-14.
	left Missouri River late in July	Initially, Orson Pratt and Horace S. Eldredge, subsequently, Ezra T. Benson and Ira Eldredge. (7)			3 Oct 1854 (Pratt and Eldredge 27 Aug)	no roster, see J.H. 8 Aug 1854, p. 2-5.

Westport, Mo.	abt. 15 Jul	William Empey (8)	43		24 Oct 1854	partial roster. JH 31 Dec 1854, Supp., p. 16
	1855					
Mormon Grove, Kan. (Near Atchison	7 Jun	John Hindley (1) (IC)	206	46	3 Sep 1855	J.H. 12 Sep 1855, and 3 Sep 1855, p. 2-12.
Mormon Grove, Kan.	13 Jun	Jacob F. Secrist (died 2 Jul) subsequently, Noah T. Guyman (2)	368	58	7 Sep 1855	J.H. 12 Sep 1855, and 7 Sep. 1855. p. 1-11.
Mormon Grove, Kan.	15 Jun	Seth M. Blair (Blair became ill, succeeded Edward Stevenson) (3) (IC)	89	38	11 Sep 1855	no roster.
Mormon Grove, Kan.	1 Jul	Richard Ballantyne (4)	402	45	25 Sep 1855	J.H. 12 Sep 1855
Mormon Grove, Kan.	4 Jul	Moses F. Thurston (5)	148	33	28 Sep 1855	J.H. 12 Sep 1855.
Mormon Grove, Kan.	24 Jul 43-turned, left again 28 Jul	Charles A. Harper (6) [P.E.F.]	305	39	29 Oct 1855	J.H. 12 Sep 1855.
Mormon Grove, Kan.	31 Jul	Isaac Allred (7) [merchandise train]	61	34-38	some 2 Nov others 13 Nov 1855	J.H. 12 Sep 1855.
Mormon Grove, Kan.	4 Aug	Milo Andrus (8) [P.E.F.]	461		24 Oct 1855	J.H. 24 Oct 1855, p. 1-13.
	1856					
Iowa City, Iowa	9 Jun	Edmund Ellsworth (1st Handcart Co.)	275	52 handcarts (hc) a few wagons	26 Sep 1856	J.H. 9 Jun 1856, p. 1; 26 Sep 1856 23-30.

LeRoy Hafen's *Handcarts to Zion* (Glendale, Calif.: A.H. Clark, 1960) for rosters on all of the handcart companies.

Iowa City, Iowa	11 Jun	Daniel D. McArthur (2nd Handcart Co.)	222	48 (hc) 4 waggons	26 Sep 1856	J.H. 11 Jun 26 Sep 1856, p. 31-16.
Iowa City, Iowa	23 Jun (left Florence, Neb. 30 Jul)	Edward Bunker (3rd Handcart Co.)	abt. 300	60 (hc) 5 waggons	2 Oct 1856	J.H. 2 Oct 1856, p. 6-12, 15 Oct 1856, p. 1.
Iowa City, Iowa	15 Jul	James G. Willie (4th Handcart Co.)	abt. 500	120 (hc) 5 waggons	9 Nov 1856	J.H. 9 Nov 18-30; J.H. 15 Oct 1856, p. 2.
Iowa City, Iowa	28 Jul	Edward Martin (5th Handcart Co.)	575	145 (hc) handcarts; 7 wagons	30 Nov 1856	J.H. 30 Nov 1856 p. 7-8, 60-76; 15 Oct 1856, p. 2,
Florence, Neb.	5 Jun	Philemon C. Merrill (1st Wagon Company)	200	50	13-18 Aug 1856	J.H. 5 Jun 1856, p. 1.

Location	Departure	Captain (Company)	Persons	Wagons	Arrival	Source
Florence, Neb. (Now Omaha)	abt. 10 Jun	Canute Peterson (2)	abt. 320	abt. 60	20 Sep 1856	J.H. 20 Sep 1856, p. 1-8, 15 Oct 1856, p. 12-13.
Florence, Neb.	Middle of June	John Banks (3) [St. Louis Company]	300	abt. 60	1-2 Oct 1856	J.H. 3 Oct 1856, p. 2-9, 15 Oct 1856, p. 3.
Iowa City, Iowa	30 Jul	William B. Hodgetts (4)	abt. 150	33	10 Dec 1856 (some later)	J.H. 15 Oct 1856, p. 3, 15 Dec 1856, p. 1-6
Iowa City, Iowa	1 Aug	Dan Jones (then John A. Hunt)(5)	abt. 300	56	10-15 Dec 1856	J.H. 15 Dec 1856, p. 7-15, 15 Oct 1856, p. 2.
Mormon Grove, Kan.	10 Aug	Abraham O. Smoot [mostly merchandise]	abt. 97	abt. 34	9 Nov 1856	some names end of 1856

1857

Location	Departure	Captain (Company)	Persons	Wagons	Arrival	Source
Iowa City, Iowa	abt. 22 May	Israel Evans (6th Handcart Co.)	149	28 h.c.	11-12 ep 1857	
Iowa City, Iowa	abt. 15 Jun	Christian Christiansen (7th Handcart Co.)[first headed by James Park, David Dille and George Thurston]	abt. 330	68 h.c. 3 wagons	13 Sep 1857	J.H. 13 Sep 1856, p. 12-26.
Florence, Neb. (Omaha)	13 Jun	William Walker's Freight Train	86	28	4 Sep 1857 (others a few days later)	no roster.
Iowa City, Iowa	early Jun	Jesse B. Martin (1st Wagon Co.)	192	34	12 Sep 1857	no roster.
Iowa City, Iowa	abt. 15 Jun	Matthias Cowley (2) [Scandinavian Co.]	198	31	13 Sep 1857	no roster.
Iowa City, Iowa	early Jun	Jacob Hoffheins (3) [New York Co. later the St. Louis Co.]	abt. 204	41	21 Sep 1857	no roster
From Texas	Jul	Homer Duncan (returning from a mission)			14 and 20 Sep 1857	no roster
Iowa City, Iowa	Jun	William G. Young	abt. 55	19	26 Sep 1857	no roster

1858

[Very few emigrants crossed the plains in 1858 due to the approaching U.S. Army which was sent to suppress a supposed rebellion in Utah]

Location	Departure	Captain (Company)	Persons	Wagons	Arrival	Source
Iowa City, Iowa	left Loupe Fork 8 Jun	Horace S. Eldredge (1st Wagon Company) men	39	13	9 Jul 1858	C.E.B. 1858.*
Iowa City, Iowa	Middle of Jun	Iver N. Iversen(2)	abt. 50	8	20 Sep 1858.	J.H. 13 Jul 1858, p. 1.
Iowa City, Iowa	19 Jun	Russell K. Homer(3) [from ship "John	abt. 60		6 Oct 1858	no roster, see Ms. History of

	Bright'']					Scandinavian Mission 21 Feb 1858, p. 3-5.

	1859					
Florence, Neb. (Omaha)	9 Jun	George Rowley (8th Handcart Company)	235	60 h.c. 8 wagons	4 Sep 1859	J.H. 12 Jun 1859, p. 4, Hafen's *Handcarts. to Zion.*
Florence, Neb.	13 Jun	James Brown, III (1st Wagon Company)	353	59	29 Aug 1859	J.H. 12 Jun 1859, p. 4.
Florence, Neb.	June	Horton D. Haight(2) [Merchandise Train]	154	71	1 Sep 1859	J.H. 12 Jun 1859, p. 4.
Florence, Neb.	26 or 28 Jun	Robert F. Neslen (3)	380	56	15 Sep 1859	J.H. 12 Jun 1859, p. 4.
Florence, Neb.	26 Jun	Edward Stevenson (4)	285	54	16 Sep 1859	no roster
Geona, Neb.		A.S. Beckwith	22		1 Aug 1859	J.H. 1 Aug 1859

Deseret News for 14 Sep 1859 notes that several small companies arrived in Salt Lake City after 1 Aug 1859. These Saints may have traveled with P.H. Buzzard's, D. Davis', J.H. Lemon's, F. Little's, and Redfield and Smith's freight trains.

	1860					
Florence, Neb.	6 Jun	Daniel Robinson (9th Handcart Co.)	233	43 (hc) 6 wagons	27 Aug 1860	J.H. 31 Dec 1860 Supp., p. 13-18.
Florence, Neb.	6 Jul	Oscar O. Stoddard (10th and last Handcart Co.)	126	22 hc 6 wagons	24 Sep 1860	J.H. Supp. after 31 Dec 1860, p. 24-37.
Florence, Neb.	30 May	Warren Walling (1st Wagon Co.)	172	30	9 Aug 1850	J.H. Supp. after 31 Dec 1860 p. 7-12.
Florence, Neb.	17 Jun	James D. Ross(2)	249	36	3 Sep 1860	J.H. Supp. after 31 Dec 1860, p. 19-25.
Florence, Neb.	19 Jun	Jesse Murphey(3)	279	38	30 Aug 1860	J.H. Supp. after 31 Dec 1860, p. 26-33.
Florence, Neb.	abt. 15 Jun	John Smith (Patriarch of of Church)(4)	359	39	1 Sep 1860	J.H. Supp. after 31 Dec 1860, p. 38-46.
Florence, Neb.	20 Jul	William Budge(5)	400	55	5 Oct 1860	J.H. Supp. after 31 Dec 1860, p. 47-57.
Florence, Neb.	3 Jul	John Taylor ["Iowa" Company]	123		17 Sep 1860	J.H. Supp. after 31 Dec 1860 p. 58-62.
Florence, Neb.	23 Jul	Joseph W. Young [merchandise]	abt. 100	50	3 Oct 1860	no roster.

Florence, Neb.	latter part June	Franklin Brown [ind. co.]	60	14	27 Aug 1860	no roster.
Florence, Neb.		Brigham H. Young [freight train]			14 Sep 1860	no roster

	1861					
Florence, Neb. (Omaha)	29 May	David H. Cannon (1st Church train)	225	57	16 Aug 1861	no roster
Florence, Neb.	7 Jun	Job Pingree [independent co.]		33	24 Aug 1861	J.H. 24 Aug 1861
Florence, Neb.	abt. 20 Jun	Peter Ranck [Independent Co.		abt. 20	8 Sep 1861	no roster.
Florence, Neb.	25 Jun	Homer Duncan(4)	264	47	13 Sep 1861	J.H. 13 Sep 1861, p. 2-5; Duncan's CEB 1861
Florence, Neb.	30 Jun	Ira Eldredge [2nd Church Train]		70	15 Sep 1861	no roster.
Florence, Neb.	July	Milo Andrus	620	38	12 Sep 1861	no roster.
Florence, Neb.	July	Thomas Woolley	abt. 150	30	Sep 1861	no roster.
Florence, Neb.	9 Jul	Joseph Horne [3rd Church Train]		62	13 Sep 1861	no roster
Florence, Neb.	13 Jul	Samuel Woolley	338	61	22 Sep 1861	J.H. 22 Sep 1861, p. 2-11.
Florence, Neb.	13 Jul	Joseph Porter [originally part Samuel Woolley Co.]			22 Sep 1861	roster for Woolley Co.
Florence, Neb.	July	John R. Murdock [4th Church Train] [mostly Scandinavian Saints from ship "Monarch of the Sea"]			12 Sep 1861	no roster, see Ms. History of British Mission, 16 May 1861
Florence, Neb.	11 Jul	Joseph W. Young and later Heber P. Kimball [5th Church Train] (Merchandise)		90	23 Sep 1861	no roster.
Florence, Neb.	11 Jul	Ansel P. Harmon [began as Joseph W. Young Co. Harmon organized 27 Jul]		40	23 Sep 1861	no roster.
Florence, Neb.	16 Jul	Sixtus E. Johnson	abt. 200	52	27 Sep 1861	no roster.

[In addition to the companies mentioned, several freight trains left Florence, Neb., during the months of July and Aug.]

	1862					
Florence, Neb.	14 Jun	Lewis Brunson (ind. co.)	212	48	29 Aug 1862	See *Deseret News* for 1861, vol. 12, p. 78. Also J.H. 20 Aug 1862, p. 2-7.*
Florence, Neb.	14 Jul	Ola N. Lijenquist (and ind. Scandinavian Co.)	abt. 250	40	23 Sep 1862	no roster.

See Ms. History of Scandinavian Mission for Apr 1862, for rosters of people that left Hamburg, Germany. Lijenquist was leader of company on ship "Athenia."

Florence, Neb.	abt. 1st week in July	James Wareham (ind. co.)	250	46	26 Sep 1862	*Deseret News* for 1862, vol. 12, p. 93. Also J.H. 16 Sep 1862, p. 1.
Florence, Neb.	22 Jul	Homer Duncan (1st Church Train)	abt. 500		24 Sep 1862	J.H. 16 Sep 1862, p. 1 *Deseret News* vol. 12, p. 93
Florence, Neb.	14 Jul	Christian A. Madsen (independent Scandinavian Company)	abt. 264	40	23 Sep 1862	No roster, see Ms. History of Scandinavian Mission, Apr 1862, for roster of ship "Franklin."
Florence, Neb.	24 Jul	John R. Murdock (2nd Church Train)	700	65	27 Sep 1862	*Deseret News* 1862, vol. 12, p. 93; J.H. 16 Sep 1862, p. 2.
Florence, Neb.	28 Jul	James S. Brown (ind. co.)	200	46	2 Oct 1862	Partial roster See *Deseret News* 1862, vol. 12, p. 113. Also J.H. 2 Oct 1862, p. 1.
Florence, Neb.	29 Jul	Joseph Horne (3rd Church Train)	570	52	1 Oct 1862	*Deseret News* 1862, vol. 12, p. 98. Also J.H. 24 Sep 1862, p. 1.
Florence, Neb.	abt. 30 Jul	Isaac A. Canfield (ind. co.)	abt. 120		16 Oct 1862	*Deseret News* 1862, vol. 12, p. 93. Also J.H. 16 Sep 1862, p. 3, and 16 Oct 1862 p. 1-14.
Florence, Neb.	early Aug	Ansel P. Harmon (4th Church Train)	abt. 500		5 Oct 1862	J.H. 24 Sep 1862, p. 2. Also *Deseret News* 1862, vol. 12, p. 98.
Florence, Neb.	8 Aug	Henry W. Miller (5th Church Train)	665	60	17 Oct 1862	*Deseret News* 1862, vol. 12, p. 92.
Florence, Neb.	early Aug	Horton D. Haight (6th Church Train)	650		19 Oct 1862	J.H. 24 Sep 1862, p. 2. Also *Deseret News* 1862, vol. 12, p. 98.
Florence, Neb.	14 Aug	William H. Dame (7th Church Train)	150	50	29 Oct 1862	J.H. 24 Sep 1862, p. 3. *Deseret News* 1862, vol. 12, p. 98.

In addition to these companies, a large number of freight trains brought small companies of LDS emigrants.

	1863					
Florence, Neb.	29 Jun	John R. Murdock (1st Church Train)	275 or 375	55	29 Aug 1863	no roster, but mentioned in J.H. 14 Jul;
Florence Neb.	6 Jul	John F. Sanders			5 Sep 1863	21, 29 Aug 1863 and *Deseret News* 1863, vol. 13. p. 57.
Florence, Neb.	30 Jun	Alvus H. Patterson (ind. co.)	abt. 200	50	4 Sep 1863	J.H. 4 Sep 1863, p. 1-3.
Florence, Neb.	9 Jul	John R. Young (ind. co.)			12 Sep 1863	no roster, J.H. 12 Sep 1863, p. 2-9. for camp history.
Florence, Neb.	9 Jul	William B. Preston (3rd Church Train)	abt. 300	55	10 Sep 1863	no roster, J.H. 5,16,24 Aug 1863, and *Deseret News*, vol. 13. p. 64.
Florence, Neb.	25 Jul	Peter Nebeker (4th Church Train)	abt. 500	70	25 Sep 1863	no roster.
Florence, Neb.	6 Aug	Daniel D. McArthur (5th Church Train)	abt. 500	75	3 Oct 1863	no roster.
Florence, Neb.	8 Aug	Horton D. Haight (6th Church Train)	abt. 200 (freight)		4 Oct 1863	no roster.
Florence, Neb.	9 Aug	John W. Woolley (7th Church Train)	abt. 200		4 Oct 1863	no roster.
Florence, Neb.	10 Aug	Thomas E. Ricks (8th Church Train)	abt. 400		4 Oct 1863	no roster.
Florence, Neb.	11 Aug	Rosel Hyde (9th Church Train)	abt. 300		13 Oct 1863	no roster.
Florence, Neb.	14 Aug	Samuel D. White (10th Church Train)	abt. 300 (freight)		15 Oct 1863	no roster.

Freight trains under the charge of Captains Canfield, Jakeman, Shurtiff, and others also left Florence, Neb. for Salt Lake City.

	1864					
Wyoming, Neb. (west bank of Missouri River about 40 miles south of Omaha)	26 Jun	John D. Chase (ind. co.)	85	28	abt. 20 Sep 1864	J.H. 20 Sep 1864, p. 2.
Wyoming, Neb.	29 Jun	John R. Murdock (1st Church Train) [large amount of freight]	78		26 Aug 1864	J.H. 26 Aug 1864.
Wyoming, Neb.	8 Jul	William B. Preston (2nd Church Train)	abt. 400	50	15 Sep 1864	*Deseret News* 17 Aug 1864. p. 369; J.H. 8 Jul, 14 Sep 19 Oct 1864.
Wyoming, Neb.	15 Jul	Joseph S. Rawlins (3rd Church Train)	abt. 400	abt. 50	20 Sep 1864	*Deseret News* 17 Aug 1864, p. 369.
Wyoming, Neb.	19 or 22	William S. Warren	abt.	abt.	4 Oct 1864	*Deseret News*

	Jul	(4th Church Train)	329	65		17 Aug 1864, p. 369.
Wyoming, Neb.	27 Jul	Isaac A. Canfield (5th Church Train)	abt. 211	abt. 50	5 Oct 1864	*Deseret News* 17 Aug 1864, p. 369.*
Wyoming, Neb.	July	John Smith (Presiding Patri- arch)[ind. co.]	abt. 150	20	1 Oct 1864	no roster.
Wyoming, Neb.	9 Aug	William Hyde (6th Church Train)	abt. 350	62	26 Oct 1864	*Deseret News* 19 Oct 1864, p. 18.*
Wyoming, Neb.	middle Aug	Warren S. Snow	abt. 400		2 Nov 1864	no roster.
Wyoming, Neb.	**1865** 31 Jul	Miner G. Atwood	abt. 45		8 Nov 1865	*Deseret News* 1865, vol. 14 p. 403, J.H. 8 Nov 1865.
Wyoming, Neb.	12 Aug	Henson Walker	abt. 200	abt. 50	9 Nov 1865	J.H. 9 Nov 1865; *Deseret News News*, 1865, vol. 14, p. 403.
Wyoming, Neb.	12, 15 Aug	William S. Will s	abt. 200	abt. 50	11 Nov 1865 others 29 Nov 1865	J.H. 29 Nov 1865, *Deseret News*, 1865, vol. 14 p. 204.
Wyoming, Neb.	**1866** 6 Jul	Thomas E. Ricks (1st Church Train)	251	46	4 Sep 1866	*Deseret News* 16 Aug 1866. Also J.H. 4 Sep 1866.
Wyoming, Neb.	7 Jul	Samuel D. White (*2nd Church Train*)	230	46	5 Sep 1866	*Deseret News 16 Aug 1866.*
Wyoming, Neb.	13 Jul	William Henry Chipman (3rd Church Train)	375	abt. 60	15 Sep 1866	J.H. 15 Sep 1866, p. 3-4.
Wyoming, Neb.	19 Jul	John D. Holladay (4th Church Train)	350	69	25 Sep 1866	J.H. 25 Sep 1866.*
Wyoming, Neb.	4 Aug	Peter Nebeker (5th Church Train)	400	62	29 Sep 1866	J.H. 25 Sep 1866.
Wyoming, Neb.	25 Jul	Daniel Thompson (6th Church Train)	abt. 500	85	29 Sep 1866	Those born and died in J.H. 29 Sep 1866.*
Wyoming, Neb.	2 Aug	Joseph S. Rawlins (7th Church Train)	over 400	65	1 Oct 1866	J.H. 1 Oct 1866.
Wyoming, Neb.	8 Aug	Andrew H. Scott (8th Church Train)	abt. 300	49	8 Oct 1866	no roster; Ms. Hist. of Wyoming, Neb.
Wyoming, Neb.	early Aug	Horton B. Haight (9th Church Train) [included 500 miles of wire for Deseret Telegraph Line]	4 families	65	15 Oct 1866	no roster.
Wyoming, Neb.	8 Aug	Abner Lowery (10th Church Train)	300		22 Oct 1866	J.H. 22 Oct 1866.
North Platte,	**1867** middle Aug	Leonard G. Rice	abt.	abt.	5 Oct 1867	no roster.

[Western Terminus of the Union Pacific Railroad]

	1868					
Laramie, Wyo.	25 Jul	Chester Loveland	abt. 400	40	20 Aug 1868	J.H. 25 Jul 1868, p. 2.
Laramie, Wyo.	25 Jul	Joseph S. Rawlins	nearly 30	31	20 Aug 1868	no roster.
Laramie, Wyo.	27 Jul	John R. Murdock	abt. 50		19 Aug 1868	no roster.
Laramie, Wyo.	27 Jul	Horton D. Haight	275	abt. 30	24 Aug 1868	no roster.
Laramie, Wyo.	1 Aug	William S. Seeley	272	39	29 Aug 1868	J.H. 1 Aug. 1868, p. 1.
Benton, Wyo.	13 Aug	Simpson A. Molen	300	61	2 Sep 1868	no roster.
Benton, Wyo.	14 Aug	Daniel D. McArthur	411	51	2 Sep 1868	no roster.
Benton, Wyo.	24 Aug	John Gillespie	abt. 500	50	15 Sep 1868	no roster.
Benton, Wyo.	31 Aug	John G. Holman	abt. 650	62	25 Sep 1868	J.H. 25 Sep 1868.
Benton, Wyo.	1 Sep	Edward T. Mumford	250	28	24 Sep 1868	J.H. 24 Sep 1868, p. 1.

1869

With the arrival of Holman's and Mumford's trains, travel across the plains with ox and mule teams was terminated. The construction of the Transcontinental Railroad from the Missouri River to San Francisco, California was completed 10 May, 1869, with the driving of the last spike at Promontory Point, Utah.

Sites on the Mormon Trail

IOWA

GARDEN GROVE — Garden Grove was the first permanent camp established in 1846 as a junction point of the trail. Fifty homes and a mill were erected for those pioneers who stayed here to raise food for themselves and for the pioneer companies that followed. Garden Grove was abandoned in 1852. There is a marker in town and a monument in the park honoring those who died here.

MT. PISGAH — Mt. Pisgah was the second permanent camp established as a way station for the pioneers in 1846. A total of 109 cabins were built and about 7,000 acres of crops were planted. This community was also abandoned in 1852. In the cemetery there is a monument honoring those who died here from 1846 to 1852.

COUNCIL BLUFFS — Arriving in 1846, the pioneers settled in the area with the name of Miller's Hollow, later changing it to Kanesville (after Thomas L. Kane). In July of 1846, 500 men joined the Mormon Battalion and left for San Diego, Calif. The First Presidency of the Church was organized here in December 1847 with Brigham Young as president. During the California gold rush in 1849, Kanesville as a natural stopping place for those heading west. Mormon pioneers left in 1852 selling their farms, stores, and homes at a sacrifice. The citizens who remained renamed the community Council Bluffs and incorporated the town in 1853.

NEBRASKA

WINTER QUARTERS (Florence, Neb.) — Winter Quarters was the fourth permanent camp and a temporary settlement of the pioneers from 1846-1848. A total of 538 homes were built during the fall and winter of 1846 to house 3,000 people. Brigham Young received Section 136 of the Doctrine and Covenants here. The pioneer cemetery contains a monument that honors 600 pioneers who are buried here. Also in the vicinity are markers on Mormon Street, Young Street, Mormon Pioneer Memorial Bridge, Old Mormon Mill, and in Florence Park.

CHIMNEY ROCK (Bayard, Neb.) — Chimney Rock was natural and one of the most conspicuous landmarks along the Mormon Trail. It's conical base with the chimney-like shaft can be seen for miles. There is a marker located some distance from the landmark.

REBECCA WINTER'S GRAVE (Scottsbluff, Neb.) — Gravesite of pioneer woman who died on the trail. Pioneers marked her grave with a wagon wheel rim engraved with her name. This gravesite represents and honors all those who died on the trail. The grave was found when the Burlington Railroad was surveying the area for the railroad tracks. The right-of-way was changed to by-pass the grave. There is a marker and the original wagon wheel rim.

WYOMING

FORT LARAMIE — Fort Laramie was built to protect the emigrants and it was a stop for stages, mail carriers, freighters, and the telegraph lines. The fort was the half-way point between Winter Quarters and Salt Lake for the Mormon pioneers. They often paused here for a few days to rest and to repair wagons.

MORMON FERRY (Casper, Wyo.) — At this site was the last crossing of the Platte River for pioneers traveling west. The first Mormon pioneer company of 1947 reached the river during its spring runoff. The company tried several methods of crossing the river but damage to their goods was great. They built a large sturdy raft big enough for one wagon and forded the river in this manner. Pioneers, not of the Mormon faith, asked to be taken across the Platte for a price. It was decided to leave men at the ferry site to maintain this prosperous business. A granite marker commemorates the establishment of this commercial enterprise.

INDEPENDENCE ROCK — Named "Register of the Desert" by Father De Smet in 1840, Independence Rock is a smooth granite rock rising 193 feet and covering more than 27 acres. The pioneers carved their names into the rock that can still be seen today. A bronze marker mounted to the rock honors these Mormon emigrants.

SOUTH PASS — South Pass is the place where the Mormon Trail crossed the Continental Divide. Expecting to find the pass in mountainous country, the pioneers were surprised to find the pass to be a gently undulating plain.

FORT BRIDGER — Established as a trading post in 1843 by Jim Bridger and Louis Vasques, the Mormons used the fort as a supply center on their way West. The pioneers bought the fort in 1855 and abandoned it in 1857 when Johnston's Army was approaching. There are several markers in the vicinity.

UTAH

THIS IS THE PLACE (Salt Lake City, Utah) — From the mouth of Emigration Canyon, the first pioneer company came into the valley in July 1847. It was here that Brigham Young, entering the valley with Wilford Woodruff a few days behind the company's first wagons, said, "This is the right place. Drive on." There is a large monument depicting those early pioneers and other individuals who contributed to the early history of Utah.

Church Publications

Title	Year	Organization or first editor	Place
The Evening and Morning Star	1832-1834	William Wines Phelps	Independence, Mo. Kirtland, Ohio
LDS Messenger & Advocate	1834-1837	Oliver Cowdery	Kirtland, Ohio
The Elder's Journal	1837-1838	Joseph Smith, Jr.	Kirtland, Ohio & Far West, Mo.
Times and Seasons	1839-1846	E. Robinson & Don Carlos Smith	Commerce (Nauvoo), Ill.
The Millennial Star	1840-1970	European Mission	Manchester, Liverpool & London, England
The Gospel Reflector	1841-1841	Benjamin Winchester	Philadelphia, Pa.

Publication	Years	Sponsor	Location
Prophetic Almanac	1845-1865	Orson Pratt	New York City, N.Y.
The Zion's Watchman	1853-1855	Australasian Mission	Sydney, Australia
The Seer	1853-1854	Orson Pratt	Washington, D.C. & Liverpool, England
Journal of Discourses	1854-1886	George D. Watt	Liverpool, England
LDS Millennial Star and Monthly Visitor	1854-1854	East Indian Mission	Madras, Hindustan, India
Juvenile Instructor (ch to The Instructor 1930)	1866-1970	Sunday School	Salt Lake City, Utah
The Woman's Exponent	1872-1914	Relief Society	Salt Lake City, Utah
The Contributor	1879-1896	MIA	Salt Lake City, Utah
Historical Record	1886-1890	Andrew Jenson	Salt Lake City, Utah
Young Woman's Journal	1889-1929	MIA	Salt Lake City, Utah
Mutual Messenger (ch to Mutual Improvement Messenger 1898)	1897-1931	MIA	Salt Lake City, Utah
Improvement Era, The	1897-1970	MIA	Salt Lake City, Utah
Southern Star	1898-1900	Southern States Mission	Chattanooga, Tenn.
Truth's Reflex	1899-1901	Southwestern States Mission	St. Johns, Kansas
Children's Friend, The	1902-1970	Primary	Salt Lake City, Utah
The Elder's Journal	1903-1907	Southern States Mission	Chattanooga, Tenn.
Liahona (ch to Liahona, The Elders' Journal 1907)	1907-1945	Central States Mission	Chattanooga, Tenn. & Independence, Mo.
Elder's Messenger (ch to The Messenger 1908)	1907-1913	New Zealand Mission	Auckland, New Zealand
Truth	1917-1956	Northern States Mission	Chicago, Illinois
Te Karare (See also Maori list)	1923-1960	New Zealand Mission	Auckland, New Zealand
Utah Genealogical and Historical Magazine	1910-1940		Salt Lake City, Utah
Messenger to the Sightless (Braille) (ch to The New Messenger 1953)	1912-75		Provo, Utah Louisville, Kentucky
Ensign Talking Book	1977-		
Relief Society Bulletin (ch to The Relief Society Magazine)	1914-1914	Susa Young Gates	Salt Lake City, Utah
Genealogical and Historical Magazine of Arizona Temple District	1924-1947	Arizona Temple District	Mesa, Ariz.
BYU Studies	1925-1937	BYU	Provo, Utah
Cumorah Monthly Bulletin (Ch to Cumorah's Southern Cross 1929; Cumorah's Southern Messenger 1933)	1927-70	South African Mission	Mowbray, South Africa
Austral Star	1929-1958	Australian Mission	Sydney, Australia
Hvezdika (See also Czechoslavakian list)	1929-1939	Czecho-Slavokian Mission	Prague, Czechoslovakia
Deseret News, Church Section (ch to Deseret News Weekly, Church Edition 1942; Church News, 1943)	1931-		Salt Lake City, Utah
BYU Studies	1959-	BYU	Provo, Utah
Week-Day Religious Education	1937-1940	Dept. of Education	Salt Lake City, Utah
Progress of the Church	1938-1943	Presiding Bishopric's Office	Salt Lake City, Utah
The Church News, LDS Servicemen's Edition	1944-1948		Salt Lake City, Utah
The Messenger	1956-1964	Presiding Bishopric's Office	Salt Lake City, Utah

The Voice of the Saints (Che Sheng Tao, see Chinese list also)	1959-	Southern Far East Mission	Hong Kong, China
The Priesthood Bulletin	1965-		Salt Lake City, Utah
Impact	1967-	BYU	Provo, Utah
The Liahona (Unified) (for American Indians)	1969-	Seminaries and Institutes	Salt Lake City, Utah
The Ensign of the Church of Jesus Christ of Latter-day Saints	1970-	The Church of Jesus Christ of Latter-day Saints	Salt Lake City, Utah
The New Era	1970-	The Church of Jesus Christ of Latter-day Saints	Salt Lake City, Utah
The Friend	1970-	The Church of Jesus Christ of Latter-day Saints	Salt Lake City, Utah

International Magazines

CHINESE
The Voice of the Saints (Che Sheng Tao; Unified, Chinese only 1967; see English list)	1959-	Southern Far East Mission	Hong Kong, China

CZECHOSLOVAKIAN
Hvezdika (See also English list)	1929-1939	Czechoslovakian Mission	Prague, Czechoslovakia
Novy Hlas	1945-1949	Czechoslovakian Mission	Prague, Czechoslovakia

DANISH
Skandinavians Stjerne (ch Den Danske Stjerne 1956) (Unified 1967)	1851-1984	Scandinavian Mission	Copenhagen, Denmark Frankfurt, Germany
Stjernen	1985-		
Ungdommens Raadgiver	1880-1887	Scandinavian Mission	Copenhagen, Denmark
Morgenstjernen	1882-1885	Andrew Jenson	Salt Lake City, Utah

DUTCH
De Ster (Unified 1967)	1896-	Netherlands Mission	Rotterdam, Holland Frankfurt, Germany

FRENCH
Etoile Du Deseret	1851-1852	French Mission	Paris, France & Liverpool, England
Le Reflecteur	1853-	French Mission	Geneva, Switzerland
Te Heheurai Api	1907-1961	French Mission	Papeete, Tahiti
L'Etoile (Unified 1967)	1928	French Mission	Geneva, Switzerland Frankfurt, Germany

FINNISH
Valkeus (Unified 1967)	1950	Finnish Mission	Helsinki, Finland Frankfurt, Germany

GERMAN
Zion's Panier	1851-1852	German Mission	Hamburg, Germany
Der Darsteller des Heiligen Der Letzten Tage	1855-1861	German Mission	Geneva & Zurich, Switzerland
Die Reform	1862-1863	Swiss, Italian & German Missions	Geneva, Switzerland
Der Stern (Unified 1967)	1869-	German Mission	Zurich, Switzerland Frankfurt, Germany
Der Wegweiser	1927-1936	Swiss-German & German-Austrian Mission	Basel, Switzerland

HAWAIIAN Ka Elele Oiaio	1908-1911	Hawaiian Mission	Honolulu, Hawaii

PORTUGUESE
A Giavota (Ch to A
  Liahona 1951) (Unified
  1967)
	1948-	Brazilian Mission	Sao Paulo, Brazil

SAMOAN O Le Liahona (Unified)	1968-	Samoan Mission	Auckland, New Zealand
SPANISH Evangelio Restaurado	1927-1930	Mexican Mission	El Paso, Texas
Atalaya (In Yaotlapiyoui) (ch to El Atalaya 1944; Liahona 1945)	1937-	Mexican Mission	Mexico
(Unified 1967)		Mexican & Spanish- American Mission	Salt Lake City, Utah
El Mensajero Desert	1937-1955	Argentine Mission	Buenos Aires, Argentina
El Candil	1951-1961	Uruguayan Mission	Montevideo, Uruguay
El Deseret Oriental	1954-1955	Uruguayan Mission	Montevideo, Uruguay
SWEDISH Nordstjarnan (Unified 1967)	1877-	Scandinavian & Swed- ish Mission	Frankfurt, Germany
ITALIAN La Stella (Unified)	1967-	Italian Mission	Frankfurt, Germany
JAPANESE Seito No Michi (Unified)	1967	Northern Far East Mission	Tokyo, Japan
KOREAN Friend of the Saints (Songdo Wi Bot, Unified 1967)	1965-	Korean Mission	Seoul, Korea
MAORI Te Karere (See also) English list)	1907-1955	New Zealand Mission	Auckland, New Zealand
NORWEGIAN Morgenstjernen	1922-1925	Norwegian Mission	Christiana, Norway
Lys Over Norge (Unified 1967)	1937	Norwegian Mission	Frankfurt, Germany
TAHITIAN Te Tiarama (Unified)	1968-70 1985-	French-Polynesian Mission	Auckland, New Zealand
TONGAN Ko E Tuhulu (Unified)	1954-1980	Tongan Mission	Auckland, New Zealand
Tuhulu	1980-		

WELSH
Prophwyd y Jubili new
  Seren y Saint (Ch to
  Udgorn Seion new
  Seren y Saint 1849)
	1846-1858	Welsh Mission	Merthyr Tydifil, Wales

CHURCH NEWSPAPERS

Upper Missouri Advertiser	1832-1833	W.W. Phelps	Independence, Mo.
Northern Times	1835-?	Frederick G. Williams	Kirtland, Ohio
The Wasp	1842-1843	William Smith	Nauvoo, Illinois
The Nauvoo Neighbor	1843-1845	John Taylor	Nauvoo, Illinois
The Prophet	1844-1845	William Smith	New York City, N.Y.
The New York Messenger	1845-1845	Parley P. Pratt and Orson Pratt	New York City, N.Y.
California Star	1847-1848	E. P. Jones	Yerba Buena (San Francisco), Calif.
Frontier Guardian	1849-1852	Orson Hyde	Kanesville, Iowa
THE DESERET NEWS	1850-	Willard Richards	Salt Lake City, Utah
Western Bugle	1852-1852	Almon W. Babbitt	Kanesville, Iowa
Saint Louis Luminary	1854-1855	Erastus Snow	St. Louis, Mo.
The Mormon	1855-1857	John Taylor	New York City, N.Y.
The Western Standard	1856-1857	George Q. Cannon	San Francisco, Calif.
Pony Dispatch (Ch to Telegraphic 1861)	1861-1864		Salt Lake City, Utah

TEMPLES OF THE CHURCH

(Listed in order of completion)

TEMPLE	LOCATION	DATE DEDICATED	BY WHOM	PAGE
Kirtland*	Kirtland, Ohio	27 Mar 1836	Joseph Smith	p. 154
Nauvoo*	Nauvoo, Ill.	30 Apr 1846 (private)	Joseph Young	p. 144
		1 May 1846 (public)	Orson Hyde	
St. George	St. George, Utah	6 Apr 1877	Daniel H. Wells	p. 132
Rededicated after remodeling		11 Nov 1975	Spencer W. Kimball	
Logan	Logan, Utah	17 May 1884	John Taylor	p. 124
Rededicated after remodeling		13 Mar 1979	Spencer W. Kimball	
Manti	Manti, Utah	17 May 1888 (private)	Wilford Woodruff	p. 131
		21 May 1888 (public)	His prayer read by Lorenzo Snow	
Rededicated after remodeling		14 Jun 1985	Gordon B. Hinckley	
Salt Lake	Salt Lake City, Utah	6 Apr 1893	Wilford Woodruff	p. 126
Hawaii	Laie, Oahu, Hawaii	27 Nov 1919	Heber J. Grant	p. 136
Rededicated after remodeling		13 Jun 1978	Spencer W. Kimball	
Alberta	Cardston, Alberta, Canada	26 Aug 1923	Heber J. Grant	p. 142
Portions rededicated after remodeling		2 Jul 1962	Hugh B. Brown	
Arizona	Mesa, Ariz.	23 Oct 1927	Heber J. Grant	p. 158
Rededicated after remodeling		15 Apr 1975	Spencer W. Kimball	
Idaho Falls	Idaho Falls, Idaho	23 Sep 1945	George Albert Smith	p. 149
Swiss	Zollikofen, near Bern, Switzerland	11 Sep 1955	David O. McKay	p. 84
Los Angeles	Los Angeles, Calif.	11 Mar 1956	David O. McKay	p. 137
New Zealand	Hamilton, New Zealand	20 Apr 1958	David O. McKay	p. 93
London	Newchapel, Surrey, England	7 Sep 1958	David O. McKay	p. 89
Oakland	Oakland, Calif.	17 Nov 1964	David O. McKay	p. 138
Ogden	Ogden, Utah	18 Jan 1972	Joseph Fielding Smith	p. 125
Provo	Provo, Utah	9 Feb 1972	Joseph Fielding Smith His prayer read by Harold B. Lee	p. 131
Washington	Kensington, Md.	19 Nov 1974	Spencer W. Kimball	p. 155

Sao Paulo	Sao Paulo, Brazil	30 Oct 1978	Spencer W. Kimball	p. 111
Tokyo	Tokyo, Japan	27 Oct 1980	Spencer W. Kimball	p. 100
Seattle	Bellevue, Wash.	17 Nov 1980	Spencer W. Kimball	p. 150
Jordan River	South Jordan, Utah	16 Nov 1981	Marion G. Romney	p. 130
Atlanta Georgia	Sandy Springs, Ga.	1 Jun 1983	Gordon B. Hinckley	p. 164
Apia Samoa	Apia, Western Samoa	5 Aug 1983	Gordon B. Hinckley	p. 92
Nuku'alofa Tonga	Nuku'alofa, Tonga	9 Aug 1983	Gordon B. Hinckley	p. 94
Santiago Chile	Santiago, Chile	15 Sep 1983	Gordon B. Hinckley	p. 120
Papeete Tahiti	Pirae, Tahiti	27 Oct 1983	Gordon B. Hinckley	p. 94
Mexico City	Mexico City, Mexico	2 Dec 1983	Gordon B. Hinckley	p. 107
Boise Idaho	Boise, Idaho	25 May 1984	Gordon B. Hinckley	p. 148
Sydney Australia	Carlingford, Australia	20 Sep 1984	Gordon B. Hinckley	p. 95
Manila Philippines	Quezon City, Philippines	25 Sep 1984	Gordon B. Hinckley	p. 103
Dallas Texas	Dallas, Texas	19 Oct 1984	Gordon B. Hinckley	p. 159
Taipei Taiwan	Taipei, Taiwan	17 Nov 1984	Gordon B. Hinckley	p. 99
Guatemala City	Guatemala City, Guatemala	14 Dec 1984	Gordon B. Hinckley	p. 108
Freiberg DDR	Freiberg, DDR	29 Jun 1985	Gordon B. Hinckley	p. 83
Stockholm Sweden	Vasterhaninge, Sweden	2 Jul 1985	Gordon B. Hinckley	p. 83
Chicago Illinois	Glenview, Ill.	9 Aug 1985	Gordon B. Hinckley	p. 142
Johannesburg South Africa	Johannesburg, South Africa	24 Aug 1985	Gordon B. Hinckley	p. 88
Seoul Korea	Seoul, Korea	14 Dec 1985	Gordon B. Hinckley	p. 99
Lima Peru	Lima, Peru	10 Jan 1986	Gordon B. Hinckley	p. 115
Buenos Aires Argentina	Buenos Aires, Argentina	17 Jan 1986	Thomas S. Monson	p. 119
Denver Colorado	Littleton, Colo.	24 Oct 1986	Ezra Taft Benson	p. 143
Frankfurt Germany	Friedrichsdorf, Germany	28 Aug 1987	Ezra Taft Benson	p. 82

* — No longer in use

Construction has been started on these temples:
Las Vegas Nevada — see p. 160
Portland Oregon — see p. 148
Toronto Ontario — see p. 155
San Diego California — see p. 138

These temples are in the planning stages:
Bogota Colombia — see p. 115
Guayaquil Ecuador — see p. 115

76 years of LDS Olympians

(Summer games participants)

Year	Name	Event	Medal
1912	Alma Richards, USA	High jump	Gold
1920	Creed Haymond,USA*	Sprints	
1932	Jesse Mortensen, USA**	Decathlon	
1936	Dale M. Schofield, USA	400-meter hurdles	
1948	Jay Lambert, USA	Boxing	
	Clarence Robison, USA	5,000-meter run	
1952	Paula Meyers Pope, USA***	Diving	Silver
	Robert Detweiler, USA***	Rowing	Gold
	Jane Sears, USA	swimming	Bronze
1956	Paula Meyers Pope, USA	Diving	Silver, Bronze
1960	Paula Meyers Pope, USA	Diving	Silver
1964	L. Jay Silvester, USA	Discus	
1968	Wade Bell, USA	800-meter run	
	Kresimir Cosic, Yugoslavia	Basketball	Silver
	Jackson S. Horsely, USA	Swimming	Bronze
	Canagasabi Kunulon, Singapore	Sprints	
	Kenneth Lundmark, Sweden	High jump	
	Keith Russell, USA	Diving	
	L. Jay Silvester, USA	Discus	
	Arnold Vitarbo, USA	Shooting	

1972	Anders Arrhenius, Sweden*	Shot put	
	Kresimir Cosic, Yugoslavia	Basketball	Bronze
	George Greenfield, USA	Gymnastics	
	Debbie Stark Hill, USA	Gymnastics	
	Kenneth James, Australia	Basketball	
	Canagasabi Kunulon, Singapore	Sprints	
	L. Jay Silvester, USA	Discus	Silver
	Usaia Sotutu, Fiji	Steeplechase	
1976	Kresimir Cosic, Yugoslavia	Basketball	Silver
	Lelei Fonoimoana, Fiji	Swimming	
	Richard George, USA	Javelin	
	Henry Marsh, USA	Steeplechase	
	Laman Palma, Mexico	Marathon	
	L. Jay Silvester, USA	Discus	
	Phil Tollestrup, Canada	Basketball	
	Tauna Vandeweghe, USA	Swimming	
	Allesandra Viero, Italy	Gymnastics	
	Wayne Young, USA	Gymnastics	
1980	Kresimir Cosic, Yugoslavia	Basketball	Gold
	Henry Marsh, USA****	Steeplechase	
	Peter Vidmar, USA****	Gymnastics	
	Danny Vranes, USA****	Basketball	
1984	Pedro Caceres, Argentina	Steeplechase	
	Paul Cummings, USA	10,000-meter run	
	Stefan Fernholm, Sweden	Discus	
	Mark Fuller, USA	Greco-Roman wrestling	
	Bo Gustafsson, Sweden	50-kilometer walk	Silver
	Lorna Griffin, USA	Discus, shot put	
	Silo Havili, Tonga	Boxing	
	Henry Marsh, USA	Steeplechase	
	Scott Maxwell, Canada	Baseball*****	
	Doug Padilla, USA	5,000-meter run	
	Viliami Pulu, Tonga	Boxing	
	Fime Sani, Tonga	Boxing	
	Cory Snyder, USA	Baseball*****	Silver
	Karl Tilleman, Canada	Basketball	
	Peter Vidmar, USA	Gymnastics	2 Gold, 1 Silver
	Walt Zobell, USA	Trapshooting	
1988	Uati Afele, Western Samoa	Wrestling	
	Lucky Agbonsevbafe, Nigeria	Soccer	
	Troy Dalbey, USA	Swimming	2 Golds
	Mike Evans, USA	Water Polo	Silver
	James Bergeson, USA	Water Polo	Silver
	Ed Eyestone, USA	Marathon	
	Tualau Fale, Tonga	Boxing	
	Mark Fuller, USA	Greco-Roman wrestling	
	Bo Gustafsson, Sweden	50-kilometer walk	
	Viliamu Lesiva, Western Samoa	Boxing	
	Henry Marsh, USA	Steeplechase	
	Asomua Naea, Western Samoa	Boxing	
	Doug Padilla, USA	5,000-meter run	
	Fred Solovi, Western Samoa	Wrestling	
	Sione Talia'uli, Tonga	Boxing	
	Troy Tanner, USA	Volleyball	Gold
	Karl Tilleman, Canada	Basketball	
	Palako Vaka, Tonga	Boxing	

*Injured, unable to compete
**Declared ineligible
***Joined Church after competition
****U.S. boycott, unable to compete
*****Demonstration sport; team finished 2nd

BOOK OF MORMON EDITIONS, TRANSLATED AND PUBLISHED

LANGUAGES	PLACE	YEAR	NOTES
English	Palmyra, New York	1830	
Danish	Copenhagen, Denmark	1851	
German	Hamburg, Germany	1852	Retranslated 1980
French	Paris, France	1852	
Italian	London, England	1852	Retranslated 1964
Welsh*	Merthyr Tydfil, Wales	1852	
Hawaiian*	San Francisco, California	1855	
English*	New York, New York	1869	Deseret Alphabet
Spanish†	Salt Lake City, Utah	1875	Selections-Full book 1886
Swedish	Copenhagen, Denmark	1878	
Spanish	Salt Lake City, Utah	1886	Retranslated 1952
Maori*	Auckland, New Zealand	1889	
Dutch	Amsterdam, Holland	1890	
Samoan	Salt Lake City, Utah	1903	
Tahitian	Salt Lake City, Utah	1904	
Turkish*	Boston, Massachusetts	1906	Armenian script Selections retranslated 1983
Japanese	Tokyo, Japan	1909	Retranslated 1957
Czech	Prague, Czechoslovakia	1933	Selections retranslated 1980 Full book reprinted in 1986
Armenian*	Los Angeles, California	1937	Selections retranslated 1983
English	Louisville, Kentucky	1939	Braille edition
Portuguese	Sao Paulo, Brazil	1940	
Tongan	Salt Lake City, Utah	1946	
Norwegian	Oslo, Norway	1950	
Finnish	Helsinki, Finland	1954	
Rarotongan	Salt Lake City, Utah	1965	
Chinese	Hong Kong	1965	
Korean	Seoul, Korea	1967	
Afrikaans	Johannesburg, So. Africa	1972	
Thai	Bangkok, Thailand	1976	
Indonesian	Jakarta, Indonesia	1977	
Aymara*†	Salt Lake City, Utah	1977	Selections-Full book 1986
Cakchiquel	Salt Lake City, Utah	1978	Selections
Croatian	Cakovec, Yugoslavia	1979	
Quechua-Peru	Salt Lake City, Utah	1979	Selections
Greek*† (Katharevusa)	Salt Lake City, Utah	1979	Selections
Hungarian	Salt Lake City, Utah	1979	Selections
Kekchi*†	Salt Lake City, Utah	1979	Selections-Full Book 1983
Quiche	Salt Lake City, Utah	1979	Selections
Bulgarian	Salt Lake City, Utah	1980	Selections
Navajo	Salt Lake City, Utah	1980	Selections
Quichua- Ecuador	Salt Lake City, Utah	1980	Selections
Arabic*†	Salt Lake City, Utah	1980	Selections-Full Book 1986
Czech*†	Salt Lake City, Utah	1980	Selections
Vietnamese*†	Salt Lake City, Utah	1980	Selections -Full book 1982
Fijian	Salt Lake City, Utah	1980	

LANGUAGES	PLACE	YEAR	NOTES
Catalan	Barcelona, Spain	1981	
Russian	Salt Lake City, Utah	1981	
Icelandic	Reykjavik, Iceland	1981	
Niuean	Salt Lake City, Utah	1981	Selections
Quechua-Bolivia	Salt Lake City, Utah	1981	Selections
Cuna	Salt Lake City, Utah	1981	Selections
Romanian	Salt Lake City, Utah	1981	Selections
Polish	Salt Lake City, Utah	1981	
Hebrew	Salt Lake City, Utah	1981	Selections
Hindi	Hong Kong	1982	
Telugu	Salt Lake City, Utah	1982	
Tamil	Colombo, Sri Lanka	1982	Selections
Cambodian	Salt Lake City, Utah	1982	Selections
Laotian	Salt Lake City, Utah	1982	Selections
Vietnamese	Salt Lake City, Utah	1982	
Swahili	Salt Lake City, Utah	1982	Selections
Guarani	Salt Lake City, Utah	1982	Selections
Mayan	Salt Lake City, Utah	1983	Selections
Sinhala	Colombo, Sri Lanka	1983	Selections
Kekchi	Salt Lake City, Utah	1983	
Mam	Salt Lake City, Utah	1983	Selections
Armenian	Los Angeles, Calif.	1983	Selections
Turkish	Salt Lake City, Utah	1983	Selections, Roman letters
Efik	Salt Lake City, Utah	1983	Selections
China-Peking	Hong Kong	1983	Selections
Kisii	Salt Lake City, Utah	1983	Selections
Greek*† (Demotike)	Salt Lake City, Utah	1983	Selections-Full book 1987
Hmong	Salt Lake City, Utah	1983	Selections
Persian	Salt Lake City, Utah	1983	Selections
Haitian Creole	Salt Lake City, Utah	1983	Selections
Marshallese	Salt Lake City, Utah	1984	Selections
Bengali	New Delhi, India	1985	Selections
Bislama	Salt Lake City, Utah	1985	Selections
Arabic	Salt Lake City, Utah	1986	
Aymara	Salt Lake City, Utah	1986	
Malagasy	Salt Lake City, Utah	1986	Selections
Akan-Fante	Salt Lake City, Utah	1986	Selections
Tagalog	Salt Lake City, Utah	1987	Selections
Greek (Demotike)	Salt Lake City, Utah	1987	
Zulu	Salt Lake City, Utah	1987	Selections
Pohnpeian	Salt Lake City, Utah	1987	Selections
Papiamento	Salt Lake City, Utah	1987	Selections
Trukese	Salt Lake City, Utah	1987	Selections
Lingala	Salt Lake City, Utah	1988	Selections

	Completed	Available
FULL BOOK OF MORMON EDITIONS	41	35
SELECTIONS FROM THE BOOK OF MORMON	48	40
TOTALS	89	75
NUMBER OF LANGUAGES	79	75
NUMBER OF NATIONS COVERED	114?	114?

* = out of print
† = replaced by later edition

People of the Doctrine and Covenants

The first reference to each person in the Doctrine and Covenants is given. Other references may also be given. Biblical names and special names are not included.

Ashey, Major N. — Missionary (75:17); H.P.; resided, Jackson Co.; in legislature, Mo.; left Church, 1838; was in mob action against Church; lived, Tallmadge, Ohio.

Babbitt, Almon W.— Aspired to presidency (124:84); repented; pres., Kirtland Stake; attorney for redress before Pres. James K. Polk; arrived S.L., 1848; was delegate to Congress, but not seated; secretary, Utah Territory, 1852; killed by Indians, Ash Hollow, Neb., Sep. 7, 1856.

Baker, Jesse — (124:137); in elders quorum presidency, Nauvoo.

Baldwin, Wheeler — Missionary (52:31); named to obtain redress documents to send to Wash. D.C.; joined with Cutlerites and Reorganized church, 1863; died, May 11, 1887, Stewartsville, Mo.

Basset, Heman — Released from responsibility (52:37); died, 1876, Philadelphia.

Bennett, John C. — Sent gospel message to kings (124:16); doctor; first Nauvoo mayor; became apostate; excommunicated, May 25, 1842; died, Aug. 5, 1867, Polk City, Iowa.

Benson, Ezra T. — In stake presidency, Quincy, Ill., 1841; moved to Nauvoo; ordained apostle, July 16, 1846; capt., 2nd 10 to S.L. (136:12); arrived, Jul. 24, 1847; early government leader; lived in Logan; died, Sept. 3, 1869 in Ogden.

Bent. Samuel — Whipped by mob, Liberty, Mo., 1836; on high council, Nauvoo (124:132); presiding elder, Garden Grove, Iowa; died there, Aug. 16, 1846.

Billings, Titus — Second person baptized in Kirtland, Nov. 1830; counselor to Bishop Edward Partridge; called to dispose of land and prepare to go to Zion (63:39); involved in Crooked River battle; reached Salt Lake Valley, 1848, settled Manti; died, Feb. 6, 1866.

Boggs, Lilburn — Gov., Missouri; issued extermination order, Oct. 27, 1838 (124: introduction); migrated to Calif.; died, March 4, 1860, Napa, Calif.

Booth, Ezra — Missionary (52:23); apostatized; wrote anti-Mormon literature (71: introduction); lived, Mantua, Ohio.

Brunson, Seymour — Missionary (75:33); on high council in Nauvoo, 1839; taken by the Lord unto himself; died, Aug. 10, 1840; Joseph Smith first spoke of baptism for dead at his funeral.

Burnett, Stephen — Missionary (75:35); apostatized by 1838; lived, Orange, Ohio.

Burroughs, Philip — Non-member; John Whitmer called to labor with him (30:10).

Butterfield, Josiah — One of Seven Presidents of Seventy, Nauvoo (124:138); worked on Kirtland Temple; missionary to Maine, 1844; later excommunicated; rebaptized; died, Apr. 1871, Monterey, Calif.

Cahoon, Reynolds — Missionary with Samuel Smith (52:30); in stake presidency, Adam-Ondi-Ahman; arrived S.L., 1848, settled Murray, Ut; died, Apr. 29, 1861.

Carter, Gideon H. — Baptized, Oct. 25, 1831, by Joseph Smith; called to ministry (75:34); killed, battle of Crooked River, Far West, Oct. 25, 1838.

Carter, Jared — Ordained priest (52:38); missionary; on high council in Kirtland; defected, 1838; disfellowshipped, 1844; lived, Chicago; died by 1850.

Carter, John S. — On high council in Kirtland (102:3); missionary with his brother Jared; died, cholera, Jun. 26, 1834, Clay Co. Mo.

Carter, Simeon D. — Mission call (52:27); collected funds for Bible translation; on high council in Far West; migrated to S.L., 1850; died, Feb. 3, 1869, Brigham City, Ut.

Carter, William — Called to Missouri (52:31); did not go; priesthood taken away, Sep. 1, 1831.

Coe, Joseph — Called to Missoiuri, (55:6); on high council in Kirtland; laid foundation stone, Kirtland Temple; helped obtain Egyptian mummies; left Church, 1837; lived in Kirtland.

Coltrin, Zebedee — Called to Missouri (52:29); one of First Seven Presidents of Seventy; in Zions Camp; in Kirtland Stake presidency; arrived Salt Lake Valley, 1847; lived, Spanish Fork; patriarch; died, Jul. 21, 1887.

Copley, Leman — Mission to Shakers (49:1); broke consecration covenant (54:4); disfellowshipped, 1834; returned, 1836; did not move West; lived in Ohio.

Corrill, John — Called to labor (50:38); second counselor in Presiding Bishopric, 1831-37; called to Missouri; keeper, Lord's storehouse; Church historian with Elias Higbee, 1838; excommunicated., 1839; lived, Quincy, Ill.

Covill, James — Baptist minister, received revelation (sec. 39); rejected baptism.

Cowdery, Oliver — Told to stand by Joseph Smith (6:18); ordained to Aaronic Priesthood (Sec. 13); one of Three Witnesses (17:3); apostle and second elder; member, first high council; excommunicated, 1838; rebaptized Nov. 12, 1848; died Mar. 3, 1850, Richmond, Mo.

Cowdery, Warren A. — Older brother of Oliver; presiding high priest, Freedom, N.Y. (106:1); moved to Kirtland, 1836; left Church 1838; died, Feb. 23, 1851.

Cutler, Alpheus — Worked on Kirtland and Far West and Nauvoo Temples; high council, Nauvoo (124:132); rejected Brigham Young as leader; moved to Iowa where he organized a church; died, Aug. 10, 1864, Manti, Iowa.

Davies, (Davis) Amos — Paid stock to Nauvoo House (124:111); did not go West with Saints, but later for California gold; returned to Ill., 1858; died, Mar. 22, 1872.

Dodds, Asa — Proclaimed gospel in West (75:15); was high priest; last known in Farmington, Ohio, 1850.

Dort, David — Converted through Lucy Mack Smith; on high council, Kirtland (124:132); in Zions Camp; died, Mar. 10, 1841, Nauvoo.

Eames, Ruggles — Missionary (75:35); last known to live in Van Buren Co., Iowa, 1840.

Foster, James — One of First Seven Presidents of the Seventy (124:138); on high council, Kirtland; lived, Jacksonville, Ill.; died, Dec. 21, 1841, Nauvoo.

Foster, Robert D. — Held stock, Nauvoo House (124:115); chief surgeon, Nauvoo Legion; in politics, education; excommunicated, Apr. 18, 1844; joined William Law group; moved to N.Y., then Ill.

Fuller, Edson — Called to Missouri

(52:28); troubled by evil spirits; excommunicated, 1831; moved to Grand Rapids, Mich., by 1850.

Fullmer, David — On high council, Nauvoo (124:132); leader, Garden Grove, Iowa; arrived Salt Lake, Oct. 13, 1850; pres., Salt Lake Stake; in territorial legislature, delegate, territorial convention; patriarch; died, Oct. 21, 1879, Salt Lake City.

Galland, Isaac — Paid stock in Nauvoo House (124:78); traveled with Hyrum Smith to obtain funds; wrote in defense of Church; became inactive; died, Sep. 22, 1858, Ft. Madison, Iowa.

Gause, Jesse — Quaker preacher; joined Church; counselor to Joseph Smith (81:intro); excommunicated, Dec. 3, 1832.

Gilbert, A. Sidney — Agent to Church (Sec. 53); established store with Newel K. Whitney; called to repentance, 1833; died, cholera in Zions Camp, Jun. 29, 1834.

Gould, John — Traveled with Orson Hyde to Missouri to seek redress; in Zions Camp; saved if obedient (100:14); one of Seven Presidents of Seventy, 1833; died, May 9, 1851, Cooley's Mill, Iowa.

Granger, Oliver — Revelation concerning duties (Sec. 117); missionary; worked on Kirtland Temple; land agent, Nauvoo; died, Aug. 25, 1841, Kirtland.

Griffin, Selah J. — To travel to Missouri (52:32); missionary with Thomas B. Marsh; blacksmith; expelled from Mo.; remained in Ill.

Grover, Thomas — On first high council, Nauvoo (124:132); body guard for Joseph Smith; in Nau. Leg.; missionary; operated ferry, Platte River; arrived Salt Lake Valley Oct. 3, 1847; on Davis Stake high council; in Utah Legislature; died, Feb. 20, 1886, Farmington, Ut.

Hancock, Levi W. — Missionary to Missouri (52:29); in Zions Camp, one of Seven Presidents of Seventy; arrived Salt Lake Valley, 1847; with Mormon Battalion; delegate, first legislative assembly, 1851; lived, Manti, Ut.; died, Jun. 10, 1882, Washington, Ut.

Hancock, Solomon — Missionary to Missouri (52:27); at Kirtland Temple dedication, 1836; sang hymn, Far West Temple site dedication; on high council in Clay Co.; died, Dec. 2, 1847, Pottawattamie, Iowa.

Harris, Emer — Brother of Martin; missionary (75:30); carpenter, Kirtland Temple; arrived Salt Lake, 1850; lived, Provo, Ut.; patriarch; died, Nov. 28, 1869, Logan, Ut.

Harris, George W. — On high council, Far West, Nauvoo (124:132); bp., high councilor, Council Bluffs, Iowa; remained in Iowa; died, 1857, Council Bluffs.

Harris, Martin — Scribe for Book of Mormon translation; lost 116 pages of manuscript (sec 3); one of Three Witnesses; on first high council; assisted in choosing the Twelve; excommunicated, 1837; came to Utah, 1870; rebaptized; died, Jul. 9, 1875, Clarkston, Ut.

Haws, Peter — Converted in Canada; helped build Nauvoo House (124:62, 70), temple; missionary; left Church, 1849; lived in Nevada, then California, where he died, 1862.

Hicks, John A. — (124:137); not sustained at conference, 1841; excommunicated Oct. 5, 1841.

Higbee, Elias — Asked questions concerning Isaiah (113:7); missionary; high priest, 1834; worked on Kirtland Temple, 1835; on high council, Far West, 1837; elected judge, Caldwell Co., Mo.; expelled from Missouri; on committee, Nauvoo Temple; with Joseph Smith to see President Martin Van Buren, 1839; died, cholera, June 8, 1843, Nauvoo.

Humphrey, Solomon — Missionary to East (52:35); assisted in laying cornerstone, Kirtland Temple; in Zions Camp; died, September, 1834, Clay County, Mo.

Huntington, William — On high council, Nauvoo (124:132) & Kirtland; protected Joseph Smith; hid Egyptian mummies in home; stone cutter, Nauvoo Temple; president, Mount Pisgah; died there, Aug. 6, 1846.

Hyde, Orson — On Kirtland high council (102:3); clerk to Presidency, 1833; in Quorum of Twelve, 1835-1878; at Kirtland Temple dedication, 1836; dedicated Holy Land; carried petition to Washington, D.C., 1844; remained at Winter Quarters until 1850; lived, Sanpete Co. Ut., 1852; died, Nov. 28, 1878, Spring City, Ut.

James, George — Ordained priest (52:38); ordained elder, Nov. 18, 1831; disfellowshipped; reinstated; remained in Ohio; died, Nov. 1864, Brownhelm, Ohio.

Jacques, Vienna — Baptized in Boston, 1832; requested expenses to Zion (90:28); married Daniel Shearer, July 25, 1845; migrated West; died, Feb. 7, 1884, Salt Lake City.

Johnson, Aaron — Ordained seventy, 1838, Far West, Mo.; on high council (124:132), Nauvoo; bishop, Garden Grove, Iowa, 1846; captain, pioneer co., Sep. 18, 1850; founder and first bishop, Springville Ward; chief justice, Utah Co.; speaker, first Legislature; died, May 10, 1877, Springville.

Johnson, John — Opened home to Joseph Smith, 1831-32; promised eternal life (96:6); on high council, Kirtland, 1834; worked on Kirtland Temple, 1835; rejected from high council, 1837; left Church, 1838; died, July 30, 1843, Kirtland.

Johnson, Luke S. — Missionary (68:7); on high council, Kirtland; in Zions Camp, 1834; in Quorum of Twelve, 1835-1838; excommunicated, 1838, Far West, Mo.; rebaptized, 1845, Nauvoo; arrived Salt Lake, 1847; bishop, St. Johns, Utah, Ward; died, Dec. 9, 1861, Salt Lake City, Ut.

Johnson, Lyman E. — Missionary (68:7); in Zions Camp, in Quorum of Twelve, 1835-1838; excommunicated, 1838; drowned in Mississippi River, Dec. 20, 1856.

Kimball, Heber C. — In Quorum of Twelve (124:129); missionary to England; arrived Salt Lake, 1847; counselor to Brigham Young, 1847-1868; first chief justice, provisional government of Deseret; in Utah Senate; introduced Perpetual Emigrating Fund; died, June 22, 1868, SLC, after a fall at Provo, Ut.

Kimball, Spencer W. — Became 12th president Dec. 30, 1973; grandson of Heber C. Kimball; born Salt Lake City, Mar. 28, 1895; lived, Arizona from youth until ordained apostle, Oct. 7, 1943; announced revelation extending priesthood to all worthy male members (declaration #2).

Knight, Joseph — Recognized (Sec. 12) for faith in Book of Mormon translation, was scribe; told to take up cross, pray (23:6); endowed, Nauvoo Temple, 1845; died, Feb. 3, 1847, Mt. Pisgah, Iowa.

Knight, Newel — Missionary (52:32); service in Ohio, (54:2; 56:6); on high council, Far West & Nauvoo; died Jan. 11, 1847, Ponca, Neb., while traveling westward.

Knight, Vinson — Asked to support Nauvoo House (124:74); bishop, Adam-Ondi-Ahman & Nauvoo; land purchasing agent; member, Nauvoo city council, 1841; died, July 31, 1842, Nauvoo, Ill.

Law, William — Requested support of Nauvoo House (124:82); counselor to Joseph Smith, 1841-44; captain, Nauvoo Legion; excommunicated, Apr. 18, 1844; died, Jan. 19, 1892, Shullsburg, Wis.

Lee, Ann — Shakers believed Second Coming had occurred and Savior appeared as woman, Ann Lee (Section 49, introduction).

Lyman, Amasa M. — In high priests quorum presidency (124:136); missionary; in Zions Camp; ordained apostle, Aug. 20, 1842; counselor, First Presidency, Feb. 1843, until Joseph Smith's death; returned to Twelve Aug. 12, 1844; deprived of apostleship Oct. 6, 1867; excommunicated May 12, 1870; died, Feb. 4, 1877, Fillmore, Ut.

Marks, William — To preside, Far West (117:1-10); on high council, Kirtland, 1837; president, Nauvoo Stake, 1839-44; sided with Sidney Rigdon; rejected as stake president; followed RLDS; died, May 22, 1872, Plano, Ill.

Marsh, Thomas B. — Subject of revelations (D&C 31, 112); missionary; physician to Church; to publish Lord's work (118:2); member of the Twelve, 1835-38; excommunicated, Mar. 18, 1839; rebaptized, July 1857, Florence, Neb; arrived Utah, 1857; died, January,1866, Ogden, Ut.

Mc Lellin, William E. — Requested revelations (D&C 66, 68); Lord not pleased (90:35); high council, Clay Co.; ordained apostle 1835; at Kirtland Temple dedication, 1836; excommunicated, 1838; died, Apr. 24, 1883, Independence, Mo.

Miles, Daniel S. — Lived, Kirtland, Far West; one of Seven Presidents of Seventy (124:138); among first settlers, Nauvoo; died, 1845, Hancock Co., Ill.

Miller, George — Ordained bishop; helped build Nauvoo Temple (124:20-23); missionary; brigadier general, Nauvoo Legion; carpenter, Nauvoo House; appointed trustee-in-trust for Church, Aug. 9, 1844; followed James J. Strang; died, 1856, Meringo, Ill. on way to Calif.

Morley, Isaac — Missionary (52:15); first counselor to Presiding Bishopric, 1831-40; persecuted, Ohio, Mo.; at Kirtland Temple dedication; patriarch; president, Lima (Ill.) Stake, 1840; settled Manti, Utah, 1849; in general assembly, provisional state of Deseret; died, Jun. 24, 1865, Fairview, Ut.

Murdock, John — To go to Missouri, (52:8); on high council, Clay Co.; missionary; bishop, Nauvoo, 1842; served, Mormon Battalion; arrived Salt Lake Valley, Oct. 12,

1847; five times captain, wagon train to valley; first bishop, 14th Ward, SLC; in first legislature, 1849; died, Dec. 23, 1871, Beaver, Ut.

Packard, Noah — On high council, Kirtland; at Kirtland Temple dedication, 1836; worked on Nauvoo Temple; counselor to Don Carlos Smith in high priest presidency, Nauvoo, (124:136); migrated to Salt Lake Valley, 1850; settled Springville, Ut.; died, Feb. 17, 1860.

Page, Hiram — Satan deceived him (28:11); one of Eight Witnesses; a founder, Far West, Mo.; left Church, 1838; died, Aug. 12, 1882, near Richmond, Mo.

Page, John E. — In Quorum of Twelve (118:6); missionary, Canada; supported James Jesse Strang, excommunicated Jun. 26, 1846; died, 1847, De Kalb, Ill.

Partridge, Edward — Sins forgiven, called to preach (36:1-8); ordained Presiding Bishop, 1831 (41:9); persecuted, tarred, feathered, 1833; at Kirtland Temple dedication; journeyed to Mo.; died, May 27, 1840, Nauvoo; received unto Lord (124:19).

Patten, David W. — High priest; worked on Kirtland Temple; in Zions Camp; in Quorum of Twelve, 1835-38; mission (114:1); killed, battle of Crooked River, Oct. 25, 1838; taken unto Lord (124:19 & 130).

Peterson, Ziba — Lamanite missionary (32:3); chastened for sins (58:60); excommunicated, 1833; moved to Placerville, Calif., where he died, 1849.

Phelps, William W. — Ordained to preach and write books for children (55:1-4); editor, printer for Church; published Book of Commandments (Section 67); assisted in publishing first hymn book; worked on Kirtland Temple; excommunicated, 1838; returned 1841; on Nauvoo city council; scribe, Book of Abraham translation; arrived Salt Lake, 1848; in state legislature; died, Mar. 7, 1872, Salt Lake City.

Pratt, Orson — Subject of revelation (Sec. 34); missionary; worked on Kirtland Temple; called to Quorum of Twelve, 1835; excommunicated, 1842; rebaptized, 1843; missionary, Great Britain; came West, 1847; established GSL base & meridian; Church historian; speaker, state legislature; died, Oct. 3, 1891, Salt Lake City.

Pratt, Parley P. — To preach to Lamanites (32:1); leader in Ohio, Mo.; at Kirtland Temple dedication, 1836; editor, *Millennial Star,* England; member, Quorum of Twelve, 1835-1857; arrived Salt Lake, 1847; in constitutional convention of Deseret; assassinated while on mission, 1857, Van Buren, Ark.

Pulsipher, Zera — One of First Seven Presidents of Seventy, 1838-1862, (124:138); persecuted in Missouri, Illinois; arrived Salt Lake, Sept. 22, 1848; partiarch; died, Jan. 1, 1872, Hebron, Ut.

Rich, Charles C. — Presidency Nauvoo Stake (124:132); in Zions Camp; brigadier general, Nauvoo Legion; missionary; arrived Salt Lake, Oct. 3, 1847; in Salt Lake Stake presidency; in territorial legislature; ordained, Quorum of Twelve, Feb. 12, 1849; colonized San Bernardino, Calif.; settled Bear Lake area; died, Nov. 17, 1883, Paris, Ida.

Richards, Willard — Doctor; missionary; called to Quorum of Twelve (118:6); on Nauvoo council; with Joseph, Hyrum Smith in Carthage Jail; Church historian; counselor to Brigham Young, 1847-1854; died, Mar. 11, 1854, Salt Lake City.

Rigdon, Sidney — Scribe to Joseph Smith for Bible translation (Sec. 35); saw vision with Joseph Smith (76:1); counselor to Joseph Smith, 1833; at Kirtland Temple dedication, 1836; held in Liberty Jail, 1838; on Nauvoo city council; with Joseph Smith in Washington, D.C.; Vice Presidential candidate of USA; rejected in claim to lead Church; withdrew; excommunicated, Sep. 8, 1844; died, Jul. 14, 1876, Friendship, N.Y.

Riggs, Burr — Missionary (75:17); ordained high priest; excommunicated, 1833; rebaptized, 1834; in Zions Camp; resided, Far West, Mo.; excommunicated, 1839; died, June 8, 1860, Adams Co., Ill.

Rolfe, Samuel — Artisan at Kirtland leader in Missouri, Illinois; bishop, Winter Quarters; reached Salt Lake, Sep. 24, 1847; joined Charles C. Rich at San Bernardino, Calif.; died, 1864.

Roundy, Shadrack — Seventy, Kirtland; expelled from Missouri; to preside over bishopric (124:141); arrived Salt Lake Valley, July 24, 1847; bishop, 16th Ward, 1849-56; on first Salt Lake Stake high council; in territorial legislature; died, July 4, 1872, high council.

Ryder, Simonds — Received calling (52:37); offended because name was misspelled in revelation, left Church; helped tar, feather Joseph Smith.

Scott, Jacob — Called to Missouri. (52:28).

Sherman, Lyman R. — Requested revelation (108:1); one of First Seven Presidents of Seventy, 1835-37; on high council, Kirtland, Far West; called to be apostle, but died Jan. 27, 1839, before ordained.

Sherwood, Henry G. — Asked to put stock in Nauvoo House (124:81); on high council, Kirtland, Nauvoo; healed of malaria; city marshal, Nauvoo; arrived Salt Lake, 1848; on high council, Salt Lake Stake; died about 1862, San Bernardino, Calif.

Smith, Alvin — Brother of Joseph Smith seen in vision (137:5); died, Nov. 19, 1823, Manchester, N.Y.

Smith, Don Carlos — Brother of Joseph Smith; president, high priests quorum (124:133); in charge of *Elders Journal*, edited *Times and Seasons* in Nauvoo; on Nauvoo city council; died, Aug. 7, 1841, Nauvoo.

Smith, Eden — Missionary (75:36); died, Dec. 7, 1851, Vermillion Co., Ind.

Smith, Emma H. — Married Joseph Smith Jan. 18, 1827; served as scribe; told will of Lord (Sec. 25); called to prepare hymn book, 1830; first Relief Society president, Mar. 17, 1842; chose not to go West; married Lewis C. Bidaman, Dec. 23, 1847; died, Apr. 30, 1879.

Smith, George A. — Joseph Smith's cousin; worked on Kirtland Temple; ordained apostle, Apr. 26, 1839; first counselor, First Presidency; mentioned in revelation (124:129); on Nauvoo city council; organized westward company (136:14); settled St. George (named for him); died, Sept. 1, 1875.

Smith, Hyrum — Joseph Smith's brother; subject of revelation (Section 11); patriarch (124:95); counselor to President 1837-41; one of Eight Witnesses; on Kirtland Stake high council; in Zions Camp; Church patriarch, assistant president to Joseph Smith; martyred, Jun. 27, 1844, Carthage Jail.

Smith, John — On high council, Kirtland (102:3); worked on Kirtland Temple; missionary; president, Adam-Ondi-Ahman Stake, 1838; Iowa Stake, 1839; Nauvoo Stake 1844; Salt Lake Stake, 1847; Church patriarch, 1849; died, May 23, 1854.

Smith, Joseph Jr. — Received First Vision, 1820; given power to translate Book of Mormon (1:29); received priesthood (13:1); ordained apostle; organized & first president of Church; directed building Kirtland, Nauvoo temples; martyred, Jun. 27, 1844, Carthage Jail.

Smith, Joseph Sr. — Father of Joseph Smith; given revelation (Section 4); one of Eight Witnesses; Church patriarch; on Kirtland high council, 1833; worked on Kirtland Temple; assistant counselor to First Presidency, 1837; died, Sept. 14, 1840, Nauvoo, Ill.

Smith, Joseph F. — Son of Hyrum Smith; missionary; on Salt Lake Stake high council; ordained apostle, 1866; counselor to John Taylor, Wilford Woodruff, Lorenzo Snow; became sixth president of the Church Oct. 17, 1901; received vision of Savior's visit to the spirit dead (Sec. 138); died, Nov. 19, 1918, Salt Lake City.

Smith, Samuel H. — Brother of Joseph Smith; called to strengthen Church (23:4); one of Eight Witnesses; first missionary for Church; on Kirtland high council, 1834-38; worked on Kirtland Temple; in Nauvoo Legion; died, Jul. 30, 1844, Nauvoo.

Smith, Sylvester — Missionary (75:34); in Zion's Camp; on Kirtland high council, 1835; at Kirtland Temple dedication, 1836; excommunicated, 1838.

Smith, William — Brother of Joseph Smith; ordained apostle, 1835; rebelled but repented, 1839; member of Twelve (124:129); in Zions Camp; member, Illinois House of Representatives; excommunicated, Oct. 12, 1845; died, Nov. 13, 1894, Osterdock, Iowa.

Snow, Erastus — Missionary; at Kirtland Temple dedication; aided Prophet in Liberty Jail; organized pioneer company (136:12); arrived Salt Lake Valley, July 24, 1847; in territorial constitutional convention; St. George city recorder; in Quorum of Twelve, 1849-88; died, May 27, 1888, Salt Lake City.

Snider (Snyder), John — Missionary in Canada, England; expelled from Missouri; on committee for Nauvoo House (124:22); in Nauvoo Legion; arrived Salt Lake, 1850; died, Dec. 19, 1875.

Stanton, Daniel — Called to preach (75:33); high priest, 1831; branch president, Jackson Co.; on high council, Adam-Ondi-Ahman Stake, 1838; pres., Quincy, Ill., Stake, 1840; settled in Springville, Ut.; died, Oct. 26, 1872, Panaca, Nev.

Sweet, Northrop — Called to preach (33:1); left Church, 1831.

Taylor, John — Member of the Twelve (118:6); missionary to England, France; editor, *Nauvoo Neighbor;* on committee to compile hymn book; on Nauvoo city council; wounded at martyrdom of Joseph Smith; arrived Salt Lake, Oct. 5, 1847; member Utah Legislature; became third president of Church, Oct. 10, 1880; died, July 25, 1887, Kaysville, Ut.

Thayre, Ezra — To preach (33:1); journeyed to Missouri; missionary; became rebellious; didn't support Twelve following Prophet's death; joined with RLDS.

Thompson, Robert B. — Promised blessings (124:12); Church recorder, 1840-41; scribe to Joseph Smith; edited *Times and Seasons;* died, Aug 27, 1841, Nauvoo, Ill.

Wakefield, Joseph — To strengthen Church (50:37); missionary; negative spirit developed; excommunicated, 1834.

Welton, Micah B. — Missionary (75:36); endowed, Nauvoo Temple, 1846.

Whitlock, Harvey — Missionary call (52:25); lived, Missouri; disfellowshipped, 1834; excommunicated, 1838; rebaptized, SLC, 1858; moved to California where he joined RLDS.

Whitmer, David — Subject of revelation (Section 16); one of Three Witnesses; called to search out Twelve Apostles; excommunicated, Feb. 13, 1838; died, Jan 25, 1888, Richmond, Mo.

Whitmer, John — Revelations to (Sec. 15, 26); one of Eight Witnesses; assisted with Book of Mormon translation; Church historian; assistant president of Church; excommunicated, Mar. 10, 1838; died, July 11, 1878, Far West, Mo.

Whitmer, Peter, Jr. — Revelation to (Sec. 16); one of Eight Witnesses; missionary; suffered Missouri persecution; died, Sept. 22, 1836, Liberty, Mo.

Whitmer, Peter, Sr. — Opened home to Joseph Smith (Sec. 14, introduction); Church organized in his home, Apr. 6, 1830, in Fayette, N.Y.; one of first members; died, Aug. 12, 1854, Richmond, Mo.

Whitney, Newel K. — To retain store (63:42); bishop, Kirtland (72:8); worked on Kirtland Temple; bishop, Adam-Ondi-Ahman, Salt Lake 18th Ward; Presiding Bishop of Church, Apr. 6, 1847; died, Sep. 23, 1850, Salt Lake City.

Wight, Lyman — Called to Missouri (52:7); in Zions Camp, 1834; at Kirtland Temple dedication; counselor, Adam-Ondi-Ahman Stake; on temple committee, Nauvoo; member of Twelve, 1841; fell away, 1844; led group to Texas, 1845; excommunicated, 1848; died, Mar. 31, 1858, Mountain Valley, Texas.

Williams, Fredrick G. — Not to sell farm (64:21); counselor to Joseph Smith, 1832; in Zion's camp; attended School of Prophets; worked on Kirtland Temple, 1834; fell from unity with Prophet; rejected from First Presidency, 1837; excommunicated, Mar. 17, 1839; rebaptized, April, 1840; died, Oct. 25, 1842, Quincy, Ill.

Williams, Samuel — Member, elders quorum presidency (124:137); came to Salt Lake Valley before 1850.

Wilson, Calves — Called to preach, Cincinnati, (75:15);

Wilson, Lewis Dunbar — On high council, Nauvoo (124:132); arrived Salt Lake, 1853; lived, Ogden where he died Mar. 11, 1856.

Woodruff, Wilford — In Zions Camp, 1834; ordained elder, 1835, seventy, 1836; missionary; called to Quorum of Twelve (118:6); presided over European mission, 1844; arrived Salt Lake, July 24, 1847; mission to England, 1848; assistant Church historian, 1856; fourth president of Church, April 7, 1890; issued "Manifesto," Sept. 24, 1890; died, Sept. 2, 1898, San Francisco.

Young, Brigham — Worked on Kirtland Temple; ordained apostle, 1835, missionary; president of Twelve (124:127); led pioneers West, arrived Salt Lake, July 24, 1847; became second president of Church, Dec. 27, 1847; died, Aug. 29, 1877, SLC.

Young, Joseph — One of Seven Presidents of Seventy (124:138); missionary; at Haun's Mill massacre; arrived Salt Lake, 1850; died, July 16, 1881, Salt Lake City.

TRANSLATIONS OF DOCTRINE AND COVENANTS, PEARL OF GREAT PRICE

1.	English	Kirtland, Ohio	1835	
	Book of Commandments	Independence, Mo.	1833	
	Braille	Louisville, Ky.	1948	
2.	Welsh	Merthyr Tydfil, Wales	1851	
3.	Danish	Copenhagen, Denmark	1852	
4.	German	Bern, Switzerland	1876	
5.	Swedish	Salt Lake City, Utah	1888	
6.	Dutch	Rotterdam, Holland	1908	
7.	French	Zurich, Switzerland	1908	Selections only
8.	Hawaiian	Honolulu, Hawaii	1914	
9.	Maori	Auckland, New Zealand	1919	
10.	Czech	Prague, Czechoslovakia	1938	Mimeographed selections
11.	Armenian	Los Angeles, Calif.	1941	
12.	Spanish	Salt Lake City, Utah	1948	
13.	Portuguese	Sao Paulo, Brazil	1950	
14.	Finnish	Helsinki, Finland	1955	
15.	Japanese	Tokyo, Japan	1957	
16.	Norwegian	Jonkiping, Sweden	1957	
17.	French	Paris, France	1958	First full French edition
18.	Tongan	Salt Lake City, Utah	1959	
19.	Samoan	Salt Lake City, Utah	1963	
20.	Italian	Salt Lake City, Utah	1965	
21.	Tahitian	Salt Lake City, Utah	1965	
22.	Korean	Seoul, Korea	1968	
23.	Chinese	Hong Kong	1974	
24.	Indonesian	Jakarta, Indonesia	1979	
25.	Thai	Bangkok, Thailand	1979	
26.	Afrikaans	Salt Lake City, Utah	1981	
27.	Vietnamese	Salt Lake City, Utah	1981	
28.	Icelandic	Reykjavik, Iceland	1982	
29.	Afrikaans	Cape Town, South Africa	1982	
30.	Polish	Salt Lake City, Utah	1984	
31.	Kekchi	Salt Lake City, Utah	1985	
32.	Greek	Salt Lake City, Utah	1986	

(Note: Bulgarian, Russian and Hungarian versions have been translated but not published.)

CHURCH STATISTICS

As of Dec. 31,	Members in Stakes	Members in Missions	Total members	Stakes	Wards, Branches	Missions	Mission Branches
1830:							
Apr. 6			6	0		0	
Dec. 31	280		280	0	4	0	
1831	680		680	0	6	0	
1832	1,318	1,313	2,661	0	27	0	6
1833	1,805	1,335	3,140	0	23	0	17
1834	3,050	1,322	4,372	2	22	0	18
1835	7,500	1,335	8,835	2	22	0	26
1836	12,000	1,293	13,293	2	25	0	29
1837	14,400	1,882	16,282	2	25	1	42
1838	15,300	2,581	17,881	2	26	1	65
1839	13,700	2,760	16,460	3	16	2	70
1840	11,962	4,903	16,865	10	18	2	69
1841	12,475	7,381	19,856	2	19	2	84
1842	13,549	10,015	23,564	2	26	2	199
1843	15,601	10,379	25,980	2	31	2	238
1844	16,374	9,772	26,146	2	33	3	239
1845	17,020	13,312	30,332	1	34	4	277
1846	18,960	15,033	33,993	0	30	5	311
1847	17,263	17,431	34,694	1	48	5	357
1848	16,749	23,728	40,477	1	55	5	426
1849	17,654	30,506	48,160	1	75	5	515
1850	18,756	33,083	51,839	1	61	9	637
1851	16,069	36,096	52,165	4	60	11	717
1852	15,627	37,013	52,640	5	65	13	795
1853	25,537	38,617	64,154	5	75	14	885
1854	30,817	37,612	68,429	6	79	13	859
1855	28,654	35,320	63,974	6	99	14	858
1856	31,762	32,119	63,881	7	124	12	841
1857	32,529	22,707	55,236	6	77	12	742
1858	33,880	21,875	55,755	4	81	9	661
1859	36,481	20,557	57,038	4	98	9	635
1860	39,338	21,744	61,082	4	110	8	611
1861	42,417	23,794	66,211	4	126	7	588
1862	45,565	23,215	68,780	4	135	7	563
1863	49,283	22,487	71,770	4	143	7	524
1864	53,006	21,342	74,348	4	161	8	471
1865	56,562	20,209	76,771	4	164	8	436
1866	59,803	18,081	77,884	4	167	8	420
1867	63,071	18,053	81,124	4	175	8	407
1868	66,589	18,033	84,622	5	178	8	385
1869	70,157	18,275	88,432	9	187	7	383
1870	73,747	16,383	90,130	9	195	7	363
1871	78,458	17,138	95,596	9	200	7	342
1872	81,821	16,331	98,152	9	206	7	347
1873	85,194	16,344	101,538	9	213	7	348
1874	88,567	15,349	103,916	10	216	7	309
1875	91,992	15,175	107,167	10	222	7	302
1876	95,773	15,338	111,111	10	230	8	307
1877	99,780	15,285	115,065	20	252	8	285
1878	109,894	15,152	125,046	21	254	9	272
1879	112,705	15,681	128,386	22	263	10	289

As of Dec 31,	Members in Stakes	Members in Missions	Total members	Stakes	Wards, Branches	Missions	Mission Branches
1880	117,773	15,855	133,628	23	272	10	287
1881	123,918	16,815	140,733	23	283	10	293
1882	128,779	16,825	145,604	24	292	10	291
1883	135,128	16,465	151,593	27	317	11	292
1884	142,417	15,825	158,242	29	340	13	296
1885	147,557	16,573	164,130	29	348	12	311
1886	150,602	16,051	166,653	30	342	12	315
1887	155,654	17,375	173,029	31	360	12	326
1888	162,464	17,830	180,294	32	373	13	336
1889	164,834	18,310	183,144	32	388	12	339
1890	170,653	17,610	188,263	32	395	12	330
1891	177,489	17,956	195,445	32	409	12	332
1892	182,623	18,338	200,961	33	439	14	350
1893	194,352	20,182	214,534	34	451	15	356
1894	201,047	21,322	222,369	34	457	15	356
1895	208,179	22,937	231,116	37	479	15	356
1896	215,514	25,913	241,427	37	489	17	348
1897	222,802	32,934	255,736	37	493	18	374
1898	229,428	37,823	267,251	40	516	20	401
1899	229,734	41,947	271,681	40	506	20	412
1900	236,628	47,137	283,765	43	529	20	438
1901	243,368	49,563	292,931	50	577	21	442
1902	249,927	49,178	299,105	50	595	22	481
1903	257,661	47,240	304,901	51	612	23	477
1904	275,681	48,608	324,289	55	619	21	475
1905	281,162	50,886	332,048	55	627	22	514
1906	289,377	55,637	345,014	55	636	22	541
1907	298,847	59,066	357,913	55	634	22	558
1908	307,308	64,164	371,472	59	666	22	595
1909	308,094	69,185	377,279	60	684	21	590
1910	327,017	71,461	398,478	62	699	21	611
1911	334,643	72,648	407,291	62	706	21	632
1912	341,278	76,277	417,555	65	716	22	647
1913	350,321	81,286	431,607	66	749	22	650
1914	371,729	82,989	454,718	68	772	21	601
1915	381,336	84,902	466,238	72	783	21	608
1916	390,449	86,872	477,321	73	808	22	559
1917	397,933	90,105	488,038	75	875	22	578
1918	404,030	91,932	495,962	75	893	22	559
1919	413,563	94,398	507,961	79	888	23	554
1920	426,167	99,820	525,987	83	904	24	623
1921	441,472	107,331	548,803	86	933	25	665
1922	451,762	114,596	566,358	87	946	25	661
1923	463,578	112,318	575,896	90	962	26	697
1924	479,498	118,363	597,861	94	969	25	716
1925	490,688	122,884	613,572	94	985	28	720
1926	494,536	129,373	623,909	96	992	28	739
1927	510,910	133,835	644,745	99	1,005	28	758
1928	516,986	138,700	655,686	101	1,004	29	813
1929	520,339	143,313	663,652	104	1,004	30	823
1930	532,877	137,140	670,017	104	1,000	30	868
1931	544,453	143,982	688,435	104	1,004	31	861
1932	554,462	149,487	703,949	104	1,012	31	867
1933	564,042	153,577	717,619	105	1,014	31	875

As of Dec 31,	Members in Stakes	Members in Missions	Total members	Stakes	Wards, Branches	Missions	Mission Branches
1934	579,118	151,620	730,738	110	1,035	31	892
1935	595,071	151,313	746,384	115	1,064	32	900
1936	607,202	153,488	760,690	118	1,081	33	933
1937	616,088	151,664	767,752	118	1,101	35	951
1938	632,994	151,770	784,764	126	1,137	36	947
1939	645,618	157,910	803,528	129	1,154	35	1,002
1940	703,017	159,647	862,664	134	1,191	35	728
1941	736,544	155,536	892,080	139	1,224	36	757
1942	754,826	162,889	917,715	143	1,242	37	776
1943	774,161	162,889	937,050	146	1,261	38	807
1944	792,362	161,642	954,004	148	1,273	38	773
1945	811,045	168,409	979,454	153	1,295	38	909
1946	823,819	172,686	996,505	161	1,340	39	959
1947	843,021	173,149	1,016,170	169	1,425	43	1,149
1948	854,099	187,871	1,041,970	172	1,451	44	1,323
1949	876,661	202,010	1,078,671	175	1,501	46	1,327
1950	898,478	212,836	1,111,314	180	1,541	43	1,370
1951	933,792	213,365	1,147,157	191	1,666	42	1,414
1952	974,118	214,935	1,189,053	202	1,767	43	1,551
1953	1,034,381	211,981	1,246,362	211	1,884	42	1,399
1954	1,079,583	222,657	1,302,240	219	1,993	42	1,476
1955	1,126,265	213,009	1,357,274	224	2,082	44	1,471
1956	1,177,856	238,875	1,416,731	239	2,210	45	1,854
1957	1,233,397	254,917	1,488,314	251	2,362	45	1,740
1958	1,292,098	263,701	1,555,799	273	2,513	47	1,757
1959	1,336,675	279,413	1,616,088	290	2,614	50	1,895
1960	1,408,722	284,408	1,693,180	319	2,882	58	1,811
1961	1,514,551	309,110	1,823,661	345	3,143	67	1,872
1962	1,626,965	335,821	1,965,786	364	3,423	74	1,802
1963	1,736,567	380,884	2,117,451	389	3,615	77	1,782
1964	1,801,571	433,345	2,234,916	400	3,749	79	2,016
1965	1,977,418	418,514	2,395,932	412	3,897	76	2,137
1966	2,032,359	448,540	2,480,899	425	4,022	75	2,053
1967	2,144,766	469,574	2,614,340	448	4,166	77	1,987
1968	2,207,976	476,097	2,684,073	473	4,385	83	2,112
1969	2,344,635	462,821	2,807,456	496	4,592	88	2,016
1970	2,485,525	445,285	2,930,810	537	4,922	92	1,943
1971	2,645,419	445,534	3,090,953	562	5,135	98	1,942
1972	2,794,731	424,177	3,218,908	592	5,394	101	1,891
1973	2,904,244	402,414	3,306,658	630	5,707	108	1,817
1974	2,999,536	410,451	3,409,987	675	5,951	113	1,822
1975	3,188,062	384,140	3,572,202	737	6,390	134	1,761
1976	3,352,535	390,214	3,742,749	798	6,903	148	1,422
1977	3,618,331	350,889	3,969,220	885	7,466	159	1,694
1978	3,829,385	337,469	4,166,854	990	8,064	166	1,790
1979	4,059,044	345,077	4,404,121	1,092	9,365	175	1,121
1980	4,333,467	311,301	4,644,768	1,218	10,324	188	2,267
1981	4,621,688	298,761	4,920,449	1,321	11,063	186	2,030
1982	4,832,158	330,461	5,162,619	1,392	11,492	180	1,979
1983	5,013,541	338,183	5,351,724	1,458	11,956	177	1,991
1984	5,278,192	362,862	5,641,054	1,507	12,421	180	2,046
1985	5,555,407	364,074	5,919,481	1,582	12,931	188	2,072
1986	5,785,100	381,650	6,166,750	1,622	13,319	193	2,070
1987	5,980,000	420,000	6,400,000	1,666	13,719	205	2,287

* — Beginning in 1986, the Church began estimating its total membership to the nearest 10,000 people.

MISSIONARY STATISTICS

Year	Set Apart During Year	Total to date	Year	Set Apart During Year	Total to date
1830	16		1870	46	
1831	58		1971	167	
1832	72		1872	132	
1833	41		1873	35	
1834	111		1874	98	
1835	84		1875	197	
1836	80		1876	211	
1837	52		1877	154	
1838	16		1878	152	
1839	67		1879	179	
Total in decade ..597		597	Total in decade ..1,371		4,889
1840	80		1880	219	
1841	100		1881	199	
1842	45		1882	237	
1843	374		1883	248	
1844	586		1884	205	
1845	84		1885	235	
1846	32		1886	209	
1847	40		1887	282	
1848	55		1888	242	
1849	58		1889	249	
Total in decade ..1,454		2,051	Total in decade ..2,325		7,212
el8					
1850	50		1890	283	
1851	44		1891	331	
1852	158		1892	317	
1853	33		1893	162	
1854	119		1894	526	
1855	65		1895	746	
1856	130		1896	922	
1857	88		1897	943	
1858			1898	1,059	
1859	18		1899	324	
Total in decade ..705		2,756	Total in decade ..5,613		12,825
1860	96		1900	796	
1861	19		1901	522	
1862	27		1902	848	
1863	50		1903	658	
1864	52		1904	699	
1865	71		1905	716	
1866	32		1906	1,015	
1867	133		1907	930	
1868	32		1908	919	
1869	250		1909	1,014	
Total in decade ..762		3,518	total in decade....8,117		20,942

Year	Set Apart During Year	Total to date	Year	Set Apart During Year	Total to date	Total in Field
1910	933		1950	3,015		
1911	822		1951	1,801		
1912	769		1952	872		
1913	858		1953	1,750		
1914	684		1954	2,022		
1915	621		1955	2,414		
1916	722		1956	2,572		
1917	543		1957	2,518		
1918	245		1958	2,778		
1919	1,211		1959	2,847		6,968
Total in decade ..7,468		28,410	Total in decade ..22,589			82,784
1920	889		1960	4,706		9,097
1921	880		1961	5,793		11,592
1922	886		1962	5,630		11,818
1923	812		1963	5,781		11,653
1924	867		1964	5,886		11,599
1925	1,313		1965	7,139		12,585
1926	1,236		1966	7,021		12,621
1927	1,017		1967	6,475		13,147
1928	1,193		1968	7,178		13,018
1929	1,058		1969	6,967		13,291
Total in decade ..10,151		38,561	Total in decade ..62,576			145,360
1930	896		1970	7,590		14,387
1931	678		1971	8,344		15,205
1932	399		1972	7,874		16,367
1933	525		1973	9,471		17,258
1934	843		1974	9,811		18,109
1935	960		1975	14,446		22,492
1936	899		1976	13,928		25,027
1937	1,079		1977	14,561		25,264
1938	1,146		1978	15,860		27,669
1939	1,088		1979	16,590		29,454
Total in decade ..8,513		47,074	Total in decade ..118,475			263,835
1940	1,194		1980	16,600		29,953
1941	1,257		1981	17,800		29,702
1942	629		1982	18,260		26,606
1943	261		1983	19,450		26,850
1944	427		1984	19,720		27,392
1945	400		1985	19,890		29,265
1946	2,297		1986	20,798		31,803
1947	2,132		1987	21,001		34,750
1948	2,161					
1949	2,363					
Total in decade ..13,121		60,195	Total in decade ..153,519			417,354

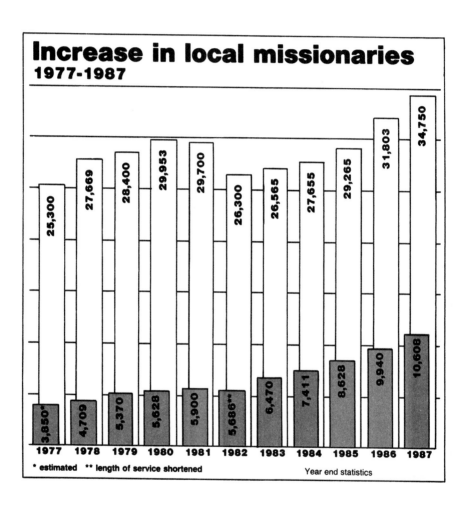

Increase in local missionaries
1977-1987

Year		
1977	25,300	3,850*
1978	27,669	4,709
1979	28,400	5,370
1980	29,953	5,628
1981	29,700	5,900
1982	26,300	5,686**
1983	26,565	6,470
1984	27,655	7,411
1985	29,265	8,628
1986	31,803	9,940
1987	34,750	10,608

* estimated ** length of service shortened

Year end statistics

STAKES, MISSIONS

STAKES OF THE CHURCH
In chronological order

NO.	NAME, LOCALITY *NAME CHANGED †DISORGANIZED ★TRANSFERRED TO	ORGANIZED	PRESIDENT	NO. IN YEAR
1	Kirtland (Ohio) †24 May 1841	17 Feb 1834	Joseph Smith Jr.	
2	Clay-Caldwell (Missouri) †1839	3 Jul 1834	David Whitmer	2
3	Adam-Ondi-Ahman (Missouri) †Nov 1838	28 Jun 1838	John Smith	1
2	Nauvoo (Illinois) †1846	5 Oct 1839	William Marks	
3	Iowa [Zarahemla] (Iowa) †6 Jan 1842	5 Oct 1839	John Smith	2
4	Crooked Creek [Ramus] (Illinois) †4 Dec 1841	4 Jul 1840	Joel J. Johnson	
5	Lima (Illinois) †1845	22 Oct 1840	Issac Morley	
6	Quincy (Illinois) †24 May 1841	25 Oct 1840	Daniel Stanton	
7	Mount Hope (Illinois) †24 May 1841	27 Oct 1840	Abel Lamb	
8	Freedom (Illinois) †24 May 1841	27 Oct 1840	Henry W. Miller	
9	Geneva (Illinois) †24 May 1841	1 Nov 1840	William Bosley	
10	Springfield (Illinois) †24 May 1841	5 Nov 1840	Edwin P. Merriam	7
1	Salt Lake (Utah)	3 Oct 1847	John Smith	1
2	Weber (Utah) †14 Jun 1970 ★Mt. Ogden (No. 87)	26 Jan 1851	Lorin Farr	
3	Provo (Utah) *Utah 1855 *Provo Utah Central 14 Jan 1974	19 Mar 1851	Issac Higbee	
4	San Bernardino (California) †1857	6 Jul 1851	David Seely	3
5	Parowan (Utah) *Parowan Utah 14 Jan 1974	May 1852	John C.L. Smith	1
6	St. Louis (Missouri) †1858	4 Nov 1854	Milo Andrus	1
7	Carson Valley (Nevada) †1858	4 Oct 1856	Orson Hyde	1
5	Nephi (Utah) *Juab 1871 *Nephi Utah 14 Jan 1974	20 Sep 1868	Jacob G. Bigler	1
6	Millard (Utah) *Fillmore Utah 14 Jan 1974	9 Mar 1869	Thomas Callister	
7	Beaver (Utah) *Beaver Utah 14 Jan 1974	12 Mar 1869	John R. Murdock	
8	Bear Lake (Idaho, Utah) *Paris Idaho 14 Jan 1974	20 Jun 1869	David P. Kimball	

NO.	NAME, LOCALITY *NAME CHANGED †DISORGANIZED ★TRANSFERRED TO	ORGANIZED	PRESIDENT	NO. IN YEAR
9	St. George (Utah, Arizona) *St. George Utah 14 Jan 1974	7 Nov 1869	Joseph W. Young	4
10	Sevier (Utah) *Richfield Utah 14 Jan 1974	24 May 1874	Joseph A. Young	1
11	Kanab (Utah, Arizona) *Kanab Utah 14 Jan 1974	18 Apr 1877	L. John Nuttal	
12	Panguitch (Utah) *Panguitch Utah 14 Jan 1974	23 Apr 1877	James Henrie	
13	Cache (Utah) *Logan Utah Cache 14 Jan 1974	21 May 1877	Moses Thatcher	
14	Davis (Utah) †20 Jun 1915 ★North Davis (No. 70), South Davis (No. 71)	17 Jun 1877	William R. Smith	
15	Tooele (Utah) *Tooele Utah 14 Jan 1974	24 Jun 1877	Francis M. Lyman	
16	Morgan (Utah) *Morgan Utah 14 Jan 1974	1 Jul 1877	Willard G. Smith	
17	Sanpete (Utah) †9 Dec 1900 ★North Sanpete (No. 42), South Sanpete (No. 43)	4 Jul 1877	Canute Peterson	
18	Summit (Utah) *Coalville Utah 14 Jan 1974	9 Jul 1877	William W. Cluff	
19	Wasatch (Utah) *Heber City Utah 14 Jan 1974	15 Jul 1877	Abraham Hatch	
20	Box Elder (Utah) †12 Dec 1944 ★North Box Elder (No. 147), South Box Elder (No. 148)	19 Aug 1877	Oliver G. Snow	10
21	Little Colorado (Arizona) †18 Dec 1887 ★Snowflake (No. 31)	27 Jan 1878	Lot Smith	1
22	Eastern Arizona (Arizona, New Mexico) †18 Dec 1887 ★St. Johns (No. 31), Snowflake (No. 31)	29 Jun 1879	Jesse N. Smith	1
23	Emery (Utah) *Castle Dale Utah 14 Jan 1974	Aug 1880	Christen G. Larsen	1
24	Maricopa (Arizona) *Mesa Arizona Maricopa 14 Jan 1974	10 Dec 1882	Alexander F. MacDonald	1
25	St. Joseph (Arizona) *Thatcher Arizona 14 Jan 1974	25 Feb 1883	Christopher Layton	
26	San Luis (Colorado, New Mexico) *La Jara Colorado 14 Jan 1974 *Manassa Colorado 31 May 1983	10 Jun 1883	Silas S. Smith	
27	San Juan (Utah, Colorado) *Monticello Utah 14 Jan 1974	23 Sep 1883	Platte D. Lyman	3
28	Bannock (Idaho) *Fremont 6 Aug 1898 *Rexburg 23 Jun 1935 *Rexburg Idaho 14 Jan 1974	4 Feb 1884	Thomas E. Ricks	
29	Oneida *Preston Idaho North 14 Jan 1974	1 Jun 1884	William D. Hendricks	2
30	Uintah (Utah) *Vernal Utah 14 Jan 1974 *Vernal Utah Uintah 10 Jun 1986	11 Jul 1886	Samuel R. Bennion	1
31	St. Johns (Arizona, New Mexico) *St. Johns Arizona 14 Jan 1974	23 Jul 1887	David K. Udall	

NO.	NAME, LOCALITY *NAME CHANGED †DISORGANIZED ★TRANSFERRED TO	ORGANIZED	PRESIDENT	NO. IN YEAR
32	Cassia (Idaho, Utah) *Oakley Idaho 14 Jan 1974	19 Nov 1887	Horton D. Haight	
31	Snowflake (Arizona) *Snowflake Arizona 14 Jan 1974	18 Dec 1887	Jesse N. Smith	3
32	Malad (Idaho, Utah) *Malad Idaho 14 Jan 1974	12 Feb 1888	Oliver C. Hoskins	1
33	Star Valley (Wyoming) *Afton Wyoming 14 Jan 1974	14 Aug 1892	George Osmond	1
34	Wayne (Utah) *Loa Utah 14 Jan 1974	27 May 1893	Willis E. Robison	1
35	Alberta (Canada) *Cardson Alberta 14 Jan 1974	9 Jun 1895	Charles O. Card	
36	Bingham (Idaho) *Idaho Falls 16 Aug 1925 *Idaho Falls Idaho 14 Jan 1974	9 Jun 1895	James E. Steele	
37	Juarez (Mexico) *Colonia Juarez Mexico 14 Jan 1974	9 Dec 1895	Anthony W. Ivins	3
38	Woodruff (Wyoming, Utah) *Evanston Wyoming 14 Jan 1974	5 Jun 1898	John M. Baxter	
39	Bannock (Idaho) *Grace Idaho 14 Jan 1974	25 Jul 1898	Lewis S. Pond	
40	Pocatello (Idaho) *East Pocatello 19 Apr 1959 *Pocatello East 29 May 1970 *Pocatello Idaho East 14 Jan 1974 *Pocatello Idaho Alameda 17 Jun 1984	7 Aug 1898	William C. Parkinson	3
41	Jordan (Utah) †8 May 1927 ★East Jordan (No. 96), West Jordan (No. 97)	21 Jan 1900	Orrin P. Miller	
42	Granite (Utah) *Salt Lake Granite 14 Jan 1974	28 Jan 1900	Frank Y. Taylor	
42	North Sanpete (Utah) *Sanpete North 29 May 1970 *Mt. Pleasant Utah 14 Jan 1974	9 Dec 1900	Christian N. Lund	
43	South Sanpete (Utah) *Sanpete South 29 May 1970 *Manti Utah 14 Jan 1974	9 Dec 1900	Canute Peterson	4
44	Alpine (Utah) *Alpine Utah 14 Jan 1974	13 Jan 1901	Stephen L. Chipman	
45	Nebo (Utah) *Payson Utah 14 Jan 1974	13 Jan 1901	Jonathan S. Page Jr.	
46	Hyrum (Utah) *Hyrum Utah 14 Jan 1974	30 Apr 1901	William C. Parkinson	
47	Benson (Utah) *Richmond Utah 14 Jan 1974	1 May 1901	William H. Lewis	
48	Big Horn (Wyoming) *Lovell Wyoming 14 Jan 1974	26 May 1901	Byron Sessions	
49	Union (Oregon) *La Grande Oregon 14 Jan 1974	9 Jun 1901	Franklin S. Bramwell	
50	Teton (Wyoming, Idaho) *Driggs Idaho 14 Jan 1974	2 Sep 1901	Don Carlos Driggs	7
51	Taylor (Canada) *Raymond Alberta 14 Jan 1974	30 Aug 1903	Heber S. Allen	1
52	Blackfoot (Idaho) *Blackfoot Idaho 14 Jan 1974	31 Jan 1904	Elias S. Kimball	

NO.	NAME, LOCALITY *NAME CHANGED †DISORGANIZED ★TRANSFERRED TO	ORGANIZED	PRESIDENT	NO. IN YEAR
53	Liberty (Utah) *Salt Lake Liberty 14 Jan 1974	26 Feb 1904	Hugh J. Cannon	
54	Pioneer (Utah) *Salt Lake Pioneer 14 Jan 1974	24 Mar 1904	William McLachlan	
55	Ensign (Utah) *Salt Lake Ensign 14 Jan 1974	1 Apr 1904	Richard W. Young	4
56	Rigby (Idaho) *Rigby Idaho 14 Jan 1974	3 Feb 1908	Don Carlos Walker	
57	Ogden (Utah) *Ogden Utah 14 Jan 1974	19 Jul 1908	Thomas B. Evans	
58	North Weber (Utah) *Weber North 29 May 1970 *Ogden Utah Weber North 14 Jan 1974	19 Jul 1908	James Wotherspoon	
59	Bear River (Utah) *Garland Utah 14 Jan 1974	11 Oct 1908	Milton H. Welling	4
60	Yellowstone (Idaho) *St. Anthony Idaho 14 Jan 1974	10 Jan 1909	Daniel G. Miller	1
61	Carbon (Utah) *Price Utah 14 Jan 1974	8 May 1910	Gustave A. Iverson	
62	Duchesne (Utah) *Duchesne Utah 14 Jan 1974	14 Sep 1910	William H. Smart	2
63	Young (New Mexico, Colorado) *Farmington New Mexico 14 Jan 1974	21 May 1912	David Halls	
64	Moapa (Nevada) *Logandale Nevada 14 Jan 1974	9 Jun 1912	Willard L. Jones	
65	Deseret (Utah) *Delta Utah 14 Jan 1974	11 Aug 1912	Alonzo A. Hinckley	3
66	Boise (Idaho) *Boise Idaho 14 Jan 1974	3 Nov 1913	Heber Q. Hale	1
67	Shelley (Idaho) *Shelley Idaho 14 Jan 1974	16 Aug 1914	Joseph H. Dye	
68	Cottonwood (Utah) *Millcreek 11 Feb 1951 *Salt Lake Millcreek 14 Jan 1974	29 Nov 1914	Uriah G. Miller	2
69	Raft River (Idaho) *Cassia East 15 Jun 1969 *Declo Idaho 14 Jan 1974	27 Apr 1915	John A. Elison	
70	Curlew (Idaho, Utah) †11 Feb 1940 ★Malad (No. 32), Pocatello (No. 40)	17 May 1915	Jonathan C. Cutler	
70	North Davis (Utah) *Davis North 29 May 1970 *Syracuse Utah 14 Jan 1974	20 Jun 1915	Henry H. Blood	
71	South Davis (Utah) *Davis South 29 May 1970 *Bountiful Utah Orchard 14 Jan 1974	20 Jun 1915	James H. Robinson	
72	Portneuf (Idaho) *Arimo Idaho 14 Jan 1974 *McCammon Idaho 19 Feb 1983	15 Aug 1915	George T. Hyde	5
73	Idaho (Idaho) *Soda Springs Idaho 14 Jan 1974	19 Nov 1916	Nelson J. Hogan	1
74	Tintic (Utah) *Santaquin-Tintic 2 Apr 1939 *Santaquin Utah 14 Jan 1974	22 Apr 1917	Erastus Franklin Birch	

NO.	NAME, LOCALITY *NAME CHANGED †DISORGANIZED ★TRANSFERRED TO	ORGANIZED	PRESIDENT	NO. IN YEAR
75	Montpelier (Idaho, Wyoming) *Montpelier Idaho 14 Jan 1974	23 Dec 1917	Edward C. Rich	2
76	Twin Falls (Idaho) *Twin Falls Idaho 14 Jan 1974	26 Jul 1919	Lawrence Gomer Kirkman	
77	Burley (Idaho) *Burley Idaho 14 Jan 1974	27 Jul 1919	David R. Langlois	
78	Blaine (Idaho) *Richfield Idaho 14 Jan 1974 *Carey Idaho 31 Oct 1977	3 Aug 1919	William Lennox Adamson	
79	Lost River (Idaho) *Moore Idaho 14 Jan 1974	18 Aug 1919	William N. Patten	4
80	Logan (Utah) *Logan Utah 14 Jan 1974	4 Jun 1920	Oliver H. Budge	
81	Franklin (Idaho) *Preston Idaho South 14 Jan 1974	6 Jun 1920	Samuel W. Parkinson	
82	Roosevelt (Utah) *Roosevelt Utah 14 Jan 1974	26 Jun 1920	William H. Smart	
83	Garfield (Utah) *Escalante Utah 14 Jan 1974	29 Aug 1920	Charles E. Rowan Jr.	4
84	North Sevier (Utah) *Sevier North 29 May 1970 *Salina Utah 14 Jan 1974	30 Jan 1921	Moroni Lazenby	
85	South Sevier (Utah) *Sevier South 29 May 1970 *Monroe Utah 14 Jan 1974	30 Jan 1921	John E. Magleby	
86	Lethbridge (Canada) †15 Nov 1953 ★Calgary (No. 211), Lethbridge (No. 189)	10 Nov 1921	Hugh B. Brown	3
87	Mt. Ogden (Utah) *Ogden Utah Mt. Ogden 14 Jan 1974	21 May 1922	Robert I. Burton	1
88	Los Angeles (California) *South Los Angeles 19 Nov 1939 *Los Angeles South 29 May 1970 †12 Aug 1973 ★Huntington Park (No. 279)	21 Jan 1923	George W. McCune	
89	Gunnison (Utah) *Gunnison Utah 14 Jan 1974	6 May 1923	Allen E. Park	
90	Oquirrh (Utah) *Magna Utah 14 Jan 1974	3 Jun 1923	George A. Little	3
91	Minidoka (Idaho) *Rupert Idaho 14 Jan 1974	11 May 1924	Richard C. May	
92	Grant (Utah) *Salt Lake Grant 14 Jan 1974	25 May 1924	Joseph J. Daynes	
93	Kolob (Utah) *Springville Utah Kolob 14 Jan 1974	23 Nov 1924	George R. Maycock	
94	Palmyra (Utah) *Spanish Fork Utah Palmyra 14 Jan 1974	23 Nov 1924	Henry A. Gardner	4
95	Lyman (Wyoming, Utah) *Rock Springs Wyoming 14 Jan 1974	18 Jul 1926	H. Melvin Rollins	
96	Nevada (Nevada) *Ely Nevada 14 Jan 1974	19 Sep 1926	Carl K. Conrad	2
96	East Jordan (Utah) *Jordan East 29 May 1970 *Ft. Union 17 Jun 1973 *Midvale Utah Ft. Union 14 Jan 1974	8 May 1927	Heber J. Burgon	

NO.	NAME, LOCALITY *NAME CHANGED †DISORGANIZED ★TRANSFERRED TO	ORGANIZED	PRESIDENT	NO. IN YEAR
97	West Jordan (Utah) *West Jordan Utah 14 Jan 1974	8 May 1927	Joseph M. Holt	
98	Hollywood (California) *Los Angeles 19 Nov 1939 *Los Angeles California 14 Jan 1974	22 May 1927	George W. McCune	
99	San Francisco (California) *San Francisco California 14 Jan 1974	10 Jul 1927	W. Aird Macdonald	4
100	Lehi (Utah) *Lehi Utah 14 Jan 1974	1 Jul 1928	Anchor C. Schow	
101	Timpanogos (Utah) *Pleasant Grove Utah Timpanogos 14 Jan 1974	1 Jul 1928	Wilford W. Warnick	2
102	Moroni (Utah) *Moroni Utah 14 Jan 1974	16 Jun 1929	James Louis Nielsen	
103	Sharon (Utah) *Orem Utah Sharon 14 Jan 1974	15 Sep 1929	Arthur V. Watkins	
104	Zion Park (Utah) *Hurricane Utah 14 Jan 1974	8 Dec 1929	Claudius Hirschi	3
105	Wells (Utah) *Salt Lake Wells 14 Jan 1974	31 Dec 1933	Thomas E. Towler	1
106	South Summit (Utah) *Summit South 29 May 1970 *Kamas Utah 14 Jan 1974	8 Jul 1934	Zach J. Oblad	
107	Gridley (California) *Gridley California 14 Jan 1974	4 Nov 1934	John C. Todd	
108	Sacramento (California) *Sacramento California 14 Jan 1974	4 Nov 1934	Mark W. Cram	
109	Oakland (California) †26 Aug 1956 ★Oakland-Berkeley (No. 227)	2 Dec 1934	W. Aird Macdonald	
110	New York (N.Y., Connecticut) *New York New York 14 Jan 1974	9 Dec 1934	Fred G. Taylor	5
111	San Bernardino (California) *San Bernardino California 14 Jan 1974	3 Feb 1935	Albert Lyndon Larson	
112	North Idaho Falls (Idaho) *Idaho Falls North 29 May 1970 *Idaho Falls Idaho North 14 Jan 1974	12 May 1935	David Smith	
113	Oahu (Hawaii) *Laie Hawaii 14 Jan 1974	30 Jun 1935	Ralph E. Wooley	
114	Highland (Utah) *Salt Lake Highland 14 Jan 1974	8 Sep 1935	Marvin O. Ashton	
115	Bonneville (Utah) *Salt Lake Bonneville 14 Jan 1974	27 Oct 1935	Joseph L. Wirthlin	5
116	Pasadena (California) *San Fernando 15 Oct 1939 *Los Angeles California Van Nuys 14 Jan 1974	19 Apr 1936	David H. Cannon	
117	Long Beach (California) *Long Beach California 14 Jan 1974	3 May 1936	John W. Jones	
118	Chicago (Ill., Ind., Wis.) *Wilmette Illinois 14 Jan 1974	29 Nov 1936	William A. Matheson	3
119	Smithfield (Utah) *Smithfield Utah 14 Jan 1974	9 Jan 1938	Alfred W. Chambers	
120	Mt. Graham (Ariz., N.M.) *Safford Arizona 14 Jan 1974	20 Feb 1938	Spencer W. Kimball	
121	Phoenix (Arizona) *Phoenix Arizona 14 Jan 1974	27 Feb 1938	James Robert Price	

NO.	NAME, LOCALITY *NAME CHANGED †DISORGANIZED ★TRANSFERRED TO	ORGANIZED	PRESIDENT	NO. IN YEAR
122	Moon Lake (Utah) †10 Nov 1957 ★Duchesne (No. 62)	24 Apr 1938	Edwin L. Murphy	
123	Portland (Oregon) *Portland Oregon 14 Jan 1974	26 Jun 1938	Monte L. Bean	
124	Seattle (Washington) *Seattle Washington 14 Jan 1974	31 Jul 1938	Alex Brown	
125	Nampa (Idaho) *Nampa Idaho 14 Jan 1974	27 Nov 1938	Peter E. Johnson	
126	Weiser (Idaho) *Weiser Idaho 14 Jan 1974	27 Nov 1938	Scott B. Brown	8
127	Provo (Utah) *Provo Utah 14 Jan 1974	19 Feb 1939	Charles E. Rowan Jr.	
128	Pasadena (California) *Pasadena California 14 Jan 1974	1 Oct 1939	Bertram M. Jones	
129	Inglewood (California) *Los Angeles California Inglewood 14 Jan 1974	26 Nov 1939	Alfred E. Rohner	3
129	Emigration (Utah) *Salt Lake Emigration 14 Jan 1974	10 Mar 1940	George A. Christensen	
130	Riverside (Utah) *Salt Lake Riverside 14 Jan 1974	24 Mar 1940	John B. Matheson	
131	Washington (D.C., Pa., Md.) *Washington D.C. 14 Jan 1974	30 Jun 1940	Ezra Taft Benson	
132	Denver (Colorado) *Denver Colorado 14 Jan 1974	30 Jun 1940	Douglas M. Todd Jr.	
133	Big Cottonwood (Utah) *Cottonwood 11 Feb 1951 *Salt Lake Cottonwood 14 Jan 1974	20 Oct 1940	Irvin T. Nelson	
134	Uvada (Utah, Nevada) *Enterprise Utah 14 Jan 1974	15 Dec 1940	David J. Ronnow	6
135	Reno (Nevada, California) *Reno Nevada 14 Jan 1974	9 Feb 1941	Nathan T. Hurst	
136	San Diego (California) *San Diego California 14 Jan 1974	9 Feb 1941	Wallace W. Johnson	
137	Southern Arizona (Arizona) *Arizona South 29 May 1970 *St. David Arizona 14 Jan 1974	2 Mar 1941	A.B. Ballantyne	
138	South Salt Lake (Utah) *Salt Lake South 14 Jan 1974 *South Salt Lake 31 May 1979	2 Sep 1941	Axel J. Andresen	
139	South Ogden (Utah) *South Ogden Utah 14 Jan 1974	7 Dec 1941	William J. Critchlow	5
140	Farr West (Utah) *Ogden Utah Farr West 14 Jan 1974 *Ogden Utah Mound Fort 23 Sep 1984	18 Jan 1942	Wilmer J. Maw	
141	Lakeview (Utah) *Hooper Utah 14 Jan 1974	22 Mar 1942	John Child	
142	Mt. Jordan (Utah) *Draper Utah 14 Jan 1974	3 May 1942	Stanley A. Rasmussen	
143	Humboldt (Nevada) *Elko Nevada 14 Jan 1974	31 May 1942	Rodney S. Williams	4
144	Sugar House (Utah) *Salt Lake Sugar House 14 Jan 1974	16 May 1943	Thomas M. Sheeler	
145	Park (Utah) *Salt Lake Park 14 Jan 1974	24 Oct 1943	J. Percy Goddard	

NO.	NAME, LOCALITY *NAME CHANGED †DISORGANIZED ★TRANSFERRED TO	ORGANIZED	PRESIDENT	NO. IN YEAR
146	Ben Lomond (Utah)	21 Nov 1943	William Arthur Budge	
	*North Ogden Utah 14 Jan 1974			3
147	Grantsville (Utah)	16 Jan 1944	Paul E. Wrathall	
	*Grantsville Utah 14 Jan 1974			
147	North Box Elder (Utah)	12 Nov 1944	John P. Lillywhite	
	*Box Elder North 29 May 1970			
	*Brigham City Utah North 14 Jan 1974			
148	South Box Elder (Utah)	12 Nov 1944	Abel S. Rich	
	*Box Elder 30 Aug 1959			
	*Brigham City Utah Box Elder 14 Jan 1974			
				3
149	West Pocatello (Idaho)	6 May 1945	Twayne Austin	
	*Pocatello West 29 May 1970			
	*Pocatello Idaho West 14 Jan 1974			
150	East Millcreek (Utah)	17 Jun 1945	L.B. Gunderson	
	*Salt Lake East Millcreek 14 Jan 1974			
151	North Carbon (Utah)	24 Jun 1945	Cecil Broadbent	
	*Carbon North 29 May 1970			
	*Price Utah North 14 Jan 1974			
152	Davis (Utah)	14 Oct 1945	Leroy H. Duncan	
	*Farmington Utah 14 Jan 1974			
153	North Rexburg (Idaho)	28 Oct 1945	Orval O. Mortensen	
	*Rexburg North 29 May 1970			
	*Rexburg Idaho North 14 Jan 1974			5
154	Hillside (Utah)	13 Jan 1946	Casper Hugh Parker	
	*Salt Lake Hillside 14 Jan 1974			
155	Temple (Utah)	13 Jan 1946	Adiel F. Stewart	
	*Temple View 14 Apr 1946			
	*Salt Lake Temple View 14 Jan 1974			
	†24 June 1979 ★Salt Lake Wells (No. 105), Salt Lake Liberty (No. 53)			
156	Palo Alto (California)	23 Jun 1946	Claude B. Petersen	
	*Menlo Park California 14 Jan 1974			
157	South Idaho Falls (Idaho)	30 Jun 1946	Cecil E. Hart	
	*Idaho Falls South 29 May 1970			
	*Idaho Falls Idaho South 14 Jan 1974			
158	East Rigby (Idaho)	7 Jul 1946	James E. Ririe	
	*Rigby East 29 May 1970			
	*Rigby Idaho East 14 Jan 1974			
159	Berkeley (California)	13 Oct 1946	W. Glenn Harmon	
	†26 Aug 1956 ★Oakland-Berkeley (No. 227)			
160	Mt. Logan (Utah)	17 Nov 1946	A. George Raymond	
	*Logan Utah Mt. Logan 14 Jan 1974			
161	Mesa (Arizona)	8 Dec 1946	L.M. Mecham Jr.	
	*Mesa Arizona 14 Jan 1974			8
162	North Jordan (Utah)	12 Jan 1947	John B. Hill	
	*Jordan North 29 May 1970			
	*Salt Lake Jordan North 14 Jan 1974			
163	Florida (Florida, Georgia)	19 Jan 1947	Alvin C. Chace	
	*Jacksonville Florida West 14 Jan 1974			
164	East Cache (Utah)	2 Feb 1947	J. Howard Maughan	
	*Cache East 29 May 1970			
	*Logan Utah East 14 Jan 1974			
165	East Provo (Utah)	13 Apr 1947	Charles E. Rowan	
	*Provo East 29 May 1970			
	*Provo Utah East 14 Jan 1974			
166	Orem (Utah)	13 Apr 1947	Walter R. Holdaway	
	*Orem Utah 14 Jan 1974			

NO.	NAME, LOCALITY *NAME CHANGED †DISORGANIZED ★TRANSFERRED TO	ORGANIZED	PRESIDENT	NO. IN YEAR
167	West Utah (Utah) *Utah West 29 May 1970 *Provo Utah West 14 Jan 1974	4 May 1947	J. Earl Lewis	
168	Spokane (Washington) *Spokane Washington 14 Jan 1974	29 Jun 1947	Albert I. Morgan	
169	South Carolina (S.C., Georgia) *Columbia South Carolina 14 Jan 1974	19 Oct 1947	W. Wallace McBride	8
170	American Falls (Idaho) *American Falls Idaho 14 Jan 1974	1 Feb 1948	George R. Woolley	
171	San Joaquin (California) *Stockton California 14 Jan 1974	25 Apr 1948	Wendell B. Mendenhall	
172	Cedar (Utah) *Cedar City Utah 14 Jan 1974	2 May 1948	David L. Sargent	3
173	South Bear River (Utah) *Bear River South 29 May 1970 *Tremonton Utah 14 Jan 1974	1 May 1949	Cliston G.M. Kerr	
174	East Riverside (Utah) †9 Oct 1955 ★Riverside (No. 130)	22 May 1949	Thaddeus M. Evans	
175	Glendale (California) *Glendale California 14 Jan 1974	4 Dec 1949	Edwin Smith Dibble	3
176	Nyssa (Oregon, Idaho) *Nyssa Oregon 14 Jan 1974	8 Jan 1950	Arvel L. Child	
177	East Long Beach (California) *Long Beach East 29 May 1970 *Long Beach California East 14 Jan 1974	12 Feb 1950	John C. Dalton	
178	University (Utah) *University 1st 30 Apr 1967 *Salt Lake University 1st 14 Jan 1974	12 Feb 1950	J. Quayle Ward	
179	East Los Angeles (California) *Los Angeles East 29 May 1970 *Los Angeles California East 14 Jan 1974	26 Feb 1950	Fauntleroy Hunsaker	
180	Richland (Washington, Oregon) *Richland Washington 14 Jan 1974	25 Jun 1950	James V. Thompson	5
181	Santa Rosa (California) *Santa Rosa California 14 Jan 1974	7 Jan 1951	J. LeRoy Murdock	
182	Wilford (Utah) *Salt Lake Wilford 14 Jan 1974	11 Feb 1951	George Z. Aposhian	
183	Murray (Utah) *Murray Utah 14 Jan 1974	11 Feb 1951	Oral J. Wilkinson	
184	Santa Barbara (California) *Santa Barbara California 14 Jan 1974	18 Mar 1951	Arthur J. Godfrey	
185	Fresno (California) *Fresno California 14 Jan 1974	20 May 1951	Alwyn C. Sessions	
186	Bakersfield (California) *Bakersfield California 14 Jan 1974	27 May 1951	E. Alan Pettit	
187	Monument Park (Utah) *Salt Lake Monument Park 14 Jan 1974	24 Jun 1951	George L. Nelson	
188	Santa Monica (California) *Los Angeles California Santa Monica 14 Jan 1974	1 Jul 1951	E. Garrett Barlow	
189	East Lethbridge (Canada) *Lethbridge 15 Nov 1953 *Lethbridge Alberta 14 Jan 1974	28 Oct 1951	Grant G. Woolley	
190	Columbia River (Oregon, Washington) *Portland Oregon East 14 Jan 1974	2 Dec 1951	R. Spencer Papworth	
191	Willamette (Oregon) *Eugene Oregon 14 Jan 1974	2 Dec 1951	Ralph B. Lake	11

NO.	NAME, LOCALITY *NAME CHANGED †DISORGANIZED ★TRANSFERRED TO	ORGANIZED	PRESIDENT	NO. IN YEAR
192	Gooding (Idaho) *Jerome Idaho 14 Jan 1974	9 Mar 1952	Ross C. Lee	
193	Bountiful (Utah) *Bountiful Utah 14 Jan 1974	23 Mar 1952	Thomas Amby Briggs	
194	El Paso (Texas, New Mexico) *El Paso Texas 14 Jan 1974	21 Sep 1952	Edward V. Turley Sr.	
195	Tacoma (Washington) *Tacoma Washington 14 Jan 1974	28 Sep 1952	Elvin E. Evans	
196	Mt. Rubidoux (California) *Riverside California 14 Jan 1974	26 Oct 1952	Vern Robert Peel	
197	Detroit (Michigan, Ohio, Canada) *Bloomfield Hills Michigan 14 Jan 1974	9 Nov 1952	George W. Romney	
198	Lorin Farr (Utah) *Ogden Utah Lorin Farr 14 Jan 1974	16 Nov 1952	Elton W. Wardle	
199	East Ogden (Utah) *Ogden East 29 May 1970 *Ogden Utah East 14 Jan 1974	23 Nov 1952	Scott B. Price	
200	East Sharon (Utah) *Sharon East 29 May 1970 *Provo Utah Sharon East 14 Jan 1974	23 Nov 1952	Henry D. Taylor	
201	Riverdale (Utah) *Ogden Utah Riverdale 14 Jan 1974	30 Nov 1952	Rudolph L. VanKampen	
202	San Jose (California) *San Jose California 14 Jan 1974	30 Nov 1952	Vernard L. Beckstrand	11
203	Layton (Utah) *Layton Utah 14 Jan 1974	25 Jan 1953	I. Haven Barlow	
204	Cannon (Utah) *Salt Lake Cannon 14 Jan 1974	1 Mar 1953	Fred H. Peck	
205	Klamath (Oregon, California) *Klamath Falls Oregon 14 Jan 1974	22 Mar 1953	Carroll William Smith	
206	North Tooele (Utah) *Tooele North 29 May 1970 *Tooele Utah North 14 Jan 1974	29 Mar 1953	Orland T. Barrus	
207	North Pocatello (Idaho) *Pocatello North 29 May 1970 *Pocatello Idaho North 14 Jan 1974	21 Jun 1953	Jared O. Anderson	
208	Butte (Montana) *Butte Montana 14 Jan 1974	28 Jun 1953	Edgar T. Henderson	
209	Houston (Texas, Louisiana) *Houston Texas 14 Jan 1974	11 Oct 1953	Jack Byron Trunnell	
210	Dallas (Texas) *Dallas Texas 14 Jan 1974	18 Oct 1953	Ervin W. Atkerson	
211	Salmon River (Idaho) *Salmon Idaho 14 Jan 1974	18 Oct 1953	Earl Stokes	
211	Calgary (Canada) *Calgary Alberta 14 Jan 1974	15 Nov 1953	N. Eldon Tanner	10
212	East Phoenix (Arizona) *Phoenix East 29 May 1970 *Phoenix Arizona East 14 Jan 1974	28 Feb 1954	Junius E. Driggs	
213	Grand Coulee (Washington) *Moses Lake Washington 14 Jan 1974	18 Apr 1954	Elmo J. Bergeson	
214	South Blackfoot (Idaho) *Blackfoot South 1 Mar 1970 *Blackfoot Idaho South 14 Jan 1974	20 Jun 1954	Lawrence T. Lambert	
215	Orange County (California) *Fullerton 14 Mar 1965 *Placentia California 14 Jan 1974	27 Jun 1954	John C. Dalton	

	NAME, LOCALITY *NAME CHANGED †DISORGANIZED			NO. IN
NO.	★TRANSFERRED TO	ORGANIZED	PRESIDENT	YEAR
216	Las Vegas (Nevada) *Las Vegas Nevada 14 Jan 1974	10 Oct 1954	Thomas Gay Meyers	
217	Taylorsville (Utah) *Taylorsville Utah 14 Jan 1974	10 Oct 1954	Wayne Charles Player	
218	West Boise (Idaho) *Boise West 29 May 1970 *Boise Idaho West 14 Jan 1974	7 Nov 1954	David Keith Ricks	
219	North Sacramento (California) *Sacramento North 30 Sep 1969 *Sacramento California North 14 Jan 1974	12 Dec 1954	Austin G. Hunt	
				8
220	Redondo (California) *Torrance California North 14 Jan 1974	29 May 1955	Leslie L. Prestwich	
221	New Orleans (Louisiana) *New Orleans Louisiana 14 Jan 1974	19 Jun 1955	Clive M. Larson	
222	Honolulu (Hawaii, Guam) *Honolulu Hawaii 14 Jan 1974	28 Aug 1955	J. A. Quealy Jr.	
222	Rose Park (Utah) *Salt Lake Rose Park 14 Jan 1974	9 Oct 1955	Joseph F. Steenblik	
223	Grand Junction (Colorado) *Grand Junction Colorado 14 Jan 1974	16 Oct 1955	Loyal B. Cook	
224	East Mesa (Arizona)* *Mesa East 29 May 1970 *Mesa Arizona East 14 Jan 1974	20 Nov 1955	Donald Ellsworth	
				6
225	Brigham Young University (Utah) *Brigham Young University 1st 14 Jan 1974	8 Jan 1956	Antone K. Romney	
226	Covina (California) *Covina California 14 Jan 1974	26 Feb 1956	Elden L. Ord	
227	Holladay (Utah) *Salt Lake Holladay 14 Jan 1974	18 Mar 1956	G. Carlos Smith Jr.	
228	Lake Mead (Nevada, Arizona, Calif.) *Henderson Nevada 14 Jan 1974	19 Aug 1956	James I. Gibson	
227	Oakland-Berkeley (California) *Oakland California 14 Jan 1974	26 Aug 1956	O. Leslie Stone	
228	Hayward (California) *Hayward California 14 Jan 1974	26 Aug 1956	Milton P. Ream	
229	Walnut Creek (California) *Walnut Creek California 14 Jan 1974	26 Aug 1956	Emery R. Ranker	
230	Reseda (California) *Los Angeles California Chatsworth 14 Jan 1974	16 Sep 1956	Hugh C. Smith	
231	Burbank (California) *Los Angeles California North Hollywood 14 Jan 1974	16 Sep 1956	James D. Pratt	
232	Flagstaff (Arizona) *Flagstaff Arizona 14 Jan 1974	23 Sep 1956	Burton R. Smith	
233	Spanish Fork (Utah) *Spanish Fork 14 Jan 1974	30 Sep 1956	Joseph Y. Toronto	
234	Kansas City (Missouri, Kansas) *Kansas City Missouri 14 Jan 1974	21 Oct 1956	Martin V. Witbeck	
235	Springville (Utah) *Springville Utah 14 Jan 1974	21 Oct 1956	Leo A. Crandall	
236	Valley View (Utah) *Salt Lake Valley View 14 Jan 1974	28 Oct 1956	Lamont B. Gundersen	
237	Canyon Rim (Utah) *Salt Lake Canyon Rim 14 Jan 1974	28 Oct 1956	Verl F. Scott	
238	Tucson (Arizona) *Tucson Arizona 14 Jan 1974	2 Dec 1956	Leslie Odell Brewer	
239	Ashley (Utah) *Vernal Utah Ashley 14 Jan 1974	2 Dec 1956	William Budge Wallis	17

NO.	NAME, LOCALITY *NAME CHANGED †DISORGANIZED ★TRANSFERRED TO	ORGANIZED	PRESIDENT	NO. IN YEAR
240	Murray South (Utah) *Murray Utah South 14 Jan 1974	28 Apr 1957	Donald W. Challis	
241	Atlanta (Georgia) *Atlanta Georgia 14 Jan 1974 *Tucker Georgia 1 Sep 1974	5 May 1957	William L. Nicholls	
242	North Seattle (Washington) *Seattle North 29 May 1970 *Seattle Washington North 14 Jan 1974	19 May 1957	Wilford H. Payne	
243	Missoula (Montana) *Missoula Montana 14 Jan 1974	16 Jun 1957	Grant K. Patten	
244	Great Falls (Montana) *Great Falls Montana 14 Jan 1974	16 Jun 1957	Victor Bowen	
245	Virginia (Virginia, North Carolina) *Richmond Virginia 14 Jan 1974	30 Jun 1957	Cashell Donahoe Sr.	
246	Midvale (Utah) *Midvale Utah 14 Jan 1974	30 Jun 1957	Reed H. Beckstead	
247	San Mateo (California) *Pacifica California 14 Jan 1974 †21 Feb 1982 ★San Francisco California (No. 99)	15 Sep 1957	Melvin P. Pickering	
248	San Luis Obispo (California) *San Luis Obispo California 14 Jan 1974	22 Sep 1957	Arthur J. Godfrey	
249	Monument Park West (Utah) *Salt Lake Foothill 14 Jan 1974	29 Sep 1957	Frank Carl Berg	
250	Albuquerque (New Mexico) *Albuquerque New Mexico 14 Jan 1974	27 Oct 1957	William J. Wilson	
251	Orem West (Utah) *Orem Utah West 14 Jan 1974 *Orem Utah Geneva Heights 5 Apr 1988	3 Nov 1957	Edward C. Bunker	
251	Santa Ana (California) *Orange California 14 Jan 1974	8 Dec 1957	Karl C. Durham	13
252	San Antonio (Texas) *San Antonio Texas 14 Jan 1974	19 Jan 1958	Roland C. Bremer	
253	Phoenix North (Arizona) *Phoenix Arizona North 14 Jan 1974	19 Jan 1958	Rudger G. Smith	
254	Shreveport (Louisiana, Texas) *Shreveport Louisiana 14 Jan 1974	26 Jan 1958	J. Milton Belisle	
255	Kearns (Utah) *Kearns Utah 14 Jan 1974	2 Feb 1958	Merrill A. Nelson	
256	Kearns North (Utah) *Kearns Utah North 14 Jan 1974	2 Feb 1958	Volma W. Heaton	
257	Orlando (Florida) *Orlando Florida 14 Jan 1974	23 Feb 1958	W. Leonard Duggar	
258	Monterey Bay (California) *Monterey California 14 Jan 1974	2 Mar 1958	James N. Wallace Jr.	
259	Utah State University (Utah) *Logan Utah University 1st 14 Jan 1974	13 Apr 1958	Reed Bullen	
260	Bountiful North (Utah) *Bountiful Utah North 14 Jan 1974	20 Apr 1958	Henry E. Peterson	
261	San Diego East (California) *San Diego California El Cajon 14 Jan 1974 *El Cajon California 30 Nov 1975	20 Apr 1958	Cecil I. Burningham	
262	Bountiful South (Utah) *Bountiful Utah South 14 Jan 1974	20 Apr 1958	Ward C. Holbrook	
263	Yuma (Arizona, California) *Yuma Arizona 14 Jan 1974	27 Apr 1958	Marion Turley	
264	Auckland (New Zealand) *Auckland New Zealand Mt. Roskill 14 Jan 1974	18 May 1958	George R. Biesinger	
265	St. Louis (Missouri, Illinois) *St. Louis Missouri 14 Jan 1974	1 Jun 1958	Roy N. Oscarson	

NO.	NAME, LOCALITY *NAME CHANGED †DISORGANIZED ★TRANSFERRED TO	ORGANIZED	PRESIDENT	NO. IN YEAR
266	Granger (Utah) *Salt Lake Granger 14 Jan 1974	8 Jun 1958	Wm. Grant Bangerter	
267	Olympus (Utah) *Salt Lake Olympus 14 Jan 1974	29 Jun 1958	Heber E. Peterson	
268	Lewiston (Idaho, Wash.) *Lewiston Idaho 14 Jan 1974	19 Oct 1958	Golden Romney	
269	Norwalk (California) *Cerritos California 14 Jan 1974	26 Oct 1958	Lewis Milton Jones	
270	Cincinnati (Ohio, Kentucky) *Cincinnati Ohio 14 Jan 1974	23 Nov 1958	Thomas Blair Evans	
271	West Sharon (Utah) *Sharon West 29 May 1970 *Orem Utah Sharon West 14 Jan 1974 *Orem Utah Cherry Hill 15 Apr 1988	30 Nov 1958	Clyde M. Lunceford	
272	Weber Heights (Utah) *Ogden Utah Weber Heights 14 Jan 1974	30 Nov 1958	Keith W. Wilcox	
273	Parleys (Utah) *Salt Lake Parleys 14 Jan 1974	7 Dec 1958	Walter J. Eldredge Jr.	22
274	Winder (Utah) *Salt Lake Winder 14 Jan 1974	25 Jan 1959	M. Elmer Christensen	
275	Granite Park (Utah) *Salt Lake Granite Park 14 Jan 1974 †31 May 1979 ★South Salt Lake (No. 138)	22 Feb 1959	Rolf Christiansen	
276	Sandy (Utah) *Sandy Utah 14 Jan 1974	12 Apr 1959	Stanley A. Rasmussen	
277	Clearfield (Utah) *Clearfield Utah 14 Jan 1974	12 Apr 1959	George Smith Haslam	
278	Pocatello (Idaho) *Pocatello Idaho 14 Jan 1974	19 Apr 1959	Roland K. Hart	
279	Huntington Park (California) *Huntington Park California 14 Jan 1974 *Downey California 18 Feb 1986	19 Apr 1959	Clifford B. Wright	
280	Whittier (California) *Whittier California 14 Jan 1974	26 Apr 1959	John Collings	
281	West Covina (California) *La Puente California 14 Jan 1974 *Walnut California 23 July 1985	3 May 1959	Mark W. Smith	
282	Torrance (California) *Torrance California 14 Jan 1974	3 May 1959	Roland Earl Gagon	
283	Indianapolis (Indiana) *Indianapolis Indiana 14 Jan 1974	17 May 1959	Phillip F. Low	
284	Yakima (Washington) *Yakima Washington 14 Jan 1974	24 May 1959	F. Edgar Johnson	
285	East Idaho Falls (Idaho) *Idaho Falls East 29 May 1970 *Idaho Falls Idaho East 14 Jan 1974	7 Jun 1959	Charles P. Birzee	
286	Cheyenne (Wyoming, Colorado) *Cheyenne Wyoming 14 Jan 1974	21 Jun 1959	Archie R. Boyack	
287	Denver West (Colorado) *Arvada Colorado 14 Jan 1974	21 Jun 1959	Thomas L. Kimball	
288	Mojave (California) *Barstow California 14 Jan 1974	16 Aug 1959	Sterling A. Johnson	
289	Tampa (Florida) *Tampa Florida 14 Jan 1974	25 Oct 1959	Edwin H. White	
290	American River (California) *Sacramento California East 14 Jan 1974	6 Dec 1959	Austin G. Hunt	17
291	University West (Utah) *Salt Lake Central 14 Jan 1974	7 Feb 1960	Lemonte Peterson	

NO.	NAME, LOCALITY *NAME CHANGED †DISORGANIZED ★TRANSFERRED TO	ORGANIZED	PRESIDENT	NO. IN YEAR
292	New Jersey (New Jersey) *Caldwell New Jersey 14 Jan 1974 *Morristown New Jersey 26 Feb 1976	28 Feb 1960	George H. Mortimer	
293	Sydney (Australia) * Sydney Australia Greenwich 14 Jan 1974	27 Mar 1960	Dell C. Hunt	
294	Manchester (England) *Manchester England 14 Jan 1974	27 Mar 1960	Robert G. Larson	
295	Brigham Young University 2nd (Utah)	17 Apr 1960	Bryan W. Belnap	
296	Brigham Young University 3rd (Utah)	17 Apr 1960	William Noble Waite	
297	Napa (California) *Napa California 14 Jan 1974	17 Apr 1960	Harry S. Cargun	
298	Tulsa (Okla., Ark., Kan.) *Tulsa Oklahoma 14 Jan 1974	1 May 1960	Robert N. Sears	
299	Puget Sound (Washington) *Bremerton Washington 14 Jan 1974	19 Jun 1960	Herbert S. Anderson	
300	Toronto (Canada) *Toronto Ontario 14 Jan 1974	14 Aug 1960	William M. Davies	
301	Pikes Peak (Colorado, New Mexico) *Colorado Springs Colorado 14 Jan 1974	11 Sep 1960	Ralph M. Gardner	
302	Taber (Canada) *Taber Alberta 14 Jan 1974	11 Sep 1960	Ray B. Evenson	
303	Riverton (Utah) *Riverton Utah 14 Jan 1974	18 Sep 1960	J. Harold Berrett	
304	Philadelphia (Penn., Del., Md., N.J.) *Philadelphia Pennsylvania 14 Jan 1974	16 Oct 1960	Bryant F. West	
305	Oklahoma (Oklahoma) *Oklahoma City Oklahoma 14 Jan 1974	23 Oct 1960	James A. Cullimore	
306	Brisbane (Australia) *Brisbane Australia 14 Jan 1974	23 Oct 1960	William E. Waters	
307	Melbourne (Australia) *Melbourne Australia Fairfield 14 Jan 1974	30 Oct 1960	Boyd C. Bott	
308	Las Vegas North (Nevada) *North Las Vegas Nevada 14 Jan 1974	6 Nov 1960	William L. Taylor	
309	Palomar (California) *Carlsbad California 14 Jan 1974	6 Nov 1960	Wallace F. Gray	
310	Hamilton (New Zealand) *Hamilton New Zealand 14 Jan 1974	13 Nov 1960	Wendell H. Wiser	
311	Miami (Florida) *Miami Florida 14 Jan 1974	13 Nov 1960	Paul R. Cheesman	
312	Edmonton (Canada) *Edmonton Alberta 14 Jan 1974 *Edmonton Alberta Riverbend 6 Nov 1983	15 Nov 1960	Leroy Rollins	
313	Hawkes Bay (New Zealand) *Hastings New Zealand 14 Jan 1974	20 Nov 1960	Joseph Alvin Higbee	
314	Ben Lomond South (Utah) *Ogden Utah North 14 Jan 1974	20 Nov 1960	Robert M. Yorgason	
315	Vancouver (Canada) *Vancouver British Columbia 14 Jan 1974	21 Nov 1960	Ernest E. Jensen	
316	Cedar West (Utah) *Cedar City Utah West 14 Jan 1974	27 Nov 1960	Franklin D. Day	
317	Minnesota (Minnesota, Wisconsin) *Minneapolis Minnesota 14 Jan 1974	29 Nov 1960	Delbert F. Wright	
318	Winter Quarters (Nebraska, Iowa) *Omaha Nebraska 14 Jan 1974	11 Dec 1960	William D. Hardy	
319	Redding (California) *Redding California 14 Jan 1974	13 Dec 1960	Albert C. Peterson	29
320	Craig (Colorado) *Meeker Colorado 14 Jan 1974	15 Jan 1961	Loyal B. Cook	

NO.	NAME, LOCALITY *NAME CHANGED †DISORGANIZED ★TRANSFERRED TO	ORGANIZED	PRESIDENT	NO. IN YEAR
321	Salem (Oregon)	22 Jan 1961	Hugh F. Webb	
	*Salem Oregon 14 Jan 1974			
322	St. George East (Utah)	5 Feb 1961	Rudger C. Atkin	
	*St. George Utah East 14 Jan 1974			
323	London (England)	26 Feb 1961	Donald W. Hemingway	
	*London England 14 Jan 1974			
	†28 May 1978 ★London England Hyde Park (No. 928), London England Wandsworth (No. 929), Staines England (No. 931)			
324	Granger North (Utah)	26 Feb 1961	Frankland J. Kennard	
	*Salt Lake Granger North 14 Jan 1974			
325	Leicester (England)	5 Mar 1961	Derek A. Cuthbert	
	*Leicester England 14 Jan 1974			
326	Holland (Holland)	12 Mar 1961	Johan Paul Jongkees	
	*The Hague Holland 14 Jan 1974			
	*The Hague Netherlands 12 Aug 1976			
327	Leeds (England)	19 Mar 1961	Dennis Liversey	
	*Huddersfield England 14 Jan 1974			
328	Roy (Utah)	26 Mar 1961	Henry Adolph Matis	
	*Roy Utah 14 Jan 1974			
329	San Leandro (California)	21 May 1961	Milton R. Ream	
	*San Leandro California 14 Jan 1974			
330	Garden Grove (California)	25 Jun 1961	James Malan Hobbs	
	*Garden Grove California 14 Jan 1974			
331	Alaska (Alaska)	13 Aug 1961	Orson P. Millett	
	*Anchorage Alaska 14 Jan 1974			
332	North Carolina (North Carolina)	27 Aug 1961	Cecil E. Reese	
	*Kinston North Carolina 14 Jan 1974			
333	Beaumont (Texas, Louisiana)	3 Sep 1961	Alden C. Stout	
	*Beaumont Texas 14 Jan 1974			
334	Berlin (Germany)	10 Sep 1961	Rudi Seehagen	
	*Berlin Germany 14 Jan 1974			
335	Greensboro (North Carolina)	13 Sep 1961	Eugene A. Gulledge	
	*Greensboro North Carolina 14 Jan 1974			
336	Cleveland (Ohio, Pennsylvania)	20 Sep 1961	E. Doyle Robison	
	*Cleveland Ohio 14 Jan 1974			
337	Canoga Park (California)	8 Oct 1961	Collins E. Jones	
	*Los Angeles California Canoga Park 14 Jan 1974			
338	Redwood (California, Oregon)	22 Oct 1961	David DeBar Felshaw	
	*Eureka California 14 Jan 1974			
339	Reno North (Nevada, California)	22 Oct 1961	Vern Waldo	
	*Sparks Nevada 14 Jan 1974			
340	Stuttgart (Germany)	26 Oct 1961	Hermann Moessner	
	*Stuttgart Germany 14 Jan 1974			
341	Swiss (Switzerland, Germany)	28 Oct 1961	Wilhelm Friedrich Lauener	
	*Zurich Switzerland 14 Jan 1974			
342	Hamburg (Germany)	12 Nov 1961	Michael Panitsch	
	*Hamburg Germany 14 Jan 1974			
343	Ammon (Idaho)	26 Nov 1961	Harold W. Davis	
	*Idaho Falls Idaho Ammon 14 Jan 1974			
344	*Mexico (Mexico)	3 Dec 1961	Harold Brown	
	*Mexico City May 1967			
	*Mexico City Mexico 14 Jan 1974			
	†8 Nov 1975 ★Mexico City Mexico Churubusco (No. 716), Mexico City Mexico Tacubaya (No. 717), Mexico City Mexico Ermita (No. 718), Mexico City Mexico Chapultepec (No. 1357)			
345	South Cottonwood (Utah)	10 Dec 1961	James S. McCloy	
	*Salt Lake South Cottonwood 14 Jan 1974			

26

346	Cumorah (New York)	21 Jan 1962	Bryant W. Rossiter	
	*Rochester New York 14 Jan 1974			

NO.	NAME, LOCALITY *NAME CHANGED †DISORGANIZED ★TRANSFERRED TO	ORGANIZED	PRESIDENT	NO. IN YEAR
347	Pomona (California) *La Verne California 14 Jan 1974	21 Jan 1962	Vern R. Peel	
348	Pearl Harbor (Hawaii) *Honolulu Hawaii West 14 Jan 1974	4 Feb 1962	George Q. Cannon	
349	Lansing (Michigan) *Lansing Michigan 14 Jan 1974	18 Feb 1962	Sylvan H. Wittwer	
350	Kaysville (Utah) *Kaysville Utah 14 Jan 1974	18 Feb 1962	Alan B. Blood	
351	Columbus (Ohio) *Columbus Ohio 14 Jan 1974	25 Feb 1962	James L. Mortensen	
352	Ft. Wayne (Indiana, Ohio) *Ft. Wayne Indiana 14 Jan 1974	4 Mar 1962	Howard W. Thompson	
353	Apia (Western Samoa) *Apia Samoa 14 Jan 1974	18 Mar 1962	Percy John Rivers	
354	Boston (Mass., N. H., R.I.) *Boston Massachusetts 14 Jan 1974	20 May 1962	Wilbur W. Cox	
355	Wichita (Kansas, Oklahoma) *Wichita Kansas 14 Jan 1974	24 Jun 1962	Lee R. Meador	
356	Glasgow (Scotland) *Glasgow Scotland 14 Jan 1974	26 Aug 1962	Archibald R. Richardson	
357	Casper (Wyoming) *Casper Wyoming 14 Jan 1974	14 Oct 1962	W. Reed Green	
358	Wind River (Wyoming) *Riverton Wyoming 14 Jan 1974	14 Oct 1962	J. Rex Kocherhans	
359	Coeur d'Alene (Idaho) *Coeur d'Alene Idaho 14 Jan 1974	14 Oct 1962	Gerald E. Browning	
360	San Diego South (California) *San Diego California South 14 Jan 1974 *Lemon Grove California 16 Aug 1983 *San Diego California Sweetwater 30 Aug 1988	21 Oct 1962	Cecil I. Burningham	
361	Butler (Utah) *Salt Lake Butler 14 Jan 1974	18 Nov 1962	James C. Taylor	
362	Mesa South (Arizona) *Mesa Arizona South 14 Jan 1974	18 Nov 1962	Stanley F. Turley	
363	Raleigh (North Carolina) *Raleigh North Carolina 14 Jan 1974	9 Dec 1962	William V. Bartholomew	
364	Scottsdale (Arizona) *Scottsdale Arizona 14 Jan 1974	9 Dec 1962	Junius E. Driggs	19
365	Sandy East (Utah) *Sandy Utah East 14 Jan 1974	13 Jan 1963	Orren J. Greenwood	
366	South Carolina West (S.C., N.C.) *Greenville 19 Nov 1972 *Greenville South Carolina 14 Jan 1974	27 Jan 1963	Ivan A. Larsen	
367	Milwaukee (Wisconsin) *Milwaukee Wisconsin 14 Jan 1974	3 Feb 1963	DeWitt C. Smith	
368	Chicago South (Illinois, Indiana) *Naperville Illinois 14 Jan 1974	3 Feb 1963	Lysle R. Cahoon	
369	Billings (Montana, Wyoming) *Billings Montana 14 Jan 1974	10 Feb 1963	Howard C. Anderson	
370	Illinois (Illinois) *Champaign Illinois 14 Jan 1974	17 Feb 1963	Ross A. Kelley	
371	Washington Terrace (Utah) *Washington Terrace Utah 14 Jan 1974	24 Feb 1963	Ernest B. Wheeler	
372	Potomac (Virginia, D.C., Md.) *Oakton Virginia 14 Jan 1974	3 Mar 1963	Miller F. Shurtleff	
373	Macon (Georgia, Alabama) *Macon Georgia 14 Jan 1974	10 Mar 1963	Rayford L. Henderson	

	NAME, LOCALITY *NAME CHANGED †DISORGANIZED			NO. IN
NO.	★TRANSFERRED TO	ORGANIZED	PRESIDENT	YEAR
374	Sunderland (England) *Sunderland England 14 Jan 1974	17 Mar 1963	Fred W. Oates	
375	South Box Elder (Utah) *Box Elder South 29 May 1970 *Brigham City Utah South 14 Jan 1974	28 Apr 1963	LeGrande Tea	
376	American Fork (Utah) *American Fork Utah 14 Jan 1974	12 May 1963	Stanley D. Roberts	
377	Alameda (Idaho) *Pocatello Idaho Alameda 14 Jan 1974 *Pocatello Idaho Highland 17 Jun 1984	12 May 1963	Homer S. Satterfield	
378	Concord (California) *Concord California 14 Jan 1974	23 Jun 1963	Ted Eugene Madsen	
379	Cascade (Washington) *Mt. Vernon Washington 14 Jan 1974	30 Jun 1963	Robert E. Jones	
380	Phoenix West (Arizona) *Phoenix Arizona West 14 Jan 1974	1 Sep 1963	Keith W. Hubbard	
381	Fresno East (California) *Fresno California East 14 Jan 1974	15 Sep 1963	Melvin P. Leavitt	
382	Brigham City (Utah) *Brigham City Utah 14 Jan 1974	22 Sep 1963	Lawrence C. Taylor	
383	Bountiful East (Utah) *Bountiful Utah East 14 Jan 1974	29 Sep 1963	Rendell N. Mabey	
384	Santa Maria (California) *Santa Maria California 14 Jan 1974	20 Oct 1963	Clayton K. Call	
385	Corvallis (Oregon) *Corvallis Oregon 14 Jan 1974	3 Nov 1963	Hugh F. Webb	
386	Portland West (Oregon) *Beaverton Oregon 14 Jan 1974	10 Nov 1963	C. Carlile Carlson	
387	San Jose West (California) *Saratoga California 14 Jan 1974	10 Nov 1963	Louis W. Latimer	
388	Seattle East (Washington) *Bellevue Washington 14 Jan 1974	1 Dec 1963	Raymond W. Eldredge	
389	North Columbia (Washington) *Columbia River North 29 May 1970 *Vancouver Washington 14 Jan 1974	1 Dec 1963	Wallace V. Teuscher	25
390	Hunter (Utah) *Salt Lake Hunter 14 Jan 1974	5 Jan 1964	Eldon Verne Breeze	
391	Tempe (Arizona) *Tempe Arizona 14 Jan 1974	2 Feb 1964	George Isaac Dana	
392	Norfolk (Virginia, North Carolina) *Norfolk Virginia 14 Jan 1974	12 Apr 1964	Walter H. Hick	
393	Mt. Olympus (Utah) *Salt Lake Mt. Olympus 14 Jan 1974	12 Apr 1964	Orin R. Woodbury	
394	Denver South (Colorado) *Lakewood Colorado 14 Jan 1974	19 Apr 1964	R. Raymond Barnes	
395	Brigham Young University 4th (Utah)	3 May 1964	William R. Siddoway	
396	Brigham Young University 5th (Utah)	3 May 1964	A. Harold Goodman	
397	Brigham Young University 6th (Utah)	3 May 1964	Wayne B. Hales	
398	Corpus Christi (Texas) *Corpus Christi Texas 14 Jan 1974	31 May 1964	Clarence Cottam	
399	Modesto (California) *Modesto California 14 Jan 1974	7 Jun 1964	Clifton A. Rooker	
400	Medford (Oregon, California) *Medford Oregon 14 Jan 1974	23 Aug 1964	Dennis R. Hassell	11
401	Las Vegas East (Nevada) *Las Vegas Nevada East 14 Jan 1974 *Las Vegas Nevada Paradise 30 Apr 1978	24 Jan 1965	Rulon A. Earl	
402	Anaheim (California) *Anaheim California 14 Jan 1974	14 Mar 1965	Max V. Eliason	

NO.	NAME, LOCALITY *NAME CHANGED †DISORGANIZED ★TRANSFERRED TO	ORGANIZED	PRESIDENT	NO. IN YEAR
403	Memphis (Tenn., Mo., Ark., Miss.) *Memphis Tennessee 14 Jan 1974	18 Apr 1965	Richard Stoddard	
404	Jackson (Mississippi) *Jackson Mississippi 14 Jan 1974	2 May 1965	Neil J. Ferrell	
405	Ricks College (Idaho) *Ricks College 1st 1 Jun 1969 *Rexburg Idaho College 1st 14 Jan 1974	7 May 1965	J. Wendell Stucki	
406	Idaho State University (Idaho) Pocatello Idaho University 14 Jan 1974	9 May 1965	Robert E. Thompson	
407	Wellington (New Zealand) *Wellington New Zealand 14 Jan 1974	12 May 1965	Keith A. Harrison	
408	Hattiesburg (Mississippi) *Hattiesburg Mississippi 14 Jan 1974	27 Jun 1965	Edwin White	
409	North Boise (Idaho) *Boise North Jan 1966 *Boise Idaho North 14 Jan 1974	26 Sep 1965	L. Alden Porter	
410	Oquirrh East (Utah) *Magna Utah East 14 Jan 1974	17 Oct 1965	William B. Martin	
411	Taylorsville West (Utah) *Taylorsville Utah West 14 Jan 1974	31 Oct 1965	Richard A. Barker	
412	Rose Park North (Utah) *Salt Lake Rose Park North 14 Jan 1974	28 Nov 1965	Joseph L. Lundstrom	
				12
413	College of Southern Utah (Utah) *Southern Utah State College 12 Oct 1969 *Cedar City Utah College 14 Jan 1974	6 Jan 1966	Robert B. White Jr.	
414	Adelaide (Australia) *Adelaide Australia 14 Jan 1974 *Adelaide Australia Payneham 23 Apr 1978 *Adelaide Australia Marion 6 Jan 1982	23 Feb 1966	Dudley Russell Tredrea	
415	Rialto (California) *Rialto California 14 Jan 1974	20 Mar 1966	Wayne A. Reeves	
416	Calgary North (Canada) *Calgary Alberta North 14 Jan 1974	17 Apr 1966	Gerald E. Melchin	
417	Sao Paulo (Brazil) *Sao Paulo Brazil 14 Jan 1974	1 May 1966	Walter Spat	
418	Butler West (Utah) *Salt Lake Butler West 14 Jan 1974	8 May 1966	Sherman M. Crump	
419	Cedar Rapids (Iowa, Illinois) *Cedar Rapids Iowa 14 Jan 1974	29 May 1966	Richard F. Hagland	
420	Huntington Beach (California) *Huntington Beach California 14 Jan 1974	5 Jun 1966	Conway W. Nielsen	
421	Hartford (Conn., Mass.) *Hartford Connecticut 14 Jan 1974	18 Sep 1966	Hugh S. West	
422	Albuquerque East (New Mexico) *Albuquerque New Mexico East 14 Jan 1974	25 Sep 1966	George Van Lemmon	
423	Buenos Aires (Argentina) *Buenos Aires Argentina East 14 Jan 1974	20 Nov 1966	Angel Abrea	
424	Sunset (Utah) *Sunset Utah 14 Jan 1974	11 Dec 1966	John L. Nicholas	
425	Fremont (California) *Fremont California 14 Jan 1974	11 Dec 1966	Francis B. Winkel	13
426	Grand Coulee North (Washington) *Quincy Washington 14 Jan 1974 *Wenatchee Washington 7 Dec 1978	29 Jan 1967	Leslie H. Boyce	
427	Utah State University 2nd (Utah) *Logan Utah University 2nd 14 Jan 1974	12 Feb 1967	Reynold K. Watkins	
428	Fair Oaks (California) *Fair Oaks California 14 Jan 1974	12 Feb 1967	Harvey Stansell Greer	

NO.	NAME, LOCALITY *NAME CHANGED †DISORGANIZED ★TRANSFERRED TO	ORGANIZED	PRESIDENT	NO. IN YEAR
429	New Jersey Central (N.J., Penn.) *East Brunswick New Jersey 14 Jan 1974	26 Mar 1967	Robert H. Daines	
430	Arlington (California) *Riverside California West 14 Jan 1974	23 Apr 1967	Clarence Leon Sirrine	
431	Brigham Young University 7th (Utah)	30 Apr 1967	Dean A. Peterson	
432	Brigham Young University 8th (Utah)	30 Apr 1967	David H. Yarn	
433	University 2nd (Utah) *Salt Lake University 2nd 14 Jan 1974	30 Apr 1967	Oscar W. McConkie Jr.	
434	Mexico City North (Mexico) *Mexico City Mexico North 14 Jan 1974 †8 Nov 1975 ★Tampico Mexico (No. 567), Mexico City Mexico Camarones (No. 719), Mexico City Mexico Satelite (No. 720)	7 May 1967	Agricol Lozano	
435	Sydney South (Australia) *Sydney Australia South 14 Jan 1974 *Sydney Australia Mortdale 15 Feb 1980	14 May 1967	John Daniel Parker	
436	Guatemala City (Guatemala) *Guatemala City Guatemala 14 Jan 1974	21 May 1967	Udine Falabella	
437	Pasco (Washington, Oregon) *Pasco Washington 14 Jan 1974	21 May 1967	David K. Barber	
438	Roy North (Utah) *Roy Utah North 14 Jan 1974	11 Jun 1967	Walter D. Bingham	
439	Long Island (New York) *Plainview New York 14 Jan 1974	20 Aug 1967	Gordon E. Crandall	
440	Olympia (Washington) *Olympia Washington 14 Jan 1974	27 Aug 1967	Herbert S. Anderson	
441	Palm Springs (California) *Palm Springs California 14 Jan 1974	27 Aug 1967	Quinten Hunsaker	
442	El Monte (California) *El Monte California 14 Jan 1974 *Hacienda Heights California 15 Jan 1978	17 Sep 1967	James Cyril Brown	
443	Ft. Worth (Texas) *Ft. Worth Texas 14 Jan 1974	24 Sep 1967	John Kelly Jr.	
444	Montevideo (Uruguay) *Montevideo Uruguay 14 Jan 1974 *Montevideo Uruguay West 17 Feb 1974	12 Nov 1967	Vincente C. Rubio	
445	Hamilton South (New Zealand) *Temple View New Zealand 14 Jan 1974	19 Nov 1967	Harry S. Peckham	
446	Texas North (Texas) *Lubbock Texas 14 Jan 1974	26 Nov 1967	Franklin S. Gonzalez	
447	Perth (Australia) *Perth Australia 14 Jan 1974 *Perth Australia Dianella 6 Jul 1980	28 Nov 1967	Donald W. Cummings	
448	Simi (California) *Simi Valley California 14 Jan 1974	10 Dec 1967	John Lyman Ballif III	23
449	Layton East (Utah) *Layton Utah East 14 Jan 1974	4 Feb 1968	Robert F. Bitner	
450	San Jose South (California) *San Jose California South 14 Jan 1974	11 Feb 1968	DeBoyd L. Smith	
451	Las Vegas Central (Nevada) *Las Vegas Nevada Central 14 Jan 1974	18 Feb 1968	Samuel M. Davis	
452	Alabama (Alabama) *Huntsville Alabama 14 Jan 1974	3 Mar 1968	Raymond D. McCurdy	
453	Newport Beach (California) *Newport Beach California 14 Jan 1974	31 Mar 1968	Ferren L. Christensen	
454	South Carolina East (South Carolina) *Columbia South Carolina East 14 Jan 1974 *Florence South Carolina 5 Feb 1978	21 Apr 1968	Clyde Elmer Black Sr.	
455	Auckland South (New Zealand) *Auckland New Zealand Manurewa 14 Jan 1974	5 May 1968	Geoffrey R. Garlick	

NO.	NAME, LOCALITY *NAME CHANGED †DISORGANIZED ★TRANSFERRED TO	ORGANIZED	PRESIDENT	NO. IN YEAR
456	Houston East (Texas) *Houston Texas East 14 Jan 1974	5 May 1968	Martell A. Belnap	
457	East Midvale (Utah) *Midvale East 29 May 1970 *Midvale Utah East 14 Jan 1974	5 May 1968	R. Kent King	
458	Weber State College (Utah) *Ogden Utah College 14 Jan 1974	12 May 1968	E. LaMar Buckner	
459	Antelope Valley (California) *Palmdale California 14 Jan 1974	12 May 1968	Sterling A. Johnson	
460	Holladay South (Utah) *Salt Lake Holladay South 14 Jan 1974	16 Jun 1968	Marvin L. Pugh	
461	Maine (Maine) *Augusta Maine 14 Jan 1974	23 Jun 1968	Olie W. Ross	
462	Marin (California) *San Rafael California 14 Jan 1974	23 Jun 1968	Weston L. Roe	
463	Nuku'alofa (Tonga) *Nuku'alofa Tonga 14 Jan 1974	5 Sep 1968	Orson Hyde White	
464	Helena (Montana) *Helena Montana 14 Jan 1974	8 Sep 1968	Ronald Rex Dalley	
465	Jacksonville (Florida) *Jacksonville Florida East 14 Jan 1974	15 Sep 1968	Louis B. Vorwaller	
466	Servicemen Stake Europe (W. Germany) *Kaiserslautern Germany Servicemen 14 Jan 1974	30 Oct 1968	Herbert B. Spencer	
467	Sao Paulo East (Brazil) *Sao Paulo Brazil East 14 Jan 1974	24 Nov 1968	Helio da Rocha Camargo	
468	Murray West (Utah) *Murray Utah West 14 Jan 1974	24 Nov 1968	Robert H.M. Killpack	
469	Mid-Michigan (Michigan) *Midland Michigan 14 Jan 1974	1 Dec 1968	E. Richard Packham	
470	Ft. Collins (Colorado) *Ft. Collins Colorado 14 Jan 1974	1 Dec 1968	Raymond Price	
471	Texas West (Texas) *Odessa Texas 14 Jan 1974	15 Dec 1968	Roland Lamar Hamblin	
472	Bend (Oregon) *Bend Oregon 14 Jan 1974	15 Dec 1968	Norman K. Whitney	
473	Hilo (Hawaii) *Hilo Hawaii 14 Jan 1974	15 Dec 1968	Rex Alton Cheney	25
474	Dearborn (Michigan) *Dearborn Michigan 14 Jan 1974 *Westland Michigan 14 Aug 1978	12 Jan 1969	Carl S. Hawkins	
475	New Zealand North (New Zealand) *Kaikohe New Zealand 14 Jan 1974	19 Jan 1969	Stanley J. Hay	
476	Baton Rouge (Louisiana) *Baton Rouge Louisiana 14 Jan 1974	26 Jan 1969	Harmon Cutler	
477	Tucson North (Arizona) *Tucson Arizona North 14 Jan 1974	2 Feb 1969	Don Hakan Peterson	
478	Brigham Young University 9th (Utah)	27 Apr 1969	Carl D. Jones	
479	Brigham Young University 10th (Utah)	27 Apr 1969	Ivan J. Barrett	
480	Ricks College 2nd (Idaho) *Rexburg Idaho College 2nd 14 Jan 1974	27 Apr 1969	Loren Homer Grover	
481	Pittsburgh (Pennsylvania) *Pittsburg Pennsylvania 14 Jan 1974	11 May 1969	William P. Cook	
482	South Jordan (Utah) *Jordan South 29 May 1970 *South Jordan 30 Nov 1970 *South Jordan Utah 14 Jan 1974	18 May 1969	Theron B. Hutchings	
483	Susquehanna (New York) *Ithaca New York 14 Jan 1974	25 May 1969	Harold R. Capener	
484	Arkansas (Arkansas) *Little Rock Arkansas 14 Jan 1974	1 Jun 1969	Deon C. Andrew	

NO.	NAME, LOCALITY *NAME CHANGED †DISORGANIZED ★TRANSFERRED TO	ORGANIZED	PRESIDENT	NO. IN YEAR
485	Hudson River (New York) *Albany New York 14 Jan 1974	8 Jun 1969	Thomas Lorin Hicken	
486	Pensacola (Florida) *Pensacola Florida 14 Jan 1974	15 Jun 1969	Stanford L. Stapleton	
487	Sacramento South (California) *Sacramento California South 14 Jan 1974	15 Jun 1969	John Henry Huber	
488	Pago Pago (American Samoa) *Pago Pago Samoa 14 Jan 1974	15 Jun 1969	Patrick Peters	
489	San Diego North (California) *San Diego California North 14 Jan 1974	22 Jun 1969	Ray Michael Brown	
490	Twin Falls West (Idaho) *Twin Falls Idaho West 14 Jan 1974	17 Aug 1969	Joel A. Tate	
491	Granger East (Utah) *Salt Lake Granger East 14 Jan 1974	24 Aug 1969	David D. Lingard	
492	Visalia (California) *Visalia California 14 Jan 1974	24 Aug 1969	Alva D. Blackburn	
493	Oregon West (Oregon) *Coos Bay Oregon 14 Jan 1974	12 Sep 1969	Edward Harold Sypher	
494	Birmingham (England) *Birmingham England 14 Jan 1974	14 Sep 1969	Derek A. Cuthbert	
495	Parramatta (Australia) *Parramatta Australia 14 Jan 1974 *Sydney Australia Parramatta 15 Feb 1980	2 Nov 1969	Stanley Owen Gray	
496	Texas East (Texas) *Longview Texas 14 Jan 1974	9 Nov 1969	Gerald C.F. Knackstedt	23
497	Granger West (Utah) *Salt Lake Granger West 14 Jan 1974	4 Jan 1970	Dwayne T. Johnson	
498	Woods Cross (Utah) *Woods Cross Utah 14 Jan 1974	4 Jan 1970	D. Hatch Howard	
499	Roanoke (Virginia) *Roanoke Virginia 14 Jan 1974	11 Jan 1970	Russell B. Maddock	
500	Fallon (Nevada) *Fallon Nevada 14 Jan 1974	18 Jan 1970	G. Verl Hendrix	
501	Val Verda (Utah) *Bountiful Utah Val Verda 14 Jan 1974	25 Jan 1970	Milton W. Russon	
502	Anaheim West (California) *Cypress California 14 Jan 1974	15 Feb 1970	Hugh J. Sorensen	
503	Lima (Peru) *Lima Peru 14 Jan 1974 *Lima Peru Limatambo 21 Nov 1976	22 Feb 1970	Roberto Vidal	
504	Blackfoot West (Idaho) *Blackfoot Idaho West 14 Jan 1974	1 Mar 1970	Alan F. Larsen	
505	Tokyo (Japan) *Tokyo Japan 14 Jan 1974	15 Mar 1970	Kenji Tanaka	
506	Transvaal (South Africa) *Johannesburg South Africa 14 Jan 1974	22 Mar 1970	Louis P. Hefer	
507	Merrimack (New Hampshire) *Manchester New Hampshire 14 Jan 1974 *Nashua New Hampshire 9 May 1980	22 Mar 1970	William A. Fresh	
508	Monterrey (Mexico) *Monterrey Mexico 14 Jan 1974 *Monterrey Mexico Mitras 8 Jun 1980	22 Mar 1970	Guillermo G. Garza	
509	Las Vegas South (Nevada) *Las Vegas Nevada South 14 Jan 1974	29 Mar 1970	Erval L. Bindrup	
510	Gettysburg (Pennsylvania) *Gettysburg Pennsylvania 14 Jan 1974 *York Pennsylvania 12 Aug 1979	19 Apr 1970	Laurence L. Yager	
511	Columbia (Missouri) *Columbia Missouri 14 Jan 1974	19 Apr 1970	Samuel D. Richards	

NO.	NAME, LOCALITY *NAME CHANGED †DISORGANIZED ★TRANSFERRED TO	ORGANIZED	PRESIDENT	NO. IN YEAR
512	Mt. Vernon (Virginia) *Annandale Virginia 14 Jan 1974	26 Apr 1970	Allen Claire Rozsa	
513	Apia West (Western Samoa) *Apia Samoa West 14 Jan 1974	26 Apr 1970	Percy J. Rivers	
514	Renton (Washington) *Renton Washington 14 Jan 1974	3 May 1970	Harris A. Mortensen	
515	Roseville (California) *Roseville California 14 Jan 1974	17 May 1970	S. Lloyd Hamilton	
516	Dayton (Ohio) *Dayton Ohio 14 Jan 1974	24 May 1970	Joseph M. McPhie	
517	Prescott (Arizona) *Prescott Arizona 14 Jan 1974	7 Jun 1970	Edward A. Dalton	
518	La Canada (California) *La Crescenta California 14 Jan 1974	7 Jun 1970	Robert C. Seamons	
519	Nuku'alofa South (Tonga) *Nuku'alofa Tonga South 14 Jan 1974	26 Jul 1970	Tevita Folau Mahuinga	
520	Nuku'alofa West (Tonga) *Nuku'alofa Tonga West 14 Jan 1974	26 Jul 1970	Orson H. White	
520	Weber (Utah) *Ogden Utah Weber 14 Jan 1974	16 Aug 1970	Nathan C. Tanner	
521	Mt. Whitney (California) *Ridgecrest California 14 Jan 1974	16 Aug 1970	AlDean Washburn	
522	West Virginia (West Virginia, Kentucky) *Charleston West Virginia 14 Jan 1974	23 Aug 1970	David L. Atkinson	
523	Sao Paulo South (Brazil) *Sao Paulo Brazil South 14 Jan 1974 *Sao Bernardo Brazil 23 May 1980	6 Sep 1970	Saul Messias de Oliveira	
524	Niagara (Canada) *Hamilton Ontario 14 Jan 1974	6 Sep 1970	Eldon C. Olsen	
525	Des Moines (Iowa) *Des Moines Iowa 14 Jan 1974	6 Sep 1970	Donald G. Woolley	
526	Chesapeake (Maryland) *Silver Spring Maryland 14 Jan 1974	13 Sep 1970	June B. Thayn	
527	London North (England) *London England North 14 Jan 1974 †28 May 1978 ★St. Albans England (No. 932), Romford England (No. 666), Staines England No. 931), London England Hyde Park (No. 928)	20 Sep 1970	Thomas Hill	
528	Cache North (Utah) *North Logan Utah 14 Jan 1974	11 Oct 1970	Charles L. Hyde	
529	Pleasant Grove (Utah) *Pleasant Grove Utah 14 Jan 1974	11 Oct 1970	Leo R. Walker	
530	Ft. Lauderdale (Florida) *Ft. Lauderdale Florida 14 Jan 1974	18 Oct 1970	Stanley C. Johnson	
531	Oklahoma South (Oklahoma) *Norman Oklahoma 14 Jan 1974	18 Oct 1970	H. Aldridge Gillespie	
532	Cascade South (Washington) *Everett Washington 14 Jan 1974	25 Oct 1970	Wesley K. Duce	
533	Orem North (Utah) *Orem Utah North 14 Jan 1974	1 Nov 1970	Eli Karl Clayson	
534	Mexico City East (Mexico) *Mexico City Mexico East 14 Jan 1974 †8 Nov 1975 ★Chalco Mexico (No. 722), Mexico City Mexico Villa de las Flores (No. 724), Mexico City Mexico Moctezuma (No. 726), Mexico City Mexico Netzahualcoyotl (No. 727), Chalco Mexico (No. 722)	15 Nov 1970	Agricol Lozano	
535	Kalispell (Montana) *Kalispell Montana 14 Jan 1974	20 Nov 1970	Roy K. Deming	
536	Holbrook (Arizona) *Holbrook Arizona 14 Jan 1974	22 Nov 1970	Jay Barder Williams	

NO.	NAME, LOCALITY *NAME CHANGED †DISORGANIZED ★TRANSFERRED TO	ORGANIZED	PRESIDENT	NO. IN YEAR
537	Nashville (Tennessee) *Nashville Tennessee 14 Jan 1974	6 Dec 1970	Robert N. Brady	42
538	Savai'i (Western Samoa) *Savai'i Samoa 14 Jan 1974	8 Jan 1971	Amuia W. Hunt	
539	Bountiful Center (Utah) *Bountiful Utah Central 14 Jan 1974	10 Jan 1971	Steven S. Davis	
540	Louisville (Kentucky) *Louisville Kentucky 14 Jan 1974	17 Jan 1971	Henry H. Griffith	
541	Edgemont (Utah) *Provo Utah Edgemont 14 Jan 1974	17 Jan 1971	Richard A. Call	
542	Mt. Rainier (Washington) *Puyallup Washington 14 Jan 1974	17 Jan 1971	Owen H. Dickson	
543	Little Cottonwood (Utah) *Murray Utah East 14 Jan 1974	21 Feb 1971	James S. McCloy	
544	Independence (Missouri) *Independence Missouri 14 Jan 1974	25 Mar 1971	Melvin James Bennion	
545	Upolu West (Western Samoa) *Upolu Samoa West 14 Jan 1974	25 Apr 1971	Tua'ifaiva O. Aiono	
546	Bountiful Heights (Utah) *Bountiful Utah Heights 14 Jan 1974	16 May 1971	Jesse Earl Godfrey	
547	Provo North (Utah) *Provo Utah North 14 Jan 1974	30 May 1971	Wayne Alvin Mineer	
548	Ventura (California) *Ventura California 14 Jan 1974	30 May 1971	Joseph F. Chapman	
549	East Anglia (England) *Ipswich England 14 Jan 1974 *Norwich England 28 May 1978	20 Jun 1971	Dennis R. Reeves	
550	Nuku'alofa East (Tonga) *Nuku'alofa Tonga East 14 Jan 1974	21 Jul 1971	Viliami Pele Folau	
551	Melbourne South (Australia) *Melbourne Australia Moorabbin 14 Jan 1974 *Melbourne Australia Dandenong 18 Mar 1986	22 Aug 1971	Bruce James Opie	
552	Curitiba (Brazil) *Curitiba Brazil 14 Jan 1974	12 Sep 1971	Jason Garcia Souza	
553	Moab (Utah) *Moab Utah 14 Jan 1974	19 Sep 1971	Leland D. Teeples	
554	Orem South (Utah) *Orem Utah South 14 Jan 1974 *Orem Utah Sunset Heights 19 Apr 1988	19 Sep 1971	Richard P. Shumway	
555	Mesa West (Arizona) *Mesa Arizona West 14 Jan 1974	10 Oct 1971	Weymouth D. Pew	
556	Spokane East (Washington) *Spokane Washington East 14 Jan 1974	17 Oct 1971	James B. Cox	
557	Mesa Verde (Colorado) *Durango Colorado 14 Jan 1974	7 Nov 1971	Del A. Talley Sr.	
558	Maricopa North (Arizona) *Mesa Arizona Maricopa North 14 Jan 1974 *Mesa Arizona North 15 Mar 1978	7 Nov 1971	Raymond L. Russell	
559	Ben Lomond West (Utah) *Pleasant View Utah 14 Jan 1974	21 Nov 1971	Jay Herbert Rhees	
560	Kaneohe (Hawaii) *Kaneohe Hawaii 14 Jan 1974	21 Nov 1971	Robert H. Finlayson	
561	Providence (Utah) *Providence Utah 14 Jan 1974	12 Dec 1971	Asa L. Beecher	
562	Tempe University (Arizona) *Tempe Arizona University 14 Jan 1974 †28 Apr 1974 ★Various stakes	12 Dec 1971	Leo Rae Huish	25

| --- | --- | --- | --- | --- |
563	Oregon City (Oregon) *Oregon City Oregon 14 Jan 1974	16 Jan 1972	James Hayward Bean	
564	Caldwell (Idaho) *Caldwell Idaho 14 Jan 1974	30 Jan 1972	Talmadge C. Blacker	
565	Chico (California) *Chico California 14 Jan 1974	6 Feb 1972	Lloyd Johnson Cope	
566	Pearl Harbor West (Hawaii) *Waipahu Hawaii 14 Jan 1974	20 Feb 1972	William E. Fuhrmann	
567	Tampico (Mexico) *Tampico Mexico 14 Jan 1974	27 Feb 1972	Guillermo Garmendia	
568	Kaysville East (Utah) *Kaysville Utah East 14 Jan 1974	27 Feb 1972	Lawrence E. Welling	
569	Cordoba (Argentina) *Cordoba Argentina 14 Jan 1974	28 Feb 1972	Arturo Palmieri	
570	Mendoza (Argentina) *Mendoza Argentina 14 Jan 1974	1 Mar 1972	Mario A. Rastelli	
571	Lexington (Kentucky) *Lexington Kentucky 14 Jan 1974	23 Apr 1972	Philip M. Moody	
572	Monterrey East (Mexico) *Monterrey Mexico East 14 Jan 1974 *Monterrey Mexico Libertad 17 Oct 1976	7 May 1972	Jose Humberto Gonzalez	
573	Tahiti (Tahiti) *Papeete Tahiti 14 Jan 1974	14 May 1972	Raituia Tehina Tapu	
574	Wilmington (North Carolina) *Wilmington North Carolina 14 Jan 1974	21 May 1972	Dean Bevin Powell Jr.	
575	Centerville (Utah) *Centerville Utah 14 Jan 1974	21 May 1972	Joseph A. Kjar	
576	Big Cottonwood (Utah) *Salt Lake Big Cottonwood 14 Jan 1974	28 May 1972	Robert B. Barker	
577	Duesseldorf (Germany) *Duesseldorf Germany 14 Jan 1974	4 Jun 1972	Kaus Fritz K. Hasse	
578	Bountiful West (Utah) *Bountiful Utah West 14 Jan 1974 *West Bountiful Utah 9 Oct 1984	11 Jun 1972	Clarence D. Samuelson	
579	Sandy West (Utah) *Sandy Utah West 14 Jan 1974	11 Jun 1972	Reed Neff Brown	
580	Meridian (Idaho) *Meridian Idaho 14 Jan 1974	11 Jun 1972	J. Richard Clarke	
581	Knoxville (Tennessee) *Knoxville Tennessee 14 Jan 1974	25 Jun 1972	Eugene H. Perkins	
582	Hunter West (Utah) *Salt Lake Hunter West 14 Jan 1974	13 Aug 1972	Evans Thomas Doxey	
583	Upland (California) *Upland California 14 Jan 1974	13 Aug 1972	Frank E. Finlayson	
584	Charleston (South Carolina) *Charleston South Carolina 14 Jan 1974	20 Aug 1972	Fred Ittner Harley	
585	San Jose North (California) *Santa Clara California 14 Jan 1974	20 Aug 1972	Lloyd M. Gustaveson	
586	Osaka (Japan) *Osaka Japan 14 Jan 1974	12 Sep 1972	Noboru Kamio	
587	Minidoka West (Idaho) *Paul Idaho 14 Jan 1974	24 Sep 1972	Keith C. Merrill Jr.	
588	Escondido (California) *Escondido California 14 Jan 1974	24 Sep 1972	Donald R. McArthur	
589	Rio de Janeiro (Brazil) *Rio de Janeiro Brazil 14 Jan 1974	22 Oct 1972	Veledmar Cury	
590	Santiago (Chile) *Santiago Chile 14 Jan 1974 *Santiago Chile Providencia 18 Apr 1976 *Santiago Chile Quinta Normal 10 Jan 1980	19 Nov 1972	Carlos A. Cifuentes	

NO.	NAME, LOCALITY / NAME CHANGED / DISORGANIZED / TRANSFERRED TO	ORGANIZED	PRESIDENT	NO. IN YEAR
591	Charlotte (North Carolina) *Charlotte North Carolina 14 Jan 1974 *Charlotte North Carolina South 21 Sep 1986	19 Nov 1972	Byron Cole Williams	
592	Rapid City (South Dakota) *Rapid City South Dakota 14 Jan 1974	10 Dec 1972	Briant LeRoy Davis	30
593	Cody (Wyoming) *Cody Wyoming 14 Jan 1974	7 Jan 1973	Parley J. Livingston	
594	Tallahasse (Florida) *Tallahasse Florida 14 Jan 1974	21 Jan 1973	Jay Nicholas Lybbert	
595	Boulder (Colorado) *Boulder Colorado 14 Jan 1974	28 Jan 1973	C. Rodney Claridge	
596	Denver North (Colorado) *Denver Colorado North 14 Jan 1974	28 Jan 1973	Gus. F. Ranzenberger	
597	Nottingham (England) *Nottingham England 14 Jan 1974	4 Feb 1973	Ernest Hewitt	
598	Taylorsville Central (Utah) *Taylorsville Utah Central 14 Jan 1974	4 Feb 1973	Richard A. Barker	
599	Columbia River West (Wash.) *Longview Washington 14 Jan 1974	4 Feb 1973	Walter Lee Robinson	
600	Southampton (England) *Southampton England 14 Jan 1974	11 Feb 1973	Reginald V. Littlecott	
601	Porto Alegre (Brazil) *Porto Alegre Brazil 14 Jan 1974	13 Feb 1973	Miguell Sorrentino	
602	Idaho Falls West (Idaho) *Idaho Falls Idaho West 14 Jan 1974	4 Mar 1973	Terry L. Crapo	
603	Butler South (Utah) *Salt Lake Brighton 14 Jan 1974	4 Mar 1973	Alvin Don Nydegger	
604	Seoul (Korea) *Seoul Korea 14 Jan 1974	8 Mar 1973	Ho Nam Rhee	
605	Lake Mead West (Nevada) *Henderson Nevada West 14 Jan 1974	11 Mar 1973	Joseph Dee Reese	
606	Jefferson (Idaho) *Roberts Idaho 14 Jan 1974	25 Mar 1973	Edwin Culter Adamson	
607	Iona (Idaho) *Iona Idaho 14 Jan 1974	15 Apr 1973	Joseph Dudley Tucker	
608	Hull (England) *Hull England 14 Jan 1974	26 Apr 1973	Ian David Swanney	
609	Bristol (England) *Bristol England 14 Jan 1974	29 Apr 1973	Donald V. Norris	
610	Ozark (Missouri) *Springfield Missouri 14 Jan 1974	29 Apr 1973	Carroll S. Claybrook	
611	Sandy North (Utah) *Sandy Utah North 14 Jan 1974	29 Apr 1973	Eugene D. Tenney	
612	Glendale (Arizona) *Glendale Arizona 14 Jan 1974	6 May 1973	Melvin L. Huber	
613	Manila (Philippines) *Manila Philippines 14 Jan 1974	20 May 1973	Augusto Alandy Lim	
614	Jordan River (Utah) *West Jordan Utah South 14 Jan 1974	20 May 1973	Max Curtis Jewkes	
615	Thames Valley (England) *Reading England 14 Jan 1974	24 May 1973	Peter B.C. Brighty	
616	Dallas North (Texas) *Dallas Texas North 14 Jan 1974 *Plano Texas 12 Apr 1981	27 May 1973	Ivan Leslie Hobson Jr.	
617	Mexico City Aragon (Mexico) *Mexico City Mexico Aragon 14 Jan 1974	27 May 1973	Agricol Lozano H.	
618	San Salvador (El Salvador) *San Salvador El Salvador 14 Jan 1974	3 Jun 1973	Mario Edmundo Scheel	
619	Savai'i West (Western Samoa) *Savai'i Samoa West 14 Jan 1974	3 Jun 1973	Fa'afoi Tuitama	

NO.	NAME, LOCALITY *NAME CHANGED †DISORGANIZED ★TRANSFERRED TO	ORGANIZED	PRESIDENT	NO. IN YEAR
620	Santos (Brazil) *Santos Brazil 14 Jan 1974	8 Jun 1973	Jose Gonzalez Lopes	
621	Campinas (Brazil) *Campinas Brazil 14 Jan 1974	9 Jun 1973	Nelson de Genaro	
622	Sao Paulo West (Brazil) *Sao Paulo Brazil West 14 Jan 1974	10 Jun 1973	Jose Benjamin Puerta	
623	Willow Creek (Utah) *Sandy Utah Willow Creek 14 Jan 1974	17 Jun 1973	Wayne E. Saunders	
624	American Fork North (Utah) *American Fork Utah North 14 Jan 1974	17 Jun 1973	Leland Forbes Priday	
624	Indianapolis North (Indiana) *Indianapolis Indiana North 14 Jan 1974	19 Aug 1973	David Val Glover	
625	Littleton (Colorado) *Littleton Colorado 14 Jan 1974	2 Sep 1973	Clinton L. Cutler	
626	Austin Texas	14 Oct 1973	Amos Luther Wright	
627	Crescent Utah *Sandy Utah Crescent 14 Jan 1974	21 Oct 1973	Allen Eugene Hilton	
628	Valle Hermosa (Mexico) *Valle Hermosa Mexico 14 Jan 1974	28 Oct 1973	Benjamin Morales	
629	Taylorsville Utah North	28 Oct 1973	LeVere Elihu Brady	
630	Auckland New Zealand Harbour	4 Nov 1973	Kenneth M. Palmer	39
631	Montevideo Uruguay East	17 Feb 1974	Ariel A. Fedrigotti	
632	Pueblo Colorado	3 Mar 1974	Louis Edward Butler	
633	Page Arizona	10 Mar 1974	J. Ballard Washburn	
634	Payson Utah East	24 Mar 1974	David R. Mangelson	
635	Reno Nevada North	24 Mar 1974	Wilford Darrell Foote	
636	Salt Lake Granger Central	31 Mar 1974	Norman H. Bangerter	
636	Rosario Argentina	5 May 1974	Hugo Ruben Gazzoni	
637	Lehi Utah North	5 May 1974	Francis Russell Hakes	
638	Pullman Washington	5 May 1974	John Leo Schwendiman	
639	Buenos Aires Argentina West	12 May 1974	May Hugo Angel Catron	
640	Tucker Georgia *Sandy Springs Georgia 1 Sep 1974 *Roswell Georgia 21 Jun 1987	12 May 1974	Richard Parry Winder	
641	Mountain Home Idaho	19 May 1974	Kenneth Herbert Johns	
642	Los Angeles California Santa Clarita	19 May 1974	Norman D. Stevensen	
643	Gresham Oregon	26 May 1974	Wilford Smith Stevenson Jr.	
644	Monclova Mexico	26 May 1974	Francisco Aragon Garza	
645	Upola Samoa South	1 Jun 1974	William Richard Schwalger	
646	Chicago Heights Illinois	2 Jun 1974	Robert E. Nichols	
647	Belfast Ireland *Belfast Northern Ireland 13 Jan 1987	9 Jun 1974	Andrew Renfrew	
648	Copenhagen Denmark	16 Jun 1974	Johan Helge Benthin	
649	Heber City Utah East	16 Jun 1974	Robert F. Clyde	
650	Globe Arizona	16 Jun 1974	Bennie Joe Cecil	
651	St. Petersburg Florida	18 Aug 1974	Bruce Earl Belnap	
652	Newbury Park California	18 Aug 1974	Lavar M. Butler	
653	Kearns Utah South	25 Aug 1974	Garth D. Mecham	
654	Las Cruces New Mexico	25 Aug 1974	Harold A. Daw	
655	Firth Idaho	8 Sep 1974	Dale Lavar Christensen	
656	Cerritos California West	8 Sep 1974	Kenneth Laurence Davis	
657	Buffalo New York	15 Sep 1974	Ronald Glen Vincent	
658	Mexico City Mexico Arbolillo	15 Sep 1974	Guillermo Torres	
659	Merced California	15 Sep 1974	Robert D. Rowan	
660	Green River Wyoming	22 Sep 1974	Ronald Clyde Walker	
661	Emmett Idaho	22 Sep 1974	David Lee Morton	
662	Yokohama Japan	27 Oct 1974	Hitoshi Kashikura	
663	Bellevue Nebraska	27 Oct 1974	Leonard Leroy Gregory	
664	Bennion Utah	27 Oct 1974	John Labrum	

NO.	NAME, LOCALITY	ORGANIZED	PRESIDENT	NO. IN YEAR
665	Edmonton Alberta East	3 Nov 1974	Bryant L. Stringham	
	*Edmonton Alberta Bonnie Doon 6 Nov 1983			
666	Romford England	24 Nov 1974	Arthur James Turvey	
667	Lethbridge Alberta East	24 Nov 1974	Bryce C. Stringham	
668	Show Low Arizona	24 Nov 1974	Elbert J. Lewis	
669	Kona Hawaii	24 Nov 1974	Haven J. Stringham	
670	Lima Peru West	1 Dec 1974	Manuel Paredes L.	
	*Lima Peru Magdelena 21 Nov 1976			
671	Vina del Mar Chile	5 Dec 1974	Jose Leyton	
672	Santiago Chile South	8 Dec 1974	Eduardo Ayala	
	*Santiago Chile La Cisterna 18 Apr 1976			
673	Wilmington Delaware	8 Dec 1974	Rulon Edward Johnson Jr.	
674	Baltimore Maryland	8 Dec 1974	Kyle W. Petersen	
675	Pleasanton California	8 Dec 1974	Dale Edwin Nielsen	46
676	Merthyr Tydfil Wales	12 Jan 1975	Ralph Pulman	
677	Newcastle-Under-Lyme England	17 Jan 1975	James Kenneth Cork	
678	Birmingham Alabama	2 Feb 1975	Fred M. Washburn	
679	Victoria British Columbia	9 Feb 1975	Howard Lowell Biddulph	
680	Puebla Mexico La Paz	16 Feb 1975	Santiago Mejia M.	
681	Puebla Mexico Valsequillo	16 Feb 1975	Ramiro Goana M.	
682	Fairfield California	16 Feb 1975	Byron Gale Wilson	
683	Guadalajara Mexico	23 Feb 1975	Emilio Garcia L.	
	*Guadalajara Mexico Union 28 Sep 1980			
684	Grand Rapids Michigan	2 Mar 1975	Glenn Goodwin	
685	Roosevelt Utah West	2 Mar 1975	Alvin Leonard Bellon	
686	Spanish Fork Utah Salem	9 Mar 1975	Kent Blaine Hansen	
	*Salem Utah 8 Dec 1976			
687	Gallup New Mexico	16 Mar 1975	Donald C. Tanner	
688	Brigham Young University 11th (Utah)	13 Apr 1975	Gregory E. Austin	
689	Brigham Young University 12th (Utah)	13 Apr 1975	Charles Verl Clark	
690	Rexburg Idaho College 3rd	13 Apr 1975	Ray Wendell Rigby	
691	Stockholm Sweden	20 Apr 1975	Evert W. Perciwall	
692	McAllen Texas	4 May 1975	Daniel Birch Larsen	
693	San Jose California East	4 May 1975	Leo E. Haney	
694	Quilmes Argentina	15 May 1975	Hugo Nestor Salvioli	
695	Ashton Idaho	18 May 1975	Horace E. Hess	
696	Akron Ohio	25 May 1975	Carmen J. Libutti	
697	Rexburg Idaho East	1 Jun 1975	Keith Lester Peterson	
698	Fayetteville North Carolina	8 Jun 1975	Leland Reid Fillmore	
699	Guatemala City Guatemala West	8 Jun 1975	Mario Antonio Lopez	
	*Guatemala City Guatemala Utatlan 31 Oct 1976			
700	Veracruz Mexico	15 Jun 1975	Leon Lopez Alavez	
701	Boise Idaho South	17 Aug 1975	Grant Ruel Ipsen	
702	Beloit Wisconsin	24 Aug 1975	Arval Lewis Erikson	
	*Madison Wisconsin 11 Apr 1982			
703	Gilbert Arizona	24 Aug 1975	Newell A. Barney	
	*Gilbert Arizona Greenfield 11 Oct 1981			
704	Los Altos California	24 Aug 1975	W. Kay Williams	
705	Springville Utah North	31 Aug 1975	F. Calvin Packard	
	*Springville Utah Spring Creek 21 Jun 1988			
706	Salt Lake Winder West	21 Sep 1975	Wayne O. Ursenbach	
707	Fullerton California	21 Sep 1975	Leon Tad Ballard	
708	Kemmerer Wyoming	12 Oct 1975	Merrill R. Anderson	
709	Vernon British Columbia	12 Oct 1975	James Ronald Burnham	
710	Hillsboro Oregon	12 Oct 1975	H. Keith Buhler	
711	Syracuse New York	19 Oct 1975	George Dale Weight	
712	Evansville Indiana	19 Oct 1975	Frank R. Fults Jr.	
713	Quetzaltenango Guatemala	19 Oct 1975	Jorge Herminio Perez Citalan	
714	Mapleton Utah	19 Oct 1975	Jay M. Smith Jr.	

NO.	NAME, LOCALITY *NAME CHANGED †DISORGANIZED ★TRANSFERRED TO	ORGANIZED	PRESIDENT	NO. IN YEAR
715	Douglas Georgia	26 Oct 1975	Roswald Mancil	
716	Modesto California North	26 Oct 1975	Charles Elwin Boice	
717	Montgomery Alabama	2 Nov 1975	Gayle Dorwin Heckel	
715	Mexico City Mexico Zarahemla	8 Nov 1975	Bonaerges Rubalcava E.	
716	Mexico City Mexico Churubusco	8 Nov 1975	Juan Casanova Cerda	
717	Mexico City Mexico Tacubaya	8 Nov 1975	Roman Gomez Ibar	
718	Mexico City Mexico Ermita	8 Nov 1975	Aurelio Valdespino Ortiz	
719	Mexico City Mexico Camarones	8 Nov 1975	Jorge Rojas Ornelas	
720	Mexico City Mexico Satelite	9 Nov 1975	Horacio Tenorio Oriza	
	*Mexico City Mexico Tlalnepantla 10 Oct 1978			
721	Cuautla Mexico	9 Nov 1975	Juan Angel Alvaradejo	
722	Chalco Mexico	9 Nov 1975	Ruben Valenzuela G.	
723	Mexico City Mexico Industrial	9 Nov 1975	Juan Roberto Alva	
724	Mexico City Mexico Villa de las Flores	9 Nov 1975	Juan Manuel Cedeno R.	
725	Tula Mexico	9 Nov 1975	Silvino Mera Uribe	
726	Mexico City Mexico Moctezuma	9 Nov 1975	Filiberto Ledezma Madrigal	
727	Mexico City Mexico Netzahualcoyotl	9 Nov 1975	Jaime Garay Morales	
728	Clinton Utah	9 Nov 1975	Albert DeMar Mitchell	
729	Kahului Hawaii	9 Nov 1975	Evan Allan Larsen	
730	Poza Rica Mexico	13 Nov 1975	Jose Luis Pichardo M.	
731	Paris France	16 Nov 1975	Gerard Giraud-Carrier	
732	Marianna Florida	16 Nov 1975	Riley Malone Peddie	
	*Panama City Florida 4 Feb 1986			
733	Houston Texas North	16 Nov 1975	Harold Elison DeLaMare	
734	Dundee Scotland	23 Nov 1975	John Keogh	
735	West Jordan Utah East	30 Nov 1975	Dale P. Bateman	
736	San Diego California East	30 Nov 1975	Philip Alma Petersen	
737	Neiafu Vava'u Tonga	4 Dec 1975	Mosese Hetau Langi	65
738	Tempe Arizona South	18 Jan 1976	Fred Dale Markham	
739	Palos Verdes California	18 Jan 1976	Merrill Bickmore	
740	Fairfax Virginia	1 Feb 1976	Ed Mordue Hayward	
741	San Salvador El Salvador East	1 Feb 1976	Alfonso Octavio Diaz	
	*San Salvador El Salvador Ilopango 3 Jun 1979			
742	Farmington New Mexico East	1 Feb 1976	Marlo L. Webb	
	*Bloomfield New Mexico 19 Sep 1982			
743	Salem Oregon North	8 Feb 1976	Jay Gerald Nelson	
	*Salem Oregon Keizer 25 Oct 1981			
	*Keizer Oregon 4 Apr 1984			
744	St. Paul Minnesota	15 Feb 1976	Thomas Albert Holt	
745	Mesa Arizona Salt River	15 Feb 1976	Elden S. Porter	
746	Gainesville Florida	29 Feb 1976	James R. Christianson	
747	Topeka Kansas	29 Feb 1976	Vahl W. Bodily	
748	Liverpool England	14 Mar 1976	Michael R. Otterson	
749	Fairview Heights Illinois	14 Mar 1976	John Odeen Anderson	
750	Blythe California	14 Mar 1976	Jerry Dean Mortensen	
751	Orem Utah East	21 Mar 1976	Mirl Blake Hymas	
752	London Ontario	11 Apr 1976	Harold Crookell	
753	Montpelier Vermont	11 Apr 1976	C. Lynn Fife	
754	Santiago Chile Republica	18 Apr 1976	Julio Jaramillo	
755	Taipei Taiwan	22 Apr 1976	I-Ch'ing Chang	
	*Taipei Taiwan West 14 Mar 1982			
756	Hong Kong	25 Apr 1976	Shiu-Tat Sheldon Poon	
	*Hong Kong Island 29 May 1980			
757	Tijuana Mexico	23 May 1976	Carlos Mendez Sullik	
758	San Antonio Texas East	30 May 1976	Archie M. Brugger	
759	St. George Utah College	30 May 1976	Peter A. Nyberg	
760	Hartlepool England	13 Jun 1976	Craig Lithgow Marshall	
	*Billingham England 10 Jun 1986			

NO.	NAME, LOCALITY *NAME CHANGED †DISORGANIZED ★TRANSFERRED TO	ORGANIZED	PRESIDENT	NO. IN YEAR
761	Toronto Ontario East	13 Jun 1976	John Bruce Smith	
	*Oshawa Ontario 22 Jun 1986			
762	Preston England	17 Jun 1976	Eric Cryer	
763	Camarillo California	8 Aug 1976	Victor Glenn Johnson	
764	Salt Lake Granger South	22 Aug 1976	Gordon Ward Evans	
765	Stuttgart Germany Servicemen	12 Sep 1976	Gary K. Spencer	
766	Frankfurt Germany	12 Sep 1976	Magnus R. Meiser	
767	Eugene Oregon West	12 Sep 1976	Robert W. Hill	
768	Dortmund Germany	19 Sep 1976	Frerich Jakob Emil Gorts	
769	Rio de Janeiro Brazil Niteroi	19 Sep 1976	Joao Eduardo Kemeny	
770	Chula Vista California	19 Sep 1976	Robert Eugene Floto	
771	Hermosillo Mexico	8 Oct 1976	Hector Ceballos L.	
772	Ciudad Obregon Mexico	10 Oct 1976	Jorge Mendez Ibarra	
773	Monterrey Mexico Roma	16 Oct 1976	Jose Humberto Gonzalez G.	
774	Monterrey Mexico Anahuac	17 Oct 1976	Lehi Garcia Lopez	
775	Sandy Utah Crescent West	24 Oct 1976	John Burton Anderson	
776	Kennewick Washington	24 Oct 1976	Elton Elias Hunt	
777	Lawton Oklahoma	31 Oct 1976	Ralph E. Siebach	
778	Guatemala City Guatemala Las Victorias	31 Oct 1976	Carlos Enrique Soto de Leon	
779	Grants Pass Oregon	31 Oct 1976	Darwin Jay Wright	
780	Leeds England	12 Nov 1976	Douglas Rawson	
781	Torreon Mexico	12 Nov 1976	David Limon Miranda	
782	Chihuahua Mexico	13 Nov 1976	Gustavo Ulises Cortez S.	
783	Ciudad Juarez Mexico	14 Nov 1976	Sergio Armando de la Mora M.	
784	Ft. Worth Texas North	14 Nov 1976	Richard W. Ragsdale	
	*Hurst Texas 12 Apr 1981			
785	Logan Utah University 3rd	14 Nov 1976	LaGrande C. Larsen	
786	Glendora California	14 Nov 1976	William Marshall Raymond	
787	Santa Ana California	14 Nov 1976	Wilbur Orion Jensen	
788	Lima Peru Lamanita	21 Nov 1976	Rafael de la Cruz	
789	Lima Peru Central	21 Nov 1976	Oscar H. Aguayo Ugaz	
790	Lyman Wyoming	21 Nov 1976	Ronald C. Walker	
791	Quilpue Chile	28 Nov 1976	Eduardo Lamartine A.	
792	Santiago Chile Nunoa	28 Nov 1976	Gustavo Alberto Barrios C.	
793	Columbus Ohio East	28 Nov 1976	Paul Frank Eastman	
794	Lancaster California	28 Nov 1976	Stephen N. Hull	
795	Madera Mexico	11 Dec 1976	Gabriel Raymundo Saldivar F.	
796	Ottawa Ontario	12 Dec 1976	Boyden E. Lee	
797	Ciudad Victoria Mexico	12 Dec 1976	Jesus Martinez T.	
798	Ogden Utah Terrace View	12 Dec 1976	Leo Neeley Harris	61
799	Poza Rica Mexico Palmas	15 Jan 1977	Angel Valle G.	
800	Veracruz Mexico Reforma	16 Jan 1977	Leon Lopez Alavez	
801	Orizaba Mexico	16 Jan 1977	Humberto Sanchez Reyes	
802	Huntington Beach California North	16 Jan 1977	Wesley Charles Woodhouse	
803	San Jose Costa Rica	20 Jan 1977	Manuel Najera Guzman	
804	Merida Mexico	22 Jan 1977	Abel R. Ordaz Rosado	
805	Bogota Colombia	23 Jan 1977	Julio E. Davila P.	
806	Concord California East	23 Jan 1977	Vern W. Clark	
	†16 Feb 1986 ★Walnut Creek California East (No. 1587)			
807	BYU-Hawaii	23 Jan 1977	Eric B. Shumway	
	*BYU-Hawaii 1st 22 Nov 1981			
808	Concepcion Chile	30 Jan 1977	Claudio Signorelli G.	
809	Taylorsville Utah West Central	6 Feb 1977	Floyd Keith Rupp	
810	Northampton England	13 Feb 1977	Michael J. Wade	
811	Sandy Utah Hillcrest	13 Feb 1977	Arnold Christensen	
812	Orem Utah Central	13 Feb 1977	Clifton M. Pyne	
813	Brussels Belgium	20 Feb 1977	Joseph Scheen	
814	Lichfield England	20 Feb 1977	Robert James Mawle	
815	Sao Paulo Brazil North	20 Feb 1977	Jorge Flavio de Moraes	

NO.	NAME, LOCALITY *NAME CHANGED †DISORGANIZED ★TRANSFERRED TO	ORGANIZED	PRESIDENT	NO. IN YEAR
816	Roswell New Mexico	13 Mar 1977	J. Allen Levie	
817	Los Angeles California Granada Hills	13 Mar 1977	Clark Spendlove	
818	Providence Rhode Island	20 Mar 1977	Morgan W. Lewis Jr.	
819	Mexicali Mexico	20 Mar 1977	Eduardo Del Rio Pulido	
820	San Pedro Sula Honduras	10 Apr 1977	Samuel Ben-Zion Ventura	
821	Provo Utah Oak Hills	10 Apr 1977	John R. Christiansen	
822	Stockton California East	10 Apr 1977	Robert Graham Wade	
	*Lodi California 3 May 1981			
823	Santa Cruz California	24 Apr 1977	Edwin Reese Davis	
824	Frankfurt Germany Servicemen	1 May 1977	Kenneth Alvin Nessen	
825	Idaho Falls Idaho Ammon West	1 May 1977	Boyd Rencher Thomas	
826	Mission Viejo California	8 May 1977	Nolan C. Draney	
827	Caracas Venezuela	15 May 1977	Adolfo F. Mayer G.	
828	Dallas Texas East	15 May 1977	Arthur Eugene Gabriel	
829	Minatitlan Mexico	15 May 1977	Ignacio Cruz Sanchez	
830	Roseburg Oregon	15 May 1977	Gary Richards Lowe	
831	Morgan Hill California	15 May 1977	Donald Russell Lundell	
832	Rivera Uruguay	20 May 1977	Ormesindo Correa	
833	Paysandu Uruguay	21 May 1977	Atilio Silveira	
834	Seoul Korea West	22 May 1977	Chang Sun Kim	
835	Oslo Norway	22 May 1977	Osvald Bjareng	
836	Minas Uruguay	22 May 1977	Alberto E. Hernandez	
837	Winchester Virginia	22 May 1977	Harold S. Harrison	
838	Culiacan Mexico	22 May 1977	Federico Fragoza Diaz	
839	Salt Lake Hunter East	22 May 1977	Merrill Dimick	
840	Santa Lucia Uruguay	23 May 1977	Hector Julio Vigo	
841	Makati Philippines	29 May 1977	Ruben Moscaira Lancanienta	
842	Quezon City Philippines	29 May 1977	Augusto Alandy Lim	
843	Friendswood Texas	29 May 1977	Newell Kenneth Hill	
844	Redmond Washington	29 May 1977	Arnold R. Parrott	
845	Hannover Germany	12 Jun 1977	Michael Schulze	
846	Newport News Virginia	12 Jun 1977	Kirk Thomas Waldron	
847	Meridian Idaho East	12 Jun 1977	Leonard E. Graham Jr.	
848	Richfield Utah East	12 Jun 1977	Warren T. Harward	
849	Billings Montana East	12 Jun 1977	Wynn J. Ferrell	
850	The Dalles Oregon	26 Jun 1977	Wayne B. Bush	
851	Kauai Hawaii	24 Jul 1977	Garner Dalthum Wood	
852	Fargo North Dakota	7 Aug 1977	John R. Price	
853	Upper Hutt New Zealand	14 Aug 1977	Trevor A. Beatson	
854	Ann Arbor Michigan	14 Aug 1977	Duane Marvin Laws	
855	Las Vegas Nevada Redrock	14 Aug 1977	E. LeGrande Bindrup	
856	Crawley England	19 Aug 1977	J.A. Casbon	
857	Piedras Negras Mexico	21 Aug 1977	Fidencio Guzman Lugo	
858	Layton Utah West	21 Aug 1977	William Clive Barney Jr.	
859	Joplin Missouri	28 Aug 1977	Kenneth Rae Martin	
860	Hobart Australia	14 Sep 1977	John Douglas Jury	
861	Auckland New Zealand Manukau	18 Sep 1977	Oscar Westerlund	
862	Orem Utah West Central	18 Sep 1977	James Edwin Mangum	
	*Orem Utah Suncrest 1 Mar 1988			
863	Salt Lake Jordan	9 Oct 1977	Robert Bennion Arnold	
864	Arcadia California	9 Oct 1977	Cree-L Kofford	
865	Helsinki Finland	16 Oct 1977	Kari Juhani Aslak Haikkola	
866	Talcahuano Chile	16 Oct 1977	Claudio Daniel Signorelli G.	
867	Orem Utah South Central	16 Oct 1977	Gordon Max Thomas	
	*Orem Utah Lakeridge 1 Mar 1988			
868	Upolu Samoa East	23 Oct 1977	Kovana Pauga	
869	Tokyo Japan North	23 Oct 1977	Ryo Okamoto	
870	Munich Germany	23 Oct 1977	August Schubert	
871	Huntington Utah	23 Oct 1977	Ira Wallace Hatch	
872	Osaka Japan North	30 Oct 1977	Noboru Kamio	

NO.	NAME, LOCALITY *NAME CHANGED †DISORGANIZED ★TRANSFERRED TO	ORGANIZED	PRESIDENT	NO. IN YEAR
873	South Bend Indiana	30 Oct 1977	Kenneth Bryan Fugal	
874	Nampa Idaho South	30 Oct 1977	Dean Ezra Beus	
875	Bennion Utah West	30 Oct 1977	Glenn A. Weight	
876	Plain City Utah	30 Oct 1977	Kent W. Calvert	
877	Ukiah California	30 Oct 1977	Robert Vernon Knudsen	
878	Tucson Arizona East	6 Nov 1977	Paul Eugene Dahl	
879	Cocoa Florida	13 Nov 1977	Cleavy Eugene Waters	
880	Goteborg Sweden	20 Nov 1977	Arne Lennart Hedberg	
881	Statesville North Carolina	20 Nov 1977	Michael Stephen Bullock	
	*Winston-Salem North Carolina 25 Nov 1979			
882	Valparaiso Chile	20 Nov 1977	Abel Correa Lopez	
883	Federal Way Washington	20 Nov 1977	Jack Lynn Smith	
884	Rotorua New Zealand	27 Nov 1977	Paul Robert Thomas	
885	Plymouth England	27 Nov 1977	Leonard Eden	87
886	Columbus Georgia	15 Jan 1978	William F. Meadows Jr.	
887	Trujillo Peru	22 Jan 1978	Teofilo Puertas Vega	
	*Trujillo Peru North 19 Aug 1984			
888	Camp Verde Arizona	22 Jan 1978	John Edward Eagar	
889	West Columbia South Carolina	5 Feb 1978	George A. Huff Sr.	
	*Augusta Georgia 21 Aug 1988			
890	Montevideo Uruguay North	12 Feb 1978	Ariel Omar Fedrigotti	
891	Salt Lake Holladay North	12 Feb 1978	John A. Larsen	
892	Brisbane Australia South	19 Feb 1978	John D. Jeffrey	
893	Curitiba Brazil South	26 Feb 1978	Albina Bruno Schmeil	
894	Pleasant Grove Utah East	26 Feb 1978	Evan Mack Palmer	
895	St. George Utah West	5 Mar 1978	Dale Gubler	
896	West Maricopa Arizona	5 Mar 1978	DeNelson Jones	
	*Phoenix Arizona West Maricopa 18 May 1978			
897	Blanding Utah	5 Mar 1978	Fred Eugene Halliday	
898	Puebla Mexico Popocateptl	12 Mar 1978	Zeferino Tlatelpa	
899	Provo Utah Edgemont South	19 Mar 1978	Keith Hale Hoopes	
900	Spanish Fork Utah West	19 Mar 1978	Clair O. Anderson	
901	Cedar City Utah North	19 Mar 1978	Robert L. Blattner	
902	Davenport Iowa	9 Apr 1978	James Earl Campbell	
903	Centerville Utah South	9 Apr 1978	Robert A. Trump	
904	Salt Lake Mt. Olympus North	9 Apr 1978	William Schaubel Partridge	
905	Orem Utah Windsor	9 Apr 1978	Dennis LeRoy Hill	
906	Carson City Nevada	9 Apr 1978	Edgar Gilbert Carlson	
907	Adelaide Australia Modbury	23 Apr 1978	Douglas E. Hann	
908	Monterrey Mexico Paraiso	23 Apr 1978	Alfredo Gallegos Lopez	
909	Kitchiwan New York	30 Apr 1978	Victor B. Jex	
	*Yorktown New York 28 Aug 1978			
910	Rochester Minnesota	30 Apr 1978	Lee McNeal Johnson	
911	Ft. Smith Arkansas	30 Apr 1978	Arthur Donald Browne	
912	Tulsa Oklahoma East	30 Apr 1978	Raleigh L. Huntsman	
913	Vernal Utah Maeser	30 Apr 1978	Venil P. Johnson	
914	Blackfoot Idaho Northwest	30 Apr 1978	Reijo Laverne Marcum	
915	Las Vegas Nevada East	30 Apr 1978	Kendall E. Jones	
916	Savannah Georgia	7 May 1978	Robert W. Cowart	
917	San Jose Costa Rica La Sabana	7 May 1978	Jorge Arturo Solano Castillo	
918	Benson Utah	7 May 1978	Dale Morgan Rindlisbacher	
919	Nagoya Japan	10 May 1978	Masaru Tsuchida	
920	Buenos Aires Argentina Banfield	14 May 1978	Heber Omar Diaz	
921	Atlanta Georgia	14 May 1978	Warren Richard Jones	
922	Bluefield Virginia	14 May 1978	Norman Perry Tyler Jr.	
923	Merida Mexico Lakin	14 May 1978	Benigno Pena Pech	
924	Huntsville Utah	14 May 1978	Marlin Keith Jensen	
925	Lynnwood Washington	14 May 1978	Robert C. Barnard	

NO.	NAME, LOCALITY *NAME CHANGED †DISORGANIZED ★TRANSFERRED TO	ORGANIZED	PRESIDENT	NO. IN YEAR
926	Hopkinsville Kentucky	21 May 1978	Robert Laurence Fears	
927	Chattanooga Tennessee	21 May 1978	Earl Eugene Callens Jr.	
928	Tooele Utah South	21 May 1978	Joel James Dunn	
929	West Jordan Utah West	21 May 1978	Robert B. Rowley	
928	London England Hyde Park	28 May 1978	Wilford M. Farnsworth Jr.	
929	London England Wandsworth	28 May 1978	John Dodd	
930	Maidstone England	28 May 1978	William J. Jolliffe III	
931	Staines England	28 May 1978	Peter Benjamin C. Brighty	
932	St. Albans England	28 May 1978	Roland Edward Elvidge	
933	Utrecht Netherlands	28 May 1978	Eugene M. Engelbert	
934	Charlottesville Virginia *Waynesboro Virginia 16 Dec 1982	28 May 1978	Wilford John Teerlink	
935	Gomez Palacio Mexico	28 May 1978	Ruben Martinez A.	
936	Salt Lake Cottonwood Heights	28 May 1978	R. Gordon Porter	
937	Cali Colombia	4 Jun 1978	Luis Alfonso Rios	
938	San Bernardino California East *Redlands California 5 May 1987	4 Jun 1978	Donald L. Hansen	
939	Guayaquil Ecuador *Guayaquil Ecuador West 22 Mar 1987	11 Jun 1978	Lorenzo A. Garaycoa	
940	Grand Blanc Michigan	11 Jun 1978	Trent Pickett Kitley	
941	Celaya Mexico	11 Jun 1978	Armando Gaona	
942	Roy Utah West	11 Jun 1978	Lewis R. Child	
943	Montreal Quebec	18 Jun 1978	Gerard C. Pelchat	
944	Bakersfield California East	18 Jun 1978	William Horsley Davies	
945	Aarhus Denmark	2 Jul 1978	Knud Bent Andersen	
946	State College Pennsylvania *Altoona Pennsylvania 31 Oct 1982	23 Jul 1978	Robert Armstrong Wood Sr.	
947	Tegucigalpa Honduras	30 Jul 1978	Jose Miguel Dominguez C.	
948	Hanford California	6 Aug 1978	Gerald Leo Thompson	
949	Sapporo Japan	13 Aug 1978	Geiji Katanuma	
950	Buenos Aires Argentina Merlo	13 Aug 1978	Enrique Alfredo Ibarra	
951	Tapachula Mexico	20 Aug 1978	Jorge David Arrevilla M.	
952	Sandpoint Idaho	20 Aug 1978	Richard William Goldsberry	
953	Christchurch New Zealand	27 Aug 1978	Bardia Pine Taiapa	
954	Alexandria Louisiana	27 Aug 1978	Jeffie Jackson Horn	
955	Sandy Utah Central	27 Aug 1978	Charles Alma Jones	
956	North Ogden Utah Ben Lomond	27 Aug 1978	Calvin J. Heiner	
957	Layton Utah Holmes Creek	3 Sep 1978	K. Roger Bean	
958	Centralia Washington	10 Sep 1978	Frank Edward Berrett	
959	Winslow Arizona	17 Sep 1978	Thomas A. Whipple	
960	Pocatello Idaho Chubbuck *Chubbuck Idaho 8 Sep 1987	17 Sep 1978	Errol Smith Phippen	
961	Hemet California	17 Sep 1978	Darrel D. Lee	
962	Anchorage Alaska North	17 Sep 1978	Wesley R. Grover	
963	Duncan Arizona	24 Sep 1978	Earl Adair Merrell	
964	Mobile Alabama	8 Oct 1978	Dean Arthur Rains	
965	Mexico City Mexico Linda Vista	8 Oct 1978	Fernando R. Dorantes T.	
966	Clearfield Utah North	8 Oct 1978	Alfred Clyde Van Wagenen	
967	Vista California	8 Oct 1978	Jack Robert Jones	
968	Sandy Utah Cottonwood Creek	15 Oct 1978	John Robert Ruppel	
969	Sandton South Africa *Pretoria South Africa 29 Nov 1987	22 Oct 1978	Johannes P. Brummer	
970	Araraquara Brazil	22 Oct 1978	Marcio Rodrigues Galhardo	
971	Pocatello Idaho South *Pocatello Idaho East 17 Jun 1984	22 Oct 1978	John Burl McNabb	
972	Sandy Utah Granite	22 Oct 1978	William Stanley Bush	
973	Brigham Young University 13th (Utah)	29 Oct 1978	Leo Preston Vernon	
974	Brigham Young University 14th (Utah)	29 Oct 1978	Curtis Nicholas VanAlfen	
975	Thayne Wyoming	29 Oct 1978	Marlow C. Bateman	

	NAME, LOCALITY *NAME CHANGED †DISORGANIZED			NO. IN
NO.	★TRANSFERRED TO	ORGANIZED	PRESIDENT	YEAR
976	Great Falls Montana East	5 Nov 1978	Howard Merle Hennebry	
977	Montrose Colorado	5 Nov 1978	Robert M. Esplin	
978	Saskatoon Saskatchewan	5 Nov 1978	Noel W. Burt	
979	Vancouver Washington West	5 Nov 1978	Earl Clifford Jorgensen	
980	Winnipeg Manitoba	12 Nov 1978	Lorne Leslie Clapson	
981	Sandy Utah Crescent South	19 Nov 1978	Marlin Alma Fairborn	
982	Salt Lake Hunter Central	19 Nov 1978	Evans Thomas Doxey	
983	Corona California	19 Nov 1978	Darvil David McBride	
984	El Dorado California	19 Nov 1978	Harold George Sellers	
985	Pittsburgh Pennsylvania East	26 Nov 1978	Garth Harrison Ladle	
986	Killeen Texas	26 Nov 1978	Stephen Brian Hutchings	
987	Novo Hamburgo Brazil	3 Dec 1978	Paulo R. Grahl	
988	Chandler Arizona	3 Dec 1978	Elone Evans Farnsworth	
989	Sorocaba Brazil	10 Dec 1978	Nelson de Genaro	
990	Kearns Utah East	10 Dec 1978	Earl M. Monson	107
991	Washington Utah	7 Jan 1979	Lorel Wynn Turek	
992	Spokane Washington North	7 Jan 1979	Dwaine E. Nelson	
993	Santa Cruz Bolivia *Santa Cruz Bolivia Canoto 15 Feb 1981	14 Jan 1979	Noriharu Ishigaki Haraguichi	
994	Cranbrook British Columbia	14 Jan 1979	Brian James Erickson	
995	Buenos Aires Argentina North	28 Jan 1979	Tomas Federico Lindheimer	
996	Salt Lake East Millcreek North	28 Jan 1979	Joel R. Garrett	
997	Mar del Plata Argentina	31 Jan 1979	Hector Luis Catron	
998	Ogden Utah Burch Creek	4 Feb 1979	James Kirk Moyes	
999	Milwaukie Oregon	11 Feb 1979	Thomas Dean Cottle	
1000	Nauvoo Illinois	18 Feb 1979	Gene Lee Roy Mann	
1001	San Nicolas Argentina	22 Feb 1979	Dedlindo Antonio Resek	
1002	Asuncion Paraguay	25 Feb 1979	Carlos Ramon Espinola	
1003	Santiago Chile San Bernardo	25 Feb 1979	Hugo Balmaceda	
1004	Tremonton Utah South	25 Feb 1979	Boyd Lee Cullimore	
1005	Wendell Idaho	25 Feb 1979	Orlo William Stevens	
1006	Guayaquil Ecuador Centenario *Guayaquil Ecuador South 22 Mar 1987	4 Mar 1979	Vincente de la Cuadra S.	
1007	La Paz Bolivia *La Paz Bolivia Miraflores 18 Jan 1981	11 Mar 1979	Jorge Leano	
1008	Bogota Colombia Kennedy	11 Mar 1979	Miguel A. Vargas	
1009	Murray Utah North	11 Mar 1979	John Mace Johnson	
1010	Kaysville Utah South	11 Mar 1979	Newell John Law	
1011	Walla Walla Washington	11 Mar 1979	David L. Hafen	
1012	Palmerston North New Zealand	18 Mar 1979	James Dunlop	
1013	Magna Utah Central	8 Apr 1979	Charles Robert Canfield	
1014	Vancouver British Columbia South	8 Apr 1979	Richard Bulpitt	
1015	Kimberly Idaho	15 Apr 1979	David LaVere Carter	
1016	North Salt Lake Utah	15 Apr 1979	Clare Anderson Jones	
1017	Seoul Korea East	18 Apr 1979	Won Yong Ko	
1018	Fukuoka Japan	20 Apr 1979	Yoshizawa Toshiro	
1019	Salto Uruguay	22 Apr 1979	Atilio Silveiro	
1020	Montpelier Idaho South	22 Apr 1979	Leonard H. Matthews	
1021	Cordoba Argentina North	29 Apr 1979	Juan Aldo Leone	
1022	American Fork Utah East	29 Apr 1979	Dale Orville Gunther	
1023	Yakima Washington North *Selah Washington 31 Aug 1982	29 Apr 1979	Robert Atwood Hague	
1024	Santiago Chile Independencia	6 May 1979	Wilfredo Lopez G.	
1025	Fairmont West Virginia	6 May 1979	David Glen Williams	
1026	Mesa Arizona Lehi	6 May 1979	Otto Stronach Shill Jr.	
1027	Kaysville Utah Crestwood	13 May 1979	Wallace Eldean Holliday	
1028	Rio de Janeiro Brazil Andarai	20 May 1979	Nelson Gennari	
1029	Dayton Ohio East	27 May 1979	Melvin Edwin Gourdin	
1030	Curitiba Brazil North	27 May 1979	Alfredo Heliton de Lemos	

NO.	★TRANSFERRED TO	ORGANIZED	PRESIDENT	NO. IN YEAR
1031	Calgary Alberta West	27 May 1979	Lynn Albert Rosenvall	
1032	Auburn California	27 May 1979	David Oliver Montague	
1033	Fairbanks Alaska	27 May 1979	Dennis E. Cook	
1033	Melo Uruguay	2 Jun 1979	Santiago Gonzalez	
1034	Montevideo Uruguay Maronas	3 Jun 1979	Jorge Washington Ventura	
1035	San Salvador El Salvador Cuzcatlan	3 Jun 1979	Franklin Henriquez Melgar	
1036	Godoy Cruz Argentina	6 Jun 1979	Salvador Molt'o	
1037	Villa Alemana Chile	8 Jun 1979	Eduardo Adrian LaMartine	
1038	Santiago Chile Cinco de Abril	10 Jun 1979	Poblibio Gonzalez Gutierrez	
1039	Santiago Chile La Florida	10 Jun 1979	Carlos G. Zuniga Campusano	
1040	Guatemala City Guatemala Mariscal	10 Jun 1979	Samuel Ramirez Abrego	
1041	Boise Idaho East	10 Jun 1979	Cecil Frank Olsen	
1042	Anderson California	10 Jun 1979	Richard Miller Ericson	
1043	Wellsville Utah	17 Jun 1979	Donald Joseph Jeppesen Jr.	
1043	Coatzacoalcos Mexico	1 Jul 1979	Raymundo Madris Carbajal	
1044	Scranton Pennsylvania	2 Aug 1979	Frederick Adelman Alderks	
1045	Apia Samoa East	5 Aug 1979	Daniel Afamasaga Betham	
1046	Hyrum Utah North	5 Aug 1979	J. Spencer Ward	
1047	Harrisburg Pennsylvania	12 Aug 1979	Charles A. Cooper	
1048	Orem Utah Timp View	12 Aug 1979	Carl Crawford	
1049	Othello Washington	12 Aug 1979	Jay L. Christensen	
1050	Valencia Venezuela	19 Aug 1979	Teodoro Hoffman	
1051	Suitland Maryland	19 Aug 1979	Thomas Bailey Kerr	
1052	Tacoma Washington South	19 Aug 1979	James Rolland Ely	
1053	Quito Ecuador	22 Aug 1979	Ernesto Franco	
	*Quito Ecuador Colon 15 Jan 1981			
1054	Cali Colombia Americus	24 Aug 1979	Libber A. Montoya O.	
1055	Kearns Utah Central	26 Aug 1979	Garth D. Mecham	
1056	Poway California	26 Aug 1979	Paul B. Richardson	
1057	Silverdale Washington	26 Aug 1979	David Junior Jones	
1058	Montevideo Uruguay Cerro	2 Sep 1979	Nester Rivera M.	
1059	Pusan Korea	6 Sep 1979	Chaewhan Chang	
1060	Seoul Korea North	9 Sep 1979	Moo Kwang Hong	
1061	Paradise Valley Arizona	9 Sep 1979	James David King	
1062	Cochabamba Bolivia	11 Sep 1979	Carlos L. Pedraja	
	*Cochabamba Bolivia Universidad 19 Feb 1984			
1063	Lima Peru Callao	16 Sep 1979	Manuel Paredes	
1064	Lima Peru San Juan	16 Sep 1979	Jorge Salazar	
1065	Lima Peru San Martin	16 Sep 1979	Rene Loli	
1066	Bozeman Montana	16 Sep 1979	Frank Wilbert Call	
1067	Riverton Utah North	23 Sep 1979	Keith LeRoy Bergstrom	
1068	Delta Utah West	23 Sep 1979	Glen Wilford Swalberg	
1069	Grantsville Utah West	23 Sep 1979	Don Henning Johnson	
1070	Mexico City Mexico Iztapalapa	14 Oct 1979	Aurelio Valdespino	
1071	Liberty Missouri	14 Oct 1979	Dell Earl Johnsen	
1072	Chino California	14 Oct 1979	Allen Clare Christensen	
1073	Quincy California	14 Oct 1979	Floyd Eugene Warren	
1074	Stevensville Montana	21 Oct 1979	Robert H. Sangster	
1075	Andalien Chile	28 Oct 1979	Pedro E. Arias	
1076	Conroe Texas	28 Oct 1979	Nylen Lee Allphin Jr.	
1077	Santiago Chile Conchali	4 Nov 1979	Juan Castro Duque	
1078	Bloomington Indiana	4 Nov 1979	Hollis Ralph Johnson	
1079	Yuba City California	4 Nov 1979	Lowell R. Tingey	
1080	Londrina Brazil	11 Nov 1979	Carlos Roberto Moeller	
1081	Panama City Panama	11 Nov 1979	Nelson Altamirano Lopez	
1082	Sao Paulo Brazil Santo Amaro	12 Nov 1979	Wilson Sanchez Netto	
1083	Talca Chile	17 Nov 1979	Emilio Diaz	
1084	Pitman New Jersey	18 Nov 1979	Victor Warren Hammond	
	*Cherry Hill New Jersey 23 Sep 1986			
1085	Sioux Falls South Dakota	18 Nov 1979	Russell Lloyd Harward	

NO.	NAME, LOCALITY *NAME CHANGED †DISORGANIZED ★TRANSFERRED TO	ORGANIZED	PRESIDENT	NO. IN YEAR
1138	Sao Paulo Brazil Perdizes	25 May 1980	Oswaldo Silva Camargo	
1139	Los Mochis Mexico	25 May 1980	Victor Manuel Soto	
1140	Ririe Idaho	25 May 1980	Arlo J. Moss	
1141	Kowloon Hong Kong	29 May 1980	Patrick Chung-hei Wong	
	*Hong Kong Kowloon 11 Nov 1984			
1142	Fernando de la Mora Paraguay	1 Jun 1980	Guillermo M. Riveros A.	
1143	Buenos Aires Argentina Castelar	8 Jun 1980	Jorge H. Michalek	
1144	Monterrey Mexico Morelos	8 Jun 1980	Carlos R. Merino D.	
1145	Chiclayo Peru	8 Jun 1980	Jorge Humberto del Carpio M.	
1146	Talcahuano Chile Hualpen	15 Jun 1980	Fernando Aguilar	
	*Hualpen Chile 26 Jul 1988			
1147	Filer Idaho	15 Jun 1980	Karl E. Nelson	
1148	Ephrata Washington	15 Jun 1980	Robert A. Hammond	
1149	Idaho Falls Idaho Lincoln	22 Jun 1980	Cleon Y. Olson	
1150	Citrus Heights California	22 Jun 1980	James Barnes	
1151	Davis California	22 Jun 1980	Peter Glen Kenner	
1152	Sacramento California Cordova	22 Jun 1980	Richard W. Montgomery	
	*Sacramento California Rancho Cordova 17 Sep 1985			
1153	Lakeland Florida	27 Jun 1980	Waymon E. Meadows	
1154	Sapporo Japan West	29 Jun 1980	Bin Kikuchi	
1155	Saltillo Mexico	29 Jun 1980	Roberto Teodoro Guzman R.	
1156	Ucon Idaho	29 Jun 1980	Joseph Dudley Tucker	
1157	Ogden Utah Mt. Lewis	29 Jun 1980	Kenneth J. Alford	
1158	Gillette Wyoming	29 Jun 1980	Marion A. Dalene	
1159	Perth Australia Southern River	6 Jul 1980	Roy B. Webb	
1160	Montreal Quebec Mt. Royal	6 Jul 1980	Ian Gillespie Wilson	
1161	Santa Fe Argentina	20 Jul 1980	Raimundo Eduardo Rippstein	
1162	Iquitos Peru	3 Aug 1980	Carlos Rojas Romero	
1163	Peoria Illinois	3 Aug 1980	Clive Edwin Ashton	
1164	Takasaki Japan	10 Aug 1980	Masataka Kitamura	
1165	Antofagasta Chile	10 Aug 1980	Octavio Araya Yeas	
1166	Villahermosa Mexico	10 Aug 1980	Jose Luis Madrigal Nieves	
1167	Highland Utah	10 Aug 1980	Merlin B. Larson	
1168	Retalhuleu Guatemala	17 Aug 1980	Manuel Efrain Barrios Flores	
1169	Pago Pago Samoa West	24 Aug 1980	William T. Geleai	
1170	Helper Utah	24 Aug 1980	Robert E. Olsen	
1171	Salem Oregon East	24 Aug 1980	William Paul Hyde	
1172	Neiafu Vava'u Tonga North	27 Aug 1980	Mosese Hetau Langi	
1173	Nuku'alofa Tonga Liahona	31 Aug 1980	Vaikalafi Lutui	
1174	Tuxtla Gutierrez Mexico	31 Aug 1980	Enrique Sanchez Casillas	
1175	Melbourne Australia Fairfield West	7 Sep 1980	Edward Anderson	
	*Melbourne Australia Deer Park 18 Mar 1986			
1176	Orem Utah Park	7 Sep 1980	Richard S. Johns	
1177	Rosario Argentina North	10 Sep 1980	Daniel Arnoldo Moreno	
1178	Buenos Aires Argentina Litoral	12 Sep 1980	Jorge Fernandez	
1179	Memphis Tennessee North	14 Sep 1980	Edward Victor Martin	
1180	Shelley Idaho South	14 Sep 1980	Kenneth P. Fielding	
1181	Maracaibo Venezuela	15 Sep 1980	Francisco Giminez Suarez	
1182	Ponta Grossa Parana Brazil	22 Sep 1980	Silvina Mendes de Jesus	
1183	Guadalajara Mexico Independencia	27 Sep 1980	Felipe Covarrubias S.	
1184	Orem Utah Lakeview	28 Sep 1980	Merrill Gappmayer	
1185	Joao Pessoa Brazil	2 Oct 1980	Jose Francisco Barbosa	
1186	Aberdeen Scotland	12 Oct 1980	William Albert Wilson	
1187	Edinburgh Scotland	12 Oct 1980	Alexander Mutter Clark	
1188	Paisley Scotland	12 Oct 1980	Alexander Cumming	
1189	Brasilia Brazil	12 Oct 1980	Daniel Alberta da Gloria	
1190	West Palm Beach Florida	12 Oct 1980	Donald Wayne Carson	
1191	Ogden Utah Weber South	12 Oct 1980	Allan T. Clarke	
1192	South Jordan Utah West	12 Oct 1980	Calvin George Osborne	

	NAME, LOCALITY *NAME CHANGED †DISORGANIZED			NO. IN
NO.	★TRANSFERRED TO	ORGANIZED	PRESIDENT	YEAR
1193	Wellington Utah	12 Oct 1980	Charles V. Bradshaw	
1194	Worland Wyoming	12 Oct 1980	David Harris Asay	
1195	Naha Okinawa Japan	23 Oct 1980	Kensei Nagamine	
1196	Kwang Ju Korea	25 Oct 1980	Bjong Kyu Pak	
1197	Machida Japan	26 Oct 1980	Koichi Aoyagi	
1198	Fredericksburg Virginia	26 Oct 1980	Douglas Lynn Marker	
1199	Magrath Alberta	26 Oct 1980	James Dickson Bridge	
1200	Hermiston Oregon	26 Oct 1980	Allen D. Alder	
1201	Recife Brazil	31 Oct 1980	Iraja Bandeira Soares	
1202	Sendai Japan	2 Nov 1980	Shigenori Funayama	
1203	Nagoya Japan West	2 Nov 1980	Take Shi Nakamura	
1204	Toledo Ohio	2 Nov 1980	Ronald Rufus Burke	
1205	Santiago Chile Huechuraba	9 Nov 1980	Juan Humberto Body B.	
1206	Bountiful Utah North Canyon	9 Nov 1980	Robert Heiner Garff	
1207	La Plata Argentina	23 Nov 1980	Hector Alejandro Olaiz	
1208	Marietta Georgia	23 Nov 1980	William K. Farrar Jr.	
1209	Provo Utah Grandview	23 Nov 1980	Laren R. Robison	
1210	Marikina Philippines	30 Nov 1980	Augusto Alandy Lim	
1211	Houston Texas South	30 Nov 1980	Leo C. Smith	
1212	Taylor Arizona	30 Nov 1980	Peter Delos Shumway	
1213	Oruro Bolivia	1 Dec 1980	J. Adrian Velasco Chavez	
1214	Columbine Colorado	7 Dec 1980	David M. Brown	
1215	San Juan Puerto Rico	14 Dec 1980	Herminio De Jesus	
1216	Santiago Chile El Bosque	14 Dec 1980	Eduardo Ayala Aburto	
1217	Santa Ana El Salvador Modelo	14 Dec 1980	Jorge Alberta Benitez M.	
1218	American Fork Utah West	14 Dec 1980	Brent Lindsay Milne	126
1219	Santa Fe New Mexico	4 Jan 1981	H. Vern Payne	
1220	Cebu City Philippines	11 Jan 1981	Jacob Torres Lopez	
1221	Guayaquil Ecuador Kennedy	11 Jan 1981	Fausto Montalvan Morla	
	†22 Mar 1987 ★Guayaquil Ecuador West (No. 939), Guayaquil Ecuador South (No. 1006), Guayaquil Ecuador North (No. 1117)			
1222	Brampton Ontario	11 Jan 1981	Cecil Malcolm Warner	
1223	San Miguel El Salvador	11 Jan 1981	Carlos Antonio Hernandez	
1224	Portoviejo Ecuador	13 Jan 1981	Jorge Vicente Salazar H.	
1225	Quito Ecuador Santa Ana	15 Jan 1981	Cesar Hugh Cacuango C.	
1226	Angeles Philippines	18 Jan 1981	Orlando D. Aquilar	
1227	La Paz Bolivia El Alto	18 Jan 1981	Victor Hugo Saravia	
1228	Durango Mexico	21 Jan 1981	Ernesto Padilla Lozano	
1229	Dagupan Philippines	25 Jan 1981	Bernardo G. Reamon	
1230	Valparaiso Chile South	1 Feb 1981	Juan Rios Rojas	
1231	San Juis Potosi Mexico	1 Feb 1981	Guillermo G. Soubervielle R.	
1232	Leon Mexico	8 Feb 1981	Armando Gaona Juan	
1233	Phoenix Arizona Deer Valley	8 Feb 1981	E. Wayne Pratt	
1234	Belo Horizonte Brazil	15 Feb 1981	Ernani Teixeira	
1235	Santa Cruz Bolivia Paraiso	15 Feb 1981	Erwin Birnbaumer	
1236	Glendale Arizona North	15 Feb 1981	Richard Johnson Barrett	
1237	Resistencia Argentina	17 Feb 1981	Leopoldo Oscar Fuentes	
1238	Caloocan Philippines	22 Feb 1981	Godofredo Hilario Esguerra	
1239	Prineville Oregon	1 Mar 1981	Heber D. Perrett	
	*Redmond Oregon 18 Feb 1986			
1240	Morgan Utah North	8 Mar 1981	Robert Warner Poll	
1241	Logan Utah Central	8 Mar 1981	Thad August Carlson	
1242	Brigham City Utah West	8 Mar 1981	Lowell Sherratt Jr.	
1243	Curitiba Brazil East	15 Mar 1981	Francisco Reguim	
1244	Renton Washington North	15 Mar 1981	Denzel Nolan Wiser	
1245	Temuco Chile	18 Mar 1981	Eleazar F. Magnere Del Rio	
1246	Managua Nicaragua	22 Mar 1981	Jose R. Armando Garcia A.	
1247	Harlingen Texas	22 Mar 1981	Leonard Moore	
1248	Phoenix Arizona Camelback	22 Mar 1981	Ernest Widtsoe Shumway	

NO.	NAME, LOCALITY	ORGANIZED	PRESIDENT	NO. IN YEAR
1249	Manteca California	22 Mar 1981	David Leon Ward	
1250	Parana Argentina	29 Mar 1981	Carlos Arturo Sosa	
1251	Marysville Washington	29 Mar 1981	Verle George Call	
1252	Caldwell New Jersey	12 Apr 1981	Weldon Courtney McGregor	
1253	Lewisville Texas	12 Apr 1981	Richard W. Ragsdale	
1254	Denham Springs Louisiana	19 Apr 1981	Stephen H. Cutler	
1255	Shizuoka Japan	21 Apr 1981	Tadachika Seno	
1256	Porto Alegre Brazil North	21 Apr 1981	Silvio Geschwasdtner	
1257	Takamatsu Japan	23 Apr 1981	Takejiro Kanzaki	
1258	Kearns Utah Western Hills	26 Apr 1981	Clarence Myron White	
1259	Quevedo Ecuador	27 Apr 1981	Pedro Jose Cantos Jimenez	
1260	Salta Argentina	29 Apr 1981	Victor Hugo Machado	
1261	Bern Switzerland	3 May 1981	Peter Lauener	
1262	Abilene Texas	3 May 1981	William E. Seegmiller	
1263	Antioch California	3 May 1981	Clifford Spence Munns	
1264	Curico Chile	10 May 1981	Jose Luis Ferreira Pais	
1265	Mesa Arizona Central	10 May 1981	Clayton H. Hakes	
1266	Bellingham Washington	10 May 1981	Eugene Clifford Hatch	
1267	Osorno Chile	17 May 1981	Raul Hernan Paredes Pena	
1268	Penco Chile	24 May 1981	Abel Poblete Flores	
1269	Bountiful Utah Stone Creek	24 May 1981	Richard Scott Lemon	
1270	Tokyo Japan South	30 May 1981	Kazutoshi Ono	
1271	Hiroshima Japan	31 May 1981	Satoshi Nishihara	
1272	Amarillo Texas	31 May 1981	Donald Eugene Pinnell	
1273	Soda Springs Idaho North	31 May 1981	Cleston Murrie Godfrey	
	†27 Apr 1986 ★Montpelier Idaho (No. 75), Soda Springs Idaho (No. 73)			
1274	Milan Italy	7 Jun 1981	Mario Vaira	
1275	Quillota Chile	7 Jun 1981	Maximo Ananias Iribarren I.	
1276	Lisbon Portugal	10 Jun 1981	Jose Manuel da Costa Santos	
1277	Stillwater Oklahoma	14 Jun 1981	C. Jay Murray	
1278	Midvale Utah Ft. Union South	14 Jun 1981	Kenneth William Kraudy	
1279	Brisbane Australia West	21 Jun 1981	John D. Jeffrey	
	*Ipswich Australia 6 May 1986			
1280	Oaxaca Mexico	21 Jun 1981	M. Ociel Bengoa Vargas	
1281	Bacolod Philippines	5 Jul 1981	Remus G. Villarete	
1282	Olinda Brazil	12 Jul 1981	Reinhold Kraft	
1283	Blanding Utah West	12 Jul 1981	Preston Gardner Nielson	
1284	Fortaleza Brazil	19 Jul 1981	Orville Wayne Day Jr.	
1285	Rancagua Chile	26 Aug 1981	Hector Verdugo Radrigan	
1286	San Pedro Chile	30 Aug 1981	Juan Cuevas I.	
1287	Hingham Massachusetts	30 Aug 1981	Brent W. Lambert	
1288	New Haven Connecticut	30 Aug 1981	Steven Douglas Colson	
1289	Concord New Hampshire	6 Sep 1981	John Tucker Hills	
1290	Portland Maine	6 Sep 1981	J. Barton Seymour	
1291	Sao Vincente Brazil	20 Sep 1981	Vicente Verta Jr.	
1292	Alegrete Brazil	20 Sep 1981	Waldomiro Siegfried Radtke	
1293	Puebla Mexico Fuertes	11 Oct 1981	Francisco Pineda Salazar	
1294	Hurricane Utah North	11 Oct 1981	Floyd Leon Lewis	
	*La Verkin Utah 30 Nov 1984			
1295	Gilbert Arizona Stapley	11 Oct 1981	Wilburn James Brown	
1296	Winnemucca Nevada	11 Oct 1981	Kenneth H. Lords	
1297	Payson Utah South	18 Oct 1981	Joe Lynn Spencer	
1298	Grants New Mexico	18 Oct 1981	Elbert Leon Roundy	
1299	Colville Washington	18 Oct 1981	Garnett Russell Port	
1300	McMinnville Oregon	25 Oct 1981	Thomas Babb III	
1301	Mante Mexico	1 Nov 1981	Humberto Noriega Farias	
	*Ciudad Mante Mexico 25 Jan 1982			
1302	Curitiba Brazil Bacacheri	1 Nov 1981	Casemiro Antunes Gomes	
1303	Kaohsiung Taiwan	6 Nov 1981	Ho Tung Hai	
1304	Auckland New Zealand Henderson	8 Nov 1981	Alan Robert Patterson	

NO.	NAME, LOCALITY *NAME CHANGED †DISORGANIZED ★TRANSFERRED TO	ORGANIZED	PRESIDENT	NO. IN YEAR
1305	Hamburg Germany North	8 Nov 1981	Karl-Heinz Danklefsen	
	*New Muenster Germany 9 Apr 1985			
1306	Inchon Korea	12 Nov 1981	Chea Huo	
1307	Davao Philippines	15 Nov 1981	George S. Lavarino	
1308	Bucaramanga Colombia	22 Nov 1981	Horacio Julio Insignarez	
1309	Paranaque Philippines	22 Nov 1981	Ruben M. Lacanienta	
1310	Payson Utah West	22 Nov 1981	Gerald M. Finch	
1311	West Jordan Utah Oquirrh	22 Nov 1981	Johannes Gerald Erkelens	
1312	Bothell Washington	22 Nov 1981	Arnold R. Parrott	
1313	BYU-Hawaii 2nd	22 Nov 1981	Herbert Kamaka Sproat	
1314	Durban South Africa	29 Nov 1981	Percy E.A. Winstanley	
1315	San Fernando Philippines La Union	6 Dec 1981	Angel B. Salanga Jr.	
1316	Otavalo Ecuador	6 Dec 1981	Luis Alfonso Morales C.	
1317	Mexico City Mexico Azteca	6 Dec 1981	Juan Alberta Ramos Barrera	
1318	Aurora Colorado	6 Dec 1981	Lawry Evans Doxey	
1319	Draper Utah North	6 Dec 1981	Richard D. Alsop	
1320	Penaflor Chile	10 Dec 1981	Sergio Venegas Pacheo	
1321	Tarlac Philippines	13 Dec 1981	Mario de Jesus	103
1322	Maceio Brazil	21 Jan 1982	Abelardo Rodrigues Camara	
1323	Bacolod Philippines North	7 Feb 1982	Rufino Alvarez Villanueva Jr.	
1324	Mannheim Germany	7 Feb 1982	Baldur H.H. Stoltenberg	
1325	McLean Virginia	14 Feb 1982	Earl John Roueche	
1325	Central Point Oregon	7 Mar 1982	Michael T. Robinson	
1326	Taipei Taiwan East	14 Mar 1982	Yuan-Hu Yen	
1327	Madrid Spain	14 Mar 1982	Jose Mario Oliveira Aldamiz	
1328	Osaka Japan Sakai	17 Mar 1982	Hiroshi Takayoshi	
1329	Tokyo Japan West	21 Mar 1982	Koichi Aoyagi	
1330	Cebu City Philippines South	21 Mar 1982	Bienvenido Pangilinan Flores	
1331	Cheltenham England	21 Mar 1982	Warrick N. Kear	
1332	Boa Viagem Brazil	21 Mar 1982	Iraga Bandeira Soares	
1333	Woods Cross Utah East	21 Mar 1982	Wayne A. Beers	
1334	Rockford Illinois	11 Apr 1982	Brent L. Horsley	
1335	Centerville Utah North	11 Apr 1982	Richard Crockett Edgley	
1336	Ferron Utah	11 Apr 1982	Jerry "D" Mangum	
1337	Kingwood Texas	18 Apr 1982	Robert Lee Ezell	
1338	Joinville Brazil	21 Apr 1982	Heins Dorival Halter	
1339	Puerto Montt Chile	25 Apr 1982	Juan Carlos Lopez Lobos	
1340	Cabanatuan Philippines	9 May 1982	Arsenio A. Pacaduan	
1341	Cardiff Wales	9 May 1982	Barry Derek Roy Whittaker	
1342	Farmington Utah North	16 May 1982	Richard J. White	
1343	Poole England	23 May 1982	Peter J. Crockford	
1344	Goldsboro North Carolina	30 May 1982	James William Dixon	
1345	Ashton England	6 Jun 1982	Brian Ashworth	
1346	Chester England	6 Jun 1982	Peter Furniss Lee	
1347	Logan Utah South	6 Jun 1982	Ronald Skeen Peterson	
1348	Sierra Vista Arizona	6 June 1982	C. Lavell Haymore	
1349	Ponce Puerto Rico	13 Jun 1982	Noah Jefferson Burns	
1350	Red Deer Alberta	13 Jun 1982	Dennis William Guenther	
1351	Providence Utah South	13 Jun 1982	Lanny J. Nalder	
1352	Geneva Switzerland	20 Jun 1982	Denis Bonny	
1353	Albuquerque New Mexico South	20 Jun 1982	Ivan Gary Waddoups	
1354	Laguna Niguel California	20 Jun 1982	Donald H. Sedgwick	
1355	Pirae Tahiti	20 Jun 1982	Lysis G. Terooatea	
1356	Mexico City Mexico Tlalpan	27 Jun 1982	Jose Alberto Rasales G.	
1357	Mexico City Mexico Chapultepec	27 Jun 1982	Jose Ismael Ruiz Guadiana	
1358	Freiberg German Democratic Republic	29 Aug 1982	Frank Herbert Apel	
1359	El Paso Texas Mt. Franklin	29 Aug 1982	Gerald Merrell Pratt	
1360	Orange Texas	29 Aug 1982	Bernard E. Packard	
1361	Santa Clara Utah	29 Aug 1982	Dale Gubler	

NO.	NAME, LOCALITY *NAME CHANGED †DISORGANIZED ★TRANSFERRED TO	ORGANIZED	PRESIDENT	NO. IN YEAR
1362	Bessemer Alabama	12 Sep 1982	Robert Henry Shepherdson	
1363	Kirtland New Mexico	19 Sep 1982	John Scot Fishburn	
1364	Gulfport Mississippi	10 Oct 1982	John Sibbald Scott II	
1365	Gresham Oregon South	10 Oct 1982	Max B. Holbrook	
1366	Savai'i Samoa South	17 Oct 1982	Malina Ropeti Ti'a	
1367	Sandy Utah Granite South	17 Oct 1982	Charles Winston Dahquist II	
1368	New Albany Indiana	24 Oct 1982	Henry Harvey Griffith	
1369	Rexburg Idaho Center	24 Oct 1982	Ronald Curtis Martin	
1370	Barcelona Spain	31 Oct 1982	Jose Lara Straube	
1371	Hickory North Carolina	31 Oct 1982	Gordon M. Thornton	
1372	Reading Pennsylvania	31 Oct 1982	Hugh G. Daubek	
1373	Cedar Mill Oregon	31 Oct 1982	Edgar Lee Stone	
1374	Kennewick Washington East	31 Oct 1982	Donald LeRoy Brunson	
1375	Huntington West Virginia	7 Nov 1982	Grant Earl Jenson	
1376	Sheffield England	14 Nov 1982	Kenneth Jones	
1377	Petropolis Brazil	14 Nov 1982	Antonio Jose Mendoza	
1378	Rio de Janeiro Brazil Madureira	14 Nov 1982	Atilio Pinto Maio	
1379	Santiago Chile Las Canteras	14 Nov 1982	Juan Castro Duque	
1380	Deland Florida *Lake Mary Florida 27 Oct 1987	14 Nov 1982	Marvin Knowles	
1381	Oklahoma City Oklahoma South	14 Nov 1982	Lawrence Andrew Jackson	
1382	Pusan Korea West	20 Nov 1982	Gil Whe Do	
1383	Comayaguela Honduras	21 Nov 1982	Jorge Alberto Sierra B.	
1384	Smithfield Utah North	21 Nov 1982	W. Noble Erickson	
1385	Seoul Korea Chong Ju *Chong Ju Korea 23 Sep 1986	28 Nov 1982	Chung Yul Hwang	
1386	Seoul Korea Kang Seo	28 Nov 1982	Do Hwan Lee	
1387	Seoul Korea Yong Dong	28 Nov 1982	Jae Am Park	
1388	Auburn Washington	28 Nov 1982	Alan Warner Bolles	
1389	Puyallup Washington South	28 Nov 1982	Dennis Tripp Sampson	
1390	Frederick Maryland	12 Dec 1982	Earl J. Wahlquist	
1391	Blackfoot Idaho East	12 Dec 1982	Franklin D. Transtrum	
1392	Lindon Utah	12 Dec 1982	Noel Thomas Greenwood	72
1393	Alvorada Brazil *Brasilia Brazil Alvorada 22 Mar 1983	9 Jan 1983	Manoel Francisco Clavery G.	
1394	Gilmer Texas	16 Jan 1983	Von Webber Freeman	
1395	Laie Hawaii North	16 Jan 1983	Willard Kaaihue Kekauoha	
1396	Richardson Texas	30 Jan 1983	Larry Wayne Gibbons	
1397	Victorville California	30 Jan 1983	Owen Dean Call	
1398	Chillan Chile	13 Feb 1983	Sergio Rios S.	
1399	Tacna Peru	13 Feb 1983	Abraham La Torre Parades	
1400	Piura Peru	16 Feb 1983	Pedro Puertas Rojas	
1401	Meridian Idaho South	20 Feb 1983	Wenden Wayne Waite	
1402	Santiago Chile Las Condes	12 Mar 1983	E. Gustavo Flores Carrasco	
1403	Santiago Chile Pudahuel	13 Mar 1983	Enrique Espinoza	
1404	Okayama Japan	20 Mar 1983	Akira Watanabe	
1405	Buenos Aires Argentina Moreno	20 Mar 1983	Carlos Domingo Marapodi	
1406	Las Vegas Nevada West	20 Mar 1983	Terry Dale Rogers	
1407	Midway Utah	27 Mar 1983	Wayne Watkins Probst	
1408	Tampere Finland	17 Apr 1983	Kari Juhani Aslak Haikkola	
1409	Silver City New Mexico	17 Apr 1983	Hal Butler Keeler	
1410	Eugene Oregon Santa Clara	17 Apr 1983	Terrel B. Williams	
1411	Unlisted			
1412	Seoul Korea Dongdaemun	24 Apr 1983	Son Awunf Ju	
1413	Nancy France	24 Apr 1983	John Keith Bishop	
1414	Maracaibo Venezuela South	24 Apr 1983	Omar Alvarez	
1415	Grand Junction Colorado West	24 Apr 1983	Andrew H. Christensen	
1416	Lehi Utah West	8 May 1983	Boyd Sabey Stewart	
1417	Lafayette Indiana	15 May 1983	Koy Eldridge Miskin	

NO.	NAME, LOCALITY *NAME CHANGED †DISORGANIZED ★TRANSFERRED TO	ORGANIZED	PRESIDENT	NO. IN YEAR
1475	Leipzig German Democratic Republic	3 Jun 1984	Hermann M. Schutze	
1476	Rupert Idaho West	3 Jun 1984	Carl B. Garner	
1477	Huntington Park California West	3 Jun 1984	Rafael Nestor Seminario	
1478	Punta Arenas Chile	10 Jun 1984	Luis Elqueda C.	
1479	Mesa Arizona Pueblo	10 Jun 1984	E. Clark Huber	
1480	Carolina Puerto Rico	17 Jun 1984	Jesus Nieves	
1481	Arimo Idaho	17 Jun 1984	Douglas Sorensen	
1482	Bennion Utah Central *Bennion Heights Utah 28 Aug 1988	17 Jun 1984	Glen Alvin Weight	
1483	Springville Utah Hobble Creek	17 Jun 1984	Donald Blaine Hadley	
1484	Pocatello Idaho Central	17 Jun 1984	Thomas William Ranstrom	
1485	Roy Utah Central	24 Jun 1984	Mark Lee Angus	
1486	Lima Peru Palao	1 Jul 1984	Rene Loli	
1487	Trujillo Peru Palermo	12 Aug 1984	Jose Neyra	
1488	Salt Lake University 3rd (Utah)	19 Aug 1984	James Stuart Jardine	
1489	Sandy Utah Alta View	19 Aug 1984	G. Scott Dean	
1490	Orem Utah College	26 Aug 1984	Charles E. Peterson	
1491	South Jordan Utah East	9 Sep 1984	Charles Elmo Turner	
1492	Santiago Chile Renca	16 Sep 1984	Eduardo Cabezas Ossa	
1493	Evanston Wyoming South	23 Sep 1984	Harold Sidney Stock	
1494	Harrisville Utah	23 Sep 1984	Robert Lynn Nielsen	
1495	Kent Washington	14 Oct 1984	Owen Edvin Jensen	
1496	Seattle Washington Shoreline	14 Oct 1984	Brent Isaac Nash	
1497	Quetzaltenango Guatemala West	24 Oct 1984	Amilcar Raul Robles Arango	
1498	San Marcos Guatemala	24 Oct 1984	Abraham Raymundo Juarez C.	
1499	Achupallas Chile	28 Oct 1984	Luis Alino Pereira P.	
1500	Ciudad Obregon Mexico Yaqui	28 Oct 1984	Jorge Mendez Ibarra	
1501	Caliche Chile	4 Nov 1984	Ricardo Manuel Palma F.	
1502	Hong Kong Kowloon North	11 Nov 1984	Fu Man Yau	
1503	Hong Kong New Territories	11 Nov 1984	Johnson Ma	
1504	Ontario Oregon	18 Nov 1984	Reed Neils Dame	
1505	Carmichael California	25 Nov 1984	Marc Earl Hall	
1506	Willard Utah	25 Nov 1984	Robert Kent Lund	
1507	Soldotna Alaska	9 Dec 1984	Merrill D. Briggs	49
1508	Iloilo Philippines	20 Jan 1985	Hannibal Delgado De Los R.	
1509	West Jordan Utah Welby	20 Jan 1985	Russell Jean Abney	
1510	Magna Utah South	20 Jan 1985	Hendrick Dorenbosch	
1511	West Jordan Utah Southeast	27 Jan 1985	Frederick James Haydock	
1512	West Jordan Utah North	3 Feb 1985	Henry Keonaona Chai II	
1513	Chandler Arizona Alma	24 Feb 1985	Martin H. Durrant	
1514	Anaheim California East	24 Feb 1985	William E. Perron	
1515	San Francisco California West	24 Feb 1985	Jeremiah I. Alip	
1516	Sao Jose Dos Campos Brazil	3 Mar 1985	Eric Brito Correa	
1517	Tucson Arizona Rincon	3 Mar 1985	Ernest G. Blain	
1518	Orem Utah Northeast *Orem Utah Canyon View 1 Mar 1988	3 Mar 1985	Jerry C. Washburn	
1519	Las Vegas Nevada Green Valley	3 Mar 1985	Roger Lee Hunt	
1520	Park City Utah	10 Mar 1985	B. Douglas Glad	
1521	Bluffdale Utah	10 Mar 1985	Michael Van Jeppson	
1522	Calama Chile	17 Mar 1985	Ivan Gonzalez Castillo	
1523	Cincinnati Ohio North	17 Mar 1985	William B. Wallis	
1524	Ephraim Utah	24 Mar 1985	Joseph C. Nielsen	
1525	Snow College Utah	24 Mar 1985	Allen P. Jacobson	
1526	Altamont Utah	21 Apr 1985	Everett Dee Roberts	
1527	Cuzco Peru	28 Apr 1985	Jose U. Coacalla	
1528	Greeley Colorado	28 Apr 1985	Gilbert I. Sandberg	
1529	Layton Utah North	5 May 1985	Lorin Winslow Hurst Jr.	
1530	Dartmouth Nova Scotia	12 May 1985	Terry Lee Livingstone	
1531	Fielding Utah	12 May 1985	Mark H. Jensen	

NO.	NAME, LOCALITY *NAME CHANGED †DISORGANIZED ★TRANSFERRED TO	ORGANIZED	PRESIDENT	NO. IN YEAR
1532	Torreon Mexico Jardin	12 May 1985	Rafael Leon Miranda	
1533	Salt Lake Hunter Copperhill	12 May 1985	Stanley Martin Kimball	
1534	Willow Creek Colorado	19 May 1985	Robert K. Bills	
1535	Cagayan De Oro Philippines	26 May 1985	Loreto Balanta Libid	
1536	Sao Paulo Brazil Interlagos	26 May 1985	Walter Guedes de Queiroz	
1537	Barranquilla Colombia	30 May 1985	Libardo Rodriguez	
1538	Nephi Utah North	9 June 1985	James Randy McKnight	
1539	Salt Lake Hunter South	9 June 1985	Morris L. Terry	
1540	Arequipa Peru Manuel Prado	20 June 1985	Efrain Jorge Rodriguez M.	
1541	Iquitos Peru Sacha Chorro	23 June 1985	Jorge Diaz Suarez	
1542	Las Vegas Nevada Lakes	23 June 1985	Dennis E. Simmons	
1543	Rochester New York Palmyra	30 June 1985	Kay R. Whitmore	
1544	Davao Philippines Buhangin	18 Aug 1985	Patrick Hartford M. Clair	
1545	Makiling Philippines	18 Aug 1985	Jose Trinidad Aguilar	
1546	Naga Philippines	18 Aug 1985	Avelino S. Babia Sr.	
1547	La Carlota Philippines	18 Aug 1985	Antonio V. Custodio	
1548	Santiago Chile Puente Alto	18 Aug 1985	Jorge A. Pedrero Martinez	
1549	Santiago Chile San Miguel	18 Aug 1985	Hector G. Carvajal Arenas	
1550	Monroe Louisiana	18 Aug 1985	John Robert Falk	
1551	Legaspi Philippines	19 Aug 1985	Jose P. Leveriza	
1552	San Pablo Philippines	20 Aug 1985	Cleofas S. Canoy	
1553	Lima Peru Villa Maria	25 Aug 1985	Juan Maguina Colquis	
1554	Pasig Philippines	15 Sep 1985	Macario Molina Yasona Jr.	
1555	Las Pinas Philippines	15 Sep 1985	Delfin T. Justiniano	
1556	Venice Italy	15 Sep 1985	Claudio E. Luttmann	
1557	Lingayen Philippines	22 Sep 1985	Oberlito R. Cantillo	
1558	Urdaneta Philippines	22 Sep 1985	Felino Caparas Ocampo	
1559	Hyde Park Utah	22 Sep 1985	Vincent Eugene Erickson	
1560	Ft. Macleod Alberta	29 Sep 1985	Heber James Beazer	
1561	Midvale Utah North	13 Oct 1985	Grant Leon Pullan	
1562	Anoka Minnesota	20 Oct 1985	Lyle T Cottle	
1563	Cape Girardeau Missouri	20 Oct 1985	David E. Payne	
1564	Enoch Utah	20 Oct 1985	Robert Louis Blattner	
1565	Lakewood Washington	20 Oct 1985	James Rolland Ely	
1566	Seneca Maryland	27 Oct 1985	David Warne Ferrel	
1567	Chiclayo Peru Central	27 Oct 1985	Franklin D. Orroyo Suarez	
1568	Fruit Heights Utah	27 Oct 1985	Newell John Law	
1569	Florianopolis Brazil	3 Nov 1985	Cesar A. Seiguer Milder	
1570	Vancouver Washington North	3 Nov 1985	Bruce A. Schreiner	
1571	Zamboanga Philippines	10 Nov 1985	Catalino A. Dugupan Sr.	
1572	Cadiz Philippines	10 Nov 1985	Carmelino M. Cawit	
1573	Baguio Philippines	17 Nov 1985	Carlos F. Chavez	
1574	New York New York East	17 Nov 1985	Mark Eliot Butler	
1575	Slidell Louisiana	17 Nov 1985	Joseph T. Kuchin	
1576	Las Vegas Nevada Sunrise	17 Nov 1985	Norman Wellington Gates	
1577	Munoz Philippines	24 Nov 1985	Juanito Wytangooy Tanedo	
1578	Fortaleza Brazil Oeste	24 Nov 1985	Antenor Silva Junior	
1579	Mexico City Mexico Valle Dorado	28 Nov 1985	Arturo Lopez Gomez	
1580	Mayaquez Puerto Rico	1 Dec 1985	Heriberto Hernandez Vera	
1581	Orem Utah Sharon South	1 Dec 1985	Wynn Howard Hemmert	
1582	Santee California	8 Dec 1985	Robert Earl Harper	75
1583	Mt. Vernon Virginia	5 Jan 1986	Keith Alan Gulledge	
1584	Fremont California South	12 Jan 1986	Jerry Valient Kirk	
1585	Guayana Venezuela	15 Jan 1986	Luis A. Aguilar Guevara	
1586	Campinas Brazil Castelo	2 Feb 1986	S. Lourenco de Oliveira	
1587	La Mesa Mexico *Tijuana Mexico La Mesa 15 Apr 1986	9 Feb 1986	Angel Luevano Cordova	
1587	Walnut Creek California East	16 Feb 1986	Williams F. Matthews	
1588	Dothan Alabama	2 Mar 1986	Ned Philip Jenne	

NO.	NAME, LOCALITY *NAME CHANGED †DISORGANIZED ★TRANSFERRED TO	ORGANIZED	PRESIDENT	NO. IN YEAR
1589	Jalapa Mexico	2 Mar 1986	Jorge Sanchez	
1590	Lake City Florida	16 Mar 1986	Ernest Robert Peacock	
1591	Turlock California	23 Mar 1986	Robert Peebles Baker	
1592	Erie Pennsylvania	23 Mar 1986	Philip Dale Baker	
1593	Santo Domingo Dominican Republic	23 Mar 1986	Jose Delio Ceveno	
1594	Arlington Texas	13 Apr 1986	Richard S. Pickering	
1595	Bangor Maine	20 Apr 1986	Paul Herald Risk II	
1596	San Miguelito Panama	20 Apr 1986	Domingo Estribi	
1596	Jeon Ju Korea	27 Apr 1986	Ju In Pak	
1597	Appleton Wisconsin	11 May 1986	Nevin Richard Limburg	
1598	Arica Chile El Morro	18 May 1986	Sergio Alberto Funes	
1599	Los Angeles Chile	1 Jun 1986	Mario Carlos Escobar	
1600	Kitchener Ontario	22 Jun 1986	Graeme K. Hingston	
1601	La Lima Honduras	22 Jun 1986	Rodolfo Arguello A.	
1602	Fontana California	22 Jun 1986	Wayne Hall Bringhurst	
1603	Mexico City Mexico Anahuac	29 Jun 1986	Luis Manuel Angel Baez	
1604	Passo Fundo Brazil	10 Aug 1986	Helio Rodrigues Severo	
1605	Brigham Young University 15th (Utah)	31 Aug 1986	H. Donl Peterson	
1606	Charlotte North Carolina Central	21 Sep 1986	Kenneth Larson	
1607	Salt Lake Eagle Gate (Utah)	21 Sep 1986	W. Herbert Klopfer	
1608	Penasquitos California	21 Sep 1986	Michael Lee Jensen	
1609	Columbus Ohio North	19 Oct 1986	D. Richard McFerson	
1610	Olathe Kansas	19 Oct 1986	Clifton D. Boyack Jr.	
1611	Guatemala City Guatemala Chimaltenango *Chimaltenango Guatemala 22 Mar 1988	26 Oct 1986	Mario Salazar Moran	
1612	Sandy Utah Granite View	26 Oct 1986	Alan Snelgrove Layton	
1613	Porto Portugal	2 Nov 1986	Alcino Pereira Da Silva	
1614	Papillion Nebraska	2 Nov 1986	Wayne Leon Mangelson	
1615	Monterrey Mexico Valle Verde	2 Nov 1986	Jose F. Torres M.	
1616	Apache Junction Arizona	16 Nov 1986	Charles Wray Squires	
1617	Melbourne Australia Waverly	7 Dec 1986	Ian Frank Davenport	
1618	Guatemala City Guatemala Atlantico	7 Dec 1986	Luis Alvarez Ovando	
1619	Guatemala City Guatemala Central	7 Dec 1986	Armando G. Diaz Lopez	
1620	Guatemala City Guatemala Florida	7 Dec 1986	Miguel A. Gomez Lopez	
1621	Iquique Chile	14 Dec 1986	Nelson C. Mondaca I.	
1622	Bakersfield California South	14 Dec 1986	Jack Ray Zimmerman	42
1623	Bloomington Hills Utah	4 Jan 1987	James Grey Larkin	
1624	Thousand Oaks California	11 Jan 1987	Grant R. Brimhall	
1625	Washington Utah West	18 Jan 1987	H. Carlyle Stirling	
1626	Mexicali Mexico Los Pinos	18 Jan 1987	Jose de Jesus Ruelas U.	
1627	Eagar Arizona	25 Jan 1987	Charles D. Martin	
1628	Mesa Arizona Mountain View	25 Jan 1987	James R. Adair	
1629	Layton Utah South	8 Feb 1987	William C. Barney Jr.	
1630	Vitoria Brazil	15 Feb 1987	Pedro J. da Cruz Penha	
1631	Peoria Arizona	22 Feb 1987	Thomas G. Jones	
1632	Hesperia California	22 Feb 1987	Larry Dale Skinner	
1633	Chihuahua Mexico East	1 Mar 1987	Humberto Enrique Serna G.	
1634	St. Louis Missouri North	15 Mar 1987	Neal C. Lewis	
1633	Irvine California	12 Apr 1987	Jack L. Rushton Jr.	
1634	David Panama	19 Apr 1987	Manuel Salvador Arauz	
1635	Kanesville Utah	19 Apr 1987	Roland B. Hadley	
1636	Hermosillo Mexico Pitic	26 Apr 1987	Carlos Pineda Ochoa	
1637	Durham North Carolina	3 May 1987	James L. Bennett Jr.	
1638	Kanab Utah South	3 May 1987	Nils G. Bayles	
1639	Sandy Utah Crescent Park	17 May 1987	Brad Jensen Sheppard	
1640	Aguascalientes Mexico	17 May 1987	Jose Luis Rios A.	
1641	Goiania Brazil	24 May 1987	Antonio Casado Rodriguez	
1642	Jujuy Argentina	7 Jun 1987	Pedro Horacio Velazquez	

NO.	NAME, LOCALITY *NAME CHANGED †DISORGANIZED ★TRANSFERRED TO	ORGANIZED	PRESIDENT	NO. IN YEAR
1643	Marietta Georgia East	21 Jun 1987	Paul A. Snow	
1644	Culiacan Mexico Tamazula	21 Jun 1987	Rosario Lobo	
1645	Ribeirao Preto Brazil	28 Jun 1987	Moises Barreiro Damasceno	
1646	Springfield Massachusetts	28 Jun 1987	David O. Sutton	
1647	La Ceiba Honduras	28 Jun 1987	Luis Alfredo Salazar V.	
1648	Cucamonga California	28 Jun 1987	Steven Thomas Escher	
1649	Lompoc California	23 Aug 1987	Billy Ray Williams	
1650	Fallon Nevada South	30 Aug 1987	Robert Floyd West	
1651	Nuremberg Germany Servicemen	6 Sep 1987	Jon Paul Baker	
1652	Setubal Portugal	6 Sep 1987	Octavio Da Silva Melo	
1653	Valle del Mezquital Mexico	13 Sep 1987	Joel Gandara Salazar	
1654	Livermore California	13 Sep 1987	Willis Arthur Sandholtz	
1655	Arapahoe Colorado	27 Sep 1987	Lawry Evans Doxey	
1656	Moreno Valley California	27 Sep 1987	David Lowell Briggs	
1657	Layton Utah Northridge	11 Oct 1987	Samuel Clair Bankhead	
1658	Pelotas Brazil	18 Oct 1987	Marco Antonio Rais	
1659	Bogota Colombia El Dorado	18 Oct 1987	Humberto Lopez Silva	
1660	Jacksonville Florida North	15 Nov 1987	Robert Edwin Bone	
1661	Gilbert Arizona Val Vista	22 Nov 1987	Craig Allen Cardon	
1662	Benoni South Africa	29 Nov 1987	Jan G. Hugo	
1663	Mexico City Mexico Ecatepec	6 Dec 1987	Juan Manuel Rodriguez C.	
1664	Auckland New Zealand Tamaki	13 Dec 1987	Clark W. Palmerstown Larkins	
1665	Idaho Falls Idaho Eagle Rock	13 Dec 1987	Michael Dean Crapo	
1666	Buckeye Arizona	13 Dec 1987	Charles Roy Rucker	46
1667	Valdivia Chile	10 Jan 1988	Armando Ambrosio Linco P.	
1668	Orem Utah Aspen	10 Jan 1988	Ross Steve Wolfley	
1669	Lille France	17 Jan 1988	Dominique Degrave	
1670	La Paz Bolivia Sopocachi	17 Jan 1988	Eduardo Gabarret I.	
1671	Chesapeake Virginia	17 Jan 1988	Joseph Craig Merrell	
1672	Long Grove Illinois	24 Jan 1988	William David Johnston	
1673	Roy Utah South	24 Jan 1988	Alonzo C Heiner	
1674	Lima Peru Las Palmeras	31 Jan 1988	Albina Isidro Chagua C.	
1675	Lima Peru Comas	31 Jan 1988	Grover Pinto R.	
1676	Lima Peru Vitarte	31 Jan 1988	Luis E. Stiglich S.	
1677	Lima Peru Las Flores	31 Jan 1988	Miguel Fernando Rojas A.	
1678	Lima Peru Maranga	31 Jan 1988	Benedicto Santiago Pacheco M.	
1679	Lima Peru Chorrillos	31 Jan 1988	Israel Antonio Gonzalez B.	
1680	Lima Peru El Olivar	31 Jan 1988	Antero Miguel Sanchez M.	
1681	Guatemala City Guatemala Escuintla	31 Jan 1988	Enrique Leveron L.	
1682	Orem Utah Northridge	31 Jan 1988	Larry V. Perkins	
1683	Long Beach California North	31 Jan 1988	V. Jay Spongberg	
1684	Brisbane Australia North	7 Feb 1988	Douglas Walter Hill	
1685	Oaxaca Mexico Monte Alban	7 Feb 1988	Valentin Cruz B.	
1686	West Jordan Utah Prairie	7 Feb 1988	J. Kim Christensen	
1687	Seville Spain	14 Feb 1988	Jesus Manuel Benitez S.	
1688	Brigham Young University 16th (Utah)	21 Feb 1988	Donald J Butler	
1689	Rexburg Idaho College 4th	6 Mar 1988	Jay Lufkin Risenmay	
1690	Bloomington Utah	6 Mar 1988	Steven Howard Peterson	
1691	Sacramento California Antelope	6 Mar 1988	Roger William Mack	
1692	Provo Utah Edgemont North	20 Mar 1988	Clayton S. Huber	
1693	Murrieta California	20 Mar 1988	Ronald Miguel Peterson	
1694	Linares Chile	24 Apr 1988	Alberto Ariosto Alveal V.	
1695	Aba Nigeria	15 May 1988	David William Eka	
1696	Salina Kansas	29 May 1988	Thomas R. Coleman	
1697	Medellin Colombia	5 Jun 1988	Arnold Porras Martinez	
1698	Saint John New Brunswick	26 Jun 1988	Blaine E. Hatt	
1699	Ciudad Juarez Mexico North	9 Oct. 1988	Luis Carlos Gomez	
1700	Manaus Brazil	16 Oct 1988	Eduardo A. Soares Contieri	

FIRST STAKE ORGANIZED
IN COUNTRIES OF THE WORLD

COUNTRY	NAME OF STAKE	DATE ORGANIZED	NAME CHANGED *-DISORGANIZED
AMERICAN SAMOA	Pago Pago (#488)	June 15, 1969	Pago Pago Samoa Jan. 14, 1969
ARGENTINA	Buenos Aires (#423)	Nov. 20, 1966	Buenos Aires Argentina East Jan. 14, 1974
AUSTRALIA	Sydney (#293)	March 27, 1960	Sydney Australia Greenwich Jan. 14, 1974
AUSTRIA	Vienna Austria (#1126)	April 20, 1980	
BELGIUM	Brussels Belgium (#813)	Feb. 20, 1977	
BOLIVIA	Santa Cruz Bolivia (#993)	Jan. 14, 1979	Santa Cruz Bolivia Canoto Feb. 15, 1981
BRAZIL	Sao Paulo (#417)	May 1, 1966	Sao Paulo Brazil Jan. 14, 1974
CANADA	Alberta (#35)	June 9, 1895	Cardston Alberta Jan. 14, 1974
CHILE	Santiago (#590)	Nov. 19, 1972	Santiago Chile Quinta Normal Jan. 10, 1980
COLOMBIA	Bogota Colombia (#805)	Jan. 23, 1977	
COSTA RICA	San Jose Costa Rica (#803)	Jan. 20, 1977	
DENMARK	Copenhagen Denmark (#648)	June 16, 1974	
DOMINICAN REPUBLIC	Santo Domingo Dominican Republic (#1593)	March 23, 1986	
ECUADOR	Guayaquil Ecuador (939)	June 11, 1978	Guayaquil Ecuador West March 22, 1987
EL SALVADOR	San Salvador (#618)	June 3, 1973	San Salvador El Salvador Jan. 14, 1974
ENGLAND	Manchester (#294)	March 27, 1960	Manchester England Jan. 14, 1974
FIJI ISLANDS	Suva Fiji (#1426)	June 5, 1983	
FINLAND	Helsinki Finland (#865)	Oct. 16, 1977	
FRANCE	Paris France (#731)	Nov. 16, 1975	
GERMAN DEMOCRATIC REPUBLIC	Freiberg German Democratic Republic (#1358)	Aug. 29, 1982	
GUATEMALA	Guatemala City (#436)	May 21, 1967	Guatemala City Guatemala Jan. 14, 1974
HONDURAS	San Pedro Sula Honduras (#820)	April 10, 1977	
HONG KONG	Hong Kong (#756)	April 25, 1976	Hong Kong Island May 29, 1980
ITALY	Milan, Italy (#1274)	June 7, 1981	
JAPAN	Tokyo (#505)	March 15, 1970	Tokyo Japan Jan. 14, 1974
MEXICO	Juarez (#37)	Dec. 9, 1895	Colonia Juarez Mexico Jan. 14, 1974
THE NETHERLANDS	Holland (#326)	March 12, 1961	The Hague Netherlands Aug. 12, 1976
NEW ZEALAND	Auckland (#264)	May 18, 1958	Auckland New Zealand Mt. Roskill Jan. 14, 1974
NICARAGUA	Managua Nicaragua (#1246)	March 22, 1981	
NIGERIA	Aba Nigeria (#1695)	May 15, 1988	
NORTHERN IRELAND	Belfast Ireland (#647)	June 9, 1974	Belfast Northern Ireland Jan 13, 1987

NORWAY	Oslo Norway (#835)	May 22, 1977	
PANAMA	Panama City Panama (#1081)	Nov. 11, 1979	
PARAGUAY	Asuncion Paraguay (#1002)	Feb. 25, 1979	
PERU	Lima (#503)	Feb. 22, 1970	Lima Peru Limatambo Nov. 21, 1976
PHILIPPINES	Manila (#613)	May 20, 1973	Manila Philippines Jan. 14, 1974
PORTUGAL	Lisbon Portugal (#1276)	June 10, 1981	
PUERTO RICO	San Juan Puerto Rico (#1215)	Dec. 14, 1980	
SCOTLAND	Glasgow (#356)	Aug. 26, 1962	Glasgow Scotland Jan. 14, 1974
SOUTH AFRICA	Transvaal (#506)	March 22, 1970	Johannesburg South Africa Jan. 14, 1974
SOUTH KOREA	Seoul (#604)	March 8, 1973	Seoul Korea Jan. 14, 1974
SPAIN	Madrid Spain (#1327)	March 14, 1982	
SWEDEN	Stockholm Sweden (#691)	April 20, 1975	
SWITZERLAND	Swiss (#341)	Oct. 28, 1961	Zurich Switzerland Jan. 14, 1974
TAHITI	Tahiti (#573)	May 14, 1972	Papeete Tahiti Jan. 14, 1974
TAIWAN	Taipei Taiwan (#755)	April 22, 1976	Taipei Taiwan West March 14, 1982
TONGA	Nuku'alofa (#463)	Sept. 5, 1968	Nuku'alofa Tonga Jan. 14, 1974
UNITED STATES	Kirtland (#1) †Salt Lake (#1a)	Feb. 17, 1834 Oct. 3, 1847	*May 28, 1841
URUGUAY	Montevideo (#444)	Nov. 12, 1967	Montevideo Uruguay West Feb. 17, 1974
VENEZUELA	Caracas Venezuela (#827)	May 15, 1977	
WALES	Merthyr Tydfil Wales (#676)	Jan. 12, 1975	
WEST GERMANY	Berlin (#334)	Sept. 10, 1961	Berlin Germany Jan. 14, 1974
WESTERN SAMOA	Apia (#353)	March 18, 1962	Apia Samoa Jan. 14, 1974

Chronological number of stake's creation, see pages 210-254
†First permanent stake

FIRST STAKE ORGANIZED
IN EACH STATE OF THE UNITED STATES

STATE	NAME OF STAKE	DATE ORGANIZED	NAME CHANGED *-DISORGANIZED
ALABAMA	Alabama (#452)	March 3, 1968	Huntsville Alabama Jan. 14, 1974
ALASKA	Alaska (#331)	Aug. 13, 1961	Anchorage Alaska Jan. 14, 1974
ARIZONA	Little Colorado (#21) †Maricopa (#24)	Jan. 27, 1878 Dec. 10, 1882	*Dec. 18, 1887 Mesa Arizona Maricopa Jan. 14, 1974
ARKANSAS	Arkansas (#484)	June 1, 1969	Little Rock Arkansas Jan. 14, 1974
CALIFORNIA	San Bernardino (#4) †Hollywood (#98)	July 6, 1851 May 22, 1927	*by 1857 Los Angeles California Jan. 14, 1974

COLORADO	San Luis (#26)	June 10, 1883	Manassa Colorado May 31, 1983
CONNECTICUT	Hartford (#421)	Sept. 18, 1966	Hartford Connecticut Jan 14, 1974
DELAWARE	Wilmington Delaware (#673)	Dec. 8, 1975	
DISTRICT OF COLUMBIA	Washington (#131)	June 30, 1940	Washington D.C. Jan. 14, 1974
FLORIDA	Florida (#163)	Jan. 19, 1947	Jacksonville Florida West Jan. 14, 1974
GEORGIA	Atlanta (#241)	May 5, 1957	Tucker Georgia Sept. 1, 1974
HAWAII	Oahu (#113)	June 30, 1935	Laie Hawaii Jan. 14, 1974
IDAHO	Bear Lake (#8)	June 20, 1869	Paris Idaho Jan. 14, 1974
ILLINOIS	Nauvoo (#2a) †Chicago (#118)	Oct. 5, 1839 Nov. 29, 1936	*by 1846 Wilmette Illinois Jan. 14, 1974
INDIANA	Indianapolis (#283)	May 17, 1959	Indianapolis Indiana Jan. 14, 1974
IOWA	Iowa (#3) †Cedar Rapids (#419)	Oct. 5, 1839 May 29, 1966	*Jan. 6, 1842 Cedar Rapids Iowa Jan. 14, 1974
KANSAS	Wichita (#355)	June 24, 1962	Wichita Kansas Jan. 14, 1974
KENTUCKY	Louisville (#540)	Jan. 17, 1971	Louisville Kentucky Jan. 14, 1974
LOUISIANA	New Orleans (#221)	June 19, 1955	New Orleans Louisiana Jan. 14, 1974
MAINE	Maine (#461)	June 23, 1968	Augusta Maine Jan. 14, 1974
MARYLAND	Chesapeake (#526)	Sept. 13, 1970	Silver Spring Maryland Jan. 14, 1974
MASSACHUSETTS	Boston (#354)	May 20, 1962	Boston Massachusetts Jan. 14, 1974
MICHIGAN	Detroit (#197)	Nov. 9, 1952	Bloomfield Hills Michigan Jan. 14, 1974
MINNESOTA	Minnesota (#317)	Nov. 29, 1960	Minneapolis Minnesota Jan. 14, 1974
MISSISSIPPI	Jackson (#404)	May 2, 1965	Jackson Mississippi Jan. 14, 1974
MISSOURI	Clay-Caldwell (#2) †Kansas City (#234)	July 3, 1834 Oct. 21, 1956	*by 1839 Kansas City Missouri Jan. 14, 1974
MONTANA	Butte (#208)	June 28, 1953	Butte Montana Jan. 14, 1974
NEBRASKA	Winter Quarters (#318)	Dec. 11, 1960	Omaha Nebraska Jan. 14, 1974
NEVADA	Carson Valley (#7) †Moapa (#64)	Oct. 4, 1856 June 9, 1912	*by 1858 Logandale Las Vegas Nevada Jan. 14, 1974
NEW HAMPSHIRE	Merrimack (#507)	March 22, 1970	Nashua New Hampshire May 9, 1980
NEW JERSEY	New Jersey (#292)	Feb. 28, 1960	Morristown New Jersey Feb. 26, 1976
NEW MEXICO	Young (#63)	May 21, 1912	Farmington New Mexico Jan. 14, 1974
NEW YORK	New York (#110)	Dec. 9, 1934	New York New York Jan. 14, 1974
NORTH CAROLINA	North Carolina (#332)	Aug. 27, 1961	Kinston North Carolina Jan. 14, 1974
NORTH DAKOTA	Fargo North Dakota (#852)	Aug. 7, 1977	
OHIO	Kirtland (#1) †Cincinnati (#270)	Feb. 17, 1834 Nov. 23, 1958	*May 24, 1841 Cincinnati Ohio Jan. 14, 1974

OKLAHOMA	Tulsa (#298)	May 1, 1960	Tulsa Oklahoma Jan. 14, 1974
OREGON	Union (#49)	June 9, 1901	La Grande Oregon Jan. 14, 1974
PENNSYLVANIA	Philadelphia (#304)	Oct. 16, 1960	Philadelphia Pennsylvania Jan. 14, 1974
RHODE ISLAND	Providence Rhode Island (#818)	March 20, 1977	
SOUTH CAROLINA	South Carolina (#169)	Oct. 19, 1947	Columbia South Carolina Jan. 14, 1974
SOUTH DAKOTA	Rapid City (#592)	Dec. 10, 1972	Rapid City South Dakota Jan. 14, 1974
TENNESSEE	Memphis (#403)	April 18, 1965	Memphis Tennessee Jan. 14, 1974
TEXAS	El Paso (#194)	Sept. 21, 1952	El Paso Texas Jan. 14, 1974
UTAH	Salt Lake (#1a)	Oct. 3, 1847	
VERMONT	Montpelier Vermont (#753)	April 11, 1976	
VIRGINIA	Virginia (#245)	June 30, 1957	Richmond Virginia Jan. 14, 1974
WASHINGTON	Seattle (#124)	July 31, 1938	Seattle Washington Jan. 14, 1974
WEST VIRGINIA	West Virginia (#522)	Aug. 23, 1970	Charleston West Virginia Jan. 14, 1974
WISCONSIN	Milwaukee (#367)	Feb. 3, 1963	Milwaukee Wisconsin Jan. 14, 1974
WYOMING	Star Valley (#33)	Aug. 14, 1892	Afton Wyoming Jan. 14, 1974

#Chronological number of stake's creation, see pages 210-254
†First permanent stake

FACTS ABOUT STAKES OF THE CHURCH

(As of October 16, 1988)

MOST STAKES IN ONE NATION
1. United States — 1,108
2. Mexico — 92
3. Brazil — 57
4. Chile — 48
5. Canada — 34
6. Philippines — 32
   England — 32
8. Peru — 31
9. Argentina — 26
10. Japan — 23

MOST STAKES IN ONE STATE
1. Utah — 382
2. California — 153
3. Idaho — 94
4. Arizona — 56
5. Washington — 46
6. Texas — 34
7. Oregon — 32
8. Colorado — 23
   Nevada — 23
10. Florida — 18

MOST STAKES CREATED IN ONE YEAR — 1980, 126 new stakes

MOST STAKES CREATED, ONE MONTH — November 1975 and May 1978, 23 each

MOST STAKES CREATED, ONE DAY — Nov. 9, 1975, Jan. 31, 1988, 10 each

PERCENTAGE OF STAKES IN THE UNITED STATES — 65 percent

PERCENTAGE OF STAKES IN UTAH — 23 percent

PERCENTAGE OF STAKES CREATED IN THE 1980S — 36 percent

PERCENTAGE OF STAKES CREATED SINCE 1950 — 90 percent

NUMBER OF YEARS NEEDED TO CREATE FIRST 50% OF STAKES — 143 years

NUMBER OF YEARS NEEDED TO CREATE MOST RECENT 50% OF STAKES — 11 years

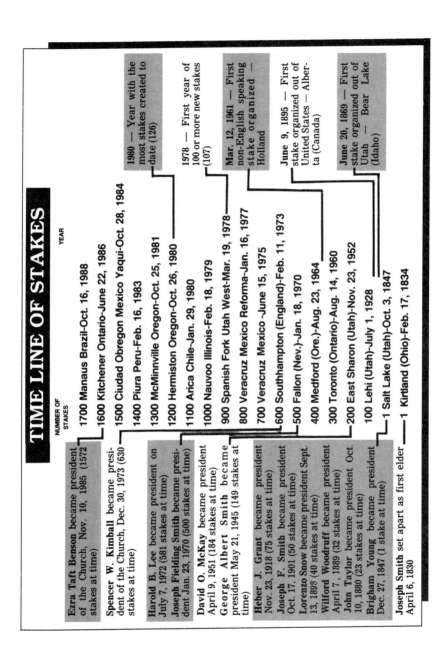

TIME LINE OF STAKES

NUMBER OF STAKES — YEAR

1700 Manaus Brazil-Oct. 16, 1988

1600 Kitchener Ontario-June 22, 1986

1500 Ciudad Obregon Mexico Yaqui-Oct. 28, 1984

1400 Piura Peru-Feb. 16, 1983

1300 McMinnville Oregon-Oct. 25, 1981

1200 Hermiston Oregon-Oct. 26, 1980

1100 Arica Chile-Jan. 29, 1980

1000 Nauvoo Illinois-Feb. 18, 1979

900 Spanish Fork Utah West-Mar. 19, 1978

800 Veracruz Mexico Reforma-Jan. 16, 1977

700 Veracruz Mexico -June 15, 1975

600 Southhampton (England)-Feb. 11, 1973

500 Fallon (Nev.)-Jan. 18, 1970

400 Medford (Ore.)-Aug. 23, 1964

300 Toronto (Ontario)-Aug. 14, 1960

200 East Sharon (Utah)-Nov. 23, 1952

100 Lehi (Utah)-July 1, 1928

1 Salt Lake (Utah)-Oct. 3, 1847

1 Kirtland (Ohio)-Feb. 17, 1834

1980 — Year with the most stakes created to date (126)

1978 — First year of 100 or more new stakes (107)

Mar. 12, 1961 — First non-English speaking stake organized — Holland

June 9, 1895 — First stake organized out of United States — Alberta (Canada)

June 20, 1869 — First stake organized out of Utah — Bear Lake (Idaho)

Ezra Taft Benson became president of the Church, Nov. 10, 1985 (1572 stakes at time)

Spencer W. Kimball became president of the Church, Dec. 30, 1973 (630 stakes at time)

Harold B. Lee became president on July 7, 1972 (581 stakes at time)

Joseph Fielding Smith became president Jan. 23, 1970 (500 stakes at time)

David O. McKay became president April 9, 1951 (184 stakes at time)

George Albert Smith became president May 21, 1945 (149 stakes at time)

Heber J. Grant became president Nov. 23, 1918 (75 stakes at time)

Joseph F. Smith became president Oct. 17, 1901 (50 stakes at time)

Lorenzo Snow became president Sept. 13, 1898 (40 stakes at time)

Wilford Woodruff became president April 7, 1889 (32 stakes at time)

John Taylor became president Oct. 10, 1880 (23 stakes at time)

Brigham Young became president Dec. 27, 1847 (1 stake at time)

Joseph Smith set apart as first elder April 6, 1830

FULL-TIME MISSIONS

Missions are listed here in chronological order and according to the name under which they were originally organized. On June 20, 1974, most of the mission names were changed under the Church's new naming system; these and other name changes are indicated on the lines beneath the "Name" column. * Denotes a name change; capital letters indicate mission's new name.

The number immediately preceding the name of the mission indicates the total number of missions in existence at the time of the organization. A letter after the number indicates that the number was reached previously; the letter is added to clarify cross references.

	NAME	ORGANIZED	PRESIDENT
1	BRITISH	20 Jul 1837	Heber C. Kimball
	*10 Jun 1970 ENGLAND EAST		
	*20 Jun 1974 ENGLAND LONDON		
	See also 4, 52, 62, 68, 79, 161		
2	EASTERN STATES	6 May 1839	John P. Green
	Discontinued Apr 1850		
	Reopened 1854 (No. 15)		
	Discontinued 1858		
	Reopened 1865 (No. 9a)		
	Discontinued 1869		
	Reopened from Northern States Jan 1893 (No. 15b)		
	*20 Jun 1974 NEW YORK NEW YORK CITY		
	See also 23a, 29, 35, 54, 77, 202		
3	SOCIETY ISLANDS	30 Apr 1844	Noah Rogers
	Discontinued 15 May 1852		
	Reopened 29 Apr 1892 (No. 13d)		
	*1907 TAHITIAN		
	*25 Nov 1959 FRENCH-POLYNESIAN		
	*10 Jun 1970 FRENCH-POLYNESIA		
	*20 Jun 1974 TAHITI PAPEETE		
4	WELSH	15 Dec 1845	Dan Jones
	Organized from British (No. 1)		
	Discontinued 26 Mar 1854, transferred to British (No. 1)		
5	CALIFORNIA	31 Jul 1846	Samuel Brannan
	Discontinued 1858		
	Reopened 23 Aug 1892 (No. 14c)		
	*20 Jun 1974 CALIFORNIA LOS ANGELES		
	See also 37, 73a, 86, 159		
5a	SCANDINAVIAN	11 May 1850	Erastus Snow
	Discontinued 1 Apr 1920, transferred to Danish (No. 23b), Norwegian (No. 24)		
	See also 22a		
6	FRENCH	18 Jun 1850	John Taylor
	Discontinued 1864		
	Reopened 15 Oct 1912 (No. 22b)		
	Discontinued 18 Sep 1914		
	Reopened 20 Aug 1923 (No. 26) from Swiss-German (No. 8)		
	*10 Jun 1970 FRANCE		
	*20 Jun 1974 FRANCE PARIS		
	See also 59, 76, 92, 121		
7	ITALIAN	1 Nov 1850	Lorenzo Snow
	Discontinued 1 Jan 1854, transferred to Swiss and Italian (No. 8)		
	Reopened 2 Aug 1966 (No. 74a) from Swiss (No. 8)		
	*10 Jun 1970 ITALY		
	*1 Jul 1971 ITALY SOUTH		
	*20 Jun 1974 ITALY ROME		
	See also 98, 123, 158		
8	SWISS	24 Nov 1850	Thomas B. H. Stenhouse
	*1 Jan 1854 SWISS AND ITALIAN		
	*1 Jan 1861 SWISS, ITALIAN AND GERMAN		
	*1 Jan 1868 SWISS AND GERMAN		
	*1 Jan 1898 SWISS		

	*22 May 1904 SWISS-GERMAN		
	*1 Jan 1938 SWISS AUSTRIAN		
	*21 Nov 1938 SWISS		
	*25 May 1946 SWISS AUSTRIAN		
	*18 Sep 1960 SWISS		
	*10 Jun 1970 SWITZERLAND		
	*20 Jun 1974 SWITZERLAND ZURICH		
	See also 6, 7, 13, 8a, 19, 26, 30, 53		
9	SANDWICH ISLANDS	12 Dec 1850	Hiram Clark
	Discontinued 1 May 1858		
	Reopened 27 Mar 1864 (No. 7a)		
	*1900 HAWAIIAN		
	*1 Apr 1950 HAWAII		
	*20 Jun 1974 HAWAII HONOLULU		
	See also 34, 178		
10	AUSTRALIAN	30 Oct 1851	John Murdock
	*1854 AUSTRALASIAN		
	*1 Jan 1898 AUSTRALIAN		
	*10 Jun 1970 AUSTRALIA EAST		
	*20 Jun 1974 AUSTRALIA SYDNEY		
	See also 20, 43c, 106		
11	EAST INDIAN	1851	Lorenzo Snow
	Discontinued 2 May 1856		
	Reopened 1 Aug 1884 (No. 12a)		
	Discontinued 10 Jun 1885		
12	MALTA	26 Feb 1852	Lorenzo Snow
	Discontinued 1856		
13	GERMAN	3 Apr 1852	Daniel P. Garn
	Discontinued 1 Jan 1861, transferred to Swiss, Italian and German (No. 8)		
	Reopened 1 Jan 1898 (No. 19) from Swiss and German (No. 8)		
	Discontinued 22 May 1904, transferred to Swiss and German (No. 8)		
	Reopened 23 Aug 1925 as German-Austrian (No. 27) from Swiss and German (No. 8)		
	Discontinued 1 Jan 1938, transferred to East German (No. 35a), West		
	German (No. 36), Swiss Austrian (No. 8)		
	See also 30		
13a	GIBRALTAR	7 Mar 1853	Edward Stevenson
	Discontinued 5 Jul 1854		
14	SOUTH AFRICAN	19 Apr 1853	Jesse Haven
	Discontinued 12 Apr 1865		
	Reopened 25 Jul 1903 (No. 23)		
	*10 Jun 1970 SOUTH AFRICA		
	*20 Jun 1974 SOUTH AFRICA JOHANNESBURG		
	See also 177a, 204, 216		
15	EASTERN STATES See No. 2	1854	John Taylor
14a	SIAM	6 Apr 1854	Elam Luddington
	Discontinued 12 Aug 1854		
15a	EUROPEAN (Administrative)	28 Jun 1854	Franklin D. Richards
	Discontinued 14 Feb 1950		
	Reopened 17 Jan 1960 (No. 51)		
	Discontinued 14 Sep 1965		
	See also 64		
14b	INDIAN TERRITORY	26 Jun 1855	Henry W. Miller
	Discontinued 23 May 1860		
	Reopened Mar 1877 (No. 9b)		
	Discontinued 12 Sep 1877		
	Reopened 20 Apr 1883 (No. 11a)		
	*29 Mar 1898 SOUTHWESTERN STATES		
	*4 Apr 1904 CENTRAL STATES		
	*10 Jun 1970 KANSAS-MISSOURI		
	*20 Jun 1974 MISSOURI INDEPENDENCE		
	See also 31, 88, 140, 153		

	NAME		ORGANIZED	FIRST PRESIDENT
7a	SANDWICH ISLANDS	See No. 9	27 Mar 1864	Joseph F. Smith
8a	NETHERLANDS		1 Nov 1864	Joseph Weiler

Organized from Swiss, Italian and German (No. 8)
 *31 Jan 1891 NETHERLANDS-BELGIUM
 *15 May 1914 NETHERLANDS
 *20 Jun 1974 NETHERLANDS AMSTERDAM
 See also 135

| 9a | EASTERN STATES | See No. 2 | 1865 | William H. Miles |
| 8b | SOUTHERN STATES | | Nov 1876 | Henry G. Boyle |

 *Jun 1971 GEORGIA-SOUTH CAROLINA
 *20 Jun 1974 GEORGIA ATLANTA
 See also 22, 29, 55, 130, 166a

| 9b | INDIAN TERRITORY | See No. 14b | Mar 1877 | Matthew W. Dalton |
| 9c | NORTHWESTERN STATES | | 6 May 1878 | Cyrus H. Wheelock |

 *20 Jul 1889 NORTHERN STATES
 *1 Jul 1973 ILLINOIS
 *20 Jun 1974 ILLINOIS CHICAGO
 *1 Jul 1980 ILLINOIS CHICAGO NORTH
 *1 Jul 1983 ILLINOIS CHICAGO
 See also 23a, 26a, 43a, 46, 97, 167, 184

| 10a | MEXICAN | | 16 Nov 1879 | Moses Thatcher |

 Discontinued Jun 1889
 Reopened 8 Jun 1901 (No. 20a)
 *10 Jun 1970 MEXICO
 *20 Jun 1974 MEXICO MEXICO CITY
 *1 Jul 1978 MEXICO MEXICO CITY SOUTH
 See also 33, 43b, 45a, 75, 125, 163, 193

11a	INDIAN TERRITORY	See No. 14b	20 Apr 1883	George Teasdale
12a	EAST INDIAN	See No. 11	1 Aug 1884	William Willis
13b	TURKISH		30 Dec 1884	Jacob Spori

 Discontinued 1 Oct 1909
 Reopened 6 Nov 1921 (No. 25)
 *23 Jan 1924 ARMENIAN
 *12 Aug 1933 PALESTINE-SYRIAN
 Discontinued 1939
 Reopened 8 Nov 1947 (No. 43)
 *25 Jan 1950 NEAR EAST
 Discontinued Jan 1951

| 13c | SAMOAN | | 17 Jun 1888 | Joseph H. Dean |

 *10 Jun 1970 SAMOA
 *20 Jun 1974 SAMOA APIA
 See also 22c, 57, 99

13d	SOCIETY ISLANDS	See No. 3	29 Apr 1892	Joseph W. Damron
14c	CALIFORNIA	See No. 5	23 Aug 1892	John L. Dalton
15b	EASTERN STATES	See No. 2	Jan 1893	Job Pingree
16	MONTANA		10 Sep 1896	Phineas Tempest

 Discontinued 12 Jun 1898, transferred to Northwestern States (No. 18)
 See also 43a

| 17 | COLORADO | | 15 Dec 1896 | John W. Taylor |

 *1 Apr 1907 WESTERN STATES
 *10 Jun 1970 COLORADO-NEW MEXICO
 *10 Oct 1972 COLORADO
 *20 Jun 1974 COLORADO DENVER
 See also 26a, 33, 43a, 132

| 18 | NORTHWESTERN STATES | | 26 Jul 1897 | George C. Parkinson |

 *10 Jun 1970 OREGON
 *20 Jun 1974 OREGON PORTLAND
 See also 26a, 36a, 43a, 78a

NAME	ORGANIZED	FIRST PRESIDENT

19 GERMAN   See No. 13   1 Jan 1898   Peter Loutensock

20 NEW ZEALAND   1 Jan 1898   Ezra F. Richards
      Organized from Australasian (No. 10)
      *10 Jun 1970 NEW ZEALAND NORTH
      *20 Jun 1974 NEW ZEALAND AUCKLAND
      See also 47, 99

20a MEXICAN   See No. 10a   Jun 1901   Ammon N. Tenney

21 JAPAN   12 Aug 1901   Heber J. Grant
      Discontinued 31 Jul 1924
      Reopened 6 Mar 1948 as Japanese (No. 44)
      Discontinued 28 Jul 1955, transferred to Northern Far East (No. 43d), Southern Far East (No. 44a)

22 MIDDLE STATES   28 Jun 1902   Ben E. Rich
      Organized from Southern States (No. 8b)
      Discontinued 7 Aug 1903, transferred to Southern States (No. 8b)

23 SOUTH AFRICAN   See No. 14   25 Jul 1903   Warren H. Lyon

22a SWEDISH   15 Jun 1905   Peter Mattson
      Organized from Scandinavian (No. 5a)
      *10 Jun 1970 SWEDEN
      *20 Jun 1974 SWEDEN STOCKHOLM
      See also 41, 145

22b FRENCH   See No. 6   15 Oct 1912   Edgar B. Brossard

22c TONGAN   8 Jul 1916   Willard L. Smith
      Organized from Samoan (No. 13c)
      *10 Jun 1970 TONGA
      *20 Jun 1974 TONGA NUKU'ALOFA
      See also 99

23a CANADIAN   1 Jul 1919   Nephi Jensen
      Organized from Eastern States (No. 15b), Northern States (No. 9c)
      *10 Jun 1970 ONTARIO-QUEBEC
      *1 Jul 1972 ONTARIO
      *20 Jun 1974 CANADA TORONTO
      See also 26a, 35, 99a

23b DANISH   1 Apr 1920   Carl E. Peterson
      Organized from Scandinavian (No. 5a)
      *10 Jun 1970 DENMARK
      *20 Jun 1974 DENMARK COPENHAGEN

24 NORWEGIAN   1 Apr 1920   Andrew S. Schow
      Organized from Scandinavian (No. 5a)
      *10 Jun 1970 NORWAY
      *20 Jun 1974 NORWAY OSLO

25 TURKISH   See No. 13b   6 Nov 1921   Joseph Wilford Booth

26 FRENCH   See No. 6   20 Aug 1923   Russell H. Blood

26a NORTH CENTRAL STATES   12 Jul 1925   John G. Allred
      Organized from Northern States (No. 9c), Western States (No. 17),
          Northwestern States (No. 18) and Canadian (No. 23a)
      *10 Jun 1970 MANITOBA-MINNESOTA
      *1 Jul 1973 MINNESOTA-WISCONSIN
      *20 Jun 1974 MINNESOTA MINNEAPOLIS
      See also 36a, 43a, 167

27 GERMAN-AUSTRIAN   See No. 13   23 Aug 1925   Fred Tadje

28 SOUTH AMERICAN   6 Dec 1925   Melvin J. Ballard
      Discontinued 25 May 1935, transferred to Brazilian (No. 31a), Argentine (No. 32)

29 EAST CENTRAL STATES   9 Dec 1928   Miles L. Jones
      Organized from Southern States (No. 8b), Eastern States (No. 15b)
      *10 Jun 1970 KENTUCKY-TENNESSEE
      *20 Jun 1974 KENTUCKY LOUISVILLE
      See also 42, 131

30 CZECHOSLOVAK   24 Jul 1929   Arthur Gaeth
      Organized from German-Austrian (No. 27), Swiss (No. 8)
      Discontinued 6 Apr 1950

NAME	ORGANIZED	FIRST PRESIDENT

31 TEXAS — 11 Jan 1931 — Charles Elliott Rowan Jr.
    Organized from Central States (No. 11a)
    *May 1945 TEXAS-LOUISIANA
    *19 Jun 1955 GULF STATES
    *20 Jun 1974 LOUISIANA SHREVEPORT
    *1 Jul 1975 LOUISIANA BATON ROUGE
    See also 33, 46a, 60, 77b, 116, 171

31a BRAZILIAN — 25 May 1935 — Rulon S. Howells
    Organized from South American (No. 28)
    *10 Jun 1970 BRAZIL CENTRAL
    Discontinued 17 Oct 1972, transferred to Brazil North Central (No. 101),
        Brazil South Central (No. 102)
    See also 48, 80

32 ARGENTINE — 14 Aug 1935 — W. Ernest Young
    Organized from South American (No. 28)
    *10 Jun 1970 ARGENTINA SOUTH
    *20 Jun 1974 ARGENTINA BUENOS AIRES NORTH
    See also 40, 50, 73, 100, 112

33 SPANISH-AMERICAN — 28 Jun 1936 — Orlando C. Williams
    Organized from Mexican (No. 20a)
    Discontinued Dec 1967, transferred to Texas (No. 60), Texas South (No. 77b),
        Western States (No. 17)
    See also 46a, 77b

34 JAPANESE — 24 Feb 1937 — Hilton A. Robertson
    Organized from Hawaiian (No. 7a)
    *14 May 1944 CENTRAL PACIFIC
    Discontinued 1 Apr 1950, transferred to Hawaii (No. 9)
    (Not related to No. 21)

35 NEW ENGLAND — 24 Sep 1937 — Carl Eyring
    Organized from Eastern States (No. 15b), Canadian (No. 23a)
    *20 Jun 1974 MASSACHUSETTS BOSTON
    See also 107, 169, 195

35a WEST GERMAN — 1 Jan 1938 — Philemon M. Kelly
    Organized from German-Austrian (No. 27)
    *10 Jun 1970 GERMANY WEST
    *20 Jun 1974 GERMANY FRANKFURT
    See also 49, 63

36 EAST GERMAN — 1 Jan 1938 — Alfred C. Rees
    Organized from German-Austrian (No. 27)
    *12 Sep 1957 NORTH GERMAN
    *10 Jun 1970 GERMANY NORTH
    *20 Jun 1974 GERMANY HAMBURG
    See also 65

36a WESTERN CANADIAN — 15 Sep 1941 — Walter Miller
    Organized from North Central States (No. 26a), Northwestern States (No. 18)
    *10 Jun 1970 ALBERTA-SASKATCHEWAN
    *20 Jun 1974 CANADA CALGARY
    See also 58, 136

37 NORTHERN CALIFORNIA — 2 Jan 1942 — German E. Ellsworth
    Organized from California (No. 14c)
    *15 Jul 1966 CALIFORNIA NORTH
    *20 Jun 1974 CALIFORNIA SACRAMENTO
    See also 85, 127, 187a

38 NAVAJO-ZUNI — 7 Mar 1943 — Ralph W. Evans
    *1 Jan 1949 SOUTHWEST INDIAN
    *10 Oct 1972 NEW MEXICO-ARIZONA
    *20 Jun 1974 ARIZONA HOLBROOK
    Discontinued 1 July 1984, transferred to Arizona Phoenix Mission (No. 179b)
    See also 78, 128, 132

39 PACIFIC (Administrative) — 7 Dec 1946 — Matthew Cowley
    Discontinued 27 Nov 1949

NAME	ORGANIZED	FIRST PRESIDENT

40   URUGUAY   31 Aug 1947   Frederick S. Williams
       Organized from Argentine (No. 32)
       *10 Jun 1970 URUGUAY-PARAGUAY
       *20 Jun 1974 URUGUAY MONTEVIDEO
       See also 50, 155

41   FINNISH   1 Sep 1947   Henry A. Matis
       Organized from Swedish (No. 22a)
       *10 Jun 1970 FINLAND
       *20 Jun 1974 FINLAND HELSINKI

42   CENTRAL ATLANTIC STATES   26 Oct 1947   Robert J. Price
       Organized from East Central States (No. 29)
       *10 Jun 1970 NORTH CAROLINA-VIRGINIA
       *1 Jul 1973 VIRGINIA
       *20 Jun 1974 VIRGINIA ROANOKE
       See also 105, 188

43   PALESTINE-SYRIAN   See No. 13b   8 Nov 1947   Badwagan Piranian

44   JAPANESE   See No. 21   6 Mar 1948   Edward L. Clissold

45   CHINESE   10 Jul 1949   Hilton A. Robertson
       Discontinued 9 Feb 1953

46   GREAT LAKES   31 Oct 1949   Carl C. Burton
       Organized from Northern States (No. 9c)
       *10 Jun 1970 INDIANA-MICHIGAN
       *1 Jul 1973 INDIANA
       *20 Jun 1974 INDIANA INDIANAPOLIS
       See also 77a, 104

43a WEST CENTRAL STATES   11 Nov 1950   Sylvester Broadbent
       Organized from North Central (No. 26a), Northwestern States (No. 18), Western States (No. 17)
       *10 Jun 1970 MONTANA-WYOMING
       *20 Jun 1974 MONTANA BILLINGS
       See also 111

43b CENTRAL AMERICAN   16 Nov 1952   Gordon M. Romney
       Organized from Mexican (No. 20a)
       *10 Jun 1970 CENTRAL AMERICA
       *20 Jun 1974 COSTA RICA SAN JOSE
       See also 76a, 79a, 177

43c SOUTH AUSTRALIAN   3 Jul 1955   Thomas S. Bingham
       Organized from Australian (No. 10)
       *Nov 1958 SOUTHERN AUSTRALIAN
       *1 Aug 1968 AUSTRALIA SOUTH
       *20 Jun 1974 AUSTRALIA MELBOURNE
       See also 82

43d NORTHERN FAR EAST   28 Jul 1955   Hilton A. Robertson
       Organized from Japanese (No. 21)
       Discontinued 31 Aug 1968, transferred to Japan (No. 82a), Japan-Okinawa (No. 83)
       See also 71

44a SOUTHERN FAR EAST   17 Aug 1955   Herald Grant Heaton
       Organized from Japanese (No. 21)
       *1 Nov 1969 HONG KONG TAIWAN
       *11 Jan 1971 HONG KONG
       See also 76b, 89, 94

45a NORTHERN MEXICAN   10 Jun 1956   Joseph T. Bentley
       Organized from Mexican (No. 20a)
       *10 Jun 1970 MEXICO NORTH
       *20 Jun 1974 MEXICO MONTERREY
       See also 56, 81, 193, 218

46a WEST SPANISH-AMERICAN   8 Mar 1958   Leland M. Perry
       Organized from Spanish-American (No. 33)
       *10 Jun 1970 WEST SPANISH AMERICA
       Discontinued 1 Jul 1970, transferred to Texas (No. 60), Texas South (No. 77b),
         Colorado-New Mexico (No. 17)

NAME	ORGANIZED	FIRST PRESIDENT
47 NEW ZEALAND SOUTH	1 Sep 1958	Alexander P. Anderson

47 **NEW ZEALAND SOUTH** — 1 Sep 1958 — Alexander P. Anderson
    Organized from New Zealand (No. 20)
    *20 Jun 1974 NEW ZEALAND WELLINGTON
    Discontinued 1 Jul 1981, transferred to New Zealand Christchurch (No. 143),
       New Zealand Auckland (No. 20)

48 **BRAZILIAN SOUTH** — 20 Sep 1959 — Asael T. Sorensen
    Organized from Brazilian (No. 31a)
    *10 Jun 1970 BRAZIL SOUTH
    *20 Jun 1974 BRAZIL PORTO ALLEGRE
    See also 80, 181

49 **SOUTH GERMAN** — 4 Oct 1959 — John A. Beuhner
    Organized from West German (No. 35a)
    *10 Jun 1970 GERMANY SOUTH
    *20 Jun 1974 GERMANY MUNICH
    See also 69

50 **ANDES** — 1 Nov 1959 — J. Vernon Sharp
    Organized from Uruguay (No. 40), Argentine (No. 32)
    *10 Jun 1970 PERU-ECUADOR
    *1 Aug 1970 PERU
    *Feb 1971 PERU ANDES
    *Apr 1971 ANDES PERU
    *20 Jun 1974 PERU LIMA
    *1 Jan 1977 PERU LIMA SOUTH
    See also 67, 75a, 79a, 93, 149, 165

51 **EUROPEAN (Administrative)** See No. 15a — 17 Jan 1960 — Alvin R. Dyer

52 **NORTH BRITISH** — 27 Mar 1960 — Bernard P. Brockbank
    Organized from British (No. 1)
    *10 Jun 1970 ENGLAND NORTH
    *20 Jun 1974 ENGLAND LEEDS
    See also 61, 72, 138

53 **AUSTRIAN** — 18 Sep 1960 — Winslow W. Smith
    Organized from Swiss-Austrian (No. 8)
    *10 Jun 1970 AUSTRIA
    *20 Jun 1974 AUSTRIA VIENNA
    See also 8, 13, 205

54 **EASTERN ATLANTIC STATES** — 16 Oct 1960 — George B. Hill
    Organized from Eastern States (No. 15b)
    *10 Jun 1970 DELAWARE-MARYLAND
    *20 Jun 1974 WASHINGTON D.C.
    See also 91a, 188b

55 **FLORIDA** — 1 Nov 1960 — Karl R. Lyman
    Organized from Southern States (No. 8b)
    *1 Jul 1971 FLORIDA SOUTH
    *20 Jun 1974 FLORIDA FT. LAUDERDALE
    Discontinued 20 Jun 1983, transferred to Florida Tampa (No. 139), West Indies (No. 178a)
    Reopened 1 Jul 1984 under Claud Darwin Mangum (No. 178b)
    See also 96, 175

56 **WEST MEXICAN** — 1 Nov 1960 — Harold E. Turley
    Organized from Northern Mexican (No. 45a)
    *10 Jun 1970 MEXICO WEST
    *20 Jun 1974 MEXICO HERMOSILLO
    See also 125

57 **RAROTONGA** — 20 Nov 1960 — Joseph R. Reeder
    Organized from Samoan (No. 13c)
    Discontinued 15 Apr 1966, transferred to New Zealand (No. 20)

58 **ALASKAN-CANADIAN** — 21 Nov 1960 — Milton L. Weilenman
    Organized from Western Canadian (No. 36a)
    *10 Jun 1970 ALASKA-BRITISH COLUMBIA
    *20 Jun 1974 CANADA VANCOUVER
    See also 114

NAME	ORGANIZED	FIRST PRESIDENT

59 FRENCH EAST — 19 Jan 1961 — Henry D. Moyle Jr.
    Organized from French (No. 26)
    *10 Jun 1970 FRANCE SWITZERLAND
    *20 Jun 1974 SWITZERLAND GENEVA

60 TEXAS — 16 Feb 1961 — Ralph J. Hill
    Organized from Gulf States (No. 31)
    *10 Jun 1970 TEXAS NORTH
    *20 Jun 1974 TEXAS DALLAS
    See also 77b, 189

61 SCOTTISH-IRISH — 28 Feb 1961 — Bernard P. Brockbank
    Organized from North British (No. 52)
    *8 Jul 1962 SCOTTISH
    *10 Jun 1970 SCOTLAND
    *20 June 1974 SCOTLAND EDINBURGH
    See also 70, 74, 147

62 CENTRAL BRITISH — 6 Mar 1961 — James A. Cullimore
    Organized from British (No. 1)
    *10 Jun 1970 ENGLAND CENTRAL
    *20 Jun 1974 ENGLAND BIRMINGHAM
    Discontinued 1 Jul 1983, transferred to England Coventry (No. 183)

63 CENTRAL GERMAN — 15 Mar 1961 — Stephen C. Richards
    Organized from West German (No. 35a)
    *10 Jun 1970 GERMANY CENTRAL
    *20 Jun 1974 GERMANY DUESSELDORF
    Discontinued 1 Apr 1982, transferred to Germany Frankfurt (No. 35a), Germany Munich (No. 49)

64 WEST EUROPEAN (Administrative) — 30 Apr 1961 — N. Eldon Tanner
    Organized from European (No. 51)
    Discontinued 14 Sep 1965

65 BERLIN — 14 Jul 1961 — Percy K. Fetzer
    Organized from North German (No. 36)
    Discontinued 31 May 1966, transferred to North German (No. 36)

66 SOUTH AMERICA (Administrative) — 25 Aug 1961 — A. Theodore Tuttle
    Discontinued 17 Jul 1965

67 CHILEAN — 8 Oct 1961 — A. Delbert Palmer
    Organized from Andes (No. 50)
    *10 Jun 1970 CHILE
    *20 Jun 1974 CHILE SANTIAGO
    *1 Jan 1977 CHILE SANTIAGO SOUTH
    See also 119, 148, 214

68 SOUTHWEST BRITISH — 1 Feb 1962 — A. Ray Curtis
    Organized from British (No. 1)
    *10 Jun 1970 ENGLAND SOUTHWEST
    *20 Jun 1974 ENGLAND BRISTOL
    See also 79

69 BAVARIAN — 4 Mar 1962 — Owen Spencer Jacobs
    Organized from South German (No. 49)
    Discontinued 10 Jun 1965, transferred to South German (No. 49)

70 IRISH — 8 Jul 1962 — Stephen R. Covey
    Organized from Scottish-Irish (No. 61)
    *10 Jun 1970 IRELAND
    *20 Jun 1974 IRELAND BELFAST
    *11 Sep 1976 IRELAND DUBLIN

71 KOREAN — 8 Jul 1962 — Gail Edward Carr
    Organized from Northern Far East (No. 43d)
    *10 Jun 1970 KOREA
    *20 Jun 1974 KOREA SEOUL
    See also 124, 170

72 NORTHEAST BRITISH — 1 Sep 1962 — Grant S. Thorn
    Organized from North British (No. 52)
    Discontinued May 1965, transferred to North British (No. 52)

NAME	ORGANIZED	FIRST PRESIDENT
73 NORTH ARGENTINE	16 Sep 1962	Ronald V. Stone

73 **NORTH ARGENTINE** — 16 Sep 1962 — Ronald V. Stone
Organized from Argentine (No. 32)
*10 Jun 1970 ARGENTINA NORTH
*20 Jun 1974 ARGENTINA CORDOBA
See also 100, 206

74 **NORTH SCOTTISH** — 24 Nov 1962 — William N. Waite
Organized from Scottish (No. 61)
Discontinued 31 May 1965, transferred to Scottish (No. 61)

75 **SOUTHEAST MEXICAN** — 27 Mar 1963 — Carl J. Beecroft
Organized from Mexican (No. 20a)
*10 Jun 1970 MEXICO SOUTHEAST
*20 Jun 1974 MEXICO VERACRUZ
See also 126, 193

76 **FRANCO-BELGIAN** — 1 Oct 1963 — Joseph T. Edmunds
Organized from French (No. 26)
*10 Jun 1970 FRANCE-BELGIUM
*20 Jun 1974 BELGIUM BRUSSELS
See also 135

77 **CUMORAH** — 26 Jan 1964 — N. Lester Petersen
Organized from Eastern States (No. 15b)
*20 Jun 1974 NEW YORK ROCHESTER

78 **NORTHERN INDIAN** — 8 Apr 1964 — Grant Roper Farmer
Organized from Southwest Indian (No. 38)
*1 Jul 1973 DAKOTA-MANITOBA
*20 Jun 1974 SOUTH DAKOTA RAPID CITY
See also 136

79 **BRITISH SOUTH** — 27 Dec 1964 — Don K. Archer
Organized from British (No. 1), Southwest British (No. 68)
*10 Jun 1970 ENGLAND SOUTH
*20 Jun 1974 ENGLAND LONDON SOUTH

76a **GUATEMALA-EL SALVADOR** — 1 Aug 1965 — Terrance L. Hansen
Organized from Central American (No. 43b)
*20 Jun 1974 GUATEMALA GUATEMALA CITY
*29 Mar 1988 GUATEMALA GUATEMALA CITY SOUTH
See also 137a, 152, 205a

73a **CALIFORNIA SOUTH** — 10 Jul 1966 — D. Crawford Houston
Organized from California (No. 14c)
*20 Jun 1974 CALIFORNIA ANAHEIM
See also 86, 87, 113, 182

74a **ITALIAN**   See No. 7 — 2 Aug 1966 — John Duns Jr.

75a **ANDES SOUTH** — 14 Nov 1966 — Franklin Kay Gibson
Organized from Andes (No. 50)
*1969 BOLIVIA
*20 Jun 1974 BOLIVIA LA PAZ
Discontinued 1 Feb 1982, transferred to Bolivia Cochabamba (No. 150)
Reopened 8 Jan 1988 under Steven R. Wright (No. 207)

76b **PHILIPPINE** — 28 Jun 1967 — Paul S. Rose
Organized from Southern Far East (No. 44a)
*10 Jun 1970 PHILIPPINES
*20 Jun 1974 PHILIPPINES MANILA
See also 110, 172, 194

77a **OHIO** — 31 Jul 1967 — E. Garrett Barlow
Organized from Great Lakes (No. 46)
*31 Aug 1972 OHIO-WEST VIRGINIA
*20 Jun 1974 OHIO COLUMBUS
See also 154, 188, 179a

77b **TEXAS SOUTH** — 10 Dec 1967 — Dean L. Larsen
Organized from Texas (No. 60), Spanish-American (No. 33)
*20 Jun 1974 TEXAS SAN ANTONIO
See also 142

NAME	ORGANIZED	FIRST PRESIDENT

78a PACIFIC NORTHWEST — 1 Jan 1968 — Joe E. Whitesides
    Organized from Northwestern States (No. 18)
    *10 Jun 1970 WASHINGTON
    *20 Jun 1974 WASHINGTON SEATTLE
    See also 166

79a COLOMBIA-VENEZUELA — 1 Jul 1968 — Stephen L. Brower
    Organized from Central American (No. 43b), Andes (No. 50)
    *1 Jul 1971 COLOMBIA
    *20 Jun 1974 COLOMBIA BOGOTA
    See also 95, 120, 215

80 BRAZILIAN NORTH — 7 Jul 1968 — Hal Roscoe Johnson
    Organized from Brazilian (No. 31a), Brazilian South (No. 48)
    *10 Jun 1970 BRAZIL NORTH
    *20 Jun 1974 BRAZIL RIO DE JANEIRO
    See also 167a, 185a

81 MEXICO NORTH CENTRAL — 5 Aug 1968 — Arturo R. Martinez
    Organized from Northern Mexican (No. 45a)
    *20 Jun 1974 MEXICO TORREON
    See also 125, 208

82 AUSTRALIAN WEST — 7 Aug 1968 — Milton J. Hess
    Organized from Southern Australian (No. 43c)
    *10 Jun 1970 AUSTRALIA WEST
    *20 Jun 1974 AUSTRALIA ADELAIDE
    See also 117

82a JAPAN — 1 Sep 1968 — Walter R. Bills
    Organized from Northern Far East (No. 43d)
    *20 Jun 1974 JAPAN TOKYO
    *1 Jul 1978 JAPAN TOKYO NORTH
    See also 90, 108, 109a, 162

83 JAPAN-OKINAWA — 1 Sep 1968 — Edward Y. Okazaki
    Organized from Northern Far East (No. 43d)
    *16 Mar 1970 JAPAN CENTRAL
    *20 Jun 1974 JAPAN KOBE
    See also 91, 108, 144, 185

84 GERMANY DRESDEN — 14 Jun 1969 — Johannes Henry Burkhart
    Discontinued Dec 1978

85 CALIFORNIA CENTRAL — 1 Jul 1969 — Wilbur Wallace Cox
    Organized from California North (No. 37)
    *20 Jun 1974 CALIFORNIA OAKLAND
    See also 118, 158a, 187a

86 CALIFORNIA EAST — 7 Jul 1969 — William L. Nicholls
    Organized from California South (No. 73a), California (No. 14c)
    *20 Jun 1974 CALIFORNIA ARCADIA
    See also 182

87 ARIZONA — 1 Aug 1969 — Clark M. Wood
    Organized from California South (No. 73a)
    *20 Jun 1974 ARIZONA TEMPE
    See also 127, 132, 179b

88 SOUTH CENTRAL STATES — 4 Aug 1969 — Albert B. Crandall
    Organized from Central States (No. 11a)
    *10 Jun 1970 OKLAHOMA
    *20 Jun 1974 OKLAHOMA TULSA
    See also 116

89 SOUTHEAST ASIA — 1 Nov 1969 — G. Carlos Smith
    Organized from Southern Far East (No. 44a)
    *20 Jun 1974 SINGAPORE
    Discontinued 1 Jul 1978, transferred to Indonesia Jakarta (No. 122)
    Reopened 1 Jan 1980 (No. 176)
    See also 109

NAME	ORGANIZED	FIRST PRESIDENT

90   JAPAN EAST   15 Mar 1970   Russell N. Horiuchi
          Organized from Japan (No. 82a)
          *20 Jun 1974 JAPAN SAPPORO

91   JAPAN WEST   18 Mar 1970   Kan Watanabe
          Organized from Japan-Okinawa (No. 83)
          *20 Jun 1974 JAPAN FUKUOKA
          See also 144

91a PENNSYLVANIA   1 Jul 1970   George M. Baker
          Organized from Delaware-Maryland (No. 54)
          *20 Jun 1974 PENNSYLVANIA HARRISBURG
          See also 129, 156

92   SPAIN   11 Jul 1970   R. Raymond Barnes
          Organized from French (No. 26)
          *20 Jun 1974 SPAIN MADRID
          See also 137, 141, 199

93   ECUADOR   1 Aug 1970   Louis W. Latimer
          Organized from Peru-Ecuador (No. 50)
          *20 Jun 1974 ECUADOR QUITO
          See also 160

94   TAIWAN   11 Jan 1971   Malan R. Jackson
          Organized from Hong Kong-Taiwan (No. 44a)
          *20 Jun 1974 TAIWAN TAIPEI
          See also 146

95   VENEZUELA   1 Jul 1971   Clark D. Webb
          Organized from Colombia-Venezuela (No. 79a)
          *20 Jun 1974 VENEZUELA CARACAS
          See also 174

96   ALABAMA-FLORIDA   1 Jul 1971   Hartman Rector Jr.
          Organized from Florida (No. 55)
          *20 Jun 1974 FLORIDA TALLAHASSE
          See also 166a, 197

97   NAUVOO   1 Jul 1971   J. LeRoy Kimball
          Organized from Northern States (No. 9c)
          Discontinued 1 Jul 1974, transferred to Illinois Chicago (No. 9c)

98   ITALY NORTH   6 Jul 1971   Dan Charles Jorgensen
          Organized from Italy (No. 74a)
          *20 Jun 1974 ITALY MILAN

99   FIJI   23 Jul 1971   A. Sherman Lindholm
          Organized from Samoa (No. 13c), New Zealand North (No. 20), Tonga (No. 22c)
          *20 Jun 1974 FIJI SUVA
          See also 178

99a QUEBEC   14 Jul 1972   John K. M. Olsen
          Organized from Ontario-Quebec (No. 23a)
          *20 Jun 1974 CANADA MONTREAL

100 ARGENTINE EAST   30 Jul 1972   Joseph T. Bentley
          Organized from Argentina North (No. 73), Argentina South (No. 32)
          *20 Jun 1974 ARGENTINA ROSARIO

101 BRAZIL NORTH CENTRAL   17 Oct 1972   Leroy A. Drechsel
          Organized from Brazil Central (No. 31a)
          *20 Jun 1974 BRAZIL SAO PAULO NORTH
          See also 190

102 BRAZIL SOUTH CENTRAL   17 Oct 1972   Owen Nelson Baker
          Organized from Brazil Central (No. 31a)
          *20 Jun 1974 BRAZIL SAO PAULO SOUTH
          See also 181

103 INTERNATIONAL   9 Nov 1972   Bernard P. Brockbank
          Organized for "unattached" members worldwide
          Discontinued 15 Aug 1987
          See also 179

104 MICHIGAN   3 Jul 1973   C. Russell Hansen
          Organized from Indiana-Michigan (No. 46)

*20 Jun 1974 MICHIGAN LANSING
    See also 164

105 NORTH CAROLINA   18 Jul 1973   Charles M. Alexander
    Organized from North Carolina-Virginia (No. 42)
    *20 Jun 1974 NORTH CAROLINA GREENSBORO
    *1 Jul 1980 NORTH CAROLINA CHARLOTTE
    See also 186

106 AUSTRALIA NORTHEAST   26 Jul 1973   Jay Martell Bird
    Organized from Australia East (No. 10)
    *20 Jun 1974 AUSTRALIA BRISBANE

107 CANADA-MARITIMES   27 Jul 1973   Thurn J. Baker
    Organized from New England (No. 35)
    *20 Jun 1974 CANADA HALIFAX

108 JAPAN-NAGOYA   1 Aug 1973   Satoru Sato
    Organized from Japan (No. 82a), Japan Central (No. 83)
    *20 Jun 1974 JAPAN NAGOYA

109 THAILAND   1 Aug 1973   Paul D. Morris
    Organized from Southeast Asia (No. 89)
    *20 Jun 1974 THAILAND BANGKOK

109a JAPAN SENDAI   1 Jul 1974   Walter Teruya
    Organized from Japan Tokyo (No. 82a)

110 PHILIPPINES CEBU CITY   1 Jul 1974   Carl D. Jones
    Organized from Philippines Manila (No. 76b)
    *1 Jul 1988 PHILIPPINES BACOLOD
    See also 157, 194

111 IDAHO POCATELLO   1 Jul 1974   Ernest Eberhard Jr.
    Organized from Montana Billings (No. 43a)
    *29 May 1979 IDAHO BOISE
    See also 132

112 ARGENTINA BUENOS AIRES SOUTH   22 Jul 1974   Juan Carlos Avila
    Organized from Argentina South (No. 32)
    See also 180

113 CALIFORNIA SAN DIEGO   1 Aug 1974   Herbert M. Butler
    Organized from California Anaheim (No. 73a)

114 ALASKA ANCHORAGE   15 Oct 1974   Weston F. Killpack
    Organized from Canada Vancouver (No. 58)

115 PORTUGAL LISBON   19 Nov 1974   Wm. Grant Bangerter
    See also 203

116 ARKANSAS LITTLE ROCK   1 Jul 1975   Richard M. Richards
    Organized from Louisiana Shreveport (No. 31), Oklahoma Tulsa (No. 88)

117 AUSTRALIA PERTH   1 Jul 1975   Bruce James Opie
    Organized from Australia Adelaide (No. 82)

118 CALIFORNIA FRESNO   1 Jul 1975   Robert B. Harbertson
    Organized from California Oakland (No. 85)

119 CHILE CONCEPCION   1 Jul 1975   Lester D. Haymore
    Organized from Chile Santiago (No. 67)
    See also 151

120 COLOMBIA CALI   1 Jul 1975   Jay E. Jensen
    Organized from Colombia Bogota (No. 79a)

121 FRANCE TOULOUSE   1 Jul 1975   George W. Broschinsky
    Organized from France Paris (No. 26)
    Discontinued 1 Jul 1982, transferred to France Paris (No. 26), Switzerland Geneva (No. 59)

122 INDONESIA JAKARTA   1 Jul 1975   Hendrik Gout
    Organized from Singapore (No. 89)
    Discontinued 1 Jan 1981, transferred to Singapore (No. 89)
    Reopened 1 Jul 1985 (No. 182a)

123 ITALY PADOVA   1 Jul 1975   John Anthony Grinceri
    Organized from Italy Rome (No. 74a)
    Discontinued 1 Jul 1982, transferred to Italy Milan (No. 98)

124 KOREA PUSAN   1 Jul 1975   In Sang Han
    Organized from Korea Seoul (No. 71)
    See also No. 191

125 MEXICO GUADALAJARA   1 Jul 1975   Isauro Gutierres
     Organized from Mexico Mexico City (No. 20a), Mexico Torreon (No. 81),
        Mexico Hermosillo (No. 56)
     See also 201
126 MEXICO VILLAHERMOSA   1 Jul 1975   Abraham Lozano
     Organized from Mexico Veracruz (No. 75)
     *1 Jul 1978 MEXICO MERIDA
     See also 193, 209
127 NEVADA LAS VEGAS   1 Jul 1975   Ronald M. Patterson
     Organized from Arizona Tempe (No. 87), California Sacramento (No. 37)
128 NEW MEXICO ALBUQUERQUE   1 Jul 1975   Stanley D. Roberts
     Organized from Arizona Holbrook (No. 38)
129 PENNSYLVANIA PITTSBURGH   1 Jul 1975   Kenneth W. Godfrey
     Organized from Pennsylvania Harrisburg (No. 91a)
     See also 188
130 SOUTH CAROLINA COLUMBIA   1 Jul 1975   Ronald L. Knighton
     Organized from Georgia Atlanta (No. 8b)
131 TENNESSEE NASHVILLE   1 Jul 1975   Emerson Taylor Cannon
     Organized from Kentucky Louisville (No. 29)
132 UTAH SALT LAKE CITY   1 Jul 1975   Ernest Eberhard Jr.
     Organized from Idaho Pocatello (No. 111), Colorado Denver (No. 17),
        Arizona Tempe (No. 87), Arizona Holbrook (No. 38)
     *1 Jul 1980 UTAH SALT LAKE CITY NORTH
     See also 187
133 YUGOSLAVIA ZAGREB   1 Jul 1975   Gustav Salik
     Discontinued 1 Jul 1976
134 IRAN TEHRAN   4 Jul 1975   Dean Burton Farnsworth
     Discontinued 1 Jan 1979
135 BELGIUM ANTWERP   16 Jul 1975   Larry Hyde Brim
     Organized from Belgium Brussels (No. 76), Netherlands Amsterdam (No. 8a)
     Discontinued 1 Jul 1982, transferred to Belgium Brussels (No. 76),
        Netherlands Amsterdam (No. 8a)
136 CANADA WINNIPEG   15 Feb 1976   Howard L. Lund
     Organized from Canada Calgary (No. 36a), South Dakota Rapid City (No. 78)
137 SPAIN BARCELONA   8 May 1976   Smith B. Griffin
     Organized from Spain Madrid (No. 92)
     See also 199
137a EL SALVADOR SAN SALVADOR   1 Jul 1976   Eddy L. Barillas
     Organized from Guatemala Guatemala City (No. 76a)
     Discontinued 1 Apr 1981, transferred to Guatemala Guatemala City (No. 76a)
     Reopened 1 Oct 1984 (No. 181a)
138 ENGLAND MANCHESTER   1 Jul 1976   O. Louis Alder
     Organized from England Leeds (No. 52)
139 FLORIDA TAMPA   1 Jul 1976   A. Sterling Workman
     Organized from Florida Ft. Lauderdale (No. 55)
     See also 178a, 197
140 IOWA DES MOINES   1 Jul 1976   Irwin E. Wirkus
     Organized from Missouri Independence (No. 11a)
141 SPAIN SEVILLE   3 Jul 1976   Hugo A. Catron
     Organized from Spain Madrid (No. 92)
     See also 220
142 TEXAS HOUSTON   3 Jul 1976   George L. Merrill
     Organized from Texas San Antonio (No. 77b)
143 NEW ZEALAND CHRISTCHURCH   5 Jul 1976   Ivan G. Radman
     Organized from New Zealand Wellington (No. 47)
144 JAPAN OKAYAMA   9 Jul 1976   William H. Nako
     Organized from Japan Fukuoka (No. 91), Japan Kobe (No. 83)
145 SWEDEN GOTEBORG   26 Jul 1976   Paul Kent Oscarson
     Organized from Sweden Stockholm (No. 22a)
     Discontinued 1 Jul 1982, transferred to Sweden Stockholm (No. 22a)

NAME	ORGANIZED	FIRST PRESIDENT

146 TAIWAN KAOHSIUNG .... 3 Aug 1976 ...... P. Boyd Hales
    Organized from Taiwan Taipei (No. 94)
    *28 Sep 1983 TAIWAN TAICHUNG
    See also 173

147 SCOTLAND GLASGOW .... 1 Nov 1976 ...... Roy W. Oscarson
    Organized from Scotland Edinburgh (No. 61)
    Discontinued 1 Jul 1981, transferred to Scotland Edinburgh (No. 61)

148 CHILE SANTIAGO NORTH .... 1 Jan 1977 ...... Berkley A. Spencer
    Organized from Chile Santiago (No. 67)
    See also 168, 214

149 PERU LIMA NORTH .... 1 Jan 1977 ...... Jose A. Sousa
    Organized from Peru Lima (No. 50)
    See also 165, 184a, 210

150 BOLIVIA SANTA CRUZ .... 1 Jul 1977 ...... DeVere R. McAllister
    Organized from Bolivia La Paz (No. 75a)
    *1 Feb 1982 BOLIVIA COCHABAMBA

151 CHILE OSORNO .... 1 Jul 1977 ...... Lester D. Haymore
    Organized from Chile Concepcion (No. 119)

152 GUATEMALA QUEZALTENANGO .... 1 Jul 1977 ...... John F. O'Donnal
    Organized from Guatemala Guatemala City (No. 76a)

153 MISSOURI ST. LOUIS .... 1 Jul 1977 ...... Norman W. Olsen
    Organized from Missouri Independence (No. 11a)
    See also 176a

154 OHIO CLEVELAND .... 1 Jul 1977 ...... Donald S. Brewer
    Organized from Ohio Columbus (No. 77a)

155 PARAGUAY ASUNCION .... 1 Jul 1977 ...... Mearl K. Bair
    Organized from Uruguay Montevideo (No. 40)

156 PENNSYLVANIA PHILADELPHIA .... 1 Jul 1977 ...... Lewis K. Payne
    Organized from Pennsylvania Harrisburg (No. 91a)

157 PHILIPPINES DAVAO .... 1 Jul 1977 ...... Layton B. Jones
    Organized from Philippines Cebu City (No. 110)
    See also 211

158 ITALY CATANIA .... 10 Jul 1977 ..... Leopoldo Larcher
    Organized from Italy Rome (No. 74a)

158a CALIFORNIA SAN JOSE .... 1 Jul 1978 ...... Lysle R. Cahoon
    Organized from California Oakland (No. 85)

159 CALIFORNIA VENTURA .... 1 Jul 1978 ...... Hyrum S. Smith
    Organized from California Los Angeles (No. 14c)
    See also 182

160 ECUADOR GUAYAQUIL .... 1 Jul 1978 ...... William J. Mitchell
    Organized from Ecuador Quito (No. 93)

161 ENGLAND LONDON EAST .... 1 Jul 1978 ...... Carl D. Jones
    Organized from England London (No. 1)
    Discontinued 1 Jul 1983, transferred to England London (No. 1), England London South (No. 79)

162 JAPAN TOKYO SOUTH .... 1 Jul 1978 ...... Delbert H. Groberg
    Organized from Japan Tokyo (No. 82a)

163 MEXICO MEXICO CITY NORTH .... 1 Jul 1978 ...... John B. Dickson
    Organized from Mexico Mexico City South (No. 20a)
    See also 193, 218

164 MICHIGAN DEARBORN .... 1 Jul 1978 ...... William R. Horton
    Organized from Michigan Lansing (No. 104)

165 PERU AREQUIPA .... 1 Jul 1978 ...... Norval C. Jesperson
    Organized from Peru Lima North (No. 149), Peru Lima South (No. 50)

166 WASHINGTON SPOKANE .... 1 Jul 1978 ...... Norwood C. McKoy
    Organized from Washington Seattle (No. 78a)

167 WISCONSIN MILWAUKEE .... 1 Jul 1978 ...... L. Flake Rogers
    Organized from Minnesota Minneapolis (No. 26a), Illinois Chicago (No. 9c)

166a ALABAMA BIRMINGHAM .... 1 Jan 1979 ...... William J. Attwooll
    Organized from Georgia Atlanta (No. 8b), Florida Tallahassee (No. 96)

NAME	ORGANIZED	FIRST PRESIDENT

167a BRAZIL RECIFE   1 Jul 1979   Harry Eduardo Klein
      Organized from Brazil Rio de Janeiro (No. 80)
      See also 200
168   CHILE VINA DEL MAR   1 Jul 1979   Gerald J. Day
      Organized from Chile Santiago North (No. 148)
      See also 214
169   CONNECTICUT HARTFORD   1 Jul 1979   Gerald L. Ericksen
      Organized from Massachusetts Boston (No. 35)
      See also 195
170   KOREA SEOUL WEST   1 Jul 1979   D. Brent Clement
      Organized from Korea Seoul (No. 71)
171   MISSISSIPPI JACKSON   1 Jul 1979   Frank W. Hirschi
      Organized from Louisiana Baton Rouge (No. 31)
172   PHILIPPINES QUEZON CITY   1 Jul 1979   Robert E. Sackley
      Organized from Philippines Manila (No. 76b)
      *1 Jan 1981 PHILIPPINES BAGUIO
      See also 192, 219
173   TAIWAN T'AICHUNG   1 Jul 1979   Frederick W. Crook
      Organized from Taiwan Kaohsiung (No. 146)
      *Oct 1979 TAIWAN TAICHUNG
      Discontinued Jul 1982, transferred to Taiwan Kaohsiung (No. 146), Taiwan Taipei (No. 94)
174   VENEZUELA MARACAIBO   1 Jul 1979   Alejandro Portal
      Organized from Venezuela Caracas (No. 95)
175   PUERTO RICO SAN JUAN   7 Jul 1979   Richard L. Millett
      Organized from Florida Ft. Lauderdale (No. 55)
      See also 178a, 188a
176   SINGAPORE   See No. 89   1 Jan 1980   J. Talmage Jones
177   HONDURAS TEGUCIGALPA   1 Feb 1980   Samuel Flores
      Organized from Costa Rica San Jose (No. 43b)
178   MICRONESIA GUAM   1 Apr 1980   Ferron C. Losee
      Organized from Hawaii Honolulu (No. 7a), Fiji Suva (No. 99)
179   AFRICA WEST   1 Jul 1980   Bryan Espenschied
      Organized from International (No. 103)
      *NIGERIA LAGOS 1 Jul 1985
      See also 183a, 221
180   ARGENTINA BAHIA BLANCA   1 Jul 1980   Allen B. Oliver
      Organized from Argentina Buenos Aires South (No. 112)
181   BRAZIL CURITIBA   1 Jul 1980   Dixon D. Cowley
      Organized from Brazil Sao Paulo (No. 102), Brazil Porto Allegre (No. 48)
182   CALIFORNIA SAN BERNARDINO   1 Jul 1980   Howard C. Sharp
      Organized from California Anaheim (No. 73a), California Arcadia (No. 86),
      California Ventura (No. 159)
183   ENGLAND COVENTRY   1 Jul 1980   Quinn G. McKay
      Organized from England Birmingham (No. 62)
184   ILLINOIS CHICAGO SOUTH   1 Jul 1980   Charles E. Petersen
      Organized from Illinois Chicago (No. 9c)
      Discontinued 1 Jul 1983, transferred to Illinois Chicago (No. 9c)
185   JAPAN OSAKA   1 Jul 1980   Shigeki Ushio
      Organized from Japan Kobe (No. 83)
186   NORTH CAROLINA RALEIGH   1 Jul 1980   Joel N. Gillespie
      Organized from North Carolina Greensboro (No. 105)
187   UTAH SALT LAKE CITY SOUTH   1 Jul 1980   Jonathan W. Snow
      Organized from Utah Salt Lake City (No. 132)
188   WEST VIRGINIA CHARLESTON   1 Jul 1980   O. Rex Warner
      Organized from Ohio Columbus (No. 77a), Virginia Roanoke (No. 42),
      Pennsylania Pittsburgh (No. 129)
188a DOMINICAN REPUBLIC SANTO DOMINGO   1 Jan 1981   John A. Davis
      Organized from Puerto Rico San Juan (No. 175)
      See also 178a, 196
178a WEST INDIES   20 Jun 1983   Kenneth L. Zabriskie

Organized from Florida Tampa (No. 139), Dominican Republic Santo Domingo (No. 188a),
    Puerto Rico San Juan (No. 175)
    See also 180a, 186a

176a Illinois Peoria   1 Jul 1983   Brent Reed Rigtrup
    Organized from Missouri St. Louis (No. 153)

177a SOUTH AFRICA CAPE TOWN   1 Jul 1984   G. Phillip Margetts
    Organized from South Africa Johannesburg (No. 23)

178b FLORIDA FT. LAUDERDALE   See No. 55

179a OHIO AKRON   1 Jul 1984   Stanley M. Smoot
    Organized from Ohio Columbus (No. 77a)

179b ARIZONA PHOENIX   1 Jul 1984   Francis M. Bay
    Organized from Arizona Holbrook (No. 38), Arizona Tempe (No. 87)

180a HAITI PORT-AU-PRINCE   1 Aug 1984   James S. Arrigona
    Organized from West Indies (No. 178a)

181a EL SALVADOR SAN SALVADOR   See No. 137a1 Oct 1984   Manuel Antonio Diaz

182a INDONESIA JAKARTA   See No. 122   1 Jul 1985   Effian Kadarusman

183a GHANA ACCRA   1 Jul 1985   Miles H. Cunningham
    Organized from Africa West (No. 179)

184a PERU TRUJILLO   1 Jul 1985   Roberto Vidal
    Organized from Peru Lima North (No. 149)

185a BRAZIL BRASILIA   1 Jul 1985   Demar Staniscia
    Organized from Brazil Rio de Janiero (No. 80)
    See also 213

186a JAMAICA KINGSTON   1 Jul 1985   Richard L. Brough
    Organized from West Indies (No. 178a)

187a CALIFORNIA SANTA ROSA   1 Jul 1985   Robert C. Witt
    Organized from California Sacramento (No. 37), California Oakland (No. 85)

188b WASHINGTON D.C. NORTH   1 Jul 1986   Dennis E. Simmons
    Organized from Washington D.C. (No. 54)

189 TEXAS LUBBOCK   1 Jul 1986   Lyle L. Wasden
    Organized from Texas Dallas (No. 60)
    *20 Jan 1988 TEXAS FT. WORTH

190 BRAZIL CAMPINAS   1 Jul 1986   Sheldon R. Murphy
    Organized from Brazil Sao Paulo North (No. 101)
    See also 213

191 KOREA TAEJON   1 Jul 1986   Moo-Kwang Hong
    Organized from Korea Pusan (No. 124)

192 PHILIPPINES QUEZON CITY   1 Jul 1986   Joel E. Leetham
    Organized from Philippines Baguio (No. 172)
    See also 219

193 MEXICO MEXICO CITY EAST   1 Jan 1987   Enrique Moreno
    Organized from Mexico Mexico City North (No. 163), Mexico Mexico City South (No. 20a),
      Mexico Monterrey (No. 45a), Mexico Merida (No. 126), Mexico Veracruz (No. 75)
    See also 217

194 PHILIPPINES CEBU EAST   1 Jul 1987   C. Elliott Richards
    Organized from Philippines Cebu (No. 110), Philippines Manila (No. 76b)
    *1 Jul 1988 PHILIPPINES CEBU

195 NEW HAMPSHIRE MANCHESTER   1 Jul 1987   Lynn E. Thomsen
    Organized from Massachusetts Boston (No. 35), Connecticut Hartford (No. 169)

196 DOMINICAN REPUBLIC SANTIAGO 1 Jul 1987   Michael D. Stirling
    Organized from Dominican Republic Santo Domingo (No. 188a)

197 FLORIDA JACKSONVILLE   1 Jul 1987   Douglas W. DeHaan
    Organized from Florida Tampa (No. 139), Florida Tallahassee (No. 96)

198 ZAIRE KINSHASA   1 Jul 1987   R. Bay Hutchings

199 SPAIN BILBAO   1 Jul 1987   Garth J. Wakefield
    Organized from Spain Madrid (No. 92), Spain Barcelona (No. 137)

200 BRAZIL FORTALEZA   1 Jul 1987   Helvecio Martins
    Organized from Brazil Recife (No. 167a)

201 MEXICO MAZATLAN   1 Jul 1987   Samuel Lara M.
    Organized from Mexico Guadalajara (No. 125)

NAME	ORGANIZED	FIRST PRESIDENT
202 NEW JERSEY MORRISTOWN	1 Jul 1987	Dan J. Workman
Organized from New York New York (No. 15b)		
203 PORTUGAL PORTO	1 Jul 1987	Dan Copeland
Organized from Portugal Lisbon (No. 115)		
See also 220		
204 ZIMBABWE HARARE	1 Jul 1987	Joseph Hamstead
Organized from South Africa Johannesburg (No. 23)		
205 AUSTRIA VIENNA EAST	1 Jul 1987	Dennis B. Neuenschwander
Organized from Austria Vienna (No. 53)		
205a GUATEMALA GUATEMALA CITY NORTH	1 Jan 1988	Gordon W. Romney
Organized from Guatemala Guatemala City South (No. 76a)		
206 ARGENTINA SALTA	8 Jan 1988	Francisco Jose Vinas
Organized from Argentina Cordoba (No. 73)		
207 BOLIVIA LA PAZ See No. 75a		
208 MEXICO CHIHUAHUA	8 Jan 1988	Victor M. Cerda
Organized from Mexico Torreon (No. 81)		
209 MEXICO TUXTLA-GUTIERREZ	8 Jan 1988	Alberto de la O
Organized from Mexico Merida (No. 126)		
210 PERU LIMA EAST	8 Jan 1988	Douglas K. Earl
Organized from Peru Lima North (No. 149)		
211 PHILIPPINES CAGAYAN DE ORO	8 Jan 1988	Rufino A. Villanueva Jr.
Organized from Philippines Davao (No. 157)		
212 LIBERIA MONROVIA	1 Mar 1988	J. Duffy Palmer
213 BRAZIL BELO HORIZONTE	1 Jul 1988	Nivio Varella Alcover
Organized from Brazil Brasilia (No. 185a), Brazil Campinas (No. 190)		
214 CHILE ANTOFAGASTA	1 Jul 1988	Carlos Ramon Espinola
Organized from Chile Santiago North (No. 148), Chile Santiago South (No. 67),		
Chile Vina del Mar (No. 168)		
215 COLOMBIA BARRANQUILLA	1 Jul 1988	Frank Berrett
Organized from Colombia Bogota (No. 79a)		
216 MASCARENE ISLANDS	1 Jul 1988	Gerard Giraud-Carrier
Organized from South Africa Johannesburg (No. 23)		
217 MEXICO PUEBLA	1 Jul 1988	George G. Sloan
Organized from Mexico Mexico City East (No. 193)		
218 MEXICO TAMPICO	1 Jul 1988	Hector Ceballos
Organized from Mexico Mexico City North (No. 163), Mexico Monterrey (No. 45a)		
219 PHILIPPINES QUEZON CITY WEST	1 Jul 1988	Robert J. Kennerley
Organized from Philippines Baguio (No. 172), Philippines Quezon City (No. 192)		
220 SPAIN LAS PALMAS	1 Jul 1988	M. K. Hamblin
Organized from Spain Seville (No. 141), Portugal Porto (No. 203)		
221 NIGERIA ABA	1 Jul 1988	Arthur W. Elrey Jr.
Organized from Nigeria Lagos (No. 179)		

HISTORICAL CHRONOLOGY,
OCTOBER 1986 – SEPTEMBER 1988
IN REVIEW

HISTORICAL CHRONOLOGY OF THE CHURCH

This chronology gives a selected listing of important dates in Church history. Among the items excluded are those that can be found elsewhere in this Almanac, including information on General Authorities and the establishment of stakes and missions. Italicized entries are world events that were taking place as Church history was being made.

1805

Dec. 23 — Joseph Smith Jr. was born in Sharon, Windsor County, Vt., the fourth child of Joseph and Lucy Mack Smith.

1811

The Smith family moved from Vermont to Lebanon, N.H. They later moved to New York, settling at Palmyra, then to a four-room log house on the family farm in nearby Manchester.

1820

Spring — In Joseph Smith's First Vision, the Father and Son answered his question about which church to join. Joseph had prayed for guidance in response to a religious revival in the area.

May 3 — *The Missouri Compromise, allowing slavery in Missouri but not anywhere else west of the Mississippi and north of Missouri, was passed by Congress.*

1823

Sept. 21-22 — In five visits with Joseph Smith, the resurrected Moroni revealed the existence of ancient metal plates and instructed him on his role in restoring the gospel and translating the Book of Mormon.

Dec. 2 — *The Monroe Doctrine, stating opposition to European intervention in the Americas, was announced.*

1827

Jan. 18 — Joseph Smith married Emma Hale in South Bainbridge, N.Y. The couple met while Joseph was working in Harmony, Pa., for Josiah Stowell and boarding with Emma's father, Isaac Hale.

Sept. 22 — Joseph Smith received the plates of the Book of Mormon from Moroni at the Hill Cumorah. He also received the Urim and Thummim, which was used to assist in translation.

1828

February — Martin Harris took a transcript and partial translation of the Book of Mormon to Prof. Charles Anthon of Columbia College and Dr. Samuel L. Mitchell of New York. Soon after Harris' return in April, he borrowed and lost 116 manuscript pages.

1829

May 15 — Joseph Smith and Oliver Cowdery received the Aaronic Priesthood from John the Baptist. The two baptized one another, as instructed.

May or June — Peter, James, and John conferred the Melchizedek Priesthood upon Joseph Smith and Oliver Cowdery near the Susquehanna River between Harmony, Pa., and Colesville, N.Y.

June — The Book of Mormon translation was completed, and the three witnesses — Oliver Cowdery, David Whitmer, and Martin Harris — viewed the plates in a vision. The testimony of eight other witnesses — J. Christian Whitmer, Jacob Whitmer, Peter Whitmer Jr., John Whitmer, Hiram Page, Joseph Smith Sr., Hyrum Smith, and Samuel H. Smith — soon followed.

1830

March 16 — *In one of the slowest trading days in Wall Street history, only 31 shares changed hands on the New York Stock Exchange.*

March 26 — The Book of Mormon was published in Palmyra by Joseph Smith. E.B. Grandin printed 5,000 copies for $3,000.

April — A revelation on church government (D&C 20) outlined procedures for organizing the Church, duties of members and officers, need for record keeping, and procedures for baptism and sacrament administration.

April 6 — Joseph Smith organized the "Church of Christ" at the Peter Whitmer Sr. home in Fayette, N.Y., with six incorporators as required by law — Joseph Smith, Oliver Cowdery, Hyrum Smith, Peter Whitmer Jr., David Whitmer, and Samuel H. Smith.

April 11 — Oliver Cowdery preached the first public discourse of the new Church at a meeting in the Whitmer home.

June — The "Visions of Moses," later incorporated in the Pearl of Great Price, were revealed to Joseph Smith. The "Writings of Moses" were added in December.

June 9 — The first conference of the Church, which now numbered 27 members, convened in Fayette. Joseph Smith was arrested on a false charge of disorderly conduct later that evening but was acquitted in a trial at South Bainbridge, N.Y. This was the first of many trumped-up charges against the Prophet.

June 30 — Samuel H. Smith left for mission to neighboring villages, including Mendon, residence of the Young and Kimball families.

Oct. 17 — Four missionaries began a mission to the Catteraugus Indians in New York, the Wyandots of Ohio, and the Shawnees and Delawares on the Missouri frontier, stopping en route to teach and baptize Sidney Rigdon and a congregation of his followers in Ohio.

1830-1833

Joseph Smith worked on an inspired revision of the Bible. As a result of the questions raised during this intensive study, the Prophet inquired of the Lord and received numerous revelations later incorporated in the Doctrine and Covenants.

1831

Feb. 4 — Edward Partridge was named "bishop unto the Church."

June 3 — At a conference in Kirtland, the first high priests were ordained, and elders were called to go to Jackson County, Mo.

June 4 — Leopold I was proclaimed as Belgium's first king after separation from Holland.

Aug. 2 — In a ceremony in Kaw Township, Jackson County, Mo., Sidney Rigdon dedicated the Land of Zion. Joseph Smith dedicated a temple site the following day.

1832

Jan. 25 — Joseph Smith was sustained president of the high priesthood at a conference at Amherst, Ohio. Sidney Rigdon and Jesse Gause were later named counselors, and this initial organization of the First Presidency was confirmed in a revelation in March. Gause was replaced by Frederick G. Williams early in 1833.

Feb. 16 — While working on the inspired revision of the Bible, Joseph Smith and Sidney Rigdon witnessed the vision that became Section 76 of the D&C.

March 24 — Joseph Smith was tarred and feathered and Sidney Rigdon beaten by a mob in Hiram, Ohio.

June 1 — The *Evening and Morning Star,* the first LDS publication, was issued at Independence, Mo., with William W. Phelps as editor.

Dec. 25 — The prophecy on the Civil War (D&C 87) was given.

Dec. 27 — The revelation known as the "Olive Leaf" (D&C 88) was presented to the Church. Included were instructions leading to the organization of the School of the Prophets.

Dec. 28 — John Calhoun became the first vice president to resign, after he won an election to fill a vacant Senate seat representing South Carolina.

1833

Feb. 27 — The revelation known as the "Word of Wisdom" (D&C 89) was recorded.

May 4 — A building committee began raising funds for a temple in Kirtland, Ohio.

July 20 — A mob destroyed the *Evening and Morning Star* printing office, interrupting publication of the Book of Commandments, a compilation of revelations to the Church.

Fall — Missionary work had extended into Canada.

November — The saints left Jackson County in response to mob threats and attacks.

Dec. 3 — Oberlin College in Ohio opened, becoming the first co-educational college in the country.

Dec. 18 — Joseph Smith Sr. was ordained the first Patriarch to the Church.

1834

Feb. 17 — A presidency and high council were chosen for the stake in Kirtland. A similar organization was created in Missouri on July 3, 1834.

May 8 — Zion's Camp commenced its march from New Portage, Ohio, to Clay County, Mo., to assist the exiled Missouri saints. The camp dispersed June 30.

June 30 — The Indian Territory was created by an act of Congress.

October — The LDS Messenger and Advocate began publication at Kirtland and continued until the Mormon evacuation of Ohio in 1837.

1835

The Church published a collection of hymns and sacred songs selected by Emma Smith. She had been appointed to the work in July 1830, but destruction of the Independence, Mo., printing press in 1833 had delayed publication.

Feb. 14 — The three witnesses to the Book of Mormon selected 12 apostles at a meeting of the members of Zion's Camp in Kirtland, and the Quorum of the Twelve was organized.

Feb. 28 — The First Quorum of the Seventy was organized and its first seven presidents were named.

March 28 — A revelation on priesthood (D&C 107) was received during a meeting of the First Presidency and Twelve in Kirtland prior to the Twelve's departure for a mission through the Eastern States.

July 3 — Michael H. Chandler exhibited Egyptian mummies and papyrus scrolls in Kirtland. Joseph Smith's work with the scrolls resulted in the Book of Abraham, later included in the Pearl of Great Price.

Aug. 17 — A general assembly of the Church in Kirtland accepted the revelations selected for publication as the Doctrine and Covenants. This volume contained the revelations gathered for the Book of Commandments in 1833 with others received since that time, along with articles on marriage and government and a series of Lectures on Faith written for the School of the Prophets.

Nov. 2-4 — *Texas proclaimed its right to secede from Mexico, and Sam Houston was named to lead the Texas army.*

1836

Feb. 23-March 6 — *Texans were held under siege in the Alamo in San Antonio by Mexican General Santa Anna's troops.*

March 27 — A solemn assembly witnessed the dedication of the Kirtland Temple, which had been under construction for nearly three years.

April 3 — Joseph Smith and Oliver Cowdery received visions of the Savior, Moses, Elias, and Elijah in the Kirtland Temple.

June 29 — A mass meeting of citizens of Clay County, Mo., asked the saints to leave. By December many had relocated in Caldwell County, located northeast of Clay County.

1837

Parley P. Pratt issued his pamphlet "Voice of Warning," the first tract published for missionary use in the Church.

June 4 — Heber C. Kimball was called to open missionary work outside North America, and he was sent with Orson Hyde to the British Isles. Elders Joseph Fielding and Willard Richards and others left for this mission June 12-13.

Nov. 8 — *Mount Holyoke Seminary in Massachusetts became the first American college founded exclusively for women.*

1838

April 23 — *The first regular trans-Atlantic steamship service began.*

July 4 — Church officials laid the cornerstones for the proposed temple at Far West, Mo.

July 6 — The exodus from Kirtland began under the direction of the First Council of the Seventy, as planned three months earlier. The Kirtland Camp arrived at Far West, Mo., Oct. 2, and at Adam-ondi-Ahman two days later. (Additional 1838 on next page.)

150 YEARS AGO — 1839

Jan. 26 — Brigham Young and the Twelve organized a committee to conduct the removal of the saints from Missouri.

Feb. 20 — *Dueling in the District of Columbia was forbidden by an act of Congress.*

March 20 — Joseph Smith wrote a letter from Liberty Jail, parts of which became Sections 121, 122 and 123 of the Doctrine and Covenants.

April 16 — Joseph Smith and four other prisoners were allowed to escape while being transferred from Daviess to Boone counties under a change in venue in their case.

April 26 — A conference was held on the temple site at Far West, Mo., in fulfillment of the revelation given July 8, 1838. At this conference a cornerstone was laid for the temple, and Wilford Woodruff and George A. Smith were ordained apostles.

April 30 — Two farms were purchased by the Church at Commerce, Ill., the first land purchases in what became Nauvoo.

June 11 — Joseph Smith began the task of compiling his History of the Church. He had the help of scribes and later Church historians. Segments of his history were published in Church periodicals in Nauvoo and later in Salt Lake City and appeared in book form beginning in 1902.

Aug. 8 — John Taylor and Wilford Woodruff left Illinois on their missions to England. They were followed within the next 2½ months by Parley P. Pratt, Orson Pratt, Brigham Young, Heber C. Kimball, and George A. Smith.

Oct. 29 — Joseph Smith left Illinois to seek redress for the persecution of the saints in Missouri.

November — The first issue of the *Times and Seasons* was published.

Nov. 29 — President Martin Van Buren told Joseph Smith the federal government could do nothing to relieve the oppressions in Missouri. Petitions were also presented to Congress, and a second interview was held with Van Buren, all to no avail.

Dec. 19 — Wilford Woodruff, John Taylor and Theodore Turley set sail from New York for England.

Aug. 6 — A scuffle at the polls at Gallatin, Daviess County, Mo., intensified the mounting tension between Latter-day Saints and other settlers.

Sept. 21 — A mob challenged the saints at DeWitt, Carroll County, Mo., and continued its threats until Oct. 11, while Gov. Lilburn W. Boggs rejected Mormon pleas for military aid.

Oct. 24 — David W. Patten and a company of militia challenged a mob in the Battle of Crooked River, winning release of three Mormon prisoners but resulting in the deaths of three others, including Patten.

Thomas B. Marsh prepared an affidavit alleging the existence of an oath-bound "Danite" band. When Joseph Smith discovered what was happening among the secret group, he put a stop to it. Marsh apostatized but later returned to the Church.

Oct. 26 — Acting upon reports of civil war and rebellion among the Mormons, Gov. Boggs issued an order to exterminate or expel the saints from Missouri.

Oct. 30 — Seventeen Latter-day Saints died in the Haun's Mill Massacre at a small settlement on Shoal Creek, 12 miles east of Far West. The attack, by the Livingston County militia, was a reaction to the extermination order of Gov. Boggs.

Nov. 1 — A court-martial ordered Joseph Smith and others shot, but Brig. Gen. A.W. Doniphan refused to carry out the order. The prisoners were then lodged in the Richmond, Mo., jail.

Nov. 2 — The militia plundered Far West, Mo.

Nov. 10 — An arraignment and two-week trial commenced, after which Joseph Smith and others were held in the Liberty jail.

1840

January — *Wilkes expedition discovered the Antarctic continent.*

April 16 — The Twelve in England named Parley P. Pratt editor of a proposed monthly periodical to be named the *Latter-day Saints Millennial Star,* which would continue until 1970.

Dec. 16 — Gov. Thomas Carlin of Illinois signed a bill creating a charter for Nauvoo, defining the city boundaries and establishing its government. Provisions included a university and a militia, the Nauvoo Legion.

1841

Jan. 19 — A revelation (D&C 124) given at Nauvoo outlined instructions for building a temple and a boarding house in Nauvoo. Baptism for the dead was introduced as a temple ordinance.

Jan. 24 — Hyrum Smith was ordained Patriarch to the Church, replacing his father, who had died Sept. 14, 1840, and also assistant president, replacing Oliver Cowdery, who had been excommunicated.

Feb. 1 — John C. Bennett was elected Nauvoo mayor, and other officers were chosen in a municipal election.

April 4 — *John Tyler was the first vice president to become U.S. president due to death of a predecessor.*

June 4 — Joseph Smith was arrested in Illinois on a fugitive warrant issued by Gov. Boggs of Missouri, but Judge Stephen A. Douglas of Quincy, Ill., ruled the writ ineffective and released the prisoner.

Oct. 24 — At a site on the Mount of Olives in Jerusalem, Orson Hyde dedicated Palestine for the gathering of the Jews.

1842

March 17 — Joseph Smith organized the Female Relief Society of Nauvoo, with Emma Smith, Sarah M. Cleveland and Elizabeth Ann Whitney as its presidency, to look after the poor and sick.

May 4 — Joseph Smith introduced the temple endowment to seven men at a meeting in the room over his store in Nauvoo. A few others received endowments before completion of a temple.

May 6 — Former Gov. Lilburn W. Boggs of Missouri was injured by an unknown gunman.

May 19 — Joseph Smith was named mayor of Nauvoo to complete John C. Bennett's term.

July 20 — Lilburn W. Boggs accused Orrin Porter Rockwell of shooting him and later implicated Joseph Smith as an accessory. The Prophet was discharged Jan. 5, 1843, under a habeas corpus writ.

Aug. 6 — Joseph Smith prophesied that the saints would be driven to the Rocky Mountains, but that he would not go with them.

Aug. 9 — *The U.S.-Canadian border was formally defined by the Webster-Ashburton Treaty, was signed by the United States and Britain.*

Nov. 8 — The *Times and Seasons* published a brief history of the Church and the Articles of Faith, written at the request of John Wentworth, editor of the Chicago Democrat.

1843

Jan. 10 — *The first impeachment resolution was introduced in Congress; Virginian*

John Botts charged President John Tyler with corruption, malconduct in office, and high crimes. It was rejected 127-83.

May 3 — The *Nauvoo Neighbor* began publication and was voice for the Church for 2½ years.

May 18 — Joseph Smith predicted Stephen A. Douglas would one day seek the presidency of the United States, and if he opposed the Latter-day Saints he would "feel the weight of the hand of the Almighty."

June 21 — Illinois agents, armed with a warrant from Illinois Gov. Thomas Ford, arrested Joseph Smith at Dixon, Lee County, Ill. He was released July 1, 1843, under a writ of habeas corpus.

July 12 — A revelation received in Nauvoo, Ill., on the "Eternity of the Marriage Covenant and Plural Marriage" (D&C 132) was recorded, giving fuller meaning to the "new and everlasting covenant," which had been mentioned as early as 1831. The Prophet had explained the doctrine to a few, and plural marriages had been performed before the official announcement.

1844

Jan. 29 — A political convention in Nauvoo nominated Joseph Smith as a candidate for the United States presidency.

Feb. 8 — Joseph Smith published his views on governmental policy, a statement of his presidential platform.

Feb. 20 — The Prophet instructed the Twelve to organize an exploratory expedition to locate a site for the saints in California or Oregon. A group of volunteers was organized for the trip in meetings over the next several days.

March 26 — Joseph Smith prepared a message for Congress asking for a law protecting United States citizens immigrating to the unorganized territories, known as California and Oregon, and offered volunteers to serve in such a protective force.

May 11 — Joseph Smith organized the Council of Fifty, a secret political body that directed the westward migration of the saints and served as a "shadow government" in Utah during the 19th century.

May 17 — *Samuel Morse transmitted the first public message by telegraph from Washington, D.C. to Baltimore.*

May 25 — An indictment was filed at Carthage, Ill., charging Joseph Smith with polygamy and perjury. The Prophet gave himself up for trial and was told of a plot to have him killed.

June 7 — The first and only edition of the *Nauvoo Expositor* appeared. The city council declared the paper a nuisance three days later, and the city marshal forced entry to the print shop and destroyed the type and papers.

June 11 — Joseph Smith and the city council were charged with riot in the destruction of the *Expositor* press. A Nauvoo court absolved them of the charge, but the complainant asked for the issue to be examined by the Carthage court.

June 22 — Joseph and Hyrum Smith crossed the Mississippi River to flee to the Great Basin. Gov. Ford had promised the Prophet safety, and so, at the pleadings of others, the pair returned to Nauvoo and turned themselves in to government agents.

June 27 — Joseph and Hyrum Smith were killed by a mob that rushed the Carthage jail. John Taylor was injured in the attack; Willard Richards escaped injury.

Aug. 4 — Sidney Rigdon advocated appointment of a guardian for the Church at a meeting in Nauvoo.

Aug. 8 — At a meeting designated for the appointment of a guardian, Rigdon again stated his views, after which Brigham Young announced an afternoon meeting. During the latter session, Young claimed the right of leadership for the Twelve and was sustained by vote of the Church.

1845

January — The Illinois Legislature repealed the city charter of Nauvoo.

May — The accused nine murderers of Joseph and Hyrum Smith were acquitted upon instructions of the court.

Sept. 9 — Church leaders stated their intent to move to the Rocky Mountains to establish a refuge for the saints.

Sept. 22 — A mass meeting in Quincy, Ill., endorsed a proposal requesting the saints to leave Illinois as quickly as possible. The Twelve's reply reiterated the Latter-day Saints' intention to move to a remote area and asked for cooperation and an end of molestation in order to prepare for the move early the following summer.

Sept. 23 — *The first U.S. baseball club, the New York Knickerbocker Club, was organized.*

1846

Feb. 4 — The Mormon migration from Nauvoo began. The same day, the ship Brooklyn left New York for California under the direction of Samuel Brannan.

April 24 — A temporary settlement of the westward-moving saints was established at Garden Grove, Iowa. Other permanent camps were established at Mount Pisgah, Iowa, on May 18; at Council Bluffs, Iowa, on June 14; and at Winter Quarters, Neb., in September.

May 1 — The Nauvoo Temple was dedicated by Apostle Orson Hyde in public services.

July 7 — *Annexation of California was proclaimed by the United States after the surrender of Mexico in the Mexican War.*

July 13 — The first of the volunteer companies of the Mormon Battalion enlisted in answer to a request delivered to Brigham Young two weeks earlier by Capt. James Allen of the United States Army. The Battalion left for Fort Leavenworth on July 20, and arrived in San Diego, Calif., Jan. 29, 1847.

Sept. 17 — The remaining Nauvoo saints were driven from the city in violation of a "treaty of surrender" worked out with a citizens' committee from Quincy, Ill. The siege is known as the Battle of Nauvoo.

1847

Jan. 14 — Brigham Young presented instructions at Winter Quarters for the westward trek, including patterns for organizing the wagon companies. (D&C 136.)

March 3 — *Congress passed an act providing for adhesive postage stamps.*

July 22-24 — Brigham Young's pioneer company reached the Great Salt Lake Valley to select a settlement site for the saints, completing a journey that began at Winter Quarters April 7, 1847.

July 28 — Brigham Young selected a site for the Salt Lake Temple and instructed surveyors to lay out a city on a grid pattern square with the compass.

Dec. 5 — The First Presidency was reorganized with Brigham Young as president and Heber C. Kimball and Willard Richards as counselors.

1848

Jan. 24 — Gold was discovered in Sutter's millrace, which was dug by members of the Mormon Battalion.

July 19 — *Delegates from numerous women's organizations met in Seneca Falls, N.Y., and issued the first "Declaration of Independence for Women." Their main goal was to win voting rights for women.*

1849

March 3 — *Congress authorized coinage of the gold dollar and $20 gold piece (double eagle).*

March 5 — A provisional State of Deseret was established and appeals made for self-government.

October — A Perpetual Emigrating Fund was established during general conference to assist the poor. The system, which was incorporated one year later, continued until it was disincorporated by the Edmunds-Tucker Act in 1887.

1850

Missions of the Church were opened overseas in Scandinavia, France, Italy, Switzerland, and Hawaii; most were discontinued after a few years. Lorenzo Snow and Erastus Snow opened missionary work in France, Italy, and Denmark.

June 15 — The first edition of the *Deseret News* was published in Salt Lake City.

September — Brigham Young was appointed governor of the Territory of Utah.

Sept. 18 — *The U.S. Congress passed the Fugitive Slave Act, permitting slave owners to reclaim slaves who had escaped into other states.*

1851-54

Missions of the Church were opened outside the United States in the South Pacific, India, Malta, Gibraltar, Germany, South Africa, and Switzerland; again, most were discontinued after a few years.

1851

Jan. 9 — Great Salt Lake City was incorporated. This city became the headquarters of the Church.

March 24 — A company of 500 settlers bound for California departed from Payson, Utah. The group settled in San Bernardino, Calif., which became the first Mormon colony outside the Great Basin since the arrival of the pioneers in 1847.

Aug. 12 — *Isaac Singer was granted a patent for his sewing machine. Singer set up business in Boston with $40 capital.*

September — Three federally appointed officials, Judge Lemuel C. Brandebury, Judge Perry C. Brochus, and Secretary Broughton D. Harris, left Utah in protest against plural marriage, as well as what they considered unjustified influence of the Church on political affairs in the territory.

1852

March 20 — *Harriet Beecher Stowe's influential novel about slavery, "Uncle Tom's Cabin," was published.*

Aug. 28-29 — At a special conference in Salt Lake City, the doctrine of plural marriage was first publicly announced, although several of the leading brethren of the Church had been practicing the principle privately since it had been taught to them by Joseph Smith in Nauvoo.

1853

April 6 — The cornerstones were laid for the Salt Lake Temple.

June 29 — *The U.S. Senate ratified the $10 million Gadsden Purchase from Mexico, which completed the modern geographical configuration of the United States.*

July 18 — The so-called Walker War began near Payson, Utah. This was one of several incidents of tension between Mormons and Indians in Utah territory. The war terminated in May 1854.

1854

Jan. 19 — The official announcement adopting the Deseret Alphabet was made in the *Deseret News.*

May 26 — *The Kansas-Nebraska bill passed, giving territories or states freedom of choice on the question of slavery.*

1855

Feb. 17 — *Congress authorized construction of a telegraph line from the Mississippi River to the Pacific.*

May 5 — The Endowment House in Salt Lake City was dedicated.

July 23 — The foundation of the Salt Lake Temple was finished.

Oct. 29 — In a general epistle, the First Presidency proposed that Perpetual Emigration Fund immigrants cross the plains by handcart.

1856

During this year a general "reformation" took place throughout the Church, in which Church members were admonished forcefully from the pulpit to reform their lives and rededicate themselves to the service of the Lord. As a symbol of renewed dedication, many saints renewed their covenants by re-baptism. The reformation movement continued into 1857.

Feb. 10 — *An important change in U.S. citizenship laws provided that all children born abroad, to U.S. citizens, were assured of citizenship.*

June 9 — The first handcart company left Iowa City. Later that year two such companies suffered severe tragedy due to an early winter. The handcart method of immigration continued until 1860.

1857

March 6 — *The U.S. Supreme Court handed down its landmark ruling that a slave, Dred Scott, could not sue in a federal court for his freedom.*

March 30 — Territorial Judge W. W. Drum-

mond, who had earlier left the Territory of Utah, wrote a letter to the attorney general of the United States charging Mormon leaders with various crimes.

May 13 — Elder Parley P. Pratt of the Council of the Twelve was assassinated while on a mission in Arkansas.

May 28 — Under instructions from President James Buchanan, the United States War Department issued orders for an army to assemble at Fort Leavenworth, Kan., to march to Utah. It was assumed that the people of Utah were in rebellion against the United States. This was the beginning of the so-called "Utah War."

July 24 — Brigham Young received word that an American army, under the command of Gen. Albert Sidney Johnston, was approaching Utah. Church leaders took the position that they had violated no laws, and they decided to allow no military "invasion" to drive them from their homes.

Sept. 7 — The tragic Mountain Meadows Massacre took place, in which Arkansas immigrants on their way to California were killed by certain misguided Mormons in Southern Utah. Twenty years later, John D. Lee was executed for his part in the crime.

Sept. 15 — Brigham Young declared Utah to be under martial law and forbade the approaching troops to enter the Salt Lake Valley. Armed militia were ordered to various points to harass the soldiers and prevent their entry. A further result of the pending difficulties was that Brigham Young called the elders home from foreign missions and advised the saints in certain outlying settlements to return to places nearer the headquarters of the Church.

1858

June 26 — After having been stopped for the winter by the delaying tactics of the Mormons, Gen. Johnston's army finally entered the Salt Lake Valley, but peacefully. The army's permanent encampment, until 1861, was at Camp Floyd in Cedar Valley in Utah County. Meanwhile, most of the saints north of Utah County had moved south, but they returned to their homes when peace seemed assured.

Aug. 5 — *The first trans-Atlantic cable was completed.*

1859

July 13 — Horace Greeley, founder and editor of the *New York Tribune* had a two-hour interview with Brigham Young, covering a variety of subjects from infant baptism to plurality of wives. The substance of his questions and the answers to them he published a year later in his *Overland Journey from New York to San Francisco.*

Aug. 27 — *The first oil well in the United States was drilled near Titusville, Pa.*

1860

Sept. 24 — The last group of saints to cross the plains by handcart entered Salt Lake City.

Oct. 13 — *The first aerial photograph in the U.S. was taken from a balloon over Boston.*

1861

April 12 — *Civil War began as Confederate forces fired on Ft. Sumter in South Carolina.*

April 23 — The first of several Church wagon trains left Salt Lake Valley with provisions for incoming saints whom they would meet at the Missouri River. This was the beginning of a new program to help immigrating saints that lasted until the railroad came in 1869.

1862

March 6 — The Salt Lake Theater, which became an important cultural center for Mormon people in the area, was dedicated. It was opened to the public two days later.

May 20 — *The Homestead Act, granting free family farms to settlers, was passed.*

July 8 — A federal law was passed defining plural marriage as bigamy and declaring it a crime. Mormons considered the law unconstitutional and refused to honor it.

1863

Jan 1 — *The Emancipation Proclamation, legally freeing all slaves, was issued by President Abraham Lincoln.*

March 10 — President Brigham Young was arrested on a charge of bigamy and placed under a $2,000 bond by Judge Kinney. He was never actually brought to trial, however.

1864

April 8 — Walter M. Gibson, who had usurped Church authority in Hawaii, was excommunicated at Lahaina, Maui.

Sept. 1 — *Union Gen. William Sherman invaded Atlanta on his relentless march through Georgia.*

Dec. 17 — Anson Call selected a site for a landing and Church warehouse on the Colorado River. The site was afterwards known as Call's Landing.

1865

A war with the Indians in central Utah, known as the Black Hawk War, commenced. It lasted until 1867.

April 10 — In a special conference, the Church agreed to build a telegraph line connecting the settlements in Utah. The line was completed in 1867.

July 5 — *William Booth founded the Salvation Army in London.*

1866

Jan. 1 — The first edition of the *Juvenile Instructor,* the official organ of the Sunday School, was published. Its name was changed to the *Instructor* in 1930, and it was discontinued in 1970.

May 16 — *The U.S. Treasury Department was authorized to put in circulation the first five-cent piece, to be called a "nickel."*

1867

July 1 — *The Dominion of Canada was created.*

Oct. 6 — The first conference to be conducted in the newly completed Tabernacle on Temple Square in Salt Lake City began.

Dec. 8 — Brigham Young requested that bishops reorganize Relief Societies within their wards. The societies had been disbanded during the Utah War.

1868

Jan. 29 — The name Great Salt Lake City was changed to simply Salt Lake City.

May 26 — *President Andrew Johnson was acquitted of impeachment charges by one vote. Johnson has been accused of "high crimes and misdemeanors."*

1869

March 1 — ZCMI opened for business. The Church-owned institution was the forerunner of many cooperative business ventures in Utah territory.

May 10 — The transcontinental railroad was completed with the joining of the rails at Promontory Summit, Utah. The railroad had great impact on immigration policy and on the general economy of the Church in Utah.

Nov. 6 — *The first official intercollegiate football game, between Rutgers and Princeton, was played.*

Nov. 28 — The Young Ladies' Retrenchment Association, later renamed the Young Women's Mutual Improvement Association, was organized by Brigham Young in the Lion House in Salt Lake City.

December — The "Godbeite" movement began to take definite shape. It consisted largely of dissident Latter-day Saints who objected to the economic and political policies of the Church in Utah, but it also took on certain spiritual overtones.

1870

Jan. 13 — A large mass meeting was held by the women of Salt Lake City in protest against certain anti-Mormon legislation pending in Congress. This and other such meetings demonstrated that, contrary to anti-Mormon claims, Mormon women were not antagonistic to the ecclesiastical power structure in Utah.

February — The "Liberal Party" was formed, which generally came to represent the anti-Mormon political interests, as opposed to the "People's Party," which generally represented Church interests until the end of the century.

Feb. 12 — An act of the Territorial Legislature giving the elective franchise to the women of Utah was signed into law. Utah became one of the first American states or territories to grant woman's suffrage.

July 24 — *The first railroad car from the Pacific Coast reached New York City, opening the way for transcontinental train service.*

1871

February — Judge James B. McKean, who had arrived in Utah in August 1870, made several rulings regarding naturalization that began a bitter and antagonistic relationship between himself and Church members.

May 10 — *The Treaty of Frankfurt ended the Franco-Prussian War.*

Oct. 2 — President Brigham Young was arrested on a charge of unlawful cohabitation. Various legal proceedings in the court of Judge McKean lasted until April 25, 1872, during which time President Young was sometimes kept in custody in his own home. The case was dropped, however, due to a U.S. Supreme Court decision that overturned various judicial proceedings in Utah for the previous 18 months.

1872

Court proceedings against various leading men in the Church continued.

June — The first edition of the *Woman's Exponent,* a paper owned and edited by Mormon women, was published. This periodical continued until 1914.

Nov. 5 — *Susan B. Anthony was fined $100 for voting in the presidential election, because women didn't have the right to vote.*

1873

May 1 — *Penny postcards went on sale for the first time.*

Oct. 1 — Zion's Bank of Salt Lake City opened its doors for its first day of business.

1874

May 8 — *Massachusetts enacted first effective 10-hour day law for women.*

May 9 — At general conference, which began on this date, the principal subject discussed was the "United Order." This resulted in the establishment of several cooperative economic ventures, the most notable of which were communities such as Orderville, Utah, where the residents owned no private property but held all property in common.

June 23 — The so-called Poland Bill became a federal law. It had the effect of limiting the jurisdiction of probate courts in Utah. These courts had been authorized to conduct all civil and criminal cases, and were generally favorable toward members of the Church, but now Mormons accused of crimes had to be tried in federal courts.

1875

March 18 — Judge James B. McKean, with whom the Mormons had been so unhappy, was removed from office by U.S. President Ulysses S. Grant.

May 19 — *The first Kentucky Derby was run at Louisville, Ky.*

June 10 — The first Young Men's Mutual Improvement Association was organized in the Thirteenth Ward in Salt Lake City. On Dec. 8, 1876, a central committee was formed to coordinate all such associations.

Oct. 16 — Brigham Young Academy, later to become Brigham Young University, was founded in Provo, Utah.

1876

March 23 — Advance companies of saints from Utah, who were called to settle in Arizona, arrived at the Little Colorado. This was the beginning of Mormon colonization activity in Arizona.

June 25 — *Gen. George Custer's troops were massacred in the Battle of the Little Big Horn in Montana.*

1877

April 6 — The St. George Temple was dedicated by President Daniel H. Wells in connection with the 47th Annual Conference of the Church that was held in St. George. This was the first temple to be completed in Utah. The lower portion of the temple had been dedicated earlier on Jan. 1, 1877, and ordinances for the dead had commenced.

April 24 — *Northern post-Civil War rule in the South ended as federal troops were removed from New Orleans.*

Aug. 29 — President Brigham Young died at his home in Salt Lake City at age 76.

Sept. 4 — The Council of the Twelve, with John Taylor as president, publicly assumed its position as the head of the Church.

1878

May 19 — The Church had previously provided for the purchase of land in Conejos County, Colo., for settlements of saints from the Southern states. On this date the first settlers arrived, thus opening Mormon settlements in Colorado.

Aug. 25 — The first Primary Association meeting was held at Farmington, Utah. The movement spread rapidly and on June 19, 1880, a Churchwide organization was established.

Dec. 1 — *The first telephone was installed in the White House.*

1879-1896

Missions outside the United States extended to Mexico, Turkey, Society Islands, and Samoa, although some missions closed after a few years.

1879

Jan. 6 — The Supreme Court of the United States, in the important Reynolds Case, upheld the previous conviction of George Reynolds under the 1862 anti-bigamy law. With such a ruling, the court paved the way for more intense and more effective prosecution of the Mormons in the 1880s.

Oct. 4 — The first edition of the *Contributor,* which became the official publication of the Young Men's Mutual Improvement Association, was issued. It was published until 1896.

Dec. 31 — *Thomas Edison first demonstrated the electric incandescent light in Menlo Park, N.J.*

1880

April 6 — At general conference, a special jubilee year celebration was inaugurated. Charitable actions, reminiscent of Old Testament jubilee celebrations, included rescinding half the debt owed to the Perpetual Emigration Fund Company, distribution of cows and sheep among the needy, and advice to the saints to forgive the worthy poor of their debts.

Oct. 10 — The First Presidency was reorganized, and John Taylor was sustained as the third president of the Church, with George Q. Cannon and Joseph F. Smith as counselors.

Dec. 20 — *One mile of Broadway Street in New York City was electrically illuminated by arc lighting.*

1881

January — George Reynolds, the secretary to the First Presidency who provided the "test case" for the constitutionality of laws outlawing plural marriage, was released from prison.

May 21 — *The American Red Cross was organized with Clara Barton as president.*

1882

Jan. 8 — The Assembly Hall on Temple Square in Salt Lake City was dedicated.

March 22 — The Edmunds Anti-Polygamy bill became law when U.S. President Chester A. Arthur added his approval to that of the Senate and House of Representatives. The law defined polygamous living as "unlawful cohabitation" and disfranchised those who continued to live that way. Serious prosecution under this law began in 1884.

July 17 — The Deseret Hospital, the second hospital in Utah and the first Church hospital, was opened by the Relief Society.

Aug. 18 — The Utah Commission, authorized in the Edmunds law, arrived in the territory. The five members of the commission, appointed by the U.S. president, had responsibility of supervising election procedures in Utah. Since the result of its activities was to enforce the disfranchisement of much of the Mormon population, Church members considered its work unfair.

Sept. 30 — *The first hydroelectric power station in the United States was opened at Appleton, Wis.*

1883

January — *Pendleton Act established the U.S. Civil Service System.*

Aug. 26 — The first permanent branch among the Maoris was organized at Papawai, New Zealand.

Dec. 26 — Thomas L. Kane, long a friend of the Church and a champion for Mormon people, died in Philadelphia, Pa.

1884

May 1 — *Work began in Chicago on a 10-story building called a "skyscraper."*

May 17 — The Logan Temple was dedicated by President John Taylor.

1885

Extensive prosecution under the Edmunds law continued in both Utah and Idaho. Many polygamists were imprisoned, while others fled into exile, some to Mexico. Mormons attempting to escape prosecution were said to be living on the "underground."

Feb. 1 — President John Taylor delivered his last public sermon in Salt Lake City, then went on the "underground."

Feb. 3 — An Idaho law was approved by the governor that prohibited all Mormons from voting through the device of a "test oath."

March 22 — The United States Supreme Court annulled the "test oath" formulated by the Utah Commission, thus restoring the franchise to a number of saints in the territory.

Sept. 5 — *Jake Gumper of Fort Wayne, Ind., bought the first gasoline pump manufactured in America.*

1886

A critical situation was evident in the Church, with many people fleeing into exile in Mexico and Canada and most of the leaders of the Church in hiding. Similar conditions continued for the next three years. These years are sometimes called the years of the "crusade."

Jan. 31 — The first meeting was held in the first meetinghouse built in Mexico on the Piedras Verdes River in a settlement named Colonia Juarez.

Feb. 14 — *The West Coast citrus industry got its start, as the first trainload of oranges left Los Angeles for eastern markets.*

March 6 — LDS women in Salt Lake City held a mass meeting to protest the abuse heaped upon them by the federal courts and to protest the loss of their vote.

Aug. 3 — The Brigham Young Academy in Provo announced that its tuition for 1886-1887 would be from $10-$20 for a 20-week semester.

1887

Feb. 17-18 — The Edmunds-Tucker Act passed Congress, and it became law without the signature of the U.S. president. Among other stringent provisions, the law disincorporated the Church, dissolved the Perpetual Emigrating Fund Company and escheated its property to the government, abolished female suffrage, and provided for the confiscation of practically all the property of the Church.

July 25 — President John Taylor died while in "exile" at Kaysville, Utah at age 78. The Twelve Apostles assumed leadership of the Church until 1889.

July 30 — Under provisions of the Edmunds-Tucker Act, suits were filed against the Church and the Perpetual Emigrating Fund Company, and their property was confiscated. A receiver for the property was ap-

pointed in November 1887, but the government allowed the Church to rent and occupy certain offices and the temple block.

Aug. 31 — *Thomas A. Edison was awarded a patent for a device he called "Kinetoscope," used to produce pictures representing objects in motion.*

1888

May 17 — President Wilford Woodruff dedicated the Manti Temple in a private service; three public dedicatory services followed, beginning May 21.

March 11 — *More than 400 people died as a snowstorm crippled the eastern United States during the "Blizzard of '88."*

---

100 YEARS AGO
1889

Jan. 5 — Clara Decker Young, widow of Brigham Young and one of the three women in the first pioneer company, died.

April 6 — The first Relief Society general conference was held in the Assembly Hall in Salt Lake City with Pres. D.H. Young presiding. Twenty stakes were represented.

April 7 — Wilford Woodruff was sustained president of the Church, with George Q. Cannon and Joseph F. Smith as counselors.

May 6 — *The Eiffel Tower in Paris was officially opened.*

Aug. 28 — Hawaiian members of the Church arrived at Skull Valley, Tooele County, Utah, and founded the Iosepa colony.

October — The *Young Woman's Journal,* official organ of the Young Ladies' Mutual Improvement Association, began publication. It was merged with the Improvement Era in 1929.

November — The Endowment House in Salt Lake City was torn down.

1890

Feb. 3 — The Idaho "test oath" was upheld by the Supreme Court of the United States.

Sept. 24 — President Wilford Woodruff issued a "Manifesto" that declared that no new plural marriages had been entered into with Church approval in the past year, denied that plural marriage had been taught during that time, declared the intent of the president of the Church to submit to the constitutional law of the land, and advised members of the Church to refrain from contracting any marriage forbidden by law.

Oct. 6 — The "Manifesto" was unanimously accepted by vote in the general conference of the Church. This marked the beginning of a growing reconciliation between the Church and the United States, which effectively paved the way for statehood for Utah.

Dec. 31 — *Ellis Island in New York Harbor was opened as an immigration depot.*

1891

March — At the first triennial meeting of the National Council of Women of the United States, the Relief Society attended and became a charter member of that council.

March 21 — *A marriage in Kentucky ended the feud between the Hatfields and McCoys.*

1892

April 19 — *Three million acres of Cheyenne and Arapaho lands in Oklahoma were opened for settlement by presidential proclamation.*

Oct. 12 — Articles of incorporation for the Relief Society were filed, after which it became known as the National Women's Relief Society. The name was again changed in 1945 to Relief Society of The Church of Jesus Christ of Latter-day Saints.

1893

Jan. 4 — The president of the United States, Benjamin Harrison, issued a proclamation of amnesty to all polygamists who had entered into that relationship before Nov. 1, 1890. The Utah Commission soon ruled that voting restrictions in the territory should be removed.

April 6 — The Salt Lake Temple was dedicated by President Wilford Woodruff.

June 27 — *The stock market crashed, resulting in four years of extreme depression.*

Sept. 8 — The Salt Lake Tabernacle Choir, while on a major tour, sang at the Chicago World's Fair and won second prize in a choral contest. This was indicative of a new image for the Mormons.

Oct. 25 — President Grover Cleveland signed a resolution, passed by Congress, for the return of the personal property of the Church. Three years later, on March 28, 1896, a memorial passed by Congress and approved by the president, provided for the restoration of the Church's real estate.

1894

March 8 — *New York became the first state to pass a law requiring dogs to be licensed.*

April — President Wilford Woodruff announced the end of the policy of adoption, under which members had been sealed to prominent Church leaders. He re-emphasized the need for genealogical research and sealings along natural family lines.

July 14 — President Grover Cleveland signed an act that provided for statehood for Utah. This culminated 47 years of effort on the part of Mormons in Utah to achieve the status of statehood.

Aug. 27 — President Grover Cleveland issued a proclamation granting pardons and restoring civil rights to those who had been disfranchised under anti-polygamy laws.

Nov. 13 — The genealogical society of the Church, known as the Genealogical Society of Utah, was organized.

1895

March 4 — The Utah Constitutional Convention met in Salt Lake City. John Henry Smith, a member of the Council of the Twelve, was elected president of that convention.

Nov. 28 — *The first automobile race in the U.S. took place from the heart of Chicago to its suburbs, 54 miles at 7½ miles an hour.*

1896

Jan. 4 — President Grover Cleveland signed the proclamation that admitted Utah into the union.

July 28 — *Miami, Fla., with a population of less than 300, was incorporated.*

1897

July 5 — *Soft coal miners, as ordered by the United Mine Workers, went on strike, eventually winning an 8-hour day and abolition of the company store.*

July 20 — The Brigham Young Monument was dedicated at the intersection of Main and South Temple streets as part of the Pioneer Jubilee celebration in Salt Lake City.

November — The *Improvement Era* began publication as the official organ of the Young Men's Mutual Improvement Association. Other Church organizations later joined in sponsoring the monthly magazine, which continued as the official voice of the Church until 1970.

1898

April 24 — *Spain declared war on the United States, and the Spanish-American War began.*

April 28 — A First Presidency statement encouraged Latter-day Saint youths to support the American war effort in the Spanish-American War. This placed the Church firmly on the side of the war declarations of constituted governments and ended a policy of selective pacifism.

Sept. 2 — Wilford Woodruff died in San Francisco, Calif., at age 91.

Sept. 13 — Lorenzo Snow became fifth president of the Church. He chose George Q. Cannon and Joseph F. Smith as counselors.

1899

May 8 — President Lorenzo Snow declared to a St. George, Utah, conference, "The time has now come for every Latter-day Saint . . . to do the will of the Lord and pay his tithing in full."

Oct. 14 — U.S. declared an "Open Door Policy" toward China, opening it as an international market.

1900

Jan. 8 — President Lorenzo Snow issued an official statement reaffirming the Church ban on polygamy.

Jan. 25 — The United States House of Representatives voted to deny Utahn B.H. Roberts of the First Council of the Seventy his seat in Congress following an investigation of the right of polygamists to hold office under the Constitution.

Aug. 14 — *Anti-saloon agitator Carry Nation began attacking bars with a hatchet.*

1901

Aug. 12 — Elder Heber J. Grant dedicated Japan and opened a mission there as a first step in renewed emphasis on preaching the gospel in all the world. Over the next two years, Elder Francis M. Lyman, also of the Twelve, dedicated the lands of Africa, Palestine, Greece, Italy, France, Russia, Finland, and Poland, though missionary work did not begin immediately in all these areas.

Sept. 6 — *U.S. President William McKinley was shot by Leon Czolgosz; he died eight days later.*

Oct. 10 — President Lorenzo Snow died at his home in the Beehive House in Salt Lake City at age 87.

Oct. 17 — Joseph F. Smith was ordained sixth president of the Church, with John R. Winder and Anthon H. Lund as counselors.

1902

The Church published in book form the first volume of Joseph Smith's *History of the Church*, edited by B.H. Roberts. Publication

continued over the next decade, with a seventh volume added in 1932.

January — The *Children's Friend* began publication as an organ for Primary Association teachers. The magazine later widened its audience to include children, then eliminated the teacher's departments.

March 6 — *The Bureau of the Census was created by an act of Congress.*

Aug. 4 — The First Council of the Seventy opened a Bureau of Information and Church Literature in a small octagonal booth on Temple Square. It was replaced by a larger building in March 1904 and by the present visitors centers in 1966 and 1978.

1903

Aug. 31 — *A Packard automobile completed a 52-day journey from San Francisco to New York, the first automobile to cross the nation under its own power.*

Nov. 5 — The Church announced purchase of the Carthage Jail as a historic site.

1904

April 5 — President Joseph F. Smith issued an official statement upholding provisions of the 1890 Manifesto and invoking excommunication against persons violating the "law of the land" by contracting new plural marriages.

July 23 — *The ice cream cone came into being in St. Louis, Mo.*

1905

Jan. 1 — The Dr. William S. Groves Latter-day Saints Hospital opened in Salt Lake City and was dedicated three days later, the first in the modern Church hospital system. When the Church divested itself of its medical facilities in September 1974, the system had grown to include 15 hospitals.

Sept. 5 — *The Treaty of Portsmouth ended the Russian-Japanese War.*

Oct. 28 — Elders John W. Taylor and Matthias F. Cowley, finding themselves out of harmony with the Church policy on plural marriage, submitted resignations from the Council of the Twelve that were announced to the Church April 6, 1906.

Dec. 23 — Church officials dedicated the Joseph Smith Memorial Cottage and Monument at Sharon, Windsor County, Vt., the site of the Prophet's birth 100 years earlier.

1906

The Sunday School introduced a Church-wide parents' class as part of an increased emphasis on the importance of the home and of the parents' role in teaching their children the gospel.

April 18 — *San Francisco was hit by an earthquake, which resulted in half the city being destroyed.*

Summer — President Joseph F. Smith visited the saints in Europe, the first such visit of a serving president to the area. President Smith also visited Hawaii, Canada, and Mexico during his presidency.

1907

Jan. 10 — President Joseph F. Smith announced payment of the last two $500,000 bond issues sold by President Lorenzo Snow in December 1899 to fund the Church debt. The first had been paid in 1903.

February — The United States Senate agreed to seat Utah Sen. Reed Smoot. The vote culminated a three-year investigation during which Church officials testified concerning polygamy and Church involvement in politics.

April 5 — A vote of the General Conference approved the First Presidency's 16-page summary statement of the Church position in the Smoot hearings. It was titled, "An Address: The Church of Jesus Christ of Latter-day Saints to the World."

Aug. 1 — *An aeronautical division, consisting of one officer and two enlisted men, was established by the U.S. Army, the forerunner of the U.S. Air Force.*

1908

April 8 — The First Presidency created a General Priesthood Committee on Outlines, which served until 1922. In fulfillment of its assignment, the committee created definite age groupings for Aaronic Priesthood offices, provided systematic programs for year-round priesthood meetings, and in other ways reformed, reactivated, and systematized priesthood work.

Oct. 1 — *Henry Ford introduced his famous Model-T Ford.*

1909

November — The First Presidency issued an official statement on the origin of man.

July 30 — *The U.S. government bought its first airplane — a Wright biplane costing $31,000.*

1910

The Bishop's Building, an office building at 50 N. Main Street for the Presiding Bishopric and auxiliary organizations, opened. It was used for more than 50 years.

January — The first issue of the *Utah Genealogical and Historical Magazine* was published. This quarterly publication served as the publication of the Genealogical Society

of Utah. It was discontinued in October 1940.

Sept. 20 — Deseret Gymnasium opened its doors in a building on the Church administration block.

Nov. 27 — *New York's Pennsylvania Station, the biggest railway terminal in the world, opened.*

1911

The Church adopted the Boy Scout program and has since become one of the leading sponsors of this movement for young men.

April 15 — *Collier's* magazine published a letter from Theodore Roosevelt refuting many charges made against Utah Sen. Reed Smoot and the Church. This action helped defuse an anti-Mormon propaganda surge of 1910-11.

Dec. 14 — *Norwegian explorer Roald Amundsen became the first man to reach the South Pole.*

1912

Aug. 14 — *The United States sent Marines to Nicarauga, which was in default of loans from the U.S. and Europe.*

Fall — A seminary at Granite High School in Salt Lake City opened, marking the commencement of a released-time weekday education program for young Latter-day Saints. As the seminary program grew, the Church phased out its involvement in academies, which were Church-sponsored high schools or junior colleges. By 1924 only the Juarez Academy in Mexico remained.

Nov. 8 — The First Presidency created a Correlation Committee, headed by Elder David O. McKay, and asked it to coordinate scheduling and prevent unnecessary duplication in the programs of Church auxiliaries. A Social Advisory Committee of the General Boards was merged with it in 1920. The combined committee issued a major report April 14, 1921, offering proposals for correlating priesthood and auxiliary activities; many of its recommendations have since been adopted.

1913

The Church established the Maori Agricultural College in New Zealand. It was destroyed by an earthquake in 1931 and never rebuilt.

Feb. 3 — *The 16th Amendment, creating the income tax, became a part of the U.S. Constitution after ratification by Wyoming.*

1914

January — The *Relief Society Magazine* appeared as a monthly publication containing lesson material for use in the women's auxiliary of the Church. The magazine carried stories, poetry, articles, homemaking helps, news, and lesson material until it ceased publication in December 1970.

The Relief Society also introduced its first uniform courses of study, organized around four general themes. The pattern was altered in 1921 to include theology, work and business meetings, literature, and social service. These developments built upon a "mother's class" started in 1902 with lesson material provided by the stakes.

Aug. 15 — *An American ship sailed from the Atlantic to the Pacific Ocean, officially opening the Panama Canal.*

1915

May 7 — *A German U-boat sank the British liner Lusitania off the coast of Iceland, killing 1,198 persons.*

September — James E. Talmage's book *Jesus the Christ* was published.

1916

Feb. 21 — *The longest and bloodiest battle of World War I, the Battle of Verdun, began in France, resulting in the death of one million soldiers.*

June 30 — The First Presidency and Council of the Twelve issued a doctrinal exposition clarifying the use of the title "Father" as it is applied to Jesus.

1917

Oct. 2 — The Church Administration Building at 47 E. South Temple was completed.

Nov. 7 — *Nikolai Lenin and his Bolsheviks overthrew the Kerensky regime in Russia.*

1918

May — Wheat that Relief Society sisters had been gathering and storing since 1876 was sold to the U.S. government, at a government price, with approval of the First Presidency and the Presiding Bishopric, to alleviate shortages during World War I.

Oct. 3 — While contemplating the meaning of Christ's atonement, President Joseph F. Smith received a manifestation on the salvation of the dead and the visit of the Savior to the world of spirits after His crucifixion. A report of the experience was published in December and was added to the Doctrine and Covenants June 6, 1979, as Section 138.

Nov. 11 — *World War I ended, as the Allies signed an armistice with Germany.*

Nov. 19 — President Joseph F. Smith died six days after his 80th birthday. Because of an epidemic of influenza, no public funeral was held for the Church president.

Nov. 23 — Heber J. Grant was sustained and set apart as the seventh president of the Church during a meeting of the Twelve in the Salt Lake Temple. He selected as counselors Anthon H. Lund and Charles W. Penrose.

1919

January — The 18th Amendment to the United States Constitution established prohibition. Church leaders supported the movement toward nationwide prohibition and opposed the amendment's repeal in 1933.

Oct. 28 — *Congress overrode President Woodrow Wilson's veto and enacted prohibition.*

Nov. 27 — President Heber J. Grant dedicated the temple at Laie, Hawaii, the first Latter-day Saint temple outside the continental United States. Construction had begun soon after the site was dedicated in June 1915.

1920-21

Elder David O. McKay of the Council of the Twelve and President Hugh J. Cannon of Liberty Stake in Salt Lake City traveled 55,896 miles in a world survey of Church missions for the First Presidency. The pair visited the saints in the Pacific Islands, New Zealand, Australia, and Asia, and then made stops in India, Egypt, and Palestine, before visiting the missions of Europe.

Nov. 25 — *WTAW of College Station, Texas, broadcast the first play-by-play account of a football game, between Texas and Texas A&M.*

1921

The M-Men and Gleaner departments in MIA were introduced Churchwide to serve the special needs of young people from ages 17 to 23.

Oct. 5 — *The World Series was broadcast for the first time.*

1922

The Primary Children's Hospital opened in Salt Lake City.

Nov. 26 — *King Tutankhamen's tomb was opened in Egypt.*

1923

The Church purchased a part of the Hill Cumorah. Additional acquisitions in 1928 gave the Church possession of the entire hill and adjacent lands.

Jan. 21 — Creation of a stake in Los Angeles illustrated the growth of the Church outside the Intermountain Area. In the post-World War I era, this growth continued rapidly.

Aug. 26 — President Heber J. Grant dedicated the Alberta Temple, which had been under construction for nearly a decade.

Sept. 29 — *Britain began to rule Palestine under a mandate from the League of Nations.*

1924

March 21 — A First Presidency statement answered criticism of unauthorized plural marriages by once again confirming the Church's policy against the practice. Over-zealous polygamist cliques within the Church were excommunicated when discovered.

June 2 — *The U.S. Congress granted citizenship to all American Indians.*

Oct. 3 — Radio broadcast of general conference began on KSL, the Church-owned station. Coverage was expanded into Idaho in 1941.

1925

July 24 — *In the famous "Scopes Monkey Trial," John T. Scopes, a Tennessee school teacher, was found guilty of teaching evolution in a public school.*

Dec. 6 — Elder Melvin J. Ballard of the Council of the Twelve established a mission in South America with headquarters in Buenos Aires, Argentina, opening the Church's formal missionary work in South America.

1926

Weekday religious education was expanded to include college students with the building of the first institute of religion adjacent to the University of Idaho at Moscow.

May 9 — *Richard Byrd and Floyd Bennett became the first men to make an airplane flight over the North Pole.*

1927

Oct. 23 — President Heber J. Grant dedicated the Arizona Temple at Mesa, completing a project begun six years before.

Nov. 12 — *Stalin became undisputed ruler of Russia, and Leon Trotsky was expelled from the Communist Party.*

1928

The YMMIA introduced a Vanguard program for 15- and 16-year-old boys. After the National Boy Scout organization created the Explorer program in 1933, patterned in part after the Vanguards, the Church adopted Explorer Scouting.

January — Priesthood quorums began meeting during the Sunday School hour for gospel instruction under a correlated experiment lasting 10 years. This Priesthood Sunday School experiment included classes for all age groups, with Tuesday evening re-served as an activity night for both priesthood and young women.

May 11 — *The first regularly scheduled television programs were begun by Station WGY in Schenectady, N.Y.*

1929

July 15 — The Tabernacle Choir and organist initiated a weekly network radio broadcast on NBC. Richard L. Evans joined the program with his sermonettes in June 1930. "Music and the Spoken Word" eventually switched with KSL Radio to the CBS network and has since become one of the longest continuing programs in broadcasting history.

Oct. 19 — *The New York Stock Market collapsed in frantic trading, the most dramatic indication of the state of the Great Depression.*

1930

April 6 — The centennial of the Church's organization was observed at general conference in the Tabernacle in Salt Lake City. Special features of the anniversary included a pageant, "The Message of the Ages," and historical articles in Church magazines. B.H. Roberts prepared his *Comprehensive History of The Church of Jesus Christ of Latter-day Saints* as a centennial memorial.

July 21 — *The U.S. Veterans Administration was established.*

1931

March 21 — A 10-reel film of the history of the Church was completed.

May 1 — *The Empire State Building was opened in New York City.*

1932

Jan. 10 — Missionary training classes were organized in wards and stakes throughout the Church.

April 2 — A campaign against the use of tobacco was launched by the Church.

May 12 — *Charles Lindbergh Jr., kidnapped on March 1, was found dead.*

May 15 — Utah Gov. George H. Dern proclaimed a special fast day in the depths of the Great Depression to gather funds for the poor.

July 16 — The first of the Mormon Trail markers were unveiled in Henefer, Utah, and Casper, Wyo.

Oct. 8 — The pageant, "The Birthright of Joseph the Seer," was performed in the Salt Lake Tabernacle. The production depicted the ancestry of Joseph Smith.

1933

Feb. 21 — The Church began a six-day

commemoration of the 100th anniversary of the Word of Wisdom revelation with special observances in every ward throughout the Church.

April 6 — President J. Reuben Clark Jr. was sustained as second counselor in the First Presidency, filling a vacancy in the Presidency that had existed for nearly 16 months.

June 1 — The Century of Progress Exposition opened in Chicago with a 500-square-foot Church exhibit in the Hall of Religions.

July 12 — *A new industrial code was established in the U.S. to fix a minimum wage of 40 cents an hour.*

July 26 — The first effort to mark the historic spots in Nauvoo, Ill., was made by the Relief Society when it placed a monument at the site of its organization in 1842 in Joseph Smith's store.

Nov. 5 — President Heber J. Grant dedicated the newly completed Washington chapel in the nation's capital in ceremonies attended by the First Presidency and four members of the Council of the Twelve.

1934

The general board of the Sunday School officially recognized the Junior Sunday School, which had been part of some ward programs for many years.

Aug. 2 — *Adolf Hitler became dictator of Germany after the death of President Paul von Hindenburg.*

1935

Jan. 11 — *American aviatrix, Amelia Earhart, became the first woman to fly across the Pacific, from Hawaii to California.*

Feb. 24 — The YMMIA general superintendency was released to allow the General Authorities serving in those posts more time for other duties. In April, Albert E. Bowen, George Q. Morris and Franklin West were sustained as the new superintendency.

March 3 — First of a series of six "Church of the Air" broadcasts sponsored by the Church was carried nationwide by the Columbia Broadcasting Co.

July 21 — President Heber J. Grant dedicated the Hill Cumorah Monument in Palmyra, N.Y.

Sept. 7 — A marker was placed on the highway in Carthage, Ill., directing the way to Carthage Jail.

1936

A separate Aaronic Priesthood program for adults, recommended by the General Priesthood Committee on Outlines 20 years earlier, was introduced.

Jan. 29 — *Ty Cobb, Walter Johson, Christy Mathewson, Babe Ruth and Honus Wagner became the first five men to be elected to the baseball Hall of Fame.*

April — The Church introduced a formal welfare program to meet the needs of indigent Church members and those unemployed in emergency situations. Called the Church Security Program at first, it was renamed the Church Welfare Program in 1938 and has continued to expand its services with the addition of local production programs.

Also in April, supervision of stake missions was given to the First Council of the Seventy, and stake missions were organized soon thereafter in all stakes. The work had been under stake presidency direction.

July 16 — Pres. Joseph F. Merrill of the European Mission presided over the afternoon session of the World Congress of Faiths in London, England. Pres. Merrill of the Council of the Twelve and Joseph J. Cannon of the British Mission were the only LDS representatives to the conference.

1937

January — The First Presidency officially adopted the practice widely utilized over several preceding decades of ordaining young men in the Aaronic Priesthood at specific ages. The recommended ages for advancement from deacon to teacher to priest to elder have changed from time to time since 1937.

April 27 — *The first Social Security payment in the U.S. was made.*

July — The Hill Cumorah pageant, "America's Witness for Christ," began on an outdoor stage on the side of the Hill Cumorah in New York. A Bureau of Information opened at the base of the hill.

1938

Aug. 14 — The first Deseret Industries store opened in Salt Lake City to provide work opportunities for the elderly and handicapped. Part of the Welfare Program, a growing network of stores still offers used furniture, clothing, and other items.

Oct. 30 — *Orson Welles' fantasy radio program "War of the Worlds," was so realistic that it caused nationwide panic.*

50 YEARS AGO
1939

Feb. 18 — Golden Gate exposition opened in San Francisco. The Church exhibit was a miniature Salt Lake Tabernacle with a pulpit and an organ.

June 19 — Wilford Wood purchased Liberty Jail in Missouri on behalf of the Church.

Aug. 24 — First Presidency directed all missionaries in Germany to move to neutral countries.

Sept. 3 — *Britain and France declared war on Germany, and World War II began.*

Oct. 6 — The First Presidency message on world peace was delivered in General Conference by President Heber J. Grant.

1940

Jan. 28 — The Mormon Battalion Monument was dedicated in San Diego, Calif.

Sept. 16 — *U.S. President Franklin D. Roosevelt signed the Selective Service Act, setting up the first peacetime military draft in the nation's history.*

1941

The Presiding Bishopric inaugurated a new membership record system. Under the new system, a master record for each member was established in the Presiding Bishopric's Office, eliminating the need for personal membership certificates.

April 6 — In general conference, the First Presidency announced the new position of Assistant to the Twelve, and the first five Assistants were called and sustained.

May — The First Presidency appointed Hugh B. Brown as the Church Army coordinator. His work with LDS servicemen and military officials led to the development of the Church servicemen's program.

Dec. 7 — *The Pacific side of World War II began with Japan's strike against Pearl Harbor, the Philippines, Singapore, Guam, Wake Island, Thailand, and Malaya. The U.S. declared war on Germany and Italy four days later.*

1942

The Girls' Activity Program of the Church was introduced.

Jan. 4 — The Church observed a special Fast Sunday in conjunction with a national day of prayer called by President Franklin D. Roosevelt.

Jan. 17 — The First Presidency asked all general boards and auxiliary organizations to discontinue institutes, conventions and auxiliary stake meetings to help members meet wartime restrictions on travel and to help reduce personal expenses under increased war taxes.

March — The Relief Society centennial, scheduled for April, was postponed because of the First Presidency's call to halt all but most essential activities.

March 23 — *The forced movement of Japanese-Americans from their homes on the U.S. West Coast to inland camps during World War II began.*

April — The annual April general conference was closed to the general membership and was confined to approximately 500 priesthood leaders. Sessions were held in the Assembly Hall on Temple Square instead of in the Tabernacle. This practice continued for the duration of the war.

April 6 — The First Presidency announced that it would call only high priests and seventies on full-time missions.

July — Church Welfare leaders urged members to plant gardens, to bottle as many fruits and vegetables as they could utilize, and to store coal.

Aug. 17 — The USS Brigham Young was christened. It was of the Liberty ship class, as was the USS Joseph Smith launched May 22, 1943.

1943

March 7 — The Navajo-Zuni Mission was formed, the first mission designated only for Indians.

May — The Church announced that a pocket-size church directory had been printed for distribution in the armed forces, along with a pocket-size Book of Mormon and a compilation titled Principles of the Gospel.

Sept. 9 — *United States troops invaded Italy.*

1944

May — The Church announced purchase of the are in Missouri known in Church history as Adam-ondi-Ahman.

May 15 — A monthly Church News for LDS servicemen began publication. To date, about 80,000 Church members had entered the armed services of their respective countries.

June 6 — *Allied forces invaded Europe, at Normandy, France, on "D-Day."*

1945

May 14 — President Heber J. Grant died in Salt Lake City at age 88.

May 21 — George Albert Smith was sustained as the eighth president of the Church, with J. Reuben Clark Jr. and David O. McKay as counselors.

August — The First Presidency authorized monthly priesthood and auxiliary leadership meetings if they could be held without violating government restrictions concerning use of gas and rubber.

September — The First Presidency began calling mission presidents for areas vacated during the war. This process continued through 1946. The sending of missionaries soon followed the appointment of mission presidents.

September — The Tabernacle was opened to the general public for the first time since March 1942.

Sept. 7 — *President Harry S Truman received the Japanese surrender papers that formally ended World War II. Germany had surrendered on May 7.*

Sept. 23 — The Idaho Falls Temple was dedicated by President George Albert Smith.

1946

January — The Church began sending supplies to the saints in Europe. This continued for the next several years.

February — Elder Ezra Taft Benson of the Council of the Twelve left for Europe to administer to the physical and spiritual needs of the members there. He traveled throughout Europe for most of the year, visiting saints who had been isolated by the war. He helped distribute Church welfare supplies and set the branches of the Church in order.

Also in February, it was announced that the First Presidency had approved the war-interrupted beautification program on a larger scale than was functioning before the war.

April 18 — *The League of Nations officially went out of existence.*

December — The Relief Society announced the creation of an enlarged social service and child welfare department.

1947

January — The First Presidency appointed Elder Matthew Cowley of the Council of the Twelve as president of the Pacific Mission, an administrative unit encompassing seven missions.

April 11 — *Jackie Robinson broke baseball's previous all-white color barrier when he began playing for the Brooklyn Dodgers.*

July 24 — Church members celebrated the 100th anniversary of the Pioneers' arrival in Salt Lake Valley.

December — Fast Day was set aside for the relief of those in need in Europe. About $210,000 was collected and then distributed to Europeans of all faiths by an agency not connected with the Church. The Church also

continued sending welfare supplies of its own to European members of the Church.

Also in December, more than a million people visited Temple Square in one year for the first time.

1948

May 14 — *Britain ended its rule in Palestine, and the independent state of Israel was proclaimed.*

June — It was announced that Ricks College would become a four-year college by the 1949-50 school year.

August — The secretary of the Genealogical Society, Archibald F. Bennett, made his second visit to Europe to consult with government and library officials in various countries concerning the microfilming of genealogical records.

1949

April 5 — At a special welfare meeting held in conjunction with general conference, the Welfare Program was declared a permanent program of the Church.

May 12 — *The Berlin Blockade ended, as the Soviets announced reopening of East German land routes.*

October — For the first time, general conference was broadcast publicly over KSL Television, although since April 1948 it had been carried by closed-circuit television to other buildings on Temple Square.

Also in October, The centennial conference of the Deseret Sunday School Union was held.

1950

July 1 — The responsibility of the LDS Girls' Program was transferred from the Presiding Bishopric to the Young Women's Mutual Improvement Association, where it remained until 1974.

September — Early morning seminaries were inaugurated in Southern California. This was the beginning of a movement that spread seminary work throughout the Church on an early morning, non-released-time basis.

Nov. 8 — *American jets were attacked by North Korean MIGs in the opening days of the Korean War.*

1951

A new edition of the Servicemen's Directory was published. In addition, it was announced that the United States armed forces had authorized the use of special "LDS" identification tags (called "dog tags") for Church members in the service.

Jan. 1 — Ernest L. Wilkinson was installed

as president of Brigham Young University, his appointment having been announced Sept. 16, 1950.

March 29 — *Julius Rosenberg and his wife, Ethel, were convicted of wartime espionage. They were executed June 19.*

April 4 — President George Albert Smith died in Salt Lake City at age 81..

April 9 — David O. McKay was sustained as ninth president of the Church, with Stephen L Richards and J. Reuben Clark Jr. as counselors.

July 20 — Because the Korean War reduced the number of young elders being called as missionaries, the First Presidency issued a call for seventies to help fill the need. Many married men subsequently served full-time missions.

1952

A Systematic Program for Teaching the Gospel was published for use by the missionaries of the Church. This inaugurated the use of a standard plan of missionary work throughout the Church, although the specific format of the various lessons was modified from time to time after this.

March 2 — The new Primary Children's Hospital in Salt Lake City was dedicated. Half the cost of the building had been raised by children of the Church through the continuing Primary penny drive.

April 5 — The Church began carrying the priesthood session of general conference by direct wire to buildings beyond Temple Square.

June — President David O. McKay took a six-week tour of European missions and branches in Holland, Denmark, Sweden, Norway, Finland, Germany, Switzerland, Wales, Scotland, and France. On this trip he announced the selection of Bern, Switzerland, as site of the first European temple.

Oct. 6 — A letter from the Presiding Bishopric introduced a new Senior Aaronic Priesthood program, with men over 21 years of age organized into separate Aaronic Priesthood quorums. Subsequently, special weekday classes were encouraged in each stake to prepare these brethren for the Melchizedek Priesthood and temple ordinances.

Nov. 1 — *The United States announced "satisfactory" experiments in developing the world's first hydrogen bomb.*

Nov. 25 — Elder Ezra Taft Benson of the Council of the Twelve was chosen Secretary of Agriculture by Dwight D. Eisenhower, newly elected president of the United States. Elder Benson served in that capacity for eight years.

Dec. 31 — A letter from the First Presidency announced that the Primary Association had been assigned the duty of establishing the Cub Scout program of the Boy Scouts of America for boys of the Church.

1953

March 25 — The First Presidency announced that returning missionaries should no longer report directly to General Authorities but, rather, to their stake presidency and high council.

May 29 — *Sir Edmund Hillary of New Zealand became the first person to reach the top of Mount Everest.*

July 9 — Organization of the Unified Church School System, with Ernest L. Wilkinson as administrator, was publicly announced.

October — The semiannual conference of the Church was broadcast by television for the first time outside the Intermountain area.

Dec. 1 — Liahona High School in Tonga was dedicated. This was only one of several Church schools established in Tonga.

1954

Utahns debated the question of ownership of Dixie, Snow, and Weber State Colleges, which had once been owned by the Church. Though the Church expressed a willingness to resume control, and the state was hard-pressed financially to operate them, voters rejected the transfer in a referendum.

Jan. 2 — President David O. McKay left Salt Lake City on a trip to London, England; South Africa; and South and Central America. He returned in mid-February, and at that point had officially visited every existing mission of the Church. He was the first president of the Church to visit the South African Mission.

May 17 — *The U.S. Supreme Court ruled that racial segregation in public schools was unconstitutional.*

July — The Church announced the inauguration of the Indian Placement Program, whereby Indian students of elementary and secondary school age would be placed in foster homes during the school year in order for them to take advantage of better educational opportunities.

July 21 — The First Presidency announced the establishment of the Church College of Hawaii. The college commenced operation Sept. 26, 1955.

Aug. 31 — The First Presidency approved a plan to ordain young men to the office of teacher at age 14 and priest at age 16. The previous ages were 15 and 17.

1955

A special program of missionary work among the Jewish people was organized. It continued until 1959 and met with only limited success.

January — The "Duty to God" award, approved by the National Council of the Boy Scouts of America, was inaugurated for the benefit of young men in the priesthood and Scouting program of the Church.

January-February — President David O. McKay took a trip to the missions of the South Pacific, where he traveled more than 45,000 miles, selected a site for the New Zealand Temple, and discussed plans for the building of a Church college in New Zealand.

April 12 — The First Presidency announced that, beginning in September 1956, Ricks College in Rexburg, Idaho, would become a two-year college instead of a four-year school.

July — The Church Building Committee was organized to supervise the now-vast building program of the Church throughout the world.

August-September — The Tabernacle Choir made a major concert tour of Europe.

Sept. 11 — The Swiss Temple, near Bern, was dedicated.

Dec. 5 — *The nation's two largest labor unions, the American Federation of Labor and Congress of Industrial Organizations, merged into the AFL-CIO.*

Dec. 27 — A letter from the Presiding Bishopric announced that students at BYU would be organized into campus wards and stakes, commencing Jan. 8, 1956. This move set the pattern for student wards to be organized at Church colleges and institutes of religion wherever their numbers warranted it.

1956

March 11 — President David O. McKay dedicated the Los Angeles Temple.

June 29 — *A bill was passed by Congress clearing the way for a nationwide Interstate highway system.*

Oct. 3 — The new Relief Society Building in Salt Lake City was dedicated.

December — A new program for training priesthood leaders was inaugurated. It included quarterly stake priesthood meetings, quarterly leadership meetings, and various special leadership sessions in connection with stake conferences.

1957

Ward education committees were orga-nized throughout the Church to encourage and enroll young people in a seminary, organize their transportation, and encourage them to attend a Church college or a college with an institute of religion. These committees functioned until 1964, when their duties were transferred to home teachers.

April — The First Presidency announced plans to move Ricks College from Rexburg to Idaho Falls, Idaho. This created much local concern and started a long debate that ended in a reversal of the decision and the announcement on April 26, 1962, of a major expansion program for the Rexburg campus.

July — The Pacific Board of Education was organized to supervise all Church schools in the Pacific area.

Sept. 22 — Richard P. Condie was appointed the 11th conductor of the Tabernacle Choir, replacing J. Spencer Cornwall. Condie continued in this capacity until July 1974.

October — For the first time in the history of the Church, the semiannual general conference was canceled due to a flu epidemic.

Oct. 4 — *The Space Age began when the Soviet Union put the first man-made satellite into orbit around the earth.*

1958

A new program for convert integration was adopted during the year, having been previously tried on a pilot basis in several stakes.

April 20 — The New Zealand Temple was dedicated by President David O. McKay.

Aug. 3 — *The world's first atomic-powered submarine, the Nautilus, made the first crossing underneath the North Pole.*

Sept. 7 — The London Temple was dedicated by President David O. McKay.

1959

April 25 — *The St. Lawrence Seaway was opened to shipping.*

November — The Tabernacle Choir received a Grammy award for its recording of the "Battle Hymn of the Republic."

1960

January — The First Presidency inaugurated a three-month series of weekly Sunday evening "fireside" programs for youth. They were carried to 290 stake centers of the Church by closed circuit radio.

Also in January, the Church began setting up the administrative framework for a large building program in Europe. By early 1961, administrative building "areas" outside North America had been established for all parts of the world where the Church existed, and the labor missionary program was utilized in each area.

March — The First Presidency requested the General Priesthood Committee, with Elder Harold B. Lee of the Council of the Twelve as chairman, make a study of Church programs and curriculum with the object of providing for better "correlation."

May 1 — *A U.S. U-2 reconnaisance airplane was shot down over the Soviet Union, typifying worsening relations between the two superpowers.*

1961

March 12 — The first non-English-speaking stake in the Church was organized at The Hague in The Netherlands.

June-July — A number of significant developments took place that revamped the missionary program of the Church. The first seminar for all mission presidents was held June 26-July 27 in Salt Lake City, at which new programs were outlined to them. Also, a new teaching plan of six lessons to be used in every mission of the Church was officially presented, as was the "every member a missionary" program. The missions of the world were divided into nine areas, and a General Authority was placed over each area.

Aug. 13 — *Communists began building the Berlin Wall, dividing East and West Germany.*

November — A Language Training Institution was established at Brigham Young University for missionaries called to foreign countries. In 1963 it became the Language Training Mission.

1962

Feb. 20 — *John Glenn became the first American to orbit the earth.*

March — The age at which young men became eligible for missions was lowered from 20 to 19.

April — At the 132nd Annual Conference, the first seminar of General Authorities and presidents of stakes outside North America was held.

October — The Church purchased a shortwave radio station, WRUL, with a transmitter in Boston and studios in New York City. It has subsequently been used to transmit Church broadcasts to Europe and South America.

Dec. 3 — The first Spanish-speaking stake was organized, headquartered in Mexico City.

1963

An Indian Education Program was inaugurated at Brigham Young University.

July — The labor missionary program was expanded to include the United States and Canada. The program originated in the South Pacific during the early 1950s, and during 1960-62 was expanded to Europe, Latin America, and Asia.

Oct. 12 — The Polynesian Cultural Center, located near the temple in Laie, Hawaii, was dedicated.

Nov. 22 — *U.S. President John F. Kennedy was assassinated while riding in a motorcade in Dallas, Texas.*

December — Church storage vaults for records in Little Cottonwood Canyon were completed. They were dedicated on June 22, 1966.

1964

January — A new program of home teaching was officially inaugurated throughout the Church after having been presented in stake conferences during the last half of 1963.

Jan. 28 — Temple Square and the Lion House were recognized as National Historic Landmarks by the federal government.

March — Two LDS schools were opened in Chile, one in Santiago and the other in Vina del Mar. During the early 1970s the Church opened an elementary school in Paraguay, one in Bolivia and one in Peru.

April — The Mormon pavilion opened at the New York World's Fair. The Church also built elaborate pavilions for subsequent expositions in San Antonio, Texas (1968); Japan (1970); and Spokane, Wash. (1974).

July 31 — *The U.S. Ranger VII spacecraft transmitted to earth the first close-up pictures of the moon.*

Sept. 18 — The Papeete Elementary School in Tahiti was dedicated.

October — The Pacific Board of Education was discontinued. Schools under its direction became part of the Unified Church School System.

Nov. 17 — The Oakland Temple was dedicated by President David O. McKay.

1965

January — The home evening program was inaugurated. A weekly home evening had been encouraged before by Church leaders, but now the Church published a formal home evening manual, which was to be placed in every LDS home. In October 1970, Monday was designated for home evening throughout the Church; no other Church activity was to be scheduled during that time.

Jan. 18 — The Tabernacle Choir sang at the inauguration of U.S. President Lyndon B.

Johnson in Washington D.C.

February — The Italian government gave permission for LDS missionaries to proselyte in the country. No missionary work had been done there since 1862.

March — The three-generation genealogical family group-sheet program was initiated.

June — The missions of the Church were divided into 12 areas, instead of nine, and the new supervisory program was centered in Salt Lake City.

June 3 — *Astronaut Ed White made the first American "walk" in space during the Gemini 4 orbital flight.*

September — A missionary quota of two per ward per year was established within the United States to comply with Selective Service requests.

October — With the appointment of President Joseph Fielding Smith and Elder Thorpe B. Isaacson as counselors, President David O. McKay announced that the First Presidency would be increased to five, instead of three.

1966

May 1 — The first stake in South America was organized at Sao Paulo, Brazil.

June 29 — *North Vietnam's capital, Hanoi, and principal seaport, Haiphong, were bombed for the first time by the U.S. in the Vietnam War.*

August — A new visitors center on Temple Square was opened to tourists in August. While this would be the most elaborate center, it represented a trend of building new visitors centers at historic sites and temples, and at various other locations during the 1960s and 1970s.

October — A branch of the Church was organized at Debnica-Kaszub, Poland.

1967

March — A unified Church magazine was launched in nine different languages.

April — For the first time, seven Mexican television and radio stations carried a session of general conference.

June 10 — *The Six-Day War in the Middle East ended with Israel holding conquered Arab territory four times its own size.*

Sept. 1 — The beginning of the Church year was changed to Sept. 1 instead of Jan. 1 in the Southern Hemisphere, to coincide with the public school year.

Sept. 29 — The new administrative position of regional representative of the Twelve was announced, and 69 regional representatives were called and given their initial training.

November — Part of the Egyptian papyri owned by Joseph Smith while he was translating the Pearl of Great Price was given to the Church by the New York Metropolitan Museum of Art.

1968

Jan. 22 — *The USS Pueblo and its 83 crew members were seized in the Sea of Japan by North Korea.*

August — A large LDS educational complex was dedicated in Mexico City. The school contained 11 grades for more than 1,200 students.

Oct. 17 — Relief Society Gen. Pres. Belle S. Spafford assumed the presidency of the National Council of Women for a two-year term.

December — The Church began microfilming Polish and Korean genealogical records.

1969

January — Two-month language training missions began. Language training for missionaries prior to their departure to their mission field first began during the early 1960s for Spanish-speaking missions.

Jan. 20 — The Tabernacle Choir sang at U.S. President Richard M. Nixon's inaugural in Washington D.C.

June — The first missionaries were sent to Spain; a little more than a year later, on July 1, 1970, Spain was made into a separate mission.

July 20 — *U.S. astronauts Neil Armstrong and Edwin Aldrin became the first men to set foot on the moon.*

Aug. 3-8 — A world conference on records was held in Salt Lake City.

Nov. 1 — The Southeast Asia Mission formally opened, with headquarters in Singapore. In January 1970, the first missionaries were sent to Indonesia, which was part of the mission.

1970

January — A computerized system for recording and reporting Church contributions went into operation.

Jan. 18 — President David O. McKay died in Salt Lake City at age 96.

Jan. 23 — Joseph Fielding Smith became the 10th president of the Church and chose Harold B. Lee and N. Eldon Tanner as his counselors.

Feb. 18 — *A federal jury found the "Chicago 7" innocent of conspiring to incite riots during the 1968 Democratic National Convention in Chicago, Ill.*

March 15 — The first stake in Asia was organized in Tokyo.

March 22 — The first stake in Africa was organized in Transvaal, South Africa.

May — The Beehive House was placed on the register of National Historic Sites.

September — A new Aaronic Priesthood Personal Achievement Program was started, which gave young men the opportunity to set their own goals in consultation with their bishop. A similar program for young women commenced in January 1971.

1971

January — Distribution of the new Church magazines began: the *Ensign* for adults, the *New Era* for youth, and the *Friend* for children.

Also in January, a bishops' training program conducted by stake presidents commenced, and a new correlated teacher development program began operation.

July — The medical missionary program (later called the health missionary program) began, as the first two missionaries were sent out.

Aug. 27-29 — The first Area Conference of the Church was held in Manchester, England, for British members.

September — All LDS women were automatically enrolled as members of the Relief Society; dues were eliminated.

Sept. 30 — *The United States and the Soviet Union signed pacts designed to avoid accidental nuclear war.*

1972

Church sports tournaments and dance festivals were directed to be held on a regional basis, instead of on an all-Church basis.

Jan. 14 — The Church Historical Department was formed in a reorganization of the Church Historian's Office. Church library, archives and history divisions were created within the new department.

Jan. 18 — The Ogden Temple was dedicated by President Joseph Fielding Smith.

Feb. 9 — The Provo Temple was dedicated by President Joseph Fielding Smith.

Feb. 27 — J. Spencer Kinard became the commentator for the Tabernacle Choir's "Music and the Spoken Word," succeeding Elder Richard L. Evans of the Council of the Twelve, who had been the program's spokesman for nearly 40 years.

July 2 — President Joseph Fielding Smith died in Salt Lake City at age 95.

July 7 — Harold B. Lee became the 11th president of the Church, with N. Eldon Tanner and Marion G. Romney as his counselors.

Sept. 5 — *The Munich Olympics massacre occurred, with 11 Israeli athletes and five Arab terrorists killed in an attack on the Olympic Village.*

November — Church departments began moving into the newly completed 28-story Church Office Building at 50 E. North Temple in Salt Lake City.

November — The MIA was realigned into the Aaronic Priesthood and Melchizedek Priesthood MIA and placed directly under priesthood leadership.

1973

A new set of missionary lessons was completed for use in all missions. This was the first change in missionary lessons since 1961.

February — The first Church agricultural missionaries to leave the United States were sent to the Guatemala-El Salvador Mission.

Feb. 4 — The Marriott Activities Center at BYU was dedicated. It was the largest such center on any campus in the United States.

March 8 — The first stake on mainland Asia, and the third in the Orient, was organized in Seoul, Korea.

April 7 — The creation of the Welfare Services Department was announced in general conference. The new organization brought the three welfare units — health services, social services, and welfare — into full correlation.

Sept. 20 — *The British-French supersonic airliner, Concorde, made its first landing in the United States at the Dallas-Fort Worth International Airport.*

Dec. 26 — President Harold B. Lee died in Salt Lake City at age 74.

Dec. 30 — Spencer W. Kimball was set apart as the 12th president of the Church, with N. Eldon Tanner and Marion G. Romney as counselors.

1974

March 23 — In an exchange of pioneer homes, the Church traded the Brigham Young Forest Farm home in Salt Lake City to the state of Utah for use in the state's Pioneer State Park. The Church acquired the Brigham Young winter home in St. George and the Jacob Hamblin home in Santa Clara, Utah, for use as visitor and information centers.

May 9 — *Impeachment hearings against U.S. President Richard M. Nixon began.*

June 23 — MIA was dropped from the name of Church youth programs, and further modifications were implemented in the administrative structure of the Aaronic Priesthood and the Young Women organizations.

July 6 — Names of all missions were changed to reflect a consistent style identifying them with the geographical area served.

Aug. 10 — A statement from the First Presidency amended the policy of the priesthood-Scouting correlation program in connection with troop and patrol leaders in Church-sponsored units of the Boy Scouts of America.

Aug. 28 — The first LDS meetinghouse in Thailand was dedicated by Elder David B. Haight in Bangkok.

Sept. 1 — Church College of Hawaii became a branch of Brigham Young University and given the name Brigham Young University-Hawaii Campus.

Oct. 3 — Seventies quorums were authorized in all stakes, and all quorums in the Church were renamed after the stake. Stake mission presidencies were also reorganized, with all seven presidents of seventies serving in the calling, instead of three of the presidents.

Nov. 19-22 — President Spencer W. Kimball dedicated the Washington Temple at Kensington, Md., with ceremonies repeated in 10 sessions. Visitors during pre-dedication tours September through November totaled 758,328, topping the record of 662,401 at Los Angeles in 1956.

1975

March 21 — The Church completed legal steps to divest itself of 15 hospitals operated by its Health Service Corporation in three western states. A non-profit, non-Church organization, Intermountain Health Care Inc., assumed ownership.

April 20 — *South Vietnam unconditionally surrendered to North Vietnam, and the bitter Vietnam War was officially at an end.*

May 3 — The First Presidency announced the creation of an area supervisory program and the assignment of six Assistants to the Twelve to oversee Church activities while residing outside of the United States and Canada. The number of areas was increased to eight later in the year.

May 17 — A supervisory program for missions in the United States and Canada was announced, along with the assignment of members of the Council of the Twelve as advisers and other General Authorities as supervisors of the 12 areas.

June 7 — Counselors in the First Presi-

dency succeeded President Spencer W. Kimball as chairmen of the board of five corporations in which the Church had substantial financial interest.

June 27 — The end of auxiliary conferences was announced during the opening session of the 1975 June Conference. These conferences would be replaced with annual regional meetings for priesthood and auxiliary leaders.

July 24 — The 28-story Church Office Building was dedicated by President Spencer W. Kimball.

Oct. 3 — President Spencer W. Kimball announced the organization of the First Quorum of the Seventy, and three members of the quorum were sustained at general conference.

Oct. 6-11 — Brigham Young University observed its 100th anniversary during homecoming week.

Nov. 18 — The Church Genealogical Department was organized with five divisions, two of which were formerly known as the Genealogical Society.

1976

Feb. 4 — Twenty-two Church members were killed and an American missionary was seriously injured in a devastating earthquake in Guatemala.

April 3 — Members attending general conference accepted Joseph Smith's vision of the celestial kingdom and Joseph F. Smith's vision of the redemption of the dead for addition to the *Pearl of Great Price*. The scriptures later became part of the Doctrine and Covenants.

May 1 — The Seoul Korea Stake established the first stake welfare farm in Asia, at a site near Seoul.

June 5 — The First Presidency published an official statement reaffirming Church policy against abortion. The statement supplemented a filmstrip placed in distribution in March.

Also on June 5, Church members in Idaho's Upper Snake River Valley suffered extensive property damage from flooding caused by the breaking of the Teton Dam.

July 4 — President Spencer W. Kimball presided at a Church-sponsored U.S. Bicentennial devotional attended by more than 23,000 people at the Capitol Centre in Landover, Md. Numerous additional activities involved Church members in the United States during the year-long Bicentennial observance.

Sept. 3 — *Viking 2, an American spaceship, made a successful landing on Mars.*

Oct. 1 — All Assistants to the Twelve were called to the expanding First Quorum of the Seventy, and the presidency of that quorum was reorganized, with Franklin D. Richards replacing S. Dilworth Young as presiding president.

1977

Jan. 1 — The First Presidency announced a new format for general conferences, with general sessions on the first Sunday of each April and October and on the preceding Saturday, and regional representative seminars on the preceding Friday.

Jan. 14 — The first Presiding Bishopric area supervisor, called to direct temporal affairs of the Church in Mexico, began work in Mexico City. Presiding Bishopric area supervisors for eight other areas outside the United States and Canada were announced June 4.

Feb. 5 — The First Presidency announced organizational steps giving the Council of the Twelve responsibility for overseeing ecclesiastical matters, including curriculum, activity programs and Scouting, and the Presiding Bishopric responsibility for temporal programs.

Feb. 21-March 11 — President Spencer W. Kimball met with heads of state in Mexico, Guatemala, Chile, and Bolivia during a month-long tour of Latin America to attend area conferences, and then visited at the White House with U.S. President Jimmy Carter.

March 27 — *The worst airliner disaster in history killed 581 people, as two jumbo jets collided on a runway in the Canary Islands.*

May 14 — A bishops central storehouse, the second in the Church and first outside of Salt Lake City, opened at Colton, Calif., to distribute welfare commodities to 10 regional and stake storehouses in parts of California, Nevada and Arizona.

May 14 — The Young Men program was restructured, and a new Young Men general presidency was called to serve under the direction of the youth division of the Priesthood Executive Committee. The Young Men presidency and general board were given responsibility for Aaronic Priesthood curriculum, leadership training, and quorum work; Young Men activities, including Scouting; and combined Young Men-Young Women activities.

May 22 — Formation of a new Church Activities Committee, with responsibility for coordinating cultural arts and physical activities, was announced. Similar groups were organized on the local level.

July 1 — In response to continued growth in membership worldwide, the geographic subdivisions of the Church, previously known as areas, were renamed zones, and the 11 zones were subdivided into areas. Members of the First Quorum of the Seventy were assigned as zone advisers and area supervisors.

July 30 — The Church Educational System was placed in the ecclesiastical line organization of the Church through an Education Executive Committee of the Council of the Twelve.

Aug. 24 — President Spencer W. Kimball dedicated the land of Poland during a ceremony at Warsaw and blessed its people that the work of the Lord might go forth there.

Oct. 1 — The Church published *A Topical Guide to the Scriptures of The Church of Jesus Christ of Latter-day Saints,* the first product of a continuing scriptural-aids project established by the First Presidency.

1978

March 31 — President Spencer W. Kimball announced that, to simplify work loads of local leaders, semiannual rather than quarterly stake conferences would be held, starting in 1979.

April — The Church published an eight-page removable insert about Church programs in the *Reader's Digest,* the first of a series aimed at nearly 50 million *Digest* readers.

May 9 — President Ezra Taft Benson dedicated the Church's Asian Administration Headquarters building in Tokyo.

June 9 — The First Presidency announced the revelation that worthy men of all races would be eligible to receive the priesthood. Reaction within and without the Church was far-reaching. On Sept. 30, members at general conference accepted the revelation by sustaining vote.

July 1 — Thousands attended the dedication of the Relief Society Monument to Women in Nauvoo, Ill.

July 22 — The United States Senate passed a bill, earlier approved by the House of Representatives, designating the Mormon Trail from Nauvoo, Ill., to Salt Lake City as a national historic trail.

Sept. 9 — A new missionary training program was announced: Missionaries to English-speaking missions would receive longer training at the new Missionary Training Center in Provo, Utah, which replaced the Language Training Mission and the Mission Home in Salt Lake City.

Sept. 16 — For the first time in LDS history, women and girls 12 years of age and over gathered for a special closed-circuit audio conference, similar to general conference priesthood broadcasts, and received counsel from President Spencer W. Kimball and women auxiliary leaders.

Sept. 30 — A new special emeritus status for General Authorities was announced, and seven members of the First Quorum of the Seventy were so designated.

Oct. 22 — *Pope John Paul II formally assumed the papal throne.*

1979

Jan. 1 — *The United States and China established diplomatic relations after decades of animosity.*

Feb. 3 — The Church Genealogical Department announced a new "family entry system" to allow submissions of names of deceased ancestors for temple work whose birthplaces and birthdates are unknown.

Feb. 18 — The Church's 1,000th stake was created in Nauvoo, Ill.

June 6 — Joseph Smith's Vision of the Celestial Kingdom and Joseph F. Smith's Vision of the Redemption of the Dead were transferred from the Pearl of Great Price to the Doctrine and Covenants, becoming Sections 137 and 138, respectively.

Sept. 12-14 — The Tabernacle Choir, which celebrated the golden anniversary of its nationally broadcast radio program in July, toured Japan and Korea, presenting 13 concerts in six cities.

Sept. 29 — A new 2,400-page edition of the King James version of the Bible, with many special features and a revolutionary footnote system, was published by the Church.

Oct. 24 — President Spencer W. Kimball, on a tour of the Middle East, dedicated the Orson Hyde Memorial Gardens in Israel.

1980

Jan. 12 — A new, automated temple recording system, using computers for greater speed and reduced costs, was announced.

Feb. 22 — The Presidency of the First Quorum of the Seventy was reorganized to strengthen the lines of administration at Church headquarters. The executive directors of the missionary, curriculum, priesthood, and genealogy departments replaced four former members of the presidency.

March 2 — U.S. and Canadian members began a new consolidated meeting schedule that put priesthood, sacrament and auxiliary meetings into one three-hour time block on Sundays.

April 5 — A new general presidency of the Primary was sustained, with Dwan J. Young

as president, and Virginia B. Cannon and Michaelene P. Grassli as counselors.

April 6 — To celebrate the Church's 150th anniversary, President Spencer W. Kimball conducted part of general conference from the newly restored Peter Whitmer farmhouse at Fayette, N.Y., where the Church was organized. The proceedings in Fayette were linked with the congregation in the Tabernacle in Salt Lake City via satellite.

May 18 — *Mt. St. Helens in Washington, one of the few active volcanoes in the United States, erupted in a violent explosion that left 10 dead and scores of others homeless.*

Aug. 1 — Dr. Jeffrey R. Holland, former Church commissioner of education, became the ninth president of Brigham Young University. He succeeded Pres. Dallin H. Oaks, who was later named to the Utah State Supreme Court.

Oct. 27 — The Tokyo Temple was dedicated by President Spencer W. Kimball.

Nov. 17 — The Seattle Temple was dedicated by President Spencer W. Kimball.

1981

Jan. 20 — The Tabernacle Choir participated in the inaugural festivities for President Ronald Reagan.

April 1 — Plans to build nine small temples in the United States, Central America, Asia, Africa, and Europe were announced by President Spencer W. Kimball.

May 5 — The First Presidency publicly voiced its opposition to the proposed basing of the MX missile system in the Utah-Nevada desert.

July 23 — Elder Gordon B. Hinckley was called as a counselor in the First Presidency, the first time since the administration of President David O. McKay that a president has had more than two counselors. Elder Neal A. Maxwell was called from the Presidency of the First Quorum of the Seventy to fill the vacancy in the Council of the Twelve.

Sept. 5 — Surgery was performed on President Spencer W. Kimball to remove blood and scar tissue from under his skull.

Sept. 12 — A smaller, less-expensive ward meetinghouse, called the Sage Plan, was announced by the First Presidency.

Sept. 26 — The first copies of a new, more readable, version of the Triple Combination (Book of Mormon, Doctrine and Covenants, and Pearl of Great Price) were made available to the public. The publication contained about 200 changes from previous editions.

Oct. 3 — A network of 500 satellite dishes for stake centers outside of Utah was announced. The receivers will link Church headquarters in Salt Lake City with members all around the United States and Canada.

Nov. 16 — The Jordan River Temple was dedicated. President Marion G. Romney, acting under the direction of President Spencer W. Kimball, read the dedicatory prayer.

1982

March 9 — The Spencer W. Kimball Tower, the tallest building on the BYU campus, was dedicated during ceremonies that featured the prophet's first public appearance in six months.

March 18 — Three new Church executive councils were created: the Missionary Executive Council, the Priesthood Executive Council, and the Temple and Genealogy Executive Council.

April 1 — Church membership reached the five million member mark.

April 2 — At general conference, major changes in financing Church meetinghouses were announced, shifting construction costs to general Church funds and utility costs to local units. Also, the term of service for single elders serving full-time missions was reduced from two years to 18 months.

June 6 — Two new stakes were created in Great Britain, marking the first time that the entire nation has come under the administration of stakes.

June 17 — Elder LeGrand Richards of the Council of the Twelve became the oldest living General Authority of this dispensation to date at 96 years, four months and 11 days.

June 30 — *The Equal Rights Amendment was defeated after a 10-year struggle for ratification.*

Sept. 5 — The Mormon Tabernacle Choir celebrated 50 years of continuous weekly broadcasts over the CBS radio network.

Sept. 10 — U.S. President Ronald Reagan visited Utah to tour a Church cannery and see the Church welfare program in action.

Oct. 3 — Elder Boyd K. Packer announced that a subtitle was being added to the Book of Mormon: "Another Testament of Jesus Christ."

Oct. 30 — The Church's newest visitors center and historic site opened its doors in the three-story Grandin printing building in Palmyra, N.Y.

Dec. 2 — Two Latter-day Saints shared the spotlight when Dr. Barney Clark, a Seattle, Wash., dentist, became the first person to receive a permanent artificial heart implantation by surgeon Dr. William C. DeVries, also LDS, at the University of Utah Medical Center in Salt Lake City.

Dec. 2 — President Marion G. Romney, who had been serving as second counselor in the First Presidency, was named first counselor, succeeding President N. Eldon Tanner. President Gordon B. Hinckley, who had been a counselor in the First Presidency since July 1981, was named second counselor.

1983

Jan. 11 — Elder LeGrand Richards of the Council of the Twelve, to date the oldest living General Authority of this dispensation, died at age 96.

Feb. 27 — The 150th anniversary of the Word of Wisdom was observed throughout the Church and at the Newel K. Whitney store in Kirtland, Ohio, where the original revelation was received.

April 28 — Food, medical supplies, and building materials were shipped by the Church to Ghana, Colombia and Tahiti, three areas of the world hit by food shortages, earthquake and hurricanes, respectively.

June 1-4 — The Atlanta Georgia Temple was dedicated by President Gordon B. Hinckley, second counselor in the First Presidency.

Aug. 5, 9 — For the first time in Church history, two temples were dedicated within a week's time: the Apia Samoa Temple on Aug. 5, and the Nuku'alofa Tonga Temple on Aug. 9; both by President Gordon B. Hinckley.

Sept. 15 — The Santiago Chile Temple was dedicated by President Gordon B. Hinckley.

Oct. 16 — The first of a series of multi-stake (later known as regional) conferences was held in London, England.

Also on Oct. 16, more than a century after the LDS exodus, President Ezra Taft Benson of the Council of the Twelve organized a new stake in Kirtland, Ohio.

Oct. 25 — *U.S. Marines and Rangers invaded the Caribbean island of Grenada, deposing the island's Marxist government.*

Oct. 27 — The Papeete Tahiti Temple was dedicated by President Gordon B. Hinckley.

Nov. 8 — LDS baseball player Dale Murphy, a centerfielder for the Atlanta Braves, became the fourth player in history to capture back-to-back National League Most Valuable Player awards.

Dec. 2 — The Mexico City Temple was dedicated by President Gordon B. Hinckley.

1984

Jan. 7 — Premier Zhao Ziyang of the People's Republic of China visited BYU-Hawaii

Campus and the adjacent Polynesian Cultural Center during the first visit of a Chinese premier to the United States since the People's Republic of China was formed in 1949.

March 25 — A new program — the Four-Phase Genealogical Facilities Program — was announced to allow wards and branches to establish genealogical facilities in their meetinghouses.

April 7 — The first members of the First Quorum of the Seventy called for temporary 3- to 5-year terms, were sustained.

May 10 — *A federal judge in Salt Lake City ruled that the U.S. government was negligent in its above-ground testing of nuclear weapons at the Nevada test site in the 1950s and early 1960s.*

May 17 — Church members in Logan, Utah, celebrated the Logan Temple's centennial with a variety of displays, seminars and firesides.

May 25 — President Gordon B. Hinckley dedicated the Boise Idaho Temple.

June 24 — Members of the First Quorum of the Seventy were appointed to serve as area presidencies in 13 major geographical areas of the Church — seven in the United States and Canada, and six in other parts of the world.

Sept. 20 — President Gordon B. Hinckley dedicated the Sydney Australia Temple.

Sept. 25 — President Gordon B. Hinckley dedicated the Manila Philippines Temple.

Oct. 19 — The Dallas Texas Temple was dedicated by President Gordon B. Hinckley.

Oct. 28 — The Church's 1,500th stake was created 150 years after the first stake was organized in Kirtland, Ohio. The new stake is the Ciudad Obregon Mexico Yaqui Stake.

Nov. 17 — The Taipei Taiwan Temple was dedicated by President Gordon B. Hinckley.

Nov. 26 — The First Presidency announced that, beginning Jan. 1, the term of full-time missionary service for single elders would again be 24 months. It had been shortened from two years to 18 months in April 1982.

Dec. 14 — The Guatemala City Temple was dedicated by President Gordon B. Hinckley.

1985

Jan. 2 — BYU's football team was voted No. 1 in the nation for the 1984 season by every major poll. The Cougars had capped a perfect 13-0 season.

Jan. 27 — Latter-day Saints in the United States and Canada participated in a special fast to benefit victims of famine in Africa and other parts of the world. The fast raised more than $6 million.

April 12 — U.S. Senator and Church member Jake Garn was a crew member aboard the space shuttle Challenger launched from Kennedy Space Center in Florida. Another Church member, Don Lind, was a crew member on a space shuttle mission that blasted off April 29.

June 29 — The Freiberg DDR Temple, located in the German Democratic Republic, was dedicated by President Gordon B. Hinckley.

July 2 — The Stockholm Sweden Temple was dedicated by President Gordon B. Hinckley.

July 31 — Li Xiannian, president of the People's Republic of China, and his wife, Madame Lin Jiamei, toured the Church's Polynesian Cultural Center in Hawaii as part of his tour of the United States and Canada.

Aug. 2 — The first LDS hymnbook published in 37 years came off the presses.

Aug. 9 — The Chicago Illinois Temple was dedicated by President Gordon B. Hinckley.

Aug. 24 — The Johannesburg South Africa Temple was dedicated by President Gordon B. Hinckley. With the dedication of this building, there was now a temple on every continent except Antarctica.

Oct. 23 — The five-story, $8.2 million Church Genealogical Library was dedicated by President Gordon B. Hinckley.

Nov. 5 — President Spencer W. Kimball died in Salt Lake City at age 90.

Nov. 10 — Ezra Taft Benson was set apart as the 13th president of the Church, with Gordon B. Hinckley and Thomas S. Monson as counselors.

Dec. 14 — The Seoul Korea Temple was dedicated by President Gordon B. Hinckley.

Dec. 27 — *Palestinian gunmen killed 20 civilians in separate attacks at airports in Rome, Italy, and Vienna, Austria.*

1986

Jan. 10 — The Lima Peru Temple was dedicated by President Gordon B. Hinckley.

Jan. 17 — The Buenos Aires Argentina Temple was dedicated by President Thomas S. Monson.

Jan. 28 — *The space shuttle Challenger exploded shortly after liftoff, killing seven people aboard.*

April 30 — Church membership was estimated to have reached the 6-million member milestone.

May 4 — A fire, believed started by an arsonist, destroyed the Kirtland Ohio Stake Center.

July 6 — New missionary discussions, which focus on "teaching from the heart," were approved for use in all English-speaking missions.

Aug. 10 — An archaeological dig at a pioneer cemetery in Salt Lake City turned up the remains of 22 children and nine adults. The site, where a large apartment complex was planned, was thought to be the pioneers' first cemetery in the Salt Lake Valley.

Aug. 31 — A major organizational adjustment in the Relief Society eliminated stake boards and allowed for ward Relief Society boards to meet local needs and resources.

NEWS IN REVIEW
October 1986-September 1988

October 1986

A historic announcement discontinuing seventies quorums in stakes of the Church and the calling of new members to the Council of the Twelve and the Presidency of the First Quorum of the Seventy highlighted the 156th Semiannual General Conference **Oct. 4-5**.

Men currently serving as seventies were to return to elders quorums or could be ordained high priests, announced President Ezra Taft Benson, and missionary-minded elders or high priests were to be called to participate in stake missionary work. The change, it was announced, would not affect members of the First Quorum of the Seventy.

Elder Joseph B. Wirthlin, 69, a member of the First Quorum of the Seventy since 1976 and an Assistant to the Twelve for a year-and-a-half before that, was called to the Council of the Twelve. He filled a vacancy in the Twelve created by the reorganization of the First Presidency after the death of President Spencer W. Kimball on Nov. 5, 1985. Elder Hugh W. Pinnock, 52, a member of the First Quorum of the Seventy since Oct. 1, 1977, was called to the seventies presidency.

Oct. 11, 1986. A group of young women at the Manti Temple join thousands of other Young Women throughout the world in releasing helium-filled balloons with messages of love and peace. It was the largest Young Women activity ever.

Also in the news during October 1986:

Oct. 5 — The First Presidency issued a strong statement opposing the legalization of gambling and government sponsorship of lotteries.

Oct. 10 — A severe earthquake in El Salvador killed an estimated 1,200 people, including two Church members. Homes of nearly 250 LDS families were destroyed or severely damaged.

Oct. 11 — In what was called the largest Young Women activity ever, some 300,000 girls around the world launched helium-filled balloons with attached messages of love, hope and peace to the world.

Oct. 12 — President Ezra Taft Benson spoke to 6,500 members of the Church in a regional conference of the Bloomfield Hills and Lansing Michigan regions at Ann Arbor, Mich.

Oct. 24 — The First Presidency and 20 other General Authorities joined with more than 28,000 Church members for the dedication of the Denver Colorado Temple, the Church's 40th in operation. Nineteen dedicatory sessions were held during five days.

Oct. 26 — Elder Joseph Anderson became the oldest General Authority ever in the 156-year history of the Church. He reached the age of 96 years and 340 days, passing Elder LeGrand Richards, who died in 1983 at the age of 96 years and 339 days.

November 1986

The Church disbursed more than $6.5 million in fast offering funds to organizations fighting hunger in Africa, it was announced **Nov. 11**. As promised by the First Presidency, all of the money went directly to benefit the needy, with none of it used for overhead costs. The money had been raised from a special Church-wide fast Jan. 27, 1985.

Also in the news in November 1986:

Nov. 2 — More than 23,000 members from the 15 BYU stakes and the Orem Utah College Stake attended the first BYU Regional Conference in the school's Marriott Center.

Nov. 6 — President Ezra Taft Benson underwent surgery for implantation of a pacemaker for his heart. He returned to his office five days later.

Nov. 9 — A satellite broadcast introducing the New Testament-based course of study for 1987 gospel doctrine classes was beamed to more than 1,000 meetinghouses in the United States, Canada and Puerto Rico.

Nov. 13-14 — Several Church leaders, including Elder Loren C. Dunn of the First Quorum of the Seventy, played prominent roles at a Religious Alliance Against Pornography conference in Washington, D.C.

Nov. 16 — President Ezra Taft Benson

Oct. 24, 1986. Pres. Ezra Taft Benson is handed tools to apply mortar during the cornerstone ceremony at at Denver Colorado Temple. Pres. Thomas S. Monson, left, and Pres. Gordon B. Hinckley await their turns.

spoke to about 16,000 members of the Salt Lake Butler and Sandy regions in the Salt Lake Tabernacle, just 10 days after surgery for implantation of a pacemaker.

Nov. 28 — Elder A. Theodore Tuttle, 67, a member of the First Quorum of the Seventy and a General Authority since April 6, 1958, died in Salt Lake City. Elder Tuttle, known for his love for and work among the people of Latin America, was eulogized in funeral services **Dec. 2**.

December 1986

"The only true test of greatness is how close one can come to being like the Master," declared President Ezra Taft Benson at the annual First Presidency Christmas devotional **Dec. 7**.

The devotional, originating from the Tabernacle on Temple Square, also featured an address by President Thomas S. Monson, second counselor in the First Presidency, and several Christmas selections by the Mormon Tabernacle Choir.

The proceedings were broadcast via satellite to meetinghouses throughout the United States, Canada and Puerto Rico.

Also in the news in December 1986:

Dec. 6 — The No. 2-ranked Ricks College football team capped a 10-0-1 season by defeating No. 3-ranked Coffeyville Community College, 26-24, at the Kansas Jayhawk Classic in Coffeyville, Kan.

Dec. 7 — Three new stakes, making a total of seven in the city, were created in a single day during a conference in Guatemala City, Guatemala, presided over by Elder Dallin H. Oaks of the Council of the Twelve.

Dec. 14 — An address by President Ezra Taft Benson highlighted a conference of the Riverside California Region in San Bernadino's Orange Pavilion, attended by more than 12,000 people.

Dec. 30 — BYU football team lost to UCLA, 31-10, in the Freedom Bowl in Anaheim, Calif.

January 1987

The First Presidency urged appropriate observances of the bicentennial of the United States Constitution in a letter sent **Jan. 15** to stake, mission, ward and branch leaders.

"An unusual opportunity to strengthen our appreciation for the great nation in which we live awaits us in America's bicentennial observance of its Constitution," the First Presidency letter stated.

"The bicentennial year affords us renewed opportunities to learn more about this divinely inspired charter of our liberty, to speak in its defense, and to preserve and protect it against evil or destruction. We encourage your participation and involvement in this worthy endeavor."

Throughout the year activities commemorating the Constitution were held in countless wards and stakes.

Also in the news in January 1987:

Jan. 3 — Hurricane Sally, called the worst storm ever to hit the island of Rarotonga in the Cook Islands, destroyed or damaged

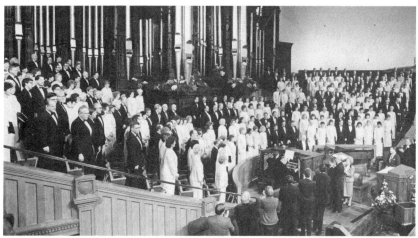

Feb.15, 1987. Dignitaries applaud the Mormon Tabernacle Choir, which celebrated its 3,000th broadcast — the longest-running network program in the free world.

homes of six LDS members. No deaths or injuries were reported.

Jan. 15 — Ten people were killed when a commuter airplane collided with a single-engine plane over predominantly LDS neighborhoods of Kearns, Utah. Although wreckage from the airplanes fell onto the densely populated Kearns Utah and Kearns Utah Western Hills stake areas, miraculously no one was injured on the ground, and little damage was done to area homes.

Jan. 18 — Homes of several Church members on American Samoa were destroyed as a hurricane packing 110-mile-per-hour winds struck the South Pacific islands. More than 100 people were injured by the storm.

Jan. 19 — President Ezra Taft Benson spoke at conference sessions of the Cottonwood and Cottonwood Creek regions, held in the Tabernacle on Temple Square.

Jan. 23 — Documents dealer Mark W. Hofmann was imprisoned after admitting in court under a plea bargain agreement that he was responsible for the bombing deaths of two people in October 1985, and that he forged the so-called Martin Harris "salamander letter." A statement from the First Presidency issued the same day expressed hope that the "healing process may now be hastened for those who have suffered from these tragedies."

Jan. 27 — The First Presidency announced the retirement of Dr. J. LeRoy Kimball, 85, who for 25 years was the director of historical restoration efforts at Nauvoo, Ill.

February 1987

The Tabernacle Choir marked its 3,000th radio broadcast **Feb. 15**, the longest-running network program in the free world. Many Church, government, CBS network and local dignitaries gathered in the Tabernacle on Temple Square for the special one-hour program honoring the choir and its 58-year broadcasting tradition.

Also in the news in February 1987:

Feb. 7 — A 3-month-old infant child of an LDS family died and 13 homes of members were destroyed or severely damaged when a hurricane struck the South Pacific island of Vanuatu.

Feb. 8 — More than 8,500 seminary and institute students and teachers filled the Anaheim Convention Center in California to hear messages from President and Sister Ezra Taft Benson.

Feb. 15 — President and Sister Ezra Taft Benson addressed 16,000 members of the Logan and Logan University regions in two sessions of conferences held at Utah State University's Spectrum.

Feb. 22 — The annual parents' fireside, highlighted by an address from President Ezra Taft Benson, was telecast over the Church satellite network.

Feb. 24 — Elder Henry D. Taylor, 83, an emeritus General Authority, died in Salt Lake City. He was called as an Assistant to the Twelve April 6, 1958, and to the First Quorum of the Seventy Oct. 1, 1976. He was eulogized in funeral services **Feb. 27**.

March 1987

Ten new missions were announced in the **March 14** issue of the *Church News*, bringing the worldwide total to 201. It also was announced that the full-time missionary force had reached 33,000, an all-time high.

The new missions are: Brazil Fortaleza, Dominican Republic Santiago, Florida Jacksonville, Mexico Mazatlan, Mexico Mexico City East, New Hampshire Manchester, New Jersey Newark, Philippines Cebu East, Portugal Porto and Zimbabwe Harare. Each of the new missions would begin functioning July 1 with the exception of Mexico Mexico City East, which began in January.

Also in the news in March 1987:

March 12, 1987. The First Presidency announced that the 76-year-old Church-owned Westin Hotel Utah would be renovated into a meetinghouse and office building.

March 11 — The U.S. House Ways and Means Subcommittee on Public Assistance heard testimony from Keith B. McMullin, managing director of Welfare Services, about how the Church's welfare program operates. The subcommittee had convened hearings to seek ways to improve government assistance programs.

March 12 — The First Presidency announced that the Church-owned Westin Hotel Utah, a landmark in downtown Salt Lake City for 76 years, would be closed as a hotel Aug. 31. Plans called for its renovation into a meetinghouse and office building to house various Church departments.

March 21 — LDS basketball coach Fred Trenkle led his College of Southern Idaho (CSI) team to the national junior college championship at Hutchinson, Kan. CSI, 37-1 for the season, defeated Midland (Texas), 69-68, in the title game.

March — Five separate avalanches of mud and rock devastated six small villages in the mountains east of Lima, Peru, in late March. Some 25,000 people, including 18 LDS families in Chosica, were left homeless.

April 1987

Eight new members of the First Quorum of the Seventy were sustained at the 157th Annual General Conference. At the conference,

April 12, 1987. Sheltered from rain dripping through a leaky roof, Pres. Ezra Taft Benson speaks in Puerto Rico. Elder Rex D. Pinegar holds an umbrella.

conducted **April 4-5**, it was also announced that the Church had surpassed 6 million in membership at the end of 1986.

The new members of the First Quorum of the Seventy are: George R. Hill III, 65, from Salt Lake City, a professor of chemical engineering at the University of Utah; John R. Lasater, 55, Pleasant View, Utah, president of the New Zealand Auckland Mission and a retired general officer in the U.S. Air Force; Douglas J. Martin, 59, Hamilton, New Zealand, plant manager for AHI Plastic Moulding Co.; Alexander B. Morrison, 56, Waterloo, Ontario, professor and chairman of the Food Sciences Department, University of Guelph; L. Aldin Porter, 55, Meridian, Idaho, president of the Louisiana Baton Rouge Mission, employed by Mutual of New York; Glen L. Rudd, 68, Salt Lake City, president of the New Zealand Temple and former director of zone operations for the Church's Welfare Services Department; Douglas H. Smith, 65, Salt Lake City, president of Beneficial Life Insurance Co. and Utah Home Fire Insurance Co.; and Lynn A. Sorensen, 67, Salt Lake City, former director of temporal affairs for the Church in Brazil.

On **April 25**, the First Presidency announced a major realignment of the Church's worldwide administrative areas. Four new areas will be created, effective Aug. 15, increasing the number from 13 to 17. New areas will be the Philippines/Micronesia Area, created from the Asia Area; the British Isles/Africa Area, [the name was later changed to United Kingdom /Ireland/Africa] created from the Europe Area; the Brazil Area, created from the South America North Area; and the North America Central Area, created from the North America Northwest and Northeast areas.

Also in the news in April 1987:

April 2 — A replica of the type of log cabin that once made up the LDS pioneer community of Winter Quarters (now within Omaha, Neb.) was dedicated at Winter Quarters.

April 4 — The *Church News* announced that the Book of Mormon had been translated into three additional languages — Greek, Arabic and Aymara (a South American Indian language) — bringing to 71 the total number of languages the book is available in.

April 12 — President Ezra Taft

Benson addressed sessions of a regional conference in Puerto Rico, attended by 2,600 people who braved a storm that dumped 3 inches of rain on the island before the day was over.

Also, Elder Boyd K. Packer rededicated the renovated Box Elder Tabernacle in Brigham City, Utah, a pioneer landmark that was originally dedicated by President Wilford Woodruff in 1890.

April 13-18 — The 49th annual "Jesus the Christ" pageant, held on the grounds of the Mesa Arizona Temple, attracted 73,000 people.

April 16 — Ricks College graduated 1,405 students in commencement exercises that featured an address by Presiding Bishop Robert D. Hales.

April 17 — President Thomas S. Monson, second counselor in the First Presidency, spoke at the 112th Commencement at BYU, which honored 4,174 graduates.

April 25 — Two new missions were announced — the Zaire Kinshasa Mission in Africa and the Spain Bilbao Mission in Europe. The new missions, which were to begin operation July 1, brought the Churchwide total to 203.

May 1987

President Ezra Taft Benson, making his first journey out of North America since becoming Church president in November 1985, traveled to Finland **May 16-17** to address members at a regional conference in

April 12, 1987. The pioneer landmark Box Elder Tabernacle in Brigham City, Utah, was rededicated by Elder Boyd K. Packer after extensive renovation.

Helsinki.

The trip was a nostalgic return for him to the nation he had rededicated for the preaching of the gospel 41 years before. More than 2,000 people attended the regional conference at the Messu Keskus convention center. The prophet made a brief stop in Sweden **May 18** to visit the Stockholm Temple and speak to temple workers there.

Also in the news in May 1987:

May 2 — Church members in western Canada began a year-long celebration, commemorating the 100th anniversary of the arrival of the first LDS settlers into western Canada in 1887.

May 3 — The annual Founders Day Devotional in the Granite Seminary in Salt Lake City, the first established in the Church, also served to mark the 75th anniversary of the Church educational program for youth. Church Commissioner of Education J. Elliott Cameron spoke at the commemorative devotional.

May 17 — President Thomas S. Monson, second counselor in the First Presidency, was featured speaker at a fireside, origi-

May 3, 1987. The seminary program celebrated its 75th anniversary. These seminary officers are among 225,000 students in 73 countries attending seminary.

May 30, 1987. Pres. Thomas S. Monson dedicates cemetery at Pioneer Trail State Park where remains of 33 pioneers, among the first pioneers in Salt Lake Valley, are buried.

nating from the Tabernacle on Temple Square, which commemorated the 158th anniversary of the restoration of the Aaronic Priesthood. The proceedings were telecast over the Church satellite network.

May 25 — President Ezra Taft Benson spoke at a conference of the Granite and Olympus regions of Salt Lake City, held in the Tabernacle on Temple Square.

May 29 — After dedication of a new baptistry at the Boise Idaho Temple by Elder James E. Faust of the Council of the Twelve, the major one-year remodeling project at the temple was officially completed.

May 30 — Elder James M. Paramore was named a member of the Presidency of the First Quorum of the Seventy, effective Aug. 15. Elder Paramore, 59, was sustained to the seventies quorum on April 2, 1977. The First Presidency also announced other changes in assignments for members of the First Quorum of the Seventy in 17 area presidencies.

Also, President Thomas S. Monson, second counselor in the First Presidency, dedicated a new cemetery area at Pioneer Trail State Park in Salt Lake City. The site would be the final resting place of some of the first pioneers to enter the valley in July 1847. The remains of 33 of these pioneers had been discovered during a recent construction project in downtown Salt Lake City.

And, the First Presidency issued a statement about what Church leaders can do to help undocumented aliens qualify for lawful immigration status under the Immigration Reform and Control Act of 1986.

June 1987

The Supreme Court ruled 9-0 **June 24** that Congress can exempt churches from laws prohibiting discrimination on the basis of religion.

The ruling, a major victory for the LDS Church and other religious groups, came in response to lawsuits brought by former employees of Deseret Gymnasium and Beehive Clothing, whose employment was terminated because they did not meet worthiness standards of the Church. The decision gives church groups that operate non-profit businesses authority to hire only members of their faith in good standing. The court said a 1972 anti-bias law exempting such employment practices is constitutional.

Also in the news in June 1987:

June 11 — LDS Business College graduated 178 students in ceremonies held in the Assembly Hall on Temple Square.

June 13 — President Thomas S. Monson, second counselor in the First Presidency, dedicated the $5.5 billion Intermountain Power Project in ceremonies near Delta, Utah. The Tabernacle Choir also participated in the program.

June 14 — President Ezra Taft Benson addressed a congregation of 8,400 members of the Heber City and Payson, Utah, regions in a conference held at BYU's Marriott Center.

June 19-20 — The Tabernacle Choir joined with the internationally known barbershop chorus "Vocal Majority" and the Constitution Symphony Orchestra for two concerts in Dallas, Texas, in commemoration of the bicentennial of the U.S. Constitution. The performances, in Dallas' Reunion Arena, were witnessed by about 25,000 people, including President Gordon B. Hinckley, first counselor in the First Presidency.

June 20 — The First Presidency sent a letter to priesthood leaders defining the organizational structure of ward Young Women presidencies and calling for consistent midweek activities for Young Women.

Also, a total of 157 graduates of BYU-Hawaii campus were instructed by Elder John K. Carmack of the First Quorum of the Seventy in commencement services in Laie, Hawaii.

June 23-26 — Eighty-eight new mission presidents, the largest group ever, heard instruction from the First Presidency and other General Authorities at the annual Mission Presidents Seminar at the Missionary Training Center in Provo, Utah.

June 25-27 — "A Frontier Story, 1833," a pageant put on by Church members in the Independence, Mo., area, attracted a record 10,000 people to this year's three performances.

June 28 — A video leadership conference instructing local Church officials how to accomplish the mission of the Church was broadcast from Church headquarters in Salt Lake City to stake centers throughout North America. Included were messages from all three members of the First Presidency and several other General Authorities.

Also, President Ezra Taft Benson addressed an audience of about 5,000 people at the rededication of the Oakland Interstake Center, adjacent to the Oakland Temple.

July 1987

With a "supreme consciousness of history," Latter-day Saints throughout the British Isles participated in three days of celebration **July 24-26** in commemoration of the 150th anniversary of the first Church missionary work in Great Britain. Thirteen General Authorities, including President Ezra Taft Benson and President Gordon B. Hinckley, first counselor in the First Presidency, were present for the festivities.

The other General Authorities were Elders Marvin J. Ashton, David B. Haight, Russell M. Nelson and M. Russell Ballard of the Council of the Twelve; Elders Marion D. Hanks and Jack H. Goaslind of the Presidency of the

July 24, 1987. Kenneth Johnson, left, Arch J. Turvey and Wendell J. Ashton deliver scriptures to 10 Downing Street to be given to British Prime Minister.

First Quorum of the Seventy; Elders Carlos E. Asay, Derek A. Cuthbert, Russell C. Taylor and Hans B. Ringger of the First Quorum of the Seventy; and Elder Bernard P. Brockbank, emeritus General Authority.

They were all in London July 24 for a gala anniversary banquet, which was attended by former British Prime Minister Edward Heath. U.S. President Ronald Reagan videotaped a message of congratulations that was shown at the banquet.

The following day, the General Authorities spread out to various parts of the island nation for an ambitious two-day series of firesides, dedications of historical sites, missionary meetings, musical events, and six Sunday conferences attended by about 35,000 people.

As part of the 150th anniversary celebration, a replica of the Book of Mormon that was given to England's Queen Victoria in 1841 and a modern quadruple combination of the four LDS scriptures were presented July 24 to Buckingham Palace and 10 Downing Street. Pres. Wendell J. Ashton of the England London Mission and Regional Representatives Arch J. Turvey and Kenneth Johnson presented the books and letters from the First Presidency to aides of Queen Elizabeth at Buckingham Palace and of Prime Minister Margaret Thatcher at her famous Downing Street address.

Also in the news in July 1987:

July 4 — President Gordon B. Hinckley, first counselor in the First Presidency, spoke to 3,500 people at services commemorating the Mormon Battalion's first raising of the

United States flag over the city of Los Angeles, Calif., 140 years earlier. The event was held at the Fort Moore Pioneer Memorial in downtown Los Angeles.

July 5 — Elder Dallin H. Oaks of the Council of the Twelve addressed more than 18,000 people in BYU's Marriott Center at a fireside commemorating the bicentennial of the U.S. Constitution. The Tabernacle Choir also performed at the fireside.

July 9-11, 14-18 — The eight performances of 21st annual Manti "Mormon Miracle Pageant" attracted 144,000 people to this small central Utah town.

July 15 — The Genealogical Department celebrated the conversion of the last card from the Genealogical Library's card catalog to computer. The project represented an estimated 1 million man-hours of effort and would give patrons around the world access to the library's vast data file.

July 24 — The annual Days of '47 Parade in Salt Lake City, featuring more than 150 entries, was witnessed by an estimated 250,000 people.

July 24-Aug. 1 — "America's Witness for Christ," the Church-sponsored pageant on the Hill Cumorah in New York, celebrated its 50th anniversary with performances attended by more than 100,000 spectators.

July 26-31 — The Mormon Youth Symphony and Chorus performed in Washington, D.C.; Philadelphia, Pa.; and New York City as part of celebrations of the bicentennial of the U.S. Constitution.

July 4, 1987. Pres. Gordon B. Hinckley lauds Mormon Battalion, which raised the first U.S. flag over Los Angeles, Calif.

August 1987

The Frankfurt Germany Temple, the fifth in Europe, was dedicated **Aug. 28** by President Ezra Taft Benson.

A total of 12,570 members from Germany, Austria, The Netherlands, Belgium and France attended the 11 dedicatory sessions held over three days. President Benson de-

Aug. 28, 1987. The Frankfurt Germany Temple, the Church's 41st temple, was dedicated by Pres. Ezra Taft Benson. A total of 12,570 attended the 11 dedicatory sessions.

livered the dedicatory prayer in the first session and spoke in the next two sessions before returning to Salt Lake City. President Thomas S. Monson, second counselor in the First Presidency, presided at the remaining sessions.

At the open house of the temple, held July 29-Aug. 8, more than 70,000 visitors toured the temple, the 41st in operation in the Church.

Also in the news in August 1987:

Aug. 1 — President Ezra Taft Benson, riding alongside his wife, Flora, was grand marshal of a parade celebrating the centennial of Cardston, Alberta, which was first settled by LDS colonists in 1887. He also spoke to 7,000 people at the Centennial Interfaith Sunrise Service **Aug. 2.**

Aug. 4 — President Ezra Taft Benson celebrated his 88th birthday.

Aug. 11-15 — An estimated 40,000 people attended five performances of the 12th annual "City of Joseph" pageant in Nauvoo, Ill.

Aug. 14 — Elder Boyd K. Packer of the Council of the Twelve addressed 2,266 graduates at commencement services at BYU.

Aug. 15 — The First Presidency announced that the Church Genealogical Department would be known as the Family History Department, and its library would be renamed the Family History Library.

Also, President Ezra Taft Benson dedicated a park in Preston, Idaho, in honor of his mother, Sarah Dunkley Benson, "and all of our beloved pioneer women."

Aug. 18-20 — The First Presidency and

other General Authorities addressed the annual Temple Presidents Seminar in the Salt Lake Temple, attended by a record 20 new presidents and their wives.

Aug. 21-22 — The Tabernacle Choir performed Mendelssohn's "Elijah" in Teton Village, Wyo., in the shadow of the world-famous Teton Mountain range. The choir's performances were part of the Grand Teton Music Festival, a seven-week series of classical music performances.

Aug. 21-22, 25-26, 28-29 — "The Man Who Knew," a pageant in Clarkston, Utah, about the life of Martin Harris, attracted 13,000 spectators for its six performances.

Aug. 23 — President Ezra Taft Benson traveled to Littleton, Colo., to speak at the missionary homecoming sacrament meeting of his grandson, David Madsen. He also addressed temple workers of the Denver Temple later the same day.

Aug. 25 — Bonneville International Corp. announced production of a one-hour television variety special on the U.S. Constitution that would receive national airing during September.

Also, a public service announcement produced for the Church's Missionary Department received a national Emmy award. It was the first time the National Academy of Television Arts and Sciences had given the award for a public service spot.

Aug. 29 — A new version of the classic missionary film, "Man's Search for Happiness," was released by the Church.

Aug. 30 — Elder Marvin J. Ashton of the Council of the Twelve dedicated the land of Zaire for preaching of the gospel in a prayer offered in the capital city of Kinshasa.

September 1987

Celebration of the 200th anniversary of the U.S. Constitution took center stage in September, and Church leaders and members played prominent roles in the activities.

President Ezra Taft Benson delivered a patriotic address to an overflow crowd of about 5,000 people from Pennsylvania, New Jersey and Delaware **Sept. 13** in a special commemorative fireside at Valley Forge, Pa.

Then on **Sept. 17**, the Tabernacle Choir helped officially commemorate the bicentennial celebration by

Sept. 18, 1987. Pres. and Sister Ezra Taft Benson enjoy dancing at the Church's Constitutional Bicentennial Ball, which was telecast over the Church satellite system as a live addition to stake constitutional balls.

singing the national anthem, signaling the start of the constitutional parade. Later that night, the choir performed during the nationally televised "We The People 200 Constitutional Gala" at the Philadelphia Civic Center. An LDS Scout troop from the Monument Ward, Colorado Springs Colorado North Stake, performed as the honor guard for the parade and constitutional gala.

That same night, the Mormon Youth Symphony and Chorus performed before a capacity audience in the Salt Lake Tabernacle. And 700 teenage Church members stood on the steps of the Jefferson Memorial in Washington, D.C., and offered a one-hour salute to the constitution entitled "Ring the Bells of Freedom." President Thomas S. Monson, second counselor in the First Presidency, spoke at the concert in the nation's capital.

President Benson returned to Salt Lake City to participate in the Church's Constitutional Bicentennial Ball at the Hotel Utah **Sept. 18**. The ball was telecast over the Church satellite system as a live addition to stake constitutional balls throughout the United States.

Also in the news in September 1987:

Sept. 2 — Elder Marvin J. Ashton of the Council of the Twelve dedicated the nation of Liberia for preaching of the gospel in a prayer offered in the capital city of Monrovia.

Sept. 4 — A letter from the First Presidency to local Church leaders announced the discontinuance of the International Mission. Areas formerly served by the mission would come under the jurisdiction of area presidencies around the world.

Also, Elder Ashton dedicated the Ivory Coast in Africa for preaching of the gospel in a prayer in the capital city of Abidjan.

Sept. 10 — President and Sister Ezra Taft Benson celebrated their 61st wedding anniversary.

Sept. 13 — More than 40,000 Utah seminary students heard messages from General Authorities and general officers of the Church in simultaneous firesides held at the Tabernacle in Salt Lake City, the Marriott Center in Provo and the Dixie Center in St. George.

Sept. 19 — President Marion G. Romney, president of the Council of the Twelve, celebrated his 90th birthday.

Sept. 26 — Women gathered to the Salt Lake Tabernacle and to 1,500 meetinghouses in the United States, Canada and Puerto Rico for the annual women's meeting, highlighted by remarks from Elder Russell M. Nelson of the Council of the Twelve and the Relief Society general presidency.

October 1987

An official Young Women logo, and mission statements and symbols for the Beehive, Mia Maid and Laurel age groups, were introduced **Oct. 18** at a Young Women satellite fireside. President Thomas S. Monson represented the First Presidency in addressing the fireside.

Also in the news in October 1987:

Oct. 1 — No injuries or major damage were reported to Church properties or members' homes from an earthquake in Los Angeles, Calif., that measured 6.1 on the Richter scale. At least seven people died from the quake.

Oct. 3-4 — President Ezra Taft Benson bore fervent testimony of the U.S. Constitution, which the nation had just given a rousing 200th birthday celebration, in opening remarks of the 157th Semiannual General Conference. Unseasonably warm weather added a peaceful accent to conference proceedings,

Oct. 18, 1987. Colored flags representing new Young Women values are displayed on Temple Square prior to Young Women fireside.

at which there were no new General Authorities or auxiliary leaders sustained.

Oct. 6 — A letter from the First Presidency to local priesthood leaders encouraged increased contributions to the General Missionary Fund, which provides assistance to many young people who otherwise would not be able to fund their own missions.

Oct. 10 — President Thomas S. Monson, second counselor in the First Presidency, and Elder M. Russell Ballard of the Council of the Twelve joined with local Church leaders to break ground for the Toronto Ontario Temple, to be located 20 miles west of downtown Toronto in suburban Brampton.

Oct. 11 — Nearly 3,500 members of the Church from three stakes in Iowa and parts of Illinois received counsel from President Ezra Taft Benson at a conference of the Des Moines Iowa Region held in the Five Seasons Center in Cedar Rapids, Iowa.

Oct. 13 — President Ezra Taft Benson emphasized the law of chastity in a devotional at BYU, attended by nearly 20,000 people.

Oct. 15 — President Ezra Taft Benson suffered a mild heart attack and was hospitalized for nine days in LDS Hospital in Salt Lake City.

Also, President Thomas S. Monson, second counselor in the First Presidency, spoke and the Mormon Tabernacle Choir sang at a meeting in the Salt Lake Tabernacle, commemorating the centennial of the United Way, a charitable organization.

Oct. 26 — The first worldwide seminar for temple engineers from the 41 operating temples of the Church began in Salt Lake City.

November 1987

A major new Church movie, "How Rare a Possession — the Book of Mormon," was shown for the first time over the Church satellite network **Nov. 8.**

The 64-minute production was produced by BYU Motion Picture Studios in conjunction with the Church Curriculum Department. It served as an introduction to the 1988 gospel doctrine class course of study — the Book of Mormon.

The movie, which portrays the coming forth of the Book of Mormon and factual accounts of how two people came to know of its truth, was filmed on location in Italy, Switzerland, London, New York City, Salt Lake City and Kanab, Utah.

Also in the news in November 1987:

Nov. 13 — Elder Franklin D. Richards of the First Quorum of the Seventy died at his Salt Lake City home at age 86. He was eulogized in funeral services **Nov. 17** at the Assembly Hall on Temple Square.

Nov. 14 — The Honolulu Tabernacle in Hawaii was reopened after 10 months of renovation work.

Nov. 21 — The BYU-Hawaii campus women's volleyball team won its second straight national championship at a tournament in Milwaukee, Wis.

Nov. 8, 1987. Scene from "How Rare a Possession — the Book of Mormon," portrays an area in New York City where young pastor from Sicily found a copy of the Book of Mormon in a barrel of ashes, which lead to his conversion.

Also, Ricks College won the inaugural Centennial Bowl for junior colleges in Pocatello, Idaho, by beating Walla Walla Community College, 42-38.

Nov. 21-22 — President Thomas S. Monson, second counselor in the First Presidency, dedicated two meetinghouses in historic Church settings — Hiram and Kirtland, Ohio. The Kirtland building had been destroyed by an arsonist's fire in May 1986.

Nov. 23 — The Church and President Thomas S. Monson were honored for their "sensitive, unselfish and ecumenical response to the needs of the homeless" by the Catholic Community Services of Utah.

Nov. 27 — Six prominent religious officials from Romania, Costa Rica, Jamaica, Nigeria and Surinam visited Temple Square as part of an extended tour of the United States.

Also, three members of the Church were killed by a typhoon that slammed into southern Luzon in the Philippines. Several Church buildings were slightly damaged.

Nov. 28 — Elder Robert L. Backman of the Presidency of the First Quorum of the Seventy was appointed to the White House Conference for a Drug-Free America by U.S. President Ronald Reagan.

December 1987

One of the first public appearances by President Ezra Taft Benson since his mild heart attack Oct. 15 highlighted the annual First Presidency Christmas Devotional **Dec. 6.**

The proceedings, carried over the Church satellite network to meetinghouses throughout the United States, Canada and Puerto Rico, featured an address by President Gordon B. Hinckley, first counselor in the First Presidency, and several Christmas musical selections from the Tabernacle Choir.

Also in the news in December 1987:

Dec. 3 — Walter and Sophi Schweiger from Salzburg, Austria, were honored as the 3 millionth visitors to Temple Square in 1987. It was the first time that Utah's most popular tourist attraction had reached that level in a single year.

Dec. 4 — A new 186,000-square-foot Church printing facility in Salt Lake City was dedicated by President Thomas S. Monson, second counselor in the First Presidency.

Dec. 8 — A new Earth Science Museum opened on the campus of BYU.

Dec. 15 — The Polynesian Cultural Center in Laie, Hawaii, announced a $7 million 25th

Nov. 21, 1987. Pres. Thomas S. Monson visits Kirtland Temple, the day before he dedicated rebuilt Kirtland stake meetinghouse, which was destroyed by arson's fire in 1986.

anniversary project that will include production of a film, "Polynesian Odyssey," and construction of a large-screen theater facility to show it in.

Dec. 19 — Seven new missions, six of them in Latin America, were announced by the First Presidency. They were: Argentina Salta, Bolivia La Paz, Guatemala Guatemala City North, Mexico Chihuahua, Mexico Tuxtla-Gutierrez, Peru Lima East and Philippines Cagayan de Oro. The missions, which will begin operations in January 1988, brought the total number of Church missions to 212.

Also, the Missionary Department announced that the number of full-time missionaries reached 35,000 in November, an all-time high.

Dec. 22 — BYU suffered a 22-16 loss to Virginia in the All-American Bowl in Birmingham, Ala.

Dec. 31 — The "rainstorm of the century" on Oahu, Hawaii, damaged the homes of 48 LDS families, 15 of which were severely damaged or destroyed. No injuries were reported.

Jan. 16, 1988. A dynamite-triggered explosion caused extensive damage to the Kamas Utah Stake Center.

January 1988

In one of the largest single-weekend stake divisions in Church history, 11 stakes became 18 on **Jan. 30-31** in Lima, Peru.

Elder M. Russell Ballard of the Council of the Twelve, returning to the continent his grandfather, Elder Marvin J. Ballard, dedicated for the preaching of the gospel some 60 years before, presided over the six conferences required to carry out the historic divisions. More than 10,500 people attended the conferences, conducted over a 28-hour span. With its 18 stakes, Lima stood second only to Mexico City (with 22) in the number of stakes in any city outside the United States.

Also in the news in January 1988:

Jan. 9 — The *Church News* announced that the Book of Mormon had been translated into six new languages in 1987 — Papiamento, Tagalog, Pohnpeian, Trukese, Akan (Fante) and Zulu. With the new translations the Book of Mormon is now in 80 languages, available to be read by 85-90 percent of the world's population.

Also, Temple Square announced that 3,408,881 people visited the historic Church site in 1987, surpassing the previous annual record by 800,000 people.

Jan. 16 — A dynamite-triggered explosion caused extensive damage to the Kamas Utah Stake Center. Authorities arrested a family of polygamists, following a 13-day standoff at the family compound that resulted in the death of an LDS law enforcement officer, Lt. Fred House.

Jan. 30 — The *Church News* reported that a Church delegation, headed by Elder Spencer H. Osborn of the First Quorum of the

Seventy, presented a copy of the Book of Mormon, newly translated into the Zulu language, to Dr. Mangosuthu G. Buthelezi, chief minister of KwaZulu and leader of 6 million Zulu people.

February 1988

In his first trip out of the Salt Lake Valley since his mild heart attack on Oct. 15, 1987, President Ezra Taft Benson broke ground **Feb. 27** for the San Diego California Temple.

President Thomas S. Monson, second counselor in the First Presidency, also spoke and dedicated the site for the temple, located in the north San Diego suburb of La Jolla. About 65,000 members live in the 15 stakes of the San Diego Temple District, including four stakes in nearby Mexico.

Also in the news in February 1988:

Feb. 2 — The 31-year-old San Jose (Calif.) stake center sustained $110,000 in damage in an arson fire.

Feb. 13 — President Gordon B. Hinckley, first counselor in the First Presidency, spoke at an unveiling ceremony for a new monument honoring the LDS founders of Mesa, Ariz. Among those who attended the ceremony were numerous descendants of members of the pioneer company that founded the city.

Feb. 13-28 — Church members in the Calgary, Alberta, area played vital roles behind the scenes as administrators and volunteers for the XV Winter Olympic Games, hosted by the city of Calgary. LDS volunteers were instrumental in providing transportation for athletes and visitors, helping with security, hosting athletic delegations, working in food services and other areas, and singing and dancing in the opening and closing ceremonies.

Feb. 14 — Both the Church and its most distinguished Scouter, President Ezra Taft Benson, were saluted in a satellite-transmitted fireside at the Salt Lake Tabernacle, commemorating the 75th anniversary of the Church's association with the Boy Scouts of America.

March 1988

The number of missions continued to grow at an unprecedented pace as nine new missions — all in developing countries — were announced **March 19**. This brought the total number worldwide to 221. At the end of 1987, an all-time high of 35,200 full-time missionaries were serving, including 10,600 from outside the United States.

Feb. 14, 1988. Scouts line up outside Tabernacle before presenting colors at fireside commemorating the 75th anniversary of Scouting in the Church.

The new missions are Brazil Belo Horizonte, Chile Antofagasta, Colombia Barranquilla, Liberia Monrovia, Mascarene Islands, Mexico Puebla, Mexico Tampico, Philippines Quezon City and Spain Las Palmas. All would begin operating July 1 except for the Liberia Monrovia Mission, which started March 1.

Also in the news in March 1988:

March 1-3 — Members of the Church played significant roles at two national conferences dealing with pressing social problems — the Religious Alliance Against Pornography, and the White House Conference for a Drug-Free America.

March 5 — Elder Marion D. Hanks of the Presidency of the First Quorum of the Seventy and Elder Vaughn J. Featherstone of the First Quorum of the Seventy were named recipients of the Silver Buffalo, the highest honor of the Boy Scouts of America for nationwide service to youth.

March 12 — The First Presidency issued a statement supporting Child Abuse Prevention Month, and encouraged members to help combat the "pernicious problem."

March 24 — President Thomas S. Monson, second counselor in the First Presidency, returned to the land of his ancestors, Sweden, to help commemorate the 350th anniversary of the first Swedish settlement in the United States.

March 26 — The *Church News* reported that an effort spearheaded by members of the Church in the Washington, D.C., area resulted in shipment of 180,000 text and library books, valued at $2.5 million, to Zimbabwe, Sierra Leone and Ghana.

April 1988

President Ezra Taft Benson, appearing to have more strength and energy than he had enjoyed since suffering a heart attack in October 1987, delivered a stirring 25-minute opening address at the 158th Annual General Conference. President Benson also addressed the Saturday evening priesthood session.

At the conference, conducted **April 2-3**, two new General Authorities and a new general Primary presidency were sustained. Called to the First Quorum of the Seventy were Robert E. Sackley, 65, a native of Lismore, Australia, who at the time was serving as president of the Nigeria Lagos Mission; and L. Lionel Kendrick, 56, of Greenville, N.C., who was serving as president of the Florida Tampa Mission.

Called as Primary general president was Michaelene Grassli, who had served as a counselor for eight years to outgoing Pres. Dwan J. Young. Called as first and second counselors, respectively, were Betty Jo Jepsen and Ruth B. Wright.

It was also announced in the annual statistical report that the number of convert baptisms for 1987 had reached an all-time high — 227,284.

Also in the news in April 1988:

April 2 — A reception with present and former Ricks College presidents at the Lion House in Salt Lake City officially kicked off the two-year college's centennial celebration. Present were current Pres. Joe J. Christensen and former presidents Bruce C. Hafen, John L. Clarke and Bishop Henry B. Eyring, now first counselor in the Presiding Bishopric.

April 2, 1988. Ricks Collge's centennial celebration begins with reception.

April 12 — Active Church member Jim Harrick, 49, was named head coach of one of college basketball's most prestigious programs — the University of California at Los Angeles.

April 21 — Ricks College awarded 1,516 degrees at its 99th Commencement, with Bishop Henry B. Eyring, first counselor in the Presiding Bishopric and former Ricks College president, as the featured speaker.

April 22 — President Thomas S. Monson, second counselor in the First Presidency, addressed 2,807 spring graduates at BYU's 113th Commencement services.

April 24 — President Ezra Taft Benson addressed more than 12,000 people at a regional conference of the Dallas and Fort Worth Texas regions.

April 28 — Elder John K. Carmack of the First Quorum of the Seventy, testified before the U.S. House Judiciary Committee's Subcommittee on Crime in favor of the Child Protection and Obscenity Enforcement Act of 1988.

April 30 — Jeanne Dunn, wife of Elder Paul H. Dunn of the First Quorum of the Seventy received the Elect Lady Award from Lambda Delta Sigma at the annual convention of the Lambda Delta Sigma sorority and Sigma Gamma Chi fraternity. A total of 1,600 women and 250 men from universities across the United States and Canada attended the convention.

May 1988

Nearly 20,000 people gathered in Manti, Utah, for the centennial commemoration **May 21** of the Manti Temple, giving a momentous welcome to the beginning of its second century. The temple was dedicated May 21, 1888.

The commemorative events included a centennial program, at which all three General Authorities in the Utah South Area presidency, Elders Vaughn J. Featherstone, Paul H. Dunn and Russell C. Taylor, gave addresses. The centennial events also included a dance festival, presented on Temple Hill, featuring 4,000 youths and adults who performed for some 15,000 spectators.

Also in the news in May 1988:

May 4 — Three explosions at a rocket fuel manufacturing plant in Henderson, Nev., which has a large population of Church members, heavily damaged homes and businesses as far as 10 miles away. Two people were killed in the blasts, which registered 3.5 on a Richter scale in Pasadena, Calif.

May 11 — President Ezra Taft Benson was honored as the most distinguished alumnus in Utah State University history as part of the institution's centennial celebration.

May 14 — A dance festival with 800 participants was presented before an audience of about 3,000 people in Wayne, N.J., kicking off a summer-long commemoration of the Church's 150th anniversary in New Jersey.

May 15 — A fireside commemorating the restoration of the priesthood was carried via satellite from the Salt Lake Tabernacle to priesthood holders throughout the United States and Canada. President Gordon B. Hinckley, first counselor in the First Presidency, gave the keynote address.

Earlier that day, President Ezra Taft Benson addressed a congregation of about 11,000 people at a conference of the Morgan, Mt. Ogden and Ogden Utah regions in the Dee Events Center at Weber State College.

Also, the first stake in western Africa, the Aba Nigeria Stake, was organized by Elder Neal A. Maxwell of the Council of the Twelve. The stake, the first in the Church in which all priesthood leaders are black, was created less than a month before the 10th anniversary of the June 9, 1978, revelation making it possible for all worthy male members to be ordained to the priesthood.

May 18 — A renewable 49-year lease for BYU's Jerusalem Center for Near Eastern Studies was signed in Jerusalem by BYU Pres. Jeffrey R. Holland. Also signing the lease, representing the BYU board of trustees, was President Howard W. Hunter, acting president of the Council of the Twelve.

May 20 — President Marion G. Romney, who was counselor to two Church presidents during his 47 years of service as a General Authority, died after a lengthy illness at age 90. The renowned Church Welfare pioneer and Book of Mormon scholar, who served the past 2½ years as president of the Council of the Twelve, was eulogized by President Ezra Taft Benson and other General Authorities in funeral services **May 23** in the Salt Lake Tabernacle.

May 25 — President Ezra Taft Benson addressed a combined group of full-time missionaries from the Utah North and Utah South missions at the Assembly Hall on Temple Square.

May 28 — The First Presidency announced the acquisition of two sites — one in Bountiful, Utah, and the other in Bogota, Colombia — as possible sites for temples.

The First Presidency also issued a statement on the subject of Acquired Immune Deficiency Syndrome (AIDS), stressing chastity before marriage, total fidelity in marriage and abstinence from all homosexual behavior.

Also, Robert M. Mills was named national director of Boy Scouts of America's Mormon Relationships, replacing John Warnick, who held the post for 12 years.

June 1988

Two events on opposite ends of the world highlighted June 1988 news.

On **June 1**, the Church received legal recognition in the Hungarian People's Republic. The recognition would allow the Church to meet, teach, and baptize without restrictions. A document granting the legal recognition was signed in Budapest, Hungary, by Dr. Imre Miklos, state secretary and president of the State Office for Religious Affairs.

Later, on **June 24**, Elder Russell M. Nelson of the Council of the Twelve, representing the First Presidency, participated in a cer-

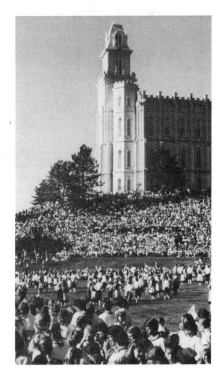

May 21, 1988. Thousands of members participate in commemorating 100th anniversary of the Manti Temple.

emony in Budapest to receive the official declaration.

And in Samoa, the 100th anniversary of the Church on these South Pacific islands was commemorated with a host of activities and meetings **June 13-26**. President Thomas S. Monson, second counselor in the First Presidency, attended the events on the island of Upolu, while Elder James E. Faust of the Council of the Twelve and Elder John Sonnenberg of the First Quorum of the Seventy presided at activities on the islands of Tutuila and Savai'i.

Also in the news in June 1988:

June 2 — President Howard W. Hunter was set apart as president of the Council of the Twelve, succeeding President Marion G. Romney, who died May 20.

June 4 — The First Presidency announced that the historic site around Carthage Jail in Illinois, where Joseph and Hyrum Smith were martyred, would undergo extensive renovation including expanded visitors center operations. The project was estimated to require three months to complete.

June 9 — Members throughout the

June 13-26, 1988. The 100th anniversary of the Church in Samoa included a parade on Savai'i, led by Elder John Sonnenberg, left, Lueli Te'o and Elder James E. Faust.

Church commemorated the 10th anniversary of the revelation opening priesthood blessings to all worthy men in the Church, regardless of race.

June 11 — President Ezra Taft Benson dedicated a gristmill at Stansbury Park, Utah, constructed in 1854 under the direction of his great-grandfather, Elder Ezra T. Benson of the Council of the Twelve. The seven-acre mill site is to be used as a historic park.

Also, LDS Business College honored 162 graduates at its 101st Commencement exercises. Elder Marvin J. Ashton of the Council of the Twelve was the commencement speaker.

June 12, 14 — Democratic presidential candidates Gov. Michael Dukakis and Jesse Jackson met with President Thomas S. Monson, second counselor in the First Presidency, and other General Authorities during a visit to Salt Lake City to address the U.S.

Conference of Mayors.

June 14-July 4 — The Tabernacle Choir made a 21-day, 19-concert tour of Hawaii, New Zealand and Australia, their second-longest tour ever. The choir traveled 25,000 miles and performed 17 concerts attended by at least 40,000 people.

The 280 singers performed in Laie and Honolulu, Hawaii; Auckland, Wellington and Christchurch, New Zealand; and Melbourne, Adelaide, Perth, Sydney and Brisbane, Australia. At the Brisbane concerts, the choir officially represented the U.S. at United States Day festivities of Expo '88, which marked Australia's bicentennial year.

June 18 — Elder Joseph B. Wirthlin of the Council of the Twelve spoke at commencement exercises of BYU-Hawaii, at which 193 graduates were honored.

June 19 — President Ezra Taft Benson addressed more than 4,500 members of the Fort Collins Colorado Region in a conference held on the campus of Colorado State University.

June 4, 1988. Architect's rendering of the historic Carthage Jail block shows a park-like appearance. The jail site is to undergo major renovation, including expansion of the visitors center.

Also, the Church, represented by President Thomas S. Monson, second counselor in the First Presidency, donated the former Salt Lake 25th Ward meetinghouse to the Salvation Army.

And, a two-page article in nationally distributed *Parade Magazine* about the Church's Family History Library resulted in thousands of telephone calls from people wanting to search their roots.

June 21-24 — President Ezra Taft Benson addressed the annual Mission Presidents Seminar at the Missionary Training Center in Provo, Utah. Other members of the First Presidency, the Council of the Twelve and First Quorum of the Seventy spoke to the 68 new mission presidents and their wives at the four-day seminar.

June 23-25 — The pageant "A Frontier Story, 1833," was viewed by an estimated 6,000 people at Independence, Mo.

June 24 — Elder Dallin H. Oaks of the Council of the Twelve unveiled a 10-foot replica of Bertel Thorvaldsen's "Christus" statue at the Washington Temple Visitors Center in Kensington, Md.

June 20, 1988. Jerold Ottley conducts Tabernacle Choir in singing at the Auckland, New Zealand, Airport.

June 25 — The Church donated $250,000 to Rotary International PolioPlus to provide more than a million polio immunizations to young people in Kenya and Ivory Coast.

Also, Elder Dallin H. Oaks of the Council of the Twelve joined 100 national leaders in signing the Williamsburg Charter at the First Liberty Summit in Williamsburg, Va. The document was drafted to reaffirm religious liberty guaranteed by the First Amendment to the Constitution.

June 27 — Flora Benson, wife of President Ezra Taft Benson, celebrated her 87th birthday.

July 1988

In its 51st year, the Hill Cumorah Pageant, "America's Witness for Christ," premiered **July 22** with a totally new production.

The pageant, which ran through **July 30**, featured a new script by Orson Scott Card of Greensboro, N.C., and a new musical score by Crawford Gates of Beloit, Wis. The new production follows the Book of Mormon in chronological sequence, and features state-of-the-art special effects and almost 10 times more props than were used in former pageants.

Also in the news in July 1988:

July 8-9, 12-16 — For the second consecutive year, the Mormon Miracle Pageant in Manti, Utah, set an attendance record —

147,000, up 3,000 from last year's total.

July 9 — A statement from the First Presidency reaffirmed the Church's neutral stance in all political races.

July 11 — President Ezra Taft Benson spoke to about 650 temple workers of the Boise Idaho Temple at a special meeting.

July 16 — Monuments commemorating the site where the Mormon Battalion was mustered and where LDS pioneers established Nebraska's first community were dedicated near Council Bluffs, Iowa, and near Florence, Neb.

July 22 — President Gordon B. Hinckley, first counselor in the First Presidency, told a group of leaders from Historic Palmyra Inc., in Palmyra, N.Y., that the Church is interested in efforts to preserve and restore Palmyra landmarks.

July 23 — A monument honoring the late President Harold B. Lee was unveiled in ceremonies at the prophet's hometown of Clifton, Idaho.

Also, more than 200 non-members of the Church gathered in Kirtland, Ohio, for the Kirtland Roots Posterity Conference, conducted by the Kirtland Ohio Stake, to better acquaint descendants of area settlers with their ancestors.

August 1988

The Church reached a milestone in temple work by performing 100 million endowments for the dead, as of **mid-August**, according to temple department estimates. In reaching that milestone number of endowments — and baptisms — for the dead, the Church is beginning to gain on its monumental task of vicarious work.

Although the 100 million-mark is miniscule compared with the estimated 75 billion in the whole family of man throughout history, it is an accomplishment, particularly considering that two-thirds of that total was completed in the past 18 years. Elder Wm. Grant Bangerter of the Presidency of the First Quorum of the Seventy and executive director of the Temple Department estimated that the next 100 million endowments might be performed within 15 years or less, as the Church grows and as members become busier in temple work.

Aug. 4, 1988. Pres. Ezra Taft Benson celebrates 89th birthday. President Gordon B. Hinckley and his wife, Marjorie, offer congratulations.

Also in the news in August 1988:

Aug. 4 — President Ezra Taft Benson was honored on his 89th birthday at a reception in the Church Administration Building.

Aug. 6 — It was announced in the *Church News* that the Tabernacle Choir would travel to Florida for a concert tour March 17-22, 1989, with highlights of concerts from the EPCOT Center at Walt Disney World videotaped and featured on the nationally televised Walt Disney World Easter Parade March 26.

Aug. 9-13 — An attendance record of 40,000 people was set at the 13th annual "City of Joseph" pageant, held at Nauvoo, Ill.

Aug. 13 — An architect's rendering of the soon-to-be-constructed Toronto Ontario Temple, the 45th temple in the Church, was published in the *Church News*. The site had been announced June 22, 1986, and ground was broken Oct. 10, 1987.

Also, the Church was presented the deed to historic Cove Fort, Utah, the only pioneer fort in the state that is still standing, by descendants of the Ira Nathaniel Hinckley family. Ira Hinckley was called by Brigham Young to spearhead construction of the stone fort in 1867. President Gordon B. Hinckley, first counselor in the First Presidency, played a dual role of giver and receiver. A grandson of Ira Hinckley, President Hinckley presented the deed in behalf of the family and received it in behalf of the Church.

Aug. 14 — President Ezra Taft Benson addressed some 6,000 Scouts and leaders at the Upper Snake River Aaronic Priesthood Scout Encampment in Island Park, Idaho.

Aug. 23 — President Ezra Taft Benson told new temple presidents at a seminar in the Salt Lake Temple that the mission of the Church "is all one great work."

Aug. 25 — To commemorate the Primary's 110th anniversary, the general Primary presidency and 1,300 children in the Farmington Utah Stake held special events at the old rock chapel in Farmington, Utah, where the Primary was organized in 1878. The children were greeted by Elder James M. Paramore of the Presidency of the First Quorum of the Seventy, and Elder Paul H. Dunn of the First Quorum of the Seventy who were dressed in 1870s-style clothing.

Aug. 26 — Republican vice presidential candidate Dan Quayle called on the First Presidency during a visit to Salt Lake City.

Aug. 30 — "Braces and Glasses," the Church's Homefront Junior community service television spot, won a prestigious Emmy, the second in two years for the Church. An estimated audience of 147 million saw the spot during the year.

September 1988

BYU's folk dancers, dressed in red-and-white checkered costumes, performed before probably a larger audience than any previous Church group as they kicked up their heels in western dance **Sept. 17** at the grandiose opening ceremonies of the 1988 Olympics at Seoul, Korea. An estimated audience of 1 billion worldwide viewed the proceedings.

The dance ensemble was one of 12 folk dance companies — and the only representative from North America — invited by the

Sept. 24, 1988. After General Women's Meeting, President Ezra Taft Benson and his counselors greet general presidents of Primary, Young Women and Relief Society: Michaelene Grassli, left, Ardeth Kapp, and Barbara Winder.

Seoul Organizing Committee to perform at the official Olympic opening.

Eighteen LDS athletes from throughout the world participated in the Summer Olympic Games.

Also in the news in September 1988:

Sept. 2-3 — LDS farmers from Idaho laid 14 miles of sprinkler pipes in West Yellowstone, Mont., to help prevent forest fires raging in Yellowstone National Park from reaching the western Montana resort town. Two days later, forest officials asked that a similar irrigation system be installed at Old Faithful, the park's most famous landmark.

Sept. 10 — President and Sister Ezra Taft Benson attended a nostalgia-filled family dinner to celebrate their 62nd wedding anniversary.

Sept. 12 — Members in the Caribbean, Mexico and Texas were spared, although a number lost homes and property in one of the worst tropical storms of the decade, Hurricane Gilbert, which had winds up to 175 miles per hour.

Sept. 17 — The Church joined an interfaith cable television network, VISN (Vision Interfaith Satellite Network), sponsored by 18 religious organizations including the Church. The network will beam "values oriented" programs nationwide.

Sept. 17 - Oct. 2 — Eighteen LDS athletes participated in the 1988 Summer Olympics in Seoul, Korea.

Sept. 20 — Richard P. Lindsay, managing director of Public Communications and Special Affairs, urged stiffer regulations of beer sales "to contain the rampant consumption," as he addressed the annual meeting of the American Council on Alcohol Problems, held in Midway, Utah.

Sept. 24 — President Ezra Taft Benson counseled women of the Church to "Realize your self-worth. Never, never demean yourself." President Benson's speech was read by his second counselor, President Thomas S. Monson, at the annual General Women's Meeting.

Also, a seven-foot Centennial Statue, representing 100 years of progress at Ricks College, was unveiled at homecoming ceremonies.

And, eight LDS Olympians at the Seoul Summer Games participated in a fireside for Korean Young Adults, sharing their testimonies of commitment to achieve goals.

INDEX

A

L

M

N

W

Y